3795

Kinkaid of the Seventh Fleet

Vice Admiral Kinkaid, Commander Seventh Fleet. Pencil sketch by Dwight Shepler, official Navy combat artist, Leyte, 1945.

Kinkaid of the Seventh Fleet

A Biography of Admiral Thomas C. Kinkaid, U.S. Navy

Gerald E. Wheeler

Naval Historical Center
Washington, D.C.

Naval Institute Press
Annapolis, Maryland

Originally published in a limited edition in 1995 by
the Naval Historical Center

Naval Institute Press edition published in 1996

Library of Congress Cataloging-in-Publication Data

Wheeler, Gerald E.
    Kinkaid of the Seventh Fleet : a biography of Admiral Thomas C.
  Kinkaid, U.S. Navy / Gerald E. Wheeler.
       p.   cm.
    Includes bibliographical references (p.   ) and index.
    ISBN 1-55750-936-0 (cloth : alk. paper)
    1. Kinkaid, Thomas C. (Thomas Cassin), 1888–1972. 2. Admirals—
  United States—Biography. 3. United States. Navy—Biography.
  4. United States. Navy. Fleet, 7th I. Title.
  V63.K57.W44   1994
  359'.0092—dc20   92-31263
  [B]

Printed in the United States of America on acid-free paper ∞

03 02 01 00 99 98 97 96   9 8 7 6 5 4 3 2

First printing

Secretary of the Navy's Advisory Committee on Naval History

William D. Wilkinson, Chairman
CAPT Edward L. Beach, USN (Retired)
David R. Bender
John C. Dann
RADM Russell W. Gorman, USNR (Retired)
Richard L. Joutras
VADM William P. Lawrence, USN (Retired)
Vera D. Mann
Ambassador J. William Middendorf II
VADM Gerald E. Miller, USN (Retired)
Clark G. Reynolds
Betty M. Unterberger

To my wife
Jean French Wheeler

Contents

		Page
Foreword		xiii
Preface		xv
Chapter 1.	Growing Up in Battleships, 1888–1919	1
Chapter 2.	The Middle Ranks, 1919–1933	27
Chapter 3.	*Colorado* and the Bureau of Navigation, 1933–1937	69
Chapter 4.	*Indianapolis*, 1937–1938	91
Chapter 5.	Rome, 1938–1941	105
Chapter 6.	Destroyer Squadron 8, 1941	123
Chapter 7.	To War, December 1941	135
Chapter 8.	Carrier Raids, January–March 1942	149
Chapter 9.	Action in the Coral Sea, May 1942	175
Chapter 10.	Midway, June 1942	203
Chapter 11.	The *Enterprise* Task Force, June–October 1942	229
Chapter 12.	The Aleutians, 1943	295
Chapter 13.	Commander Seventh Fleet, November 1943–October 1944	343
Chapter 14.	Commander Seventh Fleet, October 1944–November 1945	389
Chapter 15.	The Postwar Years, 1946–1950	449
Chapter 16.	Retirement, 1950–1972	471
Epilogue		489
Abbreviations		493

	Page
Bibliography	495
Index	515

Organization Charts

1. Destroyer Squadron 8	128
2. Task Force 17, Coral Sea Operation, 3–8 May 1942	180
3. Task Forces 16 and 17, Midway Operations, 4 June 1942	208
4. WATCHTOWER Command, July 1942	238
5. Task Force 61, October 1942	270
6. Task Force 16, November 1942	289

Maps

1. The South and Southwest Pacific, 1942	150
2. Early 1942 Carrier Raids	162
3. Battle of Coral Sea, 4–8 May 1942	183
4. Battle of Midway, 4 June 1942	214
5. Solomon Islands, 1942	232
6. Battle of the Eastern Solomons, 23–25 August 1942	254
7. Battle of the Santa Cruz Islands, 26 October 1942	272
8. Alaska and the Aleutian Islands, 1942–1944	298
9. Seventh Fleet New Guinea Operations, 1944	352
10. Battle for Leyte Gulf, 23–25 October 1944	393

Illustrations

Vice Admiral Kinkaid, Commander Seventh Fleet, 1945	ii
Thomas Wright Kinkaid and Virginia Lee Kinkaid	2
Thomas Cassin Kinkaid and his sisters Helen and Dorothy, 1892	3
Nevada (BM 8), early 1900s	6

	Page
Hartford under sail, c.1905	7
Nebraska (BB 14), junior officers' wardroom	10
Minnesota (BB 22)	15
Midshipman Kinkaid and Helen Ross	17
Pennsylvania (BB 38)	22
Scorpion (PY 3) off Constantinople	33
Isherwood (DD 284)	40
Crew of *Texas* (BB 35) mans the rail	51
General Board, 1932	67
Captain Benyaurd B. Wygant, commanding officer of *Colorado*	70
Commander Kinkaid, executive officer of *Colorado*	74
Colorado (BB 45) transits the Panama Canal	83
Indianapolis (CA 35)	100
Naval Attaché Kinkaid and his assistants	106
Admiral Husband E. Kimmel	137
Vice Admiral William S. Pye	142
Staff of Cruiser Division 6	157
Lieutenant Colonel James H. Doolittle and Captain Marc A. Mitscher	181
Lexington (CV 2) burning after the Battle of the Coral Sea	197
Yorktown (CV 5) being abandoned after the Battle of Midway	218
Rear Admiral Kinkaid on board *Minneapolis* (CA 36)	224
Kinkaid, Lieutenant Commander H. D. Moulton, and Lieutenant Commander R. H. Taylor	235
Kinkaid stands ready at the flag bag of *Enterprise*	240
Rear Admiral Richmond Kelly Turner and Major General Alexander A. Vandegrift, USMC	243
Long Island (AVG 1)	251
Vice Admiral Robert L. Ghormley and Admiral Chester W. Nimitz	267
Hornet (CV 8) under attack, Battle of the Santa Cruz Islands	277
Bomb explodes close aboard *Enterprise*, Battle of the Santa Cruz Islands	279
Kinkaid at Kodiak, Alaska	310
Joint staff, Adak, Alaska	311
Joint staff plans for invasion of Kiska	329
Vice Admiral Frank Jack Fletcher relieves Kinkaid	341
Vice Admiral Kinkaid and General Douglas MacArthur	356
Staff officers attend Pacific Strategy Conference, Pearl Harbor	359
Lieutenant David F. Freeman with New Guinea natives	369
Kinkaid with Seventh Fleet staff, Leyte-Philippine operation	380
Vice Admiral Theodore S. Wilkinson, Vice Admiral Kinkaid, and Rear Admiral Daniel E. Barbey	385

	Page
Rear Admiral Jesse B. Oldendorf, Vice Admiral Kinkaid, Rear Admiral T. E. Chandler, Rear Admiral Russell S. Berkey, and Commodore V. H. Schaeffer	396
Kinkaid watches landing operations in Lingayen Gulf	421
Liberated Navy nurses in Manila	427
Vice Admiral James L. Kauffman and Admiral Kinkaid	428
Accepting the surrender of Japanese forces in Seoul, Korea	432
Kinkaid visits with Generalissimo and Madame Chiang Kai-shek	440
Oil painting of Admiral Kinkaid by Albert Murray	465
Kinkaid receives a seventeen-gun salute	468
Retirement parade, 28 April 1950	469
Tom and Helen Kinkaid, early 1960s	472
President Eisenhower with National Security Training Commission	474
Admiral Kinkaid interviews Marine Corps recruits	476
The Kinkaids picnic with friends	479
Ceremony at WWII cemetery and memorial, Manila	481
Reunion of Southwest Pacific Area commanders, 26 January 1961	484
Kinkaid and MacArthur at the 1961 reunion	486
Christening of *Kinkaid* (DD 965)	487

Foreword

In 1976, Vice Admiral Edwin B. Hooper, then Director of Naval History, invited Gerald E. Wheeler to write this account of Admiral Thomas C. Kinkaid. The Historical Center had published Gerry Wheeler's biography of William Veazie Pratt in 1974 and we knew that study was an exceptionally able contribution to modern naval history. This biography of Thomas Kinkaid is equally distinguished. It is meticulously researched and extremely well written. In his most recent volume Professor Wheeler also demonstrates once again his deep understanding of the Navy as a professional and social institution. By judiciously weaving background information on the Navy into his narrative, Professor Wheeler allows the modern reader to comprehend the significance of Admiral Kinkaid's career.

As Professor Wheeler earned the trust and confidence of the admiral's widow, Helen S. Kinkaid, and other family members, they were more than generous in sharing their reminiscences of the admiral. Of equal importance, Mrs. Kinkaid also allowed full access to her husband's papers, which she kindly donated to the Center's archives. Eventually this collection included hundreds of personal letters that Admiral Kinkaid wrote to his wife throughout World War II.

Over the years that followed, despite long periods of poor health, Professor Wheeler undertook the often tedious work demanded by a major biographical project. He became thoroughly versed in the ancillary sources of information on Kinkaid. In 1988 the author published, in a book edited by William M. Leary of the University of Georgia, an extended essay that presented a preliminary assessment of the admiral's career. In the meantime, the author was writing and rewriting the basic biography. Eventually, in 1992, Professor Wheeler submitted the final manuscript to the Naval Historical Center. Following reviews of this work by two other notable naval biographers, Professors E. B. Potter and Clark G. Reynolds, the Center was more than happy to begin the publication process under the able guidance of editors Sandra J. Doyle and Wendy E. Karppi.

We are very grateful to Professor Wheeler for this major study of one of the key naval leaders of World War II. Although the Navy has seen fundamental changes since 1945, there are principles of military leadership, both in war and in peace, that are timeless. Of particular interest to today's readership will be Admiral Kinkaid's ability to work in harmony with his peers in the other armed services—jointness was an essential element of his personal success as well as a keystone of the American victory in the Pacific war. I hope that naval professionals and other readers interested in military affairs will benefit from learning more about the important role played by Thomas Cassin Kinkaid in shaping the modern American Navy.

William S. Dudley
Director of Naval History

Preface

This biography of Admiral Thomas Cassin Kinkaid (1888–1972) had its genesis in the mind of the late Vice Admiral Edwin B. Hooper, Director of Naval History from 1970 to 1976. As a middle grade officer, Hooper had served under Admiral Kinkaid during World War II and considered him an exceptional leader. Given Kinkaid's outstanding record as a flag officer throughout the almost four years of war in the Pacific, the admiral seemed worthy of a biography. His four Distinguished Service Medals, all won for leadership under combat conditions, clearly identified him as an exceptional commander. Though he shared the honors with Admiral William F. Halsey, Kinkaid's leadership throughout the Battle for Leyte Gulf was enough to earn him a prominent place among the Navy's wartime heroes. He is remembered in the fleet by the USS *Kinkaid* (DD 965). This 5,770-ton destroyer is a fitting reminder that its namesake was a fighting admiral.

In writing Admiral Kinkaid's biography, I have returned to an approach used in my 1974 biography of Admiral William Veazie Pratt (1869–1957). While not wanting to write a "life and times" study, it seemed important that close attention be given to Kinkaid's Navy as a professional organization and social institution. It is difficult for the civilian reader, or even those on active duty in the Navy today, to imagine how a naval officer of the nineteen twenties, thirties, or forties spent his days. Competitive gunnery training activities in the fleet, like long-range battle practice or division and force maneuvers and firing for record, which involved dozens of battleships, cruisers, and destroyers, controlled the calendar of daily and monthly routine in the fleet. But these exercises and the carefully orchestrated annual U.S. Fleet concentrations in the Gulf, Caribbean, or Hawaiian waters have long passed into history. As Tom Kinkaid rose through the ranks, these naval routines prepared him for the responsibilities of battle command. By coincidence, he arrived at flag rank at the same time that war came to the Navy.

When I began research for the biography in 1976, the Naval Historical Center held a trove of materials relevant to Kinkaid's life. The admiral had left his considerable personal papers to the center. Helen S. Kinkaid, the admiral's widow, added to the collection more than five hundred letters written to her by the admiral during the war years. Although not as insightful as personal correspondence might have been, these letters do provide a look into the daily work of a wartime flag officer. With the availability of the Kinkaid papers and official personnel records, as well as the enormous quantity of operations records preserved at the center and the National Archives, writing a biography of the admiral became feasible.

Although Admiral Kinkaid died in November 1972, he was survived by a large number of officers who had served with him during his forty-six years of naval service. Through letters and interviews thirty-six of them willingly assisted me in my work. Most of these generous officers have passed on, but their contributions are evident in this biography. Four of them wrote three or more times and several provided photographs for my use. Vice Admiral George C. Dyer shared with me his memories of Kinkaid's tour in command of *Indianapolis*; Captain Isaiah Olch described in detail Kinkaid's service as Commander Destroyer Squadron 8; Rear Admiral J. Wilson Leverton filled in many lacunae from the admiral's year in Alaska as Commander North Pacific Force; and Rear Admiral Valentine H. Schaeffer, Kinkaid's chief of staff at Leyte Gulf and after, wrote extensively about those exciting days in the Seventh Fleet. In addition, Rear Admiral Edwin T. Layton deserves special mention. He offered much valuable information on the flag commanders who served under Admiral Chester W. Nimitz. As Pacific Fleet Intelligence Officer throughout the war, Layton was a member of Nimitz's staff. He not only shared with me his observations about Admiral Kinkaid and others but also translated several accounts from Japanese naval histories dealing with the Pacific War. It is unfortunate that I can no longer thank these naval officers in person, but I do hope their families find this volume good reading.

After sixteen years of research and writing there are many others outside the circle of those who served with Admiral Kinkaid whom I wish to acknowledge for their assistance and encouragement. During 1976 and 1977 Mrs. Kinkaid welcomed me to her home in Washington, D.C., and through interviews provided a wealth of information on the admiral's career and family. The admiral's niece, Mrs. Mary Tyler Urquhart, also of Washington, provided insights into Kinkaid's relationships with his sisters (Mrs. Helen Heiner and Mrs. Dorothy Kimmel of Annapolis, Maryland) as did the admiral's nephew, Captain Thomas Kinkaid Kimmel, of Annapolis. At the Naval Historical Center, Directors Vice Admiral Hooper, Rear Admiral John D. H. Kane, Dr. Ronald Spector, and Dr. Dean C. Allard not only started me on this project but provided many years of encouragement and logistic support to see the work to its completion. Among the center's staff, past and present, Gerri Judkins, Nina Statum, Bernard Cavalcante, and Edward Marolda have met every request for assistance whether archival or editorial. Sandra J. Doyle and Wendy Karppi, the center's editors, with great patience created an orderly system of documentation and prodded the author gently to keep the manuscript on schedule. Among my professional colleagues and friends, Dr. Paola Coletta, Dr. Charles Burdick, Dr. Raymond O'Connor, Dr. Clark Reynolds, and Professor Roger Heller have been generous in sharing over the past two decades their expertise in the modern American Navy. The maps in this book were drafted by Todd Anderson and Diane Dunlap, assistants to Duilio Peruzzi and Dr. Richard Taketa of San Jose State University. For their many hours of assistance with typing, wordprocessing, and teaching me to use a computer, I have a debt of gratitude to Linda Garcia, Leslie Brand, and Emi Nobuhiro of San Jose State University. Finally I must acknowledge that this book would never have been completed without the research assistance, company, patience through several illnesses, and continuing support and encouragement of my wife, Jean French Wheeler.

Gerald E. Wheeler
San Jose State University

Chapter 1

Growing Up in Battleships, 1888–1919

When young Thomas Cassin Kinkaid of the District of Columbia raised his right hand on 7 July 1904 and swore to defend the Constitution of the United States, he did so in familiar surroundings. It was natural for this lad from the nation's capital to be at Annapolis, the common name for the United States Naval Academy. He was a Navy brat, and had even spent two years living in the Academy yard. By the time he entered high school, he had decided to become a career naval officer, a regular. He knew that the gangway to such a career was the Naval Academy.

Tom's mother had been born Virginia Lee Cassin. At the time of her marriage in 1883 to Tom's father, her father, William Deakins Cassin, was a prominent lawyer and member of the law firm of Cassin, Tree and Merritt in the Georgetown section of the District of Columbia. Her grandfather, James Luke Cassin, had emigrated from Ireland in 1802 and eventually owned a meat packing business in Georgetown, and in 1810 married Tabitha Marbury Deakins. A daughter of Leonard Deakins and Ruth Orme, Tabitha could trace her family's line to the earliest years in Maryland history. Virginia's mother, Mary Amelia (Mittie) Tyler was the daughter of Grafton Tyler, Jr., a well-known Georgetown physician, and Mary M. Bowie, the daughter of Walter Bowie, a prominent planter of Prince Georges County, Maryland. Like the Deakins family, the Tylers went back to the founding days of Maryland.[1]

Perhaps because of Virginia's strong personality the Kinkaids tended to identify with Georgetown and not Ohio, where Tom's father's family hailed from. Thomas Wright Kinkaid was born in Cincinnati, Ohio, on 27 February 1860. His father, William P. Kinkaid (1823–1914), was a New Yorker who had eventually moved west to the Queen City by way of Pennsylvania. At various times he worked as a carpenter, clerk, and traveling salesman. William's father had emigrated from Scotland around the turn of the century. Once settled in Ohio, William and his wife,

---

[1] Mary Margaret Cassin, "Genealogy of the Deakins, Cassin, Tyler and Kinkaid Families," undated manuscript in possession of Mary Tyler (Mrs. John) Urquhart of Washington, DC.

Courtesy J. Urquhart

Thomas Wright Kinkaid and Virginia Lee Kinkaid, parents of Thomas Cassin Kinkaid.

Susan Monahan Kinkaid, raised three children. The oldest, Thomas Wright Kinkaid, graduated in June 1880 as a cadet engineer from the Naval Academy,[2] and three years later married Virginia. Their first child, Helen, was born the following January.

With personnel requirements at a low, the Navy Department granted Thomas Wright Kinkaid a leave from duty so he could accept employment at the New Hampshire College of Agricultural and Mechanical Arts in Hanover. His son, Thomas Cassin Kinkaid, was born there on 3 April 1888. Fifty-six years later, when this son's name made the national news, many newspapers carried admiring stories about this "son of New England" fulfilling his nautical destiny. Little did they realize that he spoke with the soft accent of the northern Virginian and Marylander.[3]

---

[2] Lewis Randolph Hamersly, *The Records of Living Officers of the U.S. Navy and Marine Corps*, 7th ed. (New York: L. R. Hamersly, 1902), 288; "Candidates for Admission into the U.S. Naval Academy as Cadet Engineers," Record Group (RG) 405: vol. 62, National Archives (NA).

[3] Thomas W. Kinkaid's duty assignments can be traced through the annual *Register of the Commissioned and Warrant Officers of the Navy of the United States and of the Marine Corps, 1880–1920* (Washington: GPO, 1880–1920). See also article on VADM T. C. Kinkaid after the Battle for Leyte Gulf, *Boston Globe*, 29 Oct 1944.

Growing Up in Battleships 3

Author's collection

Thomas Cassin Kinkaid and his sisters, Helen and Dorothy, Washington, D.C., 1892.

Within a year of Tom's birth, Assistant Engineer Kinkaid received orders to the Mare Island Navy Yard where he was to join the gunboat *Pinta* as engineer. Based in Sitka, Alaska, *Pinta*'s mission was to help keep the peace between the settlers and Indians and to protect American vessels working the fisheries. With duty generally lasting for three or more years, officers brought their families to Sitka, and this was where the Kinkaids' third child, Dorothy, was born 31 July 1890. The Kinkaids had a Russian woman, Martha, to help in the house and thus the Kinkaid children were introduced to the Russian language and culture.[4]

After years of service that took the family to the navy yards in Philadelphia and Norfolk, the Naval Academy, and back to Georgetown when Lieutenant Kinkaid[5] was at sea, Virginia and the children settled in at the Stoddert Apartments in Georgetown in 1901. Lieutenant Kinkaid

---

[4] ADM Thomas C. Kinkaid to RADM Frank D. Wagner, New York, 1 Jul 1949. Thomas C. Kinkaid Papers, Operational Archives (OA), Naval Historical Center (NHC) (hereafter TCK Papers).

[5] In 1899 the Navy's engineering officers were integrated into the line and in most cases assigned the ranks of their classmates. Assistant Engineer Kinkaid became a lieutenant. Ralph Earle, *Life at the U.S. Naval Academy: The Making of the American Naval Officer* (New York: G. P. Putnam's Sons, 1917), 23–41.

had been assigned to the battleship *Oregon* (BB 3), where he would serve as engineering officer of the Asiatic Fleet. Tom Kinkaid attended Western High School for three and a half years before entering a Naval Academy preparatory school. Because he lived in the District of Columbia, Tom sought an at-large appointment to Annapolis from President Theodore Roosevelt. Placed on the alternate list, he was required by the President to compete by examination for the appointment. Successful, he was awarded a presidential appointment and asked to report for admission examinations.[6]

The Navy and the Naval Academy were institutions in transition when Tom Kinkaid became a midshipman in July 1904. After U.S. victory in the Spanish-American War and acquisition of colonies in the Caribbean and the Pacific, President Roosevelt believed it imperative for the nation to possess a navy capable of representing and defending its newly won status. A large start in naval construction had been made during President William McKinley's first administration, and Roosevelt pressed for continued construction, particularly in the number of heavy ships. By the close of Roosevelt's second administration in March 1909, the U.S. Navy was second only to Great Britain's in size.

To increase the number of naval officers, Congress in 1902 had authorized a ten-year increase in the number of midshipmen at the Naval Academy.[7] Each member of the Senate and House of Representatives could now sponsor two midshipmen, not one, at the Academy at any time. The number of new midshipmen admitted to the fourth class in 1903 was double the number admitted two years earlier. With 283 of the 350 who took the examination admitted in the summer of 1904, Kinkaid's class of 1908 was the largest since the opening of the Academy in 1845.[8] At 16 years of age, Tom was among the youngest.

Until academic majors were introduced into the curriculum in the 1960s, the course of instruction at the Naval Academy was almost the same for every midshipman. Only in foreign languages was there a choice to be made; for Kinkaid it was French. Classes were small, memorization and recitation were the instructional methods, and "drawing slips" and "manning the boards" were common ways of demonstrating mastery of the day's lesson. Instructors would write questions on slips of paper and lay them out on the classroom table, or leave them protrud-

---

[6] Thomas C. Kinkaid File, U.S. Naval Academy Archives, Annapolis; Admiral Thomas C. Kinkaid, "Oral History," manuscript first draft, 1961, based on interviews by John T. Mason for the Columbia University Oral History Project (hereafter TCK oral history), 5–6.

[7] VADM George Carroll Dyer, *The Amphibians Came to Conquer: The Story of Admiral Richmond Kelly Turner*, 2 vols. (Washington: GPO, 1971), 1:9–11 (hereafter Dyer, *Turner*); Jack Sweetman, *The U.S. Naval Academy: An Illustrated History* (Annapolis: Naval Institute Press, 1979), 141–43.

[8] U.S. Naval Academy (USNA) Alumni Association, *Register of Alumni, 1845–1987* (Annapolis, 1987), 134–59.

ing from closed textbooks, and invite the class to take a slip and write the answer on the blackboard. The instructor would then inspect each mid's work and assign a grade for the day.

Except for English, history, and mathematics, almost all instruction was given by officers serving a two- or three-year tour of duty at the Academy. The officers were usually those recognized as potential leaders of the department and fleet. As a midshipman, Kinkaid was taught by four future Chiefs of Naval Operations (William S. Benson, William V. Pratt, William D. Leahy and Ernest J. King) and four future Commanders in Chief, U.S. Fleet (Henry A. Wiley, Pratt, Arthur J. Hepburn, and King).[9]

The Naval Academy education was unique, narrow in its focus but suited to the Navy's needs at that time. Eleven years after retiring, and fifty-three years after leaving the Academy, Admiral Kinkaid summed up what he thought was important about his Academy education:

> I'm quite sure that I didn't learn much from a book at the Naval Academy. I was quite lucky to get through, because I got in at the age of 16. I was underdeveloped, I didn't know how to study, and I think I learned more in the next four years after I graduated than I learned in the four years down there. But I think it does help build character and undoubtedly teaches you to take orders, to do things whether you like them or not. . . . That is the main reason for having a service school.[10]

Kinkaid's three summer training cruises were spent in ships assigned to the Coastal Squadron. Unfortunately for him, all of them steamed in Chesapeake Bay, visiting the Norfolk area, and then traveling out into the Atlantic and north to Long Island Sound, Narragansett Bay, and the coast of Maine.

During his third-class (youngster) cruise in the summer of 1905 Kinkaid sailed in *Nevada* (BM 8), a coastal defense monitor commissioned in 1903.[11] In such a ship Kinkaid could learn a good deal about modern naval machinery and ordnance. He also could observe the way the Navy's officers managed the enlisted men, for Tom and his classmates would perform many of the duties of the enlisted men, including the filthy ship-coaling chores. But they would also be treated differently in address, berthing, and messing. For three more years, until becoming a passed midshipman, he would be almost "an officer and a gentleman."

---

[9] Dyer, *Turner* 1:28–29.

[10] TCK oral history, 6–7.

[11] U.S. Navy, "Nevada," *Dictionary of American Naval Fighting Ships*, 8 vols. (Washington: Naval History Division, 1970), 5:51 (hereafter *DANFS*); also LT Richard H. Webber, ed., *Monitors of the U.S. Navy, 1861–1937* (Washington: Naval History Division, 1969), 42–44.

Nevada (BM 8) from an early 1900s publication.

Nevada and the Coastal Squadron engaged in joint exercises with the Army in the Chesapeake Bay[12] and also visited Norfolk, Virginia; Rockland, Maine; and Gardiners Bay at the end of Long Island. The pace was leisurely, and there was plenty of shore leave and weekend parties for the midshipmen. At the last port, Kinkaid and his ten classmates in *Nevada* transferred to *Hartford*, Admiral David G. Farragut's flagship at the Battle of Mobile Bay during the Civil War and still an active vessel in the Coastal Squadron.[13] The six weeks spent in the old "screw sloop of war" were a unique experience for Kinkaid; never again would he serve in a man-of-war under sail. Calls to "lay aloft," "send down the royal yards," or "take a reef in the main royal" were seldom heard on ships in 1905.

As *Hartford* moved in and out of Gardiners Bay, Narragansett Bay, New London, and back to the Maine coast, the weekend parties for the midshipmen continued. So did instruction in navigation, shiphandling, signaling, gunnery, and marlinspike seamanship. Years later, overlooking some periods of seasickness, Kinkaid recalled this cruise with pleasure:

---

[12] Log of USS *Nevada* (BM 8), 11–13 Jun 1905, RG 24, NA.
[13] Ibid., 21 Jun–15 Jul 1905.

Hartford under sail, circa 1905.

I was a long-legged skinny midshipman. There were four of us on the main royal; two in my class and two in the class ahead (1907), and two of them were a little bit shy about getting out on the yardarm, so the other one in the class ahead and I did the work out on the ends of the yardarm. Standing on the footrope, I had to spread my knees wide to get a grip on the yardarm. I loved it. I could swing around like a monkey. . . . But setting sail, making sail, crossing the yards, lowering the yards, was quite a job. After six weeks of that I was as hard as nails, my muscles were, from going up and down the masts. It was wonderful training for kids.[14]

Kinkaid's other two summer training cruises were dull by comparison. The 1906 cruise was served in *Newark* (C 1), a protected cruiser commissioned in 1891 and obsolescent by 1906. Kinkaid spent the summer of 1907 in *Arkansas* (BM 7), another coastal monitor.

Commander Bradley A. Fiske commanded *Arkansas* during the 1907 cruise. Possessed of one of the most inventive minds in the Navy, Fiske was constantly testing his new inventions while at sea. That summer he tried a new optical range finder while underway. It is possible that Kinkaid had an opportunity to observe Fiske's work. A few years later, while undertaking a course in ordnance at the Naval Academy's new postgraduate school, Kinkaid spent considerable time studying optics. Once in the fleet, he became a specialist in gunfire spotting in battleships.[15]

Like all midshipmen, Kinkaid participated in intramural sports, and in his last year he earned a seat in the Academy's eight-oar racing shell. He had initially turned to rowing to develop his body so he could play football, but he did not go far in that sport. It is likely that the time devoted to athletics did not improve his academic standing. At graduation he ranked 136th in a class of 201, distinctly in the lower half. His best grades in his first class year were in experimental engineering, ordnance and gunnery, and designing machinery. Ironically, given his future attainments, his worst subjects at graduation were seamanship, languages, and navigation.[16]

In January 1907 a hearing loss had been detected in Tom's right ear; in early March 1908, when his class took its demanding graduation physicals, the impairment was too great for an officer serving on active duty. Believing that the hearing loss was due to a "throat congestion" and probably temporary, the medical director of the Naval Academy recommended that Kinkaid be graduated and then examined in two years to see if his hearing loss was still disqualifying.[17]

---

[14] TCK oral history, 7.

[15] Paolo E. Coletta, *Admiral Bradley A. Fiske and the American Navy* (Lawrence, KS: Regents Press of Kansas, 1979), 81, 86–87; Bradley A. Fiske, *From Midshipman to Rear-Admiral* (New York: Century, 1919), 400–401.

[16] USNA, Records of Naval Cadets, RG 405:8, NA; *USNA Register, 1908*.

[17] Thomas C. Kinkaid File, USNA Archives, Annapolis, MD.

Before graduation on 5 June Tom received orders to report by 1 July to the new battleship *Nebraska* (BB 14). He joined the ship and the Great White Fleet (Atlantic Fleet) in San Francisco. The fleet had left Hampton Roads, Virginia, on 16 December 1907 with personal instructions from President Roosevelt to sail to San Francisco and then across the Pacific to the American East Coast by way of the Suez Canal. It was to be a glorious fifteen months of showing the flag and circumnavigating the globe.[18]

Commissioned in July 1907 after construction in Seattle, *Nebraska* was one of the newest battleships to join the Great White Fleet. Like all battleships authorized between 1890 and 1904, *Nebraska* carried a mixed main battery of four 12-inch, eight 8-inch, and twelve 6-inch rifles plus a large assortment of lighter guns in its secondary battery. Half of the 8-inch rifles were housed in turrets superimposed above the two larger turrets, and the rest were placed in two turrets, one on each side amidships. When firing broadsides, four 12-inch, six 8-inch, and six 6-inch rifles could be brought to bear on targets. Because it was difficult to differentiate the shell splashes among the various calibers in the main battery, spotting and directing the ship's gunfire were inexact at best.[19]

If one were to judge the quality of the officer complement by their later attainments, *Nebraska* in July 1908 had an outstanding group. Captain Reginald F. Nicholson, who commanded the vessel, would later be chief of the Bureau of Navigation (BUNAV) and a rear admiral. Lieutenant Commander Robert E. Coontz was the executive officer; twelve years later he would be Chief of Naval Operations (CNO) and an admiral. The navigator was Lieutenant Commander Harris Laning, who would fly the four-star flag of the battle force commander by the end of his career. Lieutenant Walter S. Anderson, who reported on board as the gunnery officer a few months after Kinkaid's arrival, would later become a vice admiral. He was one of Tom's good friends through the years. One of the watch officers, Lieutenant Dudley W. Knox, would become a commodore and serve as the first director of the Office of Naval History. Another watch officer, Ensign John Rodgers, the descendant of a long line of navy flag officers, in a few years would be the Navy's second naval aviator. Of the eight midshipmen on board, Jonas H. Ingram reached admiral; Kinkaid's classmate and

---

[18] Robley D. Evans, *An Admiral's Log* (New York: D. Appleton, 1910), 411–15; Robert E. Coontz, *From the Mississippi to the Sea* (Philadelphia: Dorrance, 1930), 278–95; Robert A. Hart, *The Great White Fleet: Its Voyage Around the World, 1907–1909* (Boston: Little, Brown, 1965), 171–73 (hereafter Hart, *GWF*); James R. Reckner, *Teddy Roosevelt's Great White Fleet* (Annapolis: Naval Institute Press, 1988), 19–24 (hereafter Reckner, *TRGWF*); J. E. Pillsbury to MIDN Thomas C. Kinkaid, Washington, 2 Jun 1908, Thomas C. Kinkaid, Early Order File, 1908–1922, TCK Papers.

[19] *DANFS* 1:189–95; "Nebraska," *DANFS* 5:35–6; Elting E. Morison, *Admiral Sims and the Modern American Navy* (Boston: Houghton Mifflin Co., 1942), 156–75; K. Jack Bauer, *Ships of the Navy, 1775–1969: Volume I, Combat Vessels* (Troy, NY: Rensselaer Polytechnic Institute, 1969), 96–97.

Author's collection

Nebraska (BB 14), junior officers' wardroom, circa 1910. Left to right: E. J. Estess, unknown, Samuel S. Payne, Cary W. Magruder, Charles C. Soule, unknown, J. A. Logan, T. C. Kinkaid. Except for Soule and Logan, all are passed midshipmen.

close friend, Cary W. (Red) Magruder, became a commodore, as did Schuyler F. Heim; and Tom Kinkaid, of course, rose to the rank of admiral. In all, they were a talented group of shipmates.

An extended round of parties, both ashore and on board, preceded the departure of the Atlantic Fleet from San Francisco. An outbreak of scarlet fever and diphtheria, however, prevented *Nebraska* from departing with the rest of the fleet. The ship anchored off Angel Island to be fumigated. Two days later, theoretically purged of its diseases, *Nebraska* weighed anchor and stood out of the Golden Gate for Honolulu.[20]

The fleet's progress in the Pacific was slow, even majestic, and filled with long port visits highlighted by parades of the ships' crews. From the Hawaiian Islands the fleet stood south for New Zealand. En route *Nebraska* crossed the equator and "Neptunus Rex with his retinue came aboard officially at 1030 and proceeded to initiate all strangers of the ship's company into the rites of the realm." The "shellbacks" enjoyed initiating Kinkaid and at least eight hundred other "pollywogs" making their first crossing.[21]

---

[20] Log of USS *Nebraska* (BB 16), 6–9 Jul 1908, RG 24, NA; *San Francisco Examiner*, 7 and 9 Jul 1908; Roman J. Miller, *Around the World with the Battleships* (Chicago: A. C. McClurg, 1909), 56–59; Hart, *GWF*, 176; Reckner, *TRGWF*, 87.

[21] Roman J. Miller, *Pictorial Log of the Battle Fleet Cruise Around the World* (Chicago: A. C. McClurg, 1909), 17 Jul 1908; Miller, *Around the World*, 64; Coontz, *From the Mississippi*, 281.

The passage to Auckland was long and hot. The fleet's visit to the Antipodes was filled with parades, receptions, dinners, teas, and dances. There was also time for sports competitions, both between the ships and with New Zealand and Australian teams. Though there was the expected rowdiness and drunkenness by a few, the American bluejackets and their officers left a strong and positive impression on the Australians and New Zealanders.[22] While in Melbourne, Kinkaid experienced an important professional rite of passage. On the first day of September Kinkaid stood his first officer-of-the-day (OOD) watch and signed the ship's log book. *Nebraska* was at anchor in the harbor and nothing of significance occurred, but a career milestone had been passed.[23]

On 5 September Admiral Charles S. Sperry in *Connecticut* (BB 18) led the Great White Fleet out of Melbourne's harbor for the 1,400-mile passage across the Great Australian Bight to Albany at the southwest tip of the Australian continent. Arriving on 11 September, the ships spent a week awaiting the arrival of colliers and then coaling. Finally the fleet sortied from Princess Royal Harbor on 18 September and commenced the 3,500-mile, two-week voyage north to Manila. It would be thirty-five years before Tom Kinkaid returned to Australia; then he would find the people there even more ready to grasp the hand of American friendship extended to them.[24]

Anchored off Cavite on 2 October, the fleet received bad news: There would be no liberty in Manila. A cholera epidemic in Luzon made it too risky to send the crews ashore. Disappointment among the bluejackets was matched by that among the businessmen in Manila. There was a lot of money in the fleet and the Filipinos had been eager to provide hospitality and whatever goods and services the fleet desired. Instead, the ships spent eight days coaling at Cavite and engaging in gunnery exercises preliminary to firing for record. It was all hot and boring, but everyone now looked forward to the coming cruise to Japan.[25]

A typhoon dogged the fleet's progress north. At times wallowing in the stormy seaway "like a herd of swine," the battleships arrived in Tokyo Bay and Yokohama's harbor on 18 October. All of the ships had been badly battered, most had lost boats, and a few, tragically, had crewmen washed overboard, but the fleet arrived just one day behind schedule.[26]

---

[22] *Nebraska* log, 9–15 Aug 1908 (Auckland), 20–27 Aug (Sydney), 29 Aug–5 Sep (Melbourne); Hart, *GWF*, 186–201; Miller, *Pictorial Log*, 9 Aug–3 Sep 1908; Reckner, *TRGWF*, 93–102.
[23] *Nebraska* log, Sep 1908.
[24] Ibid., 5–18 Sep 1908.
[25] *Nebraska* log, 2–10 Oct 1908; Hart, *GWF*, 201–02; Reckner, *TRGWF*, 111–12; Coontz, *From the Mississippi*, 286–87.
[26] Quoted in Reckner, *TRGWF*, 112, 113; TCK oral history, 2–5.

A few officers had believed they would find a hostile Japanese fleet with guns trained outward, but they were delighted to find a column of battleships at anchor and ready to assume the role of friendly host on a ship-for-ship basis. After a week of receiving and returning entertainment, the fleet departed on 25 October to the thunder of a fifteen-gun salute from *Connecticut* and its return.[27]

The First Squadron, which included *Nebraska*, steamed to the Philippines while the Second Squadron headed for Amoy, China. The First Squadron anchored in Subic Bay six days later and spent a day calibrating the 12-inch, 8-inch, and 6-inch guns of its ships by firing from fixed locations at targets ashore. On 31 October *Nebraska* moved to Manila Bay for the annual competitive gunnery activities. The battleship did a first-class job and became a "star ship," the equivalent of an "E ship" at a later day. Despite the pressing need to finish the gunnery exercises and Admiral Sperry's doubts that the cholera outbreak had been controlled, the crews were granted time ashore. Much of their money had been spent in Japan, but there was still enough left to bring smiles along Manila's Escolta and in Intramuros.[28]

By the first of December everyone was anxious to start the last legs of the voyage. "Homeward bound" pennants streamed from the mainmasts of each ship and the pace began to quicken. The route to Colombo, Ceylon (now Sri Lanka), took the fleet through the straits of Singapore and Malacca. Passing close to Singapore's shore, Kinkaid noticed an old man and woman in a rowboat. As each ship passed, the man stood and yelled, "Give my regards to Broadway." The crews generally gave a cheer in return.[29]

The fleet departed Colombo on 20 December, crossed the Arabian Sea, and passed through the Red Sea to Suez. For Tom and *Nebraska*'s crew Christmas day was unique. Under a tropical sun gunnery prize money was awarded, and the crew participated in boxing, wrestling, and other sports. During the last three days of 1908, in a series of signaling contests, *Nebraska* was declared fleet champion.[30] In Suez, while others went sight-seeing, Tom spent many days sitting on summary court-martial panels trying cases of crew members who were absent over leave in Colombo.

Once the Suez Canal was transited on 7 January, the fleet separated into many units to visit a number of Mediterranean ports. The Second Division, including *Nebraska*, drew Marseilles and spent twelve days there. Tom and two of his classmates managed a day's leave but lacked time to visit the Cote d'Azure and the more interesting watering places of the rich. On the 27th *Nebraska* and *Georgia* got underway for Tangier,

---
[27] Coontz, *From the Mississippi*, 287; *Nebraska* log, 18–25 Oct 1908.
[28] *Nebraska* log, 25 Oct–1 Dec 1908; Coontz, *From the Mississippi*, 287–89; Hart, *GWF*, 258–60; Reckner, *TRGWF*, 138–39.
[29] *Nebraska* log, 1–20 Dec 1908; TCK oral history, 2–5; Coontz, *From the Mississippi*, 290.
[30] Coontz, *From the Mississippi*, 292; *Nebraska* log, 20 Dec 1908–1 Jan 1909.

Morocco; then Tom's ship rendezvoused in Gibraltar with the rest of the Great White Fleet. After a last week of entertainment ashore and afloat and the inevitable coaling, Admiral Sperry on 6 February set the fleet course for the Chesapeake Capes. The rough winter passage across the Atlantic shredded a few "homeward bound" pennants, cast a few boats adrift, and again washed men overboard. But it is doubtful that *Nebraska*'s crew even noticed the tossing. Home was just two weeks away.[31]

The Great White Fleet's return to Chesapeake Bay celebrated both the end of the great cruise and Washington's Birthday. On board the yacht *Mayflower* (PY 1), President Roosevelt greeted the vessels and received the traditional 21-gun salutes from each squadron flagship as he returned the ceremonial visits. These activities opened a three-week visit by *Nebraska* before departing for the New York Navy Yard in Brooklyn. Kinkaid took the opportunity to obtain leave and spent it with his parents in the Norfolk area. At leave's end on 10 March, Tom returned to the battleship, now at the Navy Yard, Tompkinsville, New York. A couple of days later *Nebraska* moved to the New York Navy Yard where it remained until mid-July.[32]

Kinkaid now learned about the tedium of spending months in drydock, at a pier, or simply anchored in a navy yard. An athletics-minded ship, *Nebraska* had regularly competed whenever possible in baseball, football, cutter rowing, boxing and wrestling, track events, and the usual professional competitions involving signaling and communications. These activities had gone on while the ship was working up in the Seattle area, and during the great cruise competitions were regularly held ashore wherever the fleet anchored. Baseball games were sought and played during the spring of 1909, but it became more difficult to keep the competitive spirit going. New York City, with all of its famous and infamous attractions, was too handy. The ship's log book began to reflect the problem as men were awarded punishments at captain's mast for disorderly conduct ashore, drunkenness, absence over liberty, absence over leave, and desertion. Although ship upkeep and overhaul were absolutely necessary, and time ashore with families was likewise needed to keep married officers and enlisted men content, it is clear that maintenance of crew discipline suffered during extended periods in a navy yard.

Relief came in mid-July when *Nebraska* finally joined the Atlantic Fleet for maneuvers in New England waters. Because the battleships carried four 21-inch torpedo tubes, drill and then firing for score took place in Cape Cod Bay. The vessels also unlimbered their 6-, 8-, and 12-inch batteries, calibrated them using marker buoys and targets ashore, and then

---

[31] *Nebraska* log, 6 Jan–22 Feb 1909; Coontz, *From the Mississippi*, 293–94.
[32] *Nebraska* log, 22 Feb–12 Mar 1909.

fired for score.³³ Kinkaid was a battery officer for the aft 6-inch guns and a year later he was specially commended for the scores made by his six gun crews. His scores were "the highest final score of this type of guns in the Navy." ³⁴ This type of positive reinforcement confirmed young Kinkaid's desire to become an ordnance specialist when he had the opportunity for advanced training.

The fleet then sailed for Hampton Roads in the Norfolk area for further maneuvers and gunnery exercises on the Southern Drill Grounds, a sea area southeast of the Chesapeake Capes. *Nebraska* spent August and September in such operations, returning north for October and November at the New York Navy Yard. December operations on the drill grounds were cut short by a collision between *Nebraska* and *Georgia* while executing a turn by divisions. The hearings that followed and the inevitable paperwork that plagued everyone involved taught Tom a serious lesson: Avoid collisions when in a position of responsibility. *Nebraska* returned to Brooklyn for repairs.³⁵

Christmas in New York for Midshipman Kinkaid meant two watches and Christmas dinner on board. It was a quiet Noel. *Nebraska* then spent the winter and spring of 1910 with the Atlantic Fleet at maneuvers and exercises in the Caribbean and the Southern Drill Grounds. While anchored at the Guantanamo naval base, Tom received orders to report ashore for the ensign's examinations on 7 March. He passed everything except navigation. He would be reexamined in December; if he passed, he would keep his standing in the class of 1908.³⁶ Kinkaid's classmates would be advanced to ensign as of 6 June, but he would remain a passed midshipman. Until reexamined in December and notified of the results in January or February, Tom might be taking orders from a classmate; he had spent too much of his time as a gunnery officer and had not paid enough attention to the navigation of *Nebraska*.³⁷

In July Kinkaid developed pleurisy. After a few weeks in the New York Naval Hospital, he was authorized to recuperate at the Naval Academy hospital. His father, now a commander, was in charge of the Navy Engineering Experiment Station across the Severn River from the Naval Academy. Tom stayed with his parents while receiving treatment. His

---

³³ Ibid., 17 Jul–4 Aug 1909.
³⁴ RADM R. F. Nicholson to TCK, Washington, 14 Jun 1909, Early Order File, TCK Papers.
³⁵ Elting E. Morison, *Sims*, 266–67; *Nebraska* log, 4 Aug–31 Dec 1909.
³⁶ S. L. Key to TCK, Guantanamo, Cuba, 1 Mar 1910; H. B. Wilson to TCK, Washington, 2 Jun 1910, Early Order File, TCK Papers.
³⁷ Thomas Cassin Kinkaid, Personnel Files, Fitness Reports section (microfilm), OA (hereafter TCK Personnel File).

NHC

Minnesota (BB 22) underway, circa 1911. As flagship of the Fourth Division, she is wearing the flag of Rear Admiral G. B. Murdoch.

convalescence had one benefit: He had the time to study his navigation intensively in preparation for the reexamination.[38]

Discharged from the hospital, Kinkaid received orders on 1 October to report to *Minnesota* (BB 22). On 6 October 1910 he crossed the quarterdeck of the new battleship and reported to Commander William S. Sims. Commissioned three years earlier, *Minnesota* was a larger battleship than *Nebraska* and more powerfully armed. It carried a single twin-gun turret fore and aft with 12-inch rifles; four twin-gun mounts, two on each broadside, with 8-inch rifles; and six casemated 7-inch guns on each broadside.[39] Kinkaid could not have found a more congenial ship to join. He was interested in gunnery and his new skipper, a classmate of his father's, was one of the Navy's best-known gunnery experts. Tom took the navigation reexamination on 7 December. He passed and was advanced to ensign on 14 February 1911 with a date of rank with his classmates of 6 June 1910.

In April 1911 Captain George R. Clark relieved Sims and the junior officers soon rotated to new assignments. For Tom this meant a move from the engineering department to gunnery. Here he would work as an 8-inch battery officer and a gunfire spotter, and he would take his turn on

---

[38] R. F. Nicholson to TCK, Washington, 24 Aug 1910, Early Order File, TCK Papers; Ibid., 15 Sep 1910; Helen S. Kinkaid, interview with author, Washington, DC, 7 Jan 1976 (hereafter Helen Kinkaid interview).

[39] "Minnesota," *DANFS* 4:374–5; Bauer, *Ships* 1:97.

the OOD watch list. On 3 September, while at sea from Philadelphia to the Southern Drill Grounds, Kinkaid stood his first "top watch" as OOD underway, an important rite of passage for a seagoing naval officer.[40]

The second most important rite of passage occurred on 24 April 1911, when Tom married Helen Sherburne Ross of Philadelphia. Not quite twenty at the time of their marriage, Helen Ross had been visiting or dating Tom Kinkaid since his youngster (second) year at the Academy. Her father, a well-to-do Philadelphia businessman, had brought his yacht to Annapolis each spring, and in 1906 Helen began attending midshipmen hops, or dances. A tall and athletic girl, she apparently caught young Kinkaid's eye at a dance, and, to her embarrassment, he insisted she dance with him. (For Tom, dancing came easily since his mother and father enjoyed music and dancing.) In 1907 Helen not only came down to the spring hops, she and other young ladies also did some visiting in Maine and the Newport area when the midshipmen cruise vessels were there. The relationship was maintained by mail during the long cruise of the Great White Fleet and was given new life during *Nebraska*'s lengthy periods in the New York Navy Yard. Tom's 1910 transfer to *Minnesota*, homeported in Philadelphia, meant that visiting became more frequent. The two had a trial run for their own marriage on 18 April when they participated as bridesmaid and groomsman in the elaborate Philadelphia wedding of Ensign Philip Houston Hammond and Miss Margaret Evans. A week later, on 24 April, Tom and Helen were married in the Silver Chapel of St. Mark's Episcopal Church in Philadelphia. Tom's classmate, Red Magruder, served as best man and Frances Ross, a cousin of Helen's, was maid of honor. The Philadelphia wedding was small, probably twenty-five at the most, and was followed by a brief honeymoon in New York City.[41]

Kinkaid's duty in *Minnesota* was not too different from his service in *Nebraska*. As an ensign he served as an assistant division officer. He received good marks for handling men and appeared to have a talent for instructing them. In *Minnesota* Captain Clark also noted that Kinkaid had "special aptitude as a ship's spotter; is very proficient in this line of work. He is also proficient in fire control (night) of a torpedo defense group."[42] The ship made the usual rounds: Hampton Roads and the Southern Drill Grounds for target practice and firing for record; the New England area for torpedo practice and mining drills; and the Caribbean and the Guantanamo naval base for maneuvers, sham battles, and firing exercises. Because of political turbulence in Cuba, Mexico, Nicaragua, Haiti, the Dominican Republic, and Panama, units of the Atlantic Fleet—often battleship divi-

---

[40] Log of USS *Minnesota* (BB 22), 3 Sep 1911, RG 24, NA.
[41] Helen Kinkaid interview, 6 Jan 1976; Mary Tyler Urquhart, interview with author, Chevy Chase, MD, 28 Jul 1976; *Annapolis Evening Capital*, 1 May 1911; *The Evening Bulletin* (Philadelphia), 18 Apr 1911.
[42] Fitness Reports, 31 Mar 1910, 30 Jun 1910, 31 Mar 1911, 30 Sep 1911, TCK Personnel File.

Courtesy J. Urquhart

Midshipman Kinkaid and Helen Ross, early 1900s.

sions—were routinely diverted to stand off Vera Cruz, Havana, Port-au-Prince, or Colón in an attempt to coerce a return to stability.

During his three years on board *Minnesota*, Kinkaid had three brief periods of detached service with state naval militias. These organizations were a cross between the state National Guard units and the Naval Reserve as it was to develop after World War I. Organized and paid by the states, the units drilled weekly ashore or in vessels provided by the Navy. Each unit was expected to spend two weeks on active duty per year on board naval vessels, usually ones that had been loaned to the states for militia use. In 1912 twenty-two states had naval militia, with about 7,500 officers and men enrolled. It was assumed that, when federalized, they would operate the ships engaged in harbor and coastline defense work. Working with these civilians in Philadelphia, the District of Columbia, and Chicago gave Kinkaid an education that was useful when mobilization for war came in five years.[43]

As his expected three-year duty in *Minnesota* was nearing its end, Tom took positive action concerning his next assignment. Due for a tour

---

[43] R. F. Nicholson to TCK, Washington, 8 Jul 1911; Philip Andrews to TCK, Washington, 22 Jun 1912 and 20 Jul 1912, Early Order File, TCK Papers; "Naval Militia," *A Compilation of the Messages and Papers of the Presidents*, vol. 20, Encyclopedic Index N–Z (New York: Bureau of National Literature, 1917).

ashore, he several times indicated on his fitness reports that he would like to be assigned to the course in naval ordnance at the Naval Academy Postgraduate School or, if that was not possible, he would prefer assignment to the target practice office in the Navy Department. This was a billet that Commander Sims had made famous.[44] In early December he formally requested postgraduate instruction in ordnance and gunnery, preferably in optics. In his first fitness reports from Captain Clark, and those from Captain Edward Simpson after 12 November 1912, Kinkaid received exceptionally high marks—almost 4.0 in every entry. In evaluating his professional ability in general, Simpson wrote: "Excellent, 4.0. Is a most excellent and dependable young officer." Concerning Tom's initiative and intelligence, he commented: "Ready to take initiative; excellent judgement; is intelligent, thorough & reliable." Under professional qualification the captain rated Kinkaid 4.0 in command, executive ability, seamanship, tactical handling of the ship, fire control, gun division officer, and watch and division officer. Given this sort of backing, it is little wonder that the recently promoted lieutenant (jg) received the orders he desired. After *Minnesota* completed its target practice on the Southern Drill Grounds in August 1913, Kinkaid was detached on 18 September to proceed immediately to the Naval Academy Postgraduate School.[45]

The course in ordnance at the Naval Postgraduate School began with four months of classroom instruction. It was followed by shorter assignments to the Bethlehem and Midvale Steel Works in Pennsylvania, electrical manufacturing companies in Schenectady, New York, and optical fabricators in Rochester, New York. Then came a three-month tour at the Navy Gun Factory in Washington, D.C., and finally four months at the Indian Head, Maryland, Ordnance Proving Grounds.[46] Because of the expense, the department insisted upon a signed agreement that students would remain in the Navy for eight years following the Annapolis phase. Tom signed without hesitation.[47]

Helen Kinkaid remembered this period in her husband's career as a "gypsy experience, living out of suitcases." In Annapolis they stayed briefly with Tom's parents until they could find a suitable apartment. During the first four months of instruction, Tom gave several lectures on fire control, optics, and munitions. He and Helen then went to Philadelphia for a three-month assignment at the Midvale Steel company.[48] International

---

[44] Morison, *Sims,* 131–47; TCK to Chief BUNAV, *Minnesota,* 9 Dec 1912, Early Order File, TCK Papers.

[45] Fitness Reports, 31 Mar 1912, 12 Nov 1912, 5 Jan 1913, 10 Aug 1913, 16 Sep 1913, TCK Personnel File; Josephus Daniels to TCK, Washington, 26 Aug 1913, Early Order File, TCK Papers.

[46] "Outline of Course of Study for Officers in Ordnance Class, Jan 1913," file 8039–18, RG 24, NA.

[47] Chief BUNAV to Chief, Bureau of Steam Engineering, Washington, 18 Feb 1914, file 8039–57, RG 24, NA.

[48] Helen Kinkaid interview, 6 Jan 1976; Josephus Daniels to TCK, Washington, 19 Jan 1914, and C. Brittain to TCK, Washington, 24 Apr 1914, Early Orders File, TCK Papers; Fitness Report, 1 Feb 1914, TCK Personnel File.

trouble intruded, and Tom's tour at Midvale was interrupted after two months. In the Dominican Republic competing factions, largely based in the northern provinces, struggled for control of the government. The Navy had blockaded Tampico in mid-April and a week later seized control of Vera Cruz. Kinkaid sent a telegram to the Navy Department, requesting sea duty: "Request duty in Mexico, prefer small command."[49] The Bureau of Navigation on 24 April ordered him to report immediately to the gunboat *Machias* (PG 5), then fitting out in the New York Navy Yard.

Machias was a small command, although perhaps not as small as Kinkaid expected. Commissioned in 1893, the gunboat had participated in the fighting in Cuban waters during the Spanish-American War. (By coincidence, Tom's father had been an assistant engineer in *Machias* during this period.) At the time Kinkaid reported, *Machias* was commanded by Commander Milton E. Reed and carried seven line officers, two assistant surgeons, and a passed assistant paymaster, plus an enlisted complement of 153. For its class, its armament was fairly heavy, with eight 4-inch guns, six lighter guns in the 6-pounder and 3-pounder category, and several machine guns. The ship was designated a third-rate war vessel (meaning it had armament less than a cruiser) assigned to the Navy's Special Service Squadron. The warships of this squadron composed the "big stick" that had been brandished in the Caribbean region by Presidents Theodore Roosevelt, William Howard Taft, and now Woodrow Wilson. Upon reporting, Tom and Oscar Smith, Jr., a classmate who had been at Midvale with him, were assigned to watch and gun division officer duties.[50]

After three weeks of yard work, coaling, provisioning, and loading ammunition, *Machias* cleared the New York area on 17 May and shaped course for Hampton Roads where other munitions were to be taken on board. Once at sea Commander Reed immediately put the crew through the traditional underway drills (fire, collision, watertight doors, abandon ship, man overboard) that are vital to a ship's integrity and survival at sea. During the run to Chesapeake Bay, new orders came by radio: after loading, *Machias* was to coal at the Guantanamo naval base and then take station off Puerto Plata in the Dominican Republic. There, on 26 May, the gunboat would join other units from the Special Service Squadron and the Atlantic Fleet in their patrol of Dominican waters.[51]

For six weeks during June and early July *Machias* and several battleships participated in skirmishes against the forces ashore. American consuls in Puerto Plata, Monte Cristi, and Samana, assisted by staff from the legation

---

[49] TCK to Chief BUNAV, Philadelphia, 20 Apr 1914, Early Order File, TCK Papers.

[50] Bauer, *Ships* 1:150–51; "Machias," *DANFS* 4:180; Log of USS *Machias* (PG 5), 27 Apr 1914, RG 24, NA; Fitness Report, 30 Sep 1914, TCK Personnel File.

[51] *Machias* log, 18 May 1914; Arthur S. Link, *Wilson: The Struggle for Neutrality, 1914–1915* (Princeton: Princeton University Press, 1960), 505–16.

in Santo Domingo, negotiated frequent cease-fires between factions only to see them violated within a day or two. Because the United States was committed to supporting the existing government, as corrupt and weak as it was, the Navy's guns occasionally were turned against groups of soldiers, or their battleworks, as they attempted to capture a government area.[52] In the early morning of 5 July *Machias* came under volleying fire from one of the rebel groups. The ship returned fire with twenty-seven rounds of 3-pounders and with machine guns. When one of the .50-caliber machine guns on the gunboat jammed while returning fire, Kinkaid took charge. His commanding officer later described what followed: "[Kinkaid] especially exposed himself to rifle fire—[he] was cool and efficient under those circumstances and assisted in clearing Colt Automatic Machine Gun and in firing same in face of volley firing directed to *Machias*."[53]

As the turbulence subsided, the Dominicans accepted a cease-fire. In August the Americans imposed a provisional government and appointed a president until elections could be held in late October. The work of *Machias* became less strenuous, and a period of hot and humid monotony began. The gunboat moved leisurely from one north coast port to another, but for everyone on board only one thought dominated—returning home. Fishing, competitive sports, swimming, picnics ashore, "smokers," and liberty in the few port cities only partially helped to relieve the tedium. The ship's log told the story as crewmen were brought daily to mast for infractions of Navy regulations. Finally, in mid-December, after a few days' visit to Port-au-Prince, Haiti, *Machias* headed north to home port in the New York Navy Yard, arriving Christmas Eve. But Kinkaid had to wait for a reunion with Helen; he had a 24-watch on Christmas.[54]

After thirty days' leave Tom returned to his postgraduate studies. His short tour in *Machias* had been professionally rewarding. He had put his previous experience as a gunnery division officer to good use, and earned his commanding officer's commendation for bravery and coolness under fire. Commander Reed's final fitness report was outstanding, all marks were 4.0. He was well liked and respected by his men. He could hardly ask for more.[55]

On 3 February Kinkaid reported to the Bausch and Lomb Optical Works in Rochester, New York. Because of his interest in spotting and fire control, the two months in Rochester were extremely valuable to Kinkaid. At the end of March he received orders to move to the Washington Navy Yard, where the syllabus called for four months of exposure to designing,

---

[52] Link, *Wilson*, 510–12.
[53] *Machias* log, 5 Jul 1914; Fitness Report, 30 Sep 1914, TCK Personnel File.
[54] *Machias* log, 1 Jul–31 Dec 1914.
[55] Josephus Daniels to TCK, Washington, 8 Jan 1915, Early Order File, TCK Papers; Fitness Report, 12 Jan 1915, TCK Personnel File; Ernest A. Cuny (an enlisted man in *Machias*) to TCK, Tawas City, MI, 22 Apr 1945, TCK Papers.

testing, and manufacturing the Navy's heaviest weapons. Quarters were not available in the navy yard, so Tom and Helen took rented rooms. Tom joined the Army and Navy Club, where he maintained his membership until ill health forced his reduction to inactive status in 1964.[56]

At the navy yard, Kinkaid was asked to write a pamphlet on fire control. He completed this assignment and then initiated a project of his own. He drew specifications and rough plans for a single-person-operated torpedo. It was not a suicide weapon. The person steering the vehicle from the mother vessel to within a thousand yards of the target would abandon the torpedo after setting its course for the final run. Despite the positive endorsement of the superintendent of the Gun Factory, the Bureau of Ordnance (BUORD) and its advisory committee on naval ordnance concluded the concept was unsound. Twelve endorsements later, it was back in Tom's hands. The new Chief of Naval Operations, Admiral William Benson, tried to be encouraging: "The Department . . . is pleased to note the interest and zeal which you have shown in this matter."[57]

Kinkaid continued his studies at the Bethlehem Steel Works, the Naval Proving Ground in Maryland, and finally at the Sperry Gyroscope Company in Brooklyn.[58] By the spring of 1916 he and Helen were both tired of living out of suitcases and looked forward to his next assignment. He requested orders to the new battleship *Arizona* (BB 39) or to her sister ship *Pennsylvania* (BB 38). In May orders came to *Pennsylvania*, due for commissioning on 12 June 1916 at the Newport News shipyard near Norfolk. Tom reported during the forenoon watch on 4 July.[59]

When Kinkaid joined the drydocked *Pennsylvania*, World War I had been blazing for almost two years, and the United States was wrestling with the problems of being an onlooker. Even in the face of daily ship sinkings by the German submarine (U-boat) fleet, the nation was insistent that its merchant vessels be allowed to trade in every European port not closely blockaded by surface ships. Rejecting the concept that submarines could create blockades, the United States persistently argued that it could carry whatever it desired into the British Isles and France, respect their ship blockades of German ports, and still remain neutral.

In hindsight, it was inevitable that German use of submarines against merchant shipping in its declared war zones would lead to direct conflict with the United States. In the summer of 1916, however, relations with Germany were reasonably stable. Following a diplomatic crisis after the

---

[56] Interview with the Manager, The Army and Navy Club, Washington, 8 Jan 1976.
[57] General Correspondence of the Navy, TCK to Chief BUORD, 3 Jun 1915 and follow-on documents, file 11804–290, RG 80, NA; Fitness Report, 30 Sep 1915, TCK Personnel File.
[58] Early Order File, TCK Papers.
[59] TCK to Chief BUNAV, Indian Head, MD, 6 Mar 1916; Josephus Daniels to TCK, Washington, 2 May 1916, Early Order File, TCK Papers; Log of USS *Pennsylvania* (BB 38), 12 Jun, 4 Jul 1916, RG 24, NA.

Pennsylvania (BB 38), at anchor in Hampton Roads, Virginia, 13 December 1916.

sinking of the French channel ferry *Sussex* in March, the Germans had pledged in May 1916 to rein in their submarines if the British relaxed their total blockade and allowed food ships to enter German ports. President Wilson accepted the "*Sussex* Pledge" but ignored the proviso.[60] The Navy, as it must in such periods, put its house in order.

Pennsylvania was the Navy's newest battleship in commission when Kinkaid logged in. With a main battery of twelve 14-inch, 45-caliber rifles; a secondary battery of twenty-two 5-inch, 51-caliber guns; and heavy armor against equivalent gunfire, the Navy had met the congressional requirement that the battleship carry "as heavy armor and as powerful armament as any vessel of its class." Congress had insisted that new construction "have the highest practicable speed and greatest desirable radius of action" for use in the Pacific Ocean. To meet this latter requirement, the Naval Acts of 1911, 1912, and 1913, which authorized construction of *Nevada* (BB 36), *Oklahoma* (BB 37), *Pennsylvania*, and *Arizona*, provided for the use of oil-fired boilers in these vessels, rather than the traditional coal.[61]

Soon after the United States entered the war on 6 April 1917, it quickly became evident to the Navy Department that there was almost nothing for the battleship fleet to do. Tom Kinkaid's service was almost

---

[60] Charles Callan Tansill, *America Goes to War* (Boston: Little, Brown, 1938), 511–15; Arthur S. Link, *Wilson Confusions and Crises, 1915–1916* (Princeton: Princeton University Press, 1964), 222–79.
[61] *DANFS* 1:195–96, "Pennsylvania," *DANFS* 5:250–51.

as tedious as his tour in *Machias*. The German High Seas Fleet was still penned in the Heligoland Bight, where it had been since the Battle of Jutland a year earlier. The British Grand Fleet had sufficient strength to ensure that the Germans did not try to break out and destroy its guards and attack the merchant shipping routes. *Pennsylvania* and the other battleships occasionally sortied for maneuvers and firing exercises in New England waters or on the Southern Drill Grounds and even massed once in the early spring of 1918 for war games in the Caribbean. Only five American battleships, all coal burners, served as a squadron attached to the Grand Fleet. More than fifty destroyers also served actively as escorts for transatlantic convoys, and all new construction in this class was assigned to such duty. With its destroyers siphoned off for war-zone duty, the Atlantic Fleet was really in no shape to operate in areas where German submarines could attack it.[62] Yet the fleet had two important missions during the war. First, it was a "fleet-in-being," available should the German High Seas Fleet, or a significant detachment from it, manage to escape the North Sea and attempt a raid against the United States or the Panama Canal. Second, it served as a floating school to prepare officers and men for service in ships at the front.[63]

As a junior officer in *Pennsylvania* Tom's primary duty was as the ship's gunfire spotter. His postgraduate study of naval optics and range-finding equipment made him highly qualified for this work. His commanding officers, the peppery Captain Henry B. Wilson, and later Captain John A. Hoogewerff, gave him high ratings as officer and chief spotter. Kinkaid's duties also called for regular watch-standing and again his fitness reports reveal that he was considered excellent in seamanship, tactical shiphandling, navigation, and piloting. Kinkaid was promoted to lieutenant in January 1917.[64]

In early November 1917 Kinkaid and Lieutenant Commander Harry A. Orr were ordered to pick up a 20-foot base range finder in the Norfolk Navy Yard and take it to England for testing in the Grand Fleet.[65] The two arrived at the London headquarters of the Commander U.S. Forces Operating in European Waters, Vice Admiral William Sims, on 29 November. While Tom was in London, the Germans launched several night air raids

---

[62] Paolo E. Coletta, *Sea Power in the Atlantic and Mediterranean in World War I* (Lanham, MD: University Press of America, 1989), 67–77; David F. Trask, *Captains & Cabinets: Anglo-American Naval Relations, 1917–1918* (Columbia: University of Missouri Press, 1972), 62–64; Hugh Rodman, *Yarns of a Kentucky Admiral* (Indianapolis: Bobbs-Merrill, 1928), 261–87.

[63] Lewis Clephane, *History of the Naval Overseas Transportation Service in World War I* (Washington: Naval History Division, 1969), 15–18. See also Admiral Harris Laning, "An Admiral's Yarn," an autobiographical manuscript in the U.S. Naval War College, Manuscript Collection, Newport, RI.

[64] Fitness Reports, 31 Mar 1917, 17 Sep 1917, TCK Personnel File; L. C. Palmer to TCK, Washington, 4 Oct 1916; H. A. Baldridge to TCK, Washington, 8 Jan 1917, Early Order File, TCK Papers.

[65] CAPT T. J. Senn to TCK, Washington, 8 Nov 1917; CAPT O. Jackson to TCK, 8 Nov 1917, Early Order File, TCK Papers.

on the British capital. Although the danger to Kinkaid was slight, he could later remind his friends in *Pennsylvania* that he had been under fire.[66]

Admiral Sims had ordered Tom to deliver some highly classified papers to Chief of Naval Operations Admiral Benson, who was then meeting with Allied naval leaders in Paris. Kinkaid was delighted with the opportunity to visit the French capital. Years later he recalled, "It was an interesting trip. I didn't dare to get into conversation with anybody on the train because my pockets were bulging with those secret papers."[67]

Once back from Paris, Sims ordered Kinkaid and Orr to visit the British Whale Island Gunnery School near Portsmouth and then the Grand Fleet at its anchorages.[68] Kinkaid spent three weeks visiting the school and testing the range finder on HMS *Excellent*. Sims then ordered him to visit optical works in London, York, and Glasgow to learn as much as possible about the manufacture of Royal Navy range-finding devices.[69] By the end of January, his mission accomplished, he returned to Washington. The Bureau of Ordnance asked him to visit the Sperry Gyroscope Company in Brooklyn and the Ford Instrument Company in New York City to consult with them concerning fire-control devices being installed in new construction.[70]

On Kinkaid's return to *Pennsylvania*, he received papers promoting him to lieutenant commander (temporary) to date from 1 February 1918. Almost ten years out of the Naval Academy, Kinkaid and his classmates were being promoted at an accelerated pace normally associated with war.[71] About six weeks after returning from Europe, orders came transferring Kinkaid from *Pennsylvania* to *Arizona*. Though considered fairly junior to be a battleship department head, Kinkaid's training and experience were enough to satisfy Commander in Chief, Atlantic Fleet (CINCLANT) Admiral Henry T. Mayo, and the Bureau of Navigation agreed.[72] Since *Arizona* and *Pennsylvania* were almost identical vessels, there was little for Tom to learn about the ship when he officially reported to Captain Josiah S. McKean on 11 May 1918. His final fitness report from Captain William L. Howard, then commanding *Pennsylvania*, was positive, with most marks in the 3.8 to 4.0 range. Howard described him as "calm, even tempered, forceful, active, painstaking," in sum, "an exceptionally fine officer."[73]

---

[66] TCK oral history, 16–17.
[67] CAPT N. C. Twining to TCK, London, 1 Dec 1917, Early Order File, TCK Papers; TCK oral history, 15.
[68] Twining to TCK, London, 3 Dec 1917, Early Order File, TCK Papers.
[69] Ibid., 27 Dec 1917, Early Order File, TCK Papers.
[70] VADM W. S. Sims to TCK, London, 13 Jan 1918; Sims to TCK, London, 30 Jan, 2 Feb 1918; Senn to TCK, Washington, 6 Mar 1918, Early Order File, TCK Papers.
[71] Josephus Daniels to TCK, Washington, 9 Mar 1918, Early Order File, TCK Papers.
[72] ADM H. T. Mayo to BUNAV, 7 Apr 1918, Early Order File, TCK Papers.
[73] Fitness Reports, 31 Mar 1918, 26 Apr 1918, TCK Personnel File.

During the remainder of the war the Atlantic Fleet continued to stand by in Chesapeake Bay. On 11 November, the day hostilities ceased, Kinkaid led a party from his ship to observe *Pennsylvania*'s night-time, long-range practice battle. *Arizona*'s deck log book does not record that World War I ended that day.[74]

A week later *Arizona*, in company with Battleship Division Six, stood out to sea on a northeasterly heading, destination Portland, England. Wartime sailing conditions were maintained during the passage, including zigzagging. From Portland *Arizona* and *Pennsylvania* escorted the transport *George Washington*, which was carrying President Wilson to the French port of Brest. By Christmas, *Arizona* was back in American waters. Tom had watch duty on Christmas, but on the 27th he finally had two weeks leave with Helen and her family in Philadelphia and then with his parents in Annapolis.[75]

The balance of Kinkaid's cruise in *Arizona* was spent "steaming as before," the phrase often used in the deck log of a man-of-war. Peacetime routines had begun. Following winter exercises in and around the Guantanamo naval base, *Arizona* received priority orders to return to Norfolk for fuel and reprovisioning and then to depart immediately for European waters. The ship entered Brest on 21 April 1919. In Brest, Tom spent four days' leave sightseeing in Paris and the French countryside. Though the city was crowded, he managed to find lodgings in the Hotel Louvre set aside by the Red Cross for visiting servicemen.[76]

Arizona had been prepositioned in European waters in case it was needed for emergency service; the emergency came to pass in early May. At the Versailles Conference, the Big Four, minus Italy, had decided that Greece should occupy the Anatolian Turkish port of Smyrna to protect the large Greek population there, with British, French, and American warships assisting. *Arizona* left Brest on 3 May and, in company with destroyers *Manley* (DD 74) and *Dyer* (DD 84), anchored before Smyrna eight days later. On the 15th the Greeks arrived in force. The occupation was not without bloodshed, but the Greek army units were in control.

Three weeks later *Arizona* set course for Constantinople and on 15 June, accompanied by the destroyers *Barney* (DD 149) and *Luce* (DD 99), began its long voyage to New York. On 3 July 1919 Kinkaid was detached from *Arizona* and ordered to the Bureau of Ordnance. He would now become a resident member of the Navy's Gun Club.[77]

---

[74] Log of USS *Arizona* (BB 39), 10–11 Nov 1918, RG 24, NA.

[75] Ibid., 18 Nov 1918–12 Jan 1919.

[76] Ibid., 4 Feb–12 Apr 1919; TCK, "Journal, 1917–1922," series 1, folder 2, TCK Papers.

[77] *Arizona* log, 21 Apr–3 Jul 1919; Marjorie Housepian, *The Smyrna Affair* (New York: Harcourt Brace Jovanovich, 1966), 46–55; Peter M. Buzanski, "The Interallied Investigation of the Greek Invasion of Smyrna, 1919," *The Historian* (May 1963), 325–43; Ray Stannard Baker, *Woodrow Wilson and World Settlement*, 3 vols. (Garden City, NY: Doubleday, Page, 1922), 2:190–94.

Kinkaid's detachment from *Arizona* brought to a close an important period in his career. Except for postgraduate school, he had spent the years from June 1908 to July 1919 in battleships. In his oral history he recalled,

> I grew up to be what we call a battleship sailor. I started out in the *Nebraska*—this is one of the 14,500 tonners that went around the world—I went from there to the *Minnesota* which was just a little bit larger, and then from the *Minnesota* I went ashore for the post-graduate course in ordnance and then to the *Pennsylvania* and then to the *Arizona*. And so I really grew up in battleships, which I never regretted and in that day the battleship was the backbone of the fleet. There was no question of it.[78]

Kinkaid had advanced from an assistant division officer to a gunnery department head and learned a great deal about managing enlisted men and officers. His final commanding officer in *Arizona*, Captain John H. Dayton, rated him 4.0 in executive ability, as the gunnery officer, and as the ship's ordnance officer. His overall evaluation was quite simple: "A most excellent officer."[79] Three months after Kinkaid's detachment Dayton recommended him for a Distinguished Service Medal for the period 11 September 1918 to 3 July 1919. He commented in his write-up, "During this time Lieutenant Commander Kinkaid displayed ability, zeal and energy in a specially meritorious degree in maintaining the battle efficiency of the Gunnery Department of the U.S.S. ARIZONA in a high degree of preparedness."[80] Kinkaid did not receive the decoration, but the letter was a nice addition to his promotion file.

---

[78] TCK oral history, 19.
[79] Fitness Report, 3 Jul 1919, TCK Personnel File.
[80] CAPT J. H. Dayton to BUNAV (Board of Awards), New York Navy Yard, 4 Oct 1919, Promotions Section, TCK Personnel File.

Chapter 2

The Middle Ranks, 1919–1933

When Tom Kinkaid crossed the quarterdeck of *Arizona* for the last time, he was leaving duty in the battleships for fourteen years. As a staff officer for the Commander in Chief, U.S. Fleet (CINCUS), he would be embarked in a battleship, but such duty was far removed from being a part of the ship's company. In the ensuing fourteen years he would spend his time as a shore-duty bureaucrat, a student, and a member of a flag officer's staff, assignments interrupted only briefly for a period in command of a destroyer.

The number of seagoing billets available to the Navy's lieutenant commanders and commanders would accommodate less than half of the officers ready for sea duty. Kinkaid made it easy for the Bureau of Navigation detailers; he did not mind shore duty in Washington or the Philadelphia area and therefore did not try to obtain shipboard billets if he was due to go ashore. The result was that, when he reached flag rank, he had the fewest number of years of sea service of any regular line officer from his class. In addition, he was separated from his wife for only about nine months in the years between 1919 and 1933.

The Gun Factory

The Kinkaids spent three years in Washington, 1919–1922. This period was one of national turmoil and naval change, but for Tom and Helen these were good years. Housing was still scarce and a bit expensive, but on a lieutenant commander's salary they could afford a good apartment in the northwest section of Washington, near 17th Street and Corcoran Avenue. They would have preferred quarters in the Washington Navy Yard, where Tom's Bureau of Ordnance office was located, but he was too junior to qualify.

Tom's annual salary as a lieutenant commander with more than ten years' service was $3,600, and he was entitled to a housing allowance of $60 per month. Helen's father had created a trust for her at the time of her marriage, and its income made life considerably easier for them. The nation experienced a period of inflation between 1918 and 1920 when the consumer price index rose 33 percent, but the Kinkaids rode it out easily. They fared even better during the recession of the early 1920s. Indeed, armed services salaries remained largely unchanged between 1918 and 1941.

People remembered the Kinkaids as a handsome, social-minded couple who were good bridge players, competent golfers (Helen eventually would win the women's golf championship for the District of Columbia in 1921 and 1922), and enjoyable company. They had no children.[1]

In coming ashore to a billet in Washington, Tom had the opportunity to observe daily the problems besetting the Navy as it moved from a wartime to a peacetime footing. As funding decreased, the Navy decreased in size. At war's end there were 32,208 officers and 494,358 enlisted men on duty and 1,362 ships in service. Three years later, on 1 January 1922, there were 6,163 officers (81 percent reduction), 100,999 enlisted (79 percent reduction), and 900 ships (34 percent reduction).[2] These cuts were to be expected, but during his last few months in Washington, Kinkaid and those about him were shocked to learn that Congress was not satisfied with the reductions. With the conclusion of the great Washington Conference on the Limitation of Armament (Washington Naval Conference) on 6 February 1922, economy-minded Congressmen concluded that the Navy would be significantly reduced and so would its needs for personnel and money. As a result, the Navy Department requested appropriations for fiscal year 1923 that would accommodate 93,000 enlisted men and 5,500 officers, a number that represented another 5 percent cut of the enlisted force.[3] By July 1922 the compromise was 86,000 enlisted men and about 6,000 officers, of whom 4,000 would be line officers.[4] It was little wonder that by 1922 Tom was looking forward to his change of duty.

Tom's work at the Bureau of Ordnance as the chief of the supply section apparently interested him. His fitness reports were all outstanding. His performance of assigned duties, plus his many collateral activities, left a strong impression on Rear Admiral Ralph Earle, the bureau chief.[5] He wrote: "Has taken hold of his work enthusiastically and with an exceptional spirit of loyalty, cooperation and helpfulness to the Chief of the Bureau, taking cheerfully and ably duties not properly pertaining to him."[6]

Admiral Earle was succeeded by an interim chief, Captain Claude C. Bloch, and then by Rear Admiral Charles B. McVay. During his last year at BUORD Kinkaid's reports were 4.0 in all of the descriptive categories

---

[1] *Washington Post*, 27 Dec 1980.

[2] U.S. Congress, House Naval Affairs Committee, *Hearings on Sundry Legislation, 1922–23*, 67th Cong., sess. 2, 3, 4, 229–30.

[3] Ibid., 229–46.

[4] U.S. Congress, Senate Naval Subcommittee of Appropriations Committee, *Hearings on Navy Department Appropriation Bill, 1923*, 67th Cong., sess. 2, 3, 4, 104–5.

[5] Fitness Reports, 30 Sep 1919, 31 Mar 1920, TCK Personnel File.

[6] Ibid., 31 Mar 1920.

(conduct, military appearance, leadership, judgment, etc.), and the written sections were loaded with superlatives occasionally stated with minimum attention to grammar: "Professional ability. Way above." His September 1921 fitness report concluded: "An excellent officer with a genius for organization." In his last report on Kinkaid, the admiral wrote: "A very capable officer, theoretically and practically. Has specialized in ordnance ashore and afloat. A good administrator."[7] With these outstanding evaluations Tom had no problem when the time came for his class to advance from temporary lieutenant commanders to permanent status. He was examined in February 1921 and was selected for permanent appointment with a date of rank of 1 January 1921.

Gun Factory duties left Tom with enough spare time to try his hand at professional writing. He published two strikingly different articles in the U.S. Naval Institute *Proceedings* on topics of current concern to the service. "Probability and Accuracy of Gun Fire"[8] was highly technical and probably warmed the hearts of the fleet's gun bosses. Once the reader waded through the eight pages of formulas and tables, the message came through: Battleships with twelve big guns had a much better chance of hitting their targets than those carrying eight or nine guns. With nine battleships and six battle cruisers under construction in the Navy,[9] the argument was important to heed. Unfortunately the Washington Naval Conference, which opened a month after the article was published, would make it almost impossible for Kinkaid's findings to be translated into new construction.

His second article, "Naval Corps, Specialization and Efficiency,"[10] argued for more education and training of specialists, the creation of more specialties within the line of the Navy, and essentially making most officers line officers by gradually reducing the civil engineers and engineering-duty-only officers in the service. Again he dealt with a timely topic. Congress was considering the possible unification of the armed services, or possibly creating a new service placing Army and Navy aviation into a separate Air Service. Within the Navy, some officers were pressing for a separate corps for naval aviators, similar to the construction corps or medical corps.

Tom's three years in Washington had only one negative event of importance. His father, Rear Admiral Thomas Wright Kinkaid, died on 11 August 1920 after several months of illness. At the time of his death the admiral was in charge of the Navy Engineering Experiment Station. He

---

[7] Ibid., 31 Mar 1921, 30 Sep 1921, 31 Mar 1922, 2 Jun 1922.

[8] LCDR T. C. Kinkaid, U.S. Navy, "Probability and Accuracy of Gun Fire," U.S. Naval Institute *Proceedings* (Oct 1921): 1543–52.

[9] Harold and Margaret Sprout, *Toward a New Order of Sea Power: American Naval Policy and the World Scene, 1918–1922* (Princeton: Princeton University Press, 1943), 51–53, 132.

[10] Kincaid [sic], "Naval Corps, Specialization and Efficiency," *Proceedings* (Sep 1922): 1491–1500.

was buried in the Academy cemetery with full military honors. One of the pallbearers was Captain Ernest J. King, head of the Naval Postgraduate School, who would have a great deal to do with the admiral's son in about twenty years.[11]

The following spring Kinkaid had to arrange his next duty assignment. A major advantage of service in Washington was the ability to deal personally with the officer detailer for lieutenant commanders. Given his seniority (number 252 among 570 lieutenant commanders), he could expect command of a destroyer or similar type unit or assignment to a flag officer's staff. Because he had served as a department head in *Arizona*, there was little likelihood of receiving a similar assignment for this next tour. While he might enjoy being executive officer of a cruiser or battleship, this was normally a commander's billet, and he lacked the rank. The evidence is not clear, but it is likely that Kinkaid's orders to the staff of Commander U.S. Forces in Turkish Waters Rear Admiral Mark L. Bristol came because the admiral requested his services. In October 1918 Bristol had tried to have Kinkaid ordered to his staff when he commanded Base Number 27 in Plymouth, England. The Navy Department had demurred because *Arizona* needed Kinkaid more than the newly minted rear admiral. Now, however, the time was ripe. Tom had regularly indicated on his fitness reports that he wanted a destroyer command in the Atlantic or Scouting Fleet; most recently he had asked for one with the forces in the Near East. The match was right. Orders came in May for detachment by 2 June 1922.[12]

Constantinople

Kinkaid's tour of duty with Admiral Bristol became one of the pivotal assignments in his career. It changed him from a fairly narrow Gun Club specialist into an officer oriented to international affairs. The tour also provided him with a senior friend and mentor who would help him move up the ladder. Yet service with Bristol had its difficult moments. For the present, however, the Kinkaids were destined for a trip that normally only the wealthy enjoyed in the 1920s. Fortunately most of Helen's travel expenses were paid by the Navy because this was a permanent change of duty, so they decided to see as much of Europe as they could while en route.

They departed New York on 6 June. On arrival at Antwerp on the sixteenth, Consul General George S. Messersmith, an old friend, gave Tom and Helen a sedan tour of the city, including a quick glance at Rubens's

---

[11] *Annapolis Evening Capitol*, 12, 13 Aug 1920.
[12] VADM W. S. Sims to BUNAV, London, 21 Oct 1918; BUNAV to Sims, Washington, 23 Oct 1918; Chief BUNAV to TCK, Washington, 4 May 1922, TCK Personnel File.

Descent from the Cross in the cathedral. At day's end they took the short train trip to Brussels and a large suite at the Hotel Grand Palais. In his journal Tom commented: "Very nice; got a real drink and had a big dinner."[13]

The next morning the Kinkaids were off to Paris and ten days of savoring Europe's grandest city. Their dollars went a long way. During their stay they took sightseeing trips; visited Navy and civilian friends; took in the Folies Bergere; ate in the best restaurants; visited the Louvre, the Pantheon de la Guerre, and the races at Auteil; and had tea daily with new or old friends, often at the Hotel Ritz. By the time they finished travel arrangements and check cashing at Cook's, and tumbled aboard the Simplon Orient Express in the early evening of 26 June, Tom and Helen were exhausted, but pleased. Paris was now *terre intime* and they would return many times in the years ahead. With lengthy stops only at Milan and Sofia, the Express took three days to cross Europe to Istanbul. Even when crossing a continent and the borders of six nations, travel interruptions were few. One wishes that Tom's observations in June 1922 were valid for the present: "Arrived at Verona 5:30 and at Venice at 8 PM. Slept through our stop at Trieste at midnight. Gave passports to porter and had no trouble with Yougo Slavia [*sic*] customs officials. They asked how much money I had and were satisfied when it was all in French francs."[14]

In 1922 ancient Constantinople (or Istanbul) was the principal city of a nation in transition. The government of Sultan Mohammed V had sided with the Central Powers in the recent war, and Turkey was now a defeated and occupied country. A vigorous nationalist movement led by Mustafa Kemal Pasha (later Kemal Ataturk) was sweeping Anatolia and clearly would control the country within months.

America's relations with Turkey had been severed when the United States declared war on Germany in April 1917, although neither country chose to go to war with the other. In the immediate postwar years dealings with the Turks were conducted by an American commissioner working through the Swedish Embassy in Constantinople. Physical protection of American nationals and their property depended on the United States Naval Detachment in Turkish Waters, commanded after January 1919 by Rear Admiral Bristol. In August 1919 the admiral became the United States High Commissioner in Turkey and commander of the naval forces. He was responsible for the conduct of diplomatic relations with Turkey, even though the usual treaty defining the basis for these relationships was lacking. By the time Tom Kinkaid reported for duty in mid-July 1922, Bristol's establishment at the American Embassy com-

---
[13] TCK, "Journal, 1917–1922," 1924, series I, folder 2, TCK Papers.
[14] Ibid.

pound was a substantial operation and the admiral an officer of considerable influence in the Middle East.[15]

Tom and Helen lived with the Bristols briefly at the embassy, but quickly obtained their own apartment in Pera in the embassy district. For Helen, the stay was a grand adventure in an exotic land.[16] An avid reader and sightseer, she took advantage of every opportunity to learn about this great cosmopolitan city. Her photograph albums from this period document their travels to Gallipoli, Angora (Ankara), Rhodes, Patmos, and Alexandria and Cairo in Egypt.[17]

Because most of the great powers had continued to keep their embassies in Constantinople even after the Sultanate was terminated in November 1922, the city had an active social life. The Admiral and Helen Bristol set a fast pace for the Americans. With no children of their own they enjoyed the company of the young staff members and their wives. Parties among the American staff members were supplemented by receptions and parties given at the other embassies; and when that type of entertainment palled, there were theatrical performances by the Greeks and Turks to be enjoyed and exquisite Russian cabarets to be visited. In season the pace of socializing was often five nights a week. And when they had been saturated with indoor entertainment, Tom and Helen could find plenty of golfers in the embassy crowd or someone ready for a picnic and swim.[18]

Because Admiral Bristol had a fairly small staff, Kinkaid served as both Assistant Chief of Staff and gunnery and engineering officer. Captain Arthur J. Hepburn was Chief of Staff, and Tom and he would serve together again in the early 1930s. Probably because duty in Constantinople was out of the mainstream and dealing with the Turks was difficult at best, naval staff and embassy personnel found themselves developing closer relationships than they might have at posts in London, Paris, or Berlin. Allen Dulles summarized the situation in a letter to his father: "I rarely have been in a place where one feels more isolated than one does in Constantinople at the present time.... Nothing is more likely to make one a confirmed pessimist regarding the future of the world in general than dealing with the hopeless muddle of the Near East."[19]

---

[15] Roger R. Trask, *The United States Response to Turkish Nationalism, 1914–1939* (Minneapolis: University of Minnesota Press, 1971), 16–36; Henry P. Beers, "United States Naval Detachment in Turkish Waters, 1919–1924," *Military Affairs* (Spring 1943), 209–14; RADM Bern Anderson, "The High Commissioner to Turkey," *Proceedings* (Jan 1957): 17–19.

[16] Helen Kinkaid interview, 7 Jan 1976.

[17] ADM T. C. Kinkaid Photograph Collection, NHC (hereafter TCK Photograph Collection).

[18] Rufus F. Zogbaum, *From Sail to Saratoga, A Naval Autobiography* (Rome, 1961), 364–66; RADM C. Julian Wheeler, interview with author, Menlo Park, CA, 2 Nov 1977; C. Julian Wheeler, interview by John T. Mason, Jr., 1969, 77–79, USNI Oral History, Annapolis (hereafter Wheeler oral history).

[19] Allen Dulles to Rev. Allen Macy Dulles, at sea, 3 Sep 1921. Allen Dulles Papers, Princeton University; Wheeler oral history, 36–38.

Scorpion (PY 3) anchored off the Dolma Bagtche Palace, Constantinople, in the early 1920s. The yacht served as the flagship for Commander, U.S. Naval Forces in Turkish Waters.

Webb Trammel, A. Stanton (Tip) Merrill, Arthur W. Dunn, and C. Julian Wheeler were among the junior officers with whom the Kinkaids socialized and with whom he would stay on one or more occasions. They remained good friends of the Hepburns and the Trammells throughout the rest of their lives.

As High Commissioner, Bristol also had a typical ambassador's staff, and Tom and Helen made many close friends among these non-Navy types. Considering their subsequent rise to importance in the State Department, it is amazing that Allen Dulles, J. Pierrepont Moffat, Howland Shaw, F. L. Belin, and Frederick Dolbeare would all be in Constantinople while the Kinkaids were there. Also attached to the High Commissioner's staff was Major Sherman Miles, an Army officer with whom Tom and Helen established an enduring relationship. Miles was a military attaché and would continue in military intelligence for most of his career.

When Kinkaid joined Bristol's staff, the admiral's naval force consisted of twenty destroyers, the tender *Denebola* (AD 12), and an old converted yacht now the gunboat *Scorpion* (PY 3). In poor condition, the flagship was scarcely capable of breasting the swift currents of the

Bosphorus when returning to Constantinople. Bristol would have preferred a cruiser with flag quarters, but none could be spared in the 1920s so the admiral made do.[20] From time to time he and his wife lived on board, and the former stationnaire worked out quite well as a center for their social life when not at the embassy.[21]

During most of his tour with Bristol, Tom's principal job was to keep track of the destroyers. He prepared their operating schedules, saw that they had periods with *Denebola* for upkeep, and scheduled training exercises so each vessel would be ready to fire its guns and torpedoes for the annual official scoring. Whereas in earlier years the destroyers spent a good deal of time actively protecting American citizens in cities situated on the perimeter of the Black Sea, by mid-1922 their work largely consisted of assisting with relief activities in the wake of the war of resistance in the Crimean region. These handy small ships also carried American businessmen and their cargoes directly to Black Sea ports, safely transported large sums of money and bullion for the businessmen, and provided a wireless communication system where none existed. Admiral Bristol firmly believed that an important part of his work was to help American business develop the Middle East as a market.[22]

Meanwhile, after several years of guerrilla operations and, finally, direct battle in the summer of 1922 with Greek forces in Turkey, the troops of Kemal Ataturk drove the Greeks westward to the port city of Smyrna. On 6 September Captain Hepburn sent naval landing parties from three destroyers ashore to protect Americans in Smyrna. Ten days later, with the Turks in the city and part of Smyrna ablaze, six American destroyers and dozens of Greek ships began evacuating Americans and more than 250,000 Greek refugees, transporting them to Athens. The Turkish victory ended foreign intervention and strengthened Turkish hands as they negotiated with their wartime enemies. Almost forty years later Admiral Kinkaid recalled those days of change in Turkey:

> During that time we saw the last Sultan and went to his last selamlik. The Calif was inaugurated on a pseudo-gold stand within a few feet of us, and he was fired out in the middle of the night by automobile caravan. He went to the border with a few of his wives and there took the Orient Express for Nice. A few days later the Republic was established. All that took place while we were there. The reoccupation by the Turks of Smyrna took

---

[20] Wheeler oral history, 79; RADM Mark L. Bristol to RADM Ashley H. Robertson, Constantinople, 11 May 1923, Mark L. Bristol Papers, Manuscript Division, Library of Congress (MD–LC) (hereafter Bristol Papers).

[21] Beers, "U.S. Naval Detachment in Turkish Waters," 218–19.

[22] Bern Anderson, "Bristol, Mark Lambert," *Dictionary of American Biography*, 20 vols. (New York: Charles Scribner's Sons, 1946), Supplement Two: 65–66; Walter Hiatt, "Admiral Mark L. Bristol, American Naval Diplomat," *Current History* (Feb 1928): 680; Anderson, "The High Commissioner to Turkey," 18–19.

place a couple of months after I got there. I didn't actually see it because I was the operations officer and somebody had to stay in Constantinople. Everybody else went to Smyrna. That was an extremely interesting thing. I had been there in 1919 as gunnery officer of the *Arizona* when the Greeks landed, so I saw the beginning and the end of the Greek occupation.[23]

Following Turkish ratification of the Lausanne Treaty in the summer of 1923, the Navy Department began reducing the number of destroyers in Bristol's command. In October the few ships remaining in Bristol's naval command shifted to Phaleron Bay, near Athens. The admiral and his staff remained in Constantinople, but the naval side of Kinkaid's work almost disappeared.[24] For Tom and Helen the reduction in workload meant more golf and more parties; they even had their portraits painted by a refugee Russian artist, Nicolai Becker. In mid-October Tom and Lieutenant Julian Wheeler boarded the destroyer *MacLeish* (DD 220) for a three-week junket. Ostensibly *MacLeish* was providing transportation for Consul General R. C. Treadwell and Consul E. L. Ives as they inspected consulates in Mytilene (Greece); Smyrna, Rhodes, and Mersin (Turkey); Alexandretta (Syria); Nicosia (Cypress); Beirut (Syria); and Alexandria (Egypt). Tom met Helen in Alexandria, and together they visited Cairo and the great pyramids.[25] In the spring of 1924 Tom and Helen, the Bristols, Julian Wheeler, and Pierrepont Moffat climbed aboard a private railway car made available to the admiral and spent eleven days touring Anatolia. This glorious trip undoubtedly sealed the bond between the Kinkaids and the Bristols.

Based on his fitness reports, it is obvious that Kinkaid had done a first-rate job on Admiral Bristol's staff. All of the admiral's reports gave Tom high marks, mostly 4.0s. In the "remarks" section of the reports he wrote:

> An officer of high professional ability and personal standards. Especially industrious, dependable, and conscientious. I especially recommend him for promotion.[26]

> An officer of exceptional ability and zeal and most dependable in every way. He performs his duties on my staff to my utmost satisfaction, but I would desire to have him under my command in any capacity. I earnestly recommend him for promotion.[27]

---

[23] TCK oral history, 1–2; Beers, "U.S. Naval Detachment in Turkish Waters," 218.

[24] Beers, 218–20; Bristol to ADM E. W. Eberle (CNO), Constantinople, 10 Oct 1923, Bristol Papers.

[25] Log of USS *MacLeish* (DD 220), 17 Oct–6 Nov 1923, RG 24, NA; Wheeler interview, 2 Nov 1977; Helen Kinkaid interview, 7 Jan 1976; TCK Photograph Collection.

[26] Fitness Report, 1 Oct 1922, TCK Personnel File.

[27] Ibid., 30 Sep 1923.

An officer of highest character and reliability, and one you would feel very satisfied on assigning to independent and difficult duty. It was with serious regret that I granted his request to be relieved from duty on my staff. I highly recommend him for promotion.[28]

Whenever the question was raised about having this officer again serve under his command, Bristol wrote that he "would especially desire to have him." The admiral's assignments had forced Bristol to become international minded. Managing the naval force was not much of a challenge and he left the ships largely to Hepburn and Kinkaid. His deep involvement was with managing American-Turkish relations and advancing American interests in the Near East. This work fascinated him and he thought he did it well. Presidents Warren G. Harding and J. Calvin Coolidge and Secretaries of State Charles Evans Hughes and Frank B. Kellogg must have agreed with him, for they left him on the job until 1927. Bristol believed that naval officers should spend more time on foreign duty stations and should become better versed in international relations.[29] Kinkaid seemed to reflect these same attitudes, though he would prefer his foreign duty to be ashore, with Helen at his side.

Tom asked for a change of duty a little earlier than he or Admiral Bristol desired. Tom's mother needed her son's assistance in getting her financial affairs in order, and Helen had developed an intestinal disease that needed medical care in Paris. By 1 July Helen had left Constantinople. Tom was detached on 17 July, with a fine fitness report and Bristol's promise to recommend him for a destroyer command. True to his word, the admiral wrote the Chief of the Bureau of Navigation: "I think Kinkaid is deserving of special consideration on account of his past record, and on account of the excellent work he did here with me. . . . If you can properly do anything to help Kinkaid, I would appreciate it." Earlier in a personal letter to Rear Admiral Shoemaker, Bristol had reminded him that Kinkaid was the son of Thomas W. Kinkaid, a flag officer known to both of them. The chief granted Tom's request for a destroyer command.[30]

Kinkaid's orders called for him to arrive in Naples, Italy, by the first of August so he could take passage in *Trenton* (CL 11) to Norfolk, Virginia. When he reported on board the light cruiser, he found there would be a 9,000-mile detour. Captain E. C. Kalbfus had been ordered to take his ship to Büshehr, Persia (Iran), so he could bring the body of Major Robert W.

---

[28] Ibid., 17 Jul 1924.

[29] Bristol to Secretary of the Navy (SECNAV) Edwin Denby, Constantinople, 22 Nov 1923; Bristol to CDR Walter S. Anderson, Constantinople, 23 Feb 1923, Bristol Papers.

[30] Bristol to RADM W. R. Shoemaker, Constantinople, 12 Aug 1924; Bristol to CAPT A. J. Hepburn, Constantinople, 15 Oct 1924; Constantine Brown to Bristol, Paris, 2 Sep 1924, Bristol Papers; Helen Kinkaid interview, 7 Jan 1976.

Imbrie, late consul in Teheran, and his wife back to Washington. Imbrie had been killed by a fanatical mob in the Persian capital. Instead of taking a ten-day trip to Norfolk, Kinkaid spent eight weeks as a supernumerary member of *Trenton*'s officer crew. Captain Kalbfus put him to work with Lieutenant Commander Vance Chapline, the cruiser's navigator. It was a blessing in disguise. Never strong on navigation, Tom had the opportunity to refresh his skills. Time also passed a little more easily because Major Sherman Miles had been detailed to the operation as an Army escort for Imbrie's body. The long trip ended at the Washington Navy Yard on 29 September. Kalbfus gave Kinkaid an excellent fitness report with a 3.9 in navigation. Admiral Bristol was amused, and he let Tom know that he was lucky to have called at ports rarely visited by the Navy.[31]

First Command

In Washington Kinkaid quickly received orders to command the destroyer *Isherwood* (DD 284), currently with Destroyer Squadron (DESRON) 9 and operating out of the Norfolk area. He reported on Armistice Day, 11 November 1924, and made the traditional inspection of the ship and crew, read his orders, and relieved Lieutenant Commander H. A. McClure. Compared with present-day destroyers or even those of World War II, *Isherwood* was a fairly small ship. Displacing 1,190 tons and with a length of 314 feet and beam of 32 feet, *Isherwood* carried twelve torpedo tubes in four triple mounts, four 4-inch guns, and one 3-inch antiaircraft gun. The ship's company consisted of 125 enlisted and 7 officers.[32] Commissioned in December 1919, the ship had spent most of its service life shuttling between the Boston, Philadelphia, and Norfolk Navy Yards, with a winter visit to the Caribbean and at least one summer cruise in New England waters for naval reservists. This routine was not to change during Kinkaid's tour as its skipper.

A few days after taking command, Kinkaid took *Isherwood*, in company with the other five vessels in Destroyer Division (DESDIV) 25, to their home port in the Philadelphia Navy Yard. It was not only *Isherwood*'s home port, but Tom's as well. When in the Philadelphia area, Tom and Helen lived at her parents' comfortable Wynnefield Avenue residence. As commanding officer he now had the advantage of not having to spend his nights on board the ship when in Philadelphia.

With winter maneuvers in the Caribbean due in January, Kinkaid used his first weeks getting *Isherwood* in shape for strenuous operations. The traditional chores of cleaning, chipping paint, wire-brushing, and paint-

---

[31] Alfred Young, USN, *The Cruise of the U.S.S. Trenton* (Privately published, [1925?]), 85–141; Bristol to TCK, Constantinople, 22 Oct 1924, Bristol Papers.
[32] Log of USS *Isherwood* (DD 284), 11 Nov 1924, RG 24, NA; *DANFS* 3:464–5.

ing went on steadily. Ship's stores were filled and ammunition brought on board. The fortnightly inspection of torpedoes was not overlooked even though the destroyer spent most of November and December at Pier 1. Shipyard periods usually result in disciplinary problems, but *Isherwood*'s log book reveals few infractions being settled at captain's mast. Overstaying leaves or violating liberties was not a problem, and there were no desertions.

Several times the division went down the Delaware River and out the Capes for exercises in the Atlantic. In mid-December an engineering observation board from the staff of Commander Destroyers, Scouting Fleet, visited and watched Kinkaid put *Isherwood* through several exercises, including the annual full-power trial. With four boilers on line the destroyer made her expected speed of 36 knots. A week later destroyer force commander Rear Admiral George W. Williams inspected the vessel and found it shipshape and ready for maneuvers.[33]

The voyage from the Philadelphia Navy Yard to the Guantanamo Naval Operating Base in Cuba began on 3 January and took four days. En route the division was joined by other ships from DESRON 9; this gave all involved the opportunity to brush up on their maneuvering board skills. Kinkaid and the other skippers had had little time to operate their commands underway while in Philadelphia, and all were a bit rusty. At this time DESDIV 25 consisted of *Breck* (DD 283), *Case* (DD 285), *Lardner* (DD 286), *Putnam* (DD 287), *Toucey* (DD 282), and *Isherwood*. Constructed and commissioned about the same time, these destroyers were nicely matched for operations.

The Caribbean operations of early 1925 were strictly for the Scouting Fleet and were designed to improve the wartime readiness of each unit and organization involved. For Kinkaid's destroyer, this meant practicing and then firing with live ammunition both day and night short-range and long-range battle practice (SRBP and LRBP), as well as battle torpedo practice (though with dummy loads only), and engaging in battle depth-charge practice. Some of the exercises emphasized single ship firing; others stressed divisional firing of guns or torpedoes. To provide plenty of sea room and not crowd anchorages too badly, the destroyer divisions of Destroyer Squadrons 9 and 14 were shuffled among three training sites: the Gulf of Gonaïves at the western end of Haiti; the Guacanayabo Bay about 170 miles west of Guantanamo; and the waters south and east of the operating base.[34]

Steaming in formation and firing live 4-inch shells at target rafts was interesting and stimulating, but the weeks of practice runs and gun

---
[33] *Isherwood* log, 15 Nov 1924–3 Jan 1925.
[34] Ibid., 7 Jan–28 Mar 1925.

pointer exercises became a bit dull. Because of limited funds available for steaming, a good many days were spent simply swinging on the hook at one of the three sites. Yet Kinkaid appears to have kept his shipmates in good spirits. He believed that team sports and exercise were good for the men. Daily swimming call was seldom missed, and Tom often led the way. He was a strong swimmer and encouraged his men to improve their skills at this survival sport. He had his ship work up a baseball team and cheered them on in the inter-ship competitions. He also took groups of men ashore for rifle training and competition. A good shot himself, he wanted as many men as possible to qualify as Navy marksmen. For pure recreation Kinkaid loved to fish. When at anchor he would spend an hour or two each day with his executive officer, Lieutenant Miles DuVal, trying to land a fresh meal for the officers mess.[35]

By 28 March the last shot had been fired, the last torpedo run down and recovered, and the last run as a target for another DESDIV completed. It was time to head north. The trip down had been on glass-like seas; the return was rough and stormy. Once out of the heaviest seas Kinkaid ordered an inventory of the topside gear. The damage was light though the sounding machine had been lost overboard. In the morning watch on 1 April the ship raised Cape Henlopen and by 1130 *Isherwood* was snugged tightly, port side to Pier 8 in the Philadelphia Navy Yard. Helen was there to welcome Tom back. After three months of steady operations, it was time to relax.[36]

Following two weeks of repairs and refilling of stores, Kinkaid took his command to the Boston Navy Yard. On 9 May a party of six officers and forty enlisted men from a naval reserve unit in the Boston area reported on board for two weeks' active duty. Because the Naval Reserve and militia units had proven invaluable in 1917 when the Navy went to war, a much-enlarged Naval Reserve had been created in the postwar years. The units normally met one night per week and occasionally for a two-day weekend, usually attached to a naval vessel in reduced commission. Each year the reserve unit would go to sea in a ship type on which it had trained. In the spring of 1925 the reserve units still had in their complements a high percentage of personnel who had served on active duty during the war. Of the six reserve officers who joined *Isherwood*, five were qualified to stand officer-of-the-day watches while underway.

The two weeks that Kinkaid arranged for the cruising reservists had a good deal of variety. After getting everyone settled in, *Isherwood* steamed overnight to Newport, Rhode Island. For three days the destroyer operated out of Narragansett Bay, with evening liberty ashore. During this

---

[35] CAPT Miles DuVal to author, Washington, 25 Sep 1976; CAPT Raleigh B. Miller to author, Rock Island, TN, 15 Jan 1977.
[36] *Isherwood* log, 28 Mar–1 Apr 1925.

NHC

Isherwood (DD 284) off Washington, D.C., May 1925. On board was a naval reserve unit from Boston.

time, including the first night out, the reserve officers took over the watch list. A regular watch officer was available if needed, but all went well. Kinkaid's trust was repaid with smart seamanship. On the 13th he shaped course for Washington, D.C., and arrived on the 16th. Tom had arranged for the reservists to visit the Naval Air Station Anacostia, the Gun Factory, and the Hydrographic Office. On the 19th a leisurely return trip got underway, with arrival in Boston on the 23d.[37]

It is clear from correspondence that Kinkaid and *Isherwood* had been exceptionally good hosts. Cameramen had recorded most of the trip, and their photos resulted in some good articles in New England newspapers. The reserve unit commanding officer, Lieutenant Commander Dudley Pray, reacted enthusiastically in writing to the naval district commandant, and Rear Admiral Louis R. DeSteiguer passed some of the praise down to Kinkaid:

> The Commandant believes that the excellent manner in which the ISHERWOOD cruise for members of the Naval Reserve Force, First Naval District,

---

[37] Ibid., 9–23 May 1924.

was carried out, and the sentiment voiced in the attached letter, reflects great credit on the officers and men of the ISHERWOOD.[38]

At the conclusion of the reservist cruise *Isherwood* remained in the Boston Navy Yard for a few days and then steamed to the New York Navy Yard in Brooklyn. Two weeks later on 6 June Kinkaid relinquished his command to Lieutenant Commander Henry T. Settle. It was to be Tom Kinkaid's only command experience until he reached the rank of captain.

The period had been briefer than one might expect, but Kinkaid appears to have made the most of his seven months. His two fitness reports from Captain Ward K. Wortman, Commander DESRON 9, were excellent. Wortman's summary remark told it all: "A most excellent destroyer captain. Has greatly improved his ship in every way since taking command." The usual question about having Kinkaid serve under him again was answered enthusiastically: "Especially desire to have him."[39] Captain Wortman's enthusiasm was based on the fact that Kinkaid had managed his crew and his ship quite well. A few days before leaving *Isherwood*, Kinkaid received an official letter from his squadron commander that praised the ship's remarkable record of no men overstaying liberty or leave during the first quarter of 1925. As a result, *Isherwood* stood number one in the Scouting Fleet. What was even more remarkable was that in the previous quarter only one man had failed to report for duty on time. The single infraction meant the vessel stood number four in the Scouting Fleet for the quarter ending December 1924. In the Navy's traditional phrasing, Captain Wortman wrote:

> The Squadron Commander is greatly pleased with the above reports and desires to heartily congratulate the Commanding Officer and all officers and crew of the ISHERWOOD for these excellent reports which speak exceedingly well for the high morale which must exist on board that ship. It is requested that this letter be read at the next general muster.[40]

BUORD Again

Upon return from Guantanamo Kinkaid took six days of leave. He and Helen stayed with his mother in Washington while he visited old friends in the Navy Department and called on his detail officer. He was due for shore duty and wanted to spend it in the capital or as a student at the Naval War College. The War College quota was filled, but there

---

[38] RADM L. R. DeSteiguer to Commanding Officer (CO), *Isherwood*, Boston, 5 Jun 1925, TCK Papers.
[39] Fitness Reports, 1 Apr 1925 and 6 Jun 1925, TCK Personnel File.
[40] COMDESRON 9 to CO *Isherwood*, New York Navy Yard, 3 Jun 1925, TCK Papers.

was a need for him in the Bureau of Ordnance so orders were written for duty again at the Gun Factory. He would now be the drafting room officer, a billet that could accommodate a senior lieutenant commander or a commander.[41] This flexibility was necessary because the rest of Tom's class was to be considered for promotion to commander in a few months, and it was anticipated that he would be among those selected.

This second tour of duty in BUORD confirmed Tom's membership in the Navy's Gun Club. Upon reporting on 10 July, he was assigned to quarters in the Washington Navy Yard. Although this assignment eliminated his housing allowance, Quarters F had spacious living accommodations that permitted the Kinkaids to entertain comfortably, something that was important to them.[42] Though most of their socializing was with their Navy associates, Tom and Helen did develop a circle of civilian friends, some going back to Tom's youth in Georgetown and the District. Helen also broadened their circle through her own activities. Not restricted by having to care for children, she began working as a volunteer at the Library of Congress in programs to assist the blind. She learned to read braille and was appointed to a committee that selected books for translation into braille. She also took an active role on the Board of Governors of the District's Home for the Incurables. (This institution would be called a nursing home today.)[43]

Unlike his activity during his previous BUORD tour, Tom published no articles, but he did initiate some official correspondence that made him the talk of the Gun Factory and even reached the staff of the Commander in Chief, U.S. Fleet. In a letter to Secretary of the Navy Curtis Wilbur dated 23 October 1925, Kinkaid raised the desirability of beginning plans for the two battleships that would replace *Utah* and *Florida* in 1932. Because the General Board and other bodies would have to agree on the new ships' characteristics, and money would have to be sought from Congress in 1928, it was time to begin the first step of soliciting service opinion. Since he had personally given some thought to the subject, Kinkaid went on to express his own ideas about the future battleships. This letter, of course, was to go via official channels, so Tom was sticking his neck out in a big way.[44]

He started with the armament. Here he returned to the theme of his gunfire article: The new battleships should mount a dozen 16-inch rifles in four triple-gun turrets. If there were displacement constraints, he would prefer twelve 14-inch rifles to eight or nine of 16-inch caliber. At that time both types of rifle could shoot beyond the distance of realistic visual fire

---

[41] TCK to COMDESRON 9, 20 Apr 1925; COMDESRON 9 to TCK, 22 Apr 1925; Chief BUNAV to TCK, Washington, 27 Apr 1925, TCK Personnel File.

[42] CAPT Thomas Kinkaid Kimmel, interview with author, Annapolis, MD, 25 Jul 1976.

[43] Helen Kinkaid interview, Washington, 12 Jul 1976.

[44] TCK to SECNAV, Washington, 23 Oct 1925, TCK Papers.

control. For a secondary battery he proposed eliminating the traditional 5-inch or 6-inch broadside guns and replacing them with sixteen 5-inch dual purpose antiaircraft (AA) guns. These 5-inch guns, he believed, would be as effective against destroyers as the regular broadside guns and would considerably increase the ship's defense against aircraft. He also recommended that the new battleships continue to mount two 21-inch torpedo tubes, though their presence in the battleships seemed vestigial rather than practical. He did call for their placement above the waterline rather than below it as had been the case in previous dreadnoughts. For protection he advocated the principle of all-or-none, that is, protection against 16-inch gunfire in the vital areas (magazines, turrets, sides, conning towers) and little in the less important between-deck spaces.[45]

Kinkaid's papers contain a copy of his letter to the Secretary and a dozen or so interoffice memoranda, letters from friends concerning his letter, and a few memoranda from staff members of CINCUS Admiral Samuel S. Robison. Almost everyone liked his ideas about the dual purpose 5-inch AA guns. Only one agreed that the torpedo tubes should be installed. Most (and a few regretfully) recognized that the 35,000-ton displacement limit of the Naval Conference's Five Power Treaty would force acceptance of the all-or-none protection principle. Even the concept of having twelve big guns on the new battleships appears to have been accepted.

Commander James L. (Reggie) Kauffman, Tom's roommate at the Naval Academy who was now on Admiral Robison's staff, wrote that "both Admiral Robison and [Commander] Nimitz thought your letter a very excellent one. . . . Admiral Robison agreed in most part with your big gun ideas but seemed to be very keen about the 16-inch gun."[46] He later sent Tom a copy of a memorandum written to CINCUS by his Chief of Staff, Rear Admiral Lusius A. Bostwick. He agreed with all Kinkaid's points, even the torpedo tubes, and commented, "I agree that twelve (12) sixteen inch (16") guns should constitute the main battery if it is possible to install such a battery on the displacement permitted."[47] A few were concerned that Kinkaid's proposals might be so challenging that the letter would focus interest on his recommendations rather than on the central proposal to get the planning process underway for the replacement battleships.

From London an old friend who previously had served with Tom at the Gun Factory wrote the most realistic response to his letter (realistic, that is, when seen with the hindsight of history). Commander Herbert Fairfax Leary had shared Tom's letter with the latter's classmate, Com-

---

[45] Ibid.
[46] CDR J. L. Kauffman to TCK, New York Navy Yard, 18 Dec 1925, TCK Papers.
[47] Memorandum for the Admiral, by L. A. Bostwick, 19 Jan 1926, TCK Papers.

mander Jerome C. Hunsaker, who was also attached to Ambassador A. B. Houghton's staff. Leary then wrote to Tom:

> However Hunsaker and I disagree with you as to the advisability of doing what you propose now. It seems to us that developments and changes in the realm of naval architecture, ordnance and marine engineering within the next five years will render such work largely valueless and that the limited expert personnel of the Design Bureaus could be better employed in putting all of their time on the question of the 10,000 ton cruisers, destroyer leaders, and submarines, types we can build now.[48]

Leary was correct, but for the wrong reason. At the time Kinkaid probably knew as much as Leary or anyone else about the prospects of serious change in the area of capital ship batteries and protection. What neither of them understood was that the Coolidge administration, and later the Hoover administration, had no intention of building any more expensive battleships. In less than a year the State Department, aided by a few reluctant naval officers, would begin planning for the 1927 Geneva Naval Conference, and for a League of Nations–sponsored World Disarmament Conference that would meet in 1932. These activities would nullify Kinkaid's proposal to start plans for a new generation of battleships.[49]

As expected Tom and almost all of the remaining members of the Class of 1908 were selected for promotion at the selection board's 1925 sitting. On 12 July 1926 he took his physical and then underwent two days of written and oral examinations. A few days later the president of the examining board wrote to Kinkaid's superior:

> I note with pleasure that Lieutenant Commander Thomas C. Kinkaid ... has passed a creditable examination for promotion to the grade of commander, his marks ranging from 3.40 in International Law to 3.89 in Strategy and Tactics, and his record has been marked excellent. Since midshipmen at the Naval Academy are given a star when they attain marks of 3.4 and over for a course, I like to notify commanding officers when any of the officers under their command attain, in any examination, marks of 3.4 and above in all subjects.

Captain Frank L. Pinney passed the letter along to Kinkaid with his heartiest congratulations. The superintendent of the Gun Factory read Kellogg's letter at the morning conference of his department heads.[50] In

---

[48] H. F. Leary to TCK, London, 8 Dec 1925, TCK Papers.
[49] Gerald E. Wheeler, *Prelude to Pearl Harbor: The United States Navy and the Far East, 1921–1931* (Columbia: University of Missouri Press, 1963), chaps. 6 and 7.
[50] CAPT E. S. Kellogg to CAPT F. L. Pinney, Washington, 16 Jul 1926; Pinney to Kellogg, Washington, 17 Jul 1926, TCK Papers.

time promotion papers came through setting his date of rank at 4 June 1926. It probably stung Tom a little when he realized that, had he been a star man at the Academy instead of eighteen years later, he would have worn his scrambled eggs (gold leaf on the visor of commanders' and captains' hats) a year earlier with the first selectees from his class.

Time passed quickly for the Kinkaids, and in the summer of 1927 Tom began arranging for his next duty. On his fitness reports he had asked for a command in the Battle Fleet, which would mean a move to the West Coast, or another Washington assignment. Instead his growing reputation resulted in a different tour of duty. Admiral Henry Wiley was due to relieve Admiral Charles F. Hughes as CINCUS in November. (It should be noted that the Class of 1888 is unique in having three members command the U.S. Fleet; perhaps it helped that Secretary Curtis Wilbur was also a graduate of that class.)

Because he had been on the General Board before being appointed to command the fleet, Admiral Wiley had to select a complete staff. The work fell largely to Captain Walter Anderson, his assistant Chief of Staff, who remembered Tom Kinkaid from previous service. It is likely that Anderson, an ordnance specialist when at the Naval Academy, checked with Captain Pinney. If so, he would have been assured that Kinkaid would make a fine fleet gunnery officer. The captain's final evaluation was decidedly favorable. He rated Kinkaid 4.0 in professional qualifications, evaluated him "superior" or "above average" in all descriptive traits, and finally concluded: "An officer of marked ability. He has performed his duties in a highly satisfactory manner and has rendered valuable service to the Naval Gun Factory."[51]

Though he had received orders well in advance, there was a little uncertainty about Kinkaid's date of departure. This lack of precision came from the fact that Admiral Hughes was to relieve an ailing Admiral E. W. Eberle as Chief of Naval Operations. Finally the Navy Department set 8 November for the change of command of the U.S. Fleet, to take place in San Pedro, California. Tom signed out of the Gun Factory on 24 October and on 27 October started his long transcontinental trip from Philadelphia—the first such trip he had made since he crossed the nation in 1908 to join *Nebraska* in San Francisco. Helen did not accompany him since the flagship was scheduled to return to the East Coast in mid-December. On arrival in San Pedro on 1 November Tom reported to Hughes's Chief of Staff, and awaited the arrival of the rest of Admiral Wiley's staff.[52]

---

[51] Fitness Report, 30 Sep 1927, TCK Personnel File; VADM Walter S. Anderson, interview by John T. Mason, Jr., 1962, 158ff, Columbia University Oral History, New York (hereafter Anderson oral history).
[52] TCK Personnel File.

CINCUS Staff

Never having served on a fleet commander's staff and lacking the requisite rank, Commander Kinkaid for the first time in his career took part in the change-of-command ceremony involving the two four-star admirals. The flag shift was scheduled for the forenoon watch on 8 November on board the battleship *Texas* (BB 35) in San Pedro harbor. Admiral Wiley and his staff, including Kinkaid, arrived early and began stowing their gear in the flag spaces. This would be home for the next eighteen months. Around 0900 and for the next hour the officer's gangway was steadily manned by side-boys and the boatswain's pipe shrilled almost constantly as subordinate flag officers arrived in their barges, most with their chiefs of staff.

First to arrive was Admiral Louis DeSteiguer, Commander in Chief, Battle Fleet; then Vice Admiral William Pratt, Commander Battleship Divisions, Battle Fleet, followed by six rear admirals and several dozen captains. It was an overcast day, but the gold braid on sleeves, cocked hats, and epaulets of the full dress uniforms flashed brightly as they all assembled on the flagship's forecastle, which also served as flag country. Admiral Wiley's staff arranged itself on the port side forward and Admiral Hughes's staff on the starboard. The two principals stood together at the bottom of the V formed by their staffs. At 1000 Admiral Hughes stepped forward and read the orders that moved him from CINCUS to Chief of Naval Operations. Admiral Wiley then stepped forward, read his orders, and told Hughes, "I will relieve you, sir." Hughes's flag was hauled down and the captain's *Texas* pennant was broken at the main. While everyone stood at attention, the ship's band played the "Admiral's March," *California* (BB 44) fired a salute of seventeen guns, and *Texas* again returned it. Following a session of handshaking and congratulations, the flagship quickly emptied of visitors and the admiral began his new duties. So did the fleet gunnery officer.[53]

Tom's duties in the beginning were fairly clear-cut. He was to schedule gunnery training for all subordinate groups within the U.S. Fleet (Battle Fleet, Scouting Fleet, Base Force, etc.) and receive reports of gunnery exercises from the same groups and the individual ships in them. The actual day-to-day scheduling of each unit for gunnery practices and live firings was left to the Battle Fleet and Scouting Fleet commanders. The gunnery training year began in the late summer and climaxed in the spring with live firing for the record. The results were carefully tabulated and those turrets (in the battleships and cruisers) and ships achieving a record of excellent would wear the coveted "E" for

---

[53] Log of USS *Texas* (BB 35), 8 Nov 1927, RG 24, NA; Henry A. Wiley, *An Admiral from Texas* (Garden City, NY: Doubleday, Doran, 1934), 274–75.

the next year. For the big ships the gunnery record was an amalgam of long-range battle practice, short-range battle practice, night firing of each, antiaircraft battle practice, and division (two or more large ships) and force (two or more divisions) firing. The emphasis was on individual ship (and turret) performance, and the rules of engagement were minutely structured to ensure that every ship fired its guns under as nearly the same conditions as possible. Reduced to its essence, an excellent gunnery record could help ensure promotion for a ship's gunnery officer and commanding officer. Those stakes were important enough in the eyes of the officers involved that they wanted no advantage to accrue to others because they had fired in better weather or did not have the sun in their faces on an approach bearing to the target.[54]

As the operations officer on Admiral Bristol's staff and later commanding officer of *Isherwood,* Kinkaid became intimately familiar with the requirements of the annual gunnery training schedule. Because training had become slack in the destroyers in Turkish waters, he had brought them back onto schedule. In *Isherwood* he had raised the standing of the ship in gunnery competition, but he detested the paperwork involved. Now he found himself in a position to effect change, and he began almost immediately to make his ideas known. Before he had completed a month on the staff, Tom wrote a lengthy memorandum for the Chief of Staff, Rear Admiral H. V. Butler, Jr., proposing to change the whole focus of the year's gunnery schedule.[55] Probably encouraged by the reception of his memorandum in the staff, he also circulated copies of it to friends at BUORD, in the CNO's office, and on other staffs in the U.S. Fleet.

Originally thirteen pages long, Kinkaid's memorandum focused on just a few points. The central theme was that current gunnery training in the fleet seemed to emphasize achievement of turret and ship gunnery competition scores rather than training a vessel for battle. In battle the concentrated effort of a division or force would be tested, not the individual gun or turret. He particularly believed that the short-range battle practice was useless, wasted steaming time and money, and contributed nothing to preparing a big ship for actual battle. Even worse, the SRBP and preliminary practices generated too much paper for the little value derived. Finally he believed that instead of the year-round practicing, rehearsals, and live firing sessions, gunnery training and firing for score could be concentrated into two six-week periods. The more important training would come in long-distance cruises, preferably to foreign ports, during which simulated engagements would be the most important type of gunnery ex-

---

[54] Wiley, *Admiral from Texas,* 287–89; Yates Stirling, *Sea Duty: The Memoirs of a Fighting Admiral* (New York: G. P. Putnam's Sons, 1939), 192–94.
[55] Memo for Chief of Staff by TCK, at sea, Nov 1927, subj: Gunnery Training, TCK Papers.

ercises. In regular home ports gunnery people would receive special training in schools established and controlled by the fleets.[56]

Tom's memorandum might have been another intellectual exercise, like his previous one on guns for the new battleships, had he not struck a responsive chord in Admiral Wiley. As it happened, the admiral had some changes he wanted to make in the U.S. Fleet, and high on the list was changing fleet gunnery training. He spelled it all out to CNO Hughes in a letter of 9 March 1929. He wanted to eliminate the SRBP and use the time for underway battle training of divisions. Gunnery training, practices, and firing for score would be concentrated in two six-week periods. During the first period individual ship gunnery training would be emphasized, and division and force training would be the focus during the second. The heart of Wiley's ideas (and Kinkaid's as well) was stated under the section "Proposed Gunnery Schedule":

> The [gunnery training] program must be so arranged that the personnel concerned will keep uppermost in their minds the application of the practices to actual battle. Battle conditions must be simulated as closely as possible. To carry out an exercise in which all of the elements such as courses, speeds, times, bearings, etc. are carefully prepared beforehand does not constitute training for battle. To approach a target at a given time, at a given speed, on a prescribed course, for firing of a definite portion of the armament in a definite way does not conform to the circumstances of battle.[57]

The admiral did not want to eliminate the competitive element in gunnery training, but he did believe that management of it could be decentralized to the fleet and its subdivisions. He also wanted to see training courses for gunnery officers established in the fleet.[58]

A few months later and after several exchanges of correspondence, Admiral Hughes forthrightly stated his view that SRBP must continue as a central feature of fleet gunnery training. He reminded Wiley that SRBP was the only practice where gun pointers proved they could hit a target. He believed that, in battle, the fire-control director equipment would eventually break down due "to the shock of gun-fire, enemy damage and inherent weaknesses which increased when handled by personnel in the excitement of battle." At that moment the gun pointers would take over from the spotters and their gun directors. It was a conservative argument and probably unanswerable given the stage of development in gunfire control equipment, but Wiley was bitterly disappointed.[59]

---

[56] Ibid.
[57] CINCUS to CNO, 9 Mar 28, subj: Training of the Fleet for War: Gunnery Training, TCK Papers.
[58] Ibid.
[59] CNO to CINCUS, Washington, 23 Aug 1928, subj: Short Range Battle Practice, TCK Papers.

Writing gunnery memos might have been intellectually stimulating for Kinkaid, but he was also in an enviable position to study battleship gunnery without responsibility for its results. In changing flagships from the old armored cruiser *Seattle* (CA 11) to *Texas*, CINCUS was removing a working battleship from the battle line. Because he believed that most gunnery training could be accomplished during regular cruising, Admiral Wiley insisted that Captain Z. E. Briggs undertake the usual practices expected of individual battleships as well as participate in division and force exercises when in a position to do so. A few years later he commented on the results:

> The *Texas*, since November, 1927, had been pretty well on the go. Her officers and men were becoming daily better seamen, better gunners, better all-round navy men. And when she went into her annual target practice she did as well as any ship of her class. On her next tests, in maneuvering, in gunnery, and in steaming, she was up among the leaders. In the meantime she kept moving. The point is she had little opportunity to jigger around sighting on towed targets. She certainly lost nothing by it, while officers and men had a touch of real sea life, with an opportunity to see something of the world, to play as well as work.[60]

Texas spent most of November 1927 at gunnery exercises out of San Diego before departing for Balboa on the 22d. That day proved a memorable one for the admiral. He and his staff informally inspected Rear Admiral Joseph M. Reeves's command, Aircraft Squadrons, Battle Fleet, and then had lunch as guests of the San Diego Chamber of Commerce. At 1627 his flagship got underway, and in eighteen minutes she was stuck on an uncharted shoal, Captain Briggs at the conn. It took forty-five minutes to work *Texas* free of the mud by using engines and anchor. Fifteen minutes after getting underway again, Admiral Wiley stumbled while walking forward and tumbled down the starboard hawse pipe. Fortunately the anchor had been hove in, and the admiral was able to grab it and prevent himself from falling into the channel. Captain Anderson, his Assistant Chief of Staff, helped to retrieve him, a bit cut up and bloody, his uniform ruined, but safe. The long cruise down to the Canal Zone gave him a chance to heal and regain his sense of humor. He later wrote, "We have often heard of officers who had reached the quarterdeck 'through the hawse pipe.' I am sure, however, that history does not record an instance of a flag officer ending his career by passing out through the hawse pipe."[61]

---

[60] Wiley, *Admiral from Texas*, 288–89.
[61] Ibid., 276–77; *Texas* log, 22 Nov 1927.

After a week in Balboa *Texas* transited the canal on 9 December and stood out of Colón two days later for New York. As a staff member, Kinkaid had had the opportunity to visit every important shore-based command in San Diego, Balboa, Colón, and Coco Solo. It was all interesting, but getting back to the East Coast and Helen was what counted with him. On Saturday, 17 December, *Texas* arrived at the New York Navy Yard and was greeted with a seventeen-gun salute from the Third Naval District's saluting battery. The battleship had been banged up rather badly transiting the canal and would need drydocking. Things obviously would slow down for the holidays, so Tom took seven days' leave to enjoy the Christmas season with Helen and her family in Philadelphia, and then made a quick trip to Washington to visit his mother.[62]

During the winter of 1927–1928 *Texas*, CINCUS, and the staff spent two very pleasant months cruising in tropical waters. In mid-January President Coolidge, Secretary of State Frank Kellogg, and former Secretary of State Charles Hughes, plus wives, aides, and a variety of government functionaries, boarded *Texas* in Key West for transportation to Havana, Cuba. The President would speak to the Pan-American Conference and return in a few days to Key West. From there the flagship steamed to Gonaïves, Haiti, to join Vice Admiral Ashley Robertson's Scouting Fleet. After a few days of inspections, official calls, and some socializing, *Texas* moved on.

The battleship arrived at the Andrew's Street Dock in New Orleans on 13 February and remained for ten days of Mardi Gras festivities. Helen was there to meet the ship and the parties began. On the 15th Mayor Arthur O'Keefe and the City Commissioners came on board for lunch. This was small return for the week of entertainment, including a ball every night, that was available to the admiral and his staff. Almost fifty years later Helen Kinkaid still remembered the enormous fun she and Tom had enjoyed in the Crescent City. The Caribbean cruise ended in early March with a visit to St. Thomas in the Virgin Islands. Not the tourist attraction they are today, to Admiral Wiley the islands seemed more a poorhouse than a paradise.[63]

Following the St. Thomas visit, *Texas* turned south again for the Panama Canal, which it transited on 14 March. After a few days of calls and inspections Wiley ordered the flagship north to San Diego, then on to San Francisco, where they arrived on 5 April. Three weeks later, in company with the Battle Fleet, *Texas* headed out the Golden Gate and shaped course for Pearl Harbor. (Slightly less than twenty years earlier Tom had joined *Nebraska* and the Great White Fleet for a similar voyage.)

---

[62] *Texas* log, 11–28 Dec 1927.
[63] Ibid., 12 Jan–23 Feb 1928; Wiley, *Admiral from Texas*, 278–86.

NHC

The crew of *Texas* (BB 35) mans the rail in honor of President Coolidge during the presidential review of the fleet at Hampton Roads, Va., September 1927.

A half-dozen of the staff wives, including Helen Kinkaid, followed their husbands by commercial liners in order to enjoy a month's vacation in Uncle Sam's tropical garden. Although fleet problems and exercises occupied the attention of Wiley and his staff, there was plenty of time for recreation, and the Kinkaids made the most of it. On 21 May the fleet exercises ended and *Texas* again headed for San Francisco. Here Admiral Wiley would leave the ship to travel overland by train to Washington. He had orders to chair the annual selection board. Tom and most of the staff remained in *Texas* to continue by way of the Panama Canal to the New York Navy Yard, where they would arrive at Pier 4 on 27 June. As usual Helen was dockside when Tom stepped ashore.[64]

While *Texas* received its annual maintenance in the New York Navy Yard in Brooklyn, CINCUS and his staff began several months of leave-taking. With the admiral taking most of August to vacation in Canada, Tom and Helen spent the month attending the eighth annual session of the Institute of Politics held on the campus of Williams College at Williamstown, Massachusetts. Located in the Berkshire Mountains the

---

[64] *Texas* log, 9 Mar–27 Jun 1928.

Williams campus was an ideal place to spend a New England summer. Daily reading, lectures, and round-table seminar discussions proved exciting. Both were able to bring a great deal of personal insight and some expertise to the round-table conference dealing with "Modern Turkey and Its Problems."[65] The relaxed schedule permitted a daily round of at least nine holes of golf, and that made the institute almost idyllic. Helen had been a reading enthusiast most of her life, and she enjoyed books on international relations, politics, and travel. By the end of the month Tom was a convert. Building on their experience in Constantinople, they became ardently internationalist in their outlook, following in the steps of Tom's senior mentors, Admirals Bristol and Wiley.[66]

After the month at Williamstown, Kinkaid returned to *Texas* and his duties on Wiley's staff. The month of September was largely spent at sea on the Southern Drill Grounds where Captain J. R. Defrees put his ship through the various required firing exercises. The battleship's log book bristles with daily notations concerning SRBP, LRBP, AA practice, and their night variants. Probably sensitive to Wiley's views on gunnery drills, Defrees exercised his crew at battle stations during routine departures and entries through the Chesapeake Capes and during practically any other evolution involving his ship's movement. It was necessary of course, since the battleship was not currently a part of the Battle Fleet or of a battleship division. Once the practices were completed, CINCUS made an official visit to Havana and the ship's crew enjoyed nine days of recreation in Cuba's capital. The month of October ended with *Texas* visiting the Naval Academy for Navy Day (October 27). Following another month on the Southern Drill Grounds and at the Hampton Roads anchorages, *Texas* and her admiral returned to the Navy Yard in Brooklyn for replenishment and the Christmas holidays before heading south for the U.S. Fleet concentration in Panamanian waters.[67]

Despite the skimpy naval budgets of the period, Admiral Wiley convinced CNO Hughes that a full U.S. Fleet concentration was needed in the winter of 1928–1929. The previous year the Scouting Fleet had held its concentration in the Guantanamo area and the Battle Fleet had drilled in Hawaiian waters. As CINCUS, Wiley commanded most of the Navy's vessels, but he would be an active commander of the two main fleets (battle and scouting) and their trains only when they were concentrated. So he called for the two fleets, plus fleet trains and the Control Force (submarines), to concentrate on the Pacific side of the isthmus in

---

[65] *The Institute of Politics at Williamstown, Massachusetts: Its First Decade* (Williamstown, MA: The Institute of Politics, 1931), 58.
[66] TCK Personnel File; *Texas* log, 31 Jul–31 Aug 1928; Helen Kinkaid interview, 7 Jan 1976.
[67] *Texas* log, 1 Sep–31 Dec 1928.

mid-January 1929. Included in the concentration for the first time would be the new giant aircraft carriers, *Lexington* (CV 2) and *Saratoga* (CV 3).[68]

The war games and exercises took three weeks and concluded with a carrier task force raid by *Saratoga*'s aircraft against the canal. The concept of a carrier raid was not new, but the range, speed, and striking power of the ship's squadrons had previously been unappreciated. Kinkaid's eyes were opened. Within a few months he would apply for flight training at Pensacola with the hope of joining several other senior officers who were coming late to naval aviation. Unfortunately the hearing impairment first discovered at Annapolis prevented his being accepted.[69] Both CINCUS and the Battle Fleet commander, Admiral Pratt, were deeply impressed by the performance of Rear Admiral Reeves's squadrons. Twelve years later Tom Kinkaid would be participating in carrier task force raids in the southwest Pacific, and a few months after that would be commanding his own carrier task force.[70]

At the conclusion of Fleet Exercise IX *Texas* sailed north with the Battle Fleet for visits to San Diego and San Francisco. The latter city was always popular with the Navy, and the payroll of the ships' companies was certainly appreciated by the San Franciscans. By 15 April the Battle Fleet was again in San Pedro and ready to begin six weeks of practice and firing for record. As usual, CINCUS and his staff were interested observers, simply along for the ride. During these months Tom again had to think about a new assignment. The President and Secretary of the Navy had already decided that on 21 May Admiral Wiley would be relieved by Admiral Pratt, then commanding the Battle Fleet. Tom had indicated on both his fitness reports and in a separate letter to the Bureau of Navigation that he wanted to attend the Naval War College or be assigned as an executive officer in a battleship. He got his first choice; he and Helen were to spend a year in Newport, Rhode Island.[71]

It is clear that Tom Kinkaid had been a satisfactory member of Admiral Wiley's staff. In three of the last four fitness reports the admiral gave his gunnery officer the highest marks that could be given. The remarks section on the last report was typical:

---

[68] Wiley, *Admiral from Texas*, 297–302.

[69] TCK Personnel File.

[70] Eugene E. Wilson, *Slipstream: The Autobiography of an Air Craftsman* (New York: McGraw-Hill, 1950), 135–48, describes the maneuvers of 1929. See also Wiley, *Admiral from Texas*, 297–300; Gerald E. Wheeler, *Admiral William Veazie Pratt, U.S. Navy: A Sailor's Life* (Washington: Naval History Division, 1974), 274–75; Archibald D. Turnbull and Clifford L. Lord, *History of United States Naval Aviation* (New Haven, CT: Yale University Press, 1949), 270–72; Scot MacDonald, "Flattops in the War Games," *Evolution of Aircraft Carriers* (Washington, 1964), 28–33.

[71] TCK to Chief BUNAV, 7 Oct 1928; Chief BUNAV to TCK, Washington, 9 Feb 1929, TCK Personnel File.

An unusually fine type of officer and gentleman, exceptionally qualified professionally. Intelligent, industrious, loyal and of strong military character. Well balanced and of very pleasing manner. Fully qualified for promotion and strongly recommended therefor. Thoroughly qualified for independent command or any other duty for which he may be eligible.[72]

The strength of these remarks and Wiley's generally positive attitude toward Kinkaid probably stemmed from the meshing of their views on gunnery training. It is quite evident that Tom's early views on fleet and ship gunnery were his own; by coincidence the admiral had been thinking along parallel lines. Under such conditions it was simple and natural for Kinkaid to write the Wiley memoranda that were used to try to change the CNO's views on gunnery exercises. It is also clear that at this point in his career Kinkaid was a smooth staff member. Wiley highlighted the characteristics that repeatedly showed up on fitness reports written by others. Kinkaid was industrious, loyal, pleasing, and at all times a gentleman. He was also well qualified in ordnance and gunnery and entertained views of his own on training that stood outside the mainstream thinking of the 1920s and 1930s.

On 21 May, at 1105, the change-of-command scenario played eighteen months earlier was again enacted. Admiral Pratt brought his staff on board *Texas* in San Pedro harbor and relieved Admiral Wiley. Within a few days Tom would be heading east by train for a month of leave and the move to Newport. He and Helen were again invited to spend August at Williamstown with the Institute of Politics, but the War College course precluded such a pleasant diversion. August in Newport, however, was not a bad alternative to the Berkshires.

The Naval War College

Like the majority of naval officers before and after him who attended the Naval War College, Kinkaid's year in Newport was a unique experience. He had not served there earlier and he would not return again, except briefly as a visitor. By 1929 the view of Admiral William Sims and a few other senior officers—that attendance at a war college (preferably the Navy's) should be mandatory for promotion to flag rank—had almost become writ. A few captains were still becoming rear admirals without completion of the course at the Army college at Fort McNair in Washington, D.C., or the Navy's in Newport, but they were becoming rarer.[73] To prepare himself for Newport while serving in *Isherwood* and at the Gun Fac-

---

[72] Fitness Reports, 31 Mar and 21 May 1929, TCK Personnel File.
[73] Michael Vlahos, *The Blue Sword: Naval War College and the American Mission, 1919–1941* (Newport, RI: Naval War College Press, 1980), 91–5; Wheeler, *Pratt*, 245–47.

tory, Tom had completed the War College correspondence course in "Strategy and Tactics." It had taken him almost two and a half years, but complete it he did "With Great Credit."[74] That experience, followed by staff duty with CINCUS, had been a good tune-up for a year of study.

The Kinkaids rented a house on Greenough Place in Newport and dug in for a year of intellectual improvement. Helen became a devotee of the Redwood Library and kept busy for the year. When the weather permitted, she and Tom continued golfing at the local courses. But his routine at the War College controlled the pattern of their social activities. The college then operated Monday through Saturday, with Wednesday and Saturday afternoons free. The Kinkaids made a few friends among the civilians of Newport, but by and large their evening and weekend social activities were confined to their service friends. As might be expected, Christmas leave was spent in Philadelphia with Helen's parents; a quick trip was made to Washington to visit Tom's mother and to make sure Tom's detailer understood clearly his preference for assignment after completion of the War College course.[75]

The routine of the War College had not been changed significantly since 1919. Reading and lectures provided a common basis for education in international relations, international law, logistics, communications, strategy, and tactics. What was learned then formed the basis for problem solving in the form of operations exercises and war games. By the time the Class of 1930 began its war games activities, the overwhelming amount of time was spent on problems involving the theoretical enemy: Japan. Blue (U.S.)-Orange (Japan) war games exposed Kinkaid and his classmates to the realities of moving an American fleet across the Pacific Ocean to confront the Imperial Navy. The year proved to be both an education and an indoctrination. Not having served in the Asiatic Fleet or the Pacific Fleet (Battle Fleet), Tom's natural outlook was Europe centered. He was well aware of the size and composition of the Japanese navy, but he was not well informed about Far Eastern international relations, nor about the Japanese as a people and a culture, although he could talk at length about the British, the Turks, the Greeks, or the affairs of France. The result was that the year of emphasis on potential Blue-Orange operations left him better educated about managing a naval operation or campaign in the far Pacific, but not much more knowledgeable about the Japanese people except in terms of the stereotypes presented by his instructors.[76]

---

[74] President Naval War College to TCK, Newport, 23 Jul 1927, TCK Personnel File.

[75] John B. Hattendorf, B. Mitchell Simpson, and John R. Wadleigh, *Sailors and Soldiers: The Centennial History of the U.S. Naval War College* (Newport, RI: Naval War College Press, 1948), 137–40; Helen Kinkaid interview, 7 Jan 1976.

[76] Vlahos, *Blue Sword*, 113–130; Wheeler, *Prelude to Pearl Harbor*, 60–69; Hattendorf, *Sailors and Solders*, 140–46; Thomas B. Buell, *The Quiet Warrior: A Biography of Admiral Raymond A. Spruance* (Boston: Little, Brown, 1974), 50–53, 71–72.

At the end of their year of study the students of the Senior Course were expected to choose from a few broad topics and write a thesis of about one hundred pages. Tom chose national foreign policies, and titled his paper "The Present Foreign Policies of the United States." Students were encouraged to be as original as possible in their thinking, but Kinkaid was not. In a bit more than one hundred pages he simply listed and described the basic foreign policies of the United States in 1930. His work was little more than a distillation of several textbooks in diplomatic history and international relations, perhaps lightly spiced with the contents of a few lectures by university professors working in the New England area. It was probably dreary work putting the thesis together, but no more dreary than analyzing a basket full of gunnery reports from the Battle Fleet. It met the requirement for graduation and Tom got his diploma on 26 May 1930.[77]

Because he was still an active-duty naval officer while attending the War College, Kinkaid received a fitness report at the time of his detachment. In many ways it was his report card for the year in Newport. In 1930 there were five broad grades for each personal quality evaluated, ranging from superior to unsatisfactory, and each grade was further divided into five subdivisions, with 1 the highest and 5 the lowest. Tom was evaluated superior in all qualities, but he received a 1 in only five of them: initiative, cooperation, attention to duty, industry, and neatness of person and dress. He received a 2 for loyalty and aptitude for the service; a 3 for intelligence, judgment, force, leadership, tact, presence of mind, and military bearing; and a 5 for endurance. This last mark, the only 5 he got, probably reflected the fact that Kinkaid suffered more from colds and sinus infections than the average officer and probably had more absences than his instructors thought reasonable for a superior evaluation. Captain Joseph K. Taussig, in charge of the War College's new advanced course, prepared the report and concluded it with the remarks, "A superior officer in every respect. Industrious and intelligent. His work in Strategy and Tactics has been generally above the average. Recommended for promotion when due."[78]

Given his penchant for carefully managing his career, Kinkaid did not leave his next duty assignment completely in the hands of his detailer. On 1 November he wrote to Rear Admiral Mark Bristol, then in Washington, and asked that he be considered as a relief for the secretary of the General Board, Captain Robert L. Ghormley, who was slated for sea duty in June. He believed, as did the rest of the Navy, that Bristol was to be the new senior member (presiding officer) of the board once Rear Admiral Andrew

---

[77] TCK, "Senior Class, 1930, Thesis: The Present Foreign Policies of the United States," Newport, 26 Apr 1930, TCK Papers.
[78] Fitness Report, 28 May 1930, TCK Personnel File.

T. Long moved onto the retired list. The next day Tom officially requested the Bureau of Navigation to consider him for duty as secretary of the General Board.[79] At the end of the month Bristol answered Tom's letter, and told him that he would relieve Ghormley. This was not news. The admiral had seen Helen Kinkaid in Washington a few days earlier and gave her the same information; but it was nice to get it in writing. On 8 February, the bureau made it all official: Kinkaid would relieve Ghormley and could delay reporting until 30 June. For Tom and Helen this was all perfect. They would even be able to get in a month's vacation before reporting for duty. Unfortunately Admiral Bristol decided he needed Tom's services more than Tom needed a vacation. Tom reported on 2 June.[80]

Tom Kinkaid's year at the Naval War College might be considered as simply getting a required "punch in his ticket." Because he stood in the lower half of his class, he needed to take advantage of every opportunity to improve the odds in his favor when he next faced a selection (promotion) board. Considered in those terms, he made a good decision. Of the 201 graduates of the Class of 1908, only thirty-one attended war college; of these, seventeen became flag officers, and fourteen were passed over as captains. On the other hand eight of his classmates achieved flag rank without war college experience. Seen with the benefit of hindsight the year in Newport was one pleasantly spent, and a good job became available at the right time. This type of luck was to become more common in the years ahead.[81]

The General Board

Unlike his previous Washington tour, Kinkaid could not live in government quarters, so he and Helen leased a house on 18th Street not too far from Dupont Circle and the embassies along Massachusetts Avenue. (Twenty years later they would return to this locality for retirement.) From his house Tom could walk to Main Navy in twenty minutes to a half hour, or, in less time, could visit his mother at the Wyoming Apartments. It was also a fairly brief walk to the Army and Navy Club if the Kinkaids felt like dining out.

The General Board in 1930 was a well-established and respected Navy institution. Created during the Spanish-American War to advise on strategy, it became a permanent body for advising the Secretary of the Navy. Its scope of activities was spelled out in executive orders. The board con-

---

[79] TCK to Bristol, Newport, RI, 1 Nov 1929. Bristol Papers; TCK to Chief BUNAV, Newport, 2 Nov 1929, TCK Personnel File.
[80] Bristol to TCK, Washington, 31 Jan 1930, Bristol Papers; Chief BUNAV to TCK, Washington, 8 Feb 1930, 15 May 1930, TCK Personnel File.
[81] Statistics drawn from USNA Alumni Association, *Register of Alumni, 1845–50*.

cerned itself with naval policy, fleet organization and reorganization, naval construction plans, and ship and aircraft design characteristics. Originally created to develop war plans and strategies, the board in the 1930s left that aspect of naval operations to the War Plans Division in the CNO's office. Its membership has been described as a "receiving ship for admirals," and that was not an inappropriate phrase.[82] The full board was presided over by the Chief of Naval Operations; in June 1930 it was Admiral Hughes, and in September 1930, Admiral Pratt. In addition to the CNO, there were three other ex officio members: the President of the Naval War College, the Director of Naval Intelligence, and the Commandant of the Marine Corps. The full board met monthly, usually on the last Tuesday. Between meetings of the full board the executive committee carried on the work of the board under the leadership of the senior member, Rear Admiral Bristol. The working members of the board (the executive committee) varied in number depending on the needs of the Navy. Bristol, for instance, had just completed a tour as an admiral and Commander in Chief, Asiatic Fleet and had fleeted down to his permanent rank of rear admiral. On the other hand Rear Admiral J. V. Chase reported in mid-May and was detached in mid-September 1930 to become CINCUS with the rank of admiral. Following a year in the fleet's top command, Chase stripped two gold stripes from his dress blues and returned to the board as a rear admiral. In April 1932 he succeeded Bristol as senior member and remained there until retirement in January 1933. A board assignment was often used by the Department's top leadership to park a new rear admiral until an appropriate billet opened for him. The board also became, unfortunately, a final resting place for a few rear admirals who never possessed the superior abilities needed to fill the few vice admiral and admiral slots in the fleet. At almost any time, there would be one rear admiral among the six or seven members of the executive committee waiting to reach age sixty-four and statutory retirement.[83]

Kinkaid's motivation in seeking the secretary's position on the General Board is not clear. As a commander he was still a bit junior to claim an executive officer billet in a battleship or cruiser. He was too senior for a destroyer command and too inexperienced to be a destroyer division commander. He could have gotten a seagoing job somewhere, perhaps commanding an auxiliary type ship (cargo, refrigerator, ammunition, transport, oiler), but he wasn't that eager to go to sea. So he sought a po-

---

[82] Wheeler, *Pratt*, 174–75; ADM James O. Richardson, *On the Treadmill to Pearl Harbor: The Memoirs of Admiral James O. Richardson, USN (Ret.) as Told to Vice Admiral George C. Dyer, USN (Ret.)* (Washington: Naval History Division, 1973), 8–9.

[83] Wheeler, *Pratt*, 174–75; James Leutze, *A Different Kind of Victory: A Biography of Admiral Thomas C. Hart* (Annapolis: Naval Institute Press, 1981), 132–33; Ernest J. King and Walter Muir Whitehill, *Fleet Admiral King: A Naval Record* (New York: W. W. Norton, 1952), 295–305.

sition he believed would be career enhancing. Well aware that his lower-half position in the Class of 1908 was going to influence his chances to make captain, he took shelter in a familiar lee. He knew Bristol quite well and probably expected that several years of strong fitness reports from him would not hurt his chances for advancement. He also knew that the Navy's most important officers, either on their way up or returning from top commands, sat on the General Board. Some of the board members also sat on the captain and rear admiral selection board. Although the board's secretary was always present, he rarely contributed to its discussions. His job was to schedule, arrange, facilitate, and keep the record.[84] He could probably help himself professionally in such a position; but he also could bring his career to a sudden halt should he perform poorly.

Tom quickly mastered the routines of the board. The executive committee met daily at 1000. If there was business to be concluded or a hearing to be held, the members worked until noon. On a busy day or when facing a deadline, the board would recess for lunch and return to work into the afternoon. But it was fairly common for the members to meet, have a cup of coffee, and adjourn until the next day. Each member would be working on some question, usually together with another member or specialist ordered to the board for temporary duty, so they could keep busy. After two months and with Admiral Bristol on leave, Kinkaid requested and received permission to take a month's leave to attend the Institute of Politics at Williams College. Once again Tom and Helen enjoyed fleeing the Washington summer and refreshing themselves intellectually in the Berkshires.[85]

Upon his return from Williamstown, Kinkaid found an interesting surprise waiting. He was to be ordered to the State Department for temporary additional duty as a technical advisor to the "American Delegation to the Second Part of the Sixth Session of the Preparatory Commission for the Disarmament Conference." The assignment was temporary, and he would continue as secretary to the General Board.[86] Meeting in Geneva, the preparatory commission was an agency of the League of Nations; the United States participated hesitantly.

Since 1925 the commission had been struggling to create a draft convention to reduce or eliminate armaments (land, sea, and air) for submission to a World Disarmament Conference. The conference was expected to convene in early 1932. There was little to interest the Navy in the proceedings of the Preparatory Commission. The navies of the major sea powers (Great Britain, United States, Japan, France, and Italy)

---

[84] Observations about the work of the General Board and the duties of the board secretary are based on reading the minutes, proceedings, hearings, and reports of the board. The records of the General Board are stored at the Operational Archives, Naval Historical Center.

[85] General Board Proceedings, 1930, vol. 22, 29 Jul–2 Sep 1930.

[86] Assistant Secretary of State W. R. Castle, Jr. to TCK, Washington, 14 Oct 1930, TCK Papers.

had been limited by the Washington Naval Treaty of February 1922, and the United States, Great Britain, and Japan were further limited by the London Naval Treaty of April 1930. The Navy's leaders believed that more naval limitation should only be considered after a convention had been accepted that would limit armies and air forces.[87] But because technical data was needed concerning the U.S. Navy and those of other powers, the department was willing to supply officers to assist the delegation. The General Board was asked to name an officer, and Bristol chose Kinkaid. He probably did not think a flag officer was needed, and it would be useful to the board to have a member keeping an eye on the delegation. Kinkaid would know the mind of the board and of Mark Bristol when naval questions were raised in the delegation. The other naval technical advisor, Captain William W. Smyth, had been with the delegation for several years and would continue in that post.

Helen went with Tom, and they arrived in Cherbourg on the 24th. Moving immediately to Paris, the Kinkaids began ten splendid days of enjoying the City of Light. Between the social whirl of Paris, similar to that of 1922, and the fine restaurants of Geneva, Tom admitted later to Bristol that "I have taken on about ten pounds of light wine and beer."[88] Finally on 5 November Tom reported to the chairman of the American delegation, Hugh Gibson. A confidant of President Hoover and Ambassador to Belgium, Gibson was a career diplomat with perhaps the greatest experience in arms-limitation matters of anyone in the Foreign Service. He not only was a member of the 1930 delegation, he would serve as cochairman of the delegation to the World Disarmament Conference fifteen months later.

This last meeting of the Preparatory Commission labored mightily but had little to show for its efforts. The draft convention that emerged possessed few ideas that were totally accepted. In terms of naval matters it stated little more than the agreements reached by naval treaties in 1922 and 1930. There were no further reductions in existing navies and no plans to limit replacements as they came due. Kinkaid had been reasonably busy keeping tables up to date, but he probably profited most from lunches with the technical advisers of the other powers. Ambassador Gibson spoke for the Americans at any session, but Tom benefited greatly from learning all he could about the views of the other naval powers. Here his developing interest in international affairs paid dividends. A lengthy letter from Kinkaid, written to Bristol a few weeks before the meeting ended, reads like one of Hugh Gibson's or Pierrepont Moffat's gossipy exchanges, but it reveals some of the sophistication he was developing:

---

[87] Merze Tate, *The United States and Armaments* (Cambridge, MA: Harvard University Press, 1948), 75–78, 83–86.

[88] TCK to Bristol, Geneva, 22 Nov 1930, Bristol Papers.

The whole proceedings, of course, have been of great interest to me. I suppose I should have known better but I expected that some of the questions would be discussed and decided on their merits. However, the merits of the case have nothing to do with the decisions reached. The whole atmosphere is political. . . . France and Italy oppose each other almost consistently and each is supported by his respective satellites [sic]. . . . In discussing naval questions in sub-committees and outside of the Commission, the French cannot be depended upon to take any particular position. They jump about in an effort to get on the opposite side from Italy. After agreeing to C.P.D./230 they completely ditched us in regard to the tables. The British also went back on their agreement in one instance, but Mr. Gibson forced [Lord] Cecil to reverse his stand. The Japanese Delegation can be relied upon more than any other to keep its agreements.[89]

The Kinkaids left Geneva on 9 December and arrived in London the 11th. They spent an enjoyable five days visiting this great city before departing Southampton on the 16th, on board *Leviathan*. The passage was rough, but the Kinkaids traveled well. Arriving at New York on the 22d they returned immediately to Washington where Tom reported to the General Board the next day.[90]

Ambassador Gibson appreciated Kinkaid's work and showed it in a letter to Secretary of the Navy Charles Francis Adams:

Commander Kinkaid was attached to the delegation for the first time during the last session, and showed himself a hard worker and careful thinker. I have only commendation for his work. I should add that it has been a source, not only of official satisfaction, but of personal pleasure, to have had Captain Smyth and Commander Kinkaid members of the delegation.[91]

Because Captain Smyth was the senior naval officer in the delegation, he too evaluated Kinkaid's work. It is evident that Tom was not hurt by this temporary duty:

Commander Kinkaid was very industrious and painstaking, showed a liking for this kind of work, quickly grasped the points of discussion and showed good judgment in his handling of his duties. His professional ability and experience, his knowledge of French, and his personality render him an excellent officer for this duty.[92]

---

[89] Ibid.
[90] Kinkaid's itinerary can be found as endorsements to his basic orders. Castle to TCK, Washington, 14 Oct 1930, TCK Papers.
[91] Hugh Gibson to SECNAV C. F. Adams, 8 Dec 1930, TCK Papers.
[92] Fitness Report, 23 Dec 1930, TCK Personnel File.

It is evident that Kinkaid had done his usual first-class job. If he was interested in attending the World Disarmament Conference due to convene in February 1932, he had created a record that should help him get consideration.

Assignment again to the State Department was not long coming. Those nations preparing the draft convention had recommended the early convening of the widely anticipated World Disarmament Conference, but February 1932 was the earliest month possible. And while it disliked dealing with the matter, the General Board quickly began discussions of the draft convention.[93]

To meet the needs of the State Department for a technical advisor, Kinkaid was assigned temporary additional duty to the office of the CNO in early March for further assignment to the State Department, but he continued his basic work as the board's secretary.[94] For the next eight months he worked one or more days a week with an interdepartmental (Army, Navy, State Departments) committee; the rest of the time he tried to keep up his work for the board. His fitness reports from Admiral Bristol continued to be superior in their evaluations, so we must conclude that he could serve two masters quite competently.[95]

While working with the interdepartmental committee in the spring of 1931, Tom again ventured into the area of professional publication. He had been vexed by an article appearing in the April issue of *Foreign Affairs* by the Royal Navy's Admiral Sir Herbert Richmond.[96] The admiral opined that the previous naval limitation efforts had been inadequate. Furthermore he argued that the preparatory work for the World Disarmament Conference had simply applied the same tired approach of previous meetings. From his point of view each nation should be free to determine how many ships it needed; the only real restriction should be on size. Rallying precedents from history and invoking the shade of Mahan, he concluded that no fighting vessel need exceed the Versailles Treaty limit placed on Germany's naval vessels—10,000 tons displacement. He really thought 6,500 tons would be adequate.[97]

Kinkaid had heard these arguments in person at Williamstown the previous summer. Rear Admiral Hepburn had chaired a round-table discussion on problems of naval disarmament, and Tom had been the recorder for the group. He had not confined himself to minuting the discussion

---

[93] SECNAV to Senior Member General Board, Washington, 3 Feb 1931, TCK Papers.
[94] SECSTATE to SECNAV, Washington, 5 Mar 1931; Chief BUNAV to TCK, Washington, 10 Mar 1931, TCK Papers.
[95] Fitness Reports, 30 Sep 1930, 31 Mar 1931, 30 Sep 1931, TCK Personnel File.
[96] ADM Sir Herbert W. Richmond, "Immediate Problems of Naval Reduction," *Foreign Affairs* (Apr 1931): 372–88.
[97] Ibid., 379–81.

but spoke in opposition to Admiral Richmond.[98] The admiral had reached a national audience, although a fairly select one, and Kinkaid tried to do likewise. Unsuccessful in placing his article in the *Saturday Evening Post, Collier's,* or the *New York Herald Tribune Sunday Supplement,* he settled for the Naval Institute's *Proceedings,* which paid the author $37.[99]

In preparing his reply, Kinkaid clearly had several audiences in mind.[100] He wanted above all to convince the State Department, particularly Secretary Henry L. Stimson, that Richmond's arguments were nonsense.[101] The capital ships (battleships) should not be eliminated or reduced in tonnage or gun caliber. Repeating a decade of General Board and Bureau of Ordnance nostrums, he wrote:

> The capital ship is the center from which radiate the light surface forces, the undersea forces, and the air forces in exercising control of the sea. Likewise, it is the rallying point on which all other types focus for mutual support. The battleship's "power of survival" makes it, as it has always been, the backbone of the fleet.[102]

He hoped to convince the reading public that the approaches used at past naval conferences were sound enough to be continued. To Kinkaid they were not useless international gatherings; rather, he praised their work: "As a result of these labors all political and technical considerations have been brought to light and the attitude of the various powers with respect to each question is recorded in the minutes of the sessions of the preparatory commission . . . all of which have been widely distributed throughout the world."[103]

It is also likely that Kinkaid's article was designed to convince the General Board that he had not been tainted by his association with Admiral Pratt, the CNO. At meetings of the board and with State Department personnel charged with preparing for the World Disarmament Conference, Pratt had expressed a willingness to see battleship guns reduced to 12 inches in caliber and the number of vessels brought down from fifteen to thirteen. In time and with all naval powers concurring, he also believed the battleship could be standardized at 27,500 tons with 12-inch rifles.

---

[98] TCK oral history, 10–12.

[99] Letters to periodicals dated 29 Apr 1931, 6 May 1931, 11 May 1931, 25 May 1931, TCK Papers.

[100] CDR Thomas C. Kinkaid, U.S. Navy, "Present Problems of Naval Reduction," *Proceedings* (Jul 1931), 949–54.

[101] Memos for CNO, by TCK, 23 May 1931, 1 Jun 1931, Bristol Papers. In his 1 June memorandum Kinkaid concluded: "I respectfully suggest that it is extremely important that the question of the future of battleships be settled now in the mind of the Secretary of State in order that he not publicly take a stand from which he could not later recede."

[102] TCK, "Present Problems," 953.

[103] Ibid., 950.

Less imaginative than his senior, Kinkaid could not picture a fleet without battleships.[104] Neither could the General Board. The board and Kinkaid believed the battleship discussions in 1931 and 1932 were inappropriate and should not be taken up until the projected 1935 naval conference.[105]

Tom's work for the CNO, State Department, and General Board continued through the summer and fall of 1931. In mid-October the pace quickened when Secretary of the Navy Charles Francis Adams directed that "[Commander Kinkaid] would continue as liaison officer with the State Department and would keep the Board informed of everything that occurs in this connection." In deference to Admiral Bristol's wishes the Secretary further ordered that Kinkaid "will act under the instructions and advice of the Board."[106] Bristol had assumed that the General Board would be consulted concerning the appointment of the Navy's technical advisors to the delegation, but here he was to be disappointed. On 13 November Secretary Stimson informed the press that Rear Admiral Arthur Hepburn would head the naval advisory group and would be assisted by Captain Alexander H. Van Keuren, Commander Richmond K. Turner, and Commander Thomas Kinkaid. What bothered Bristol about this group was that Hepburn was a close friend of Admiral Pratt and had supported his views through the years. The head of the Western European Division of the State Department, Pierrepont Moffat, commented about the appointments in his diary: "The Navy, I am told, is very resentful in the matter of the selection of their delegates. . . . I fear the General Board will attempt to make trouble."[107] Fortunately for Tom Kinkaid, neither Admiral Bristol nor his successor, Admiral J. V. Chase, showed any lack of confidence in him.

Once the civilian members of the delegation were selected and an arrangement made for a chairman, the technical advisors and State Department people began two months of intense effort to work out an American position on anticipated military and naval questions. Secretary Stimson was to be the formal head of the delegation, but he was too busy to do the work. Appointed cochairman, Hugh Gibson took charge. Other delegates were the Minister to Switzerland, Hugh Wilson; Senator Claude Swanson, a Democrat and chairman of the Senate Naval Affairs Committee; Norman H. Davis, a prominent Democrat and League of

---

[104] Department of State (D/S), File 500.A15A4, American Commission Minutes/8, dated 25 May 1931, RG 59, NA. See also U.S. Department of State, *Papers Relating to the Foreign Relations of the United States, 1931* (Washington: GPO, 1946), 1:496–8; General Board Hearings, 1931, "Reduction in Displacement and Armament of Capital Ships," 31 Mar 1931.

[105] D/S File 500.A154A, American Commission Minutes/6, dated 1 Jun 1931, RG 59, NA; General Board Hearings, 1931, "Preliminary Discussions for 1932 Disarmament Conference," 7 Jul 1931.

[106] General Board Proceedings, 1931, 12 Oct 1931.

[107] J. Moffat Diary (carbon), 13–16 Nov 1931, box 37, Hugh Gibson Papers, Hoover Institution, Stanford, CA.

Nations enthusiast; and Dr. Mary Emma Woolley, a prominent women's peace movement leader and president of Mount Holyoke College. Kinkaid enjoyed working with all of them. He admired the professionalism of the "Two Hughs" and Senator Swanson's nationalistic devotion to the Navy. Mary Woolley's open mind and willingness to be educated about the Navy appealed to Kinkaid and Turner, particularly since most of her private briefing fell to them.[108] As might be expected, she inspired a good deal of private and public humor because of her (for the time) incongruous position. Yet by the conclusion of the delegation's labors, Hugh Gibson would write to his mother:

> I confess I trembled when I heard about the selection of an eminent woman pacifist as a Delegate, but can tell you that Dr. Woolley is a grand girl, and that if there were any effort to send her home there would be a loud protest from our entire delegation. She is all full of idealism and soars, and soars, and soars—but always with her feet on the ground. She saves me any amount of anguish, because the cranks look to her . . . instead of bothering me, and I am perfectly easy in my mind because I know she will give them lots of sympathy and not commit poor old Uncle Sam to anything.[109]

The delegation, including Tom and Helen, left New York on 20 January 1932 on board *Leviathan*. The Depression-driven parsimony of the Hoover administration was reflected in its allowances to the delegation for expenses. Tom had been authorized $20 per diem once in Europe during his 1930 trip, but the rate was now $15. But to the Kinkaids the trip and stay at the Hotel De Bergues in Geneva was well worth the personal cost. Old friends from Constantinople days, such as Allen Dulles and H. C. Pell, were working with the State Department advisory team headed by Theodore C. Marriner. Tom's personal friendships among the State Department people made it possible for him to help put across the Navy's view when there seemed to be misunderstandings within the delegation.

Seen in retrospect, the World Disarmament Conference was doomed from its opening day in early February. The nations attending were simply freighted down with too many other concerns that inhibited disarmament activity. In his memoirs written a decade later, Minister Hugh Wilson recalled that dismal period in international history:

> Fighting was going on between Japan and China, economic dislocation was widespread, in Germany the Communists and Fascists had just gained enormously in the last elections, in France an extreme Right Government

---

[108] TCK oral history, 22–36; Jeannette Marks, *Life and Letters of Mary Emma Woolley* (Washington, 1955), 144.
[109] Hugh Gibson to "Lucy," Geneva, 16 Mar 1932, box 32, Gibson Papers.

under Tardieu could be expected to make little concession to the modern Bruening government of Germany. . . . We know these things but we were powerless to stop or postpone the endeavor. The thing ground on with steady deterioration, one could only hope that a miracle would reverse the trend that seemed inevitable.[110]

Though lasting more than six months until 23 July, the Disarmament Conference achieved nothing during its first session. On 22 June President Hoover, despite serious reservations by the State and Navy Departments, tried to prod the delegations to concrete achievement by proposing a one-third reduction in the world's navies and abolition of such offensive weapons as tanks, heavy mobile artillery, and bombardment aircraft. Although discussing the plan at length, it was clear that the British, French, and Japanese could not accept such a radical proposal.[111] In his diary Secretary Stimson privately admitted his worry about Hoover's plan: "This is the point . . . I am afraid, and I have always been afraid, that the effect of the proposal would be to force us into a position where we would have to discuss changes in our Navy which would weaken us against Japan."[112] Given Japan's actions in Manchuria and Shanghai during 1932, it is easy to understand the secretary's uneasiness. It is also easy to understand why the British, with their eastern interests, could not accept a serious diminution in the size of the Royal Navy.

After six months in Geneva the return to the General Board must have been a considerable let-down for Kinkaid. Commander Theodore S. (Ping) Wilkinson had relieved him at the end of November 1931, so he became supernumerary on the board. The State Department continued to use him in the afternoons, but the mornings were spent assisting Wilkinson (his junior) or providing expertise when the board discussed plans for the next session of the Disarmament Conference. Tom received strong letters commending his work from both Hugh Gibson and Brigadier General George S. Simonds, the head of the Army's advisory group. Admiral Hepburn's fitness report was as good as those previously received from Bristol. The usual phrases were still there: "A very conscientious, industrious, competent officer. . . . Thoroughly dependable in any kind of duty."[113]

---

[110] Hugh R. Wilson, *Diplomat Between Wars* (New York: Longmans, Green, 1941), 264; Raymond G. O'Connor, *Force & Diplomacy: Essays Military and Diplomatic* (Coral Gables, FL: University of Miami Press, 1972), 22–23.

[111] F. Walters, *A History of the League of Nations*, 2 vols. (New York: Oxford University Press, 1952), 2:508–9; Nancy Harvison Hooker, ed., *The Moffat Papers: Selections from the Diplomatic Journals of Jay Pierrepont Moffat, 1919–1943* (Cambridge, MA: Harvard University Press, 1956), 72–775; Tate, *U.S. and Armaments*, 104–7.

[112] Henry L. Stimson, Diary, 25 Jul 1932, Henry L. Stimson Papers, Yale University, New Haven, CT.

[113] Hugh Gibson to Secretary of State, Geneva, 25 Jul 32; Chief BUNAV to TCK, Washington, 1 Sep 32 (enclosing Simonds's comments), TCK Papers; Fitness Reports, 31 Mar 1932, 6 Aug 1932, TCK Personnel File.

Members of the 1932 General Board, seated left to right: Rear Admiral M. L. Bristol, Rear Admiral C. B. McVay, Captain J. W. Greenslade, Commander T. S. Wilkinson, Rear Admiral J. V. Chase, Captain C. W. Cole; standing: Lieutenant Colonel L. C. Lucas, USMC, Commander E. M. Williams, USN.

One obvious advantage for Kinkaid in returning to the General Board was his ability to work closely with his Bureau of Navigation detailer, Captain J. M. Smeallie. Between 3 December 1931 and 30 September 1932 Smeallie found four different executive-officer billets for Tom. Captain J. O. Richardson (a future CINCUS) let him know in December that he was looking forward to his reporting on board the Scouting Force flagship, *Augusta* (CA 31). At the end of January while Kinkaid was en route to Geneva, these cruiser orders were modified; he would return to battleships as the executive officer of *Arkansas* (BB 33). Two weeks later, again to accommodate his stay in Geneva, he was scheduled for heavy cruiser *Northampton* (CA 26). Once back in Washington the cruiser orders were canceled. The billet had been filled. In September Captain Smeallie wrote his last set of orders for Kinkaid. Unless ordered otherwise he would be detached from the General Board in January and report as executive officer of the battleship *Colorado* (BB 45) with the Battle Force at San Pedro, California. He was detached on 7 January 1933 and immediately began a cross-country trip to California. Admiral Chase showed his appreciation for Tom's services by giving him a first-class fitness report.[114]

The fourteen years, 1919 to 1933, had been good years and important ones for Kinkaid's career. He had drawn interesting assignments abroad that had widened his knowledge of international affairs. His two tours at the Gun Factory established his credentials as an ordnance expert, not a bad specialization for an upwardly mobile naval officer. His tour had been brief, but he had demonstrated in *Isherwood* that he could handle a small ship command—another important benchmark. Finally duty on the staff of CINCUS and the General Board had brought him into contact with the service's top leadership. He made a good impression because he did his work well, and he could expect to be remembered when his class came up for selection for captain. His next assignment, as he knew quite well, would be deadly serious. If he could handle an executive officer's billet in a capital ship with his usual competence, it would be clear sailing to four stripes.

---

[114] Kinkaid's many aborted assignments can be followed in the orders section of his personnel file. See also Fitness Report, 7 Jan 1933, TCK Personnel File.

Chapter 3

Colorado and the Bureau of Navigation, 1933–1937

The years on the General Board, with additional duty in the State Department, had been very satisfying both to Tom and Helen. London, Paris, Geneva—it had been grand revisiting those cities they enjoyed when Tom was attached to Admiral Mark Bristol's staff in Constantinople. It was time to move on; the well-managed career dictated a return to sea duty.

Now with six years in grade as a commander with only eighteen months of sea duty, and that on the staff of CINCUS, Tom needed line experience afloat in one of the forces. His classmates had been positioning themselves in various units in the fleet while he had worked with the General Board and the disarmament commission. So Kinkaid sought an executive officer billet in a battleship or cruiser to meet one of the unstated requirements for a major command at a later date. Since the turn of the century the Navy's top leadership had regularly expressed its belief that a successful tour as executive officer in a major combatant unit was prerequisite to being a commanding officer in a battleship or cruiser.[1]

It was equally important from Kinkaid's viewpoint to serve in a ship attached to the Battle Force. Given the location of his and Helen's families, he might have preferred an old battleship or light cruiser in the Scouting Force, normally based on the East Coast, but he wanted to be where the action was, and that was in the Pacific Ocean's Battle Force. Maneuvering in the battleship divisions was demanding and the fleet exercises were more complicated. And there were more senior officers to impress; many of them would be on selection boards in the years ahead. His patience (and the detailer's) paid off when he reported to *Colorado* (BB 45), one of the newest and largest battleships in Battleship Division Four. It was the plum of the Battle Force. *West Virginia* (BB 48), flagship for Commander Battleship Divisions, Battle Force, and *Maryland* (BB 46) were fast company for *Colorado*, but that was the type of challenge that Tom Kinkaid wanted.

---

[1] Buell, *Quiet Warrior*, 57; Zogbaum, *Sail to Saratoga*, 359, 386–87; Richardson, *Treadmill to Pearl Harbor*, 178; CDR C. M. Cooke to TCK, Washington, 29 Nov 1935, Cooke Papers, Hoover Institution.

Captain Benyaurd B. Wygant, commanding officer of *Colorado*.

The delay in release from further duty with the State Department had resulted in one boon for Kinkaid; he was spared a trip to San Pedro by government transportation. Helen decided to stay behind for a month or two to look after Tom's mother in Washington and to visit her own parents in Philadelphia. She would join him after he had shaken down in his new billet.

On arrival in San Pedro, Kinkaid found *Colorado* swinging on the hook in berth A–5 of Los Angeles harbor. Captain Benyaurd B. Wygant in command and Commander Red Magruder, the executive officer, met him at the quarterdeck. Red Magruder, of course, was an old friend; they had been classmates at the Academy and had served together in *Nebraska* as passed midshipmen. Red had been best man at Kinkaid's wedding. Fortunately for Tom their orders permitted almost three weeks together before he would formally relieve his friend on 3 February. He used this time to familiarize himself with the battleship and its problems and to get his sea legs in shape.

Kinkaid found almost the entire U.S. Fleet in Long Beach. After Battle Force maneuvers in the Hawaiian area during the winter of 1931–1932, President Herbert Hoover had ordered the Scouting Force to transit the Panama Canal and join the Battle Force for an extended stay in the Pacific. The Japanese had invaded Manchuria the previous September and attacked Shanghai in January 1932. No one was sure how the trouble between China and Japan would end. Secretary of State Henry Stimson believed the presence of the U.S. Fleet on the Pacific Coast might help slow down the Japanese. The Navy's top leadership was not as sanguine as the Secretary of State.[2] After a year of drills, exercises, and limited fleet maneuvers, the Scouting Force's officers and crews wanted their ships to return to their home ports. Many had not seen their families for a year. National strategy interests, however, were fairly remote for Kinkaid. His job was to master the routines of *Colorado* and Battleship Division Four as quickly as possible.

Like her sister ships in the division, *Colorado*'s construction had been authorized by the Navy Act of 29 August 1916. In that momentous naval law Congress attempted to prepare the nation for the possibility that Germany might emerge victorious from the world war, with its navy intact. The Navy Act was followed by appropriations for ten battleships (*Colorado* and *South Dakota* classes), six battle cruisers (*Lexington* class), ten scout cruisers (*Omaha* class), and a plethora of destroyers, submarines, and other naval auxiliaries. With existing capital ships and the sixteen new

---

[2] Armin Rappaport, *Henry L. Stimson and Japan, 1931–33* (Chicago: University of Chicago Press, 1963), 119–20; Gerald E. Wheeler, "The United States Navy and War in the Pacific, 1919–1941," *World Affairs Quarterly* (Oct 1959), 210–12; Wheeler, *Pratt*, 347–49.

big-gun vessels, Congress believed the nation would possess a Navy "second to none." When Kinkaid reported on board, *Colorado* mounted a main battery of eight 16-inch, 45-caliber rifles, a secondary battery of twelve 5-inch, 51-caliber guns, and an antiaircraft battery of eight 5-inch, 25-caliber guns. To help with spotting for its big guns, four Vought O3U–1 seaplanes and pilots of VO–4B were attached to the ship. With its 624-foot length and 97-foot beam, *Colorado* was on the portly side and worked hard to make its 21-knot designed speed. Commissioned in August 1923, it still was one of the newest battleships in the Navy list.[3]

For some years *Colorado* had carried the reputation of a hard-luck ship—so much so that younger officers preferred duty elsewhere. Wardroom talk had it that Magruder had been ordered to help straighten out the ship, and like most new brooms he had been a bit stiff and abrasive. He had come to *Colorado* from executive department duty at the Naval Academy; thus he quickly was able to get the ship's lively junior officers in hand. An ensign who tried to repair a previous night's damage with a midday nap would often be roused by the executive's heavy hand calling him to duty. Uniforms became regulation and not even a visiting admiral's aide was free of Magruder's insistence that he wear his hat squared away. With the crew he was firm but consistent, the type of leader respected in a ship. One department head considered him to be a "driver," yet he did get results. His relief had the opportunity to observe his style, but he would do things his own way.[4]

Kinkaid moved swiftly into the routine of an executive officer. Like Magruder his job was to manage the ship in the name of Captain Wygant. He set out the day's work in the plan-of-the-day, supervised the department heads (navigation, engineering, gunnery, communications, and first lieutenant), maintained discipline, and regularly conned the ship when getting underway or coming to anchor. A contemporary of Kinkaid's wrote that a battleship executive officer was "a housekeeper as well as a manager of a corporation, the standard of up-keep and performance depend largely on him. If he is alert, conscientious, and energetic he is rewarded by enthusiastic cooperation by the crew. If he is fussy and pedantic he can ruin the morale of a ship's company."[5] It had been almost eight years since he had had to deal with a crew, but Kinkaid quickly showed that he had learned a good deal about managing people in his twenty-five years since graduation.

---

[3] George T. Davis, *A Navy Second to None* (New York: Harcourt, Brace, 1940), 222–31; James C. Fahey, *The Ships and Aircraft of the United States Fleet, 1939* (Annapolis: Naval Institute Press, 1976), 4–5; William T. Larkins, *U.S. Navy Aircraft, 1921–1941* (Concord, CA: Privately printed, 1961), 124, 128, 146, 158–59.

[4] RADM G. R. Luker, USN (Ret.) to author, Carmel, CA, 26 Sep 1977; Commodore Russell M. Ihrig, USN (Ret.) to author, Carmichael, CA, 20 Oct 1977.

[5] Zogbaum, *Sail to Saratoga*, 390.

Because of his personality Kinkaid soon began decreasing the tension among the officers that had been omnipresent under Magruder. He learned the names of his officers quickly and used them. He visited their spaces and observed them at work. Although formal in manner, he had a pleasant smile and interest in their departments and divisions that left his subordinates feeling at ease. His department heads began to recognize that, when called to his office, he wanted to discuss matters, not to inform them of his desires. He expected first-class performance, but he understood that perfection was not always attainable. He paid close attention to materiel, yet he never overlooked personnel. He insisted on cleanliness, good upkeep, and smart appearances, and he soon made these desired traits for his division officers. In these early months, probably because Helen wasn't ashore in Long Beach, he worked long hours without creating the impression that he was a "sun-downer." As president of the officer's mess, he used the wardroom to strengthen his leadership.

Although observing customary protocol and dress standards, Kinkaid abandoned some of Magruder's refinements. Mess jackets were no longer required at the evening meal on Fridays and the two after-dinner speeches were abandoned. Kinkaid was not fond of public speaking, so this change came naturally. He made it a point to visit from group to group before meals in the wardroom, asking about wives and children and keeping the conversation informal. He insisted that business not be conducted in the mess; meals were to be a period of relaxation.[6]

As he did with his officers, Kinkaid tried to develop a spirit of mutual trust and concerned interest in the affairs of the enlisted men. Responsible for the ship's discipline, he used the executive officer's mast to improve performance, not merely to punish. From his earliest commissioned years he had believed that hard work and hard play were good ways to relieve tension and hold down disciplinary problems. He was not one to lead the crew in exercise or participate in ship's athletics, but he did encourage such activity. He still played golf and tennis when convenient and swam when possible.

By this time he was beginning to be concerned with his waistline. When on board he enjoyed the boxing and wrestling matches that were a prelude to fleet competition. At age forty-five he was better able to enjoy watching rather than participating in rigorous athletics. His encouragement of athletics, it should be noted, struck a warm response in Captain Wygant. Buzzing Benny (or Bicycle Benny) was a true sports enthusiast who insisted on daily deck tennis whenever possible, sometimes despite division maneuvering.

---

[6] Ihrig to author, 20 Oct 1977; RADM Bosquet N. Wev, USN (Ret.) to author, Boynton Beach, FL, 11 Oct 1977.

Commander Kinkaid, executive officer of *Colorado*.

Though the whole U.S. Fleet currently was based on the West Coast, the annual routines of the ships, divisions, squadrons, flotillas, and forces continued in the pattern followed since the world war. Drills and exercises were designed to prepare the ship for type competition in gunnery, engineering proficiency, and communications. In gunnery the prize would be an E for the best turrets and prize money for the crews. Engineering efficiency involved achieving the best steaming for the least amount of fuel use. It would be called cost-effectiveness today. Prize-winning results were regularly noted in the fitness reports of the engineering officers and occasionally by letters of commendation from division commanders or the Bureau of Engineering.

But all this training was limited by two important factors: the shortage of money to pay for fuel and yard maintenance, and the natural desire of the crews to have as much time as possible ashore with their families. For the battleships of the Battle Force, including *Colorado* and Battleship Division Four, these limitations meant daily sorties commencing around 0800 and a return to the buoy by 1630. Sometimes five days at sea, from Monday through Friday, would be spent south and west of Santa Catalina and San Clemente islands with nights at anchor in Pyramid Cove (San Clemente) or off tiny Santa Barbara Island. A week at sea often would be followed by a week or more of housekeeping at anchor off Long Beach. When not tied to the ship by duty sections, married officers and enlisted men streamed ashore in small craft at the close of work, not too differently than civilians leaving their offices. In the morning while their civilian counterparts were still rousing or at breakfast, the fleet landing witnessed a return stream of craft headed for the cruisers and smaller ships in the inner harbor behind the breakwater or to the battleships rolling at their berths in the more exposed anchorages. Many flag officers lamented this pattern of behavior in the fleet but most were unwilling to attempt serious change.[7]

Kinkaid joined *Colorado* at the period in the gunnery year when final rehearsals and live firing for score were underway. During his first week on board, while he was still a supernumerary, *Colorado* fired long-range and short-range battle practices, towed target rafts, and sent its senior officers to observe the firing of *Tennessee* (BB 43) and *New York* (BB 34). Because the exercises were competitive, observers made sure that all ships approached the firing position on the same bearing, at the same speed, under similar conditions of visibility, and at the same distance from the target. Only a fixed period of time was permitted for firing.

---

[7] Wheeler, *Pratt*, 262; Wiley, *Admiral From Texas*, 237–39; Harvey M. Beigel, *Battleship Country: The Battle Fleet at San Pedro-Long Beach, California—1919–1940* (Missoula, MT: Pictorial Histories, 1983), 14–17.

What counted was the number of hits per gun per minute, but all had to fire under as close to the same conditions as was possible on board a battleship at sea. Kinkaid understood the system intimately from his previous service as U.S. Fleet Gunnery Officer on Admiral Henry Wiley's staff, and he still considered such exercises too artificial to be of genuine value. He had pressed unsuccessfully for changes in the rules governing long-range battle practice; now he was bound by them.[8]

On 3 February 1933 Commander Magruder was piped over the side in Long Beach Harbor, and Kinkaid assumed the responsibilities of executive officer.[9] Six days later *Colorado* sortied with the rest of the battleships to participate as part of the Blue Fleet in Fleet Problem XIV. Admiral Luke McNamee, Commander Battle Force, commanded the Blue Fleet and was charged to defend the Pacific Coast, from San Diego to Puget Sound, against a raiding Black Fleet. Vice Admiral Frank H. Clark's (Commander Scouting Force) Black Fleet consisted of two aircraft carriers, *Lexington* and *Saratoga*, commanded by Rear Admiral Harry E. Yarnell (Commander Aircraft Squadrons, Battle Force), seven new heavy cruisers, twelve destroyers, and two fleet oilers.

During the eleven days of war games the Black Fleet proved to be a dangerous adversary for Admiral McNamee's defending forces. Admiral Yarnell divided his carrier force, with the intention of *Saratoga's* task group attacking Los Angeles and *Lexington's* raiding San Francisco Bay's installations. The *Lexington* group was intercepted and "destroyed" off Point Reyes while trying to position itself for attack. To the south *Saratoga's* aircraft launched a deckload strike in darkness and held reveille for Los Angeles and its defenders. Turning north Yarnell again launched a predawn strike and from the Point Sur area successfully attacked naval installations in the San Francisco Bay area on 17 February.[10] Yarnell had pulled off a similar attack against Pearl Harbor a year earlier.

Colorado had participated in the destruction of *Lexington* but had been ineffective in preventing the *Saratoga* raid. At a closed fleet critique two weeks later in the Long Beach civic auditorium, several important points were made: (1) Aircraft carrier attacks could be devastating, but the loss of a single carrier would be a critical loss. It was absolutely necessary to build the rest of the allowed carriers under the London Naval Treaty. (2) Carrier task forces needed larger destroyers, with better sea-keeping capabilities, in order to operate effectively with the carriers. (3) The Navy needed some fast big-gun ships that could intercept and engage carrier task forces. If fast battleships or battle cruisers could not be con-

---

[8] Ibid.
[9] Log of USS *Colorado* (BB 45), 3 Feb 1933, RG 24, NA.
[10] *Los Angeles Times*, 3–5 Mar 1933.

structed, then the heavy cruisers had to remain with the Battle Force and its carrier force. (4) The carriers needed larger aircraft capable of striking with heavier bomb loads. Obviously the carrier task force was here to stay and the Navy had to learn to use it even more effectively. Equally obvious was the fact that the fleet had to learn to defend itself against attacks by carrier task forces.[11]

Fleet Problem XIV ended with the attack on San Francisco Bay and a parade through the Golden Gate by the fleets. For ten days San Francisco hosted nine battleships, three aircraft carriers, fourteen cruisers, and dozens of destroyers, submarines, and fleet train vessels. The city opened its hearts, clubs, dance halls, recreational facilities, and private homes. The fleet opened its ships and its pocketbooks. For the Depression-ridden Bay area a fleet concentration of this size was an economic godsend.

Despite the splendid time in San Francisco the fleet had other tactical exercises to undertake in the San Diego–San Pedro area and annual gunnery exercises to complete. In the forenoon watch on 27 February *Colorado* and Battleship Division Four weighed anchor, sortied through the Golden Gate, and shaped course for their berths in Long Beach. Wives who had followed the fleet to northern California now boarded the Southern Pacific Daylight from San Francisco to Los Angeles. For most Battle Force wives this parallel movement was a familiar excursion.

Upon return to Long Beach the fleet began another week of vigorous exercises that culminated in a general fleet engagement between Red and Black forces. Again Admiral Yarnell's carriers demonstrated their striking power against the battle line. Equally interesting, at least to the naval correspondent of the *Los Angeles Times*, was a coordinated destroyer-aircraft attack, under the cover of destroyer and aircraft smoke screens, launched against the battleships.[12] Despite the successes of Rear Admiral William Leahy's destroyer forces against the battle line and the spectacular dive-bombing attacks from the carriers, correspondent Waldo Drake earned his passage with the Battle Force: "Etched in carbon silhouettes against a silver mirror of a windless sea, 130 ships and 238 aircraft in battle exercises off San Clemente Island today strikingly demonstrated the existing United States Fleet's instant readiness for its business of war."[13]

The tactical exercises of 6–9 March concluded with the most spectacular fleet review ever staged in the Los Angeles area. The shores, headlands, highways along the ocean, and every possible viewing point along the route into the Los Angeles harbor area were lined with people the

---

[11] Ibid., 3 Mar 1933; "Last of the Fleet Problems," in Scot MacDonald, *Evolution of Aircraft Carriers* (Washington: Chief of Naval Operations, 1964), 36–37.
[12] *Los Angeles Times*, 8 Mar 1933.
[13] Ibid., 7 Mar 1933.

afternoon of the 9th. CINCUS Admiral R. H. Leigh led his fleet in *Pennsylvania*. On board were one hundred specially invited guests headed by California Governor James (Sunny Jim) Rolph. *Pennsylvania* anchored first, then the fleet passed with parade-ground precision. There was a massive fly-over by carrier aircraft squadrons and Navy and Marine Corps units from North Island. Following dive-bombing attacks on the battleships by the carrier squadrons, *Saratoga* and *Lexington* recovered aircraft while passing in review—a real eye-opening feat for the spectators. Destroyers, cruisers, battleships, and submarines followed one another into San Pedro and Long Beach harbors. It was marvelous public relations for the Navy, and the Californians loved it. In that Depression year it was also a flash of cheer to accompany the new administration of President Franklin Delano Roosevelt, sworn into office a few days earlier. In support of the Navy the *Los Angeles Times* editorialized on the value of holding the U.S. Fleet on the West Coast and building the Navy immediately to the strength allowed by the 1930 London Naval Treaty. With an eye to affairs in Asia, the editorial writer concluded: "The disturbed condition in the Near West continues, and while there is no intention on the part of this country of becoming involved in that disturbance, remote contingencies must be provided for and the Navy must be held where it is most apt to be needed."[14]

By one of those providential coincidences the U.S. Fleet was exactly where it would be most needed the next week. In the early evening of the day following the fleet review, a devastating earthquake struck the Los Angeles area. Long Beach was most heavily hit, with more dead and injured than in any of the surrounding communities. Because *Colorado* was lying at anchor in the outer harbor, nothing was felt on board during the first shocks. It wasn't until 2041 that the log book entry was made: "Slight quake felt." Within an hour ten men with radio equipment were sent ashore. Soon a steady flow of information came to the battleship. Hotels and apartments in Long Beach and San Pedro had been damaged, hundreds were injured and many killed, and some families from *Colorado* were without housing. By midnight *Colorado* was sending a stream of emergency medical supplies, blankets, stretchers, and cots ashore.

Kinkaid was on board and authorized bringing enlisted and officer families to the ship. Tarpaulins and signal flags were rigged in the crew's berthing areas to create family areas. Officers took their families into their cabins. It was crowded, but it was safe. Some families stayed for a week before they could find replacement housing ashore. One junior officer brought his young child and pregnant wife for a week's stay. He noted that "Tommy Kinkaid was a most gracious host to all of our

---

[14] Ibid., 9 Mar 1933.

guests."¹⁵ Captain Wygant had not liked the idea of bringing families to the ship, but Kinkaid convinced him that such a move was necessary.¹⁶

Early the next morning *Colorado*, along with the other large ships in the harbor, sent an armed landing force of eighty sailors and marines to help in the Long Beach area. Two days later the shore parties were increased to 110. During the first three days after the quake and its many aftershocks, the U.S. Fleet kept 4,000 sailors and Marines ashore in Long Beach, San Pedro, Compton, Los Angeles, and several other cities. They assisted the injured, set up feeding stations and temporary shelter areas, and patrolled constantly to prevent looting. In a few instances they helped fight fires.¹⁷ Kinkaid went ashore during the first day of the emergency to see what else could be done to assist the stricken and to make his sailors more efficient in their duties.¹⁸ Admiral Leigh let the mayors of the cities know that the fleet would remain as long as it was needed. By the 12th the Navy and Army were feeding at least 1,000 people in the area. By the time the crisis was over, the U.S. Fleet had suspended its exercises for ten days to devote its resources to humanitarian operations. The Navy had often assisted foreign countries, particularly in Central America and the Caribbean, in times of natural disaster, but this was the first major operation on the West Coast since the catastrophic San Francisco earthquake of April 1906.

On 20 March *Colorado* and most of the Battle Force sortied from Long Beach for five days of intense drills preparatory to final gunnery exercises for the fiscal year. The earthquake and the assistance rendered by the Navy had upset the closely scheduled activities, but there was nothing that could be done to regain lost ground. At last during the period 27 March–7 April, force battle practice took place with firing at targets with the main batteries and the secondary 5-inch guns during the first week. *Colorado*'s eight 16-inch rifles fired seven rounds apiece, standard for the times and about all the budget would allow. During the second week antiaircraft firing drills were stressed, with live firing at towed sleeves. By Friday, 7 April, the battleships were back at their anchorages and all hands in *Colorado* turned to preparation for the ship's annual inspection. It came in the forenoon watch of 12 April, when Commander Battleships Vice Admiral D. F. Sellers came aboard with his staff to inspect the ship and crew. *Colorado* came through with flying colors. Kinkaid's job was to see that *Colorado* left nothing to be desired, and he did his job superbly. Captain Wygant showed his approval and appreciation by rating his executive officer superior in every section of his June fitness report.¹⁹

---

¹⁵ Wev to author, 11 Oct 1977.
¹⁶ CDR K. E. Brimmer, USN (Ret.) to author, Staatsburg, NY, 28 Sep 1977.
¹⁷ *Los Angeles Times*, 11–14 Mar 1933.
¹⁸ Ihrig to author, 18 Oct 1977.
¹⁹ Fitness Report, 3 Jun 1933, TCK Personnel File.

The morning following Admiral Sellers's annual inspection, *Colorado* got underway for the Puget Sound area and the vessel's annual overhaul in the navy shipyard at Bremerton. Helen Kinkaid, now in Long Beach, took the train north to be with her husband during the two months the ship would be away from its home port. Bremerton was not the liveliest city on the West Coast, but it was better than Long Beach without her husband.

Normally the annual overhaul at Bremerton would have been little different from those of the previous ten years. This time, however, there was a modicum of concern in the battleship fleet that not all of the big ships would be returned to full duty once the drydockings were completed. During the spring of 1933 Chief of Naval Operations Admiral William Pratt proposed that one-third of the U.S. Fleet, including the battleships, be placed in a rotating reserve as a means of saving money. This period in reserve would last six months and include the overhaul period. The CNO planned to limit operating ship complements to 80–85 percent, with 60 percent complements on board those vessels in reserve. He really would have preferred to shut down many shipyards on the East and Gulf Coast rather than creating a rotating reserve, but Congress would not accept the closures. Such action would mean even more unemployment in those districts with shipyards; no Congressman wanted to face such an eventuality during the depths of the Great Depression.[20] In the end, responding to congressional pressure and genuine concern in the fleet, Pratt rescinded his plan for a rotating reserve.[21]

During the stay in Bremerton *Colorado* received a new skipper. On 3 June 1933, Captain Ralph P. Craft relieved Captain Wygant as commanding officer. Before leaving the ship Wygant sent in a splendid fitness report on his executive officer. All of his marks fell within the superior section, and twelve of the fifteen were the highest marks possible, with only initiative and military bearing marked 2 and force rating a 3. Wygant's statement on the report noted:

> Commander Kinkaid is an officer of the very highest type. He is extremely efficient, industrious, and with such excellent judgment as to make him a very valuable executive officer. He handles the *Colorado* with confidence and ability and is, in my opinion, thoroughly qualified for promotion. I heartily recommend him for such promotion.[22]

In the section evaluating Kinkaid's performance of his duties, he received 3.9s in all but one category, executive duties, for which he re-

---
[20] CNO to Bureaus, Offices, and Divisions of the Office of CNO, 3 Apr 1933, file FF1(1934)/A4–3(320510), box 2141, RG 80, NA; *Army and Navy Journal* 15 Apr 1933: 649, 658.
[21] Wheeler, *Pratt*, 367.
[22] Fitness Report, 3 Jun 1933, TCK Personnel File.

ceived 3.8. Most important, in his present assignment (executive officer) and deck and watch officer duties he was rated 3.9. He had proven himself to be a good shiphandler, and such recognition was vital if he ever expected a major ship command at sea.

With the completion of the overhaul period on 12 June, Captain Craft took *Colorado* back to her home port for the start of another yearly training cycle. Throughout the fleet the officer personnel began its annual turnover of billets. Among the junior ranks about a third moved ashore in time for families to find housing and place their children in the appropriate schools. The more senior officers, lieutenant commanders and above, usually stayed in a seagoing billet for two years or a bit more; then they had to move on so that others could qualify for promotion. Kinkaid and Craft, if fortunate, could expect no more than two years in a shipboard position. Then they would be detailed to a staff afloat or an office and desk ashore.

In practical terms the turnover meant that a vessel's operational readiness and efficiency declined considerably during the first quarter of the new fiscal year. On the other hand, if officer personnel were to be trained for larger responsibilities, they could not be held static in one billet on board a single class of vessel.[23] When a gunnery officer and several turret officers left a ship, it was inevitable that the quality of its gunnery would sag. Those vessels with good training routines usually made sure that assistant gunnery officers and assistant turret officers thoroughly learned the jobs of the officers directly over them.[24] It was part of Kinkaid's duties to see that officer turnover did not create a catastrophic situation in *Colorado*.

During the summer and fall of 1933 *Colorado* continued to operate out of Long Beach. With normally good weather and afternoons free of fog and haze, the battleship divisions worked on antiaircraft drills and firing and then, later in the summer, on short-range battle practice with the 5-inch batteries. By October the turret crews were again competent to begin serious big gun drills and spotting exercises with aircraft. The usual routine of a series of four- or five-day periods at sea, followed by weekends in port and then a couple of weeks to clean ship for inspections, had become *de rigeur*. The tedium of such scheduling was broken by holiday port visits. *Colorado* spent the Fourth of July in Laguna Beach with open house for the local populace. In August there was a week's visit to San Francisco. For Navy Day on 27 October *Colorado* dressed ship and sent a landing force into Long Beach for a parade. In November the Battle Force visited San Francisco for the inevitable Armistice Day parade. The visit was unusually "wet" because national prohibition had just

---

[23] Richardson, *Treadmill*, 42–43, 177–78.
[24] Ibid., 186–87.

been repealed on the day the fleet arrived. Because of the limited operating budget for the Navy during most of 1932 and 1933, there was no fleet concentration in the Panama Canal area or the Caribbean, but there was plenty of showing-the-flag along the Pacific Coast.[25]

In the late fall and early winter of 1933–1934, the training pace began to quicken in the Battle Force. Long-range battle practice with the 16-inch batteries commenced in earnest. In January force battle practices were held, and on the 25th the battleship divisions fired both SRBP and LRBP. *Colorado*'s log recorded the only major interruption to this intense activity on 25 December. At 1330 the officer of the deck noted: "Santa Claus received on board with full side honors and distributed gifts to all the children."[26] The Christmas party for the crew's children was one of those traditions in the Navy that helped remind all on board that the larger society still depended very much upon them.

During these months of gunnery drills and firing exercises, Kinkaid took more than a casual interest in the operations at hand. As executive officer he supervised the work of the department heads and was expected to work impartially with all of them. Given his ordnance background, it would have been unusual if he had not looked in on "the gun boss" a little more frequently than on the rest. He deepened his friendship with Lieutenant Commander Ralph O. Davis, the gunnery officer, and they were to serve together a few more times in the years ahead. Several of the turret officers remembered him donning dungarees and assisting them with boresighting, gun alignments, and trunion adjustments. Lieutenant (jg) B. N. Wev (later a rear admiral) thought Kinkaid's extra assistance "aided my turret to make an 'E' for our next target practice." *Colorado*'s plotting room officer found the executive officer "very understanding in our gunnery operations" and considered him "very responsive to our needs."[27] But, although gunnery might have interested Kinkaid deeply, the ship competition system of the times created a dilemma requiring Solomon-like judgment. In its efforts to achieve a high level of fuel economy, the engineering department resisted the gunnery department's desire to operate its turrets when it saw fit to do so. Extra electrical power use required extra generator activity, and that cost fuel. Kinkaid held the gunners at bay, and in time the engineering department and several turrets won their coveted Es. The executive officer, of course, won plaudits from both departments.[28]

Following the Battle Force practices at the end of January, *Colorado* again was ordered north to Bremerton for a two-month overhaul and drydock-

---

[25] *San Francisco Chronicle*, 8 Nov 1933.
[26] *Colorado* log, 25 Dec 1933.
[27] Wev to author, 11 Oct 1977; VADM Harold D. Baker, USN (Ret.) to author, Washington, 18 Oct 1977.
[28] Brimmer to author, 28 Sep 1977.

Author's collection

Colorado (BB 45) in the Gaillard (Culebra) Cut while transiting the Panama Canal, April 1934.

ing. The U.S. Fleet was scheduled to leave for the Caribbean and East Coast in early April, so Helen went East for a round of family visits. She was to meet Tom in New York when *Colorado* and the rest of the fleet arrived.

With its overhaul and yard trials completed on 29 March, Captain Craft took *Colorado* south to San Pedro. After a week of provisioning and inspections *Colorado* and the U.S. Fleet sortied from Long Beach on 9 April and began a nine-day cruise to Balboa, the Pacific Coast anchorage for the Canal Zone. The passage south featured plenty of tactical maneuvering exercises to get the big ships ready for the operations in the month ahead. Finally at 1343 on 21 April the fleet anchored in the harbor at Balboa. Whereas most logbook entries list the other naval vessels present when a ship comes to anchor, *Colorado*'s quartermaster of the watch saved himself a bit of effort by simply noting, "In company with the whole U.S. Fleet." Three days later Kinkaid made his first passage through the canal. Except for scraping off the lips of a few scuppers, and stranding a junior officer in Balboa, the transit to Cristobal was without incident.

Colorado's month of operations in the Caribbean began with the ship's annual inspection by Vice Admiral W. R. Sexton, Commander Battleship Division. The crew put extra effort into its preparation because the admiral was accompanied by his Chief of Staff, Captain Wygant, *Colorado*'s former skipper. Kinkaid's efforts in preparing the ship were rewarded by a special letter of commendation from the admiral lauding his "administrative efficiency and energy which resulted in the COLORADO passing an excellent annual inspection."[29]

From 28 April until 25 May Admiral Sellers put the U.S. Fleet through a long series of tactical exercises in the vicinity of Guantanamo, Culebra, and Gulf of Gonaïves (Haiti). All went well until 15 May when *Colorado* suffered a cracked propeller blade from a destroyer torpedo whose air flask exploded on impact. Divers ascertained that the damage was not crippling, but Captain Craft had to prepare for the worst during future operations. The fleet maneuvers concluded with a final visit to Gonaïves on 24 May. Early the next morning, with Kinkaid at the conn, *Colorado* shaped course for New York and a grand fleet review.

The Presidential review of the U.S. Fleet was a spectacular occasion for the Navy and nation alike. A quarter century earlier Passed Midshipman Kinkaid had returned with *Nebraska* to a review of the Great White Fleet by President Theodore Roosevelt. Now Roosevelt's nephew, Franklin, was welcoming the U.S. Fleet back to the Atlantic Coast after almost three years in Pacific waters. With President Roosevelt on board *Indianapolis* (CA 35) were CNO Admiral W. H. Standley and CINCUS Admiral D. Sellers.[30] Passing honors were rendered by a twenty-one-gun salute from each passing vessel, manning the rail, and the ship's band playing the national anthem. New Yorkers were treated to a cannonading equivalent to a major naval engagement. In addition, the giant carriers *Lexington* and *Saratoga* launched their squadrons for an aerial parade once the big ships passed their Commander in Chief.[31] The naval review was a unique and interesting experience for Kinkaid, but Helen's presence in New York made anchoring in the North River a much more significant event. Separations during their married years had been few and four months seemed like four years to them. Despite the warmth of the civic welcome and the chance to enjoy the great city, the Kinkaids slipped away for a week.[32] They visited Helen's parents briefly in Philadelphia and then continued on to Washington for a stay with Captain Frank Jack Fletcher and his wife. They enjoyed the whirl of parties and visiting in the capital, but Tom had one serious bit of business to set-

---

[29] Kinkaid Promotion File.

[30] Also with the President on board *Indianapolis* was former SECNAV, and now Ambassador to Mexico, Josephus Daniels. In December 1918 Roosevelt and Daniels had reviewed the Atlantic Fleet upon the return of its major units from European waters. The difference then was that Daniels was Secretary and Roosevelt, his assistant.

[31] *New York Times*, 1 Jun 1934; Zogbaum, *Sail to Saratoga*, 458–64.

[32] TCK to CAPT R. P. Craft, 6 Jun 1934, TCK Papers.

tle with his detailer in the Bureau of Navigation. Normally Kinkaid would have remained on board *Colorado* until January 1935, and he had made his plans along those lines. In October 1933 the President of the Naval War College, Rear Admiral Luke McNamee, had asked him to accept a billet on the staff the following July. He had declined—carefully, of course, but firmly. Kinkaid explained that his previous tour ashore had been overly long, and he needed a solid two years as executive officer before his name came up to the captain selection board.[33]

Now in June 1934 an opportunity appeared that interested Kinkaid and his wife. The senior detailer was due to be detached in October, and the chief of the Officer Personnel Division invited Kinkaid to be his relief. The professional advantages of such a position were too obvious to be ignored, so Kinkaid accepted. If all went well, he would be promoted to captain during this tour ashore; he could then select his own ship to command once he returned to sea. With his mother still living at the Wyoming Apartments, he could keep an eye on her as well as on his career. The hitch was President Roosevelt's insistence that, except in special cases, officers not be assigned to the Navy Department for successive tours ashore. Captain David W. Bagley made a case for special consideration; on 1 October CNO Admiral Standley noted that Secretary Claude Swanson had approved the request.[34] The commander was running a bit of a risk in accepting detachment three months early, but it didn't seem too serious in June 1934.

Kinkaid and *Colorado* spent June 1934 in the North River and the New York Navy Yard. At the yard the battleship was dry-docked and the cracked propeller blade repaired. Once the work was completed, *Colorado*'s crew had its chance to contribute to the Fourth of July celebration in Brooklyn. The vessel then rejoined the battleship divisions for a summer of operations in the waters between the Chesapeake Capes and Portland, Maine. The U.S. Fleet operated out of Narragansett Bay for several weeks in July, with enough shore leave to make it worthwhile for Helen Kinkaid to enjoy an extended visit with old friends in Newport. From Newport *Colorado* visited the Charleston Navy Yard outside Boston for ten days of minor work and more visiting by the Kinkaids. On 9 August *Colorado* rejoined the battleship fleet and headed south for Hampton Roads and almost two months of intense gunnery exercises over what years before had been called the Southern Drill Grounds.

Kinkaid's days on board *Colorado* were now drawing to a close. The vessel moved from the Chesapeake Bay down to Guantanamo Bay in late

---

[33] RADM Luke McNamee to TCK, Newport, RI, 10 Oct 1933; TCK to McNamee, San Pedro, CA, 23 Oct 1933, TCK Papers.

[34] Memo, CAPT D. W. Bagley to Chief BUNAV (RADM W. D. Leahy), 24 Sep 1934; Leahy to Bagley, 1 Oct 1934, TCK Personnel File; Richardson, *Treadmill*, 66–67, 121–26.

September, but Kinkaid would not become immersed in the Caribbean drills. He had seen the vessel through two full gunnery training cycles and twice had brought the ship back to complete readiness after the summer depletion of the crews. Captain Wygant had been very pleased with his work; Captain Craft was even more so. The commanding officer marked his executive's fitness reports 4.0 in every evaluative category and rated him the highest possible in every descriptive quality. The remarks sections in his three reports are strewn with such phrases as "an officer of exceptional ability"; "there is combined all of those traits of military character desirable and essential to successful high command"; "his grasp of strategical and tactical dispositions is excellent"; "his untiring energy and devotion to duty has contributed in a major degree to the efficiency of this command"; "he is a good seaman." In signing and delivering Kinkaid's detachment orders on 20 October 1934, Craft wrote after the terse statement of detachment: "and with regret."[35] It was with equal regret that the officers and crew saw Kinkaid detached. Though frowned on officially, the crew purchased their executive a suit of luggage as a farewell remembrance. In keeping with an old tradition reserved for senior officers they genuinely admired, junior officers manned a whale boat and rowed Kinkaid from *Colorado*'s anchorage to the landing at Guantanamo Base. One of those pulling at the oars remembered that Kinkaid had tears in his eyes as he was piped over the side. He also recalled, "We felt we were losing a father."[36]

That Kinkaid should have been remembered as a father to the young officers of *Colorado* should not be surprising. The age spread between them and a senior commander was more than twenty years, and there were members of the Class of 1908 who were four years older than Tom Kinkaid. He had managed the ship with a spirit of friendliness and trust, and the younger officers appreciated this. He was sufficiently low-key so that he did not leave a strong impression as one who would eventually reach the top of the naval pyramid. He was not flamboyant; he preferred to solve problems quietly, but permanently. If he entertained any doubts that he was still fit for sea duty and command at sea, his *Colorado* cruise should have eliminated that concern. As a member of the Gun Club, he had paid his dues by service in the largest and newest class of battleships. He had had the opportunity to observe the integration of aviation into the fleet and to learn the danger posed to capital ships by carrier aircraft in the war games of 1933. Though he would not again serve in the big ships, in less than a decade he would find much use for the lessons of 1933–1934.

---

[35] Fitness Reports, 30 Sep 1933, 31 Mar 1934, 20 Oct 1934, TCK Personnel File; Chief BUNAV to CO *Colorado*, 3 Oct 1934, TCK Personnel File.
[36] Burt C. Jacobson to TCK, Seattle, WA, 7 May 1950, TCK Papers; Luker to author, 26 Sep 1977.

Detached from *Colorado*, Commander Kinkaid boarded the naval cargo vessel *Sirius* (AK 15) at Guantanamo Naval Operating Base for a fairly rapid passage to Norfolk. Within ten days of detachment he reported to Rear Admiral William Leahy for duty as an assistant detail officer in Captain David Bagley's Officer Personnel Division. His immediate superior, the head of the officer detail section, was Captain Isaac C. Kidd, an old friend and graduate of the Class of 1906. Because it was Kinkaid's fourth tour in Washington since the war, settling in was no problem. He and Helen found an adequate apartment and quickly reestablished the social routines that had made previous assignments in Washington so enjoyable.

At the bureau Kinkaid's duties were routine, but they did require close attention and an uncommon amount of patience and good humor. His most important work was sending a steady stream of lieutenant commanders and commanders to billets afloat and finding an almost equal number of new billets afloat or ashore for those being relieved. Compared to the present the numbers involved were not large but the work was continuous with a heavy build-up in the spring of each year. His principal job was to place 828 lieutenant commanders and 461 commanders in billets appropriate to their rank, training, and experience; he also had to assist these officers in maintaining steady progress toward qualifying for promotion. Theoretically each new assignment for an officer should be a step up in responsibilities and should present new opportunities for developing a sound service reputation. (Today one would say that each new assignment should be career enhancing.) After a few years in rank most officers hoped their reporting seniors would write that they "were fully qualified for promotion in rank when due" in the remarks section of their fitness reports. For promotion to commander a lieutenant commander was expected to command a small vessel like a destroyer or submarine or an aviation squadron, or to have served as a department head on board a cruiser, battleship, or aircraft carrier. A commander expecting promotion to captain, of course, needed command experience in a minor vessel or service as executive officer in a cruiser or capital ship. The pattern was slightly different for naval aviators, but even they were expected to serve a part of their sea duty requirement in the ship's company of a major vessel.

To carry out his work as a detailer, Kinkaid maintained a large correspondence with officers due to be moved. He also corresponded regularly with a large number of flag officers who wanted specific officers assigned to their commands or who wanted to unload someone who hadn't worked out too well. Kinkaid saw his job as trying to provide maximum assistance to both groups. Because of his position, he became familiar with the records of a large number of middle-grade officers, a competence that was to serve him well in later years. He also became known, favorably in most instances, to a large portion of the flag officers seeking good officers. A steady correspondent was Rear Admiral E. C. Kalbfus, President of the Naval War College, who constantly sought certain outstanding officers to add to his staff. He wrote to "Dear Tom" and usually got the ones he wanted. Kinkaid also had to manage correspondence, both delicately and honestly, from officers who did not want to accept so-called opportunities to serve with certain officers. Having had to use the good offices of a detailer to avoid a tour of staff duty at the War College just a few years before, Kinkaid appreciated the sensitiveness of this part of his job.[37] Probably the best measure of Kinkaid's effectiveness in his billet can be found in Rear Admiral Adolphus Andrews's fitness report evaluation: "This task [as assistant detail officer] has been performed with unfailing courtesy, consideration, tact and justice."[38]

Officer detailing was the principal work in Kinkaid's day, but he also regularly served on a variety of Bureau of Navigation boards selecting officers for schools or other special duties. A few officers were selected each year to attend law school, usually in Washington, D.C. These officers, as might be expected, were later to serve on the staff of the Navy's Judge Advocate General or in legal billets in the bureaus or the staffs of naval district commandants. Occasionally boards would choose a few for designation as engineering-duty-only officers, normally after they had completed advanced degrees in some of the nation's most prestigious schools of engineering. Kinkaid also had to help select officers annually to be sent for a year in the School of the Line, located with the Navy's Postgraduate School at the Naval Academy, and officers to attend the Navy War College in Newport. These tasks took a few days at a time, but they gave Kinkaid the opportunity to review the records and become better acquainted with officers in the middle grades.

It was during this tour in Washington that Tom Kinkaid's class finally came up for selection for captain, and he faced a major crisis in his career. In January 1935 there were still sixty-three members of the Class of 1908 on active duty in the grade of commander. Most had been in rank nine to ten years; the most senior was Kelly Turner, whose date of rank was 4 January 1925. Kinkaid ranked from 4 June 1926; thus he was seventeen months junior to Turner. Kinkaid's position in the lower half of his class had almost dictated that he would be promoted a year later than those above him. And at the same time 1908 was to be considered, a handful of members of 1907 were still hoping that the selection board would remember them.

---

[37] RADM E. C. Kalbfus to TCK, Newport, RI, 31 Oct 1936, ADM E. C. Kalbfus Papers, Naval War College, Newport, RI; McNamee to TCK, Newport, RI, 10 Oct 1933, TCK Papers.
[38] Fitness Report, 31 Mar 1936, TCK Personnel File.

By this time most of those from 1908 had managed to arrange their tours of duty so that they met the basic qualifications for promotion. Kinkaid had commanded a destroyer, served on several staffs afloat, had been executive of a battleship, and had had three tours in Washington. Compared with many of his class he was short on sea duty, but not markedly so. In the end it appears that, once more, the key determinant for selection (actually nonselection) was Kinkaid's class standing. The new captain's list had fourteen from the Class of 1907 and thirty-seven from the Class of 1908. Of the thirty-seven selected in January 1935, Kelly Turner headed the list, and Willis Augustus Lee ended it. Technically speaking, Kinkaid had not been passed over since no one junior to him had been promoted; but in reality he had been, because those from his class not selected in January 1935 would receive one more consideration in January 1936.

Many naval officers in Kinkaid's position might have panicked or showed some evidence that they were deeply concerned. The usual pattern for such an officer was to seek counsel of someone quite senior, possibly a member of the selection board, and then take some remedial action if the situation were not completely hopeless. Someone short of sea duty, lacking expected experience an as executive officer, or not having a minor command, often would ask for immediate orders to a new billet that might remedy the deficiency. Kinkaid had handled enough requests of this type to know what should be done. What he did was sit tight and concentrate on the job at hand. His record was satisfactory in terms of having touched all the usual bases. His work in BUNAV had satisfied Admiral Leahy, and he had said so on two fitness reports: "Especially desire to have him." "He is hard working, thorough and efficient in the performance of his duties. He is well qualified for promotion and so recommended."[39] Leahy's relief, Rear Admiral Andrews, was even stronger in his marks and remarks: "Commander Kinkaid is an excellent officer of the highest personal and military character. . . . He is strongly recommended for selection to the grade of Captain when due." Kinkaid was due.[40]

The 1936 captain selection list was considerably shorter than in 1935. A dozen commanders from 1908, including Kinkaid, had made the grade; so had sixteen from 1909, with Ping Wilkinson at the head of the new group. Of the 201 who had graduated in June 1908, 49 had survived to be selected for captain. Compared with post–World War II Naval Academy classes, 24.3 percent was a remarkably good record. Those from 1908 not making the list, some fourteen in number, were retired by the start of the new fiscal year.

---

[39] Ibid., 31 Mar 1935, 30 Jun 1935.
[40] Ibid., 30 Sep 1935.

Selected in January 1936, Kinkaid had a year to wait before he could be examined for promotion and officially sew on his fourth stripe. By the time he was notified that there was a vacancy and he could take his physical and professional examinations on 11 January 1937, he was serving as the director of the Officer Personnel Division. Because Kinkaid's work was demanding and he could not spare the time to study for the professional exam, Rear Admiral Andrews requested that the formal examination be waived and that Kinkaid be examined "on his record only." The Secretary of the Navy approved this departure from standard procedures, and Kinkaid did not take the regular professional examination.[41] The physical examination revealed that his hearing had continued to deteriorate, but the impairment was not severe enough to disqualify him for sea duty.

Now a captain and overseeing the Officer Personnel Division, which included detailers, Tom Kinkaid picked out an attractive command and saw that appropriate orders were written. It was not common for a "fresh-caught" captain to receive a major command at sea during his first year, but Kinkaid had decided early that he wanted to prove as quickly as possible that he was worthy of selection to flag rank. Success in a seagoing command was vital for selection, so he moved directly toward that objective. On 20 March he was ordered to report to Commander Cruisers, Scouting Force, for duty in command of heavy cruiser *Indianapolis*, and to report by 7 June 1937.

---

[41] Chief BUNAV to TCK, Washington, 8 Jan 1937; Chief BUNAV to SECNAV, 8 Jan 1937, TCK Personnel File.

Chapter 4

Indianapolis, 1937–1938

Kinkaid's detachment from the Bureau of Navigation required an evaluation, and the chief supplied a ringing reaffirmation that the captain selection board had made no mistake. Admiral Adolphus Andrews assigned 4.0 marks for performance and the highest ratings for all descriptive traits such as intelligence, judgment, initiative, leadership, perseverance, reaction in emergencies, and military bearing. He concluded his written statement with these encomia: "An energetic officer, of fine presence and personality, tactful to a high degree and possessed of insight and judgment. Has the qualities necessary for high command and is well qualified for promotion to flag rank when due." After such a fitness report it is not surprising that the admiral concluded: "It is with extreme regret that I see Captain Kinkaid leave the Bureau of Navigation."[1]

Tom and Helen decided to drive to Long Beach, the home port of *Indianapolis*. He enjoyed driving and there was much of the country, particularly the Midwest and the West, that they had never seen. After a few days with Helen's parents in Philadelphia, they headed West. The Kinkaids arrived in Long Beach on 21 June and moved into the Villa Riviera, that splendid apartment-hotel they had lived in while Tom was executive officer of *Colorado*. Following two weeks of visiting and play in southern California, Captain Kinkaid reported to Vice Admiral William T. Tarrant, Commander Scouting Force (COMSCOFOR), on Saturday morning, 5 June.[2]

Two days later he started the morning by reporting to Rear Admiral E. B. Fenner, Commander Cruisers, Scouting Force (COMCRUSCOFOR) and then officially reported on board *Indianapolis* to relieve Captain H. Kent Hewitt. The ceremony was brief. After the traditional inspection of the ship, officers, and crew, Kinkaid read his orders and relieved Hewitt. Once in command Kinkaid informed Chief of Naval Operations Admiral William Leahy that "I find the material condition of the ship and the efficiency of the crew to be most satisfactory." He did note that the galley ranges needed yard work and that the vessel currently was immobilized while the tubing was replaced on condensers one and three.[3]

---
[1] Fitness Report, 1 May 1937, TCK Personnel File.
[2] TCK to Chief BUNAV, Philadelphia, 5 May 1937, TCK Personnel File.
[3] TCK to CNO, Long Beach, 7 Jun 1937.

At the time Kinkaid took command of *Indianapolis*, a substantial portion of the U.S. Fleet was in Pacific waters. International tensions in Asia had relaxed little since the Scouting Force had moved to the West Coast in 1932, so its vessels were now using the Long Beach–San Diego area as their home ports. The Battle Force had moved to the Pacific in 1921 and since then had been based in southern California, though it occasionally visited the East Coast. Now, in June 1937, there were nine battleships (out of fifteen) in Long Beach, with Admiral E. C. Kalbfus, Commander Battle Force (COMBATFOR), flying his four stars in *California*. In *Indianapolis* was COMSCOFOR Vice Admiral Tarrant. Nearby, within the breakwater, was *Chicago* (CA 29), which flew the two stars of Rear Admiral Fenner, COMCRUSCOFOR. Kinkaid's immediate boss was Rear Admiral F. H. Sadler, Commander Cruiser Division (COMCRUDIV) 6. There were at least another dozen flag officers within the two forces, but Admirals Tarrant, Fenner, and Sadler were the ones who would deal directly with Captain Kinkaid, evaluate his work, and create the written record on which he would be judged for future assignments and promotion. In mid-1938 Sadler would be relieved by Rear Admiral Royal E. Ingersoll, Fenner by Joseph Taussig, and Tarrant by Kinkaid's old friend, Adolphus Andrews.[4]

Kinkaid's command, the heavy cruiser *Indianapolis*, was to many "the most beautiful ship in the Fleet."[5] Built between March 1930 and August 1932 in the New York Shipbuilding Corporation Yard at Camden, New Jersey, *Indianapolis* was commissioned in November 1932 with Captain Smeallie as her first skipper. The cruiser carried nine 8-inch rifles in her main battery and eight 5-inch dual purpose antiaircraft guns as a secondary battery. Displacing 9,950 tons, with a cruising range in excess of 13,000 miles and a designed speed of 32.7 knots, *Indianapolis* and the other 1924 and 1929 heavy cruisers were built to operate with the battleships and aircraft carriers in the broad reaches of the Pacific Ocean. *Indy* had already achieved some notoriety as a showboat or presidential cruiser because of carrying President Franklin Roosevelt on special occasions during 1933, 1934, and 1936. Built as a flagship and thus carrying cabin space for an additional fourteen officers, *Indy* could easily host a presidential party or the commander of the Scouting Force and his staff. The exceptionally clean condition of the vessel when Kinkaid took over was probably attributable to the fact that six months earlier the President had used the flagship for a trip to and from Charleston to attend the 1936 conference of the Pan-American states in Buenos Aires.[6]

---

[4] U.S. Navy Department, *Navy Directory*, Jul 1, 1937; VADM Walter S. DeLany, interview with author, Washington, 28 Jun 1977.

[5] RADM Clayton R. Dudley, USN (Ret.) to author, Seattle, 8 Apr 1977.

[6] "Indianapolis," *DANFS* 3:432–34; Fahey, *Ships and Aircraft of the U.S. Fleet, 1939*, 10–11.

It is hard to tell whether or not Tom Kinkaid was confident at the time he relieved Hewitt. It had been twelve years since he last had a ship command, and the small *Isherwood* was a pale shadow compared with *Indianapolis*. On the other hand, as executive officer in *Colorado,* he had managed considerably more officers and enlisted men than *Indy* carried. As is the case with any large vessel he had to put the operation of his ship in the hands of others, but Navy regulations left no doubt about who was responsible. Except in the rare case of new vessels coming into service, a commanding officer inherits the crew from the person he relieves. Captain Smeallie had selected his own department heads while he was a BUNAV detailer, but Kinkaid brought only his communications officer with him. Yet, because of their positions, the executive officer and department heads held the success of Kinkaid's command in their hands. He was fortunate because he did have an experienced, energetic, and intelligent executive to carry the burden of daily management. Commander Oscar C. Badger had served Hewitt and would spend a year with Kinkaid. He was loud, abrupt, forceful, and a driver. He was a good shiphandler, though he kept the bridge in a state of tension when he was about. He was an excellent complement to Kinkaid's style of command. Badger readily accepted and exercised authority. Kinkaid believed strongly in delegation of authority, but he never shirked responsibility.[7]

Within *Indianapolis* the change from Hewitt to Kinkaid was not considered sharp nor particularly noteworthy. Both were older men—Hewitt, fifty, and Kinkaid, forty-nine—and to their crew they may well have seemed father figures. They were reserved in manner, formal with their officers, and insistent on quality performance. Officers who served with both remember Hewitt as a bit more direct, a little warmer in personality, and a better shiphandler, but not strikingly so. Fairness and evenness in handling people characterized both of them. Because he was taller and sparer in build, Kinkaid seemed to possess a better military bearing and was judged much neater in his personal dress.[8]

The life of a commanding officer, of course, was not all work, and the Kinkaids made certain there was plenty of relaxation in their routine. They did the usual entertaining associated with their position: teas, receptions, returning of calls, and attendance at wardroom parties. Helen

---

[7] Dudley to author, 8 Apr 1977; VADM George C. Dyer, USN (Ret.) to author, Annapolis, 17 Apr 1977; RADM Charles C. Hartman, USN (Ret.) to author, San Diego, CA, 12 Apr 1977; VADM George C. Dyer, interview by John T. Mason, Jr., 1969–1971, 173–77, USNI Oral History, Annapolis, MD (hereafter Dyer oral history).

[8] RADM Edward C. Forsyth, USN (Ret.) to author, Pebble Beach, CA, 29 Apr 1977; RADM Chester W. Nimitz, Jr., USN (Ret.) to author, Norwalk, CT, 13 Apr 1977; CAPT H. H. Connelley, USN (Ret.) to author, San Diego, CA, 14 Apr 1977; Hartman to author, 12 Apr 1977; Dyer to author, 19 Apr 1977.

Kinkaid was considered by many to be a splendid hostess and an ideal role model for the wives of *Indy*'s officers. Truly sociable types (though Tom was more a listener than a participant during evenings of conversation), the Kinkaids enjoyed being with people. They also enjoyed sports for just the two of them. They were good swimmers; they played golf whenever possible, and, occasionally, tennis. Helen was still a good golfer; Tom's game stayed in the 90s.[9]

As had been the case with *Colorado* the activities of *Indianapolis*, daily and annual, were determined by the U.S. Fleet's training schedules. When Kinkaid came on board on 7 June, the Scouting Force cruisers had recently completed their battle practices and live firing for score. The ship was now cleaning up and preparing to begin the next cycle of training, which would start while the Scouting Force visited Seattle and the Puget Sound area. The trip to the Northwest was becoming an annual ritual for both the Scouting Force and the Battle Force. At least a portion of the ships would celebrate the Fourth of July in Seattle's Elliott Bay, and then most of the cruisers and some destroyers would visit Portland, Oregon, for the annual Rose Festival. For the Fourth of July detachments of the two forces would show the flag in other Northwest port cities such as Tacoma, Everett, Bellingham, Aberdeen, Astoria, and Coos Bay. Since the nation was still struggling with the Great Depression, their spending could help the various port cities.

During the forenoon watch on 28 June *Indianapolis* slipped her mooring at buoy G and stood out of Long Beach with CRUDIVs 4, 5, and 6, destination Seattle. It was Kinkaid's first chance to take his ship out, and he handled the chore himself. In time he let his executive or the senior watch officer handle the ship when unmooring or coming to anchor, but in the beginning he needed the experience himself. En route the cruiser divisions engaged in minor maneuvering, and the crew of *Indy* had the opportunity for loading, pointing, and training drills with the turrets and antiaircraft guns. After three days' steaming *Indy* and two other cruisers joined *Saratoga*, *Langley* (AV 3), and *Vestal* (AR 3) at anchor off Seattle.[10]

Once the national birthday had been appropriately celebrated, the Scouting Force began ten days of maneuvers and battle practices. When the practices began, the cruisers shifted to Port Angeles for operations and returned to Seattle for weekends. On 10 July, Admiral C. C. Bloch, now COMBATFOR, brought most of his Battle Force for five days of combined exercises with Vice Admiral Tarrant's command. Finally, on

---

[9] Hartman to author, 12 Apr 1977; Dyer to author, 19 Apr 1977; Nimitz, Jr., to author, 13 Apr 1977; Dudley to author, 8 Apr 1977.
[10] Log of USS *Indianapolis* (CA 35), 28 Jun–5 Jul 1937, RG 24, NA

15 July, CRUDIV 6, plus two other heavy cruisers from CRUDIV 7 and four light cruisers from the Battle Force, left the Puget Sound area and proceeded independently to Portland. Kinkaid's luck gave out; after several weeks of good weather *Indy* approached the channel through the Columbia River bar in a dense fog. His night vision wasn't good enough to pick up the marker buoys, but his navigator was able to set a safe course into the channel despite the presence of other shipping. It was probably with considerable relief that Kinkaid welcomed a river pilot on board at Astoria, who then took the ship to its pier in Portland.[11]

The two weeks in the Rose City were reasonably relaxing for Kinkaid and his crew. At the end of the stay Admiral Tarrant gave a dinner for some of the city's leaders attended by two state governors. Governor Charles H. Martin of Oregon, a graduate of the Military Academy and then a retired major general, and Governor Lloyd C. Stark of Missouri, a classmate of Kinkaid's from the Naval Academy, added a bit of uniqueness to the occasion.[12]

On 29 July Kinkaid took *Indianapolis* downriver to the ocean, then turned south for San Francisco Bay. The next day he put his ship through its annual full power run. With a team from *Astoria* (CA 34) on board to verify the results, the cruiser reached 31.7 knots at 348 rpm.[13] Reaching the Golden Gate on the last day of July, the sixteen cruisers were welcomed as the advance guard of the U.S. Fleet. Within the next week Admiral Claude Bloch brought in his Battle Force and swelled the number of ships present to seventy-nine. The city celebrated Harbor Day with an assist from the Navy, but more important, 11,000 bluejackets celebrated payday in the finest liberty port on the Pacific Coast.[14]

After ten superb days in San Francisco *Indianapolis* joined a grand sortie through the Golden Gate. Admiral Bloch in *California* had taken Assistant Secretary Charles Edison on board for the passage to Long Beach and was determined to give him his money's worth. On the first night out the cruisers engaged in screening exercises with the battleships and beat off a destroyer "attack" in the early morning. As a part of the Green Fleet, Kinkaid and his fellow skippers were put through four days of intense maneuvers, drills, torpedo attacks, aircraft attacks, and plenty of scouting and screening missions. For the first time in his career Kinkaid was required to conduct a burial at sea for a fireman killed in a shipboard accident. By the time *Indy* made buoy G, the commanding officer was ready for relaxation; but the pace was just beginning to increase.

---

[11] Hartman, 12 Apr 1977; *Indianapolis* log, 16 Jul 1937.
[12] Anderson oral history, 213–23; *Indianapolis* log, 28 Jul 1937.
[13] *Indianapolis* log, 30 Jul 1937.
[14] *San Francisco Chronicle*, 31 Jul–9 Aug 1937.

For the next two months, beginning in mid-August 1937, Kinkaid and *Indianapolis* spent most of their time away from Long Beach. The cruiser divisions would usually leave their moorings in Long Beach on Monday morning and return on Friday afternoon. Evenings normally were spent at anchor in Pyramid Cove at the south end of San Clemente Island, about 75 miles southwest of Long Beach. During most of August the emphasis was on short-range battle practice with the turrets and secondary batteries, but practice with target rafts was interspersed with plenty of antiaircraft drill as well. *Indy*'s five planes (Curtiss SOC–1s) were given regular exercise in spotting shellfire as well as scouting for the cruisers. After days of firing rehearsals and then "official rehearsals" with observers from other ships, Kinkaid took his ship through live SRBP for record on 24 August. The whole exercise took three hours; each turret had only three minutes for each run and fired a total of eighteen 8-inch projectiles per three-gun turret. The eight 5-inch guns used up sixty-eight bullets in their share of the firing.[15] Kinkaid was proud of his ship and crew, but he was not really satisfied with its gunnery record. Because he was an ordnance specialist, he probably expected more than could be delivered. One turret did wear a gunnery E, but he undoubtedly wanted all of his turrets to reach this level.[16] The SRBP emphasis of August was followed by night firing drills, spotting drills, and live firing at towed sleeves at night as well as during the day. Kinkaid was getting much more gunnery activity under a larger variety of conditions than he had in *Colorado*.

In late October *Indianapolis* was scheduled to leave for its annual drydocking and overhaul at Mare Island. Before departure, however, Rear Admiral Sadler, assisted by officers from *Houston* (CA 30), came on board for the semiannual inspection. Officers, crew, and ship were found to be in first-class condition. Pleased with what he saw, Commander CRUDIV 6 submitted a special letter of commendation for Kinkaid. Vice Admiral Tarrant also liked what he had observed since Kinkaid had taken command. In two fitness reports submitted in early October, Tarrant rated his flagship commander 4.0 in "present assignment," "ability to command," "administration," and "shiphandling." In his written comments he sprinkled in such phrases as "exceptionally able officer," "high standards," "clear grasp of profession," "excellent shiphandler," "maintains high standards of efficiency, discipline, and morale," and above all "well-qualified for promotion."[17]

A few days after the semiannual inspection, Kinkaid took *Indianapolis* to Oakland for the Navy Day celebration. After three days of open house

---

[15] *Indianapolis* log, 24 Aug 1937.
[16] Dyer to author, 19 Apr 1977.
[17] Fitness Reports, 30 Sep 1937, 14 Oct 1937, TCK Personnel File.

Indy moved up to San Pablo Bay and the Mare Island Navy Yard. The three months at Mare Island might have been uneventful had the Navy transport *Henderson* (AP 1) not swung into *Indy*'s stern and damaged a starboard propeller guard. The damage was light, but an extra drydocking was needed to inspect the vessel. The tedium of a yard overhaul was broken by a Christmas party for the crew and the generous granting of leaves. The midwatch on New Year's Eve left to naval historians and their readers this bit of doggerel in the ship's log:

> Moored as before,
> On this twelve to four,
> With nine strong lines. In berth assigned.
> Boilers secured at Mare Island we lay,
> With a port brow to our berth "J".
> And from the dock we receive brine,
> Electricity, fresh water, steam and telephone line.
> Among ships present besides our own boat.
> The *New Orleans*, S.O.P. Afloat.
> Des Div Twenty Four, *Brant, Arctic* and *Borie*.
> *Pampano, Porpoise, Nautilus* and *Henley*.
> In closing this log.
> A word of good cheer.
> We hope you enjoy
> A "Happy New Year."

Following two weeks in dry dock 2 and a full power test outside the Golden Gate, Kinkaid and *Indianapolis* returned to Long Beach on 4 February 1938. A week was spent allowing the crew to reestablish home ties; two weeks of intensive drills and exercises then led to live firing at towed sleeves by the antiaircraft batteries and a live day-battle practice with observers on board from *Chester* (CA 27). The firing exercises were followed by two weeks of preparations for an extended cruise, interrupted by two days of intensive inspections by parties from *Tuscaloosa* (CA 37) and *Pensacola* (CA 24). Again *Indianapolis* was found to be in outstanding condition. Finally on 15 March Vice Admiral Tarrant led his Scouting Force (now designated White Fleet) out of Long Beach and shaped a fleet course for the Hawaiian Islands. Fleet Problem XIX was commencing.

For two weeks while en route to Hawaiian waters and once in that area, *Indianapolis* and the U.S. Fleet engaged in continuous operations that closely simulated actual wartime conditions. The cruiser scouted and screened, drove off destroyer attacks, engaged in gun duels with other cruisers, and fought in line-of-battle actions. Ships were darkened at night and buttoned up during general quarters periods. Not only were carrier aircraft attacks encountered, but once the fleets moved into the islands, the forces were snooped by land-based patrol planes and, when in range, attacked by land-based aircraft. Whereas earlier the carriers had attacked the fleets, now the exercises had them defending the fleets from the land-based marauders. Vice Admiral Ernest King, then Commander Aircraft, Battle Force, took a task group built around *Saratoga* and *Ranger* (CV 4) and launched a surprise attack against Pearl Harbor. Like the Japanese four and half years later he held his carriers within a frontal storm and approached the islands without detection. Unable to operate effectively in such weather, the Army's long-range bombers and the Navy's patrol squadrons failed to detect the carrier aircraft until it was too late. A similar attack with equally devastating surprise had been staged six years earlier by Admiral Harry Yarnell.[18]

After two weeks at sea the White and Green Fleets stood into Pearl Harbor for a brief stay, then commenced another five days of exercises. The second period of activity, concentrated in the Maui and Hawaii area, featured work with the carriers *Lexington*, *Saratoga* and *Ranger* and further exercises involving shore-based attacks. The two periods of maneuvers so far and the ten days of maneuvering while returning to Long Beach impressed on Kinkaid the fact that fleet tactics were changing significantly. In earlier years while he was with Admiral Wiley's staff and when in *Colorado*, cruisers served principally in scouting and screening roles when working with the battleships. Now it was clear that the antiaircraft batteries of the cruisers would be important in helping provide air attack defense for the battle line. The cruiser captain also found another employment for his vessel in special task forces built around the aircraft carriers. During the return to Long Beach, *Indianapolis* fueled four destroyers (30,000 gallons apiece) while in normal cruising formation. This task was new to Kinkaid, but it would not be the last time. Although he could not clearly see the direction these new departures in operations were taking, it is obvious that Kinkaid and his command were engaged in the type of operations he would be pursuing against the Japanese in less than five years.[19]

The return to its home port on 28 April did not lead to a long period of inactivity for *Indy*. After a brief respite for cleaning and painting, practice began for more competitive firing. In mid-May there was fleet battle practice, advanced day practice, and SRBP with live firing. The routine of five days out, usually near San Clemente, and back for weekends was followed. In the middle of this activity after a Friday night return to port, Admiral Sadler brought a group of officers from *Minneapolis* (CA 36) for a surprise

---

[18] *Indianapolis* log, 15 Mar–1 Apr 1938; King and Whitehill, *Fleet Admiral King*, 280–83; Thomas B. Buell, *Master of Sea Power: A Biography of Fleet Admiral Ernest J. King* (Boston: Little, Brown, 1980), 110–13; "Last of the Fleet Problems," in MacDonald, *Evolution of Aircraft Carriers*, 37–38.

[19] Dyer oral history; Anderson oral history; *Indianapolis* log, 15 Mar–28 Apr 1938.

inspection the next morning. If Kinkaid and his crew were discomfited, it didn't show. Commander CRUDIV 6 reported to Vice Admiral Tarrant:

> The condition of the *Indianapolis* shows the result of careful inspection, work-planning and constant supervision. All of the Heads of Departments are worthy of special mention but particularly noteworthy is the work of the First Lieutenant and Damage Control Officer [Lieutenant Commander G. C. Dyer] and, the leader of the ship, Captain Thomas C. Kinkaid.

Commander Scouting Force (Tarrant) sent this report along to Admiral Bloch, Commander in Chief, U.S. Fleet. Bloch sent to Kinkaid his own letter of commendation:

> The Board which conducted the subject inspection found the material condition of the *Indianapolis* to be uniformly excellent. Commander Scouting Force . . . stated that the *Indianapolis* was in an outstandingly good material condition and was an extraordinarily well administered ship.

Kinkaid could not have been more pleased. He sent the letter from Admiral Bloch and its attachments from Sadler and Tarrant to his department heads with an attached note that was a gem of understatement: "This is a nice kind of letter to get."[20]

The smooth administration and splendid material condition of *Indianapolis* was the result of constant attention by Kinkaid; his executive, Commander Badger; and his first lieutenant and damage control officer, Lieutenant Commander George C. Dyer. Badger had run the ship in a no-nonsense manner since he had been on board. His battles with the department heads to maintain standards and meet commitments had been frequent and often wound up in the commanding officer's office. If Badger was being unreasonable, Kinkaid normally was able to find a middle ground that would not only leave his executive's feelings and authority intact, but also meet the needs of the department head. If Badger was correct, he got his way without his subordinate fearing his career would go out the scuppers when the next fitness report was submitted. Kinkaid managed to infuse his officers with the concept that he was more interested in results than in fault-finding. Because of this attitude, he received loyalty and, most important, honest reports. Kinkaid had been ordered to the ship because Admiral Tarrant had heard he was of the best at maintaining a ship, and the admiral wanted a first-class flagship. If *Indianapolis* was the "most beautiful ship in the Fleet," a good part of the reason was the incessant activity of its first lieutenant; Dyer was a bear for work and

---

[20] Commander in Chief U.S. Fleet (CINCUS) to CO *Indianapolis*, San Pedro, CA, 24 May 1938, TCK Papers.

NHC

Indianapolis (CA 35) passes under the Golden Gate Bridge, San Francisco, 1938.

he never let up. Forty years later his shipmates remembered the quality of his work. Another did note that Commander Cruiser Divisions Rear Admiral Joseph Taussig had once commented about the fine material condition of *Indianapolis*: "She ought to look good—she costs more to maintain than any other ship under my administration!"[21]

About a month before Kinkaid was due to take *Indianapolis* north for the usual operations in the Puget Sound area, Commander Badger was relieved as executive officer by Commander Ralph Davis. Badger went ashore to the War College and was followed by a strong fitness report. He had served Kinkaid well. Davis was no stranger to his new skipper; he had been gunnery officer in *Colorado* while Kinkaid had been executive. It is probable that Kinkaid's connections in officer detailing had brought Davis to this new berth. Of a different personality than his predecessor, Davis quickly established his authority and kept the ship operating as smoothly as it had under Badger.

The summer of 1938 commenced with CRUDIVs 4, 5, and 6 leaving Long Beach for Seattle. There they joined Commander Battle Force with a few battleships, the seaplane tender *Langley*, and a handful of destroyers. After a few days of operations out of Port Angeles *Indy* dropped her

---

[21] Dyer oral history; Dudley to author, 8 Apr 1977; Hartman to author, 12 Apr 1977; Forsyth to author, 29 Apr 1977.

hook in Elliott Bay to celebrate the Fourth by sending a landing force ashore for a parade through Seattle's business district. On the 9th the cruisers headed south to San Francisco Bay for ten days of activities in that delightful area. On 13 July the citizens of the Bay Area were treated to the booming salutes that accompanied changes in flag commands. In the morning, on board *Indianapolis*, Vice Admiral Adolphus Andrews relieved Vice Admiral Tarrant of command of the Scouting Force. Kinkaid now had an old friend on board during his last couple of months on *Indy*. Andrews had written to him earlier and said he would soon take over the Scouting Force. He noted a bit wistfully that he wished Tom could stay longer, but he knew that his younger friend had to move on.[22] Following the change in Scouting Force commanders, Kinkaid was taken to *Chicago* to see Rear Admiral G. J. Rowcliff relieve Rear Admiral Taussig as Commander Cruisers, Scouting Force. Again the windows in San Francisco were rattled by the booming salutes. Three days later he went on board *Minneapolis* to witness the change in commanders for CRUDIV 6 as Rear Admiral Royal Ingersoll relieved Sadler. But the real show took place on 14 July with the President in the starring role.

President Roosevelt made a cross-country political trip in July 1938 and followed it with a vacation cruise in *Houston*. After visits throughout the West speaking on behalf of Democratic Party candidates who supported his New Deal programs, the presidential train pulled into the Bay Area. He spent 14 July politicking in San Francisco, lunching with the local Democratic leaders, and giving the usual press interviews. In the late afternoon the President boarded *Houston* and reviewed the sixty-seven ships anchored in four columns from the San Francisco–Oakland Bay Bridge to Hunter's Point, a distance of three miles. Led by the destroyer *McDougal* (DD 358), *Houston* moved down the four columns and received a full twenty-one-gun salute as it passed each major vessel. At 1647, with rails manned and all hands saluting, *Indianapolis* fired its twenty-one-gun salute and *Houston* returned the honors with its band playing the national anthem. The President, with Commander in Chief, U.S. Fleet Admiral Claude Bloch at his side, enjoyed the review from a special stand built on the cruiser.[23] A few days after the presidential review, Vice Admiral Andrews with CRUDIVs 4 and 5, plus *Indianapolis*, sailed north again, this time to pay the annual visit to Portland. The routine was little different than the previous year except that Kinkaid was able to enter the Columbia River channel without the anxiety caused by a dense fog. The cruisers remained for ten days and finally, at 0448 on 1 August, Kinkaid took *Indy* back to San Francisco for another week. The

---

[22] *Indianapolis* log, 13 Jul 1938, 16 Jul 1938; RADM Adolphus Andrews to TCK, Washington, 8 Jun 1938, TCK Papers.

[23] *San Francisco Chronicle*, 9–15 Jul 1938.

captain might have enjoyed the visit more, but he now had orders to a new duty station and was anxious to move along. While in the Bay Area he did have the opportunity for a short visit with his brother-in-law, Rear Admiral Husband E. Kimmel. As COMCRUDIV 4 Kimmel had come on board *Indianapolis* to make an official call on Vice Admiral Andrews and his flag captain.[24]

Kinkaid and *Indianapolis* returned to Long Beach on 12 August. The next day Admiral Andrews gave a personnel inspection to both. As usual ship and crew were clean and well-rigged. Ten days later the captain took *Indianapolis* out for a quick trip to San Diego. Four days later, on 27 August at 0935, Captain Jack F. Shafroth inspected the ship and crew and then relieved Kinkaid. "Big Jack" was a classmate of Tom's. In his notice to the CNO that he had relieved Kinkaid, Shafroth wrote: "I find the material condition of the ship and the efficiency of the crew to be excellent in all respects."[25]

Kinkaid received two fitness reports during the last six months of his command. Vice Admiral Tarrant, at the time of his detachment, wrote a report that was outstanding in every respect. He concluded with a phrase dear to a captain's heart: "Captain Kinkaid is . . . well fitted for promotion to Flag rank." Though he had been on board *Indianapolis* about seven weeks, Vice Admiral Andrews filed a complete fitness report and awarded the highest marks possible in every category of evaluation. He closed the remarks section with these paragraphs:

> I have found him to be an outstanding officer of the highest character in every way. He is an excellent seaman and possesses marked ability, coolness, initiative, and other attributes of the highest type naval officer. He would make a splendid flag officer and I strongly recommend his selection for flag rank when due. Upon inspection I have found the *Indianapolis* to be a smart, efficient, and happy ship, all reflecting great credit upon her commanding officer, Captain Kinkaid.[26]

As previously noted, Tom Kinkaid was not one to leave his career to chance. He deliberately chose a ship command as his first captain's duty afloat in order to prove early to his seniors that he was flag officer material. His fitness reports bore out his confidence in himself. He now had to come ashore, but he could not return to Washington, normally his first choice for shore duty, because he had served there too often. Because he and Helen had so thoroughly enjoyed duty in Constantinople, and the short tours in Geneva with the State Department, he had left word with

---

[24] *Indianapolis* log, 20 Jul–9 Aug 1938.
[25] Ibid., 27 Aug 1938; CAPT J. F. Shafroth to CNO, San Diego, CA, 27 Aug 1938, TCK Papers.
[26] Fitness Reports, 13 Jul 1938, 27 Aug 1938, TCK Personnel File.

his detailer and on every fitness report that he wanted naval attaché duty in London. There was another possible factor at work as well. Naval attaché duty would remove him from the day-to-day scrutiny of senior naval officers. The Ambassador would be his immediate supervisor and the Director of the Office of Naval Intelligence (ONI) would write his fitness reports, though these would do little more than comment on his diligence. After thirty years of active service Kinkaid probably believed he had made his mark and would be willing to stand for selection on what he had accomplished. We do get a bit of insight in this ambition from a rather candid letter he wrote to his detailer, Captain A. S. Sharp, in January 1938. He laid out his career plan for the next few years:

> My whole interest now is in command of this fine ship, which I want to retain as long as possible. For the future I have only three things in mind— (1) Naval Attaché, London. (2) Chief of the Bureau of Navigation and (3) Commander-in-Chief. Everyone shoots at (3) though few arrive; I would like (2) because of the opportunity for constructive work and real service; and at present I am concentrating on (1).[27]

Tom thought he would get the London billet because the timing would be right, but others were as diligent as he in planning. A good friend, Alan Kirk, got the London slot and Tom was offered Rome. The director of ONI, Rear Admiral R. S. Holmes, explained that London was out and hoped that he would accept Rome. Holmes had been there and strongly recommended it. Kinkaid accepted the offer but closed with the comment: "I still have a hankering to go to London and hope you will keep me in mind."[28] In time orders came for Kinkaid calling for detachment on 27 August for a month of temporary duty in Washington at the spaces of ONI, and his billet in Rome by early November.

---

[27] TCK to CAPT A. S. Sharp, Mare Island Shipyard, 10 Jan 1938, TCK Papers.
[28] RADM R. S. Holmes to TCK, Washington, 1 Feb 1938; TCK to Holmes, Long Beach, CA, 12 Feb 1938, TCK Papers.

Chapter 5

Rome, 1938–1941

Assignment to Rome pleased the Kinkaids, particularly Helen. Constantinople had been exciting and the international society dazzling, with much that was new to see and do throughout the Middle East. Tom's career had been advanced, if for no other reason than his close association with Admiral Mark Bristol. The duty in Geneva in 1930 and 1932, when Tom was attached to the State Department, had introduced them to sophisticated officials from a variety of European states and broadened their circle of friends in the Foreign Service.

Now in Rome they would move outside the Navy and become a part of the official family in what was becoming an important embassy in Europe. Tom was fifty and Helen, a few years younger, was as attractive, charming, intelligent, articulate, and vigorous as ever. With a captain's pay and the allowances that went with an attaché's position, plus Helen's own income, they could live gracefully and well. A naval attaché's work could be fairly heavy, but they anticipated enough time and opportunity to enjoy this unique tour of duty.

Returning from leave after detachment, Kinkaid began his month of briefings and study in Washington preparatory to departure. He read attaché reports, both for background and as examples of the type of reporting he was expected to do. He also visited the Division of European Affairs at the State Department and was briefed by its head, Pierrepont Moffat, and his staff. Tom had first worked with Moffat in Constantinople, and again when assisting the State Department for the World Disarmament Conference. A few years earlier he had described Moffat as "keen, intelligent, and extremely well informed, . . . not a pacifist; friendly toward the Army and Navy."[1] It was comforting in 1938 to know that one of Secretary of State Cordell Hull's most important advisors was this same man. Kinkaid also managed to squeeze in twenty-five lessons in conversational Italian at the Washington Berlitz school. He considered himself slow at learning languages, but he completed the accelerated course and continued his studies with a tutor once he was settled in Rome.[2]

---
[1] TCK to CDR T. S. Wilkinson, Bremerton, 26 Feb 1934, TCK Papers.
[2] CNO to Chief BUNAV, Washington, 21 Feb 1938, TCK Papers.

Author's collection

Commander James B. Sykes, Assistant Attaché (Air), Commander Proctor Thornton, Assistant Attaché, and Captain Thomas Kinkaid, Naval Attaché, Rome, circa January 1940.

He reported in Rome on 8 November. It took little time for the new attaché to meet his staff, inventory the files and ciphers, count the funds in the attaché's custody, and relieve Captain Thaddeus Thomason. The assistant naval attaché, Commander Proctor M. Thornton, had reported several months earlier. He and his wife were able to help the Kinkaids find temporary quarters and begin learning the social ropes.

Kinkaid took up his duties at a time of enormous tension in European affairs. Only six weeks earlier virtually the whole continent had been transfixed in terror at the prospect of a major war as Nazi Germany insisted that Czechoslovakia yield its western mountain region, the Sudetenland. Wanting to resist if England and France would support them, the Czech government of Eduard Benes yielded when it was obvious that Prime Minister Neville Chamberlain and Premier Edouard Daladier were not ready to face down Adolf Hitler. Italian Prime Minister Benito Mussolini won plaudits from most Europeans and Americans by a last-minute appeal to Hitler to hold his fire and negotiate. Politically bound to the Germans by the Rome-Berlin Axis of 1936, Il Duce was not interested in seeing a war involving Germany commence.

In Washington and now in Rome, Kinkaid learned that Italy was a great deal more than an observer of the European scene. Determined to enhance his reputation as a leader and restore the reputation of Italy as the dominant power in the Mediterranean, Mussolini had led his country into a war of territorial conquest against Ethiopia in 1935–1937. When a rightist revolt erupted against the newly elected government in Spain in July 1936, Hitler and Mussolini provided material assistance and later "volunteer" armies and air units as their contribution to support the proto-fascist rebels. Though shaken when Hitler incorporated Austria into the Third Reich in March 1938 and German troops manned the border crossing at the Brenner Pass, Il Duce maintained a wary friendship with Der Fuhrer.

The American Embassy's role was to observe, report, and, within the limits of American policies, try to influence the course of Italian foreign affairs in directions consistent with American ends. Ambassador William Phillips was a career officer of great experience. He had served every President except Herbert Hoover since Theodore Roosevelt's time. Before Rome, his most recent post was Under Secretary of State. Because of his experience, and his regular correspondence with his friend, President Franklin Roosevelt, it was expected that Phillips could keep the Italian foreign ministry well informed on a day-to-day basis about American views on matters that might affect Italian-American relations. When critical issues or crises arose, he was instructed directly by the President or Secretary of State Cordell Hull. Although American policy was not always easy to decipher, the Roosevelt administration was clearly interested in seeing Europe remain at peace. Further territorial conquests by Germany or Italy could jeopardize the perilous peace in Central Europe, so American policy was to counsel moderation in the foreign relations of Italy. Unwilling to commit itself to the democratic states in Europe because of a fundamental public insistence on an isolationist stance, the United States could do little more than urge that all live by the Golden Rule.

Captain Kinkaid, when appointed to Rome, was designated naval attaché and naval attaché for air. In early 1939 the Navy Department requested that he also be accredited as naval attaché to the American legation in Belgrade, Yugoslavia.[3] Kinkaid's mission was to support Ambassador Phillips and provide a steady flow of information to the Navy Department about Italian naval and military matters. His reports were based on personal observations and those of the other naval attachés, official data supplied by the Italian naval ministry, information derived from the press, and information he acquired from the naval attachés of other countries. Personal contact with Italian officials and civilians also generated information. In time he developed

---

[3] CNO to SECSTATE, Washington, 2 Feb 1939, TCK Papers.

a number of covert sources who provided political and naval information, some of enormous value and some totally worthless. All this information was sorted into predetermined subject categories and reported to the Navy Department by diplomatic pouch almost daily. From time to time and eventually on a weekly schedule, he sent lengthy reports, often titled "Current Events and Comments." In these summaries he not only provided raw data but also tried his hand at interpreting what it all meant.[4]

Kinkaid's official movements and activities were largely prescribed by years of customary practice. He could visit ships, naval bases, shipyards, factories, and other naval, military, and aviation facilities to the extent that Italian naval attachés could do the same in the United States. Certain naval bases, reservations, and operating areas were off limits, and he scrupulously adhered to the rules. He soon discovered he was under regular surveillance when traveling outside Rome. About 95 percent of Kinkaid's work consisted of collecting intelligence from overt sources—not a very dramatic occupation but vital to U.S. development of a clear picture of a potential enemy's naval and military capabilities.

During his stay in Rome Kinkaid moved in a variety of official and social circles that helped him do his job. He and Helen were brought into the embassy's society early in the tour of duty. They were hampered for almost six months by having to live in a hotel suite, but they were still able to do most of the entertaining expected of them. The embassy crowd was like an extended family, providing a social refuge from culture shock. Ambassador Phillips and his wife had rented a large and opulent estate more magnificent than the embassy. Their entertaining set a standard that none in the embassy could match, and they weren't expected to try. Cocktail parties, dinners, bridge, poker sessions (men only), golf and tennis, and bathing parties at the embassy's cabana at the beach provided the basic entertainment. The musical arts flourished in Rome under Mussolini, and Rome's opera had become the most magnificent in Italy, with the exception of Milan's La Scala. The summer outdoor performances at Baths of Caracalla were spectacular. Kinkaid had resisted his predecessor's request to take over his opera box, but he and Helen still managed to see occasional performances.[5]

Because they were basically social types, the Kinkaids found it easy to make friends with people in the Italian government. Tom was immediately introduced to the officials at the naval ministry and officers from the Italian fleet. A few became fairly close friends, but most could not af-

---

[4] U.S. National Archives, "Selected Naval Attaché Reports Relating to the World Crisis, 1937–1943" [Microfilm] M975, roll 1 (hereafter Naval Attaché Reports, M975:1).

[5] Helen Kinkaid interview, 7–8 Jan 1976; CAPT and Mrs. (Louise) Proctor Thornton, interview with author, San Francisco, 13 Oct 1977 (hereafter Thornton interview); William Phillips, *Ventures in Diplomacy* (London: John Murray, 1955), 115–16.

ford to be seen too often with the Kinkaids—or any other Americans. Because of his fondness for golf Tom played regularly with government people at the Golf Club, an exclusive establishment designed by Count Galeazzo Ciano, the foreign minister and Mussolini's son-in-law. It was on the links that Kinkaid received his first definite assurance from Count Ciano that Italy would enter the war between 10 and 15 June 1940.

The Kinkaids also socialized with the attachés from other nations. Despite their cultural differences, they shared a common interest and profession with Tom Kinkaid. They visited one another in their offices regularly and often shared what they had learned. Once war began in September 1939 Kinkaid often found himself acting as a social go-between for the British, French, and German attachés. Following the defeat of the German pocket battleship *Admiral Graf Spee* by three English cruisers at the Battle of the River Plate, the German commanding officer, Captain Hans Langsdorff, committed suicide. The British attaché, Captain Bowyer-Smith, asked Kinkaid to pass the word to the German attaché, Captain Lowisch, that Langsdorff had not disgraced himself by his conduct of the battle. Lowisch was touched and assured Kinkaid that Langsdorff's widow would receive the message.[6] When Italy declared war on Great Britain and France in June 1940, the American Embassy took charge of British and French affairs and property. Kinkaid himself bought out the British attaché's liquor stock and had the American attaché in London settle the account generously once Rear Admiral Bevan returned to the admiralty.

Kinkaid's reports to the Office of Naval Intelligence had a large number of memoranda of conversations resulting from visits with his colleagues. Occasionally the sum of several visits provided interesting insights into official Italian attitudes. Once war was declared, the British and French attachés had to call on the Italian chief of the naval general staff, Admiral Somigli, to discuss naval matters that would concern Italy as a neutral party. Both were astounded to find that Somigli was clearly pro-English in his sympathies. Kinkaid had suspected as much from his own dealings with the admiral.[7]

After many months of searching, the Kinkaids located a satisfactory, furnished apartment owned by Lady Caroline, the widow of a Scot, Sir Robert McClure. The furnishings were elegant, the library enormous, and the site spectacular. Located below the Trinita dei Monti and beside the Spanish steps, it was on the fifth floor (reached by elevator) and overlooked the Sacred Heart Convent. Lady Caroline's cook and butler were included. The Kinkaids could now do the entertaining they desired

---

[6] Naval Attaché Reports, M975:2, "Italy's Present Position, 29 May 1940"; TCK oral history, 99–100.

[7] Naval Attaché Reports, M975:2, "British Naval Attaché, Conversation with . . . Somigli, 1 Sep 1939"; "French Naval Attaché, Conversation with . . . Somigli, 2 Sep 1939."

in the manner they thought proper. In time the Kinkaids were fluent enough in Italian to enjoy visiting with other than Italian officialdom. Combined with a good deal of shopping for their necessities, the contacts helped them see another part of Rome's population. Yet such socializing did not really enhance their understanding of the Italian people. Their Italian friends were from an educated upper class and did not represent the viewpoints and attitudes of the masses. The newspapers they read were American or English, or Roman and censored, though Kinkaid could read an analysis of the local press sent in by the consular officials throughout the country. Therefore when he ventured analyses, Kinkaid's views on public opinion in Italy were not drawn from the most useful sources, a fact he didn't quite recognize. In the end his most important reports concerned ships, aircraft, factory production, and the number of Germans to be seen in Rome, and not public opinion in Italy.

During Kinkaid's first six months in Rome tension again began to build in Europe as Adolf Hitler proceeded to absorb more territory into his Third Reich and violate more German promises that he had committed to paper. In mid-March 1939 he ordered the remainder of Czechoslovakia placed under German control. A month later President Roosevelt sent Hitler and Mussolini a formal plea that they assure the thirty-one nations he listed that they would be free from future attack. In return, these listed nations would refrain from menacing the Axis powers. No formal reply was given, but on 28 April Adolf Hitler addressed the Reichstag, derided the President's message, and denounced the German-Polish Non-Aggression Pact of 1934 and the Anglo-German Naval Agreement of 1935.[8]

A May meeting in Milan between Count Ciano and German Foreign Minister Joachim von Ribbentrop was followed by the signing of an Italian-German Pact, the so-called Pact of Steel of 22 May 1939. By this agreement Mussolini pledged Italian support should Germany find itself at war. On the basis of von Ribbentrop's assurances, Il Duce believed there would be no war for at least three years; by then Italy might be ready. It was probably well for the nerves of all involved that the terms of the Pact of Steel were secret.

Against this background of increasing tension Kinkaid went about his naval attaché duties in a businesslike manner. Most of his reports in those first months concerned the Italian air force and aircraft production in Italy. Because of concern in Europe and America that aerial bombardment would be used in a future war, particularly after the grim demonstration of Luftwaffe effectiveness against the Spanish city of

---

[8] Robert Dallek, *Franklin D. Roosevelt and American Foreign Policy, 1932–1945* (New York: Oxford University Press, 1979), 185–87; Nancy Harvison Hooker, ed., *The Moffat Papers: Selections From the Diplomatic Journals of Jay Pierrepont Moffat* (Cambridge, MA: Harvard University Press, 1956), 239–41; William L. Shirer, *The Rise and Fall of the Third Reich: A History of Nazi Germany* (New York: Simon & Shuster, 1960), 469–79.

Guernica, Kinkaid's superiors wanted to know about Italian capabilities in this field. Through visits to aircraft factories by his assistants, Kinkaid concluded that production was slowing down because the government could not provide enough support to keep production at a high level. Ironically, foreign sales to Italy, including those from American companies, had forced cutbacks in Italian factory output.[9]

Kinkaid and Commander Thornton took a trip through southern Italy and Sicily to observe the naval bases in that region. They would have liked to look in on the submarine base in western Sicily, but wisely followed Italian instructions and avoided the region. Later Tom mentioned to a naval ministry official that they had been in Sicily but had avoided the base area. The officer said he knew; an Italian naval intelligence officer had been following them.[10]

Since he had been accredited as naval attaché for Yugoslavia, Kinkaid determined to visit Belgrade and Minister Arthur Bliss Lane in April and establish contact with the Yugoslav naval ministry. Tom and Helen had decided many years before that they would try to never have an international boundary between them, so Helen joined her husband for the trip. The Lanes were marvelous hosts, and Minister Lane introduced Kinkaid to the people he should know. After four pleasant days in Belgrade, Arthur and Cornelia Lane took the Kinkaids to Smederevo on the Danube. From there Tom and Helen started their return to Rome.

While in Trieste on the return trip Tom received a summons to return to Belgrade. The minister had mentioned Kinkaid's visit to Prince Paul, the regent for young King Peter. The prince wanted to meet Kinkaid. At a splendid dinner laced with wines from one of the finest cellars in Europe and hosted by the Lanes, the Oxford-educated Prince Paul began a fairly sophisticated discussion of naval matters. Kinkaid warmed to the subject. He spoke for more than an hour about ships, guns, armor, power plants, and anything else that interested the prince. He concluded that the regent had not had the opportunity to talk with an expert outside his own country. Such evenings would occur several more times before Kinkaid left his post in Rome.[11]

It is possible, of course, that Prince Paul wanted to know more about navies in case Mussolini decided to follow his conquest of Albania the week before with a move against Yugoslavia. By the time Kinkaid wrote his bread-and-butter letter to Minister Lane, Albania was completely controlled by the Italians, and King Zog had gone into exile. In his reports

---

[9] Naval Attaché Reports, M975:1, "Report on Aircraft Production for Mar 1939, 31 Mar 1939."
[10] TCK oral history, 57–8; Thornton interview, 13 Oct 1977.
[11] TCK oral history, 63–70; Arthur Bliss Lane Correspondence File, box 94. Arthur Bliss Lane Papers, Yale University (hereafter Lane Papers).

to ONI on the invasion, the attaché noted that the Italian air force did little more than put on an intimidating aerial display over Tirana while the Italians were negotiating with the Albanians. It was rumored, he noted wryly, that the air force had transported some troops to Tirana "to provide a nice looking guard of honor at the airport upon the arrival of Count Ciano." The naval bombardment and amphibious assault against Durrazo was amateurish. He closed this report by observing: "The fact remains that reports show that the fundamental principles governing landing forces were completely violated."[12]

The procession of events was interrupted on 12 March by the coronation of Pope Pius XII. The Kinkaids made it a point to get tickets and attend. Warned by old-timers, Tom, Helen, and Commander Thornton's wife, Louise, dressed warmly and took sandwiches, chocolate, and brandy to sustain them. They spent almost six hours at St. Peter's, viewing the pontifical procession, mass, and finally the coronation itself. As the triregnum was placed on the Pontiff's head, its three tiers symbolizing his absolute authority within the Church as the Vicar of Christ, his authority as Bishop of Rome, and his traditional power over all princes on earth, many who understood this symbolism must have regretted that Pius XII possessed little power to check the catastrophic course of history. Packed in with a crowd that might have reached a quarter million, including those outside in the square, the Kinkaids considered themselves fortunate to have witnessed the event and even luckier to have survived it.[13]

In the summer the Eternal City began to empty as its denizens sought vacation in more salubrious places. Tom was lonely after Helen left to visit her parents in Philadelphia. Because of the heat he worked early in the morning, took a long break at midday, and worked in the early evening if necessary, with considerable attention to the question of whether Italy would be going to war soon. Unconsciously Kinkaid answered the question to his own satisfaction by taking a working vacation in Yugoslavia in mid-August.

Before packing his bags for the trip he spent two weeks helping the diplomatic community welcome his new assistant attaché, Commander James B. Sykes. He acquainted the Sykes family with the local scene, including the beach, the Golf Club, and the Sulphur Baths. There was the almost interminable round of welcoming cocktail parties, lunches, and somewhat formal dinners. Tom described one luncheon to his wife: "It was the usual affair with a table laden with food from which we got up at 3:15.... At 6:30 went to Blakes' for KT's [cocktails], also for the Sykes,

---

[12] Naval Attaché Reports, M975:1, "Italian Aviation Participation in Conquest of Albania, 13 Apr 1939;" "Report of the Italian Expeditionary Force's Actions against Albania, 14 Apr 1939."

[13] TCK oral history, 60–62; Thornton interview, 13 Oct 1977; *New York Times*, 13 Mar 1939.

so you see my figure is having difficulty changing for the better. . . . This week of celebrations of the Sykes' arrival have caused a setback." Between rounds of entertainment Kinkaid took his new assistant to the Italian naval and air ministries to meet the Italian officials associated with his work. Commander Sykes was a naval aviator and thus was expected to provide a level of expertise that Kinkaid lacked.[14]

Kinkaid left Rome for Yugoslavia on 7 August. Because of the heat in Belgrade, almost the whole legation migrated with its minister to summer in Bled, a small vacation spa in the foothills of the Alps almost at the Austrian border. Lane owned a villa on a lake outside the city, and Tom had a room with a magnificent view. He had brought his golf clubs and within an hour he was touring the local course with the minister. For five days he golfed each morning with Lane, usually shooting in the upper 80s.

After a week of vacation, Kinkaid paid his first visit to Yugoslav naval facilities. On 15 August he took the train from Bled to Zagreb and transferred to a night train to Split, a port city on the central Yugoslavian coast. He visited with Admiral Mariasevic, who commanded the naval base at Split, and was given a tour of the city and countryside by the admiral's aide. After dining with the senior officers he took the train south to visit the naval facilities in Dubrovnik. Kinkaid completed his visit with the firm conviction that the Yugoslavs were friends of the United States and disliked the Germans and Italians, in that order of intensity.[15]

While visiting and golfing in Bled, Kinkaid and Minister Lane were not unaware of the world scene; it just didn't seem too important. With a bit of introspection about the German absorption of Austria, the actions on behalf of the Sudetan Germans, and the current campaign concerning the German people in the Polish corridor, the naval attaché might have wondered about the popularity of Ljubljana and Bled with vacationing Germans. But in writing to Helen his only observation was that his Italian, French, and English did not help much around Bled, and that 68 percent of the tourists were German.[16]

Returning to Rome on 22 August he found an atmosphere of anxiety. The radio, cables, and mail were bringing in news of the deepening crises concerning Poland. Barring a miracle or total capitulation by the Poles, Germany seemed ready to declare war. From mid-August, after meetings with von Ribbentrop and Hitler in Salzburg, Ciano and Mussolini knew that the German Wehrmacht would march against Poland at the end of the month, but no one else knew of this.[17]

---

[14] TCK to Helen S. Kinkaid [HSK], Rome, 22, 24, 27, 29 Jul; 1, 3 Aug 1939, TCK Papers.
[15] Ibid., 10, 12, 15, 17, 21 Aug 1939, TCK Papers; Appointment Books, Lane Papers.
[16] TCK to HSK, Bled, Yugoslavia, 14 Aug 1939, TCK Papers.
[17] Shirer, *Rise and Fall of the Third Reich*, 509–12.

Expecting the worst, President Roosevelt had Ambassador Phillips deliver a personal appeal to King Victor Emmanuel II that he use Italy's influence with Adolf Hitler in the cause of peace. Expressing his impotency as a constitutional monarch, the king refused to act. Not even Mussolini's admission that Italy could not join in the conflict served to stop the German juggernaut. It would be Deutschland uber Alles, with or without their faithless ally.[18]

War commenced on 1 September with the German attack on Poland. England and France entered two days later. The American Embassy's principal job now was to monitor Italy's activities closely and try to anticipate any move toward its entry into the conflict. Kinkaid's reports in turn began to focus on reported strengths of the Italian armed forces, their distribution, and aircraft production. Conversations with other naval attachés were reported when they produced new information.

His relations with these colleagues also began to shift in subtle ways. The German attaché, Captain Werner Lowisch, became less communicative and more defensive about his country's actions. Kinkaid suspected that Lowisch was being evasive when he asked him about the torpedoing of the British passenger liner *Athenia*. On the other hand Lowisch sought out Commander Thornton to assure him that he had spoken honestly though ignorantly when he had told him a few weeks earlier that Germany would not attack Poland. At the close of a visit with Kinkaid the German attaché asked Kinkaid to tell the British (Bowyer-Smith) and French (De Larosiere) naval attachés "that he had no enemy feeling toward them but only a feeling of personal friendship."[19] Captain Lowisch outlasted all of the other attachés in Rome.[20]

Kinkaid also regularly submitted analyses of current events in Italy and often some estimates on the likelihood of Italy entering the war. But Kinkaid's judgment about possible actions the Italian government might take were flawed because his sources were poor. Count Ciano was quite outspoken in social gatherings, doing little to hide his contempt for the Germans, and tending to say things and reflect attitudes that pleased Americans. Kinkaid and others knew that Mussolini did not share these views, but it was tempting to place more importance on Ciano's utterances than warranted. When Helen's hairdresser, Tom's barber, the local vegetable vendor, and no end of civilian acquaintances also indicated contempt for the Nazis and friendship for Americans, it was difficult for the naval attaché not

---

[18] Phillips, *Ventures in Diplomacy*, 127–30; Shirer, *Rise and Fall*, 553–55, 564–68.

[19] Naval Attaché Reports, M975:1 & 2; Thornton interview, 13 Oct 1977.

[20] Because of his expertise in Balkan affairs, Captain Lowisch was advanced to flag rank in 1943 and placed in charge of naval matters in the Adriatic. He stayed on in Italy through 1944 and survived the war as the commander of German naval forces in the south. Information from Professor Charles B. Burdick, San José State University.

to conclude that Italy's nonbelligerency, actually technical neutrality and support for Germany, would be as far as the nation would go. Because he was a professional naval officer, and above all a person trained to think and act in a rational manner, it is little wonder that Kinkaid and many others in the embassy found it hard to believe that Italy would ever enter the war as an ally of the demonic Adolf Hitler. They ignored the control Benito Mussolini had over his government and his equally demonic personality that directed him into actions lacking logic or a sense of national prudence. Thus on 12 April 1940, just three days after Hitler reopened hostilities by invading Denmark and Norway, Kinkaid reviewed Italy's international position and concluded, "All things considered, one is constrained to believe that Italy will maintain her attitude of blustering 'non-belligerency' as long as possible and will endeavor to profit at the peace conference by a strong military readiness to fight for her claims."[21]

A few days after this report a fairly vitriolic press campaign opened against the Allies, and Kinkaid began to shift his ground. He thought the Italian army was doing little, but the fleet was being mobilized. He noted that for Italy to go to war was "to fly in the face of common sense. [But] . . . it must be remembered that the final issue may not be decided by what seems to be common sense. . . . If Mussolini gives the order, Italy will march." Finally by 25 May it was fairly clear that Italy would attack someone. Anti-Allies posters were up, the press campaign was in high gear, troops were concentrating, antiaircraft batteries were in evidence at the ports, and submarine nets were being emplaced in many harbors. In his report of 29 May Kinkaid noted that, while golfing, Ciano had said that Italy would enter the war between 10 and 15 June. On the 10th Il Duce hurled his armies against France.[22]

Italy's decision marked the opening of eighteen months of steadily deteriorating Italian-American relations. In the six weeks prior to Italy's action President Roosevelt addressed four pleas to Mussolini to stay his hand. On 27 May he offered mediation and promised that Britain and France would cooperate. On 31 May he simply asked that Mussolini carefully consider the consequences of any move and warned that if Italy entered the war the United States would begin a rearmament program that the enemies of the democracies could not match. Ciano was impressed; Mussolini was not. Ciano informed Ambassador Phillips, orally, that the die was cast—another Caesar had crossed the Rubicon.[23]

With the declaration of Italian belligerency, it was natural that relations with America would worsen; if nothing else, President Roosevelt's

---

[21] Naval Attaché Reports, M975:2, "Italy's Present Position, 12 Apr 1940."
[22] Naval Attaché Reports, M975:2, "Italy's Present Position, 25 and 29 May 1940."
[23] Phillips, *Ventures in Diplomacy*, 155–63; *Moffatt Papers*, 305–7; Thomas G. DeCola, "Roosevelt and Mussolini: The Critical Years, 1938–1941" (Ph.D. diss., Kent State University, 1967), 256–66.

actions had been scorned. But the Italian dictator had realized that the United States was already assisting the Allies to the limit of its abilities. The addition of another hostile power to the President's list could not make much of a difference to the Axis powers. Like Hitler, Mussolini assumed that Great Britain would crumple before the United States could take decisive action. He was wrong, of course, because the German invasion of the Low Countries, following the conquest of Denmark and Norway, and now Italy's entrance into the war, had awakened all Americans and their Congress to the extreme peril of the nation. Within the next twelve months the neutrality laws were revised, national conscription instituted, the armed forces dramatically increased, fifty destroyers traded to Great Britain, and a massive lend-lease program legislated to assist those nations resisting Axis aggression.

The war did not significantly change the work of the naval attaché, but the lifestyle of the Kinkaids was definitely altered. Helen had been in the United States for two months when Germany attacked Poland in September. The State Department was undecided as to whether she would be permitted to sail for Italy. Fortunately Ambassador Phillips's wife, Caroline, had been snared by the same situation, and the waves made by the ambassador's wife were considerably larger than Helen's. After a two-month delay they were permitted to leave. While Helen was away, Tom had lunch with the wife of Admiral Alberto Lais, who mentioned that her husband expected certain imported foods to become scarcer in the near future. Always one to plan ahead, Kinkaid began to purchase extra kilos of coffee and boxes of lump sugar. He suggested that Helen bring back with her a good supply of soap, toothpaste, toothbrushes, shaving cream, and his brand of razor blades.[24] The liquor supply was no problem for the international community until Italy joined the fighting and the supply of British gin and whiskey dried up. With the addition of Admiral Bevan's supply, the Kinkaids were able to make it until Tom's detachment.

When Helen arrived in Rome, the social season was again in full session. The Kinkaid guest book, an autograph album they kept to log in their visitors, shows quite clearly that the war did not seriously diminish the rounds of entertainment until June 1940. They did have to be selective: Germans could not be entertained with the French, English, or Poles, and later the Danes or Norwegians. They also tried not to mix anti-Nazi Italians with their pro-German fellows, but were not always successful. Their guest book shows an interesting scattering of royalty, international luminaries, journalists, and an occasional artist or critic of international standing. Cecil Brown, Joseph C. Harsch, Herbert Matthews,

---
[24] TCK to HSK, Rome, 28 Jul 1939.

Cyrus L. Sulzberger, and Constantine Brown were all well-known newspapermen who had KTs with the Kinkaids. Princess Marie of Greece, Queen Victoria Eugenia of Spain, and Prince Jaime de Borbon of Spain signed in at Kinkaid parties, and the Spanish Queen regularly entertained them. Of all the guests that Tom and Helen entertained at their Trinita dei Monti apartment, the one who most impressed Helen, even forty years later, was Bernhard Berenson, the internationally renowned art critic. He visited them on several occasions and entertained them at I Tatti, his villa outside Florence. Because of his Jewish blood and despite his American citizenship, Berenson was harassed by petty Italian regulations and forced to go into hiding after 7 December 1941.

There was a touch of irony attached to the last party the Kinkaids held in Rome, on 2 March 1941. It was for the naval attachés, but this group had shrunk after Italy's declaration of war. The most prominent names were the Japanese, German, Romanian, and Swedish attachés. By now the most trusted in this group from Tom's point of view was Captain Henning Hammargren of the Swedish navy. He proved to be insightful concerning both the German and Italian navies; official conversations with him invariably gave Kinkaid some information worth reporting. In the years after the war Commodore Hammargren and Admiral Kinkaid regularly exchanged cards and notes.

In his work as attaché Kinkaid visited Yugoslavia twice during 1940. At the end of February he and Helen traveled to Belgrade and again stayed with Minister Lane and his family. The minister had arranged in advance for Kinkaid to visit with the senior officers in the naval ministry. Because so many had served in England at one time or another, he was able to carry on his conversations in English. After five days in Belgrade Helen left for Florence to visit the Berensons, and Tom went to Sibenik, a major Yugoslavian naval base about 25 miles north of Split. He called on the admiral commanding the forces afloat, visited several of the vessels, inspected the training station and the radio school, and had lunch with ten of the commanding officers on board Admiral Pavic's flagship *Zmaj*. He later wrote to Lane that "my trip to Sibenik was very successful."[25]

In mid-May 1940 Kinkaid paid his last visit to Belgrade. Again Minister Lane housed him and saw that he was included in his official entertaining. Prince Paul dined twice with the minister while Kinkaid was there. The regent wanted to talk about naval matters, but he also wanted to know about the rumors that Italy would enter the war by attacking Yugoslavia. We don't know what Kinkaid communicated, but the question became moot when Italy turned against France rather than Yugoslavia. Because he was needed in Rome, the naval attaché did

---

[25] TCK to Arthur Bliss Lane, Rome, 30 Jan 1940, 8 Mar 1940, boxes 18, 94, Lane Papers.

not return to Belgrade or the Yugoslavian naval bases during his last ten months on the job.[26]

Kinkaid now paid special attention to Italy's wartime activities. Based on social contacts with a variety of people he believed that many in the professional classes were ashamed of the jackal-like behavior of their government. But he was realistic enough to recognize that these people were not too numerous. He closed a report on 25 June with this observation:

> Then there is the Italian, and there are many of them, who some months ago feared the effect upon Italy of going to war and disliked the idea of siding with Germany but who today sees Italy in a position to grab something without danger or cost to herself and whose avaricious nature is pleased.[27]

Three months later he thought he detected a growing pessimism among "the common people." The cost of living was rising and there were shortages of those staples dear to the Italian diet: bread and pasta. He believed the public was losing faith in the controlled press. Despite steady predictions to the contrary England was not folding under the heavy bombardment of the Luftwaffe. Italians were equally disillusioned when Genoa and other Italian cities in the north were attacked by British squadrons.[28]

Until Italy entered the war, Kinkaid was reasonably respectful of the Italian navy's capabilities. He considered its officers competent though tending to be "cocky." Most American naval officers had overestimated the speed of Italy's cruisers and expected they would have trouble in combat due to their light armor, or thin skins; but few would have predicted just how ineffective the Italians would prove to be. Kinkaid recognized that the Italian fleet had some severe problems, national in scope, that would hinder its effectiveness. A shortage of steel made it difficult to repair battle damage. This situation and a shortage of fuel held the Italian fleet at its anchorages. Sorties against the British were rare and usually disastrous for the Italians. On the day the Tripartite Pact was signed (27 September 1940) binding Japan, Italy, and Germany to a common struggle, Kinkaid reported the rumor that the Italian naval ministry had ordered its fleet not to accept battle with the British. The steel shortage also prevented the Italians from finishing two battleships under construction, *Roma* and *Impero*, and from providing adequate antisubmarine and antitorpedo nets in fleet anchorages.[29]

---

[26] Ambassador Phillips to Lane, Rome, 22 May 1940, box 18, Lane Papers; A. B. Lane Appointment Books, 1939–1941, Lane Papers; Winston S. Churchill, *The Second World War*, vol. 2, *Their Finest Hour* (Boston: Houghton Mifflin, 1949), 128–29.

[27] Naval Attaché Reports, M975:2, "Italy's Present Position, 25 Jun 1940."

[28] Naval Attaché Reports, M975:1, "Italy's Present Position, 27 Sep 1940."

[29] TCK oral history, 102–4.

During the last few months of his stay Kinkaid developed a large amount of useful information through informants within the Italian government and armed services. One of his covert contacts, simply referred to as Signor X, was connected with censorship and press-control activities. He provided accurate ship battle-damage reports when the Italians were in action. He also passed along political tidbits concerning Italian dealings with the Russians, Bulgarians, Rumanians, and Turks. His information about the Italian timetable for attacking Greece proved accurate and may well have been used to help prepare the furious resistance they encountered. One report concerning Signor X noted that he had just returned from several days in Florence where he had helped organize censorship activities and "discover subversion there."[30] From meetings with a senior air force officer and a ship constructor Kinkaid obtained a detailed report on the damage the battleship *Littorio* received in the British attack on Taranto in November 1940. The aviator provided information on Italian views of aircraft engines, experiments with self-sealing gas tanks and armor for aircraft, aircraft torpedoes and launching techniques, and operational doctrine in Italian bombing squadrons. Kinkaid concluded a full report with the information that the Italians blamed British success at Taranto on spies and not their own poor defenses: "Whether they are as sure of their present security as declared, is doubted, but their pride would not let them admit any major fault in their own command, and consequently they are mentally open to other Tarantos."[31]

As the Italians began to bungle their campaign in Greece and failed to provide secure convoys across the Mediterranean to Africa, the Germans moved their own air units into the country and turned Sicily into a maze of Luftwaffe air bases. Kinkaid reported the size of the German buildup as accurately as possible, but his ability to move south of Rome had been limited. He estimated there were 2,300 German pilots and 10,000 air support personnel in Italy at the beginning of 1941. He also noted that the Germans were working as advisors and were helping to reorganize the Italian armed forces. In one of the last reports, he drew a fairly grim picture of life in Italy and said the people were becoming restive due to mounting losses in Africa, the disaster at Taranto, the ineffective campaign in Greece, the shortages of food, and above all the presence of the Germans: "To sum up, Italy's armed forces have failed miserably, morale is sub-zero, the people are hungry and are on the verge of revolt. Mussolini has been forced to turn to Germany to keep

---

[30] Naval Attaché Reports, M975:2, "Signor 'X', 14 and 22 Oct 1940."
[31] Naval Attaché Reports, M975:1, "Items from Conversation with Air Force Lieutenant Colonel and Lieutenant Naval Constructor, 7 Jan 1941."

himself in power and Italy in the war, and German domination of Italy grows stronger every day."[32]

A week before Tom was due to be detached, the Kinkaids witnessed one of those historical events that provided conversational anecdotes the rest of their lives. Queen Victoria of Spain called them in the morning of 28 February 1941 and asked that they come visit her in her husband's suite at the Grand Hotel. The king had just died and she needed some friends to comfort her. Tom and Helen had visited her regularly; in fact, she enjoyed calling Tom her "naval advisor." When they got to the hotel, they found Alfonso XIII laid out on the floor, covered by a large mantle with a candle burning at each corner, and attended by nuns and priests. There was little the Kinkaids could do except to offer condolences and promise whatever assistance they could render.[33]

While in Rome, Kinkaid had kept in close touch with his detailer, Captain H. C. Train. He reminded Train that his cruise in *Indianapolis* had been shortened and he therefore needed to get back to sea before the selection board started work on his class in 1942. Kinkaid wanted to leave after two years in Rome rather than the usual three. Train told him that he knew his situation and was already making plans for his relief. He also said that it appeared that Kinkaid's class would face selection in December 1941, rather than 1942. As it turned out, the 1940 selection board picked four from Kinkaid's class to be rear admirals: Captains Kelly Turner, A. T. Bidwell, A. S. Carpender, and W. R. Munroe. On 23 January 1941 the Chief of BUNAV sent Kinkaid orders for detachment upon the arrival of his relief.[34]

With his orders on his desk Tom began notifying his superiors and friends that he was due for transfer. To Arthur Lane he wrote:

> We both regret leaving Rome but we realize that it is time to go. Although it is not the same Rome that we came to, it is still interesting. Helen will be glad to see her family and, naturally, I want to get back to sea. I have been told that I will have command of a squadron of destroyer leaders (1850 tons) and that sounds like an interesting job to me.

He concluded with regrets that they could not see the minister and his wife before leaving: "I particularly regret that I will not be able to see His Highness Prince Paul who has been kind enough to receive me when I have been in Belgrade."[35] Had Kinkaid known that Prince Paul

---

[32] Naval Attaché Reports, M975:2, "Italy's Present Position, 3 Feb 1941;" M975:1, "Current Events and Comment, 31 Jan–7 Feb 1941;" "Italian Intelligence Items, 10 Mar 1941."

[33] Helen Kinkaid interview, 7 Jan 1976; TCK oral history, 121–7; *New York Times*, 28 Feb 1941.

[34] TCK to CAPT H. C. Train, Rome, 5 Oct 1939; Train to TCK, Washington, 24 Oct 1939, TCK Papers; Dyer to author, Annapolis, 30 May 1977.

[35] TCK to Arthur Bliss Lane, Rome, 18 Feb 1941, box 18, Lane Papers.

would be the victim of a coup d'etat in less than six weeks because he had signed the Tripartite Pact and invited German control of his country, he might have left this penultimate paragraph out of his letter.

Ambassador Phillips showed his appreciation for the work of his naval attaché in a special letter of commendation for Kinkaid's record. He noted in the report:

> It is my considered opinion that he has been the most efficient Naval Attaché with whom I have even been associated. The fact that he and Mrs. Kinkaid have been personae gratae not only in Italian naval circles but in all circles, has given him an unusual position from which the Embassy as a whole has greatly benefited. Captain Kinkaid has kept in constant touch with me personally and with other members of my staff, and has been in fact one of the associates upon whom I have most relied for information of a naval character, as well as for more general information.[36]

Kinkaid had, of course, received regular fitness reports during his tour in Rome, but they consisted only of "remarks," rather than the point-by-point evaluation in the customary reports. Director of ONI Rear Admiral Holmes wrote the first evaluation, which was quite brief and noncommittal. The next four were written by Holmes's relief, Rear Admiral W. S. Anderson. His reports stressed Kinkaid's diligence, effectiveness, good judgment, interpretive skill, and ability to acquire technical information that was difficult to obtain. In most cases he concluded with remarks urging promotion. His report of 30 September 1939 was typical: "Character excellent in all respects. Definitely recommended for promotion. Will make a fine flag officer."[37]

Kinkaid's service record contains an interesting letter recommending him for the Legion of Merit based on his service in Rome. Written in July 1948 by Chief of Naval Operations Louis E. Denfeld, the letter to the Secretary of the Navy commented on Kinkaid's fine intelligence work while in Rome. Denfeld stated that, though the United States was not at war, Kinkaid acquired significant operational information about the Italian fleet that was passed along to the British, presumably by others senior to Kinkaid. The vital information helped to make the November 1940 attack at Taranto a success and helped the British intercept and defeat the Italians at the Battle of Cape Matapan in March 1941. The CNO's letter was passed along to the Navy's awards board, but no action was taken.[38]

---

[36] William Phillips to SECSTATE, Rome, 28 Feb 1941, TCK Personnel File.
[37] Fitness Reports, 9 Jun, 30 Sep 1939, 30 Sep 1940, 15 Jan 1941, TCK Personnel File.
[38] CNO to SECNAV, Washington, 6 Jul 1948, TCK Personnel File.

The Kinkaids' return to the United States began on 3 March and was long on time and short on comforts; they found it both fascinating and depressing. Because passenger liners were not operating in the Mediterranean, they traveled overland by train through Vichy France and then to Barcelona. Their party of six included Commander Thornton's wife and the wife of newsman Cecil Brown. All were struck by the poverty in Spain and the miserable condition of the Spanish railroads. Well briefed before leaving Rome, they wore warm clothing and carried food and drink for the whole trip. An overnight stay in Barcelona permitted some sightseeing but did nothing to prepare them for the horror of riding a packed and filthy train to Madrid. Once in the capital, the American naval attaché rescued Tom and Helen from a hotel and had them housed at the embassy. Because the United States and Great Britain were working closely at this time, Tom paid for this hospitality by visiting the British Embassy and briefing the ambassador and the attachés on affairs in Italy. He noted that air raids in the north, although fairly light in tonnage of bombs dropped, had brought the war home to the Italian people. The British naval bombardment of Genoa on 9 February had been destructive; the best testimony to its effectiveness was the suppression of news concerning it in the Italian papers.[39]

From Madrid the Kinkaids traveled overnight to Lisbon to wait for space on a Pan American clipper flight to the United States. Because it was the winter season, the clipper route was south to Bolama in Portuguese Guinea (Guinea-Bissau), then across the South Atlantic to Belém in Brazil, north to Trinidad, Puerto Rico, and then finally to New York. They arrived on 22 March at LaGuardia after a snowstorm; the air was clear, crisp, and, above all, American. The war was now behind Helen, for the time being at least. For Tom, new and serious work lay ahead. He would be preparing himself and his new command for active participation in a war at sea.[40]

---

[39] TCK, "Four Years of War in the Pacific: A Personal Narrative" (manuscript), chap. 1, TCK Papers (hereafter TCK, "Four Years of War").

[40] Ibid.

Chapter 6

Destroyer Squadron 8, 1941

The America to which the Kinkaids returned in March 1941 was strikingly different from the country which they had left in October 1938. Although the nation was not at war, it almost seemed so to Tom when he reported to Naval Operations two days after his arrival in New York. The offices at the Navy Department building (Main Navy) were as busy as those at the Italian naval ministry in wartime Rome. Classmates and shipmates everywhere, but no one had time for visiting as they had three years earlier during his tour in the Bureau of Navigation. Lodging was in short supply, and the number of visitors, all on business it seemed, was almost oppressive. The armed forces and their civilian support bases were burgeoning. Finding a hotel room or apartment would be a major operation; even finding a chair in some offices would test a senior captain's patience. Fortunately for the Kinkaids there were friends and relatives who could help for a few days.

Kinkaid had not yet received a final assignment, but he did need to debrief on affairs in Europe at the Office of Naval Intelligence. Above all, he and Helen wanted to take forty-five days' leave to relax after the pace of the past year. The routine in 1941 called for returned naval attachés to file a few final reports, summarizing their tour and presenting a final evaluation, perhaps brief interested officers in ONI or Naval Operations, and then await further assignment. Captain Alan Kirk, recently returned from an attaché tour in London, was temporary director of ONI. Tom made several attempts to visit Kirk, even by appointment, but the director was swamped. Eventually Tom managed a quick visit with Kirk and Brigadier General Sherman Miles when both were meeting in the director's office. Miles, head of the Military Intelligence Division in the Army, was an old friend from Constantinople. Kinkaid could see that Kirk did not want to discuss affairs in Rome and took his leave. Later he wrote, "How strange.... Neither of the heads of our two intelligence services were [sic] interested in such news as might have been brought from Rome by a Naval Attaché just returned in the month of March 1941."[1]

---

[1] TCK, "Four Years of War," chap. 1, 23.

Kinkaid was given a desk in the Italian section of ONI, and he began reading the reports he had filed from Rome and the latest ones coming in from his successor, Captain Laurance N. McNair. Curious about how useful his information had been to ONI, particularly since he knew his reports were "dependable and the information usually accurate," he traced them through a junior officer to their final repose in locked file cabinets. No one wanted to discuss his reports. Kinkaid later discovered that the assistant director of ONI considered information from Rome "none too accurate and that no great importance was attached to them."[2] Despite this judgment on his reports, Kinkaid did formally brief an attentive General Board the day after he arrived. A few weeks later the superintendent of the Naval Academy, Rear Admiral Russell Willson, invited the captain to speak to a round-table group of active-duty officers concerning the European scene and Italy in particular. Perhaps these talks and a few others he gave in the Washington area soothed his ego, which had been bruised by ONI.[3] If not, it didn't show, probably because he was caught up in the pleasures of leave and preparing for his next command.

Kinkaid also visited the officer-detailing section in BUNAV to see what was available for his next assignment. There were plenty of captain billets available, but few fit Kinkaid's needs. His tour in *Indianapolis* had been cut short in order to meet the necessary reporting date in Rome. He did not therefore have the number of months in command at sea that captains normally needed to be considered qualified for promotion. Because Kinkaid and his classmates had already had their chance at large ship commands in the Atlantic, Pacific, or Asiatic Fleets, it was unlikely that he would be assigned to a battleship or cruiser command, particularly since the next flag rank selection board would meet in the fall. It did not make sense to assign a captain to a ship command and have him detached after only six months. Kinkaid understood these facts, since he had served as a detailer, and he must have been uneasy with the situation.

The head of officer detailing was a classmate, Captain Arthur S. (Chips) Carpender, a recent selectee to rear admiral. Carpender understood the problem and found a satisfactory solution for Kinkaid. Destroyer Squadron 9, a part of the Pacific Fleet, needed a commanding officer. It was an active sea command, normally made up of several destroyer divisions, each with three or four destroyers. Tom was rather senior for this type of assignment, but Chips had come ashore from such duty and could speak well of it. As usual, Kinkaid would have preferred an East Coast assignment but was willing to go to Pearl Harbor since that was where most of the U.S. Fleet was operating.[4]

---

[2] Ibid., chap. 2, 24.
[3] TCK Personnel File.
[4] TCK, "Four Years of War," chap. 1, 21.

The Kinkaids spent a part of their leave in Washington looking after Tom's mother and clearing up a sinus infection that had plagued Tom since the trip from Rome. He was reluctant to visit the naval hospital at Bethesda because a severe condition might cause him to be passed over by the flag selection board. Helen suggested seeing a civilian doctor for a full physical. Tom was found to be in general good health, and the infection was traced to a tooth. Extraction quickly ended the problem. Kinkaid's consultation and treatment by a civilian doctor was not an uncommon practice in the prewar Navy. Aviators and senior line officers concerned that an official examination could lead to an undesired grounding or early medical retirement often sought private treatment.[5]

By the time Kinkaid returned from leave in mid-May, he had orders to DESRON 9. He was to go, via the SS *Acadia*, from New York to Hawaii. Apparently there was no sense of urgency for him to report, since the *Acadia* wouldn't sail until early June and the sea voyage would be long. But fate, or good luck, again intervened. His orders to DESRON 9 were replaced by orders to command DESRON 8, which had moved along with DESRON 9 from the Pacific Fleet to the Atlantic and would soon be in Philadelphia.[6] Needless to say, the Kinkaids were pleased. Helen's parents in Philadelphia now needed more of her attention, and would have felt the separation keenly had Tom gone to Pearl Harbor as a squadron commander and taken Helen with him.

Kinkaid's change in orders was the result of the new emphasis on naval operations in the Atlantic that had commenced with the creation of the Atlantic Fleet on 1 February 1941. Before that and continuing until July 1941 the United States assisted the British in their struggle with Nazi Germany by keeping the Atlantic area west of Iceland a neutral zone. British convoys from Canadian ports were protected to the extent that the U.S. Navy could keep German submarines (U-boats) and surface raiders out of the Western Hemisphere Neutrality Zone. The mission of the American Neutrality Patrol (later Patrol Force) was to locate and inform anyone, particularly the British, of U-boats or raiders encountered within the American neutrality area.[7]

---

[5] Ibid., 20–22.

[6] Chief BUNAV to TCK, Washington, 3 Jun 1941, TCK Personnel File, OA.

[7] Patrick Abbazia, *Mr. Roosevelt's Navy: The Private War of the U.S. Atlantic Fleet, 1939–1942* (Annapolis: Naval Institute Press, 1975), 144–47, 153–57, 213–16; Samuel Eliot Morison, *History of United States Naval Operations in World War II*, vol. 1, *The Battle of the Atlantic, September 1939–May 1943* (Boston: Little, Brown, 1947), 13–6, 49–55, 174–79; E. B. Potter and Chester W. Nimitz, eds., *The Great Sea War: The Story of Naval Action in World War II* (New York: Bramhall House, 1960), 79–83; Thomas A. Bailey and Paul B. Ryan, *Hitler vs Roosevelt: The Undeclared Naval War* (New York: Free Press, 1979), 41–42, 59, 109–11, 127–28, 156–57; Walter Karig, Earl Burton and Stephen L. Freeland, *Battle Report*, vol. 2, *The Atlantic War* (New York: Rinehart, 1946), 4–6, 12–13; Theodore Roscoe, *United States Destroyer Operations in World War II* (Annapolis: U.S. Naval Institute, 1953), 27–35.

Looking ahead to future operations, in March 1941 Admiral Ernest J. King, Commander in Chief, Atlantic Fleet, created a Support Force (Task Force 4) under the command of Rear Admiral Arthur L. Bristol. Its task would eventually be to escort convoys across the Atlantic to United Kingdom ports. Originally given three destroyer squadrons and four aviation patrol squadrons, Bristol's Support Force was to grow steadily as America ventured farther into the dangerous waters of an undeclared naval war with Germany.

Bristol's units immediately began intensive antisubmarine warfare (ASW) training in the Norfolk and Narragansett Bay areas. Admiral King anticipated that convoy duties would begin in April, but President Franklin Roosevelt delayed this until the United States took over the defense of Iceland on 8 July 1941. Once the First Marine Brigade under Brigadier General John Marston was established ashore, it became necessary to protect American shipping bringing supplies to the Marines. This task became the basis for forming American convoys and inviting Canadian and British shipping to join them for escort eastward. At a "mid-ocean meeting point" south of Iceland the American vessels turned north with their Support Force escorts, and the British and Canadian ships continued to the British Isles under Royal Navy protection. This operation saved the British the need to escort convoys the full distance across and allowed them to concentrate their all too few corvettes and destroyers in the eastern half of the ocean.

With the passage of the Lend-Lease Act on 11 March 1941, the volume of war supplies shipped to England (and Russia after 21 June) steadily increased, as did the number of ships requiring naval vessels to protect them. The Support Force's requirements were met by new construction authorized in past years and now coming into commission, and by transfers from the Pacific Fleet. Citing "the existing and prospective strategic situation in the Atlantic Ocean . . . [that would require] a greater initial strength in order to perform effectively the tasks that will be assigned to it in war," on 7 April 1941 the CNO ordered the Commander in Chief, Pacific Fleet (CINCPAC), Admiral Husband E. Kimmel, to transfer three battleships of Battleship Division 3, one aircraft carrier, Cruiser Division 8's four light cruisers of the 10,000-ton *Brooklyn* class, and four destroyer divisions (DESDIVs 3, 15, 17, 18) from Destroyer Squadrons 8 and 9. The transferred destroyers were all 1,850-tonners capable of performing ASW escort and screening operations from American bases to Iceland without refueling.[8]

---

[8] CNO to CINCUS, Washington, 4 Jul 1941, U.S. Congress, Joint Committee on the Investigation of the Pearl Harbor Attack, *Pearl Harbor Attack*, vol. 11, 5502–5.

The battleships *Idaho* (BB 42), *Mississippi* (BB 41), and *New Mexico* (BB 40); the cruisers *Brooklyn* (CL 40), *Philadelphia* (CL 41), *Savannah* (CL 42), and *Nashville* (CL 43); and the carrier *Yorktown* (CV 5) were distributed as reinforcements to other divisions of the Atlantic Fleet, which, in addition to the Support Force (TF 4), consisted of the Ocean Escort Force (TF 1) made up of the battleships, two cruisers, and thirteen destroyers, all under the command of Rear Admiral Arthur B. Cook; and the Scouting Force (TF 3) of four cruisers and four destroyers under Rear Admiral Jonas H. Ingram.[9]

Kinkaid's temporary duty in the office of the CNO ended on 14 June 1941. Rear Admiral Royal E. Ingersoll, as Acting CNO, sent him on his way with a glowing fitness report covering the three months since his detachment in Rome. All evaluative statements were checked "outstanding" and under the remarks section Ingersoll commented, "He was very helpful in correcting office records, etc., through his personal knowledge of the situation [in Italy]. An officer of inspiring personality."[10] Although fitness reports for temporary duty between assignments were not critical to promotion, it didn't hurt to have one more strong report in the file, particularly since Ingersoll was one of the Navy's most important officers and would become even more so in the years ahead.

Following a weekend with Helen's parents, Kinkaid drove to the Philadelphia Navy Yard on Tuesday, 17 June, and boarded *Wainwright* (DD 419). The destroyer was at a pier, but the rest of DESRON 8 was in the back channel of the navy yard. Kinkaid spent the morning discussing operational matters with his predecessor and old friend from Constantinople, Captain A. S. (Tip) Merrill, and becoming acquainted with *Wainwright*, which was to be his squadron flagship. The change-of-command ceremony was held at 1400. Commanding officers from the squadron's vessels gathered with *Wainwright*'s crew and the squadron commander's staff for the brief ceremony. Merrill read his detachment orders and had his command pennant hauled down. Kinkaid then read his orders to the command of DESRON 8 and ordered his blue and white broad command pennant broken at the truck. It wasn't the tidiest command, or one that he would have preferred, but it met Kinkaid's needs.[11]

During May and early June, DESRONs 8 and 9 had left the Pacific Fleet at Pearl Harbor and made the long shift to the Atlantic. Though all of DESRON 8's boats had been commissioned in 1936 or later, most of them needed some type of yard work to make them effective for convoy duty. In

---

[9] Abbazia, *Mr. Roosevelt's Navy*, 145; Morison 1:51, 67–9, 78–9, 81–4.
[10] Fitness Report, 14 Jun 1941, TCK Personnel File, OA.
[11] Log of USS *Wainwright* (DD 419), 17 Jun 1941; CAPT Isaiah Olch, USN (Ret.) to author, Nice, France, 2 Feb 1977.

a few cases the number of gun houses or torpedo tubes was reduced in order to accommodate depth-charge tracks on the stern. Sonar gear was added to some to make them capable of tracking submarines. Because all were needed immediately for duty with the Support Force's convoying operations, only a few were taken out of service at a time to be upgraded. The end result of the shifts was that DESRONs 8 and 9 lost their original identities and their component divisions were mixed, as were the boats within them. The magnitude of these changes can be seen by listing the destroyers of DESRON 8 at the time Kinkaid took command and at the time he was relieved five months later. It should be noted that Merrill's flagship had been *Winslow* (DD 359) until he reached the East Coast.

Destroyer Squadron 8

17 June 1941
Wainwright (DD 419), flagship

DESDIV 3	DESDIV 15
Anderson (DD 411)	*Lang* (DD 399)
Hammann (DD 412)	*Stack* (DD 406)
Mustin (DD 413)	*Sterrett* (DD 407)
Rowan (DD 405)	*Wilson* (DD 408)

November 1941
Wainwright (DD 419), flagship

DESDIV 16	DESDIV 17
Mayrant (DD 402)	*McDougal* (DD 358)
Rhind (DD 404)	*Moffett* (DD 362)
Rowan (DD 405)	*Winslow* (DD 359)
Trippe (DD 403)	*Sampson* (DD 394)

SOURCES: U.S. Congress, Joint Committee on the Investigation of the Pearl Harbor Attack, *Hearings*, 79th Cong., 1st sess., 1945–1946, 11:5502–5; Theodore Roscoe, *United States Destroyer Operations in World War II* (Annapolis, 1953), 41; Log of USS *Wainwright*, 11–19 November 1941.

Unlike flag officers, who usually brought their staffs with them when they assumed a command, a destroyer squadron commander normally kept the small staff that was available when he took over. Kinkaid had three staff officers on board *Wainwright*, the senior being Lieutenant Donald T. Eller who served as the senior staff officer and squadron gunnery officer. Lieutenant Francis S. Stich was the squadron engineering officer; and Lieutenant Jacob A. Lark, the squadron radio officer. There was also a squadron medical officer and a disbursing officer, but these two were berthed on other boats in the squadron. The staff officers were experienced and served Kinkaid well during his short tour. *Wainwright's* commanding officer, Lieutenant Commander Thomas L. Lewis, had put the destroyer in commission fourteen months earlier. In fact, most of the boats in the squadron had their original commanding officers on board when Kinkaid took over.[12]

Kinkaid and his squadron spent ten days in the Philadelphia Navy Yard before moving to Norfolk. Besides refit work and loading ammunition stores, there was little time for socializing. Tom and Helen were "at home" for those who wished to make social calls, and many of the squadron's officers did. The Kinkaids used the home of Helen's parents to receive callers, despite its being far out on the Main Line. One destroyer skipper recalled taking a street car to the end of the line and then a taxi to the Wynnefield Avenue address. Not only did he enjoy cocktails and a pleasant visit, but Tom drove him back to the car line. Kinkaid's officers knew that their "commodore" was more accustomed to the wardroom manners and social ways of battleships and cruisers, and they accepted his slightly formal behavior. He was not as gregarious as Tip Merrill, but he did enjoy working with competent people and left a strong impression that he both knew his job and respected his officers and men. The commanding officer of *McDougal*, Lieutenant Commander Dashiell L. Madeira, probably captured the image of Kinkaid at this time when he described him as "somewhat courtly."[13] Tom might have grimaced had he heard this, but he and Captains Alan Kirk and Walden L. (Pug) Ainsworth were the oldest destroyer squadron commanders in either ocean, and they laughingly described themselves as part of the "nine old men."[14]

On 27 June, as directed by Kinkaid's Operation Order 3–41, *Wainwright*, *Mustin*, *Hammann*, *Sterrett*, and *Stack* departed the Philadelphia yard to commence training operations out of Norfolk and other East Coast bases. For three weeks the squadron worked with Admiral Cook's Strike Force, engaging in screening operations with the carrier *Yorktown* and the cruisers *Vincennes* (CA 44) and *Quincy* (CA 39). Although the ASW work of *Wainwright* and the other destroyers was more appropriate to a destroyer division, it did give Kinkaid experience with the operations of a carrier task group.[15] In less than a year he would see action in the Coral Sea and at Midway with many of these same ships. Interspersed with the exercises came days of torpedo battle practice for those squadron vessels available

---

[12] CAPT Francis S. Stich, USN (Ret.) to author, Delaware, OH, 10 Feb 1977; CAPT Jacob A. Lark, USN (Ret.) to author, Marion Station, PA, 3 Feb 1977; RADM D. T. Eller, USN (Ret.) to author, Key Colony Beach, FL, 15 Jan 1977; CAPT Thomas L. Lewis, USN (Ret.) to author, New Orleans, 4 Dec 1976; RADM Thomas V. Cooper, USN (Ret.) to author, Media, PA, 2, 18 Oct 1976.

[13] RADM D. L. Madeira, USN (Ret.) to author, Virginia Beach, VA, tape recording, 22 Nov 1976; CAPT Olch, 2 Feb 1977, 1 Mar 1977.

[14] ADM Alan G. Kirk, interview by John T. Mason, Jr., 1961, 186, Columbia University Oral History, New York (hereafter Kirk oral history); TCK, "Four Years of War," chap. 1, 5–6.

[15] *Wainwright* log, 27 Jun–13 Jul 1941.

for such activity. Although DESRON 8's future operations would probably be convoy-escort duty, *Wainwright* and other boats in her class carried eight 21-inch torpedo tubes that might someday be used.

On 13 August, after the workout with Admiral Cook's force and several weeks in drydock at Norfolk, *Wainwright* and the squadron moved north for training operations out of Provincetown, Boston, and Casco Bay (Base Sail), Maine. Here the destroyers worked with submarines in ASW training and also served as targets for the subs. In early September Kinkaid visited Argentia in Placentia Bay, the operating base of the Ocean Escort Force. Though his squadron was not considered ready for escort duty, individual ships were being taken for such work. Kinkaid was titled a squadron commander, but he was finding that he had little control over divisions or individual boats within his command.[16]

From 10 September to 10 October *Wainwright* and a few boats from the squadron returned to Norfolk and commenced training exercises again with *Yorktown* and the cruisers *Brooklyn* and *Nashville*. On the Southern Drill Grounds Kinkaid's destroyers engaged in more ASW exercises with submarines interspered with torpedo drills, live antiaircraft firing at sleeves, depth charge attack drills, and plenty of tactical exercises with the carrier. The task group then moved out to Bermuda and spent almost three weeks of work and recreation operating from the new naval operating base. During nine days at anchor in Port Royal Bay, Kinkaid visited several times with his classmate, Captain Jules James, who had put the base into commission and was experiencing considerable difficulty pleasing both the Bermudans and the Navy Department. Fortunately for James's future, Admiral King felt he was handling his job in a highly satisfactory manner.[17]

Kinkaid's last six weeks with the squadron were spent operating in and out of Casco Bay. By this time DESDIVs 3 and 15 had been replaced by DESDIVs 16 and 17, but a few of the squadron's original boats continued with the new divisions. The squadron was now ready for escort duty and there was a fascinating assignment at hand. On 1 September Prime Minister Winston Churchill approached President Roosevelt about borrowing twelve liners and twenty cargo ships, manned by American crews, to move two British Army divisions to the Middle East. Because the passage through the Mediterranean was too hazardous for troop convoys, the borrowed vessels would have to go to Alexandria, Egypt, by way of the Cape of Good Hope, Indian Ocean, and Red Sea. The President immediately replied, "I am sure we can help with your project to reinforce the Middle East Army." A month later, on 7 October, Roosevelt notified

---
[16] Ibid., 13 Aug–13 Sep 1941.

[17] Ibid., 10 Sep–10 Oct 1941; Abbazia, *Mr. Roosevelt's Navy*, 103–105; King and Whitehill, *Fleet Admiral King*, 340–41.

Churchill that there would have to be a major change in the plans. He was asking Congress for "sweeping amendments" to the existing neutrality laws and feared that, were an American vessel sunk in British waters while carrying British troops, the incident would kill attempts to modify the laws. Roosevelt proposed that the British bring their troops to Halifax and transfer them to American liners. The U.S. Navy would then escort this convoy to the Middle East. Churchill readily agreed to this plan and the movement began in late October.[18]

In the early hours of 6 November Kinkaid led DESRON 8 out of Casco Bay to intercept the Halifax-bound convoy with its troop transports loaded with more than 20,000 British soldiers. Rear Admiral Kent Hewitt was commanding the escort and Captain Pug Ainsworth, the destroyer screen. Rough seas plus a good deal of running down U-boat sonar contacts had left Ainsworth's DESRON 2 dangerously low on fuel, so Kinkaid's squadron had to bring the convoy almost to Halifax. Once the Canadians took over, DESRON 8 dashed back to Casco Bay for a quick refueling and at 1444 on 9 November it sortied again to join convoy WS–124. The escort force (TF 14) was commanded by Rear Admiral Cook in the aircraft carrier *Ranger* (CV 4) and consisted of cruisers *Quincy* and *Vincennes*, the oiler *Cimarron* (AO 22), and the ASW screen provided by DESRON 8. The troops were carried in Navy transports *Mount Vernon* (AP 22), *Leonard Wood* (AP 25), *Joseph T. Dickman* (AP 26), *Orizaba* (AP 24), *Wakefield* (AP 21), and *West Point* (AP 23). Kinkaid led the convoy in *Wainwright* and *Rhind* (DD 404) brought up the rear.

The passage to Port of Spain, Trinidad, was uneventful except for a steering casualty in *Joseph T. Dickman* that almost caused a collision with *Orizaba*. On 17 November the convoy anchored in the Gulf of Paria, Trinidad, to refuel and there Kinkaid found orders awaiting him. Two days later he hauled down his broad pennant and turned over command of the squadron to Commander Lyman K. Swenson, Commander DESDIV 17. Kinkaid was surprised to be relieved in the middle of the operation; but he did know that he could not stay much longer in his billet since he had been selected for promotion to rear admiral.[19]

Kinkaid's service as Commander DESRON 8 had certainly not hurt his chances for promotion. Despite his brief assignment with the squadron he had received four fitness reports from Rear Admiral Ferdinand (Dutch) Reichmuth, Commander Destroyers, Atlantic Fleet. All of the reports contained the highest marks possible and the second had

---

[18] Francis L. Lowenheim, Harold D. Langley, and Manfred Jonas, *Roosevelt and Churchill: Their Wartime Correspondence* (New York: Saturday Review Press/E. P. Dutton, 1975), 155–61; Abbazia, *Mr. Roosevelt's Navy*, 352–54.

[19] *Wainwright* log, 6–19 Nov 1941; Morison 1:109–11; Abbazia, *Mr. Roosevelt's Navy*, 352–54; Roscoe, *Destroyer Operations*, 41–42; TCK Personnel File.

been a special report to the rear admiral selection board. The remarks section of the special report concluded:

> While he has not been under my direct observation . . . there is every evidence that he has taken hold of the administration and operation of his new command in a manner that is characterized by firmness, energy and good judgment. Based upon this recent observation taken together with many years of association with this officer, I believe him outstandingly qualified for flag rank and so recommend him.[20]

Admiral Reichmuth's reports simply confirmed the service reputation that Kinkaid had built in the thirty-three years since graduation.

Four of Kinkaid's classmates had been selected for promotion to rear admiral the year before (Richmond Kelly Turner, Abel T. Bidwell, Chips Carpender, William R. Munroe). In August 1941 the board had reviewed the rest of the Class of 1908 and also picked an additional three from 1909. Of the fifty captains from Kinkaid's class eleven had reached rear admiral before Pearl Harbor. Kinkaid was the last one chosen from his class in 1941.[21]

Seen from today's perspective, there was much about his record to suggest that he would not be selected for flag rank in the summer of 1941. Standing 136 among the 201 graduates of 1908 had already lost him a year and half of seniority as a captain, when compared with Kelly Turner, who was a rear admiral by August 1941. Except for William R. (Spec) Purnell, who in 1941 was senior to Kinkaid on the captain's list, no one standing lower than Kinkaid at graduation became a rear admiral before retirement, though Worrall R. (Nick) Carter was promoted to commodore during the war. The career pattern that Kinkaid followed did not usually lead to selection. By 1 September 1941 his command tours (*Isherwood, Indianapolis,* DESRON 8) had been short, totaling no more than twenty-four months. His total sea duty since becoming a lieutenant commander, including staff duty, added up to approximately eight and one-half years. His time in shore billets since April 1918, including his time in Rome, was approximately fourteen and one-half years, and three of his tours had been in Washington. To some crusty types this alone was enough to suggest that he was a bureaucrat—a "fixer," in Ernie King's vocabulary—and not the type who had built his service reputation at sea.[22]

---

[20] Fitness Reports, 31 Jul 1941, 11 Aug 1941, 30 Sep 1941, 19 Nov 1941, TCK Personnel File.

[21] U.S. Department of the Navy, *Register of the Commissioned and Warrant Officers of the Navy of the United States and of the Marine Corps to January 1, 1942* (Washington: GPO, 1942), 16–18; Dyer, *Turner* 1:123; Dyer to author, 30 May 1977.

[22] Buell, *The Quiet Warrior,* 68.

On the other hand the evaluations in Kinkaid's fitness report file showed him to be an excellent officer worthy of promotion. He never displayed the brilliance nor irascibility of Kelly Turner, but whatever he undertook was completed, done well, and normally with good humor. He was a long-standing member of the Gun Club, yet he recognized that his strength was in personnel, not in ordnance. Kinkaid was not an innovator, at least not since he had tried to change the fleet gunnery exercises and failed. He worked well with people and believed that the best way to administer in the Navy was to support capable subordinates as they went about their work. Admiral King's admonition to the Atlantic Fleet in January 1941, "Exercise of Command-Excess of Detail in Orders and Instructions," fit Kinkaid's approach better than its author's.[23]

Finally it must be noted that he had the good fortune to serve under several of the Navy's most prestigious leaders and he served them well. Strong fitness reports from Henry Wiley, Mark Bristol, William Leahy, Walter Anderson, Adolphus Andrews, and William Tarrant had to impress a flag officer selection board. Kinkaid showed strong leadership qualities, and that was what the Navy obviously needed in the fall of 1941.

---

[23] Buell, *Master of Sea Power*, 131–32, 521–33.

Chapter 7

To War, December 1941

Tom Kinkaid was eager to return to the Navy Department to see what orders he would receive, but transportation in 1941 was slower than today. He waited two days in Port of Spain and finally took passage on a Pan American Airways clipper to Miami by way of Puerto Rico. He met the island's governor, Rex G. Tugwell, on board the clipper from San Juan and shared a hotel room with him in Miami. They departed Miami by train and arrived in the capital the morning of Monday, 24 November.

At the Navy Department Kinkaid learned that he was to join the Pacific Fleet at Pearl Harbor and take command of Cruiser Division 6. The need for flag officers was increasing steadily as new construction was commissioned. The Chief of the Bureau of Navigation, Rear Admiral Chester W. Nimitz, had already asked the Chairman of the Senate Naval Affairs Committee to present Kinkaid's name to the Senate for approval of his promotion. Action came quickly on 27 November. Equally promptly, Tom shed his four stripes. Following an old custom in the Navy, he passed his captain's shoulder marks along to Commander John L. McCrea, who had just accepted his promotion to four stripes.[1]

The new assignment would be permanent duty, so Helen could accompany Tom to Honolulu. Although everyone in the department believed war would come at any time, peacetime travel rules still applied and dependent travel was authorized for her. Kinkaid took a few days of leave to help his wife organize their affairs in Philadelphia and Washington. His mother was still living in the Wyoming Apartments in Washington, but she was not well and the prognosis was not good. Helen's parents were also frail and her mother was doing poorly. It was likely that Helen would have to return in the near future, but she was determined to stay with her husband as long as possible.

With their trunks packed and their short-term needs provided for in several large pieces of hand luggage, the Kinkaids returned to Washing-

---

[1] RADM C. W. Nimitz to Senator David I. Walsh, Washington, 22 Nov 1941, TCK Personnel File; U.S. Congress, Senate, *Journal of the Executive Proceedings of the Senate of the United States*, vol. 83, 77th Cong., 1st sess., 19, 27 Nov 1941.

ton for final instructions and a round of bon voyage parties. They were scheduled to leave San Francisco on board *Lurline* on 11 December. The day they left Washington, Tom and Helen had lunch with old friends, head of Army Intelligence Brigadier General Sherman Miles and his wife. When it was time to leave for Union Station and their train for Chicago, Miles joked that Tom had better hurry, or he might not get to his command before war began. The date was Saturday, 6 December.[2]

After an overnight trip to Chicago, the Kinkaids had the afternoon free before the Overland Limited left in the early evening, so they went to a movie. When they emerged from the theater, newspaper vendors were shouting that Japan had struck the Pacific Fleet at Pearl Harbor—war had come. Kinkaid checked in with the Commandant of the Ninth Naval District in Chicago, informing him of his orders and travel plans. The next day at North Platte, Nebraska, he received telegraphic notice that Helen's travel beyond San Francisco had been canceled. Upon arrival in San Francisco on the 10th the Kinkaids registered at the St. Francis and Tom visited the Commandant of the Twelfth Naval District. He learned *Lurline's* sailing had been canceled for the time being; he had no way to get to Pearl Harbor. The next afternoon he was told he could leave that evening on a Pan American clipper if he could make it. He and Helen reduced his luggage to the fifty-five pounds allowed, had a last dinner together, and made the 2100 departure from the Pan Am terminal on Treasure Island. Tom was off to war; Helen returned to Philadelphia. Almost a year would pass before they would meet again.[3]

Except for spotting a Japanese submarine and reporting its position several hundred miles northeast of Oahu, Kinkaid's flight to Pearl Harbor was uneventful. As the clipper approached the naval base, the admiral was able to survey the catastrophe wrought by the Japanese assault. He had read the secret dispatches at Com 12 about the attack and its damage, but they could not communicate the scene below him. The East Loch was still covered with stinking oil; damaged and destroyed ships filled the view. It was hard to imagine that a navy had survived the attack five days before. Captain Charles H. (Soc) McMorris, Admiral Kimmel's war plans officer, met Kinkaid and drove him to CINCPAC headquarters. A decade later Kinkaid recalled his arrival:

> If I had been shocked by the sight of Pearl Harbor from the air, I was doubly shocked by the appearance of the members of CincPac's staff and of the senior officers of the Fleet whom I saw at headquarters. Each of them looked

---

[2] TCK, "Four Years of War," chap. 1, 26; Roberta Wohlstetter, *Pearl Harbor, Warning and Decision* (Stanford, CA: Stanford University Press, 1962), 305.

[3] TCK, "Four Years of War," chap. 1, 27–28; TCK oral history, 20–21.

Admiral Husband E. Kimmel, Commander in Chief, U.S. Fleet and Pacific Fleet, 1941. Admiral Kimmel was Admiral Kinkaid's brother-in-law.

as though he had not had a wink of sleep in the five days which had elapsed since the Japanese attack. All were in a defiant mood, but at the moment none could produce a concrete plan as to how we would "get those ———."[4]

Admiral Kimmel invited his brother-in-law to stay with him, and Tom accepted. Senior officer quarters were scarce ashore because so many ships were out of service, and everyone was doubling up. From his stay with Kimmel and his association with the admiral's staff, Kinkaid came to believe that CINCPAC was the last person to blame for the success of the Japanese. There were plenty of dispirited people and some defeatism, but the majority of the senior officers at Pearl Harbor probably agreed with the analysis of Captain Arthur C. Davis (later vice admiral) when he wrote a classmate about morale in headquarters:

Of course I am speaking only for myself, but I am certain that everybody here feels exactly the same way. Eager is the best way to express it. We think only of things that are next and not of those that are past. Wonders have already been accomplished. As a matter of fact, there has been no time for anything but action and planning, anyhow. We ain't going nowhere but to victory.[5]

Kinkaid's orders were to relieve Rear Admiral Frank Jack Fletcher of command of CRUDIV 6, but there was to be a two-week delay in executing them. Preparations were already underway to send a relief expedition to Wake Island and Fletcher was to command it. To Kimmel and his staff it seemed best to have Fletcher carry out the mission. Kinkaid could go along for on-the-job training and a chance to become familiar with his command and cruiser captains, without the burden of responsibility. As the Navy became more familiar with the South Seas and its Pidgin argot later in the war, they would describe an admiral in Kinkaid's position as a "makee learn."

The Japanese had been hammering at Wake since the war began, and their attacks had taken a heavy toll. The defense of the island was in the hands of Major James P. S. Devereux's Marine defense battalion and VMF–211, a Marine fighter squadron of twelve Grumman Wildcats (F4F–3s) commanded by Major Paul A. Putnam. Because the long-term plan was to make Wake a naval air station for patrol plane operations, a civilian construction company with 1,146 employees was at work when the war began. There were also seventy Pan American Airways workers who provided facilities and personnel for the twice-weekly stops of clip-

---

[4] Ibid.; TCK, "Four Years of War," chap. 1, 29–30.
[5] CAPT A. C. Davis to CAPT R. W. Bates, Pearl Harbor, 18 Dec 1941, RADM Richard W. Bates Papers, Naval War College, Newport, RI (hereafter Bates Papers).

pers en route to or returning from points farther west. The island also had a small contingent of Army communications people and sixty-eight naval personnel who were to start up the air station when the seaplane facility was completed. All were under the control of Commander Winfield Scott Cunningham, the island's commanding officer.[6]

Though the United States had claimed Wake in 1899, nothing had been done to develop it as an operating base until Pan American Airways commenced trans-Pacific flight operations with its seaplane "clippers" in the late 1930s. The company's development was followed in 1940 by a Navy decision to build an airfield and seaplane operating base. With a fully developed base on Wake it would be possible to fly land-based aircraft to the Philippines with the longest flight being from the mainland to Honolulu, around 2100 miles. More important, with patrol planes operating from Wake toward Midway, it would be difficult for an enemy naval force to approach the Hawaiian Islands without being detected. Because the Japanese could use the island in a similar manner against the United States, Admiral Kimmel believed that Wake should be vigorously defended against capture.

Bombing attacks on Wake Island by the Japanese 24th Air Flotilla were launched from the Marshall Islands to the south, commencing on 8 December (7 December at Pearl Harbor) at noon and continuing almost on a daily basis. On 11 December a naval task force under Rear Admiral Sadamichi Kajioka launched an amphibious assault but was beaten off by the Marine defenders. This attempt cost the Japanese two sunken destroyers; hits on many of the other ships, including the transports; more than 400 casualties; and at least 3,400 dead. Although deadly effective with his few 5-inch guns and 3-inch antiaircraft batteries, Major Devereux could not continue to work miracles without reinforcements. His fighter squadron was down to two planes, though it would get two more in the air a few days later. Without a warning radar, another fighter squadron, more heavy guns, and an American naval force for support, it was obvious the Japanese could take Wake with a larger and more determined effort.[7]

Concern about Wake had intensified soon after the Japanese bombings began, but the atmosphere in CINCPAC headquarters made it difficult to produce sound plans. Once the shock wore off in Pearl Harbor and Washington, the desire to strike back quickly manifested itself. In a communication to all Naval Forces, Secretary of the Navy Frank Knox at 0900 Hawaii time (12/07 1930 GCT) ordered the Navy to "execute WPL

---

[6] Robert Sherrod, *History of Marine Corps Aviation in World War II* (Washington: Combat Forces Press, 1952), 34–38; Morison, vol. 3, *The Rising Sun in the Pacific, 1931–April 1942* (Boston: Little, Brown, 1948), 223–29.

[7] Sherrod, *Marine Corps Aviation*, 38–43; Morison 3:229–35; Paul S. Dull, *A Battle History of the Imperial Japanese Navy (1941–1945)* (Annapolis: Naval Institute Press, 1978), 22–26.

forty-six [War Plan 46] against Japan." A few hours later Admiral Harold R. Stark added his own refinement: "Execute unrestricted air and submarine warfare against Japan."[8]

When Admiral Kimmel's description of the damage at Pearl Harbor arrived in Main Navy at about midnight on that fateful December Sunday, it was evident that WPL46 could not be executed. From then on the pressure for retaliatory operations mounted steadily. The American people and their naval leadership wanted revenge for the treacherous attack, but a strategic prudence began to control decisions.[9]

By mid-afternoon the day after the attack Admiral Kimmel received instructions to modify WPL46. Almost all the modifications set defensive tasks for CINCPAC with the clear emphasis being to hold the Hawaiian Islands at all costs. Midway, Johnston, and Palmyra islands were to be defended as sturdily as the Hawaiians. Wake Island, on the other hand, was placed in a less significant defense category. Probably to suggest what might be done with the surviving portion of the Pacific Fleet, one offensive task was stated: "Raid enemy sea communications and positions."[10]

By 10 December CINCPAC's staff had generated a fourteen-page "briefed estimate" that summarized the situation and stated some possible courses of action. Although noting that the battleship losses forced a commitment to the "strategic defensive until our forces can be built up," there did exist "a very powerful striking force" of carriers, cruisers, and destroyers. "These forces must be operated boldly and vigorously on the tactical offensive in order to retrieve our initial disaster." Despite these bold phrases, the document emphasized defensive activities. Three carrier task forces could be organized around *Lexington, Saratoga,* and *Enterprise* (CV 6), and later a fourth with *Yorktown,* but they would operate largely in defense of the Midway-Johnson-Palmyra line. CINCPAC doubted that attempts would be made to take the Hawaiian Islands, but further raids and amphibious assaults did seem possible against Wake and Samoa.[11]

While Admiral Kimmel and his staff grappled with the Wake Island problem, another factor was introduced that did little to assist planning. Secretary Knox flew in on 11 December to examine personally the situation in Pearl Harbor. Though he stayed just a day and a half, and saw only a few people, he returned to Washington with the private convic-

---

[8] CNO to CINCPAC, 7 Dec, 2252 Greenwich Civil Time, CINCPAC Summary, 5, Chester W. Nimitz Papers, OA (hereafter radio communications cited as CNO to CINCPAC, 12/072252Z, Command Summary. The year will be omitted unless it is not obvious in the narrative. The "Command Summary" is often referred to by other authors as "Captain Steele's Running Estimate," or simply as the "Grey Book").

[9] CINCPAC to CNO, 12/080450Z, Command Summary, 5.

[10] CNO to CINCPAC, 12/090139Z, Command Summary, 6.

[11] "Briefed Estimate as of 10 December," Command Summary, 8–21.

tion that Admiral Kimmel and Major General Walter C. Short had been derelict in the performance of their duties. They had to be replaced immediately. CINCPAC's "briefed estimate" further convinced Knox that the Navy needed someone in Pearl Harbor who could instill confidence and eliminate what Knox considered to be a defeatist attitude. It appears that the Secretary saw only enough to confirm his own preconceptions. As a former newspaper publisher, he would be sensitive to public opinion, and apparently concluded that the American people wanted those responsible for the losses at Pearl Harbor removed. It is clear from the actions taken that he did not think anyone in Washington was to blame. Kimmel and his staff could only wait for the other shoe to drop.

Knox's arrival in Washington on 15 December led to a flurry of activity, much of it further complicating the work of Kimmel's staff. Following a meeting with the President on the 16th, the Secretary's report to the press presented a limited account of the damage to the fleet and noted that a commission of inquiry would be appointed to establish the facts and fix responsibility for the losses. By then Knox had decided that Rear Admiral Chester Nimitz, Chief of BUNAV, should replace Kimmel as CINCPAC. The President agreed, and decided that the change should be made as soon as possible.[12] Two days later Knox and Secretary of War Henry Stimson announced that Kimmel and Short were to be relieved and that a unified command under CINCPAC would be established for the defense of the Hawaiian Islands and the prosecution of the Pacific war. It also became known that Nimitz was to be the new CINCPAC. Within the Navy Department it was understood that Admiral Ernest King, Commander in Chief, Atlantic Fleet, would become Commander in Chief, U.S. Fleet (COMINCH). Until Admiral Nimitz arrived to take command of the Pacific Fleet, as of 17 December Vice Admiral William S. Pye would be acting CINCPAC. The other shoe had dropped in Pearl Harbor.[13]

Against this background Kimmel's staff completed the final plans for the relief of Wake Island and organized the task forces to do the job. These first plans called for Vice Admiral Wilson Brown's *Lexington* task force (TF 12) to escort the seaplane tender-transport *Tangier* (AV 8), which would carry about 300 Marines of the Fourth Defense Battalion, ground personnel of VMF–221, plus additional guns, munitions, provisions, and radar sets. The plans also called for TF 14, commanded by Rear Admiral Aubrey W. (Jake) Fitch in *Saratoga*, to make a diversionary raid against Jaluit, a Japanese air base in the Marshall Islands. Expected

---

[12] Martin Melosi, *The Shadow of Pearl Harbor: Political Controversy over the Surprise Attack, 1941–1946* (College Station, TX: Texas A&M University Press, 1977), 20–30; Gordon W. Prange, *At Dawn We Slept: The Untold Story of Pearl Harbor* (New York: McGraw Hill, 1981), 584–91.

[13] Melosi, *Shadow of Pearl Harbor*, 29–30; E. B. Potter, *Nimitz* (Annapolis: Naval Institute Press, 1976), 8–11; King and Whitehill, *Fleet Admiral King*, 349–50; Buell, *Master of Sea Power*, 151–54.

Vice Admiral William S. Pye, Acting Commander in Chief, Pacific Fleet, 1941. Admiral Pye previously commanded the Battle Force.

to arrive on 14 December, *Saratoga* would be bringing VMF–221 from San Diego with its eighteen F2A–3 Buffalo fighter planes. Once dockside in Pearl these planes were to be loaded onto *Lexington*. Finally, Vice Admiral William F. (Bull) Halsey's TF 8, built around the carrier *Enterprise*, would enter Pearl Harbor for refueling once Task Forces 11 and 14 had sortied and then steam in the area southwest of Midway, positioning itself to assist the Wake Island force should it need support.

Because of delays in bringing *Lexington* and *Saratoga* into Pearl for refueling and sending them on their way, the operation order for the Wake Island expedition was changed and more delays followed. Admiral Brown's TF 12 was renumbered TF 11 and given the Jaluit raid mission. *Lexington* and its cruisers and destroyers finally cleared Pearl Harbor in the afternoon of 14 December. Because *Saratoga* was slow to arrive, *Tangier*, *Neches* (AO 5), and a division of destroyers headed west on the 15th, expecting the faster ships of TF 14 to overtake them en route to Wake. At 1115 on 16 December, TF 14 stood out of Pearl Harbor and turned west. In changing the carrier in the relief task force from *Lexington* to *Saratoga*, Admiral Kimmel had created a problem in command. The commander of CRUDIV 6, Rear Admiral Frank Jack Fletcher, was senior to Rear Admiral Fitch. The command was therefore placed with Fletcher, a nonaviator, who was on board *Astoria*. CINCPAC could have given the command of TF 14 to Fitch by simply asking Fletcher to stand aside, but Pye chose to follow regulation practice. Of course Fitch's carrier division command experience was not lost to TF 14; he simply did not command it. It should be noted that had *Lexington* remained with the Wake Island task force, Admiral Brown, also a nonaviator, would have had the task force command and no aviation flag officer would have been in the force. Once TF 14 overtook *Tangier* and *Neches*, it consisted of *Saratoga*; CRUDIV 6 heavy cruisers *Astoria* (F), *Minneapolis* (CA 36), and *San Francisco* (CA 38); and DESRON 4 destroyers *Selfridge* (DD 357) (F), *Mugford* (DD 389), *Jarvis* (DD 393), *Patterson* (DD 392), *Ralph Talbot* (DD 390), *Henley* (DD 391), *Blue* (DD 387) and *Helm* (DD 388).[14]

Except for the part played by Admiral Halsey's TF 8, nothing in the Wake Island operation went as planned. Once Admiral Brown's TF 11 was underway to raid Jaluit, pressures began to mount to abort the operation. Intelligence estimates in CINCPAC headquarters began to convince the staff that TF 11 might be steaming into a trap. Finally in midafternoon on 20 December (Hawaii time), Admiral Pye directed TF 11 to reverse course and move north to a position where it could offer support to

---

[14] Except for the despatches cited from the "Command Summary," the basic information in the paragraphs concerning the Wake Island relief expedition was drawn from Lloyd J. Graybar, "American Pacific Strategy after Pearl Harbor: The Relief of Wake Island," *Prologue* (Fall 1980): 134–50; TCK, "Four Years of War," chap. 2, 40–49; TCK oral history, 75–6, 130–4; Morison 3:223–54.

TF 14 as it closed on Wake. Because CINCPAC had heard from Wake that it was under dive-bombing attack by aircraft from an unknown number of carriers, he directed Fletcher to bring *Saratoga* no closer than 200 miles to the island. Halsey was directed to bring TF 8 to a position to assist, but he was much closer to Midway than to Wake when he received his instructions. In reporting the new plan to the CNO, Pye explained, "In view of indicated increased air activity [in the] Marshalls, with assurance one and possibly two carrier groups, and evidence of extensive offshore lookout and patrol, now consider surprise attack improbable. I have reluctantly abandoned proposed carrier attack on Marshalls." Admiral Pye's prefatory statement to this message revealed his true priorities: "In view disclosed weakness of Army defense of Hawaiian Islands, and reduced battleship strength, consider maintenance of most of present fleet strength essential to insure defense of islands."[15]

From this message it is clear that the Acting CINCPAC decided his carrier task forces could not be risked in the Wake operation because of their importance to the defense of the Hawaiian Islands. The operation could continue only if TF 14 could succeed in assisting Wake from an attack position 200 miles to the east. These decisions by Pye were based on a warning by Admiral Stark on 16 December that "Knox is not yet satisfied that Hawaiian Islands are safe from capture. CNO considers it possible for Japanese carriers again to destroy a large part of the shore-based aircraft." Two days later Pye replied to this admonition: "First, concur Hawaiian Islands not yet safe from capture by major operation. Second, concur possibility enemy carriers may again raid Oahu, but question probability of destroying large percentage of planes on the ground."[16]

At sea, TF 14 was beset by its own problems. Slowed by the oiler's speed of 12.7 knots, the *Neches-Tangier* group was overtaken by *Saratoga* and the rest of TF 14 on the 17th. Three days later, now 21 December at Wake, the dateline was crossed. The next morning Admiral Fletcher began a fueling operation that would take two days because of the heavy seaway. The operations orders to both Fletcher and Brown had given them the discretion to top off the destroyers before commencing combat operations.

Wake reported dive-bombing attacks by carrier planes on the 21st and again on the 22d while TF 14 was refueling. We now know the Japanese planes had come from the carriers *Hiryu* and *Soryu*, but at the time neither CINCPAC headquarters nor Fletcher knew the number of carriers involved. It was clear that the twin-engine horizontal bombers attacking Wake had probably come from the Marshall Islands to the south or Marcus Island to the northwest. Although there was no evidence yet of a

---

[15] CINCPAC to CNO, 12/210147Z, Command Summary, 71.
[16] CNO to CINCPAC, 12/170115Z; CINCPAC to CNO, 12/191037Z, Command Summary, 70, 84.

Japanese invasion force, there was little doubt that Admiral Fletcher recognized that the presence of carrier aircraft presaged some sort of larger operation, and was not just another harassing raid.

In fact, the Japanese had come back in force. Rear Admiral Kajioka was again entrusted with the command of the invasion force, but he now had four more heavy cruisers under Rear Admiral Aritomo Goto (*Kinugasa* [F], *Aoba*, *Kako*, and *Furutaka*) to act as a covering force to the east of Wake; and two carriers (*Hiryu* and *Soryu*), two cruisers, and several destroyers, all commanded by Rear Admiral Hiroaki Abe, positioned to the northwest. The carriers began their softening-up attacks on 21 December; the first wave of assault boats hit the beaches before dawn on 23 December.[17]

With the advantage of hindsight and extant Japanese records, naval historian Samuel Eliot Morison and others have recognized that, if Admiral Fletcher had wanted to engage the Japanese before they began their assault, he should have refueled on the 21st. With calmer seas the fueling operation could have been concluded in daylight; he could then have steamed the 625 miles (the distance to Wake at 2000 on the 21st) at sufficient speed to arrive off the island in time to meet the Japanese. Or Fletcher could have abandoned the idea of refueling during the morning of 22 December when he saw the adverse weather conditions, and he still could have made the run to Wake in time to challenge the Japanese. But instead he refueled on the 22d and was recalled by Admiral Pye at about daybreak the next morning. At that time TF 14 was still more than 400 miles from Wake and the Japanese were ashore.

From his vantage point as a "makee learn" with Admiral Fletcher in *Astoria*, Kinkaid received an interesting education in the problems of flag command. Ten years later, he wrote:

> After Fletcher had reversed course to return to Pearl Harbor he told me that some of his staff thought he should continue on toward Wake but he felt bound to obey Pye's order. He said, "I could do nothing else, could I?" My reply was that two-letter word "No" which is clear, distinct and conclusive.
>
> Today I am extremely glad that Pye and Fletcher made what I consider to be sound decisions in those very difficult circumstances. . . . By their decisions they prevented the useless sacrifice of valuable ships which later saw action with our enemy in circumstances of vital importance.[18]

In 1951, when he wrote about this operation, Admiral Kinkaid had read Morison's account and responded with the same omniscience that hindsight confers. He believed it would have been dangerous for TF 14

---
[17] Dull, *Battle History IJN*, 26; Morison 3:244–49.
[18] Kinkaid, "Four Years of War," chap. 2, 48.

to have risked running into Admiral Goto's cruiser line to the east of Wake, particularly at night; *Saratoga* might have been badly mauled in such an action and the risk to the carrier was not worth it.

But *Saratoga* was escorted by three heavy cruisers and a destroyer squadron, and the carrier did carry eight 8-inch rifles in four turrets. The situation might not have been as critical as Kinkaid later believed. It is possible, of course, that in 1951 Kinkaid was also recalling the prowess displayed by Japanese cruisers at night on several occasions around Savo Island in August 1942. At the time, however, Fletcher and Kinkaid knew no more about the Japanese assault force and covering units than did Admiral Pye. All they knew for sure was that carrier aircraft were attacking Wake and that a Japanese carrier task force was undoubtedly present to assist an assault force bent on taking the island. Task Force 14's mission was to bring VMF–221's eighteen aircraft to a launch position and protect *Tangier* as it went in to deliver her cargo of marines and equipment.

While Fletcher and TF 14 had their mission to reinforce Wake, Pye had missions of his own to consider and had Admirals Stark and King coaching from Washington. There was no doubt in CINCPAC headquarters that the Hawaiian Islands had to be protected and that this defense currently lay with the three task forces at sea. It was also clear that Wake occupied a lesser level of importance after Hawaii, Midway, Johnston, Palmyra and Samoa. Protecting these island outposts and the communications line to Australia by way of Samoa was central to the whole strategy of the Pacific war as it was understood two weeks after the attack at Pearl Harbor. While the Wake Island operation was being planned and carried out, CINCPAC's staff was deeply engaged in managing reinforcement and development planning for Samoa and other islands that would be important for future operations in the South and Southwest Pacific. The task forces built around *Saratoga*, *Lexington*, and *Enterprise* (and later *Yorktown*) would be the principal means of covering and protecting these strategically vital outposts.[19]

Once it became clear that Wake could not be reinforced without a fight, the choices available to Admiral Pye narrowed considerably. The easiest course to follow would have been to let Fletcher continue on to Wake without further guidance from CINCPAC. As task force commander he was closest to the scene of action and presumably would be the best informed from his own search activities. Whatever CINCPAC or CNO might learn through communications intelligence analysis could be forwarded to TF 14. But based on decisions already made and actions taken, TF 14 was more than 400 miles from Wake when the island fell. It would have taken at least eight more hours of steaming before strike sor-

---
[19] Command Summary, 50–73.

ties could have been launched by *Saratoga*. Undoubtedly scouting aircraft from Admiral Goto's cruisers would have located the task force during its daylight approach. How Admiral Abe, with two carriers northwest of Wake, would have reacted to a sighting is just further conjecture. Pye, of course, did not allow Fletcher to continue on to Wake. In the early morning of 23 December at Wake, Admiral Pye and two of his staff drafted formal estimates of the situation. Pye and his chief of staff, Rear Admiral Milo F. Draemel, decided that the risk of losing a carrier and possibly the whole task force by seeking an engagement was not acceptable. Only Pye's operations officer, Captain Soc McMorris, believed that what happened to Wake was of secondary importance, though he thought it should be retaken soon. What he recognized was that "there is an enemy force (possibly weaker) that we can get at." He urged that Fletcher be ordered to seek an engagement.[20]

While these estimates were being drafted, a message came from the CNO about Pye's decision to recall TF 11 from the Jaluit raid and have it move to support TF 14. Admiral Stark, with Admiral King concurring, agreed to the recall and then noted that "general considerations and recent developments emphasize that Wake is now and will continue to be a liability. You are authorized to evacuate Wake with appropriate demolition. Efforts to strengthen and hold Midway should continue."[21] Coming while Pye was trying to reach a decision, this message must have produced a large sigh of relief. The authorization to evacuate Wake relieved Pye of the burden of trying to defend or retake the island immediately. The stress on Midway in the CNO's message fit in with paragraph six in Pye's estimate: "The danger to damaged ships 2000 miles from base must not be under-estimated. A loss of a large part of our forces would make possible a major operation against the Hawaiian Islands. We cannot afford such losses at present."[22] By the time Pye finished his estimate at 0700 on 23 December (Hawaii time) and McMorris his at 0800, there was no possibility of evacuating Wake unless the assault force and its supporting and covering forces were completely defeated. Not willing to chance the possibility of losing TF 14, and uncertain (due to radio silence) of the exact location of Admiral Brown's *Lexington* TF 11, Pye reluctantly recalled Task Forces 14 and 11 and ordered Halsey's TF 8 to continue its operations in the vicinity of Midway.[23]

Many writers and historians have commented on the disappointment and frustration, even outrage, that were expressed in TF 14 and at Pearl

---

[20] Ibid., 78–81.
[21] CNO to CINCPAC, 12/221706Z, Command Summary, 72.
[22] Command Summary, 77–78.
[23] CINCPAC to CNO, 12/222256Z, Command Summary, 72.

when Admiral Pye recalled the Wake task forces. The pilots, both Marine and Navy, on board *Saratoga* were the most sorely tried. They wanted at least a Parthian shot at the Japanese invaders, but it was not permitted. It is probable that, had *Saratoga* run in and launched VMF–221 on a one-way flight to Wake, those gallant pilots in their obsolescent Buffaloes would have been decimated by the Zeros from *Hiryu* and *Soryu*. In the end, VMF–221 was wiped out defending Midway against those same Japanese pilots, now strengthened by two more carriers.

Admiral Kinkaid, as an interested observer, described the impact of the recall decision on Pye:

> Shortly after we returned to Pearl Harbor, I was present when Admiral Pye discussed the expedition to relieve Wake and his decision to break it off. With an apologetic expression on his face he said that he and members of staff had carefully considered all of the circumstances in the light of the information available and that he had decided to recall Fletcher. He added that he did not know whether or not that was the correct decision, but was in accordance with his best judgment. I am sure that the decision was sound. Pye's orders to Fletcher followed the intelligent and courageous course rather than the one most likely to be popular.[24]

Task Force 14 took a week to return to Pearl Harbor. During the return a swing north was made and on Christmas Day *Saratoga* launched VMF–221 to its new home on Midway. The task force finally entered Pearl on 29 December. The next day Kinkaid relieved his friend Frank Jack Fletcher of command of CRUDIV 6. The ceremony was brief and held on board *Astoria*. Later Admiral Kinkaid was to note that he never flew his personal two-star flag at sea as a rear admiral or vice admiral. Because the blue flag would attract attackers under battle conditions, most admirals left their stars in the flag bags during operations at sea. The first time Kinkaid had his flag broken at sea it had four stars and the war was over.

Immediately after the change of command Frank Jack flew to San Diego, and on New Year's Eve took his staff on board *Yorktown*, flagship for his new command, Task Force 17. In a few weeks he and Tom Kinkaid would meet again, though this time it would be deep in the Southwest Pacific, in the corner called the Coral Sea.[25]

---

[24] Kinkaid, "Four Years of War," chap. 2, 49, 54.
[25] Patrick H. H. Frank and Joseph D. Harrington, *Rendezvous at Midway: U.S.S. Yorktown and the Japanese Carrier Fleet* (New York: Stein & Day, 1967), 11, 49.

Chapter 8

Carrier Raids, January–March 1942

Though it is a part of America's culture to plan personal renewal on the first day of a year, to sweep away the past and promise improvement during the next 365 days, the Navy's leadership launched its campaign to defeat Japan slightly earlier. A few hours before Rear Admiral Tom Kinkaid read his orders to his staff on board *Astoria* on December 30, Admiral King, the newly appointed Commander in Chief, U.S. Fleet, officially took charge in Main Navy and broke his four-star flag in the yacht *Vixen* (PG 53), his temporary flagship, now tied to a dock in the navy yard. The next day, 5,000 miles from Washington, Admiral Nimitz briefly boarded the fleet submarine *Grayling* (SS 209) to relieve Vice Admiral Pye as CINCPAC. Having spent a week reviewing the situation, he was ready to take command. Unlike Admiral King, who had to build a complete staff to assist him, Nimitz decided that the Kimmel-Pye staff was well selected and competent and should not be immediately replaced. He invited those who wished to stay to get to work; those desiring transfer could see him privately. Nimitz's statement of confidence raised morale among these officers and created a spirit of loyalty that rode out many storms of doubt in the months ahead.[1]

In Pearl Harbor, and in Main Navy as well, the pressing question was: What could be done to stop the surging Japanese? Before 7 December a grand strategy had been agreed upon between Britain and America. Should Japan attack, the United States and the British Empire would stand on the defensive in the Pacific and turn almost all of their resources toward the defeat of Germany and its European allies. Once the Nazi menace was removed, it was assumed that Japan could be quickly defeated. Not only had President Roosevelt and Prime Minister Churchill accepted this grand strategy a year earlier, but Admiral Stark and General George C. Marshall, the Army Chief of Staff, had directed that the national war plans be reconstructed toward this end.[2] No one,

---

[1] Potter, *Nimitz*, 19–21.
[2] Forrest C. Pogue, *George C. Marshall: Organizer of Victory, 1943–1945*, vol. 3 (New York: Viking Press, 1973), 123–29; William Love, Jr., *The Chiefs of Naval Operations* (Annapolis: Naval Institute Press, 1980), 125–26; Louis Morton, *United States Army in World War II: The War in the Pacific: Strategy and Command, The First Two Years*, Subseries volume 10 (Washington: Office of the Chief of Military History, 1962), 79–86.

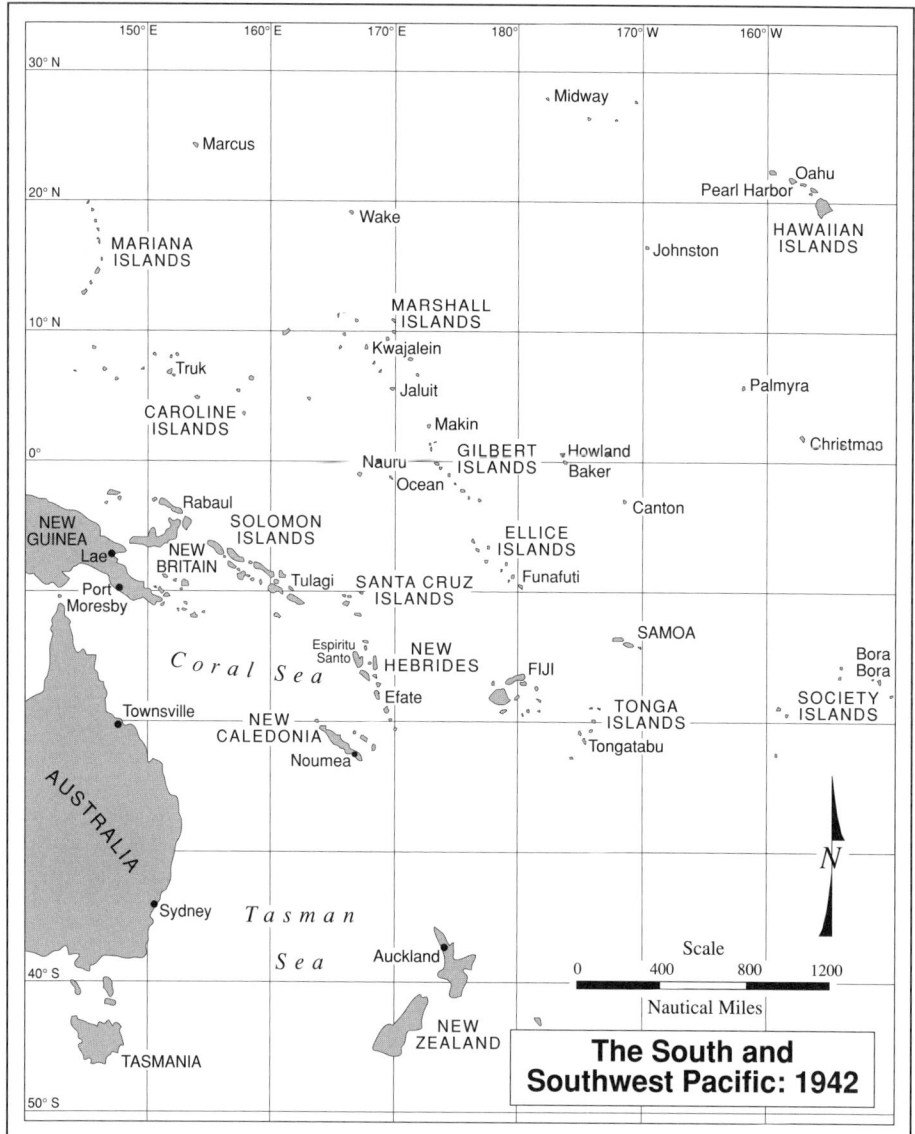

of course, anticipated that the Japanese would immobilize the Pacific Fleet at Pearl Harbor and then proceed to overrun the Philippines, British Malaya, Burma, and the Dutch East Indies (Indonesia) with their own version of the blitzkrieg. Given the naval needs of the Atlantic war, and the necessity to press convoys through to Britain and the Soviet Union, it was evident to all at CINCPAC headquarters that they would have to stop the Japanese with the ships that had survived the Japanese attack of 7 December plus whatever could be spared from Admiral Royal Ingersoll's Atlantic Fleet. It was also evident in Pearl Harbor and Washington that new plans would have to be made for the guidance of Admiral Nimitz as he tried to stem the Japanese *tsunami* that all feared was racing toward American Samoa and the Antipodes.

Upon assuming command of all naval forces, Admiral King sent his Pacific Fleet commander two signals for guidance. In the first he stated his philosophy of command, an approach he had developed throughout his career and more recently enunciated as CINCLANT:

> It is my intention that command shall be exercised by the issue of general operating plans and or directives and that pertinent direction and responsibility shall be vested in appropriate principal subordinates in chain of command.[3]

His second message spelled out two immediate tasks for CINCPAC:

> First covering and holding line Hawaii-Midway and maintaining its communications with West Coast; second and only in small degree less important, maintenance of communication West Coast-Australia, chiefly by covering, securing, and holding line Hawaii-Samoa which should be extended to include Fiji earliest practicable date.[4]

Nimitz was undoubtedly pleased to receive the broad grant of authority that came in the first message. He could hardly expect less if he were to be a true Commander in Chief. The tasks in the second message were already being carried out. It was good to know that his plans officers were not wasting their time.

Nimitz's tasks were not solely the product of his own planning staff. On 23 December the British Prime Minister and his military chiefs of staff had begun meeting with their American counterparts in Washington to determine the opening strategies for the coming year. Foremost in the minds of Churchill and his colleagues was to persuade America to adhere to the earlier "Germany first" decision. Though Adolf Hitler had

---

[3] COMINCH to CINCPAC, 12/301701Z, Command Summary, 121; see also King and Whitehill, *Fleet Admiral King*, 324–26.

[4] COMINCH to CINCPAC, 12/301740Z, Command Summary, 121.

conveniently declared war on the United States on 11 December, following Congress's declaration against Japan on 8 December, newspapers left little doubt that the American public believed the nation's first job was to settle the score with Japan. But at the joint British-American meetings logic rather than emotion controlled the discussions and decisions. By the 14 January close of the conference, ironically named ARCADIA (meaning a place of contentment) by the Prime Minister, agreement had been reached on many points. Some of the most important were:

1. The reaffirmation of the "Germany First" decision;
2. The establishment of the combined Chiefs of Staff for strategic direction of the war;
3. The acceptance of the principle of "unity of command" in the combat areas;
4. The decision to use Australia as the major base for launching the counterattack against Japan;
5. The appointment of General Sir Archibald P. Wavell to the ABDA [American-British-Dutch-Australian] Command.[5]

During the three weeks that the British and American military leadership conferred, the situation in Southeast Asia and the Southwest Pacific moved from critical to catastrophic. At about the same time Churchill and his party came ashore in Norfolk, the Japanese landed a major invasion force on Luzon, at Lingayen Gulf. By the first of the year Manila had been taken and General Douglas MacArthur and the Philippine political leadership driven into the tunnels of Corregidor Island. Although Filipino and American troops resisted throughout the archipelago, most had withdrawn to the Bataan Peninsula to wait vainly for a relief expedition from the United States. In early January the Japanese declared war on the Netherlands and moved to occupy the Netherlands East Indies with initial landings in Dutch Borneo and Celebes Island. To General Wavell in his headquarters in Java, it seemed unlikely that he could continue to defend the Malay Barrier against the surging Japanese. And if the Netherlands East Indies were to fall, could the Japanese be kept from the Eastern Dominions—India, Burma, Australia, and New Zealand?

Defense of the Malay Barrier and the Eastern Dominions was a combined responsibility of all the Allies. If the Japanese were to be beaten back in the East Indies and Malaya, an early relief of the Philippines was

---

[5] King, *Fleet Admiral King*, 360–64; Ronald H. Spector, *The American War with Japan: Eagle Against the Sun* (New York: Free Press, 1985), 123–27; Grace Person Hayes, *The History of the Joint Chiefs of Staff in World War II: The War Against Japan* (Annapolis: Naval Institute Press, 1982), 36–60; Morton, *Strategy and Command*, 158–66.

possible. Unfortunately the ABDA Command could not accomplish its mission. With the early elimination of American air power in the Philippines, and the rapid decimation of British and Dutch aviation in Malaya and the East Indies, the Japanese navy and army were free to move when and where they desired. Singapore fell on 15 February, and the Battle of the Java Sea (27 February–1 March) ended Allied naval resistance in the East Indies. On 8 March the Netherlands East Indies government surrendered. On the same day Rangoon, the major port in Burma, was occupied by the Japanese and landings began in Lae and Salamaua, New Guinea, by the Japanese navy and army. The menace to Port Moresby, New Guinea, and the northwest coast of Australia was now desperately obvious.

Following the abortive effort to relieve the Wake Island garrison, Kinkaid in Pearl Harbor followed events as they unfolded in the Southwest Pacific. But there was little he or the other Pacific Fleet officers could do to influence them. During this period of waiting, Kinkaid began to shape his Cruiser Division 6 into a smoothly operating organization. Yet its operations would not be what he might have expected when he left Washington a few weeks before.

The traditional role of a cruiser division in the fleet had been to generate information for the main body. Using their scouting aircraft and accompanying destroyers, the cruisers would scout ahead in search of enemy forces. At the same time, they were prepared to screen their own forces from prying destroyers and cruisers. With their 8-inch batteries the cruisers were expected to turn back the enemy's scouts and fight for the information they desired. Because of their endurance and firepower cruisers were designed to protect lines of communication at sea. They could escort transoceanic convoys and defend them against marauding surface craft. Accompanying destroyers would be expected to take care of hostile submarines. As commanding officer of *Indianapolis* and while "commodore" of DESRON 8, Kinkaid had been schooled in these traditional cruiser and destroyer operations. But times had changed, and so had cruiser operations.

With the battleships out of business and the war plan projecting a fleet movement west to relieve a siege of the Philippines scrapped, the aircraft carrier became the Navy's major striking weapon. The carrier task force, normally built around a single fast carrier, now contained two or more cruisers and a division of destroyers. The cruiser role was to defend the carriers against attacking cruisers and destroyers, but more important, their antiaircraft batteries were expected to provide an active defense for the carriers and themselves. As a task force all could travel and maneuver at speeds in excess of 28 knots, though the destroyers had problems if the seas were rough or the operations were of extended duration. Finally, given the island environment of the South and Southwest Pacific Areas, cruiser divisions were regularly expected to bombard Japanese shore installations during raiding expeditions or provide covering fire during the assault phase of amphibious attacks against enemy-held islands.

As a cruiser commander the admiral was allowed a small staff. Under peacetime conditions Kinkaid would have contacted officers of the appropriate rank and invited them to serve on his staff. But given the rapidity of his transfer from DESRON 8 to Pearl Harbor, he had to take his staff from those available at Pearl Harbor. For chief of staff and flag secretary, he took Lieutenant Commmander Donald W. Gladney from *Astoria*. A Naval Academy graduate in the Class of 1930, Gladney had been a Rhodes Scholar at Oxford University for his first three years after graduation. Kinkaid's aide and flag lieutenant, Lieutenant Commander Robert H. Taylor, also came from the Class of 1930. He had served previously with the staff of Rear Admiral S. Ralston Holmes, a good friend of Kinkaid's when Holmes had been Commander Destroyers, Battle Force. Taylor served with Kinkaid for the next two years. The rest of the admiral's staff was drawn from *Minneapolis*'s ship's company. Lieutenant Leland G. (Jake) Shaffer became the division radio officer. Ensign R. W. Swearingen, a reservist, was his assistant. And Lieutenant Commander Myron T. Evans served as the staff's senior aviator and also as commanding officer of VCS–6, the division's scouting squadron of eighteen SOC–1 and SOC–2 Seagulls.[6]

The day after relieving Rear Admiral Fletcher, Kinkaid and a few of his cruisers and destroyers departed Pearl with TF 14 for several weeks of "covering operations" along a line from Midway to Johnston Island. Rear Admiral Herbert Fairfax Leary commanded the task force from *Saratoga*. In *Astoria*, Kinkaid was responsible for that cruiser, *Minneapolis*, and six destroyers from DESRON 4. Leary's most important task was to ensure that another Japanese raiding force did not surprise Midway or the Hawaiian Islands. *Saratoga* had another task to complete during this cruise. The task force was slowly working its way south to meet *Enterprise* and TF 8. The two task forces were to exchange fighter aircraft (different models of the F4F–3 Wildcat) so that each carrier's fighter squadron would be equipped with a single model. Due to Japanese interference, this exchange never took place.[7]

A covering operation was despised by almost all involved because it was boring, but it did have some value for those participating. The scouting and bombing squadrons' pilots flew 200- to 300-mile sector searches from *Saratoga* as a part of their daily operations. Although the risk of losing a plane and crew was always present, the discipline of carrier opera-

---

[6] Logs of USS *Astoria* (CA 34) and *Minneapolis* (CA 36), January 1942; USNA Alumni Association, *Register of Alumni, 1987 Edition* (Annapolis, 1986).

[7] John B. Lundstrom, *The First Team: Pacific Naval Air Combat from Pearl Harbor to Midway* (Annapolis: Naval Institute Press, 1984), 60.

tions developed competence and confidence in the pilots that would prove invaluable in the months ahead. Kinkaid's cruisers carried out their share of the task force's flight operations by launching their Seagulls for close-in antisubmarine surveillance. Were it not for the presence of the cruiser pilots, this inner patrol would have been flown by carrier fighter pilots, a task they truly detested. The fighter role during flight operations was to provide a continuous combat air patrol (CAP) over the task force and to investigate every "bogey" (unknown-identity aircraft) that appeared in the vicinity of the force.

Throughout the working day the cruisers exercised their gun crews with simulated and live firing of their antiaircraft weapons. But after a few days of "conforming to the movements of the flagship" as *Saratoga* launched and recovered its planes, exercising the gun crews at general quarters, and having pilots bore holes in the clouds, the covering operations became tedious. Tom admitted in a letter to his wife, "I'm getting a little bored with our present operation, as I did with some of those on the East Coast." He was also feeling a little queasy from the constant rolling of the *Astoria* in the long Pacific swells west of Midway. Yet he found that the space in a cruiser, compared with a DESRON commodore's lodgings, made life more bearable. He was also getting plenty of fresh air and catching up on his reading; but it was all deadly dull.[8]

The tedium of this cruise ended abruptly at 1915 on 11 January when a torpedo struck *Saratoga* forward on the port side. Belching smoke, the carrier turned hard to starboard and increased speed. With everyone in the task force at general quarters and the destroyers combing the area for the Japanese I-boat, Captain Archibald H. Douglas got the fire under control and the ship's trim restored.[9] Badly holed, the carrier needed to be drydocked and patched, and then returned to a navy shipyard for major repairs and reconstruction. Unable to carry out his mission, Admiral Leary had TF 14 shape course for Pearl, 450 miles distant, at best available speed. Two days later, Kinkaid's first outing as commander of CRUDIV 6 was completed. More important for him, mail call brought "six lovely letters from my sweetheart."[10]

The admiral's delight at receiving a handful of mail was undoubtedly repeated throughout the crews of *Astoria*, CRUDIV 6 and TF 14. Little could take the place of a letter from home in capturing the attention of the sailor. Recognizing the importance of mail to maintain morale among the fighting forces, both the War and Navy Departments exercised great ingenuity to see that mail got to the advanced areas. Any ship departing westward from Pearl

---

[8] TCK to HSK, *Astoria*, 2, 6, 9 Jan 1942, TCK Papers.
[9] TCK oral history, 135–36.
[10] Morison 3:250; TCK to HSK, Pearl Harbor, 14 Jan 1942.

Harbor carried mail for the vessels with which it would rendezvous. If a ship was headed for an island base like Bora Bora, Samoa, or Noumea, its mail would be carried from a base to the cruising task forces by other vessels moving to an advanced area. Fleet oilers regularly brought mail as well as fuel to the task forces at sea. For those willing to accept the delays of surface mail, letters to and from servicemen could be sent postage-free. But most in the armed forces found the expense of a six-cent air mail stamp worth the investment. Those at home usually felt the same way.

In his eagerness for letters from Helen, Tom was little different from the greenest seaman second class in his ship. When at sea he wrote Helen three or four letters a week, sometimes numbered serially. She, of course, would receive these in batches once the ship's mail finally left. Each assured the other that there was little to write about, but the letters flowed anyway. Tom regretted regularly that he could not write about operations, but he felt he had to abide by the rules. From his sea cabin he wrote, "My letters are as dull as dishwater and I am sorry I have no interesting bits to put in them." Often he noted, "I am thriving on fresh air, food with plenty of fruit, and backrest and it is the same day after day."[11] Occasionally he would drop in a clue: "Yesterday was Sunday 4 Jan., today is Tuesday 6 Jan. and tomorrow will be the same date. Figure that out."[12]

Helen must have once lamented that her letters were trivial, for Tom replied, "The things you call 'trivia' all are important and interesting by the time your letters get here."[13] She did try to add interest by including clippings and letters she had received from others. Because Tom's mother was in poor health, Helen visited Washington regularly to assist her. Tom appreciated hearing about these trips, but it is clear that he appreciated even more the Navy Department news. Helen never failed to call old friends and classmates to find out for Tom how the real war along the Potomac was progressing.

As with many Navy people in wartime, Kinkaid's pay records from *Wainwright* (DESRON 8) did not catch up with him for several months. He was paid regularly in the interim, but everything was temporary until the records arrived. Once his records were in hand, he arranged for a monthly allotment to be paid Helen from his account. This arrangement would provide her with a regular income in case he were taken prisoner or declared missing in action. After the allotment was deducted, Tom's basic salary was available to him, but he touched little of it. He found that his food allowance covered the expenses of his flag officer's mess, and a bit more took care of his needs. Since he didn't gam-

---
[11] TCK to HSK, *Minneapolis*, 23 Jan 1942.
[12] TCK to HSK, *Astoria*, 6 Jan 1942.
[13] TCK to HSK, *Minneapolis*, 23 Jan 1942.

Author's collection

Staff of Cruiser Division 6, on board *Minneapolis* in 1942. Rear Admiral Kinkaid kept Lieutenant Commander R. H. Taylor (to Kinkaid's left), Lieutenant Commander D. W. Gladney (center, rear) and Lieutenant L. G. Shaffer (behind Taylor) with him during several of his important command periods. Taylor spent the longest period of time as a member of the admiral's staffs.

ble and there was little to buy at sea, Helen received a steady flow of $200 to $300 checks.[14] Tom left the family expenses in her hands, but he suggested she purchase government war bonds: "I think you should buy some of them and you can go as far as you like with my full approval. The last time [World War I] we bought our first car on war savings stamps and dime banks, so perhaps this time we can save enough to buy a ranch."[15] How and where they would live after retirement was a subject to which they would return regularly during the next three years.

The day after returning to Pearl Harbor Kinkaid shifted his flag from *Astoria* to *Minneapolis*, the regular flagship of CRUDIV 6. His staff accompanied him in the move. This ship would be home until July when the admiral would move to the carrier *Enterprise*, leaving his staff behind. In

---

[14] TCK to HSK, Pearl Harbor, 15 Jan 1942.
[15] TCK to HSK, *Astoria*, 6 Jan 1942.

158   *Kinkaid of the Seventh Fleet*

moving to *Minneapolis*, Kinkaid also saw the last of TF 14. With *Saratoga* going to the Bremerton Navy Yard for repair and refit, its task force was broken up and the cruisers were assigned to *Lexington*'s TF 11 under Vice Admiral Wilson Brown.[16] During the next five days Kinkaid spent a lot of time conferring with his new boss, meeting with his four cruiser captains, and becoming better acquainted with all the senior officers who would work with him at sea. Conferences on board *Minnie* or *Lex* were only one way he met with other officers. Strolling in Waikiki and swimming at the Moana and Royal Hawaiian combined exercise and socializing. Some of the senior officers still had wives on Oahu, though the number was dwindling with each transport departure east. Admiral Brown's chief of staff, Captain C. Turner Joy, owned a house near Waikiki and he and his wife provided drinks and recreation for Kinkaid and other senior types.[17]

On 19 January Vice Admiral Brown took Task Force 11 to sea as a part of the Pacific Fleet's first offensive operation. Around the first of February Vice Admiral William Halsey's TF 8 (*Enterprise*) was due to raid the Marshall Islands. He would be joined by TF 17 (*Yorktown*), now commanded by Rear Admiral Fletcher, in the Samoan area. Task Force 17 would escort a convoy of transports bringing a Marine regiment to defend the developing naval base in the Samoans. Once free of escort duties TF 17 would move north with TF 8 for a 1 February dawn attack on Roi, Taroa, Kwajalein, and Wotje (TF 8) and Jaluit, Makin and Mili (TF 17). Brown's TF 11 was assigned a covering role during the Marshalls raid. His force would be on the Johnston-Palmyra-Christmas Island line, ready to defend against any Japanese counteraction aimed at Hawaii or move to the aid of Halsey or Fletcher should they need assistance that would otherwise take two or three days to arrive.[18]

The overriding purpose of the Marshalls raid was to pressure the Japanese to ease up in Malaya and the East Indies and perhaps reconsider any anticipated moves against the New Hebrides, Fiji or Samoan islands. As suggested by Admiral King, CINCPAC increased the pressure on 21 January by ordering TF 11 to attack Wake Island once Halsey and Fletcher were clear of the Marshalls. Two days later and a thousand miles closer to Wake Island, Brown's orders were canceled. Because "the factor of safety was too small" for TF 11 to raid Wake without an oiler to greet it on returning, *Neches* was dispatched toward a rendezvous, Point Mike (20°N, 179°50′W), without the usual destroyer escort. During the midwatch on 23 January, while about 135 miles west of Oahu, *Neches* was torpedoed and sunk by the Japanese submarine *I–72*. The inevitable followed. Task Force 11 was or-

---

[16] Morison 3:260–61.
[17] TCK to HSK, Pearl Harbor, 14, 18 Jan 1942.
[18] Command Summary, 156; Morison 3:260–65.

dered back to Pearl Harbor and arrived there on 25 January.[19] The cruise had provided more drills for Kinkaid's cruisers, plenty of carrier operations for *Lex*'s squadrons, and a large amount of boredom for all involved.

More frustrations awaited Kinkaid when *Minneapolis* tied up in Pearl. The weather between Hawaii and the mainland had been wretched, so no clipper mail had come for many days. Then there was the news that the Roberts Commission—established to investigate the attack on Pearl Harbor—had filed its report and found Admiral Kimmel and General Short lacking. Tom was "sorry that it [the report] crucified Kimmel and Short. . . . Everyone out here thinks it pretty awful and feels that the Board was looking for a scapegoat to stave off a Congressional investigation." And to finish off the day, the movie projector became a casualty as Tom was settling down in *Minnie's* aircraft hangar to enjoy Fred Astaire and Rita Hayworth in "You'll Never Get Rich." Probably the irony of the title escaped him that evening.[20]

Task Force 11 had six days in Pearl before setting out on what proved to be an extended cruise. While the ships were provisioning, the admiral was doing likewise. He and his staff laid in a stock of magazines to trade among themselves and with *Minnie's* officers. Tom also received one of the bottles of "pep pills" (vitamins) that Helen regularly mailed to him. Expecting to be gone more than a month (the ships were provisioned for forty-two days), the admiral sent his entire last paycheck to Helen. "As I have some cash in my pocket and not much use for it, I am sending you the whole pay check this time. (Enclosed $299.00) . . . My semimonthly check should be about this size each time."[21]

Vice Admiral Brown and TF 11 departed Pearl Harbor on 31 January with only general orders, probably because neither CINCPAC's nor COMINCH's staff could decide what its mission should be. The force would escort the oiler *Neosho* (AO 23) as it steamed southwest to meet Halsey's force after its raid on the Marshalls, but beyond that TF 11 would continue toward the line between Canton Island and Samoa.

At Nimitz's headquarters there had been a difference of opinion concerning TF 11's next moves. On 28 January Vice Admiral Pye, now an advisor to CINCPAC, had proposed that two carrier groups operate in the Suva (Fiji Islands)–Samoa area. This plan would preposition two carrier striking groups to respond to any Japanese move against Noumea on New Caledonia or Fiji. Pye suggested sending either TF 8 (*Enterprise*) or TF 17 (*Yorktown*), probably the latter, to Suva and TF 11 (*Lexington*) to operate west of Samoa.

---

[19] Command Summary, 135, 156; Lundstrom, *First Team*, 72–73.
[20] TCK to HSK, Pearl Harbor, 25 Jan 1942.
[21] Ibid., 27, 28, 30 Jan 1942.

Nimitz's war plans section demurred. It believed that such a move was "too eccentric for our primary task of protecting Hawaii and the Mainland; that is [the task forces] would be considerably weaker than the force the enemy is employing in that area; and that the logistic situation of our forces would be most precarious." Not wanting to leave TF 11 unemployed, the planners suggested that Brown might hit Wake or even the Marshalls again. Either strike, following the Halsey-Fletcher attack on the Marshalls, might deflect the Japanese from current offensive plans.[22]

Nimitz favored his planning staff's suggestion and so informed COMINCH, but King didn't agree. On 31 January after TF 11 had sailed, he ordered Nimitz to keep one task force in the convoy routing area, south of Samoa and east of 180 degrees longitude (the international date line). On 4 February CINCPAC finally ordered TF 11 to pick up three convoys and escort them to Samoa.[23] A few days later Brown sent CINCPAC an outline of his future operations from Samoa: Task Force 11 would operate between Fiji and New Caledonia and looked forward to being reinforced by Vice Admiral Leary's ANZAC Squadron (TF 44). Brown, Nimitz, and King were unsure what TF 11 should do once it began "covering" the Suva-Noumea area, but each had a staff that would work it out.[24]

There is little evidence that Kinkaid concerned himself with what TF 11 would do next. His job was to protect *Lexington* with the firepower of *Minneapolis, Indianapolis, Pensacola,* and *San Francisco,* plus ten destroyers. Admiral Brown could do little more than monitor the radio circuits tying him to Pearl Harbor, Washington, and Melbourne and keep a continuous patrol searching for any Japanese forces at sea. He had no special intelligence access to Japanese plans; thus he could only react to information received by radio or from *Lexington's* scout planes. He could plan a raid against Japanese-held island bases, but his plans actually received their intelligence annexes from COMANZAC (Leary) or CINCPAC, and this information could cause the plans to be scrapped in their early phase.

There was confusion in Pearl Harbor because CINCPAC did not have complete control over the task forces sent to the Southwest Pacific Area (SWPA). Admiral King insisted on retaining operational control of the forces even after they arrived in Samoan waters. This meant that Nimitz might send them south, but once they turned west, King might step in and exercise his authority as COMINCH. This problem began to stultify planning in Pearl Harbor once it became clear that CINCPAC and COMINCH's staff were not in agreement on the strategy that was being followed.

---

[22] Command Summary, 194.

[23] Ibid., 205, 207–8.

[24] Ibid., 208–10. ANZAC (Australia–New Zealand Army Corps) is a World War I term, which was applied in World War II to any military unit in which Australians and New Zealanders served.

By the first of February CINCPAC was still committed to two tasks laid down early by COMINCH: protect the Hawaiian Islands from invasion and maintain the security of the shipping routes from the mainland to Australia. But with the deployment of a Marine regiment to Samoa, and obvious plans to garrison Noumea, Suva, Tongatabu, Bora-Bora, and probably other locations like Efate and Espiritu Santo, it appeared that Admiral King had more far-reaching plans for the South and Southwest Pacific Areas than just making it a secure transit route. If Noumea was to become the departure point for rooting the Japanese out of Rabaul, then New Caledonia would obviously attract the attention of the Imperial Navy. If this were the strategy, several carrier task forces would certainly be needed in the area. But CINCPAC was not aware that he was supposed to be moving from the defensive to the offensive. Given this murky background, and prodding by COMINCH, the planners at Pearl began considering the possibilities of TF 11 and TF 8 raiding Rabaul and TF 17 hitting Wake at about the same time.[25]

In a pair of dispatches to Nimitz on 6 February, COMINCH's staff conveyed its own anxieties to Pearl Harbor. Washington believed that the "enemy would soon strike all along the Southwest line, including Noumea and the New Hebrides. They also might well raid Midway, Oahu, West Coast and Canal Zone." To meet these possible attacks, King called for Pacific Fleet action: "Expedite dispositions and operations of your forces to seize this opportunity for making detached enemy ventures costly for him."[26] Task Force 11 had been underway for a week to meet whatever forces the Japanese might send into the South Pacific Area, but Admiral King now gave it specific instructions. Admiral Brown was to proceed to a rendezvous with the ANZAC Squadron and then, under the direction of Vice Admiral Leary in Melbourne, engage in active operations in the New Hebrides–New Caledonia area. The rendezvous was set for a point 300 miles west of Suva on 13 February. A rendezvous at sea was planned because Admiral Brown considered Noumea unsafe against submarine attack, and *Lexington* was too valuable to risk.

While TF 11 steamed toward its meeting with the ANZAC Squadron and operations in the Southwest Pacific, Admiral Nimitz responded to COMINCH pressure by sending Admiral Halsey and TF 16 (*Enterprise*) on another raiding mission. Halsey was to hit Wake Island around 24 February and then blast Marcus Island, some 900 miles to the northwest. It was hoped by those in Washington and Pearl Harbor that the combined activ-

---

[25] Command Summary, 212; John B. Lundstrom, *The First South Pacific Campaign: Pacific Fleet Strategy, December 1941–June 1942* (Annapolis: Naval Institute Press, 1976), 31–32; H. Willmott, *The Barrier and the Javelin: Japanese and Allied Pacific Strategies, February to June 1942* (Annapolis: Naval Institute Press, 1983), 147–51.

[26] COMINCH to CINCPAC, 2/161513Z and 2/062352Z, Command Summary, 209, 220–21.

162 *Kinkaid of the Seventh Fleet*

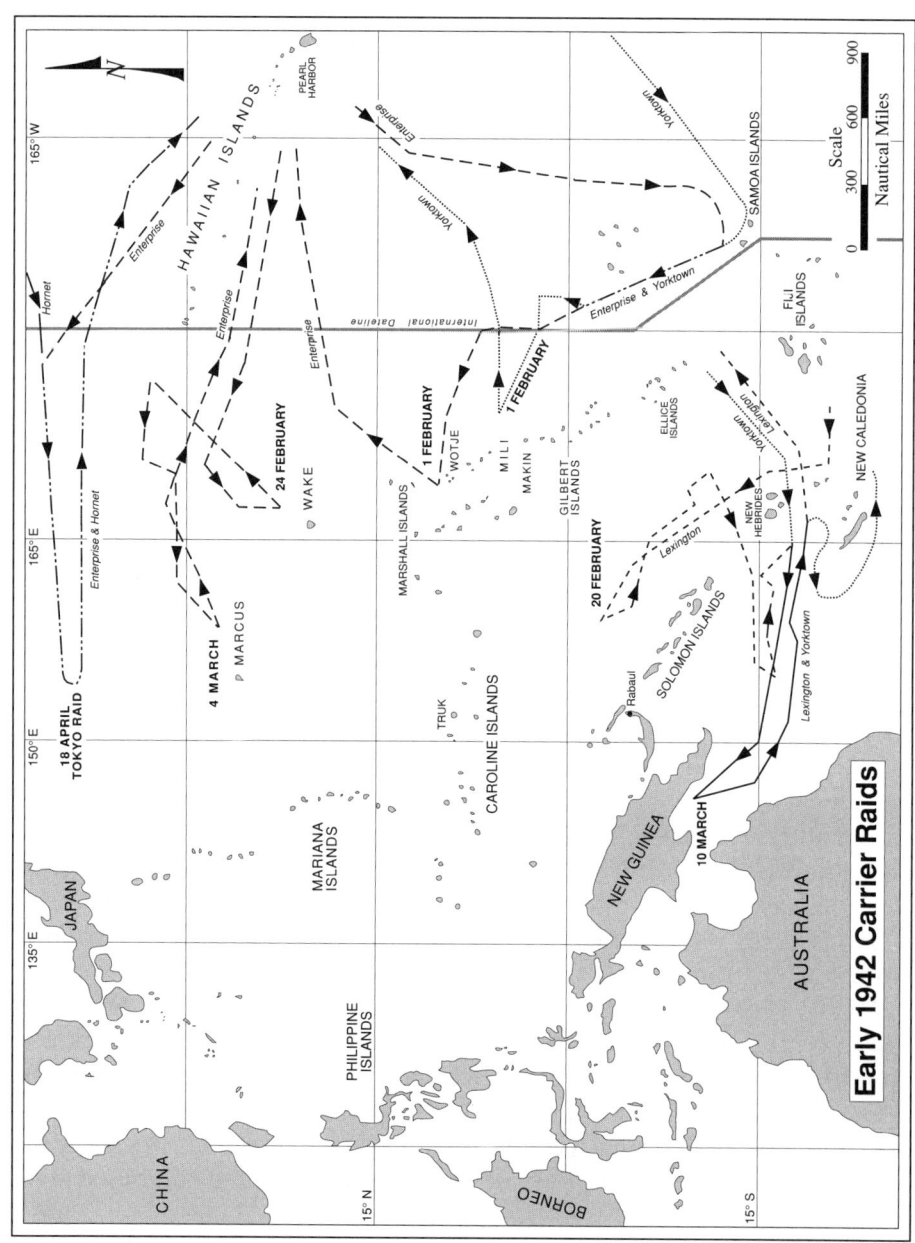

ities of Brown and Halsey would slow down enemy attacks in the direction of Australia and New Guinea.[27] There is good evidence that these pin-prick attacks by Brown's and Halsey's carrier forces did buy some valuable time for the beleaguered Allies in the Southwest Pacific.

The potential outcome of this cruise did not occupy much of Tom Kinkaid's attention in early February as the task force approached the equator. Not since July of 1908, during his passed midshipman cruise in *Nebraska*, had he ventured into the realm of Neptunus Rex. Now, as a shellback, he watched in amusement from his flag bridge as *Minnie's* old salts initiated the pollywogs into the fraternity of line-crossers. A half-mile away on board *Lexington* all rates and ranks, if they could not prove they were shellbacks, experienced a full initiation, including a flight deck gauntlet. Needless to say, Admiral Brown did not spend the day at the line engaging in parade ground maneuvers with the vessels in TF 11 while initiation rites were carried out.

Tom's letters to Helen early in the cruise reflected the boredom that had begun to set in. "I have been sizzling" was a phrase that appeared often. The heat was oppressive, particularly when there was a following wind, but at least Kinkaid enjoyed whatever breezes came across the bridge. He had a cabin below, but except for a morning shower he rarely visited it. The sea cabin, opening onto the bridge, was a much more comfortable place to rest or sleep. While reading or dozing, he could keep up with the activity on the bridge and respond immediately to any problems that arose. In his sea cabin Kinkaid preferred reading magazines and short stories that demanded little sustained attention. All around him knew he enjoyed detective stories and mysteries, but he had exhausted the supply within two weeks. He then turned to the ship's library, which was quite good. Because he slept in the sea cabin, with ports open and no lights showing, he turned in early and rose with the sun or even before it. If he wanted to read or work on reports at night, he had to do so in his hot and stuffy cabin below. Although bored, the admiral had too many people around him to be lonely. His good humor showed through as he punned to his wife: "I am glad that I have a very nice group of youngsters with me as it helps to keep from getting ship-bored(?)."[28]

Kinkaid's boredom ended on the 13th when the task force arrived at the rendezvous and found *Neosho* ready to replenish its depleted bunkers. *Lexington* was filled completely, as were the destroyers, but the remaining fuel could only bring the cruisers to 75 percent capacity. This

---

[27] Potter, *Nimitz*, 41–43; E. B. Potter, *Bull Halsey* (Annapolis: Naval Institute Press, 1985), 53–55; James M. Merrill, *A Sailor's Admiral: A Biography of William F. Halsey* (New York: Thomas Y. Crowell, 1976), 30–31; Fleet Admiral William F. Halsey and LCDR J. Bryan III, *Admiral Halsey's Story* (New York: Whittlesey House, McGraw-Hill, 1947), 97–101.

[28] TCK to HSK, *Minneapolis*, 8, 11 Feb 1942.

insufficiency was to prove troublesome in the days ahead as offensive operations were undertaken. While at the rendezvous Admiral Brown flew staff members to Suva where messages could be sent to Pearl Harbor, Washington, and Melbourne without revealing the presence of his force in the area. Brown's visiting staff also checked at Suva for the latest reports on Japanese activities and for information about fuel and supplies that the task force might need. Two days later, Rear Admiral John G. Crace, RN, hove into sight with the cruisers *Australia, Leander, Achilles,* and *Chicago,* and the destroyers *Lamson* (DD 367) and *Perkins* (DD 377). *Chicago* and the two destroyers were American vessels assigned to the ANZAC Squadron. Despite rough boating, Kinkaid and Crace plus several members of their staffs boarded *Lexington* to confer with Admiral Brown and plan their next move, a raid on the Japanese naval base at Rabaul on New Britain Island in the Bismarck Archipelago.[29]

The operation plan for the raid was simple and straightforward. The task force would steam northwest from the rendezvous area, passing to the east of the Santa Cruz Islands, and then turn to approach Rabaul from the northeast. A dawn air raid was planned for 21 February, with a cruiser bombardment of the base if it seemed feasible. As an extra punch, and also a distraction to the Japanese, a dozen B–17s were to move from Noumea to Townsville on the northeast coast of Australia. From this advanced base the Flying Fortresses could attack Rabaul in coordination with *Lexington's* squadrons. Admiral Crace wanted to join TF 11, but his ships (except *Australia* and *Chicago*) were too short-legged for the operation. He was asked to remain behind as a covering force for Noumea and Suva and, more important, to escort a second oiler that was to meet the task force as it returned from Rabaul.[30] Unfortunately, Admiral Brown's operation fell apart due to reports from a rather imaginative Japanese lookout at least 750 miles from the task force.

There is little doubt that Admiral Halsey's raids of 1 February had caught the attention of the Japanese high command. By the 14th Japanese operational intelligence sources were reporting a heavy increase in radio traffic at Pearl Harbor that they correctly believed presaged another carrier raid. Halsey took TF 16 to sea on 14 February with plans to visit Wake and Marcus. Two days later Fletcher headed south with TF 17 to eventually rendezvous with TF 11. Intercepting these signals, the Japanese ordered their forces in Rabaul and the Mandates Area (Caroline, Gilbert, and Marshall islands) on a "strict alert" condition. At 1335 on the 19th, a lookout on Mortlock Island (Satawan Atoll, 160 miles

---

[29] Commander Task Force 11, Action Report, "Report of Operations with ANZAC Force," 23 Mar 1942, OA (hereafter CTF 11 Action Report, 23 Mar 1942).
[30] Ibid.

southeast of Truk) reported that he had sighted two destroyers heading north. Two hours later the same lookout again reported sighting a destroyer mast, this time headed west. These reports were checked by air reconnaissance from Truk, but the planes arrived after sunset and were unable to verify the sightings. The Commander South Seas Force at Truk ordered long-range flying boat searches early the next morning from Truk, Rabaul, and Kwajalein with medium bombers and fighters standing by to attack any contacts. Although the eager lookout on Mortlock had seen nothing, he did trigger such Japanese responses that the *Lexington* task force was snared in the search net.[31]

At 1030 (local time) the Commander 24th Air Flotilla, Rear Admiral Eiji Goto, was galvanized into action by a contact report. A "Mavis" flying boat (Kawanishi Type 97) searching sector 075–090 degrees radioed: "Large enemy force sighted, 075 degrees, 460 miles from Rabaul, course 315." Lieutenant (jg) Noboru Sakae had found TF 11, but he too had been spotted. A few minutes later Lieutenant Commander John S. Thach, commanding officer of VF–3, flying CAP from *Lexington*, shot down the snooper and commenced a string of aerial victories that would soon make him one of the Navy's earliest aces.[32] But Sakae's contact report had been worth the loss of the flying boat and crew. From Rabaul, the Air Flotilla Commander snapped out orders: Other flying boats were to maintain contact with the intruders; eighteen "Bettys" (Mitsubishi Type 1 land attack plane) of the Fourth Air Group, loaded with bombs, were to attack the task force; remaining patrol boats were to carry out twilight torpedo attacks; and eighteen "Nells" (Mitsubishi Type 96 land attack plane) were to attack, if within range, from Kwajalein.

In all a warm reception had been set into motion by the Rabaul command, but there were problems. The distance was too great for the Japanese bombers to be escorted by available fighter aircraft. The Bettys would have to fight their way through *Lexington*'s defending force of sixteen Wildcats (Grumman F4F–3). The attack potential of the Bettys was also compromised by a lack of torpedoes at Rabaul. Though experienced at medium-level bombing, the attacking squadron was specially trained to attack naval targets with the deadly 21-inch aerial torpedo. Finally, Admiral Brown's task force was outside the combat radius of the twin-engine Nells in Kwajalein; thus the Bettys from Rabaul would have to attack TF 11 without assistance. Despite these deficiencies the Japa-

---

[31] Translation for author by RADM E. T. Layton, USN (Ret.), of an extract from [Japanese] *Navy Operations in the Southeast Area* (Nanto homen kaigun sakusen), vol. 49, pt. 1 of *Compilation of War Histories* (Senshi sosho), prepared by War History Section of the Defense Research Division of the Japanese Defense Agency (Boeicho Kenshujo Senshishitsu): chap. 10, "The Battle of 20 February 1942 (Counterattack Against the American Carrier Task Force)" (hereafter Layton Translation 1).

[32] Lundstrom, *First Team*, 113–14.

nese squadron's pilots were confident that their previous combat experience would bring them to victory.³³

Once spotted by the Japanese, there was little that Admiral Brown and TF 11 could do but prepare to meet them. Two weeks earlier, while en route, the admiral had signaled his force:

> We are moving into an area where an opportunity may offer to attack enemy naval forces at sea. Commanding officers are directed to give meticulous attention to every detail of armament, fire control. . . . There must be no failure to shoot fast. Enemy air attacks require earliest possible development of high volume of fire by ships in sector from which an attack is launched.³⁴

There had been plenty of drills coming down from Pearl Harbor; now the time had come to "clear for action." Kinkaid's four cruisers were on station off the four quarters of *Lexington,* ready to provide high-volume antiaircraft fire, and beyond the cruisers were the destroyers, prepared to contribute with .50-caliber and 1.1-inch firepower. Though the Japanese obviously knew they were coming, Admiral Brown held the task force to its northwesterly course while he and his staff made a quick re-estimate of the situation. Given their distance from Rabaul and Kwajalein, they could expect an attack on the task force any time after 1330. Should they beat off these attackers, there was little doubt that their squadrons would be fiercely received when they arrived for their dawn strike. Lacking the element of surprise and probably recognizing that Rabaul's harbor would have been emptied, the admiral decided to abort the operation and informed King and Leary of his decision. *Lex's* commanding officer, Captain Frederick C. (Ted) Sherman, wanted to continue the raid, but he did not prevail. To confuse the Japanese, Admiral Brown did decide to feint toward Rabaul until dark and then reverse course.³⁵ Kinkaid did not participate in this decision. When the task force turned southwest to begin the feint toward Rabaul, he knew they were not serious, but he also knew the distance to the Japanese would now be shortened with every turn of *Minnie's* screws.

The expected attack lighted *Lexington's* radar screen at 1611 and by 1630 the first wave of nine Bettys was almost overhead. Thach's Wildcats, the task force's antiaircraft barrage, and superb shiphandling by Captain Sherman completely frustrated the seven Japanese planes that reached

---

³³ Layton Translation 1; "Airview" Staff, *General View of Japanese Military Aircraft in the Pacific War* (Tokyo: Kanto-Sha, 1948), 53–57, 62–63

³⁴ CTF 11 to TF 11 Despatch, Lexington, 7 Feb 1942, Wilson Brown Papers, USNA Archives.

³⁵ Lundstrom, *First Team,* 115–16; ADM Frederick C. Sherman, *Combat Command: The American Aircraft Carriers in the Pacific War* (New York: Bantam Books, 1982), 58–61.

the drop point. All bombs missed and none of the aircraft survived the engagement. At the height of the attack by the first wave, the second wave arrived on *Lexington*'s radar and by 1700 was within ten miles. The eight Bettys in the second wave were first intercepted by Lieutenant (jg) Edward H. (Butch) O'Hare and his wingman, Lieutenant (jg) Marion W. Dufilho. Attacking alone because his wingman's guns were jammed, O'Hare shot down three bombers and mortally wounded two more. Four arrived at the drop point, but again they were totally ineffectual. Of the seventeen bombers that attacked the task force, only two managed to return to their home at Rabaul's Vanakanau aerodrome; thirteen planes and their crews were totally destroyed. Group Four of the 24th Air Flotilla had been needlessly sacrificed. The sightings by the two Mavis flying boats had been cause enough for Admiral Brown to scrub the planned attack on Rabaul.[36]

Kinkaid had a grandstand view of the action. *Minneapolis* earned its first battle star by contributing to the antiaircraft barrage, but not even in the inflated rhetoric of the ship's cruise book could any kills be claimed. Although he felt unable to provide any specific information on what became known as the action off Bougainville, the admiral did entertain his wife with a personal reaction to the air attacks on the task force: "When I saw them coming out from behind a cloud I thought of you in your berth on the night of 7 Dec. muttering to yourself 'those bastards.' According to 'Time' that is the expression that was used throughout the country on that day." Tom's jar of Brillantine was a casualty of *Minnie*'s violent maneuvering and the concussions from her secondary batteries. He noted that he was now "a devotee of Vitalis'. If you will read the magazine advertisements you will probably expect me back with a full head of hair."[37]

The action off Bougainville was Tom Kinkaid's first battle action in World War II, but it was not his first exposure to enemy fire. Some twenty-eight years earlier guerrilla forces in Haiti had brought *Machias* under small-arms fire while Kinkaid was on deck. Then he had manned a machine gun and repaid his attackers in kind. On board *Minnie* the admiral remained on the flag bridge to observe the action. In an interview twenty years later, he commented honestly about his feelings when the Japanese Bettys reached their drop point: "As I looked up and saw those four planes wobbling like this [he wiggled both hands together] I wondered who was more scared, those pilots or we who were directly under their bombs there."[38]

---

[36] Layton Translation 1; Lundstrom, *First Team*, 115–32; Stanley Johnston, *Queen of the Flat-Tops: The U.S.S. Lexington and the Coral Sea Battle* (New York: E. Dutton, 1942), 89–101.

[37] TCK to HSK, *Minneapolis*, 21 Feb 1942; A. T. Luey and H. Bruvold, *The "Minnie" or War Cruise of the U.S.S.Minneapolis* (Elkhart, IN: Bell Printing, 1946), 12–13.

[38] TCK oral history, 136–41.

As planned, Admiral Brown held TF 11 to its course toward Rabaul until darkness, then reversed course. By daybreak on the 21st the task force was beyond surveillance by the ubiquitous Japanese flying boats and headed for a badly needed refueling rendezvous with its tankers. Brown's action report presented the logic of his abandoning the Rabaul attack and noted a problem that would plague future carrier task force operations. There never seemed to be enough fuel for the number of high-speed operations that inevitably came with surprise attacks and evasion of counterattacks. The admiral doubted that he would have had adequate fuel for the high-speed run toward Rabaul, evasive maneuvers when counterattacked, and then the high-speed dash out of danger. He concluded that the gain of a successful raid was less important than the possible loss of *Lexington*: "The loss of the carrier or a bungled attack would have been still another calamity to the Allied cause."[39]

Once the Rabaul raid was aborted, planners in Washington, Pearl, and on board *Lexington* began again to consider how best to employ TF 11. Admiral Brown let Nimitz know that another attack on Rabaul should only be attempted by a task force with at least two carriers. That said, Brown turned his refueled task force southwest for an offensive patrol of the Coral Sea. It seemed likely to all that the Japanese were planning to attack either New Guinea or the Solomons, or possibly the New Hebrides; Brown hoped to intercept them somewhere. Meanwhile, taking TF 11's commander at his word, Nimitz proposed to King that TF 17 leave its covering position in the vicinity of Canton Island, rendezvous with TF 11, and then proceed to attack Rabaul. Listening in, Admiral Brown let CINCPAC know that a successful raid on Rabaul might be difficult even with two carriers. Ignoring Brown's lukewarm attitude, COMINCH ordered the joint TF 11 and TF 17 attack. On 2 March he set 10 March as the date for an attack in the New Britain–Solomons area.[40] King's choice of 10 March was carefully considered, for on 11 March a convoy would arrive in Noumea from Australia, bringing American troops to reinforce the New Hebrides base.[41]

Following the offensive patrol into the Coral Sea, during which nothing was encountered, TF 11 again rendezvoused with its tanker, and in the morning of 6 March Admiral Fletcher's TF 17 signaled its arrival. In a conference on board *Lexington* a plan was devised to have the joint task force attack both Rabaul and Gasmata, the Japanese air base on the southern periphery of New Britain Island. *Lexington*'s air group would

---

[39] CTF 11, "Report of Action of Task Force Eleven with Japanese Aircraft on February 20, 1942," CTF 11 to CINCPAC, 24 Feb 1942, OA.

[40] Command Summary, 243–47, 260; Lundstrom, *First Team,* 134, 151–53.

[41] CTF 11 Action Report, 23 Mar 1942.

take on Rabaul; *Yorktown*'s would hit Gasmata and help with Rabaul if needed. The eight cruisers would have divided chores. Kinkaid's TG 11.2, consisting of *Minneapolis, San Francisco,* and *Indianapolis,* would stay with *Lexington* to defend against counterattacks. Rear Admiral William W. (Poco) Smith, who had brought his cruisers down with TF 17, would lead *Astoria, Pensacola,* and *Louisville* (CA 28) and the destroyers *Dewey* (DD 349) and *Dale* (DD 353), in a bombardment of Rabaul. Rear Admiral Crace, with the heavy cruisers *Australia* and *Chicago* and the destroyers *Patterson* and *Bagley* (DD 386), was assigned the task of bombarding Gasmata.[42] Brown preferred a night attack, but *Yorktown*'s air group was not night qualified, so the attacks were set for daybreak on 10 March. Smith and Crace must have been uncomfortable knowing that their shipboard bombardments were planned in part to draw the shore-based aircraft away from the carriers that would be 125 miles from their target.[43]

As the task forces turned into the Coral Sea and began their approach to Rabaul from the south, the operation order was once again overtaken by events already underway. At the end of January the Japanese Imperial General headquarters had issued orders to the Commander Combined Fleet to seize as quickly as possible Lae and Salamaua on the north coast of New Guinea and also to establish a seaplane operating base at Tulagi in the Solomon Islands. Gathering at Rabaul in early March, the landings were completed at Lae and Salamaua in the early hours of 8 March. Harassing attacks by Australian Lockheed Hudsons commenced on the 8th, and Admiral Leary informed TF 11 of the presence of the Japanese invasion force.[44]

Informed that the Japanese were at Lae and Salamaua, Admiral Brown and his staff decided that this force presented a more attractive target than Rabaul and Gasmata. It was quickly decided that an attack should be made from the south, launching from an offshore position in the Gulf of Papua to the south of New Guinea's eastern region. Because the operation would require the attacking squadrons to cross the Owen Stanley Mountains to reach New Guinea's north coast, Brown sent two planes to Townsville and two others to Port Moresby to obtain firsthand information about the terrain. Once Commanders Walton W. Smith (Townsville) and William B. Ault (Port Moresby) returned, plans were completed to hit the Japanese in the morning of 10 March. To prevent any Japanese force from surprising them by rounding the eastern end of New Guinea, Admiral Crace with the

---

[42] CTF 11, Operation Order 5–42, 6 March 1942, Wilson Brown Papers.
[43] CTF 11 Action Report, 23 Mar 1942.
[44] "Eastern New Guinea Invasion Operations: Japanese Monograph No. 96," in Donald S. Detwiler and Charles B. Burdick, eds., *War in Asia and the Pacific, 1937–1945,* 15 volumes (New York: Garland Publishing, 1980), vol 5, 1–5.

heavy cruisers *Australia, Chicago, Astoria,* and *Louisville* and the destroyers *Anderson* (DD 411), *Hammann, Hughes* (DD 410), and *Sims* (DD 409) was to patrol off the Louisiade Archipelago. Admirals Kinkaid and Smith would keep the rest of the cruisers and destroyers with their respective task forces to provide the usual antiair and antisubmarine defenses.[45]

The operation went smoothly and complete tactical surprise was achieved. Lieutenant Commander Thach and most of Fighting Three arrived over the target area at 0920. By 1015 *Lexington's* and *Yorktown's* torpedo and dive-bomber pilots had finished their attacks and were headed back to their carriers. Harassment of the Japanese continued with eight AAF B–17s from Townsville and eight RAAF Hudsons from Port Moresby pounding the Japanese vessels. As was true of all of these early raids, the reported results were considerably more optimistic than reality. Admiral Brown believed that five transports or cargo ships, two heavy cruisers, one light cruiser, one destroyer, and probably a minelayer had been sunk. The actual damage, as reported by the Japanese after the war, was three transports sunk (*Yokohama Maru, Tenyo Maru, Kongo Maru*), an ex-minesweeper (*Tama Maru No. 2*) damaged severely enough that it sank two days later, and medium to light damage to another thirteen ships. The Japanese were not driven out of New Guinea, nor were the airfields at Lae and Salamaua knocked out of commission. At Pearl Harbor the raid was recorded in the war diary with this less than sanguine comment: "Even with damage inflicted, it is doubtful if enemy will be greatly retarded."[46]

Actually the Lae-Salamaua raid proved more useful to the Allied cause in the Southwest Pacific than Admiral Nimitz's staff anticipated. In his action report Admiral Brown concluded, "It seems probable that our appearance off RABAUL on February 20 and our overwhelming attack at SALAMAUA on March 10 have caused them [the Japanese] to proceed with caution quite apart from the losses they have suffered in ships and planes."[47] The two actions had caused little damage to TF 11 and TF 17, but the same could not be said about the Japanese. They had been caught at Lae and Salamaua without any fighter aircraft to defend their beachheads. This situation occurred because the Combined Fleet's fast

---

[45] CTF 11 Action Report, 23 Mar 1942; Office of Naval Intelligence (ONI), *Early Raids in the Pacific, February 1 to March 10, 1942*, Combat Narratives series, (1943), 57–68, ONI, WWII Command File, OA; Sherman, *Combat Command*, 62–65; Johnston, *Queen of the Flat-Tops*, 103–16; Lundstrom, *First Team*, 153–56.

[46] Command Summary, 267; ONI Combat Narrative: *Early Raids*, 57–68; translation for author by RADM E. T. Layton, USN (Ret.), of an extract from [Japanese] *Navy Operations in the Southeast Area* (Nanto homen kaigun sakusen), vol. 49 of *Compilation of War Histories* (Senshi sosho), prepared by War History Section of the Defense Research Division of the Japanese Defense Agency (Boeicho Kenshujo Senshishitsu): chap. 10, "Background of the Battle of 10 March 1942" (hereafter Layton Translation 2); Lundstrom, *First Team*, 162.

[47] CTF 11 Action Report, 23 Mar 1942.

carrier task force, the *Kido Butai*, was operating in the Indian Ocean and there were no extra carriers to use in New Guinea waters.

Because of the damage inflicted at Salamaua and Lae, the Japanese decided that the invasion of Port Moresby and Tulagi, planned for early April, should be put off until May. By then Admiral Nagumo's carriers would again be ready to cover operations in an area where American carrier task forces might appear. Though not apparent at the time, this month was desperately needed by the Pacific Fleet.

It is even possible that the Lae-Salamaua raid, when combined with Halsey's raids in the Gilbert, Marshall, Wake and Marcus islands, brought Admiral Yamamoto and his Combined Fleet staff to the conclusion that the U.S. Pacific Fleet had to be lured into a showdown battle. Their projected plan to invade Midway seemed to be the vehicle to achieve this goal.[48]

With the recovery of the air groups on their return from the Lae-Salamaua area, TF 11 and TF 17 set course for their rendezvous with Crace's group at "Point Pig" (15°S, 159°E). Though occasionally "snooped" by unidentified planes, no Japanese counterattack developed. Without a carrier force in the area there was little they could do against the withdrawing Americans. On 14 March Admiral Crace's cruiser-destroyer force hove into sight, accompanied by the fleet oilers *Kaskaskia* (AO 27) and *Neosho*. Though steaming at economical speeds, both task forces were thirsty for fuel. During the next three days the oilers were drained, and provisions were distributed among the ships to enable all of TF 11 to make it back to Pearl. Aircraft were traded between *Lexington*'s squadrons and those of *Yorktown* so that the latter's pilots would be flying the best planes available. All of this activity took place while the two forces were steaming on a general northeasterly course. Admiral Brown commented in his action report:

> These issues were effected while under way at fifteen knots at times, in a moderate sea. I consider this transfer of stores at sea one of the finest exhibitions of resourcefulness and seamanship I have witnessed in my entire naval experience. The fact that Task Force ELEVEN has been able to operate at sea under war conditions for a period of nearly two months, away from any port, is a tribute to the intelligence, skill and seamanship of every officer and man in the force.[49]

As might be expected, all hands in both task forces were delighted to see mail bags had been brought by the oilers. Kinkaid's share of *Minnie*'s

---

[48] Lundstrom, *First South Pacific Campaign*, 27, 39; Lundstrom, *First Team*, 163–64; James H. and William M. Belote, *Titans of the Seas: The Development and Operations of Japanese and American Carrier Task Forces During World War II* (New York: Harper & Row, 1975), 62; RADM E. T. Layton, USN (Ret.) "Early Carrier Raids of World War II," Naval History Symposium Paper, Annapolis, MD, Sep 1983.

[49] CTF 11 Action Report, 23 Mar 1942.

trove included eleven letters from Helen, the last one dated 18 February. Not bad, given the fact that TF 11 had been at sea since 31 January. Tom's own letters, piling up in *Minnie*'s mail sacks, detailed his hardships of the last month. It had been hot constantly; the sea had been unsettling due to distant typhoons, and *Minnie* had plenty of roll built into her. The detailers at the Bureau of Navigation had gotten under his skin. His staff was a good one, young and anxious to please, but now the bureau wanted to send them to other duties. One can almost read the unwritten complaint, common to all commanders west of Pearl Harbor: "Don't they know there's a war on?" Fortunately CINCPAC did understand and Kinkaid's staff remained intact for another three months.

Helen's letters, although eagerly anticipated, also reminded Kinkaid of the burdens placed on his wife. His mother, now quite frail, continued to live alone in the Wyoming Apartments in Washington, but she needed more attention than Helen could provide from Philadelphia. Mrs. Kinkaid's sister, Fannie Marby Cassin, helped, but she too was long on years. Tom's older sister, Helen Heiner, had suffered a stroke and could do nothing; in fact, she was to die before TF 11 returned to Pearl. His younger sister, Dorothy Kimmel, could do little to assist their mother, so Helen Kinkaid and Aunt Fannie did their best, with occasional assistance from nieces and nephews when in the Washington area. Helen's mother, Mrs. Ross, was also having health troubles. Tom was as supportive as he could be through letters, but he suffered the same frustrations and guilt of anyone at war and away from their family. For both Helen and Tom there was the ultimate frustration—they were separated and getting no younger. This, of course, was true for everyone in America's armed forces in the early spring of 1942.

The return trip to Pearl Harbor was uneventful, but memorable. The task force had taken on provisions for forty-two days at sea, but the trip lasted almost eight weeks. The ships ran out of fresh vegetables and meats, and most of them almost exhausted their dry stores. Fortunately *Lexington* had taken on ninety days of dry stores and thus could provision the destroyers and help out with the cruisers. By 15 March all vessels in the force found it necessary to start reducing the daily ration for all hands. Between the tropical heat and the reduced rations, there was a general weight loss throughout the task force. Kinkaid rarely weighed himself, but his belt told him that he had lost a couple of inches off his waist. He summarized the shortages in *Minnie* a week before the force entered Pearl: "After this letter I will have left one air mail envelope and one sheet of paper and the Ship's Store is completely sold out. Fortunately I have enough soap and toothpaste to last and apparently cigarettes will hold out."[50] Finally on 26

---

[50] Ibid.; TCK to HSK, *Minneapolis*, 18 Mar 1942; TCK oral history, 142–43.

March TF 11 entered Pearl for a three-week rest and substantial repairs and refitting to its ships. During this outfitting period, Admiral Kinkaid would have a chance to review carefully his command experiences and try to deduce a few lessons that might make his next contact with the enemy even more successful. In his action report as Commander Task Force 11 Admiral Brown warned his superiors that carrier task forces were best used against Japanese naval forces and shipping, not against shore bases protected by land-based aircraft.

> Since carrier planes have shorter radii then [*sic*] shore-based planes, carrier attacks on enemy shipping in defended ports will be successful only when the attack arrives as a complete surprise to the enemy, and that even then, when surprise is successful the carrier will run serious risks of heavy attacks by surviving enemy planes. In other words the evergrowing importance and effectiveness of aircraft has not changed the old truism that ships are at a disadvantage in attacking strongly defended shore positions.[51]

Halsey's recommendations after attacking the Marshall Islands and now Brown's admonitions did result in more antiaircraft firepower being added to TF 11's ships. During this stay in Pearl Harbor, *Minneapolis*'s antiaircraft weapons were increased and their effectiveness upgraded by new automatic weapons directors and a new search radar.[52] *Lexington* underwent even more extensive modifications. Its four 8-inch gun turrets were replaced with numerous heavy-caliber automatic weapons and directors. The Southwest Pacific Area was a hostile environment for U.S. task forces, but technical changes in antiaircraft weapons, fire control directors, and search radars were improving the chances of survival for the carriers and their consorts. Within five weeks Kinkaid's cruisers would get their most severe testing to date.

---

[51] CTF 11 Action Report, 23 Mar 1942.
[52] Luey and Bruvold, *The "Minnie,"* 13–14.

Chapter 9

Action in the Coral Sea, May 1942

April and May had normally been happy months for the Kinkaids, with both their birthdays and their wedding anniversary to celebrate. There had always been presents and parties, but not in 1942. The task force had arrived at Pearl Harbor on 26 March and was due to stay in port almost three weeks. Kinkaid was bored and lonely, as were most of the several thousand that sailed with him in Task Force 11. While Oahu might have been a tropical paradise for the few who could afford to vacation there in prewar years, it was just an island without Helen as far as Tom was concerned.

The unexplained delays in the mail were frustrating. The Pan American clippers did not fly in either direction for ten days in early April; thus there was no air mail. Kinkaid continued to write every other day but he couldn't respond to Helen's letters, and his correspondence became repetitious and filled with trivia. His pay had now risen to $658 per month. The magazines that Helen had ordered for him were arriving: *Time, Life, Red Book, Reader's Digest,* and *Colliers.* He found that reading them, starting with the most recent, was as informative as starting with the oldest. Rear Admiral Jake Fitch was now his new boss. Vice Admiral Wilson Brown had given a farewell dinner at the Moana Hotel for his flag officers, staff, and captains. Kinkaid usually ate dinner in the captain's cabin of the *Minnie* because Captain Frank J. Lowry's wife was still in town and the captain went home every day. About every other day he and a few staff members took an afternoon swim on the Moana beach in Waikiki. *Minnie*'s wardroom gave a dance at the navy nurses' quarters, from 1700 till 2000, and he had enjoyed himself so much that he had stayed for the whole evening.

> It was a great success and there were no casualties in spite of the fact that the punch was well spiked. The nurses were a remarkably attractive group and not the type that we all expected. . . . I danced twice with the Chief Nurse who, while not exactly a riot, was a little less stiff-necked than most Chief Nurses.[1]

---

[1] TCK to HSK, Pearl Harbor, 1, 3, 5–6, 9 Apr 1942.

While TF 11 was being overhauled, Admiral Chester Nimitz and his staff were deciding how to use it during its next deployment. There was little doubt that it would be sent back to the South Pacific, probably to relieve Fletcher's TF 17, which was still cruising among the Fiji, New Hebrides, and New Caledonia islands. TF 11's orders would depend on what the combat intelligence units at Pearl Harbor, Washington, and Melbourne learned about Japanese intentions for the near future.

Much has been written about the Navy's radio communications intelligence operations during the war. At Pearl Harbor, in spaces adjacent to CINCPAC's staff, "Station Hypo," under the command of Lieutenant Commander Joseph J. Rochefort, worked furiously at trying to read Japanese radio communications traffic picked up by receivers in the islands. Similar work was performed in Washington at OP–20–G or "Station Negat" and in Melbourne (formerly "Station Cast" on Corregidor in Manila Bay). But Rochefort and the team he had assembled at Pearl Harbor became the most proficient in reading the Japanese naval codes. Information gleaned by Rochefort's crew went to Commander Edwin T. Layton, Nimitz's Fleet Intelligence Officer, to use in his daily intelligence briefings and estimates. This same information and any sent on from OP–20–G in Washington was used by CINCPAC's staff to prepare estimates of Japanese intentions and plans to thwart them.[2]

Where the Japanese would go and what they would do next were still being decided at the highest levels of the Japanese military staffs. The landings at Lae and Salamaua in early March were to be preliminaries to the capture of Port Moresby in New Guinea and Tulagi in the southern Solomon Islands. Both bases would be important for controlling the Coral Sea to the northeast of Australia's east coast. The Japanese anticipated that the Port Moresby operation would be as easy as the capture of Rabaul, but the American carrier raid against Lae and Salamaua convinced them that a strong force, including several aircraft carriers, would be necessary to ensure success. By mid-March 1942 the Port Moresby Operation (Operation Mo) was set for late May. In mid-April the Japanese planned the operations to follow the capture of Port Moresby. By then the *Kido Butai* had returned from its campaign of destruction against British bases and shipping in the Indian Ocean. Surfeited with successes since Pearl Harbor, the Japanese Combined Fleet and its leader Admiral Isoroku Yamamoto insisted that the next campaign be an

---

[2] W. J. Holmes, *Double-Edged Secrets: U.S. Naval Intelligence Operations in the Pacific During World War II* (Annapolis: Naval Institute Press, 1979), 57–73; Ronald Lewin, *The American Magic: Codes, Ciphers and the Defeat of Japan* (New York: Farrar, Straus, Giroux, 1982), 85–91; RADM Edwin T. Layton, USN (Ret.), with CAPT Roger Pineau, USNR (Ret.) and John Costello, *"And I Was There": Pearl Harbor and Midway—Breaking the Secrets* (New York: William Morrow, 1986), 357–82; Lundstrom, *First South Pacific Campaign*, 45–47, 75–77; Potter, *Nimitz*, 63–67. For the Coral Sea battle, see John Winton, *Ultra in the Pacific* (London: Leo Cooper, 1993), 32–48.

assault on Midway. The island would be useful for controlling the North Pacific, but more important, such an invasion would surely draw the U.S. Fleet into the showdown battle (and defeat) so necessary to force a successful conclusion to the Pacific war. In planning the Midway campaign, the Japanese strategists decided that Tulagi should be taken around 3 May and Port Moresby a week later.[3]

Using the minimum of hard data available and a lot of intuition, Admiral King warned Vice Admiral Leary and Rear Admiral Fletcher on 13 March that "enemy activities against Port Moresby and/or secure base sites in Solomon Islands are indicated as objectives."[4] By this date Rochefort's cryptanalysts were beginning to suspect that the Japanese were planning a new campaign. The movement of ships, air units, and personnel toward Truk and Rabaul suggested that something was brewing. A CINCPAC staff conference on 2 April decided that TF 11 should join TF 17 in the Coral Sea to oppose anticipated Japanese moves against New Guinea and the Solomons.[5] A week later Commander Layton provided Nimitz's staff with an intelligence briefing that also predicted the Japanese would attempt to capture Port Moresby sometime around the end of April. A few days later Rochefort responded to a formal request from Admiral King with an estimate similar to Layton's.[6] Given the closeness of Layton and Rochefort, one should not be surprised that their analyses were similar.

Finally on 22 April, a week after TF 11 had begun working its way to the South Pacific, Layton attended a CINCPAC staff conference that he described as "one of the most critical Cincpac staff meetings of the war."[7] Here he again stated with complete confidence that the Japanese would soon launch an attack in the New Guinea–New Britain–Solomons area. Layton's briefing and a detailed estimate of the situation (EOS), more than thirty pages in length, provided the basis for the staff decision to have TF 11 join TF 17 on 30 April and then position themselves in the Coral Sea to stop the Japanese. It was anticipated that Vice Admiral Halsey, with the *Hornet* (CV 8) and *Enterprise* task forces, would not be back from the Tokyo raid in time to join Task Forces 11 and 17. Because of their need to replenish at Pearl Harbor, the earliest they could arrive in the Coral Sea would be 13 May.[8]

---

[3] Samuel E. Morison, *History of United States Naval Operations in World War II*, vol. 4, *Coral Sea, Midway and Submarine Actions, May 1942–August 1942* (Boston: Little, Brown, 1949), 5–12; Lundstrom, *First South Pacific Campaign*, 65–74.

[4] COMINCH to COMANZAC and Commander Task Force (CTF) 17, 3/131535Z, Command Summary, 288.

[5] Command Summary, 2 Apr 1942, 308.

[6] Potter, *Nimitz*, 65–66; Holmes, *Double-Edged Secrets*, 66, 69–72; Lewin, *American Magic*, 90–91; Layton, *"And I Was There,"* 375–83.

[7] Layton, *"And I Was There,"* 390.

[8] Command Summary, 22 Apr 1942, 371–407; Lundstrom, *First South Pacific Campaign*, 83–86.

In preparation for the move south Admiral Fitch, now TF 11's commander, had Kinkaid spend four days in gunnery exercises with all of the vessels except *Lexington*. Temporarily organized as TF 2, the cruisers and destroyers fired away at rafts during the day and night. Cruiser SOCs were launched for inner air patrol around the task force, but they also spent time spotting the 8-inch fire against the rafts and towing sleeves for antiaircraft practice by all ships. Though the cruisers and destroyers seemed destined to serve only as antiaircraft defenders of the carriers, Kinkaid and Fitch recognized that their commands could get into a gunfire duel with the Japanese, and it was imperative that their captains be prepared.

On 15 April *Lexington* sortied from Pearl Harbor and joined Kinkaid's group at sea. Just prior to departure fourteen F2A–3 Buffaloes were hoisted on board to be flown to Palmyra by the Marine pilots of VMF–211. Once at sea the carrier's air group flew on board and the newly reformed TF 11 shaped course almost due south for Palmyra and Christmas islands.[9] Once the Marines were launched to Palmyra, Fitch's orders were to have TF 11 rendezvous with TF 1 in the vicinity of Christmas Island, some 450 miles to the southeast, and then engage in tactical exercises with the old battleships. This meeting might have been interesting for Kinkaid, but the rendezvous never took place. The Marines departed *Lexington* on the 17th and at 2315 the next day CINCPAC ordered TF 11 to head immediately toward Fiji and a rendezvous with TF 17. As yet there was no urgency in the orders; the task force was to proceed at an economical speed, which was 15 knots.[10]

Again Kinkaid settled into the routine of a south seas cruise. He stayed on the flag bridge most of the time because it was cooler than below, and it kept him close to communications. About the only times he went below were to eat and shower, and occasionally to wrestle with paperwork. From his space in *Minnie*'s superstructure he could see his boss in *Lex*, his other cruiser, the "No Boat" (*New Orleans* [CA 32]), and the seven destroyers that provided antisubmarine protection, antiaircraft firepower, and plane guard service when *Lex* was launching or recovering aircraft. In all the task force vessels' gunnery drills (without live firing) were carried out en route to the rendezvous. Zigzagging during daylight hours was standard, and SOCs were launched for close-in antisubmarine patrols. By the 19th, *Lex*'s SBD Dauntlesses (scout bombers) began distant patrols to 250 miles, and its fighters began tactical drills on a daily basis. Zigzagging also began around the clock. Though aircraft were launched and a high degree of readiness was maintained in each ship, the shellbacks did see that the fresh-caught pollywogs were properly initiated after TF 11 crossed the

---
[9] Commander Cruiser Division 6, War Diary, 1–15 Apr 1942, OA (hereafter COMCRUDIV 6, War Diary).

[10] Ibid., 17–18 Apr 42; Lundstrom, *The First Team*, 203–4.

equator on 21 April at 164°30′W. Most in the crews were old salts, but there were enough new arrivals to make for a lively day.

As usual there was little that Kinkaid could report to his wife, but he continued to write. One complaint that appeared regularly, besides the scarcity of incoming mail, was the problem of getting enough exercise. There wasn't enough space in a cruiser to get the sort of workout he craved. He loathed the boring "setting up exercises," but he feared he would be driven to them shortly. After a few days at sea he commented that all his rheumatism-type pains and sinus discomforts had disappeared, probably the result of sailing in warm, moist air. In his letter of 18 April Tom revealed that even flag officers when in Pearl Harbor were not always privy to Pacific Fleet operations. His ship had heard from an armed forces news broadcast that Tokyo had been bombed. He commented to Helen, "That is a good beginning and I hope will become a regular proceeding. It depends of course upon where the planes came from whether it can be frequently repeated. Perhaps the radio will tell us more about it today." Two days later he wrote, "The radio still does not give us full details of the bombing of Tokio. Of course we can guess a lot but we would like to know." Eventually Kinkaid and Helen both learned that sixteen B–25s, led by Lieutenant Colonel James H. (Jimmy) Doolittle from the flight deck of TF 16's *Hornet*, had bombed military targets in Tokyo and other areas. Then most had flown on to China where the crews were forced to crash-land or parachute from their planes into the darkness. It was an operation that cheered the American public and many like Kinkaid in the Pacific area, but the military cost would be brought home to Task Forces 11 and 17 in a very short time.[11]

The task force's first fueling rendezvous came on 24 April when the fleet oiler *Kaskaskia* and its destroyer escort, *Sims*, met TF 11 about 250 miles north of the Fiji Islands. The group crossed the dateline a few hours later while steaming westward at a leisurely refueling speed of 13 knots. Once all fuel tanks had been topped off, Admiral Fitch headed southwest toward the New Hebrides and the Coral Sea for a rendezvous with Admiral Fletcher and TF 17. During the morning watch on 1 May, *Yorktown* and TF 17 hove into sight. Six hours later the fleet oiler *Tippecanoe* (AO 21) and then the heavy cruiser *Chicago* and its escort, *Perkins*, joined the gathering as fueling again commenced in the vicinity of 16°S, 162°E (Point Butternut).

As May began, Admiral Fletcher's command expanded daily. Even before the rendezvous with Fitch's TF 11 Fletcher had radioed to CINCPAC his proposed organization of the enlarged Task Force 17, and then on 1 May he sent the organization to his commanders.

---

[11] TCK to HSK, *Minneapolis*, 18, 20, 22 Apr 1942; Morison 3: 389–98.

Task Force 17, Coral Sea Operation, 3–8 May 1942

Commander Task Force 17
RADM Frank J. Fletcher (Flag, *Yorktown*)

CTG 17.2 Attack Group RADM Thomas C. Kinkaid (Flag, *Minneapolis*)
    CTU 17.2.1 RADM Kinkaid
        Minneapolis (CA 36), *New Orleans* (CA 32)
    CTU 17.2.2 RADM William W. Smith
        Astoria (CA 34), *Chester* (CA 27), *Portland* (CA 33)
    CTU 17.2.4 CAPT Alexander R. Early
        Phelps (DD 360), *Dewey* (DD 349), *Farragut* (DD 348),
        Aylwin (DD 355), *Monaghan* (DD 354)

CTG 17.3 Support Group RADM John G. Crace, RN (Flag, HMAS *Australia*)
    CTU 17.3.1 RADM Crace
        HMAS *Australia* (CA), *Chicago* (CA 29), HMAS *Hobart* (CA)
    CTU 17.3.4 CDR Francis X. McInerney
        Perkins (DD 377), *Walke* (DD 416)

CTG 17.5 Carrier Group RADM Aubrey W. Fitch (Flag, *Lexington*)
    CTU 17.5.1 CAPT Frederick C. Sherman
        Lexington (CV 2)
    CTU 17.5.2 CAPT Elliott Buckmaster
        Yorktown (CV 5)
    CTU 17.5.4 CAPT Gilbert C. Hoover
        Morris (DD 417), *Anderson* (DD 411),
        Hammann (DD 412), *Russell* (DD 414)

CTG 17.6 Fueling Group CAPT John S. Phillips
    Neosho (AO 23) CAPT Phillips
    Tippecanoe (AO 21) CDR Atherton Macondray, Jr.
    Sims (DD 409), *Worden* (DD 352)

CTG 17.9 Search Group CDR George H. DeBaun
    Tangier (AV 8) CDR DeBaun
    VP–71, VP–72

SOURCE: CTF 17 to CINCPAC, 4/280925Z, Command Summary, 287, OA.

Other forces existed but were not always available to Fletcher as he waited at the eastern edge of the Coral Sea. Six-hundred-mile searches from Noumea to the northwest were carried out daily by Catalinas (PBY–5s) of VP–71 and VP–72, now under his tactical command. It was hoped that these patrols would spot any Japanese task forces that might round the southeast end of the Solomons chain. Using medium bombers (B–25s, B–26s) from Townsville, the Army Air Force searched about 300 miles to sea, but the Japanese were not really expected in that

NHC

Lieutenant Colonel James H. Doolittle, left, and Captain Marc A. Mitscher on board *Hornet* (CV 8) surrounded by some of the Army pilots who would participate in the historic bombing of Tokyo, April 1942.

area. Shuttling through Port Moresby from their heavy bomber base at Townsville, B–17s flew missions against Rabaul and other targets in New Britain and provided information about naval activity in the waters between eastern New Guinea and Rabaul. Unfortunately the B–17 crews were not skilled when it came to ship recognition.

Finally Australian medium bomber and patrol squadrons, flying Lockheed Hudsons and Catalinas and operating from Port Moresby, Tulagi, and other Australian bases, reported a steady flow of sightings as the Japanese Port Moresby Operation got underway. Although Admiral Leary, now Commander Naval Forces, Southwest Pacific Area, had promised to lend Fletcher maximum assistance, he could only request service from the Army and Australian squadrons, and those requests had to be routed through General Douglas MacArthur's headquarters, which was still in its shakedown phase in Melbourne.[12]

---

[12] COMANZAC to CTF 17, 3/130025Z, Command Summary, 287.

The combined task forces spent the first two days of May in fueling operations within a fairly limited area. By good luck, rather than good planning, they were not ambushed by enemy submarines, and their location and composition were not made known to the Japanese. By 2 May Japanese intelligence was estimating that only one American carrier force was in the Southwest Pacific. At Pearl Harbor Rochefort's code breakers were turning up steady information that confirmed their previous estimates had run hot and true. The Japanese were refining the broad outlines of the plan, and this information was radioed to Fletcher's staff. There was no doubt that the Japanese were aiming to take Port Moresby and a Solomon Island base, but the timing was still unknown. Anticipating the report of an action or sighting that would tell them when the Japanese would attack, the admiral held his forces just beyond the search radius of the Japanese patrol squadrons and kept his ships fueled to capacity.

On 2 May Fletcher decided to start moving. Incorrectly anticipating that it would take Fitch until 4 May to complete TF 11's fueling, he ordered Fitch to continue fueling and then move to a 4 May daybreak rendezvous at 15°S and 157°E. Here TF 17, TF 11, and Rear Admiral John Crace with *Australia* and *Hobart* would form the combined task force. With just *Yorktown* and TF 17, plus the oiler *Neosho*, Fletcher started moving slowly first south, then west, then in a northwest direction while sending planes 200 miles ahead to scout for enemy forces. Late the next day, 3 May, he received information based on a B–17 sighting that a Japanese invasion force had moved into Tulagi harbor on Florida Island, an Australian seaplane base across the sound from Guadalcanal in the southern Solomon Islands. Deciding to attack at dawn the next day, Fletcher sent *Neosho* and *Sims* to his previously arranged rendezvous with TF 11 to inform Fitch of the actions he was taking. He now wanted TF 11 and the Australian force to meet him at daylight on 5 May at 15°S, 160°E, oiler rendezvous Point Corn. Fitch's use of a fleet oiler as messenger was unusual, but he did not want to break radio silence, particularly since he was planning a surprise party for the Japanese at Tulagi. Some feel that he took an unnecessary risk in planning to attack the Japanese without assistance from TF 11. He could have sent the plan to *Lexington* by plane, but that would have necessitated a night flight to a carrier whose position was not precisely known. Fletcher probably considered the risk to be reasonable since no Japanese carriers were reported in striking distance of Tulagi.[13]

The Japanese force that *Yorktown*'s squadrons attacked at 0815 on 4 May was one of five forces that the Japanese had created to capture Tu-

---

[13] U.S. Naval War College, *The Battle of the Coral Sea, May 1 to May 11, inclusive, 1942: Strategical and Tactical Analyses*. NAVPERS 91050 [Microfilm] (1950), 30–31 (hereafter NWC, *Coral Sea*).

Action in the Coral Sea 183

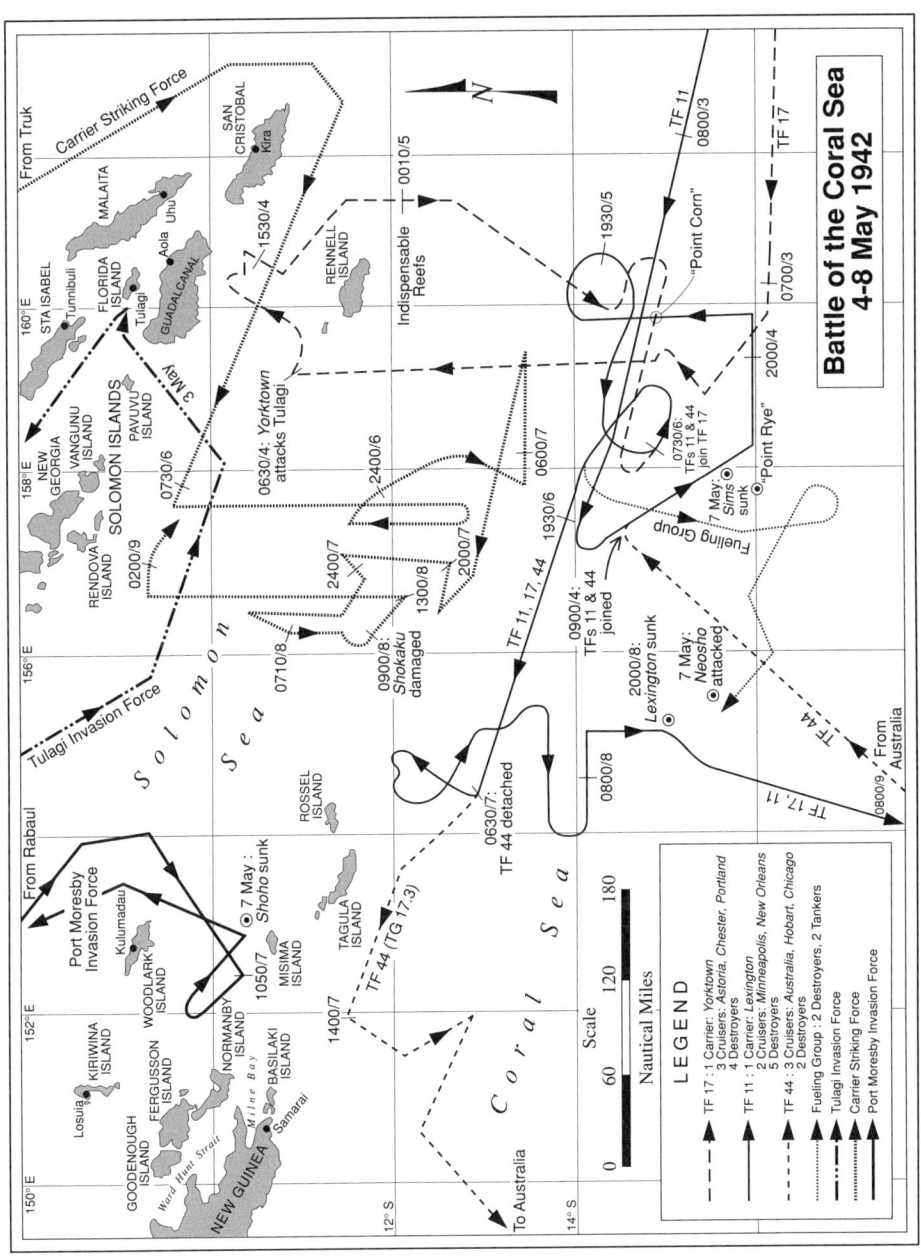

lagi and Port Moresby. Commanded by Rear Admiral Kiyohide Shima, the Tulagi Invasion Force consisted of a dozen light craft, the largest being the flagship minelayer *Okinoshima*. The Port Moresby Invasion Force, with Rear Admiral Sadamichi Kajioka commanding, centered on eleven transports carrying more than 4,500 army and special naval landing force troops plus a handful of naval auxiliary vessels. Direct escort for the transports was provided by Kajioka's command ship, the light cruiser *Yubari*, and six accompanying destroyers. Additional firepower for the Port Moresby Invasion Force came from a Support Force under Rear Admiral Kuninori Marumo, which had two light cruisers (*Tenryu*, *Tatsuta*), a seaplane carrier, and three gunboats. Commanding both invasion forces and a strong Covering Force was Rear Admiral Aritomo Goto in the heavy cruiser *Aoba*. In addition to his flagship, Goto had three other heavy cruisers (*Kako, Kinugasa, Furutaka*) and the light aircraft carrier *Shoho* with twenty-one planes aboard.

Although the naval strength of the three forces associated with the Port Moresby expedition was considerable (seven cruisers, eight destroyers, and a light carrier), it was not really prepared to defend itself against an attack by a carrier task force. To meet this contingency, Vice Admiral Shigeyoshi Inouye, the overall commander of Operation MO, convinced the Japanese high command that a striking force of two fast carriers should be added to his operation. Carrier Division 5 (*Zuikaku, Shokaku*), Cruiser Division 5 (*Myoko, Haguro*), six destroyers, and an oiler comprised the striking force. It was placed under the command of Vice Admiral Takeo Takagi, with Rear Admiral Tadaichi Hara directly commanding the carrier division. If concentrated, the Japanese would have had a powerful naval force to deal with any American interference; but concentrated they were not.[14]

Yorktown's squadrons achieved complete surprise when the SBDs from VS–5 and VB–5, each carrying a 1,000-pound bomb, screamed down in a dive bombing attack against the Tulagi beachhead. Following the SBDs came a dozen TBD (torpedo bombers) Devastators of VT–5, each packing an Mk 13 torpedo. Following their first attack, the squadrons returned to *Yorktown* for a reload and struck again. A third strike was launched at 1400, and on this one, four F4Fs went along to clear out a few seaplane fighters that had been reported in the area. Despite a Japanese antiaircraft barrage, American losses were light: two fighter planes lost, their pilots recovered; one TBD and crew lost; eight aircraft damaged by gunfire. Based on reports from his returning pilots Admiral Fletcher notified CINCPAC of these results:

---

[14] Ibid., 11–16; Dull, *Battle History IJN*, 118–20.

Positively sunk: two destroyers, four gunboats, one cargo ship

Beached and sunk: one light cruiser

Badly damaged: one light cruiser, one seaplane tender, one cargo ship, one transport

Aircraft destroyed: five seaplanes, one 4-engine flying boat[15]

The actual score was considerably lower: the destroyer *Kikuzuki* holed, beached, and sunk; two light minesweepers sunk; and the merchant minesweeper *Tama Maru*, damaged in the attack, sank a week later en route to Japan.[16]

In the three attacks *Yorktown*'s aircraft expended twenty-two torpedoes, seventy-six 1,000-pound bombs, and more than 82,000 rounds of machine-gun ammunition. Though applauding their fighting spirit, Admiral Nimitz suggested that *Yorktown*'s pilots needed some target practice.[17]

Task Force 11 and Admiral Kinkaid had no part in Fletcher's attack on Tulagi. At 0635 on 4 May *Neosho* and *Russell* fell in with TF 11 and informed Admiral Fitch of Fletcher's plan, then being carried out. Two hours later Admiral Crace joined TF 11 with *Australia, Hobart,* and *Whipple* (DD 217). The day was spent leisurely cruising on various courses that would allow TF 11 to rendezvous with TF 17 the next morning. It is unclear why Fitch did not move toward the northeast during the 4th so that he could provide emergency support to Fletcher's task force should it be needed.

For Kinkaid and most of the crews in TF 11 it was a particularly irritating day because *Neosho* was loaded with mail bags that weren't being transferred. Mail call finally came the next day when *Farragut* (DD 348) began shuttling guard mail and the U.S. mail between *Neosho* and the various vessels of TF 11. *Minnie*'s turn came around 1800 and Tom received six letters from Helen dated between 25 March and 8 April. There were other letters and a lot of second-class mail still on *Neosho* that, because of later events, were never delivered.[18]

Task Force 11 rendezvoused with Fletcher's TF 17 at about 0900 on the 5th and the usual fueling operations commenced. During that day and the next communications from Melbourne and Noumea informed Fletcher of the movements of the various Japanese forces. By the 6th it was clear that the Port Moresby invasion force would try to round the

---

[15] Command Summary, 4 May 1942, 435; ONI Combat Narrative: *Coral Sea*, 5–9.
[16] Morison 4:25–27; Dull, *Battle History IJN*, 121; Robert Cressman, *That Gallant Ship: U.S.S. Yorktown (CV 5)* (Missoula, MT: Pictorial Histories, 1985), 79–85.
[17] ONI Combat Narrative: *Coral Sea*, 5–9.
[18] TCK to HSK, *Minneapolis*, 9 May 1942; War Diary, *Minneapolis*, 5 May 1942; *Minneapolis* log, 3–5 May 1942.

eastern end of New Guinea and head for its destination on the 7th or possibly the 8th. At 0735 on the 6th Fletcher signaled Operation Order 2–42 to all ships and established a single TF 17. Meanwhile, Admiral Takagi's Striking Force had sailed to the southeast along a course north of the Solomons. It rounded San Cristobal Island around 1900 on the 5th and spent the 6th not too distant from TF 17. Neither Fletcher nor Takagi was aware that they were within 70 miles of each other during the evening of the 6th. As the historian Morison has noted, had Takagi or Fletcher sent out scouts in the correct directions, the Battle of the Coral Sea would have occurred two days earlier.[19]

By noon on 6 May Fletcher had begun clearing his task force for action at any time. *Neosho* and *Sims* were detached and sent to fueling rendezvous Point Rye (16°S, 158°E) to be available there on the 7th and subsequent odd-numbered days, and at Point Corn (15°S, 160°E) on even-numbered days. Inner antisubmarine warfare patrols were being flown by the cruiser aircraft, and intermediate ASW patrols likewise came from the cruisers. A carrier air patrol was either in the air over the task force or fighters were warmed up and ready for launch, and scouts were searching far ahead for enemy forces. Contact with the Japanese Striking Force was almost made in the morning of the 6th. Because the task force was snooped several times during the day, Fletcher had to assume the Japanese knew his position. Fortunately the long-range flying boats that found TF 17 were not reporting directly to Admiral Takagi's Striking Force. The contact reports were not relayed by Admiral Inouye's Fourth Fleet in Rabaul until they were too late to be useful.[20]

At dawn on 7 May TF 17 was approximately 115 miles south of Rossel Island, the easternmost of the Louisiade Archipelago and about 210 miles east of the tip of New Guinea. The Port Moresby Invasion Force, its Support Force, and the Covering Force had by this time arrived in the area between Misima Island and Woodlark Island, about 125 miles northwest of Rossel Island. At dawn the Striking Force bore about 210 miles due east of TF 17.

Yorktown had the duty for advanced scouting and sent ten SBDs from VS–5 to search 250 miles between compass bearings 325 degrees and 085 degrees, roughly from the northwest, through north, to the east. At the same time Admiral Takagi ordered the Striking Force to concentrate its search to the south. Unfortunately the *Yorktown* scout assigned to search a bearing of 067 degrees was forced to return to the carrier due to bad weather. It is possible that, had he persisted, he would have located the Striking Force's two carriers, *Shokaku* and *Zuikaku*.[21] But at 0735 another

---

[19] Morison 4:28–32; NWC, *Coral Sea*, 15.
[20] Morison 4:33; NWC, *Coral Sea*, 8–11.
[21] NWC, *Coral Sea*, 53–54.

Yorktown scout radioed TF 17 that he had sighted two heavy cruisers at 10°40′S, 153°15′E, steaming at 12 knots on course 310 degrees. At almost the same time one of the Striking Force scouts spotted *Neosho* and *Sims* and reported them as a carrier and cruiser.[22]

Admiral Takagi ordered full deck-load strikes launched immediately from his two carriers against the American "carrier and cruiser." Between 0900 and 1200 the Japanese attacks pounded the two luckless ships. *Sims* was sunk first and then the dive bombers turned *Neosho* into a floating shambles. Because her fuel tanks were almost dry, the oiler wouldn't sink. Four days later a destroyer out of Noumea located the hulk, rescued the 123 survivors from both ships, and gave the sturdy *Neosho* a decent burial. The loss of these two vessels actually served TF 17 well. Had those two deckloads of attack aircraft been directed at *Lexington* and *Yorktown* while their forces were attacking to the north, the consequences could have been tragic for the Pacific Fleet. When the radio came in disclosing the loss of *Neosho* and *Sims*, the war diarist in Pearl Harbor wrote into the Grey Book (Command Summary), "The loss of a new tanker makes the fuel supply to forces in that area more difficult than ever. And the loss of a DD, when we are already very short of that type in the Pacific, is a hard blow indeed."[23]

Because of the distance from TF 17 to the 0735 contact, Fletcher held his attack squadrons at their blocks on board *Lex* and *Yorktown*. At 0815 another *Yorktown* scout reported that it had sighted two carriers and four heavy cruisers at 10°3′S, 152°27′E. The distance between the two contacts was around 70 miles. After continuing north for another hour at 20 knots, *Lexington* began launching its squadrons at 0926, and *Yorktown* began at 0944. The morning scouts were then recovered and it was discovered that the 0815 report had been in error: he had seen two old cruisers and two gunboats, no carrier. Like Admiral Takagi, Fletcher had apparently sent a massive strike to swat some flies. The decision was made to let the strike continue in the hope that it would stumble on the main invasion force. Some comfort came at 1022 when MacArthur's headquarters radioed that at 0748 a B–17 had bombed an enemy fleet at 103°34′S, 152°36′E, just north of the Jomard Passage through the Louisiades. This fleet consisted of one carrier, sixteen warships, and ten transports, close enough to the 0815 combat report that TF 17's squadrons could hardly miss sighting them.[24]

Up to this point Kinkaid and his cruisers were simply "conforming to the movements of *Lexington*," as *Minnie*'s log book read. Although he was

---
[22] Ibid., viii.
[23] Command Summary, 6 May 1942, 442; Morison 4:33–37.
[24] NWC, *Coral Sea*, viii, 55–58; Morison 4:40.

not invited on board *Yorktown* to confer with Fletcher and Fitch about battle plans, it took no stretch of imagination to realize that TF 17 would soon encounter the enemy. During this approach to battle *Minneapolis* occupied its usual position, broad on *Lexington*'s starboard bow, bearing 045 degrees at 3,000 yards from the carrier. At this time the two carriers were operating together, and all cruisers and destroyers formed a circular screen around the two. In theory any torpedo plane approaching the formation would be forced to fly directly (or almost so) at a screening cruiser or destroyer to reach the carriers inside the circle. Such an approach offered at least one ship the opportunity to fire without deflection at the attacker, thus increasing the likelihood of bringing it down. The circular screen also allowed the guns on the unengaged (inside) side of the screening vessel to concentrate on the dive bombers that might be simultaneously attacking with the torpedo planes.[25]

Kinkaid's role as an unengaged observer continued throughout the daylight hours of 7 May. Along with everyone else in the task force he waited eagerly by the radios for information from *Lexington*'s and *Yorktown*'s aircraft. Just after 1100, VB-2's leader sighted the light carrier *Shoho* and the battle began. Within forty minutes the ninety-three attacking aircraft had finished off *Shoho* and Lieutenant Commander Robert E. Dixon's jubilant report, "Scratch one flat-top," excited the task force into believing that a major naval victory was at hand. Later analysts, far removed from that corner of the Pacific Ocean, would wonder if a few of the attackers' torpedoes and 1,000-pounders could not have been directed at some of the escorting cruisers and destroyers, or at the transports. When Admiral Fitch and other air admirals reviewed the results, the decision was made to designate a strike leader in the future who would "direct traffic" and see that more than one ship received the aviators' attention.[26]

By 1400 the attack on *Shoho* was history, and the aircraft from the strike had been recovered. During the early afternoon another portion of TF 17 came under vigorous attack, this time Admiral Crace and his Task Group 17.3 (*Australia, Chicago, Hobart, Perkins, Walke,* and *Farragut*). Fletcher had detached Crace at 0625 that morning to head northwest and intercept any Japanese ships attempting to penetrate or round the Louisiades. Without air cover and operating within 100 miles of land, Crace's ships were in serious danger from land-based Japanese aircraft as well as whatever *Shoho* might send. At 0815 the force was snooped by a twin-float Japanese seaplane and later overflown by two groups of U.S. Army aircraft out of Australia.

---

[25] NWC, *Coral Sea*, 123.
[26] Ibid., 55–58.

Finally at about 1400 eleven single-engine land-based Nell bombers attacked. A second assault followed, consisting of twelve twin-engine Bettys carrying torpedoes. Crace's small task group repulsed or destroyed all attacking aircraft; no hits registered on TG 17.3. A third attack now came from nineteen Nells flying at high altitude. Again, as in the previous attacks, nimble maneuvering and a curtain of shrapnel frustrated the Japanese, though they did straddle *Australia* with a 500-pound bomb pattern. A final attack came at 1457, a few minutes after the previous three. This time Crace's tormentors were three U.S. Army B–26s from Townsville who unsuccessfully tried to blast *Australia* with five bombs. The Army Air Corps commander in *Australia*, Major General George H. Brett, vigorously denied the attack, but a *Farragut* photographer had the evidence on film. With the attacks defeated and the invasion force withdrawing toward Rabaul, TG 17.3 remained south of the Louisiades until midnight, then turned to Sydney for a spot of rest and recreation for the crews.[27]

Although the attacks on TG 17.3 had little tactical significance—except to those who sweated through them—it does appear that the Japanese had early reported these ships as a carrier, battleship, and cruiser force. This misidentification resulted in the Japanese shore-based squadrons concentrating on Admiral Crace's TG 17.3 and leaving *Lexington* and *Yorktown* safe while blowing *Shoho* out of the water. This error was like the one committed by Admiral Takagi's Striking Force with similar results.[28]

Throughout the 7th Admiral Fletcher recognized that more damage could be done to the Japanese forces to the north, but he had not located the Striking Force and its two carriers. Attack groups were spotted on the flight decks of *Lex* and *Yorktown*, but Fitch held them in place, waiting for a report on the Japanese. But nothing came in during the afternoon of the 7th. Takagi's force was too far north and west for the Catalinas out of Noumea to spot it, and almost 300 miles beyond the usual search radius for the Army Air Corps planes operating out of Townsville.[29] With weather deteriorating and the likelihood that any strike launched against the Japanese would have to be recovered at night, Fletcher kept his CAP aloft but decided that he would wait until the next day to seek further action with the Japanese.

Task Force 17's commander might have decided to wait until 8 May to engage the Japanese, but Admiral Takagi had other ideas. Although his information was faulty concerning the location of the American carriers,

---

[27] Ibid., viii–ix; Morison 4:37–39; Wesley Frank Craven and James Lea Cate, eds., *The Army Air Forces in World War II*, vol. 1, *Plans and Early Operations, January 1939 to August 1942* (Chicago: University of Chicago, 1948), 450.
[28] Lundstrom, *First Team*, 240.
[29] NWC, *Coral Sea*, 105a.

the admiral pressed his carrier force commander to seek action that afternoon. At 1600, estimating Fletcher's force to be at least 300 miles to the west, Admiral Hara launched a strike force of fifteen "Kate" torpedo planes (Nakajima Type 97) and twelve "Val" dive bombers (Aichi Type 99) from *Shokaku* and *Zuikaku*. The distance to TF 17 was actually closer to 200 miles, but Fletcher's carriers were under an overcast and operating in and out of local squalls. Given this overestimation Hara's attackers never sighted TF 17 as they flew outbound on a course of 277 degrees, but they were picked up on the task force radars. At about 1800 Wildcats from *Lexington* and *Yorktown* intercepted the Japanese attacking force and commenced destroying it. Mostly Japanese dive bombers were engaged and they proved easy targets. Eight dive bombers and one torpedo plane were shot down. By 1815 the Japanese decided to abort the mission, dump their bombs and torpedoes, and return to their carriers. Then an incident occurred that left a deep impression on Tom Kinkaid.

One group of Japanese torpedo planes that had overflown TF 17 set a return course to their carriers that had them recross Fletcher's force. Since it was about 1900, murky, and after sunset, the Japanese mistook TF 17's carriers for their own. Kinkaid had just finished a quick dinner brought to his emergency cabin on *Minneapolis*'s bridge. Standing outside with a few others, he observed a group of aircraft cross the task force and turn into *Lexington*'s landing circle. At the last second the planes were recognized as Japanese. *Lexington*, *Minneapolis*, and others in the force opened fire. None of the Japanese were shot down, but there were plenty of surprised people on both sides. The Japanese did, however, radio a report of TF 17's position to Takagi's force. Fletcher and Takagi each considered a night cruiser-destroyer attack, but abandoned the idea in favor of morning aircraft strikes.[30]

While Admirals Fletcher and Takagi groped for one another during the daylight hours of 7 May and three forces were brought under attack, a plethora of information was bombarding Commander Fourth Fleet Admiral Inouye in Rabaul—a good deal of it wrong. Most important, the Japanese scouts and four-engine snoopers had given the impression that three American carrier task forces were at sea. Admiral Crace's cruiser-destroyer force was described at one time as having a carrier and a battleship; *Neosho* and *Sims* had been described as a carrier and battleship force; only TF 17, which had battered *Shoho*'s force, was correctly identified as a carrier task force.

Given these reports in the morning, Inouye ordered his Port Moresby Invasion Force to pull back to the north until the Japanese had won con-

---

[30] TCK, "Four Years of War," 96–100; Lundstrom, *First Team*, 263–74; Morison 4:43–45.

trol of sea and air along the invasion route.³¹ By midday Admiral Takagi knew that *Neosho* was not a flat-top, but somehow this vital information failed to reach the Fourth Fleet commander, his superior in Rabaul. And by nightfall Inouye still believed that there were two carrier forces, totaling two or three carriers, to the west of Takagi's Striking Force. With *Shoho* gone, and the invasion force standing to the north, Admiral Inouye at 2300 rescheduled the landing at Port Moresby for 12 May. He hoped that by that time his plan of hammering the Americans with land-based bombers and *Shokaku*'s and *Zuikaku*'s air groups would have cleared the way for a successful completion of Operation Mo.³²

During the night of 7 May Fletcher and Fitch decided that dawn searchers would be launched to cover 360 degrees because it was possible that the Japanese could have passed them to the south. It was *Lexington*'s duty day for searches, so Captain Ted Sherman ordered VS-2 to use twelve planes to comb the northern sectors to 200 miles and VB-2 to send six planes to search the less likely area 150 miles to the south. More certain of the general area where the Americans might be and wanting to save as many planes as possible for an attack force, Admiral Hara sent just seven planes to search the area between 140 and 230 degrees to a distance of 250 miles from the Striking Force. *Lexington* launched its searches at 0625, the Japanese at 0600. For Kinkaid and the crew in *Minneapolis* this was to be a very long day.³³

The battle that developed in the Coral Sea the morning of 8 May 1942 was early described by the Office of Naval Intelligence as "the first major engagement in naval history in which the issue was decided without surface ships having exchanged a shot." The writer of the 1943 Combat Narrative which dealt with the Battle of the Coral Sea further noted, "It was purely an air action, with each opponent seeking to gain the upper hand by depriving the other of naval air support. Adding to the novelty was the fact that both forces sought to accomplish the same thing at the same time by the same means."³⁴

The parallel activity that had begun with the morning launches of search aircraft continued two hours later when both forces were sighted. At 0820, Lieutenant (jg) Joseph G. Smith of *Lexington*'s Scouting Two broke radio silence and electrified Fitch's flag bridge: "Contact, 2 enemy CVs, 4 CAs, many DDs, bearing 006 degrees, distance 120 miles from Point Zed, course 120, speed 15." To save time Smith sent his message by voice and uncoded. It undoubtedly electrified the Japanese as well to

---

[31] Lundstrom, *First South Pacific Campaign*, 108; NWC, *Coral Sea*, 172–73.
[32] Lundstrom, *First South Pacific Campaign*, 110; NWC, *Coral Sea*, 78.
[33] TCK, "Four Years of War," 100; Lundstrom, *First Team*, 279–80.
[34] ONI Combat Narrative: *Coral Sea*, 1.

know they had been spotted. "Point Zed" was a map reference point to be used to avoid giving the Japanese the location of the American task force. Actually the Striking Force was 175 miles distant from TF 17 on bearing 028 degrees.[35] A few minutes after Lieutenant Smith's sighting report a Japanese scout from *Shokaku* located the American carriers and radioed their position; this report was intercepted by *Yorktown*'s radio operators. Thus both sides knew they could expect attacks that morning.[36]

Admiral Kinkaid in *Minneapolis* probably got his first indication that action was imminent when the carriers turned into the wind and *Yorktown* commenced launching its strike force at 0900, followed by *Lex* at 0907. The two air groups took departure from the area at 0925. To protect the task force, about half of the fighter planes in each carrier's squadrons remained behind for CAP duty. Admiral Fitch ordered the fighter coverage supplemented with eight SBDs each from VS–2 (*Lexington*) and VS–5 (*Yorktown*). It was hoped that the SBDs, although not in a class with the Wildcats, could intercept the attacking torpedo planes while F4Fs took on the Japanese dive bombers.[37] On board all ships, of course, a condition of full readiness for immediate action was maintained. Finally, Admiral Fletcher passed tactical command of the force to Fitch at 0908.

This first carrier-against-carrier battle opened at 1057 when *Yorktown*'s dive bombers dove on *Shokaku* and ended about fifty minutes later when *Lexington*'s squadrons began withdrawing. In that period almost every bomb carried to the scene of action was directed toward *Shokaku*, with her sister ship, *Zuikaku*, receiving very little attention. Despite this concentration and heavy damage from three bomb hits, *Shokaku* survived and eventually returned to the Kure shipyard for repairs. *Zuikaku* was undamaged, but her squadrons were so badly decimated that she was out of action for several months. Because of the visible fires and smoke, the pilots returning to *Yorktown* and *Lex* reported that *Shokaku* was "settling fast" at the conclusion of their attacks.[38]

About twenty minutes after *Shokaku* had been attacked by *Yorktown*'s squadrons, Fletcher's task force was put to the test. Arriving en masse, the aircraft from the Striking Force completely concentrated their attacks on the two American carriers. At the beginning *Yorktown* and *Lexington* were at the center of a circle of destroyers and cruisers, of which *Minneapolis* was a part, but this single formation quickly broke into two groups as the carriers began maneuvering independently. As each carrier desperately strove to evade attacking dive bombers and torpedo planes, its 30-knot

---

[35] Lundstrom, *First Team*, 281, 284.
[36] Ibid.
[37] ONI Combat Narrative: *Coral Sea*, 28; Sherman, *Combat Command*, 84, 86.
[38] Morison 4:51–52.

twists and turns were matched by the cruisers and destroyers normally associated with that carrier. *Lex*'s screen now consisted of cruisers *Minneapolis* and *New Orleans,* and destroyers *Morris, Anderson, Phelps,* and *Dewey.*

Tom Kinkaid had an unobstructed view of the attacks.[39] With Admiral Fitch now in tactical command of both carriers and their screens, Kinkaid became little more than a two-starred passenger in Captain Lowry's *Minneapolis.* He later wrote:

> My flagship, the heavy cruiser Minneapolis, was with the Lexington group and our station was on the northern side of the circle, from which direction the Jap planes approached. We had a ringside seat for a remarkable performance lasting only 9 or 10 minutes but seemingly much longer. Strangely enough, we in the Minneapolis were not greatly concerned about our own ship, although the Jap torpedo planes flew at us and around us and over us. We know that, in the circumstances, the carrier was the logical target, not the vessels of the screen. We knew that, but the thought crossed my mind that possibly all the Jap pilots did not know it and I watched with apprehension a plane which headed for us at low altitude and then zoomed up and past our stern to drop its torpedo at the Lexington.[40]

During the seventeen minutes the task force was under attack (1116 to 1133), Kinkaid remained on *Minnie*'s bridge. Wearing what he called his "tin hat," he observed the attempts of the screening vessels to destroy the attackers with antiaircraft fire. Long after the action, when asked about being on the bridge during an air attack and whether he had experienced fear, he remembered, "You haven't got time to emote.... There isn't time.... A commanding officer... may be scared—in fact, if he has sense, he's scared—but he can't show it, with all the men around."[41]

From his observation post he saw *Minnie*'s gunners shoot down at least four aircraft as the attackers passed over or around the cruiser en route to the carrier. Captain Lowry believed two torpedoes had been aimed at his cruiser, but both had been evaded. *New Orleans* had less luck with its gunfire; it bagged none of the Japanese planes. Although *Dewey* had knocked down at least one plane, it was heavily strafed and bombed. Fortunately no direct hits were made with bombs, but the crew suffered five casualties from the strafing. Most of the vessels in the screens had also received gunfire, including 5-inch, from the ships around them.[42]

Though damage to the ships and personnel of the screen was light, the same could not be said for the carriers. Kinkaid's cruiser was close

---

[39] Combat Narrative: *Coral Sea,* 25–6; Edwin Hoyt, *Blue Skies and Blood: The Battle of the Coral Sea* (New York: Paul S. Ericksson, 1975), 104–8.
[40] TCK, "Four Years of War," chap. 5, 106.
[41] TCK, *Oral History,* 157.
[42] ONI Combat Narrative: *Coral Sea,* 35–37; TCK, "Four Years of War," 106–7; Hoyt, *Blue Skies,* 105–6.

enough to *Lexington* that he could see and hear the results of the attacks. Nine years later he wrote:

> From the Minneapolis, about 2,000 yards away, the situation did not look good. We had heard the thu-u-u-mp of too many bombs and the deeper tone of the torpedoes exploding under water against her sides. I turned to look at the Yorktown and as my glance fell upon that ship a huge column of smoke and flame shot up from her port side amid ships. She, too, began to turn in tight circles and I walked into the chart house to consult the chart. If Fletcher and Fitch were to be out of the picture, command would devolve upon me and I wanted to know what course was best "to get the hell out of there," as the saying goes.[43]

What the admiral had heard were two torpedoes ripping the port side of *Lex* and five bombs of various sizes blasting the flight deck and internal areas of the ship. Yet despite these wounds the vessel's list was soon corrected and flight operations continued. On board *Yorktown* a single 800-pound bomb had penetrated the flight deck and exploded deep within the carrier. Although casualties were heavy, flight operations there also remained uninterrupted.

At 1247, as Admirals Fletcher and Fitch were reviewing the situation and considering another strike against the Japanese carriers, *Lexington* suffered a massive gasoline explosion below the hangar deck level. It appeared for a time that the carrier might be saved, and, incredibly, enough control existed to recover a large portion of its aircraft as they returned from battle. But the damage was terminal. By 1415 further explosions and spreading fires forced *Lex*'s crew to concentrate on saving the ship rather than launching further flight operations.

Admiral Kinkaid in *Minneapolis* and the rest of the *Lexington* screen continued to follow the carrier's increasingly erratic movements as the fires ate away at the ship's communication and control systems. Earlier *Lex*'s flag hoist had informed the task force that the ship had been torpedoed, then at 1445 that "this ship has had a serious explosion." At 1452 the carrier's signalmen bent on the message, "stand by, this ship needs help." Admiral Fletcher quickly directed the destroyers *Phelps*, *Morris*, and *Anderson* to render what assistance they could to Captain Sherman. But at 1538 the ominous signal snapped out that the fires were out of control. Unable to conduct further offensive operations and having informed CINCPAC that he was pulling back, Fletcher now had to worry about being attacked while others tried to manage the catastrophe on board *Lexington*.

---

[43] TCK, "Four Years of War," 108–9.

Before explosions and fires had terminated *Lexington*'s ability to launch aircraft, Fletcher had ordered a large number of its planes transferred to *Yorktown*. By merging the remnants of the two air groups, he hoped to have enough planes to attack the remaining Japanese carrier (if it remained in the area) the next day. But consultation with Admiral Fitch and some second thoughts by his staff revealed that the task force could do little more than defend itself. There simply were not enough fighter aircraft to defend the force and also escort a strike against the Japanese. Furthermore with *Lexington* no longer able to operate aircraft and with *Yorktown*'s forward elevator damaged, it was obvious that TF 17 could not meet *Zuikaku*'s air groups on equal terms. And if there was a possible third Japanese carrier present, as many believed, Fletcher could lose his whole force by seeking further battle. Given this situation, Fletcher divided his task force at 1601. Kinkaid was ordered to take *Minneapolis, New Orleans, Hammann, Anderson,* and *Morris* and stay with *Lexington*, which was now dead in the water. He was to provide protection and fire-fighting assistance. If the carrier had to be abandoned, Kinkaid was to manage the rescue operation. Fletcher and the rest of TF 17 pulled away a few miles and prepared to repel a possible second Japanese attack. Fortunately the Japanese had decided to return to Rabaul and Truk.[44]

By 1600 preparations had begun among Kinkaid's vessels to receive the crew of *Lexington* once the order to abandon ship was given. All ships put cargo nets and lines over their sides and lowered available boats. The general plan was that the destroyers would close the carrier to retrieve whoever was in the water; then the bulk of those picked up would be transferred to the cruisers. At 1610 *Lex*, using her own boats, began transferring the wounded to *Minneapolis* on the starboard quarter and to *New Orleans* off the port bow. For an hour the crew of the carrier gradually assembled on the flight deck while the wounded were transferred. Finally at 1706 *Lexington* gave the dreaded signal: "I am abandoning ship." A few minutes earlier, Admiral Fitch had leaned over the side of the flag bridge and called down to Captain Sherman, "Well Ted, let's get the men off." With that, an amazingly orderly abandonment of the furiously burning carrier began.

From his perch in *Minneapolis* Kinkaid choreographed the rescue operation. *Morris* had been sent alongside *Lex*'s starboard (lee) side to help with fire fighting. Now the crew packed in as many men as possible and then moved to *Minnie*'s starboard side and unloaded all but the number that could be accommodated for several days. *Morris* then returned to *Lex*

---

[44] Commander Task Group (CTG) 17.2 [Kinkaid] to CTF 17 [Fletcher], "Report of Loss by Fire of USS *Lexington*," 24 May 1942, WWII Action Reports, OA; Command Summary, 8 May 1942, 452; Lundstrom, *First Team*, 352–59; Sherman, *Combat Command*, 88–91; Hoyt, *Blue Skies*, 127–44.

to pick up a few more from the port (windward) side and moved to join the *Yorktown* group. *Morris*'s skipper, Commander Harry B. Jarrett, displayed superb seamanship and courage maneuvering *Lex*'s lee. Not only was he aware that the carrier's munitions could momentarily explode and take the destroyer down with it, but he also had to work his ship constantly to prevent crushing men in the water between the hulls of the two vessels. Once Jarrett backed *Morris* clear of *Lexington*, Commander Arnold E. True brought *Hammann* in to take its place. True had been filling his destroyer with men from *Lex*'s stern. Now on the starboard side *Hammann* quickly filled to its limit and stood clear. While still within a ship's length of the carrier, *Hammann* and most of the other vessels in the operation were showered with burning debris from a particularly violent explosion on *Lexington*. As *Morris* and *Hammann* worked in the carrier's lee, Lieutenant Commander John K. B. Ginder in *Anderson* worked the port and then starboard sides of *Lex*. These three destroyers were joined by *Dewey* (Lieutenant Commander Charles F. Chillingworth) and then *Phelps* (Lieutenant Commander Edward L. Beck). When the last man was plucked from the water, 2,685 members of *Lexington*'s crew had been rescued, and no one alive was left behind in the carrier or the sea. The last three to leave *Lex* were a Marine orderly; Commander Morton T. Seligman, the executive officer; and last of all, the skipper, Captain Sherman. Admiral Fitch and his staff had left earlier by ship's boat to *Minneapolis.*

Now empty, fires and explosions brilliantly illuminated *Lexington*'s burning hulk. Having been previously instructed by Admiral Fletcher, at 1853 Kinkaid directed *Phelps* to give "Lady Lex" a coup de grace with torpedoes. After four shots and one dud the carrier turned over to port and sank just before 2000. She rests in 2,400 fathoms at 15°12′S and 155°27′E.[45]

During the rescue operation Fletcher had time to decide on his next course of action. With his remaining carrier damaged and possessing a melange of crippled squadrons from both flat-tops, it was unlikely that *Yorktown* could be an effective fighting ship. And three cruisers and four destroyers were almost immobilized by overcrowding from *Lex*'s crew. In this situation Fletcher could see no reason to question Admiral Nimitz's order to withdraw from the Coral Sea. Furthermore the *Yorktown* task force had been in the South Pacific Area since 16 February and a return to Pearl was badly needed by ships and men alike. So the task force headed south during the night of 8–9 May and then pulled around to the southeast late in the morning watch. Although every turn of the ships' screws made it less likely that TF 17 would again come under attack, Fletcher knew that it was too early to sound "all clear."

---

[45] CTG 17.2 to CTF 17, 24 May 42; TCK, "Four Years of War," 111–5; Sherman, *Combat Command*, 89–92; Johnston, *Queen of the Flat-Tops*, 252–64; Hoyt, *Blue Skies*, 147–61.

Lexington (CV 2) burns while being abandoned after the Battle of the Coral Sea, 8 May 1942. Destroyers *Morris, Anderson* and *Hammann*, and cruiser *Minneapolis* stand by.

Morning searches were launced northward and one of the planes reported an enemy carrier force about 175 miles northwest and in hot pursuit. Dauntlesses were armed and sent unescorted to attack the Japanese carrier. With only thirteen fighters available, all were held to defend TF 17. As an extra safety measure Fletcher sent his staff gunnery officer in one of VS–5's Dauntlesses to Rockhampton, Australia, 350 miles to the west. This emissary was to ask General MacArthur to order a strike against the Japanese by bombing squadrons under his command. Fletcher sent the plane in order to maintain radio silence.

The task force remained at general quarters and moved south at 25 to 27 knots until it was concluded that the morning searchers had mistaken surf pounding over Lihou Reefs for enemy vessels. Then at 1630 the ships slackened speed. By then the destroyer skippers were becoming concerned about their fuel shortages. For the rest of the 9th and until around 1630 on the 10th, when fueling operations began, the destroyer captains reported their fuel status to the flagship every four hours, a significant departure from the usual daily reports.[46]

---

[46] TCK, "Four Years of War," 115–16; Morison 4:60–61; Lundstrom, *First Team*, 360–61.

The fueling plan that Kinkaid signaled to the cruisers required first-class seamanship. Time was at a premium because of fuel shortages in the destroyers, and it was necessary to redistribute *Lexington*'s survivors and get the wounded into better sick quarters. It was therefore decided to refuel the destroyers and make personnel transfers at the same time and at night. At 1647, on a signal from *Minneapolis*, the cruisers *Portland* (CA 33), *Chester, Minneapolis,* and *New Orleans* formed a line abreast on course 220 degrees at 8 knots. Destroyers then moved alongside each cruiser and fueling began at 1700. *Russell* refueled from *Minnie* at the same time 173 survivors were transferred to the destroyer by way of coal bags. In all seven destroyers were fueled and several hundred men were redistributed from the cruisers. The entire operation had been accomplished at night without lights, and with the danger of a sudden submarine attack always present. Kinkaid's later comment is understandable: "I was much pleased by the smooth handling of the ships and gear, and much relieved when the somewhat difficult operation was completed."[47]

In *Minneapolis* every effort was made to make the survivors comfortable. Where possible men and officers from the various divisions in *Minnie* shared their spaces and personal gear with similar groups from *Lex*. Kinkaid shared his cabin with Jake Fitch, Captain Lowry took in Ted Sherman, the signalmen and quartermasters found their opposite members, and so it went down to "black gangs" (engine and fire room ratings) on both vessels. Lowry overlooked restrictive regulations and opened up *Minnie*'s small stores so that the survivors could receive a minimum bag of replacement clothing. The editor of *Minnie*'s newspaper, with assistance from *Lex*'s newspaper staff, put out a special eight-page edition for the carrier's crew. The cover carried the Concord and Lexington Minute Man superimposed on a silhouette of *Lexington*, plus the modified Latin quote, *Sit Tibi Mare Levis*—"Light lie the sea upon thee." Captain Sherman wrote for all of the survivors: "I have never experienced such hospitality and warm-hearted treatment as we have received on the U.S.S. *Minneapolis*. I speak for all of us from the *Lexington* in saying we are deeply grateful. Our sorrow at the loss of our ship is softened by the reception we have received."[48]

On 11 May Fletcher again divided his force. Kinkaid was to take *Minneapolis, New Orleans,* and *Astoria* plus four destroyers to Noumea. Here he would land *Lexington*'s healthy survivors who were going home on leave. He was to shift the seriously injured to *Astoria* for further transfer to the hospital ship *Solace* (AH 5), then in Tongatabu. The wounded would be

---
[47] TCK, "Four Years of War," chap. 5, 116; VADM William W. Smith, *Midway: Turning Point of the Pacific* (New York: Crowell, 1966), 48–49; Morison 4:60.
[48] Johnston, *Queen of the Flat-Tops*, 269–73.

transferred dockside in Noumea to avoid the rigor of shifting them while underway. Once *Minneapolis* and *New Orleans* had landed their *Lexington* personnel, Kinkaid was to take the two cruisers plus the destroyers *Phelps, Worden,* and *Dewey* and steam north to a rendezvous with TF 16. Here he would come under Vice Admiral Halsey's command.[49]

Although the Battle of the Coral Sea was "something to write home about," Tom Kinkaid followed the censorship rules. Thus his letters disappointed Helen, particularly since the American newspapers were trumpeting that the Navy had won a great victory. However, Tom did include hints. The day after the battle he commenced his letter, "I brought this letter up to the bridge four days ago and I just now am getting down to writing you. . . . They have been full four days." He mentioned several times that Jake Fitch was on board, "as are many others." He had been sharing his cabin with Jake since the 8th. Upon arrival in Noumea on the 12th he sent a cablegram to Helen: "Well and happy. Tom." Though no geographical location was given, the *sans origine* in its place told Helen that her husband was on a French island, and she correctly deduced it was French New Caledonia. The cable arrived on her fiftieth birthday, 13 May.

If Admiral Kinkaid was aware that he had been in a history-making naval engagement, he didn't reveal it in his letters. Nor did his action reports, written several weeks after the battle, suggest that the 7th and 8th of May might have a dramatic effect on the course of the war. The impression from his postwar writing, his oral history, and the war diaries of his command and flagship *Minneapolis* is one of retreat from the Coral Sea. The loss of *Lexington* (and earlier *Neosho* and *Sims*) had cast a pall over TF 17 that was difficult to dispel. Certainly Admiral Nimitz's ebullient message, "Congratulations on your glorious accomplishments of the last two days," must have boomed hollowly in Frank Jack's ears.[50]

Yet the Battle of the Coral Sea deserves a place of prominence in the history of World War II in the Pacific. The Office of Naval Intelligence, in its 1943 Combat Narrative *The Battle of the Coral Sea,* a classified pamphlet written to provide naval officers with an accurate account of major naval operations, described the battle as "a victory with decisive and far-reaching consequences for the Allied cause."[51] Seven years later a research team at the Naval War College studied the battle in great depth and commented on the different ways one could interpret the action.

> Victories at sea are not necessarily always based on ships lost or tactical successes gained. They are more often based upon the effect such losses

---

[49] TCK, "Four Years of War," chap. 5, 117; Smith, *Midway,* 48–49.
[50] Potter, *Nimitz,* 75–76.
[51] Combat Narrative: *Coral Sea,* 46.

or tactical successes may have upon ultimate victory; upon the extent to which such losses or tactical successes contribute to the accomplishment of the strategical plan.

The War College study concluded that, from an American viewpoint, the battle had been a tactical loss but a great strategic victory because "the Allies by the Coral Sea action had succeeded in checking further Japanese advances by sea in the New Guinea–Solomons area. This was a cardinal objective in the allied strategical plan for the Pacific War."[52]

In his action report of the battle on 8 May Kinkaid made ten recommendations without assigning priority. The majority dealt with defense of a task force against aircraft attack. Along with practically every ship captain writing an action report the admiral said that antiaircraft gunfire needed improvement. The weapons available in the screen—5-inch, 20mm, .50 caliber, and 1.1s—had demonstrated that they could bring down torpedo planes, but "it is vitally important that all machine gun crews be thoroughly trained and experienced." It was also important that all equipment be tested and in top operating condition before action. The need for remote direction of the 1.1 and 20-mm batteries by automatic (radar) directors was also specified in many of the action reports. The 5-inch batteries were valuable in bringing down a torpedo plane before it reached a normal drop point, but they trained too slowly in tracking fast-moving aircraft. Against dive bombers the 5-inch guns had been almost useless.[53]

While Kinkaid was still learning the lessons of defending a force with gunfire, those in the carriers recognized that the best defense of a carrier task force came from its aircraft. Admiral Fitch and Captain Sherman pointed out that their carriers needed larger fighter squadrons and better fighter aircraft. These improvements would allow more planes in the task force CAP and give them a better chance of repulsing or destroying an incoming raid. Although no one criticized individual fighter-director officers in the carriers, it was recognized that better fighter direction might have prevented the loss of *Lexington*. The Japanese were first picked up on the radar at 68 miles, but they were not intercepted until almost within 5-inch gun range. The twenty or so fighters available to meet the enemy were too few, they lacked the military performance necessary to intercept in a timely manner, and they had been held too close to the carriers for effective defense. Since the radar on the ships did not give altitude readings in 1942, there was no way to accurately direct the fighters to the Japanese planes. Given these developments, it was inevitable that the air defense of the task force was above it rather

---

[52] NWC, *Coral Sea*, 113–14.
[53] CTG 17.2 to CTF 17, "Action Report: Battle of the Coral Sea," 28 May 1942, WWII Action Reports; ONI Combat Narrative: *Coral Sea*, 35–37, 46–47.

than at 30 or 40 miles distance. It was likewise inevitable that enemy dive bombers or torpedo planes would hit both carriers. Because VF–2 and VF–42, supplemented by the SBDs from VS–2 and VB–2, proved unable to repel the attacks, it was only nimble maneuvering of *Yorktown* and Captain Elliot Buckmaster's superb shiphandling that saved that carrier from *Lexington*'s fate.[54]

Once Kinkaid's TG 17.2 had landed *Lex*'s survivors in Noumea and replenished its fuel and stores, it was time to move on. Admiral Halsey had left Pearl on 30 April with *Enterprise* and *Hornet*, too late for the Battle of the Coral Sea but spoiling for a fight. His TF 16 was scheduled to meet Kinkaid's cruiser force on the 16th north of the New Hebrides Islands. On the 14th Halsey changed the rendezvous to a point farther north and well within the search radius of Japanese seaplanes flying out of Tulagi and Makin. Kinkaid did not like being within attack range of Japanese land-based squadrons, but Halsey was calling the shots. Kinkaid might have felt more comfortable as he steamed north had he known that CINCPAC, using TF 16, was playing a game of bluff with the enemy. Originally Halsey had been positioned to break up an anticipated Japanese attempt to capture the two British guano islands, Ocean and Nauru. Later Nimitz decided that simply allowing TF 16 to be spotted in the target area would be enough to cause the Japanese force to withdraw, particularly since it was unaccompanied by aircraft carriers. Once his force was spotted, Halsey was instructed to head east, out of range of Japanese observation.

On the 15th, still steaming northward, Kinkaid intercepted a CINCPAC message to Halsey informing him that his force had been snooped and his position accurately reported to Rabaul. Halsey of course knew he had been sighted and his own Japanese-language specialists had given him the content of the Japanese contact report. A second report from Pearl notified Halsey that the snooper had now reported that the task force was headed east. On hearing this report, Kinkaid ordered *Minnie*'s helmsman to turn to course 090 degrees. A few minutes later Halsey instructed Kinkaid to head east for a new rendezvous. Once spotted, Halsey no longer worried about radio silence.[55]

The next morning, 16 May, Kinkaid's cruiser force joined the TF 16 screen and came under the direct command of Rear Admiral Raymond A. Spruance. *Vincennes* was added to Kinkaid's charges, now TG 16.2.2. Spruance commanded not only the screen, but also TG 16.2.1, *Northampton, Salt Lake City* (CA 25), and *Pensacola*, plus a handful of destroy-

---

[54] CTF 11 to CINCPAC, 5/112100Z, Command Summary, 463; ONI Combat Narrative: *Coral Sea*, 26; Sherman, *Combat Command*, 117; Lundstrom, *First Team*, 310–17.

[55] TCK, "Four Years of War," 125–9; TCK oral history, 162–65; Lundstrom, *First South Pacific Campaign*, 150–58; Potter, *Bull Halsey*, 72–77.

ers. The force remained east of the New Hebrides, replenished from an oiler on the 18th, and then turned north for Pearl Harbor. Having intercepted Admiral Inouye's order canceling the occupation of Ocean and Nauru islands, Admiral Nimitz felt comfortable in recalling TF 16. His only caveat to Halsey was to make sure he was not spotted leaving the area. CINCPAC wanted the Japanese to continue believing that they had sunk *Yorktown* as well as *Lexington* and that *Hornet* and *Enterprise* were operating in the South Pacific. Perhaps this belief would make them less cautious in their approach to Midway.[56]

Once TF 16 turned north and shaped course for Pearl Harbor, it would take eight or nine days to arrive. Halsey saw this as a time to sharpen the skills of the squadrons in *Enterprise* and *Hornet*, so on nonduty (flying searches and CAP) days the squadrons engaged in gunnery and air-to-air combat exercises. Ironically these exercises cost *Enterprise* six lost or damaged fighter aircraft in just two days of drills.

The trip back to Pearl gave Kinkaid a chance to catch up on his reports, do some recreational reading, and relax after the tension of combat operations. Gladney and Taylor, his flag secretary and flag lieutenant, gathered materials for the action reports and drafted parts of them, but the final reports are clearly based on Kinkaid's observations. Once he had caught up on his sleep, Tom considered himself reasonably healthy. As he explained it to Helen, "Perhaps it is the vitamin B, or the sunshine or the fresh air; but whatever it is, I manage to keep in good shape except that I am soft as mush."[57] He was a bit concerned with his waistline, but figured he could swim it off once he was in port. His reading included Gifford Pinchot's travel odyssey, *To the South Seas* and *Mr. Churchill* by Phillip Guedalla. The last three letters to Helen, before arrival at Pearl Harbor on 26 May, were written on official bond because the ship's supply of air mail stationery and stamps had been exhausted. With everything running out, including the crews' patience about the lack of recreation ashore, everyone was relieved to reach Pearl. But time on the beach would again be brief for there were battle clouds boiling up to the northwest.

---

[56] Lundstrom, *First Team*, 372–74; Potter, *Bull Halsey*, 76.
[57] TCK to HSK, *Minneapolis*, 15 May 1942.

Chapter 10

Midway, June 1942

While Task Forces 11 and 17 were defeating the Japanese thrust at Port Moresby in the Battle of the Coral Sea, the staff of the Commander in Chief, Pacific Fleet turned to the basic question, What would the Japanese do next? The Commander in Chief, U.S. Fleet had regularly radioed warnings from Washington that New Caledonia, Fiji, and Samoa were vulnerable to attack. Loss of these bases could be devastating to the line of communication to Australia,[1] and Admiral Nimitz had kept task forces in the South Pacific area to meet threats to these strategically vital bases. But by the first part of May the cryptanalysts of Station Hypo were beginning to assemble a different interpretation of Japanese intentions. As they saw it, the enemy was now aiming at Midway.[2]

Unknown, of course, to Commander Rochefort and his colleagues was the fact that the Japanese naval high command had heatedly quarreled about future operations, but by 5 April had accepted Admiral Yamamoto's plan to have the Combined Fleet capture Midway. Exhibiting symptoms of what Japanese writers later diagnosed as the "victory disease," the Japanese opted for the Midway plan, starting the many logistical activities to support it before the forces had set sail for Port Moresby. Yamamoto's objective was to provoke the Pacific Fleet to battle and then smash it. Once the fleet and its carriers were destroyed, Yamamoto was sure the Americans would seek a negotiated settlement.[3]

By the time Kinkaid and Halsey's TF 16 reached Pearl Harbor, Nimitz and his staff were committed to the premise that the Japanese would launch an assault against Midway, probably commencing in the early light of 4 June. It had taken the first two weeks of May to convince Admi-

---

[1] Command Summary, 6 Feb 1942, 209; Buell, *King*, 170–71, 188–89; Buell, *Quiet Warrior*, 98–99.
[2] Holmes, *Double-Edged Secrets*, 85–89; Layton, "*And I Was There*," 405–406; Lewin, *American Magic*, 94–105; Potter, *Nimitz*, 78–82; Winton, *Ultra in the Pacific*, 49–58.
[3] U.S. Naval War College, *The Battle of Midway, Including the Aleutian Phase, June 3 to June 14, 1942: Strategical and Tactical Analyses* [Microfilm] (1948), 3 (hereafter NWC, *Midway*); Mitsuo Fuchida and Masatake Okumiya, *Midway: The Battle that Doomed Japan* (Annapolis: Naval Institute Press, 1955), 60–61, 245–48; John Costello, *The Pacific War* (New York: Wade Publishers, 1981), 214–21; Layton, "*And I Was There*," 406–13; Lundstrom, *First South Pacific Campaign*, 45–7; Dull, *Battle History IJN*, 134; Spector, *Eagle Against the Sun*, 150–56.

ral King that the code-breakers were not wrongheaded or being cleverly misled. By the 17th CINCPAC's war diarist could report, "COMINCH substantially agrees with the estimate of CINCPAC of present enemy intention. . . . Steps were taken to organize a force for the defense of Alaska and to expedite the return of Task Forces 16 and 17."[4] Following a visit to Midway early in May Nimitz had started a flow of Marines; munitions; antiaircraft guns; and Navy, Marine, and Air Corps aircraft to build up the island's defenses. On the 14th, at the direction of Admiral King and Army Chief of Staff Marshall, CINCPAC announced a "state of fleet-opposed invasion," which effectively placed all military resources within the Hawaiian area under his command.[5] On the 16th Nimitz ordered Halsey and Fletcher to bring their task forces to Pearl Harbor as quickly as possible. Finally on 21 May Nimitz created TF 8, to be commanded by Rear Admiral Robert A. (Fuzzy) Theobald. Two heavy cruisers, *Indianapolis* and *Louisville*; two light cruisers, *Honolulu* (CL 48) and *St. Louis* (CL 49); and five destroyers were sent to Alaskan waters with Theobald. There he found the light cruiser *Nashville* and eight more destroyers. This destroyer-cruiser force, assigned submarines and smaller surface craft plus two squadrons from Patrol Wing Four, made up the North Pacific Force, Theobald's administrative command.[6]

While Halsey's task force was anchoring in Pearl Harbor, Nimitz's staff completed a sixteen-page estimate of the situation. Developed many years before at the Naval War College, this formal planning document was structured to encourage a commander's staff to examine a problem from all sides. By carefully inventorying and evaluating the military assets of the enemy, particularly those forces that could play a role in a battle, a staff was forced to plan realistically. The EOS of 26 May clearly revealed that the Japanese forces being assembled for an assault against Midway would far outnumber those that CINCPAC could muster to oppose it. Not only were ships counted, but a frank evaluation of quality was also made. Concerning carrier aircraft, for example, the EOS stated, "Their planes are, generally speaking, of greater range than ours. The fighters out-perform ours. . . . They have amply demonstrated their ability to use their carrier air with great ability. We can no longer under-estimate their naval air efficiency."[7]

---

[4] Command Summary, 16–17 May 1942, 482–83; Potter, *Nimitz*, 78–84; Layton, "*And I Was There,*" 418–30.

[5] Stetson Conn, Rose C. Engelman, and Byron Fairchild, *United States Army in World War II: The Western Hemisphere: Guarding the United States and Its Outposts* (Washington: Office of the Chief of Military History, 1964), 221 (hereafter Conn, *Guarding the US*).

[6] Morison 4:83.

[7] Command Summary, "Estimate of the Situation, 26 May 1942," 508.

Because American forces would be inferior to the enemy's, the EOS spelled out the required tactics:

> Not only our directive from Commander-in-Chief, U.S. Fleet, but also common sense dictates that we cannot now afford to slug it out with the probably superior approaching Japanese forces. We must endeavor to reduce his forces by attrition—submarine attacks, air bombing, attack on isolated units. The principle of calculated chance is indicated, as set forth in a letter of instructions [on 21 May] to Task Force Eight. If attrition is successful the enemy must accept the failure of his venture or risk battle on disadvantageous terms for him.[8]

Once TF 16 arrived at Pearl, it quickly became evident that the stay in port would be brief. Because of the high level of readiness being maintained almost all personnel were being held on the base or on board their ships. But the returning crews from TFs 16 and 17 were allowed daylight liberty. Nimitz knew that many of them had been at sea for almost three months and morale had to be a concern for all commanding officers.

There was a noticeable improvement in Kinkaid's disposition when he found six letters from Helen waiting. He was pleased that his wife had solved a serious problem that had nagged at him since leaving the East Coast. His mother's health had been declining alarmingly, and she was no longer able to care for herself in the Wyoming apartments. Nursing assistance was both scarce and expensive. Helen and Tom's sister, Dorothy Kimmel, had finally been able to arrange for her admission to a nursing home in Washington, the Home for Incurables. Despite its ominous name Mrs. Kinkaid would receive excellent care. The trip to Washington to make arrangements meant that Helen also saw many of their friends and was able to pass along the latest information and gossip. Flag selections, new assignments, conditions of health, and marital fidelity among their friends and acquaintances all found their way into Helen's correspondence. Because she was reading first-class newspapers, there was also news from abroad, particularly in Italy. A certain self-congratulatory tone often crept into the admiral's replies: "Herbert Matthews' article on Italy was very interesting and very sound. It is not difficult for you and me to understand what he is talking about [but] the average reader will not get it all by a long shot."[9]

That first day in port resulted in a shift in command that took many by surprise. Admiral Halsey had a severe case of dermatitis that covered his body. The medical staff in *Enterprise* (the *Big E*) had been able to do little for him; hospitalization was needed. Halsey suggested to Admiral

---

[8] Ibid., 520.
[9] TCK to HSK, Pearl Harbor, 26, 27 May 1942.

Nimitz that Rear Admiral Raymond Spruance, his cruiser screen commander, be given the command of TF 16. He was not concerned about Spruance's lack of aviation experience because his own staff would stay with *Enterprise*. Nimitz accepted the recommendation and Spruance immediately shifted his flag from *Northampton* to the *Big E*. He brought his own flag lieutenant with him, Lieutenant Robert J. Oliver, and Halsey's (Lieutenant William H. Ashford) stayed ashore with his boss. Kinkaid now took charge of the cruiser screen assigned to TF 16. For the second time he would be working with two carriers, *Enterprise* and *Hornet*, but this time he would be going into battle with them.[10]

The next day, 27 May, Kinkaid and the rest of the flag officers plus a few Army generals received their formal introduction to the problem at hand.[11] The Japanese attack on Midway would be a major effort and, in the Japanese tradition, fairly complicated. One segment would make a diversionary attack against the Aleutians or western Alaskan bases, probably on 3 June. Carrier Division Four (*Ryujo* and *Junyo*) plus cruiser-destroyer forces would be in this segment. Admiral Theobald was to meet this attack with assistance from the Eleventh Air Force units that were within range. The assault on Midway would come from three different groups: the Carrier Striking Force was expected to have at least four carriers, possibly five, and the usual cruiser-destroyer screen; the Midway Occupation Force would consist of battleships, cruisers, destroyers, and a transport group, but the exact numbers and types were not definite; and the Main Body was expected to consist of battleships, cruisers, destroyers, and possibly another carrier. The Japanese forces would far outnumber anything Nimitz could organize by early June to meet them. The Pacific Fleet had only two significant advantages: Midway itself could be used as a stationary aircraft carrier with plenty of patrol, attack, and bombing aircraft to throw at the advancing Japanese; and the Pacific Fleet, through superior communications intelligence, knew the enemy plans and could make dispositions in advance to counter them.[12]

Nimitz's battle plan was fairly simple. He would retain broad tactical direction of all forces in the Midway area, but allow considerable freedom of action to the carrier task force commanders and Captain Cyril T. Simard, the commanding officer of the Naval Air Station, Midway.[13] To detect the incoming Japanese early enough to concentrate his forces against them, starting on 30 May PBY Catalina patrols were to be flown

---

[10] Buell, *Quiet Warrior*, 119–22; Potter, *Bull Halsey*, 78.
[11] Command Summary, 27 May 1942, 543–44.
[12] Morison 4:74–93.
[13] VADM E. P. Forrestel, *Admiral Raymond A. Spruance, USN: A Study in Command* (Washington: Naval History Division, 1966), 35.

to 700 miles from Midway in sectors from 200 to 020 degrees. To protect against forces that might approach from the Marshall Islands, 500-mile patrol sectors were ordered from the air station on Johnston Island, about 700 miles southwest of Pearl Harbor.[14] In addition to aerial patrols Nimitz's staff also provided for submarines to defend Midway. The nineteen boats that Rear Admiral Robert H. English, Commander Submarine Force, Pacific Fleet, could muster were placed on bearings from the southwest to north about 150 miles from Midway. Their task was to scout for the Japanese, report them when sighted, and then attack. Four subs were held back from the Midway patrol force and positioned to the north of Oahu in order to provide warning should a portion of the Japanese force approach Hawaii from that direction.[15]

Finally Nimitz set an ambush for the unsuspecting Japanese. Task Force 16 (Spruance) with *Enterprise* and *Hornet* and TF 17 (Fletcher) with *Yorktown* were directed to lie in wait about 200 miles northeast of Midway. Cruising on the flank of the approaching Carrier Striking Force, the three American flat-tops would be in the optimum position to launch a surprise attack once the Japanese were located. The key to the ambush was to find the enemy Striking Force before its commander realized that there were American carriers at hand.

Despite their expectation of achieving tactical surprise the stakes were exceptionally high for both Nimitz and Fletcher, the admiral in tactical command. The Japanese had to be met, but the Pacific Fleet could not afford to trade losses with them on a ship-for-ship basis. The enemy's forces had to be whittled down by attrition tactics consisting of submarine and Midway-based aircraft attacks, and then they had to be destroyed by the squadrons from TF 16 and TF 17.

In his Operation Plan 29–42 dated 27 May 1942, Nimitz set the tasks and assigned the forces to accomplish them, but in his personal letters of instruction to Spruance and Fletcher, and to Theobald a week earlier, the admiral set the limits to which they could go in risking their forces.

> In carrying out the task assigned in OP Plan 29–42, you will be governed by the principle of calculated risk, which you will interpret to mean the avoidance of exposure of your force to attack by superior enemy forces without good prospect of inflicting, as a result of such exposure, greater damage to the enemy.[16]

---

[14] NWC, *Midway*, 50.
[15] Ibid., 62, 66–67; Clay Blair, Jr., *Silent Victory: The U.S. Submarine War Against Japan*, 2 vols. (Philadelphia: Lippincott, 1975), 1:211–13, 217.
[16] Morison 4:83–84; Potter, *Nimitz*, 87; Buell, *Quiet Warrior*, 123–24; Forrestel, *Spruance*, 38; Walter Lord, *Incredible Victory* (New York: Harper & Row, 1967), 35–36; Gordon W. Prange, with Donald M. Goldstein and Katherine V. Dillon, *Miracle at Midway* (New York: McGraw Hill, 1982), 98–100.

Task Forces 16 and 17, Midway Operations, 4 June 1942

Commander Task Force 16
Raymond A. Spruance (Flag, *Enterprise*)

CTG 16.2 Cruiser Group RADM Thomas C. Kinkaid
    CTU 16.2.1 CAPT William D. Chandler
        Northampton (CA 26) CAPT Chandler
        Pensacola (CA 24) CAPT Frank L. Lowe
        Atlanta (CL 51) CAPT Samuel P. Jenkins

    CTU 16.2.2 RADM Thomas C. Kinkaid
        Minneapolis (CA 36) CAPT Frank J. Lowry
        New Orleans (CA 32) CAPT Walter S. DeLany
        Vincennes (CA 44) CAPT Frederick L. Riefkohl

CTG 16.4 Destroyer Screen CAPT Alexander R. Early
    Phelps (DD 360), *Worden* (DD 352), *Monaghan* (DD 354),
    Aylwin (DD 355), *Balch* (DD 363), *Conyngham* (DD 371),
    Benham (DD 397), *Ellet* (DD 398), *Maury* (DD 401)

CTG 16.5 Carrier Group CAPT George D. Murray
    Enterprise (CV 6) CAPT Murray
    Hornet (CV 8) CAPT Marc A. Mitscher

CTG 16.6 Oiler Group CAPT Ralph H. Henkle
    Platte (AO 24) CAPT Henkle
    Cimarron (AO 22) CDR Russell M. Ihrig
    Dewey (DD 349), *Monssen* (DD 436)

Commander Task Force 17
RADM Frank J. Fletcher (Flag, *Yorktown*)

CTG 17.2 Cruiser Group RADM William W. Smith
    Astoria (CA 34) CAPT Francis W. Scanland
    Portland (CA 33) CAPT Laurence T. DuBose

CTG 17.4 Destroyer Screen CAPT Gilbert C. Hoover
    Hammann (DD 412), *Morris* (DD 417), *Russell* (DD 414),
    Anderson (DD 411), *Hughes* (DD 410), *Gwinn* (DD 433)

CTG 17.5 Carrier Group CAPT Elliott Buckmaster
    Yorktown (CV 5) CAPT Buckmaster

SOURCES: Forrestel, *Spruance*, 248–50; Commander Cruisers, TF 16 to CTF 16, "Report of Action, 4 June 1942, Battle of Midway," 11 Jun 1942, OA; Commander Cruisers, TF 17 to CINCPACFLT, "Report of Action, 4 June 1942," 12 Jun 1942, OA.

In private oral instructions to Spruance, Nimitz went even further. If the issue was in doubt, Spruance was not to risk his force. It would be better to withdraw and let Midway be taken. The Japanese would not be able to hold it, and the Pacific Fleet could retake it at a future date.[17]

Task Force 16 was scheduled to sortie the next morning, but first Kinkaid called his wife in Philadelphia. They had concluded that it was worth the expense, about $15.00, for him to telephone her occasionally. As before, the call was carefully monitored, and it was irritating to be interrupted several times when the conversation strayed onto forbidden topics. Operations, ship names, and even the mention of senior commanders were all to be avoided at the risk of a disconnect. A few days later Tom wrote, "I am still enjoying having talked to you over the telephone. It is nice to hear your voice and helps to reduce the feeling that we are so far from each other."[18]

Zero hour for TF 16's sortie was set for 28 May at 2030Z (Greenwich Civil Time), which was 1100 Hawaiian Daylight Saving Time. The destroyers would move out at minus one hour (1000); Kinkaid's cruisers would weigh anchor at zero hour and sortie at five-minute intervals. *Minneapolis* would lead the way. Finally, at zero plus 35 minutes, *Enterprise* and *Hornet* would head for sea. Five hours later, at 21°N and 158°40′W, the two air groups would rendezvous with their carriers and once on board proceed to the Midway area.[19] Fletcher's TF 17 was expected to depart Pearl two days later, depending on repairs to *Yorktown*.

One of the ironies concerning the Battle of Midway is the number of flag officers on each side. Counting only those Japanese surface forces directly involved in the attack on Midway, Admiral Yamamoto brought sixteen flag officers (including himself) to command aspects of the operation. Among the sixteen were one admiral, two vice admirals, and thirteen rear admirals. In contrast there were only four American flag officers at sea for the battle, all of them rear admirals.

Once the air groups were on board *Enterprise* and *Hornet*, Spruance had TF 16 shape course for its ambush station, about 350 miles northeast of Midway. For the first two days long-range air searches from Oahu covered the area ahead of the force so only intermediate and inner air patrols were flown by carrier and cruiser aircraft. On the 31st, now beyond practical coverage by remaining Oahu PBYs, *Enterprise* launched searches to 200 miles by its scout bombers. As the duty carrier for the day it also sent aloft Fighting Six (VF–6) for the combat air patrol over the task force. That same day TF 16 fueled from its two oilers. It would be the last

---
[17] Buell, *Quiet Warrior*, 121.
[18] TCK to HSK, Minneapolis, 29 May 1942.
[19] CINCPAC to CTF 16, 5/280105Z, Command Summary.

opportunity for the carriers and cruisers to replenish their bunkers before meeting the Japanese. In fact it would be six days before *Cimarron* (AO 22) and *Guadalupe* reappeared with badly needed fuel. On 2 June, during the forenoon watch, two SBDs from *Yorktown* buzzed TF 16 and dropped instructions to Spruance for a rendezvous with Fletcher's TF 17 later that day.[20] At 1630 the bridge watch on board *Minneapolis* informed Kinkaid that TF 17 was in sight to the southeast. Now that the two task forces were together, a seemingly interminable period of waiting began.

Early that day Admiral Spruance sent the ships in his task force blinker messages about the operation they were undertaking. Although Kinkaid and the other flag officers already knew the plans, not all of the commanding officers did. So that everyone, including the crews, would understand clearly that a battle was at hand, Spruance signaled:

> An attack for the purpose of capturing Midway is expected. The attacking force may be composed of 311 combatant types including four or five carriers, transports and train vessels. If presence of Task Force 16 and 17 remains unknown to the enemy we should be able to make surprise flank attacks on enemy carriers from a position northeast of Midway. Further operations will be based on results of these attacks, damage inflicted by Midway forces, and information of enemy movements.

In one of the grandest understatements in a career filled with them, the admiral concluded his signal, "The successful conclusion of the operation now commencing will be of great value to our country."[21] No one could guess how important this battle would be, but Kinkaid and his fellow flag officers did understand that the stakes were very high.

Though a rendezvous at Point Luck (32°4′N, 172°45′W) had been effected, Fletcher as senior officer present took no action to combine the two task forces into a single tactical unit. He had good reasons for his decision. Most obvious was the fact that Fletcher and Spruance had never worked together when each was in command of a carrier task force. During the previous five months Fletcher had commanded a carrier task force, but Spruance had been a cruiser group commander. More important, Admiral Halsey's staff, now working for Spruance, ran his operations quite differently from Fletcher's and, at the time, there were no mandatory fighting instructions for carrier task forces in the Pacific Fleet. This lack would be remedied in a few weeks, but on 2 June each admiral managed his task force as he saw fit.

There was a reason for this apparent tactical anarchy. To date task force commanders and carrier captains were undecided about the best

---

[20] Lundstrom, *First Team*, 404.
[21] Forrestel, *Spruance*, 39–40; Morison 4:98–99.

tactics for protecting their carriers when under air attack. Some believed that evasive maneuvering was the most effective way to avoid enemy dive bombers and torpedo planes. For such activities flat-tops needed sea room and task forces required a separation of several miles. Others were convinced that all ships in a task force should be concentrated in concentric rings around a core consisting of all the carriers. Although such a concentration made the job of attack simpler for the enemy, it also made it more hazardous. With all gunfire concentrated over the carriers, and all fighters from the carriers likewise concentrated, the possibilities of enemy aircraft penetrating to the target carriers should have been considerably reduced. But Fletcher had learned from the Coral Sea experience that competent fighter director officers, first-class radars, and much larger squadrons were absolute necessities if the carriers were to be effectively protected by their fighters. During the turn-around at Pearl Harbor a few more fighters were added to each carrier, but there had not been the time to make the needed improvements in fighter direction. It was clear to Kinkaid, who was a gunnery specialist, that the 1.1-inch and .50-caliber machine guns all needed replacement with 20- and 40-mm guns in twin and quadruple mounts. Once such changes were completed, the airspace over the carriers would truly become almost impenetrable. But at the time it seemed prudent to Fletcher to leave plenty of room for maneuvering. So, while in tactical command, Fletcher maintained 10 to 15 miles between the two task forces, with TF 17 normally operating to the west of TF 16. It was to be a fateful decision.[22]

Fletcher held the two task forces in an area roughly 300 miles to the northeast of Midway. Frank Jack had considerable faith in Nimitz's intelligence briefing and therefore did not expect the Japanese to be within striking distance of Midway—about 250 miles—until the early morning of the 4th. Nonetheless, as a precaution, he ordered the carriers to fly regular 200-mile searches on sectors from the southwest through north to the northeast. On the third, *Yorktown* launched scouts at first light and again at 1500. Midway was also sending out PBYs on 700-mile searches. So unless the Japanese were trying to approach from the east, it was unlikely they could come close to Midway without being detected by the scouts. In reality, given the Japanese Striking Force's approach from the southwest until 1530 on 3 June when it turned to a southeast approach course, the distance between Admirals Chuichi Nagumo and Fletcher made it impossible for their task force scouts to sight one another.

The first detection of the approaching Japanese came shortly before 1100 on the third. One of Midway's twenty-two searching PBYs located a portion of the Occupation Force at 700 miles headed eastward. Because of the large

---

[22] NWC, *Midway*, 63; Smith, *Midway*, 70; Lord, *Incredible Victory*, 65.

number of transports and escorts, including a destroyer squadron, cruiser, and two seaplane transports, the pilot signaled that he had found "the main body." A few minutes later he radioed, "Bearing 262, distance 700."[23] Because all flagships were tuned to the PBY communication channel, Kinkaid picked up the flash reports at the same time that Fletcher and Spruance received them. Given CINCPAC's estimate and battle plan, there was probably some controversy among the staffs of the four American flag officers until a message from Nimitz arrived in flag cipher. He clarified the identify of the Japanese force immediately: "That is not repeat not the enemy striking force—stop—That is the landing force. The striking force will hit from the northwest at daylight tomorrow."[24] It was obvious to all that the Transport Group could not arrive at Midway for another two days, but this was not the case with the fast-stepping Striking Force.

For the balance of the third, while Midway-based B–17s and PBYs attempted to bomb and torpedo the Transport Group, Fletcher's task forces rode back and forth across the 176th meridian (west) between latitude 32 and 34 degrees north. During the first watch at 2150 the admiral finally made his move to close the approaching enemy. The task forces wheeled from a northwest course to 210 degrees and set the revolutions to hold about 14 knots. Fletcher hoped to be within 200 miles and positioned on the flank of the Japanese carrier force by 0900. With luck his scouts might even discover its location before the Japanese were aware he was in position to strike them. Fletcher and the rest of his flag officers felt the long night would never end.[25]

On board *Minneapolis* Kinkaid followed his usual routine. With evening dark he retired to his sea cabin adjacent to the bridge, read briefly, and then tried to sleep. He was up again by first light, having his morning coffee and beginning to work on his daily two packs of Camels. In keeping with shipboard operations throughout the task force all general quarters stations were manned at 0539, an hour before dawn on 4 June. Because of danger from submarine attack with the eastern horizon beginning to lighten, all ships would continue their zigzagging pattern until sunrise. At 0621 *Yorktown* launched ten Dauntlesses to search the northern sectors, from west to east, to 100 miles. Fletcher was taking no chances on being surprised by Nagumo's carriers. According to the battle plan he had communicated to Spruance, *Yorktown* took the morning search. Its air group would be held in reserve once *Enterprise* and *Hornet* launched against the enemy—provided there was an enemy out there.[26]

---

[23] Prange, *Midway*, 162.
[24] Smith, *Midway*, 73–74; Potter, *Nimitz*, 92; Prange, *Midway*, 162, 170; Layton, "*And I Was There*," 436–37.
[25] *Minneapolis* log, 3–4 Jun 1942; Smith, *Midway*, 76–78; Lord, *Incredible Victory*, 87; Morison 4:102.
[26] NWC, *Midway*, 51–52.

At 0734 any doubts concerning Nimitz's battle plan dissolved when Lieutenant Howard P. Ady signaled from a PBY that he had spotted "enemy carriers." Eleven minutes later he warned the Midway people, "Many enemy planes heading Midway, bearing 320 degrees distant 150." At 0803 another PBY pilot amplified Ady's contact report: "Two carriers and battleships bearing 320, distance 180, course 135, speed 25." Although all the anticipated enemy carriers had not been reported, Fletcher and Spruance had something to attack. It now made even more sense for Fletcher to hold back *Yorktown*'s air group until the rest of the Japanese flat-tops were located. It took Frank Jack only five minutes to signal Spruance: "Proceed southwesterly and attack enemy carriers. Will follow as soon as search planes recovered."[27]

Fletcher's instructions gave Spruance an enormous responsibility. At 0800 the Japanese were about 175 miles from TF 16 on a bearing of 240 degrees. This distance was about the maximum from which an American carrier air group could launch and expect to have a fighter (Wildcat or F4F-3,4) escort both en route and on return. If Spruance held back his attack for two hours, there would be no problem of range for any of his squadrons. After a moment of thought he directed his chief of staff, Captain Miles R. Browning, to launch everything they had at 0900. By striking as quickly as possible, he hoped to hit the Japanese carriers while they were recovering, servicing, and rearming the strike they had sent against Midway. He was also reducing the possibility of the Japanese attacking his ship while the flight decks were loaded with aircraft.[28]

Once the launch was set for 0900, *Enterprise* and *Hornet* separated and remained that way for most of the day. Kinkaid with *Minneapolis, New Orleans, Atlanta* (CL 51), and a handful of destroyers formed their protective circle around Captain Marc A. Mitscher's *Hornet* and got on with the business they had been sent to accomplish. To eliminate any possible command confusions should the Japanese hit their task group, Kinkaid had the bridge signalman flash a message to the *Hornet*'s captain: "Screen will conform to your movements. Operate without reference to me." The admiral was recognizing that maneuvering was still central to the protection of the carrier and Mitscher would have to call the tune. Though he was still actively in command of *Hornet*, Mitscher had taken his oath a few days earlier and was promoted to rear admiral. It is highly doubtful that this fact entered the mind of either of the two as they prepared for action.[29]

---

[27] Smith, *Midway*, 79; Prange, *Midway*, 238–39.

[28] Buell, *Quiet Warrior*, 130–32; Lord, *Incredible Victory*, 136.

[29] Commander Cruisers, TF 16 [Kinkaid] to CTF 16 [Spruance], "Report of Action, June 4, 1942, Battle of Midway," 11 Jun 1942, WWII Action Reports, OA; TCK, "Four Years of War," 151–52; Prange, *Midway*, 135; Theodore Taylor, *The Magnificent Mitscher* (New York: W. W. Norton, 1954), 122.

214 Kinkaid of the Seventh Fleet

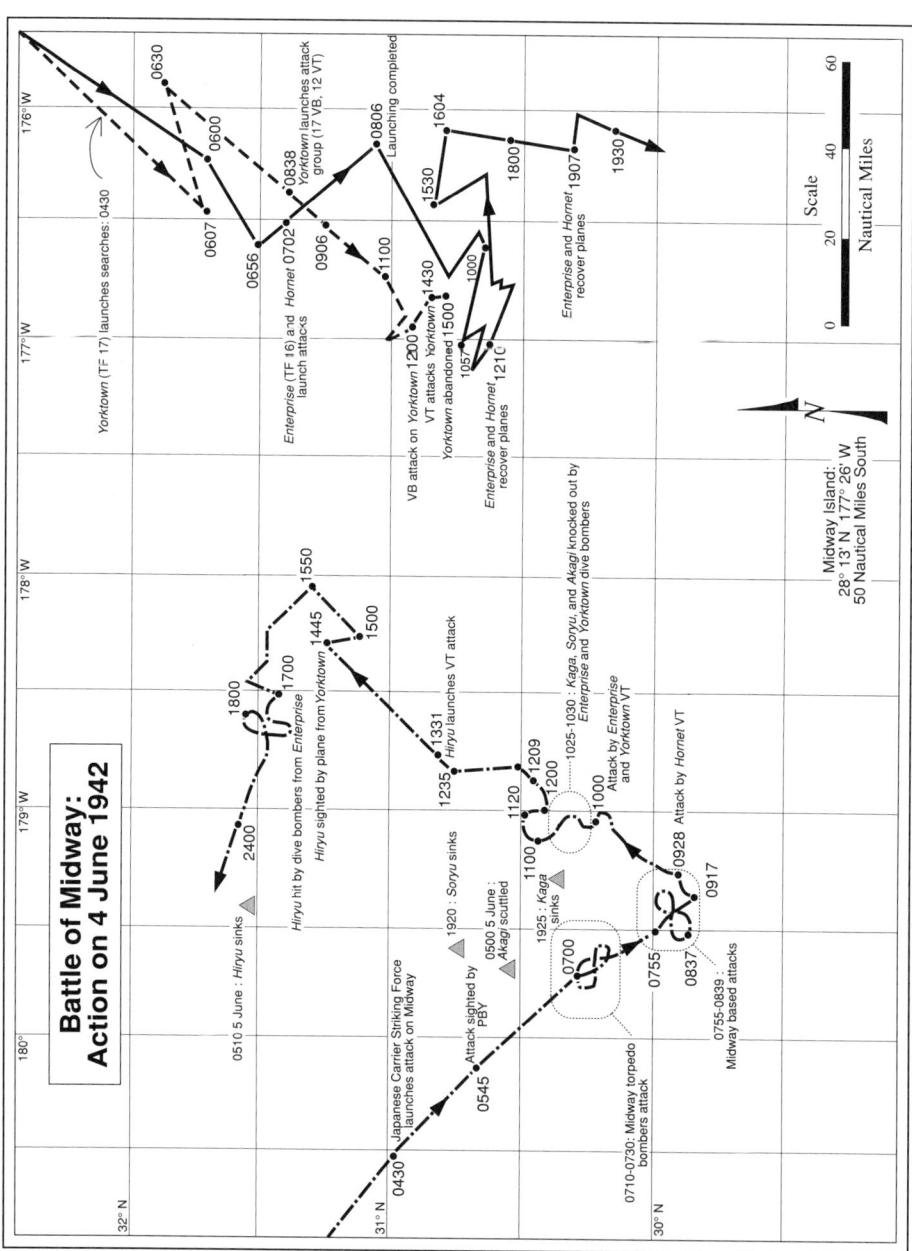

Once the squadrons from *Enterprise* and *Hornet* departed to attack the Japanese carriers, there were hours of anxious waiting in TF 16. It was hard to believe they hadn't been spotted, so a high degree of alertness was maintained in all ships. About an hour after the last plane from *Hornet* cleared the area, *Northampton* broadcast on TBS (talk between ships) at 1015, "Bandit bearing 185 degrees, distance 30 miles. Bandit is single engine float seaplane." This scout plane from the Japanese cruiser *Tone* had already reported the presence of TF 17, but it had not yet seen and reported TF 16. Twelve minutes later Spruance signaled his force, "Prepare to repel enemy aircraft," but none came. *Tone*'s scout hung on tenaciously, even providing continuous radio signals so that Japanese attack squadrons could follow his signals to the Americans, but nothing happened. With good reason.[30]

Spruance's plan of attack had worked almost to perfection. Bombing squadrons from *Enterprise* and *Yorktown* reached the Japanese at the anticipated critical moment. Carriers *Kaga, Akagi,* and *Soryu* all had deckloads of aircraft, recently returned from attacking Midway and now being serviced and rearmed for another strike. The dive bombers had also found the airspace over the Japanese carriers clear because the Japanese fighter planes had been decimating the three torpedo squadrons sent against them: VT–6 (*Enterprise*), VT–8 (*Hornet*), and VT–3 (*Yorktown*). The Americans therefore had almost unimpeded dives against the Japanese flattops. All three were struck repeatedly and all were left in a sinking condition. The attacks had been made at approximately 1230 and so far no enemy attack aircraft had approached TF 16 or TF 17. Of course none would come from the three carriers that had been mortally damaged. But there was a fourth carrier, *Hiryu*, to consider.

In *Minneapolis* Admiral Kinkaid was mostly unaware of the successes of the squadrons from TFs 16 and 17. Occasionally his radios would pick up chatter from the squadrons. He heard *Enterprise*'s air group commander's startling announcement: "There is no combat patrol over the enemy fleet. We have been flying over the enemy fleet for the past half hour. They are 8 DDs, 2 BBs and 2 carriers." He also heard Captain Browning's frantic reply to Lieutenant Commander Wade McClusky: "Attack immediately!" But the tragic losses of Lieutenant Commander John C. Waldron's VT–8 (fifteen planes, twenty-nine pilots and crewmen lost), Lieutenant Commander Eugene E. Lindsey's VT–6 (ten of fourteen planes lost), and Lieutenant Commander Lance E. Massey's VT–3 (twelve of thirteen planes lost) were unknown by the ships in TF 16 until losses could be confirmed in the next couple of days. Instead Kinkaid would write in his action report for 4 June 1942, "The cruisers of the *Hornet* group did not

---

[30] COMCRUDIV 6, War Diary Notes, 4 Jun 1942, in COMCRU Action Report, 11 Jun 1942; Prange, *Midway*, 231.

at any time engage the enemy, and were occupied solely with maintaining close contact with the *Hornet* as she launched and recovered aircraft." He did not mention that the *Hornet* group had been lucky.

Because the Japanese carriers had separated when reversing course following the attacks upon them by aircraft from Midway, *Hiryu* was not spotted by the bombing squadrons from *Enterprise* and *Yorktown*. *Hiryu's* commanding officer, of course, had picked up the location of TF 17 from *Tone's* scout. He was thus able to launch a dive bomber strike in retaliation for the catastrophe overtaking *Kaga, Akagi,* and *Soryu*. These aircraft—eighteen Val dive bombers and six Zero fighter escorts—took off at 1240 and were able to trail returning U.S. aircraft to the vicinity of their carriers.[31] By 1400 the Japanese attackers were lighting up the radar screens in both task forces, and a few minutes later the word was passed to all ships, "Prepare to repel air attack."

The first vessels sighted by the Japanese belonged to Fletcher's TF 17. Like a magnet attracting iron filings, *Yorktown* drew in the dive bombers. Of the incoming eighteen Vals only eight successfully fought their way through the wall of defending Wildcats and the gunfire barrage to dive against the carrier. Three hits were made, stopping *Yorktown* dead in the water. The attack was over by 1415 and the five bomber pilots who escaped to *Hiryu* were convinced that they had mortally damaged the flat-top.[32] But such was not the case. Within two hours damage control parties in *Yorktown* had repaired much of the destruction wrought by the three hits, and the carrier was making 18 knots. As a precautionary measure Admiral Fletcher and his staff shifted his flag to *Astoria*. With *Yorktown's* radios and radar out of commission, the carrier was no longer a suitable flagship. To further protect his ship, at 1435 Fletcher moved the cruisers *Vincennes* and *Pensacola* and the destroyers *Benham* (DD 397) and *Maury* (DD 401) from the TF 16 screen to TF 17's.

As it became clear that three Japanese carriers had been knocked out, it also became apparent that the fourth carrier, anticipated in CINC-PAC's operation plan, had been the one to attack *Yorktown*. At about 1345, 20 minutes before the Japanese struck, Fletcher had sent a search to locate any missing carriers, and now, three hours later, an SBD pilot radioed the key information. He had found "one carrier, two battleships, three heavy cruisers, four destroyers" at a position about 100 miles west and north of TF 17.[33] Unfortunately *Yorktown* was now in no condition to respond. However Admiral Spruance had ordered a strike group assem-

---

[31] Fuchida, *Midway*, 190–2; *Minneapolis*, War Diary, 4 Jun 1942; Action Reports CTF 16 and CTF 17, 11–12 Jun 1942.
[32] Lord, *Incredible Victory*, 193; Fuchida, *Midway*, 192.
[33] Smith, *Midway*, 125; Buell, *Quiet Warrior*, 138–40; Prange, *Midway*, 288.

bled from the remnants of the squadrons in TF 16, and at 1730 he launched twenty-four SBDs from *Enterprise*. Included in the twenty-four were fourteen planes from *Yorktown*. Spruance expected *Hornet*'s dive bombing units to join the strike, but his staff didn't get orders to Mitscher in time. More than a half hour later, *Hornet* finally launched sixteen SBDs to attack the *Hiryu* task force.[34]

The radio report of *Hiryu*'s location arrived at 1645, only minutes after its torpedo squadron. Again *Yorktown* was the first carrier spotted and thus became the focus of the attack. Escorted by a half dozen Zeros, the ten Kates split up at 1640 and commenced their runs. Fighters from *Yorktown* and *Enterprise* put up a spirited defense, but the Japanese were ably led. At 1642 *Yorktown* was struck on the port side by two torpedoes, slowed, then went dead in the water. Twenty minutes later, with the carrier listing 25 degrees to port, the "Hypo, Love" flags were bent on the flag hoist, and *Yorktown*'s crew began abandoning ship.[35]

In *Minneapolis* Kinkaid was merely an interested observer of these dramatic events. His duty was to screen *Hornet* and *Enterprise*, mostly by mimicking the movements of Mitscher's flat-top. When both carriers were together in a cruising formation, the *Big E* shared the gunfire protection from *Minneapolis*. But when under attack the two carriers separated, and Kinkaid's staff kept their eyes trained on *Hornet*'s flag hoist. During the two attacks on *Yorktown*, *Enterprise* and *Hornet* were about 15 miles apart and the *Hornet* group, including *Minneapolis*, remained about 15 to 20 miles from *Yorktown*. Though the crew on Kinkaid's ship was at general quarters and all guns that would bear were trained outward at the Japanese, the torpedo planes stayed out of gun range. Again *Minneapolis*'s weapons never opened fire. *Hornet*'s fighter squadron provided CAP over TF 16, but they also managed to work themselves into the fight against the Japanese attackers. The 1642 attack by *Hiryu*'s Kates proved to be a deadly Parthian shot.

The dive bombers launched by Spruance at 1730 arrived over *Hiryu* at 1903 and promptly turned Nagumo's last carrier into a floating inferno. By the time *Hornet*'s SBDs were ready to attack, it was obvious that *Hiryu* was finished, so they concentrated on its screen. Though the battleship *Haruna* and the heavy cruisers *Tone* and *Chikuma* received a lot of attention, they escaped being hit. *Hiryu* remained afloat during the night and was sent to the bottom early the next morning by torpedoes from destroyers *Kazagumo* and *Yugumo*.[36]

---

[34] Morison 4:136–37; Buell, *Quiet Warrior*, 138–39; Prange, *Midway*, 283, 288.

[35] CTF 17, "Report of Action, 4 June 1942," and enclosures of *Astoria* and *Portland* action reports, 12 Jun 1942; Fuchida, *Midway*, 192–95; Lundstrom, *First Team*, 502–16; Prange, *Midway*, 284–88; Foster Hailey, *Pacific Battle Line* (New York: Macmillan, 1944), 176–77.

[36] Action Reports for 4 Jun 1942 by CTF 16 and TF 17; Morison 4:136–37; Fuchida, *Midway*, 196–99; Prange, *Midway*, 389–91.

Yorktown (CV 5) being abandoned on 4 June 1942 after being hit by Japanese air attack during the Battle of Midway. *Balch* (DD 363) stands by.

When Captain Elliott Buckmaster ordered "abandon ship," it appeared to him and most of the captains around *Yorktown* that the carrier was in imminent danger of capsizing. But it didn't. Fortunately the sea was calm with almost no wind in the early evening. The flat-top hung with the port edge of its flight deck almost touching the water. Concerned about a possible submarine attack, the four cruisers under Rear Admiral Poco Smith (including two from TF 16) warily circled the carrier outside 2,000 yards. Eventually the destroyers moved closer and plucked 2,280 of *Yorktown*'s crew from the water. As at Coral Sea there was severe overcrowding in the rescuing ships, but all who survived were on board a vessel within two hours. Destroyers *Benham* (725 passengers), *Balch* (DD 363) (541 passengers), and *Russell* (508 passengers) carried the largest numbers. Admiral Fletcher ordered the destroyer *Hughes* (DD 410) to guard the carrier until relieved. If the Japanese tried to capture it or if heavy fires were to start, the commanding officer of *Hughes* was to sink the carrier. With those orders Fletcher pulled TF 17 into cruising formation and at 1945 turned east at 15 knots.[37]

---

[37] Action Report for 4 Jun 1942 by CTF 17, 12 Jun 1942; Smith, *Midway*, 119, 123, 131–32.

After Admiral Fletcher shifted his flag from *Yorktown* to *Astoria*, he recognized that he was in a poor position to operate as the officer in tactical command (OTC) for the two task forces. When Admiral Spruance had assembled the strike against *Hiryu*, he asked Fletcher if he had any instructions. Fletcher signaled in reply, "Negative. Will conform to your movements." In the argot of his airmen Frank Jack was tapping his helmet, pointing at Spruance, and thus "passing the lead" to his junior. Spruance was now OTC and would remain so for the next few days.[38] The long day of battle finally ended for TF 16 at 2040. It had been a glorious 4th of June and would remain so in American naval annals.[39]

The SBDs that had attacked *Hiryu* returned at sunset and the fighter CAP was finally brought on board. Spruance had decided not to pursue the Japanese groups during the night. Instead he would steam east and then begin a return route during the night that would place him in a position to defend Midway at dawn or launch searches for the Japanese if the Midway patrol planes had not been able to find them. Leaving *Yorktown* and a lonely guard astern, TF 16 sailed east. Once Fletcher had decided to try to save the carrier, he also turned TF 17 east, planning to overtake and sail in company with Spruance. The latter's plan not to offer battle that evening certainly evoked no contrary suggestions from Frank Jack when he overtook Spruance around 2100. There is little doubt that Kinkaid also agreed with Spruance's action at the time. Years later he told an oral history interviewer:

> Spruance had to think about following up the action. He didn't want to head right on west at night and run into surface ships, and so he made a wise decision and headed east. He's been criticized for that. . . . I think Spruance did exactly the right thing.[40]

The next day Kinkaid wrote briefly to his wife. As usual he stayed within the censorship rules, but read in retrospect, his letter said a great deal:

> Yesterday was a long day and when I turned in about 10 p.m. having been up since 5 a.m. and on my feet most of the time, my dogs were tired. The Jap stuck his neck out. That is about all I can say about "operations." You will have plenty of headlines to read today or during the next day or so. . . . This also is going to be a long day and possibly tomorrow. . . . Perhaps what is happening now will have a great effect on the war, even to shortening it.[41]

---

[38] Buell, *Quiet Warrior*, 139; Smith, *Midway*, 125–26.

[39] The British celebrate Admiral Lord Richard Howe's 1794 naval victory over the French as the "Battle of the Glorious First of June."

[40] TCK oral history, 173–74; RADM R. A. Spruance to ADM Chester W. Nimitz, *Enterprise*, 8 Jun 1942, Nimitz Papers, OA.

[41] TCK to HSK, *Minneapolis*, 5 Jun 1942; Smith, *Midway*, 131–32.

Finally convinced that the enemy had been soundly defeated, Nimitz radioed his task force commanders late in the evening: "You who participated in the Battle of Midway today have written a glorious page in our history. I am proud to be associated with you." But the battle wasn't over. As befits an aggressive commander in chief, CINCPAC believed in pursuit and destruction of a defeated foe. He closed his congratulatory message with a direct suggestion: "I estimate that another day of all out effort on your part will complete the defeat of the enemy." At dawn TF 16 was steaming west at 14 knots to take up the task at hand, but the day was to prove frustrating.[42]

During the previous afternoon and evening, while still assessing the damage to his carriers, Admiral Yamamoto had ordered his forces to rendezvous in the early morning of the 5th. He hoped that the American task forces would steam westward during the night and thus come under the guns of his battleships and cruisers in a night engagement. But wary of such an eventuality Spruance had taken TF 16 and TF 17 east, north, south, and finally west, but not until 0400. By then Yamamoto knew that *Hiryu* had been sunk and that only one U.S. carrier out of three had been immobilized. He realized that his ships would come under air attack at daylight without their effective Zeroes to fend off the Yankees. At 0255 he signaled for a general withdrawal to the northwest. But again fate dealt him a wretched hand. Two of his heavy cruisers, *Mogami* and *Mikuma*, collided while maneuvering in the inky darkness and were unable to join the general retreat.[43]

When Kinkaid arose at first light on the 5th, he found TF 16 still steaming westward with no clear idea of the disposition of the Japanese forces. Visibility was good, the sky overcast, and the sea relatively smooth. During the morning and forenoon watches sighting reports began to arrive that helped clarify what the enemy was doing. At 0415 *Tambor* (SS 198), a submarine patrolling 90 miles west of Midway, vaguely reported the presence of "many unidentified ships." Actually these were four cruisers (including *Mogami* and *Mikuma*) and two destroyers that Yamamoto had ordered to bombard Midway preliminary to an amphibious assault. At 0800, with full visibility, the submarine informed Nimitz and Spruance that there were two damaged cruisers and a destroyer escort almost due west and 115 miles from Midway. An hour later a PBY reported five ships at 200 miles, bearing 325 degrees from Midway. These were later identified incorrectly as a crippled carrier and two battleships plus supporting cruisers and destroyers, all heading northwest.[44] Spruance later wrote to Nimitz:

---
[42] CINCPAC to CTF 16, CTF 17, 6/060801Z, Nimitz Papers.
[43] COMCRUDIV 6, War Diary, 5 Jun 1942; Dull, *Battle History IJN*, 162–64; Lord, *Incredible Victory*, 256–58.
[44] ONI Combat Narrative: *Midway*, 35–38; Blair, *Silent Victory*, 1:222–33.

We had reports of two groups, either of which contained good targets. One was to the west of Midway, the other to the northwest. I chose the one to the northwest. It was farther away, but it contained the crippled CV and 2 BBs, one of them damaged.

We stood to the northwestward at 25 kts., using the position reported during the forenoon by a VP. There were no trailing reports, and, as the day wore on, this position began to grow rather cold, but it was the best we had.[45]

At 1700, with no clear location of their target, *Enterprise* and *Hornet* launched all of the SBDs they had on a search and strike mission. The only vessel located was the destroyer *Tanikaze*, which managed to evade forty-two bombs and shot down one of its attackers. Another Dauntless was lost while the carriers were recovering their aircraft long after sunset. After their splendid successes of the previous day the fruitless afternoon mission of 5 June was a letdown. The problem was the lack of a long-range morning search out of Midway. Had the PBYs gone out 700 miles in sectors between 200 and 340 degrees, almost all of Yamamoto's fleet would have been discovered. By confining their searches to 250-mile sectors the Catalina pilots denied Spruance the vital information he needed. On the other hand had Spruance used some of his SBDs for searches, or even had he catapulted some of the two dozen cruiser aircraft on board, he might have been able to make the 5th another blazing success. The long day ended with another encouraging message from CINCPAC:

> The efforts and sacrifices of the Army, Navy and Marine Corps forces involved in the Battle of Midway have been crowned with glorious success and I firmly believe have already changed the course of the war in the Pacific in our favor. The enemy is attempting to withdraw his wounded ships. If you follow up your successes vigorously he will be so crushed that his total defeat will be inevitable.[46]

At dawn on Saturday the 6th Spruance decided to make every effort to finish off any Japanese ships within reach of his carriers. *Enterprise* launched eighteen SBDs, each armed with a 500-pound bomb, to search to 200 miles in sectors to the west between 180 and 360 degrees. At 0845 a Dauntless pilot made contact and reported a battleship and five destroyers about 130 miles to the southwest. Other sightings of cruisers and destroyers were reported, and another of a battleship, a cruiser, and destroyers. Frustrated by conflicting reports and undecided whether

---

[45] Spruance to Nimitz, 8 Jun 1942, Nimitz Papers.
[46] CINCPAC to CTGs, Midway, COMGEN Hawaiian Dept., 6/060801Z, CINCPAC Message Files, Records of the Office of the CNO, RG 38, NA; NWC, *Midway*, 214; Buell, *Quiet Warrior*, 141.

there were one or two groups of ships, Spruance ordered Kinkaid to use his cruiser aircraft to verify what the carrier scouts had reported. *Minneapolis* and *New Orleans* each launched two Sea Gulls (SOCs) with instructions to stay with the Japanese ships once they were located. By staying on station until relieved by other cruiser planes, the SOC pilots would ensure that the Japanese did not escape this time. At 1014 *Hornet* launched twenty-three SBDs, with fighter escorts, to attack the Japanese force. They found the cruisers *Mogami* and *Mikuma*, both damaged from their collision, and two escorting destroyers. Unable to sink the cruisers, the *Hornet* pilots returned to their flat-top.

At 1310 *Enterprise* took up the fight, sending thirty-one SBDs, three torpedo planes, and twelve fighters to help suppress the antiaircraft fire for the torpedo pilots. Again the Japanese cruisers were pounded, but they remained afloat. At 1546 Spruance called on *Hornet*'s pilots a second time to finish the hardy Japanese cruisers. Success at last. A few hours after Mitscher's pilots left the scene, *Mikuma* rolled over and plunged under. *Mogami*, completely shattered above the waterline and with a portion of its bow bent at a 45-degree angle, escaped into the gloom with its more nimble escorts. Tom Kinkaid would get another shot at that hardy survivor a couple of years later at the Battle for Leyte Gulf.[47]

With the recovery of *Hornet*'s aircraft Spruance concluded that it was time to terminate the pursuit. His task force was moving into the range of the Japanese bombers on Wake Island and there was no need to risk his two precious carriers to land-based attack. More important, his destroyers were dangerously short on fuel and the tankers were a day or two behind them. And the pilots were badly frayed; three days of continuous air operations had taken their toll. Though not a pilot himself, Spruance understood the problems that could arise if tired aviators were pushed beyond their limits. Casualties to pilots and material had already been heavy; there was no reason to go on. At 2100 TF 16 moved into cruising disposition 10V, the two carriers again to the center of the formation, and shaped course for a fueling rendezvous.

The Battle of Midway was over. The Japanese Striking Force had lost four fleet carriers, all of their aircraft, a cruiser, and a high percentage of the pilots and aircrews. Another cruiser and two destroyers had been severely damaged. The Pacific Fleet had lost another carrier (*Yorktown* sank on 6 June) and the destroyer *Hammann*, both to the skillful attack of submarine *I–168*. Pilot and aircrew losses in Spruance's carriers had been devastating, but replacements were in the pipeline. For the Japanese there was no real pipeline in operation. Admiral Yamamoto and his

---

[47] COMCRUDIV 6, War Diary, 6 Jun 1942; Spruance to Nimitz, 8 Jun 1942, Nimitz Papers; Buell, *Quiet Warrior*, 144–47.

commanders had gambled that a smashing victory at Midway would force the Americans out of the war. It was a gamble the Japanese lost.[48]

All those involved in the Battle of Midway probably believed that it was time to return to Pearl Harbor for a rest, but CINCPAC saw things differently. While TF 16 was steaming toward its fueling rendezvous, Admiral Theobald in Alaskan waters called for reinforcements. The attacks on Dutch Harbor on 3 and 4 June had not led to an amphibious landing but the admiral and his opposite number, Major General Simon Bolivar Buckner, USA, knew that the Japanese could have landed almost anywhere had they chosen to do so.[49] The intelligence from CINCPAC's staff had informed Theobald that the Alaskan attacks were diversionary movements by the Japanese in support of their Midway operation. The admiral, on the scene, was not sure this was true. His ships and PBY squadrons had had little success in tracking the enemy, and the Air Corps had been pitiful in its inability to find or hit anything at sea. Theobald warned CINCPAC on 7 June that the Japanese were trying to wear out his patrol squadrons preliminary to an "all out attack." He then commented dramatically that "the reasonable safety of Pearl . . . may warrant quick reinforcement of Alaska from there. Consider need approaches desperation." Unknown to the admiral, the Japanese had just captured Kiska and Attu at the end of the Aleutian chain. They then left Aleutian waters with no intention of invading any more Aleutian or Alaskan territory.[50]

Before Nimitz could reply to Theobald, Admiral King made his own views known: "In view situation COMNOWESTSEAFRON [Commander Northwest Sea Frontier] 071611 with indications of continued presence of Orange force in Aleutians suggest you consider sending northward a strong task force formed on *Saratoga*. You are authorized to strip West Coast of patrol planes if you do not plan to send any from Hawaii."[51]

As a good subordinate, CINCPAC understood that COMINCH's suggestions should be taken seriously. Eight and a half hours later orders flashed to Commanders Task Forces 8, 16, and 17. Task Force 17 was to resupply TF 16's *Enterprise* and *Hornet* with surviving aircraft and pilots and *Saratoga* would provide additional aircraft. Once the transfers were completed, TF 17 would return to Pearl and TF 16 would head north to rendezvous with Admiral Theobald's TF 8 at Point Blow (48°N, 172°W) and pass under his command. The task of Theobald's command was to

---

[48] Edwin Hoyt, *Japan's War: The Great Pacific Conflict, 1853 to 1952* (New York: McGraw Hill, 1986), 300–301.

[49] Brian Garfield, *The Thousand-Mile War: World War II in Alaska and the Aleutians* (Garden City, NY: Nelson Doubleday, 1983), 49–52.

[50] COMNORWESTSEAFRON to CINCPAC, 6/071611Z, CINCPAC Files, OA; Garfield, *Thousand-Mile War*, 96–99; Morison 4:180–81.

[51] COMINCH to CINCPAC, 6/071954Z, Command Summary.

Rear Admiral Kinkaid on board *Minneapolis* (CA 36), June 1942.

drive the Japanese navy away from the Aleutians area.[52] *Saratoga* ("*Sara*" to her crew), with the new light cruiser *San Diego* (CL 53), five destroyers, and the oiler *Kaskaskia*, would sail northwest from Pearl and join the remnants of Admiral Fletcher's TF 17, now reduced to two cruisers, *Astoria* and *Portland*, and three destroyers. The *Saratoga* group (TG 11.1) and Fletcher's group would become TF 17 under Fletcher's command. Rear Admiral Jake Fitch was supposed to command TF 11, but *Saratoga* had to leave San Diego and later Pearl Harbor without him. Captain DeWitt C. Ramsey, the skipper of *Saratoga*, commanded TG 11.1 by default until it was absorbed under Fletcher's command.[53]

Tom Kinkaid and *Minneapolis* were still assigned to TF 16. Though their progress northward had not really begun in earnest, by the time his ships arrived at the fueling rendezvous he was beginning to note the coolness in the air. To Helen he confided that he was "glad to have my rubber boots, rain coat and wind breaker." The task force was still below 32°N, but Tom was probably cool from fog and rain that surrounded his cruisers. He did tell his wife that he might have "lots of need for his foul

---

[52] CINCPAC to CTF 8, 16, 17, 6/080429Z, Command Summary, 556–57; Forrestel, *Spruance*, 55; Buell, *Quiet Warrior*, 148; Lundstrom, *First Team*, 543–47.

[53] Lundstrom, *First Team*, 544, 546.

weather gear in the near future." Had he greater prescience, Kinkaid might have taken much greater interest in the operations ahead in Alaskan waters. But neither he nor his bosses in Pearl Harbor and Washington could guess that in just six months he would be forced to deal with the Aleutians firsthand.[54]

Once *Cimarron* and *Guadalupe* completed fueling TF 16 on the 9th, the task force continued on to its rendezvous with *Saratoga* and TF 17. By 0930 the next day, 10 June, *Saratoga* and its consorts were barely visible due to the wretched weather, so the transfer of aircraft had to wait until the following morning. Finally fifteen planes were flown to *Enterprise* and another nineteen to *Hornet*. By 0900 Fletcher, now riding *Saratoga*, had departed for Pearl while Spruance and TF 16 shaped course for Point Blow. Fletcher didn't mind returning; he had experienced plenty of fighting and there was more ahead. Ramsey's squadrons on the other hand were eager for action, but it was not to be. Nimitz and his air advisors believed that *Sara*'s squadrons needed more training before they could be committed to a high-risk environment such as the Alaskan waters.[55]

Spruance had barely turned TF 16 to a northerly heading when radio orders arrived from CINCPAC canceling his previous instructions. Task Force 16 was to return immediately to Pearl Harbor. The new orders were received with considerable enthusiasm. Spruance, never too demonstrative, later commented candidly, "I was not looking forward to extensive carrier operations in the climate of the Aleutians and was glad when . . . we were ordered back to Pearl." Kinkaid was looking forward to again calling Helen.[56]

During the week following TF 16's pursuit of the Japanese, Kinkaid gave a lot of thought to the actions that had taken place and what could be learned from the Battle of Midway. In his action report concerning 4 June, the admiral made a dozen observations and suggestions. One (paragraph 7) concerned the disposition of the screen when action was imminent. He recommended that cruisers and destroyers move immediately to their battle positions in the screen once it was clear the formation was to be attacked. It was too difficult to break up a single two-carrier formation and establish their separate defensive arrangements when the enemy planes were at hand. A second recommendation (paragraph 8) came from his (and Spruance's) dismay at the amount of time it took to get squadrons launched and on their way to attack the enemy. He observed, "On June 4 the attack groups appeared, to a non-aviator, to take considerable time after launching before proceeding toward their objec-

---

[54] TCK to HSK, *Minneapolis*, 8 Jun 1942.
[55] CINCPAC to COMINCH, 6/082029Z, Command Summary; NWC, *Midway*, 185–89.
[56] Forrestel, *Spruance*, 55; TCK to HSK, *Minneapolis*, 12 Jun 1942.

tive." He recommended, "It is of great importance that attack groups launched from a carrier proceed promptly to their objective, complete the attack immediately and return to base to prepare to launch a second attack as soon as possible." As a nonaviator, Kinkaid was revealing that he did not understand the complexities of flight deck management, but he did have a point. In a few months, when Grumman TBF–1 Avengers were added to the air groups, the problem of escorting the slow torpedo planes would be solved. The TBFs and SBDs would be closer to the speed of the escorting Wildcats than had been the terribly slow Devastators, which had suffered so tragically in the fruitless attacks of VT–8 and VT–6.

Along with Spruance Kinkaid had keenly felt the lack of clear information coming from carrier and land-based scouting aircraft. He noted, "Reports from our own planes, both shore based and ship based, were in many instances incomplete, inaccurate and misleading." He recognized that the scouting plane's being under attack was part of the problem. Since Japanese patrol planes had been easily shot down by his task force's Wildcats, he believed the PBY Catalinas were equally vulnerable. The solution, as he saw it, was for the Navy to use B–17s for long patrols since they could climb above the Zero's operational ceiling. The B–17s were also armed well enough to drive off enemy fighters. Remembering how several squadrons had missed finding the Japanese carriers on their first outing, Kinkaid also recommended that every group of planes have some among them equipped with YE–ZB homing devices so that planes could home in on the aircraft that were in direct contact with the enemy.[57]

In an oral history interview nineteen years after the Battle of Midway, Admiral Kinkaid talked about the meaning of that engagement. He pointed out that the department called almost every successful battle a turning point. But there was considerable truth in the statement when applied to Midway. "Just taking those four carriers out made all the difference in the world." Because his memory was fuzzy on the details and perhaps because Japanese-American relations had been rehabilitated by 1961, Kinkaid told the interviewer that he thought the Japanese could have taken Midway had they not lost their aggressive spirit. They could have used the carriers from the Aleutian operation plus the small ones that had remained with Yamamoto to put together a successful assault on Midway. He concluded, "They'd have had three carriers against our two, and three fresh ones. They'd have had a landing force that was very strong. They had the surface ships needed for bombardment, and they could have gone in the next day and taken Midway—undoubtedly, in my mind." When asked why the Japanese lost their aggressive attitude,

---

[57] CTF 16, "Report of Action June 4, 1942, Battle of Midway," 11 Jun 1942.

Kinkaid opined, "Because of their losses, undoubtedly. I don't think they knew exactly what our situation was."[58]

No time was lost once TF 16 received orders on 11 June to return to Pearl. At 1600 on the 13th *Enterprise* and *Hornet* led the way to the anchorages. The air groups had flown off just after noon, and their squadrons had landed to beer welcomes at Naval Air Station Kaneohe and Marine Corps Air Station Ewa. For Kinkaid and those in the ships' companies there was good reason to celebrate, but the needs of intelligence had to be observed. Parties included few outsiders, and the press was held in check by the censors. It wasn't until 14 July that the Navy Department issued communiqué number 97, giving a fairly full report of the battle. But for the ships and their crews the traditional Navy "well done" had come from COMINCH and CINCPAC, and that had been enough. Or nearly enough—decorations and medals would soon follow. But no one could fill the empty seats in the wardrooms and ships' messes where squadron mates had previously sat. Tom Kinkaid had been lucky so far, but the time was coming when he too would feel the sickening jolt as his flagship rocked under a dive-bombing attack. But for the present, he was "home" again. Pearl Harbor had become such for him.

---

[58] TCK oral history, 175–76, 180–81.

Chapter 11

The *Enterprise* Task Force, June–October 1942

With Task Force 16 back in Pearl Harbor, Tom Kinkaid had two tasks to complete. The first was to finish his action reports and associated documents. He enjoyed this kind of work because of the professional challenge involved, but so much had been happening, it was not quick and easy to accomplish. The second was to call Helen. The news reporting about the Battle of Midway had been quite positive, with little of substance concerning the Navy's losses. But he knew she would be relieved to hear from him by telephone. Mail was helpful, in fact critical to his mental well-being, but it was pure pleasure to talk to his wife, even with a censor monitoring the call.

From Helen he learned that his mother was living comfortably at the Home for the Incurables. He was also pleased to hear that the $500 per month allotment was now arriving at Wynnefield Avenue in a timely manner.[1] Since Helen was living with her father, this income was sufficient for her during the war years.

Because Admiral Nimitz wanted to rest his badly battered carrier task forces as much as possible, Kinkaid could look forward to at least a month in port with only occasional training sorties after the first of July. Captain James M. Steele, in his daily command summary entry for 16 June, created his own "Three R's" to describe this period of reduced activity: "Task Forces 16 and 17 are utilizing the present period at Pearl Harbor to rest, refit, and replenish depleted and exhausted personnel and ships."[2]

Based on the hard lessons learned in the Coral Sea and at Midway, many of the ships, where possible, had their antiaircraft batteries and fire control systems upgraded. Because of the rapid development of radar technology almost every large ship received some type of improved installation for search or fire control purposes.

For the crews there was plenty of work each day, but there was also liberal liberty in most ships to help reduce tensions and rejuvenate spirits.

---
[1] TCK to HSK, Pearl Harbor, 15 Jun 1942.
[2] Command Summary, 16 Jun 1942.

Honolulu was not San Francisco or New York City, but it was a better liberty port than Noumea and certainly better than remaining on board a hot ship in early summer. After a couple of weeks in port, yard work began in earnest on *Minneapolis,* so Kinkaid moved into senior officer quarters ashore. With little to do, he devoted the afternoons to reducing his waistline. Concerned that he was becoming "soft as mush," the admiral tried to swim and get in a good walk daily. With members of his staff or occasionally flag officers such as Mahlon S. Tisdale or Poco Smith, he visited the Waikiki beaches and closed the day with a preprandial highball at the Moana or Royal Hawaiian Hotel. There was also a villa on Kaneohe Bay where tired flag officers and captains could escape the incessant noise of the navy yard. Although this regimen might have been restful, even restorative, it didn't satisfy Tom Kinkaid, as he wrote to his wife, "I am astonished when I look at the date. It seems like I have been out here a thousand years but at the same time it is hard to realize that six months have slipped by. If only we could see civilization occasionally, it would be a lot easier."[3] Civilization, obviously, had to include "the lovely Helen."

While in Pearl Harbor part of the admiral's daily routine included a visit to the offices of CINCPAC to see if any decisions had been reached concerning the next operations. As commander of TF 16 since 30 June when Rear Admiral Spruance had become Nimitz's chief of staff,[4] Kinkaid had a natural curiosity about his future. In early July he wandered into a conference room where a small group of very senior officers were huddled around some charts. Among those present was his classmate Rear Admiral Richmond Kelly Turner, now Admiral King's war plans officer. Admitted to the group, a bit reluctantly it seemed to him, Kinkaid found them discussing the next big operation—amphibious landings on Tulagi and Guadalcanal in the Solomon Islands.[5] The plan had originated with Turner and his boss, Ernest King.

Following the victory at Midway American naval leaders and General Douglas MacArthur in Australia began to press the Joint Chiefs of Staff (JCS) for a change in strategic priorities. The Japanese carrier fleet, the awesome *Kido Butai,* had obviously suffered catastrophic losses in ships, aircraft, and experienced flight personnel and the Combined Fleet had retreated to its anchorages to reconsider future operations. Admiral Yamamoto and his admirals still had at least six operational fleet carriers and a couple of auxiliary carriers (CVEs) plus a large battleship and cruiser fleet that were capable of overwhelming Nimitz's Pacific Fleet.[6]

---

[3] TCK to HSK, Pearl Harbor, 17 Jun 1942.
[4] TF 16, War Diary, 30 Jun 1942.
[5] TCK, "Four Years of War," 189–90; "Estimate: An Offensive for the Capture and Occupation of TULAGI and Vicinity, 6 Jul 1942," in Command Summary, 709–43.
[6] Dull, *Battle History IJN,* 343, 348.

Before the battle at Midway the Japanese had been thinking of seizing New Guinea, the Solomon Islands, the New Hebrides, New Caledonia, and the Fiji and Samoa islands. Japanese occupation of these islands, astride the communication lines from Hawaii, San Diego, or Panama to Australia, could make the American reinforcement of Australia extremely costly. The Allies would be forced to send their precious transport and cargo vessels over ever-longer routes to the Antipodes.[7] Admirals King and Nimitz had no idea how the Japanese plans would change after 4 June, but they did know the enemy still had the capability of driving the U.S. Navy out of its bases in New Caledonia (Noumea) and the New Hebrides (Espiritu Santo, Efate), particularly if they could build airfields in the lower Solomons at Tulagi and Guadalcanal. To avoid this development, King had begun planning a preemptive action. In mid-April he gained the Joint Chiefs' approval on a general plan proposed by Admiral Turner. That plan called for a buildup of ground, air, and naval forces by America, Australia, and New Zealand, and then a movement through the Solomons to the Japanese-controlled Bismarck Archipelago with its great naval and air base complex at Rabaul. Once the Bismarcks were captured, the goals of Orange Plan to take the Marshall and Caroline islands would be pursued. Finally an advance into the East Indies or the Philippines would begin.[8]

In late April at the first of his bimonthly meetings with Admiral King in San Francisco, Nimitz fell in with King's thinking. He agreed to order Vice Admiral Robert L. Ghormley, now en route to become Commander South Pacific Area (COMSOPAC), to begin planning a Solomons operation.[9] But before any action could be taken, the JCS and the Combined Chiefs of Staff would have to give their blessings. Standing in the way, of course, was the grand strategy agreed upon by the Allies to stand on the defensive in the Pacific while first concentrating offensive efforts on the defeat of Germany and Italy. On the other hand, King was assisted by the fact that there was no British-American agreement on when or where in Europe the first blow against the Axis would be struck in 1942.

As a member of the JCS and a participant in all the meetings of the Combined Chiefs of Staff, Admiral King was aware that the British were dragging their heels over an invasion of the German-controlled continent. General Marshall was ready to begin using the American Army that had been raised and trained. President Roosevelt, representing the public's point of view, wanted action against Germany in 1942. The Russians, now engaged in a death struggle with Adolf Hitler's forces deep within the So-

---

[7] Dyer, *Turner* 1:254–55; Lundstrom, *First South Pacific Campaign*, 41.
[8] Dyer, *Turner* 1:261–62; Hayes, *History Joint Chiefs*, 139; Richard B. Frank, *Guadalcanal* (New York: Random House, 1990), 15–16.
[9] Dyer, *Turner* 1:261–62.

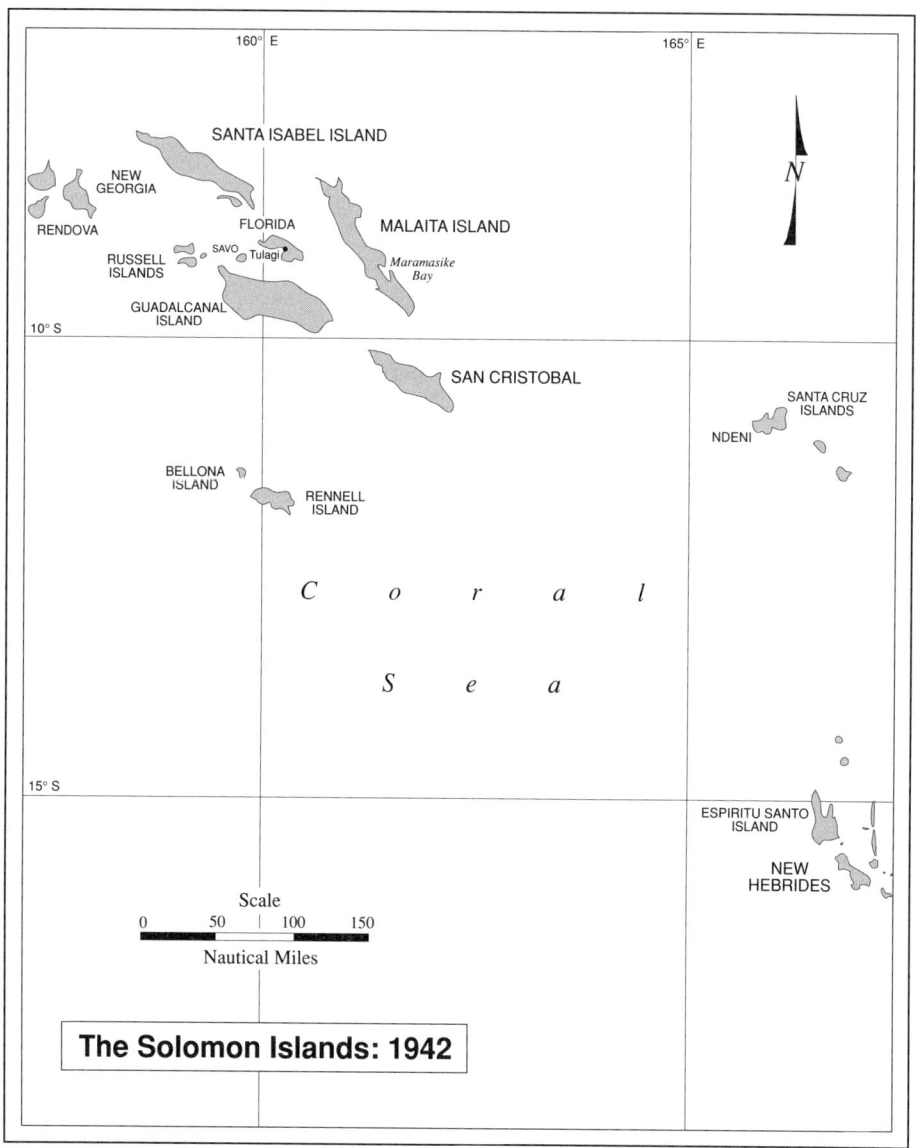

The Solomon Islands: 1942

viet Union, badly needed a second front opened to force the Germans to reduce the pressure on them.[10] Given this situation, on 5 May King asked the JCS to think seriously about strengthening American bases in the South Pacific to forestall further Japanese moves. Six weeks later, now somewhat supported by General MacArthur, he proposed to the JCS that the troops, ships, and material waiting in Britain be used to dislodge the Japanese.[11] General MacArthur had already proposed a campaign against Rabaul on 9 June. With some 40,000 amphibious troops (mostly Marines) in the United States and two carrier task groups to cover his landings, he thought the Japanese could be dislodged from the north coast of New Guinea; then the Bismarcks, including Rabaul, could be seized.[12]

There was a substantial difference between Admiral King's thinking and that of General MacArthur. King envisioned a Pacific Fleet-controlled operation with Nimitz or Ghormley planning and directing an assault in the Solomons. MacArthur considered an assault in the Solomons or New Guinea to be an operation in his domain, the Southwest Pacific Area, and thus his business.[13]

Admiral King and General Marshall worked out a compromise that satisfied MacArthur and Nimitz, though the timing left Ghormley and his staff with many doubts. It became the JCS order of 2 July to open a campaign for the capture of Rabaul. To meet the complaint of the SWPA commander that most of the Solomons lay west of 160°E, the boundary between the SWPA and the South Pacific Area was shifted to the 159th meridian. Tulagi and Guadalcanal would now lie in Ghormley's area. It was further agreed that the Pacific Fleet, through Ghormley, would initiate and control Task I, the seizure of Tulagi, Guadalcanal, and the Santa Cruz Islands. The next move, Task II, would be against Lae, Salamaua, and the northeast coast of New Guinea and would be under MacArthur's command. The final action, Task III, would be MacArthur's assault of the Bismarcks. A D-day for landings in the Solomons was set for 1 August 1942.[14] The lower Solomons operation was to be called PESTILENCE and the attacks against Tulagi and Guadalcanal to be operation WATCHTOWER. Because Admiral King had ordered Nimitz and Ghormley to begin their planning in April and May, this complicated operation, a logistical nightmare to some, was somewhat manageable.

---

[10] King and Whitehill, *Fleet Admiral King*, 390–96; Richard M. Leighton, "OVERLORD Revisited: An Interpretation of American Strategy in the European War, 1942–1944," *The American Historical Review* (Jul 1963): 927–28.

[11] Dyer, *Turner* 1:255–56; King and Whitehill, *Fleet Admiral King*, 386–87.

[12] COMSWPA to CINCPAC, 6/080731Z, 6/080733Z, 6/080735Z, Command Summary; D. Clayton James, *The Years of MacArthur*. vol. 2, *1941–1945* (Boston: Houghton Mifflin, 1975), 186–87.

[13] Hayes, *History Joint Chiefs*, 141–43; James, *MacArthur* 2:186–89.

[14] Hayes, *History Joint Chiefs*, 146–48; King and Whitehill, *Fleet Admiral King*, 387–88; Frank, *Guadalcanal*, 34–35.

During the first couple weeks that TF 16 had been in port, the inevitable command shifts occurred and Kinkaid had been a part of them. *Hornet* replaced the destroyed *Yorktown* in the roster of Striking Forces Pacific Fleet and became the centerpiece of TF 17.[15] Marc Mitscher, now a rear admiral, left his beloved *Hornet* and relieved another old-time naval aviator, Rear Admiral P. N. L. (Pat) Bellinger as Commander Patrol Wing Two on Oahu. Mitscher's relief as Commander TF 17 was another fresh-caught rear admiral, George D. Murray, the previous skipper of *Enterprise*.[16] Now considered an experienced carrier task force commander, though a nonaviator, Frank Jack Fletcher relieved Jake Fitch of *Saratoga's* TF 11. The *Enterprise* group, TF 16, was still Vice Admiral Halsey's command, but it had been led by Rear Admiral Spruance at Midway while Halsey was receiving medical treatment. Although Halsey was not ready for sea duty as yet, Nimitz needed a new chief of staff. Spruance was ordered ashore, and much to Kinkaid's surprise, Nimitz tapped him to take over TF 16 until Halsey could return, probably in mid-September. On 30 June on board *Enterprise*, Kinkaid read his orders to the assembled staff and relieved Spruance. Thus began what was to become the most memorable command of his naval career. Kinkaid was relieved as Commander Cruisers, TF 11 by Rear Admiral Frank Lowry, another newly minted flag officer, who had previously commanded *Minneapolis*.[17]

The records do not explain Kinkaid's assignment to a carrier task force command, but a few reasons do seem obvious. Since becoming a cruiser division commander, the admiral had seen steady employment as a cruiser-destroyer screen commander with the carrier task forces. From his vantage point on *Minneapolis*'s flag bridge he had been able to observe and learn about task force operations. By now Kinkaid also knew a great deal about the antiaircraft defense of a task force. Furthermore, Nimitz knew that Fletcher and Spruance had been successful task force commanders even though neither was a naval aviator. Spruance had been prepared for his command in the same way Kinkaid had, by following in the wakes of the carriers. Halsey had recommended Spruance to be his relief in *Enterprise*; it is probable that Fletcher or possibly Spruance recommended Kinkaid for Spruance's job. Fletcher was to command the Guadalcanal expeditionary force and therefore would normally have been consulted about the task force commanders to serve under him. Finally in late June 1942 there was a shortage at Pearl Harbor of battle-tested flag officers with carrier task force command experience. Kinkaid was in the right place at the right time.

---

[15] CINCPAC to PACFLT, 6/160131Z, Command Summary.

[16] Taylor, *Magnificent Mitscher*, 139; Paolo E. Coletta, *Patrick N. L. Bellinger and U.S. Naval Aviation* (Lanham, MD: University Press of America, 1987), 314–15.

[17] COMCRU 6, War Diary, 16 and 30 Jun 1942.

Rear Admiral Kinkaid, Lieutenant Commander H.D. Moulton, and Lieutenant Commander R. H. Taylor on board *Enterprise* (CV 6), fall 1942. Moulton had been a member of Admiral Halsey's TF 16 staff and was "loaned" to Kinkaid while he commanded TF 16.

A week after relieving Spruance, Kinkaid took his new command to sea for tactical drills. The *Enterprise* squadrons needed a great deal of work before they could again function with the competence displayed at Midway. New pilots had been assigned to replace those lost in action or sent stateside to instructor duty, and these new pilots needed intensive training. The ship's new air boss, Commander John G. Crommelin, oversaw the air operations and made sure that every training opportunity was utilized. Not only did the squadrons sharpen their operational skills, they also helped the ships' companies throughout the task force improve their gunnery. Towing target sleeves for the antiaircraft batteries was both tedious and dangerous for the pilots, but they appreciated the need to develop shipboard gunners who could bring down enemy dive bombers and torpedo planes before they disabled the *Big E*.[18]

These training sorties also provided Kinkaid with an opportunity to work with his new staff. In moving to *Enterprise*, he had brought with him only

---

[18] TF 16, War Diary, 8–11 Jul 1942. See also John B. Lundstrom, *The First Team and the Guadalcanal Campaign* (Annapolis: Naval Institute Press, 1994), 5–7, 23–27.

Lieutenant Commander Robert Taylor, still his flag lieutenant. From Spruance he inherited part of the staff that Halsey had left behind when he went ashore for medical treatment. Because of the relatively small size—five lieutenant commanders and five junior officer communicators—there was no designated chief of staff, but Lieutenant Commander Sherman E. (Sherm) Burroughs took charge on an interim basis. Lieutenant Commander Leonard J. (Ham) Dow became the task force fighter director officer (FDO). He was to have a good deal of work ahead of him. The five senior members of the staff messed with Kinkaid, who quickly came to recognize their competence. Unlike Halsey, who had developed a free and easy relationship with his staff, Kinkaid continued to keep his distance. Taylor was probably the only one with whom he was socially comfortable. Burroughs later remembered the admiral to be direct, fair, quiet, and somewhat aloof.[19]

During the two weeks Kinkaid was trying his sea legs as a carrier task force commander, CINCPAC's staff completed its plans for the Solomons operation. Built upon the estimate that Admiral Turner had carried to Pearl Harbor,[20] it was clearly a move to the offensive and involved considerable risk. In attacking at Tulagi and Guadalcanal, Fletcher's naval force would be sailing within attack range of aircraft based at Rabaul and any air bases the Japanese might possess in the Solomons. To meet this problem, Nimitz's planners (and Ghormley's as well) were counting on General MacArthur's bombing squadrons to neutralize enemy bases at Rabaul and in the upper Solomons. Turner had recognized this dependency: "In any plan, the air support which General MacArthur can give from AUSTRALIA and from PORT MORESBY is essential to the success of the operation. If adequate air from PORT MORESBY is not available we will be unable to neutralize the enemy at a very critical time."[21] That critical time would be when the transports were unloading their troops and supplies onto the beaches at Tulagi and Guadalcanal. The stakes were high, but the basic philosophy of Admirals King and Turner suffused the plan and was stated in the estimate:

> The sooner we accomplish the Second Stage [moving to the offensive in the Solomons], the sooner the war, and its terrific drain on our national resources, will be brought to successful conclusion. This point is stressed here because there is too often the tendency of the military profession to wait until everything is absolutely perfect before any operation can commence. Conditions will never be perfect, and we cannot afford to miss any chance while waiting for perfection.[22]

---

[19] TCK to HSK, *Enterprise*, 9 Jul 1942; RADM Sherman E. Burroughs, USN (Ret.), interview with author, Coronado, CA, 27 Dec 1988.
[20] "Estimate Jul 6, 1942," Command Summary, 709–43.
[21] Ibid., 727.
[22] Ibid., 713.

The King-Turner attitude toward risk taking was not shared by Admiral Ghormley and General MacArthur. As ships and material began to flow southwest to support WATCHTOWER, the two met in Melbourne to discuss the support the Southwest Pacific Area commander could provide. The result of this meeting was a seven-part message addressed on 8 July to King and Nimitz that was designed to derail the Solomons operation. As they saw it, the largest obstacle to success would be their inability to gain command of the air in the operation area. Their message painted a grim picture:

> The air force now in sight for the Southwest Pacific Area is not adequate to interdict hostile air or naval operations against the Tulagi area. The carrier task groups themselves will be exposed to attack by land-based air while unprotected by our land-based aviation and it is extremely doubtful that they will be able to render fighter support to the transport area, especially should hostile naval forces approach.[23]

Ghormley and MacArthur concluded that in their "considered opinion" the "successful accomplishment of the operation is open to the gravest doubts." They counseled postponement until they had air bases on the north coast of New Guinea, more naval vessels, and more trained troops.[24]

The message from Ghormley infuriated Admiral King. He complained to General Marshall about MacArthur's *volte face* after suggesting a campaign against Rabaul. The admiral was seriously concerned about the information that had arrived within the week from CINCPAC that the Japanese were constructing an airfield on Guadalcanal. There was no doubt. The code-breakers had detected the information first, and then aircraft had photographed the Japanese in action. If the enemy were allowed to finish the field and fortify Guadalcanal, American positions in New Caledonia and the New Hebrides would be at risk. WATCHTOWER had now become a race between the Japanese construction crew and CINCPAC's forces.[25]

Without responding directly to the seven-part message of 8 July, Nimitz informed Ghormley the next day that COMSOPAC would be the overall commander for the Solomons operation and that he was to "exercise strategic command in person in the operating area, which is interpreted initially to be the New Caledonia, New Hebrides area."[26] It settled the matter. On 16 July Ghormley issued his Operations Plan 1–42 for the capture and occupation of Tulagi and adjacent areas (Guadalcanal, Santa Cruz Islands, etc.).[27]

---

[23] COMSWPA to COMINCH, CINCPAC, COMSOPAC, 7/081015Z, Command Summary.
[24] Ibid., 7/081021Z, Command Summary; Frank, *Guadalcanal*, 36–38.
[25] Potter, *Nimitz*, 179; Buell, *King*, 219–20.
[26] CINCPAC to COMSOPAC, 7/090633Z, Command Summary.
[27] COMSOPAC to CTF 11, 16, 18, 44 and COMPHIBFORSPAC, 7/170602Z, Command Summary.

WATCHTOWER Command, July 1942

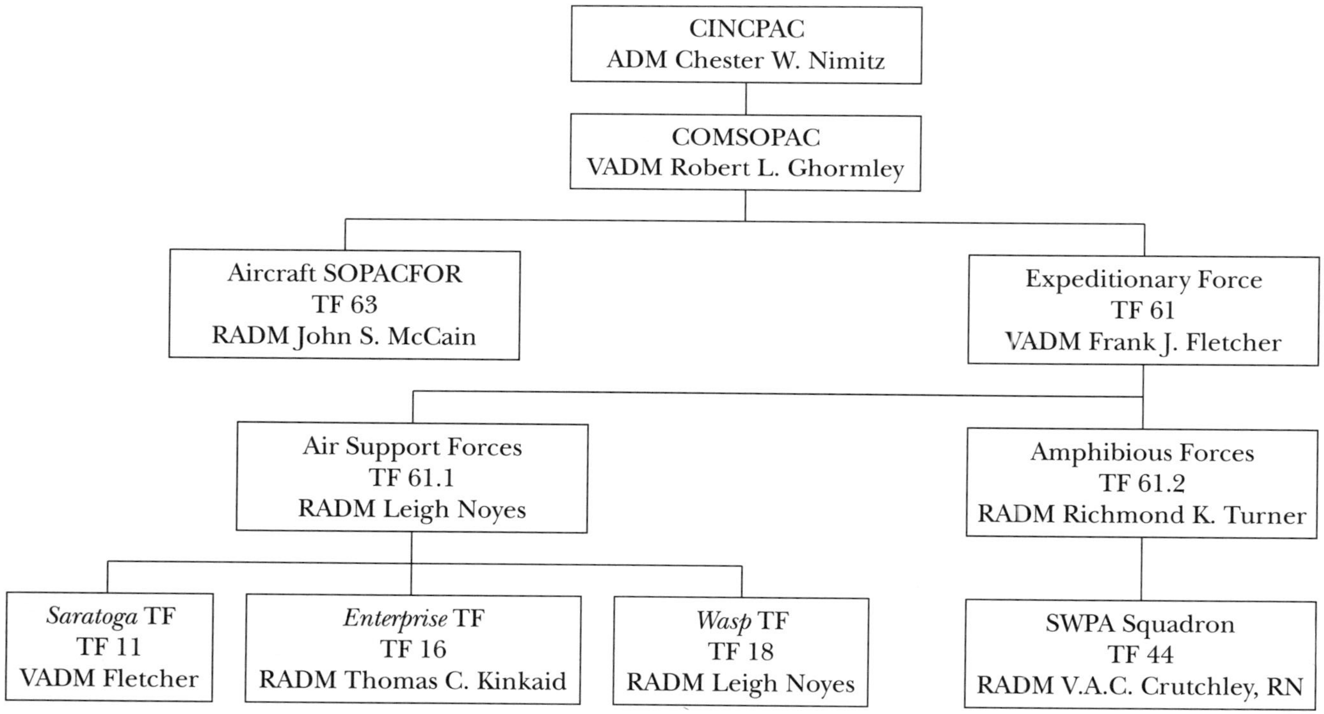

- CINCPAC — ADM Chester W. Nimitz
  - COMSOPAC — VADM Robert L. Ghormley
    - Aircraft SOPACFOR, TF 63 — RADM John S. McCain
    - Expeditionary Force, TF 61 — VADM Frank J. Fletcher
      - Air Support Forces, TF 61.1 — RADM Leigh Noyes
        - Saratoga TF, TF 11 — VADM Fletcher
        - Enterprise TF, TF 16 — RADM Thomas C. Kinkaid
        - Wasp TF, TF 18 — RADM Leigh Noyes
      - Amphibious Forces, TF 61.2 — RADM Richmond K. Turner
      - SWPA Squadron, TF 44 — RADM V.A.C. Crutchley, RN

SOURCE: Dyer, *Turner*, 1:291–93.

The command arrangements for WATCHTOWER were relatively simple. With four carrier task forces available to him during July, Admiral Nimitz chose three for WATCHTOWER and retained one (*Hornet*) in Hawaiian waters. Based on the condition of readiness of the flat-tops and their air groups TF 11 (*Saratoga*), with Vice Admiral Fletcher embarked, headed south first on 7 July. Finally awarded his third star on 15 July, Fletcher was now clearly senior to all of his task force commanders, including classmate Rear Admiral Leigh Noyes.[28] Fletcher's group would be joined in the Fiji area by Noyes's *Wasp* (CV 7) task force (TF 18), which was escorting the transport group carrying the Second Marine Regiment from San Diego. On 15 July Admiral Kinkaid took TF 16 with *Enterprise* out of Pearl Harbor and shaped course for Fiji. Once together Fletcher would meld the three carrier task forces into one, TF 61.

After two previous trips to the South Pacific area, the route and the task force routines were familiar to Kinkaid. With the first stop being the Navy's fueling base at Tongatabu in the Tonga Islands, the sailing directions from Pearl could have read "south along 160W and turn right at Rarotonga." From his flag bridge high in *Enterprise*'s island he had a splendid view of the eleven vessels in TF 16. Broad on the bows were *Portland* and the fairly new antiaircraft cruiser, *Atlanta*. The task force screen commander, Rear Admiral Mahlon Tisdale, flew his blue flag in the heavy cruiser. Riding the wake of the *Big E* was the newest battleship addition to the Pacific Fleet, *North Carolina* (BB 55). Commissioned in the spring of 1941 and following its East Coast shakedown, it had arrived at Pearl Harbor just in time for assignment to the *Enterprise* task force. With her twenty 5-inch, 38-caliber antiaircraft guns and a large assortment of smaller automatic weapons, *North Carolina* enormously strengthened the protective ring around the carrier.[29] At the outer reaches of the circular formation were Captain Edward P. Sauer's seven destroyers: *Balch, Benham, Ellet, Grayson* (DD 435), *Gwin* (DD 433), *Maury,* and *Monssen* (DD 436).[30] Except for *Grayson* and *North Carolina*, Kinkaid's ships had battle experience and most of them had fought with him at Coral Sea and Midway.

The fast, new battleship brought with it some questions. A basic one was where to place the ship in the operating formations. Were it given a cruiser's normal position, 45 degrees relative on the bow or stern, the battleship would have problems maintaining station during turning battle maneuvers. The great displacement of the vessel, upwards of 35,000 tons, created enormous momentum and thus a skidding motion (advance) when formation turns were ordered. Kinkaid's solution was to have *North*

---

[28] Dyer, *Turner* 1:293.
[29] "North Carolina," *DANFS* 5:108–10.
[30] TF 16, War Diary, 15 Jul 1942.

Rear Admiral Kinkaid stands ready at the flag bag of *Enterprise*, fall 1942. Normally the admiral did not wear a necktie while at sea in the tropics.

Carolina move in the carrier's wake at the 180-degree station. Later the admiral was to learn that, when *Enterprise* moved to flank speed under attack, she began to pull away rapidly from the battleship's protective gunfire.[31]

Kinkaid's schedule called for a 1400 (local time), 26 July rendezvous of the task forces at 23°15′S on the 180th meridian, about 430 miles south of Koro Island in the Fijis.[32] Previously the daily advance of the task force had been someone else's problem, now it was Tom's. Within two days it became obvious that his task force was falling behind schedule. Steaming at 17 knots, a comfortable and economical speed for all of the ships, would not get them there on time.

Delays were caused by daily air operations. Two or three times a day *Enterprise* turned into the prevailing wind to launch aircraft and later repeated the operation to recover them. Each morning around 0630 torpedo planes or scout bombers were launched to search 150 to 200 miles ahead of the force, to the south and west. Several planes from the early launch would spend the morning circling the force watching for signs of a submarine, the feathering wake of a periscope moving through the water, or the telltale track of bubbles from a torpedo moving at 40 knots. In late morning the inner patrol planes would be relieved by scout-observation aircraft from the heavy cruisers and battleship. In midafternoon the morning searches were repeated, and the fighters and dive-bombers were also launched for gunnery and attack exercises. Because the winds normally blew from the southeast around to the northeast in these latitudes, and the task force course was to the west of south, air operations cost heavily in terms of miles lost. The admiral therefore considered the miserable weather on 21 July a blessing because it forced a cancellation of flight operations. The cancellation was doubly appreciated because the force had to slow to 8 knots the previous day as *Portland* and *North Carolina* spent several hours fueling the destroyers. By the 22d Kinkaid had increased task force speed to 25 knots to make up distance.[33]

On 23 July, while a day's steaming from Tongatabu, Kinkaid sent two torpedo planes to the island to make arrangements for fueling in the port of Nukualofa. His chief of staff, Sherm Burroughs, made the trip as the admiral's representative. Early the next morning the task force anchored in the harbor and began taking oil from a couple of tankers. When Burroughs returned on board *Enterprise*, he startled the admiral by informing him they were a whole day behind schedule. No one on

---

[31] TCK, "Four Years of War," 190–91.
[32] ONI Combat Narrative: *Solomon Islands*, 1:2.
[33] TF 16, War Diary, 15–24 Jul 1942; TCK, "Four Years of War," 191–93; LT Frederick Mears, *Carrier Combat* (Garden City, NY: Doubleday, Doran, 1944), 85–88.

the staff had remembered that the rendezvous point at Tonga and the Fiji Islands were west of the international dateline.[34] It was 25 July, not the 24th. Instead of departing the next morning, *Enterprise* and her brood weighed anchors and steamed hurriedly from Nukualofa at 1530.[35] Task Force 16 made the rendezvous, but its admiral came closer to fouling the operation than he cared to remember.

The next day, Sunday, 26 July, at 1400 almost the whole WATCHTOWER force laid to at the rendezvous. Delivered by high line to *Saratoga*, Kinkaid joined a conference of senior officers to work out the details of the WATCHTOWER rehearsal, which was code-named DOVETAIL. Koro Island would be the rehearsal target. All of the activities associated with WATCHTOWER would be carried out against the island between 28 and 31 July. The dawn attack by carrier fighters and bombers against gunnery installations, a ship bombardment of the beach and hinterlands, and the full ship-to-shore amphibious movement of troops would all be a part of DOVETAIL. Fletcher informed his senior commanders that the carrier force would be available for support and covering operations at Tulagi-Guadalcanal for only two days. Because of anticipated fuel shortages the three carrier groups would have to withdraw from the area on 9 August to meet their oilers. No one present was pleased with this decision, and several challenged its necessity or wisdom, but Fletcher held fast to it. He recognized, as did most carrier task force commanders, that keeping flat-tops tied to areas that could be reached by land-based attack aircraft put the ships at great risk. Given the shortage of carriers in the Pacific Fleet, Fletcher believed no other course was open to him. According to later interviewers Kinkaid agreed with Fletcher's decision. As might be expected, the Amphibious Force commander, Kelly Turner, and the Marine commander, Major General Alexander A. Vandegrift, both saw the situation quite differently.[36]

The rehearsal exercises were completed on 31 July and the replenishment of magazines and oil bunkers began. Always concerned about fuel logistics, Fletcher had kept the pressure on Ghormley and Nimitz to see that the precious black oil flowed to his expeditionary force. A few days before departing Koro Island, he informed COMSOPAC that he would be short approximately 50,000 barrels after emptying the available oilers on the 31st. He considered it imperative that his ships be topped off again between Koro and the Solomons area. Ghormley did his best, but a portion of TF 61, the cruisers and destroyers of Turner's escort force, had to fuel from the transports and cargo ships. Although not obvious to

---

[34] TCK, "Four Years of War," 191–93; Mears, *Carrier Combat*, 89.
[35] TF 16, War Diary, 25 Jul 1942.
[36] Dyer, *Turner* 1:299–303; Lundstrom, *First Team and Guadalcanal*, 28–29.

Rear Admiral Richmond Kelly Turner, left, and Major General Alexander A. Vandegrift, USMC, on the flag bridge of *McCawley* (AP 10) during the Guadalcanal operation, July–August 1942.

all, WATCHTOWER's deadlines pressed on Ghormley by Admirals King and Nimitz had created a situation that could imperil the operation. Fletcher's force had almost outrun its logistics pipeline.[37]

During the three weeks his task force was steaming first to the Fiji Islands and then the Solomon Islands, Tom Kinkaid wrote regularly to Helen even though the letters only piled up in the ship's mail sacks. At Tongatabu mail left the ship, but none came on board to cheer the crew. Adhering strictly to censorship regulations, despite his own mail not being censored, Tom filled his one-page letters with trivia. Now in the world of carrier aviation he wrote that he had purchased and was wearing an overseas cap with his khaki uniform. It stayed on better in the brisk wind that usually blew around his station high in the carrier's superstructure. To keep his face and ears from getting sunburned, he usu-

---

[37] CTF 61 to COMSOPAC, 7/280201Z, Command Summary; Dyer, *Turner* 1:311–14.

ally wore his "summer bonnet," a flak helmet liner, if he was out in the sun very long. Because his task force was moving south of the equator, down to almost 20°S, Tom regularly wore a leather flight jacket with a fur collar (from the clothing he described in his letters, Helen understood where he had been). Throughout *Enterprise*'s officers and crew, particularly the married ones, there must have been many who echoed the admiral's sentiments when he lamented:

> I look at the date in astonishment and I hate to see the months slipping by while we are not together. Just think how much we would have enjoyed each other during the past eight months! There are so many things that I can think of that I would like to do with you and nothing seems much fun without you.[38]

The most direct route from the Fijis to the Guadalcanal area would have required a course of 300 degrees, roughly a west-northwest heading, but Fletcher did not turn in that direction. Instead the expeditionary force shaped course slightly to the south of west in order to pass through the New Hebrides between Efate and Eromanga islands. It was hoped that this route, if spotted by enemy submarines, would deceive the Japanese as to the ultimate destination of the ships.

At Pearl Harbor and Washington other deceptions had been planned to draw attention away from the Solomons. On 27 July the light cruiser *Boise* (CL 47) slipped out of Pearl Harbor on a solitary mission to raid the Japanese "sampan patrol line" some 500 to 800 miles east of Tokyo. By using its scout planes to attack enemy picket ships and by cluttering the radio circuits with unnecessary traffic, CINCPAC's staff hoped to create the impression that a major American raid was in progress. Nimitz also asked the Army to lay on a B–17 raid against Wake Island, again to convince the enemy that serious action was about to commence.

Boise contacted no picket ships, but in trying to locate two of its lost scouts, the cruiser created enough radio traffic for a task force. For its part the Army's Hawaiian Department sent a single B–17 on a successful photo reconnaissance of Wake Island on 31 July. Whether it caused the Japanese to worry about a seaborne attack in the near future is questionable. In Washington, Admiral King convinced the British that they should make a naval feint in the Bay of Bengal in order to direct Japanese attention to that area. On 1 August naval groupings left Vizagapatam, Madras, and Trincomalee on courses aimed at the Andaman Islands. These movements were distantly covered by a battleship-carrier task force that sailed from Colombo a day earlier. Though the Eastern

---

[38] TCK to HSK, Enterprise, 1 and 2 Aug 1942.

Fleet movements lasted just one day before they reversed course, this activity did cause the Japanese to move minor forces to Sabang at the opening into the Strait of Malacca, and to spend several days worrying about a possible assault on their holdings in the eastern Bay of Bengal.[39]

Once through the New Hebrides the task forces continued on a heading of about 290 degrees until they reached the 159th meridian in the early morning of 5 August. From there it was due north to Guadalcanal. The day before turning north *Enterprise*'s search radar made contact several times with enemy patrol planes from Tulagi. Correctly believing the force was still undetected, Fletcher kept his fighters reined in and made no effort to destroy the snoopers.[40] He was not eager to reveal his force's position and then have to fight his way through to the Tulagi-Guadalcanal landing sites. To do so could have been disastrous; at the least it would have led to a serious fuel shortage. Kinkaid's staff estimated that, as of 0800 on the 4th, "heavy ships have fuel for 3 days at 15 knots plus 4 days at 25 knots." That wasn't bad. It meant the carrier, cruisers, and battleship could reach Guadalcanal and still be able to engage in battle maneuvering for four days. But the same estimate revealed a major problem: "Destroyers have fuel for 3 days at 15 knots plus 2 days at 25 knots."[41] It would be necessary to fuel the destroyers soon after arrival at their destination. If they drew their oil from the larger ships, they would all have less time before refueling became mandatory.

The expeditionary force's luck held. Rain showers and low visibility in the region of the intertropic front kept the ships hidden from the enemy. On the 6th more radar contacts were made with enemy patrolling aircraft, but the Japanese did not spot them. Had the patrol planes been equipped with radar sets, it might have been a very different story. But Turner's amphibious force arrived at the western end of Guadalcanal in darkness undetected. The three carrier task forces took station about 75 miles south and west of Guadalcanal and awaited the dawn.

With first light at 0530, *Enterprise, Wasp,* and *Saratoga* commenced their aerial assault against targets on Tulagi, Gavutu, Tanambogo, and Guadalcanal. It was immediately evident that tactical surprise had been achieved. There was no opposition. Because the most experienced fighter director officer was in *Enterprise,* that carrier was given the responsibility of providing combat air patrol over the task forces and of controlling the actions of their Wildcats. A fighter direction team from *Saratoga* moved on board *Chicago* and provided control for aircraft as-

---

[39] CINCPAC to COMINCH, 7/280329Z, Command Summary; Mike Stankovich, "The Hardest Choice," *Naval History* (Winter 1988): 30–33; COMINCH to CINCPAC, COMSWPA, 7/301601Z, Command Summary; ADMIRALTY to CINCPAC, 8/101418Z, Command Summary.
[40] TF 16, War Diary, 4 Aug 1942.
[41] Ibid.

signed to close support duties with the troops as they moved ashore and inland. Because of first-class staff work by Rear Admiral Noyes's planners the three carrier groups went into action with assigned targets, required munitions, communications frequencies to be used, and even the fuel loads for each type of aircraft.[42] There was not a great deal left for Kinkaid to do. His principal duties were associated with the air defense of TF 16 and much of that work was the concern of his screen commander, Rear Admiral Tisdale. Yet when an air attack did occur the signal, "Follow my movements," would be snapped onto Kinkaid's flag hoist in *Enterprise*. The carrier, of course, would be maneuvered by its commanding officer, Captain A. C. (Art) Davis.

Turner's assault force had the morning to enjoy the benefits of surprise, but everyone knew the Japanese would soon react. The distance from Rabaul was about 575 air miles and there were plenty of attack aircraft there that could cover the distance in three-plus hours. The first wave of counterattackers arrived at 1330 and was greeted by Wildcats from *Saratoga* and *Enterprise*. Flying with parade-ground precision in three nine-plane Vs, the twenty-seven Bettys and their Zero escorts were badly mauled by the F4Fs and obtained no hits on the transports or escorts off the beaches of Tulagi and Guadalcanal. Most of the attacking bombers managed to escape the combat air patrols, but all were thoroughly riddled with bullet holes. An hour and a half later a second attacking group arrived from Rabaul. Consisting of nine Vals—the fixed-gear carrier dive bombers then in use by the Japanese—this attack proved as ineffective as the first. The fighters downed six of the Vals in the vicinity of Guadalcanal and the remaining three ditched during the return flight to Rabaul.

The cost to the Japanese that day had been five Bettys, nine Vals, and a couple of escorting Zeros. Fletcher's pilots had not had an easy time of it; eight Wildcats and one Dauntless had been shot down.[43] But the invasion had been a success. The Marines now controlled the airfield on Guadalcanal and were rapidly achieving control of Tulagi, Gavutu, and Tanambogo. However there was concern that the ships were not being unloaded as rapidly as Turner and Vandegrift desired.

During the attacks on the invasion fleet, Kinkaid and the other carrier task force commanders were interested but distant spectators. Tom could follow the approaching enemy flights on *Enterprise*'s radar and could see the intercepting blips on the screen as the CAP made contact, but the carriers were too far away for the admirals to observe the action directly. When *Enterprise* secured from flight operations at 1915, there was a collec-

---

[42] ONI Combat Narrative: *Solomons* 1:17–18.

[43] Thomas G. Miller, Jr., *The Cactus Air Force* (New York: Harper & Row, Bantam Books, 1981), 5–6; Eric Hammell, *Guadalcanal: The Carrier Battles* (New York: Crown Publishers, 1987), 16–32; CDR Edward Stafford, *The Big E* (New York: Random House, 1962), 110–14.

tive sigh of relief. There was no doubt in anyone's mind that the next day would see further attacks, perhaps with the carriers as the targets.

Again with first light on 8 August air operations began where they had left off the previous day. Fighters were launched for CAP and Dauntlesses began an intermediate patrol around the task force area to make sure no submarines were setting up for attacks while the ships were silhouetted by a rising sun. Fighters also darted among the ships, looking for enemy subs that might have worked inside the screen. Later when the first group of fighters had to be recovered, the float planes from the cruisers took over the inner patrol duties. During these same early hours Wildcats, Dauntlesses, and Avengers were being launched for strikes against targets ashore as the Marines encountered isolated strong points or artillery batteries revealed themselves. And on board every ship in the area antiaircraft batteries were unlimbered, ready ammunition stocks filled, and gun drills begun. Everywhere there was a high degree of readiness, particularly among those ships lying off Guadalcanal and Tulagi. Their crews knew they were the bull's-eye in the target area.

The expected attack hit the transports and cargo ships a few minutes before noon. Though warned by an Australian coast watcher on Bougainville that a large number of bombers were headed their way, the radars of *Chicago* and the carriers failed to pick up the Japanese. Coming down the north side of the Solomons chain, the twenty-three torpedo-carrying Bettys and their escorts came into sight of the shipboard gunners only as they flew over Florida Island and bore down on the ships off Guadalcanal. Once sighted, they were immediately engaged by fighters from *Enterprise* and by the antiaircraft batteries of every ship that could bring its guns to bear. The Bettys and their escorts were decimated. In return they made a torpedo hit on *Jarvis* (DD 393) and a Zero, in extremis, crashed into the transport *George F. Elliott* (AP 13), setting it afire and causing its loss. Eighteen of the attacking Bettys with their crews of seven were destroyed. Figures are still inexact, but at least forty Japanese aircraft and their crews had been shot down in these first two days of WATCHTOWER.

The cost to TF 61 had not been insignificant, however. Admiral Fletcher reported a loss of twenty-one fighters in combat or operations accidents, a 21-percent reduction in Wildcats from his squadrons. The Japanese losses, mostly in land-based bombing planes, had been much heavier, but replacements could be sent from the Marianas and Truk. Except for limited replacement planes carried triced up above the hangar deck, the American carriers, for the time being, could not replace the aircraft they had lost.[44]

---

[44] Norman Polmar, *Aircraft Carriers: A Graphic History of Carrier Aviation and Its Influence on World Events* (Garden City, NY: Doubleday, 1969), 246; Miller, *Cactus Air Force*, 7–8; Hammell, *Carrier Battles*, 32–34; Stafford, *Big E,* 114–15; ONI Combat Narrative: *Solomons* 1:75–77.

With the close of air operations on the 8th Kinkaid and TF 16 were very tired. Even more tired, if possible, were the personnel in *Enterprise*. Air operations had been strenuous both days, particularly the 7th, invasion day. The historian of the *Big E* found that "during the two-day period there had been 372 take-offs and 366 landings, 236 take-offs and 229 landings on the single day of the seventh to establish a new record for flight operations in combat." Even more telling had been the stress on the pilots; ninety-one had flown a total of 1,000 hours.[45] Carrier flight operations involved constant risk and worry for the pilots. Wrestling a loaded Grumman Avenger or Douglas Dauntless off a flight deck required absolute concentration and enormous skill. Most of the squadron losses in these types came from flight-deck launches, not enemy action. The return to the carrier deck required equal concentration and skill, often after a tiring four- to five-hour mission. And the wardroom messes in the carriers no longer brought relief from the tension of operations. The twenty-one lost fighters and a half-dozen other types of aircraft meant missing faces at meals. The losses weren't as dramatic as those suffered by VT–8 and VT–6 at Midway, but the pilots deeply felt the loss of a wingman, a roommate, an acey-deucey opponent, or a friend.

Yet there could be no letting up in vigilance on board any ship. Admiral Fletcher was convinced that enemy carriers were within striking distance, and he sent Kinkaid's scouts out 260 miles in the afternoon of the 8th, searching to the north from 270 to 090 degrees. He also pressed Rear Admiral John S. McCain, Commander Aircraft, South Pacific Area, to extend his patrol searches up the Solomons chain and toward the north to locate any enemy task forces approaching from Rabaul or Truk.[46]

By midday on the 8th, Kinkaid's staff was becoming concerned about the fuel situation in TF 16. With the noon position, the force war diary commented, "Continuing support air operations this afternoon. Fuel situation this force becoming critical. It is estimated the destroyers have fuel for about three days at 15 knots and the heavy ships have little more."[47]

As noted before, consumption based on 15 knots was an optimum figure. If the task force were to come under air attack or have to deploy and engage in surface battle, the rate of consumption would more than double. Furthermore, if a Japanese submarine sank an oiler that had been dispatched to refuel TF 16, Kinkaid's force could be in desperate straits. By the 8th *Enterprise* had fuel for about five days at 15 knots, *Atlanta* and *Portland* were good for seven and nine days, respectively, but *Grayson* had just two and a half days in her bunkers, and *Benham* and *Balch* each had

---
[45] Stafford, *Big E*, 115.
[46] TF 16, War Diary, 8 Aug 1942; Dyer, *Turner* 1:369–71, 385–87.
[47] TF 16, War Diary, 8 Aug 1942.

three and a half days, provided they could average 15 knots.⁴⁸ However, flight operations, which involved the whole task force, usually meant increasing the force speed to at least 25 knots, and such operations were continual while the task forces were on station. Task Forces 11 and 18 also faced fuel shortages. Aware of the problem, but more concerned about further attacks from land-based bombers against Turner's ships and possibly his own TF 61, Fletcher decided to implement the decision he had made on 26 July. He would move his task forces to the southeast, away from possible attack by land-based bombers.

The *Big E*'s afternoon searches were on board by 1800 and reported no contacts with any enemy surface forces. Content that nothing could steam into the area and disrupt the unloading of Turner's cargo vessels during the coming night, Fletcher requested permission from COMSOPAC to withdraw his carriers from the Tulagi-Guadalcanal area. He noted that he was short on fighter planes and that his task forces were low on fuel. Implicit was his desire not to expose the carriers to a day of possible land-based bomber attacks.⁴⁹ Apparently Kinkaid was not consulted concerning the retreat of his task force. At the end of the day, his war diarist merely recorded the information that "due to enemy air attacks and reduction of fighters in our force . . . together with critical fuel situation, has caused CTF 61 to recommend to Comsopac that carriers be withdrawn."⁵⁰

Three and a half hours after the war diary entry of 2330, the first information concerning the Battle of Savo Island was entered somewhat innocuously by the flag secretary: "0300. Heard first flash report indicating some type of surface action in the Tulagi-Guadalcanal Area."⁵¹ A half hour later came Admiral Ghormley's approval for the carriers to retire. At 0430 the entry read, "Changed course to right to 140, commencing retirement from the area."⁵² It is not at all evident in reading the Task Force 16 war diary that Turner's TF 62 had engaged in a night action with seven Japanese cruisers. Four heavy cruisers (*Vincennes, Astoria, Quincy, Canberra*) had been lost and another (*Chicago*) had been severely damaged. No enemy cruisers had been sunk and only one, *Chokai*, had suffered any damage.

Because of communication difficulties and the "fog of war," information came slowly to Turner and Fletcher, the latter now pulling away steadily to the southeast in *Saratoga*. At 0800 Kinkaid's war diary reported that there had been a surface action in the Tulagi-Guadalcanal area, but "no definite information has been received upon which to base a decision." Two hours later, with the return of the Dauntlesses that had

---

[48] Dyer, *Turner* 1:389–90.
[49] CTF 61 to COMSOPAC, 8/081807W (8/090707Z), Command Summary.
[50] TF 16, War Diary, 8 Aug 1942.
[51] Ibid.
[52] Ibid.

searched the battle area, the diarist laconically stated, "Pilots of VSB planes . . . saw no evidence of surface action there or enemy vessels."[53]

By midday on the 9th Turner and then Fletcher knew the dimensions of the disaster that had overtaken TF 62. Unloading what he could for the Marines ashore, Kelly Turner decided not to test this luck any further. In late afternoon (1608 local time) he informed Admiral Ghormley that he was withdrawing his transports, cargo vessels, and naval support forces, and by 1830 the last units were underway.[54] General Vandegrift and his Marines were on their own, on short rations and with limited munitions and weapons, until they could prepare the Japanese airfield for some squadrons to return and help them defend the island. Ghormley, somewhat after the fact, blessed Turner's withdrawal, told McCain to pull his PBYs out of Malaita northeast of Guadalcanal and the Santa Cruz Islands east of Guadalcanal, and asked Fletcher to use his task forces to cover the Marines as best he could once he had finished refueling.[55] In a "most secret" dispatch to Nimitz, Ghormley wound up business on the 9th with his own summary. It was still not clear to him what had happened at Savo Island.

> The carriers [were] short of fuel and [are] proceeding to fueling rendezvous. Am withdrawing other naval surface forces and patrol planes until such time as I have shore-based aircraft in such strength that I can protect my lines of communication to CACTUS [Guadalcanal] and supply CACTUS with sufficient aviation for effective defense. Request immediate air reinforcement, especially long range fighters and heavy bombers.[56]

Unfortunately, there were no planes immediately available. Nimitz replied indirectly to his South Pacific commander in a dispatch "to be handled with utmost secrecy." A Marine fighter squadron was being brought to the area on board *Long Island* (AVG 1), but it would not arrive until the 13th. (It actually flew ashore on the 20th.) Another Marine fighter squadron would leave Pearl Harbor on 15 August and arrive the 25th at the earliest. Finally a carrier replacement fighter squadron should be ready to leave Pearl Harbor around the first of September. Ironically the Marines had the airfield ready on the 11th; all they needed were occupants.[57] *Long Island* was doing more than Nimitz had noted. Along with VMF–223 she was bringing VMSB–232, a dive-bombing unit equipped with SBD–3s. These two squadrons constituted half of

---

[53] Ibid.
[54] CTF 62 to CTF 61, COMSOPAC, 8/090508Z; CTF 62 to COMAIRSOPAC, COMSOPAC, CTF 61, 9/090725Z, Command Summary.
[55] COMSOPAC to CTF 61, 62, 63, 8/090750Z, Command Summary.
[56] COMSOPAC to CINCPAC, 8/090830Z, Command Summary.
[57] CINCPAC to COMINCH, info COMSOPAC, 8/091957Z; COMSOPAC to CINCPAC, 8/102230Z, Command Summary.

Long Island (AVG 1) moored at Naval Air Station, North Island on 2 June 1942. Aircraft from VGS–1 are on deck.

Marine Air Group 23. The other half, VMF–224 and VMSB–231, was to leave Hawaii in mid-August.[58]

Once clear of the immediate Guadalcanal area Fletcher took his three task forces on a two-week leisurely cruise of the eastern Coral Sea. Kinkaid's TF 16, of course, was a part of this odyssey. At 1700 on the 10th the *Enterprise* task force began a day of fueling from *Platte* (AO 24) and *Kaskaskia*, and then TF 18 and TF 11 brought the hoses on board. It took a full two days to replenish the three groups. Most of this time was spent in the vicinity of 17°S, 164°E. To stay this long in a fairly restricted area could have been extremely dangerous, but the carriers maintained a heavy antisubmarine patrol out to 50 miles while other aircraft scouted 200 miles to the north and west. On the 12th a couple of *Enterprise* Dauntlesses surprised a surfaced Japanese submarine and sank it. As usual, the cruiser aircraft and destroyers maintained a constant sweep for submarines closer to the task forces. A good deal of the two weeks was spent in the waters between New Caledonia and the New Hebrides

---

[58] Miller, *Cactus Air Force*, 22–23; Sherrod, *History of Marine Corps Aviation*, 74, 79–80; William T. Y'Blood, *The Little Giants: U.S. Escort Carriers against Japan* (Annapolis: Naval Institute Press, 1987), 13–15.

Islands. Here it was safe to refuel because the ships were covered by patrol aircraft from Noumea, Efate, and Espiritu Santo. Finally it was time to move back to the Guadalcanal area. CINCPAC and COMSOPAC had concluded that the Japanese were on the move.

Fortunately for the Marines stranded on Guadalcanal, the Japanese were not prepared to challenge their occupancy with any large operations. The planes destroyed in attacking the original landings had forced the enemy to resort to less effective bombing missions. At the same time the Japanese operations in New Guinea, from Buna along the Kokoda Trail toward Port Moresby, had forced a delay in sending large numbers of troops to Guadalcanal. Ghormley and Vandegrift were pleased with the distraction, though it is doubtful that General MacArthur shared this feeling. Although there were no large armadas bringing in Japanese troops, those that did arrive made each day one of desperate combat for the embattled Marines. The island simply could not be secured until American forces had command of the sea around it and control of the air overhead.

While Fletcher's carriers were cruising some 400 miles southeast of the Solomons, CINCPAC's intelligence staff was keeping track of the Japanese navy. As early as 10 August the Command Summary began to predict with amazing accuracy the next enemy operation: "The possibility exists that the Japs are forming a typical BB, CV [battleships, carriers] striking force for employment in the Bismarck-Solomons area. . . . A rough guess is that such a force could arrive in that area about August 24th."[59]

A couple days later CINCPAC warned COMSOPAC ("Treat as Ultra Secret") that the Japanese were getting ready to attack and that he should get his carriers in a position to repulse the enemy fleet. Ghormley in turn pressed Admiral McCain to get aviation established in Guadalcanal and to use some speedy destroyer transports (APDs) to move up support personnel, munitions, and supplies for the squadrons that would be based there.[60] Ghormley also turned to MacArthur for assistance. He wanted the general to step up his reconnaissance in the northern Solomons and Bismarcks, particularly at Rabaul, and to bomb the harbor when there were naval ships present.[61] Recognizing the crisis developing at Guadalcanal, even Admiral King tried to help. He suggested that Nimitz send three to five of his old battleships, currently based at Pearl Harbor, down to BLEACHER (Tongatabu) to help beef up Ghormley's command. Nimitz appreciated COMINCH's interest, but stated that Ghormley was in no position logistically to support such a battleship squadron. What was needed in the South Pacific were shore-

---

[59] Command Summary, 10 Aug 1942.
[60] CINCPAC to COMSOPAC, 8/112209Z; COMSOPAC to CTF 63, 8/120216Z, Command Summary.
[61] COMSOPAC to COMSWPA, 8/120316Z; 8/121056Z, Command Summary.

based aircraft, carriers, and fast surface forces, including the new fast battleships of the *North Carolina* or *South Dakota* (BB 57) classes.[62]

Following another Ultra Secret message from CINCPAC, describing the Japanese naval order of battle and advising that they could hit the Guadalcanal area as early as the 20th, though probably a few days later, Ghormley ordered Fletcher to bring his carrier task forces up to the Solomons. Although CINCPAC had not located the enemy carriers, Ghormley expected they would be coming down from Truk. In Operation Order 2–42 he set the mission for TF 61: Be in position by the 20th to intercept and destroy the Japanese forces.[63]

Fletcher responded by fueling his carriers once more on the 18th and then wheeling northwest. On board *Enterprise* at the close of the 18th Kinkaid's flag secretary commented that TF 16 was standing north to cover *Long Island* as it ferried aircraft for Guadalcanal. He concluded the entry, "Indications are that the enemy intends to attack the Tulagi-Guadalcanal area in force in near future, probably to attempt recapture."[64] Kinkaid got off a quick note to his wife on the 18th because the oilers were receiving mail bags from TF 16. Not having received any letters for almost a month, he had little to say. "Except for that [no mail], I am bearing up but we would all like to see a little civilization occasionally. There is not a chance in a thousand, however, of our doing so in the near future. As always, I do not like being separated from my sweetheart."[65]

By the 20th TF 61 was cruising in an area about 100 miles southeast of the eastern tip of San Cristobal Island, the easternmost of the Solomons. From this area the carriers covered *Long Island*'s launch of two Marine squadrons for Guadalcanal. A modest beginning for the CACTUS Air Force, the nineteen Wildcats and twelve Dauntlesses were wildly welcomed by General Vandegrift's troopers, who had begun to believe they had been completely forgotten by their leaders.[66] That night the newly arrived airmen learned that the Japanese had not forgotten the Marines. A recently landed reinforcement group, the 900-strong Ichiki Detachment, made a rash assault against the emplaced Marines. By morning every soldier in this elite unit, including Colonel Kiyorao Ichiki, was dead. While this battle was winding down, two more destroyer loads of troops came ashore to partially replace the slaughtered Japanese.[67] Farther to the north another

---

[62] COMINCH to CINCPAC, 8/121750Z; CINCPAC to COMINCH, 8/122337Z, Command Summary.
[63] CINCPAC to COMSOPAC, 8/172047Z; COMSOPAC to CTF 61, 62, 63, 8/180916Z, Command Summary.
[64] TF 16, War Diary, 18 Aug 1942.
[65] TCK to HSK, *Enterprise*, 18 Aug 1942.
[66] Spector, *Eagle Against the Sun*, 195; Miller, *Cactus Air Force*, 28.
[67] Raizo Tanaka, "The Struggle for Guadalcanal," in David C. Evans, ed., *The Japanese Navy in World War II* (Annapolis: Naval Institute Press, 1986), 160–64; Miller, *Cactus Air Force*, 34–35; TF 16, War Diary, 21 Aug 1942.

254 *Kinkaid of the Seventh Fleet*

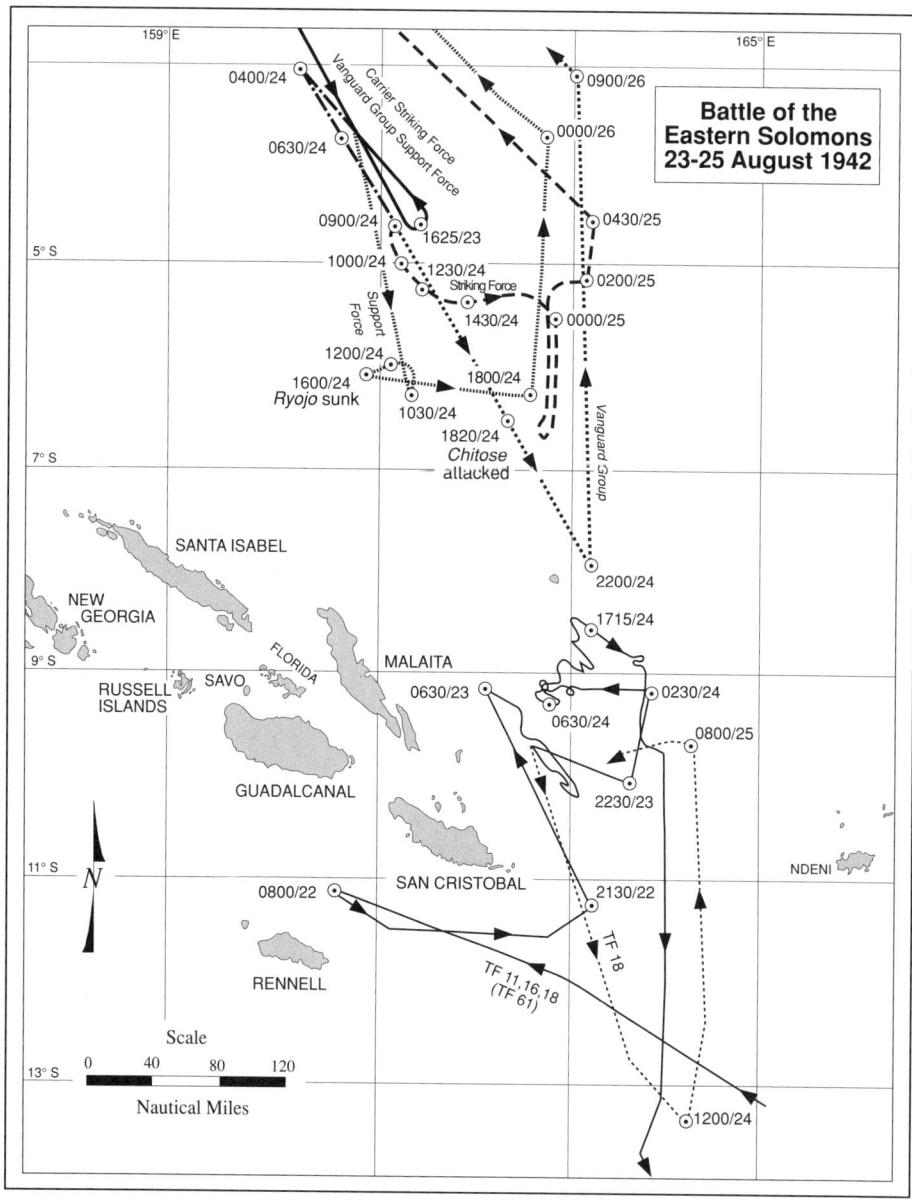

1,500 troops loaded into the transport *Kinryu Maru* and four Japanese-style APDs in Truk and sailed for Guadalcanal. The number of soldiers seemed adequate to the Japanese since their high command had consistently estimated that only 2,000 Marines had landed on the island. Covering and escorting the transports would be a substantial naval force since the Japanese hoped to draw Fletcher's carriers into a major engagement.[68]

By the 23d it was becoming obvious to Kinkaid and Fletcher that the enemy was on the move. Snoopers, usually the big four-engine Kawanishi flying boats, had begun to illuminate *Enterprise*'s radar regularly, and the CAP had shot down one or two of these planes daily since the 20th. In the early afternoon of the 21st, four Japanese cruisers and a destroyer were sighted about 300 miles north of Tulagi by one of McCain's long-range patrols. The next day an *Enterprise* Wildcat bagged a Kawanishi and later in the day a torpedo broached between *Portland* and the *Big E*. On the 23d *Enterprise* sent out 180-mile morning searches that covered the northern sectors from west to east. No task forces were sighted, but two of the SBDs attacked submarines they had surprised. Since the Japanese usually positioned a scouting line of submarines ahead of their fleets, Kinkaid knew the Japanese were coming toward them.[69] Given the regular presence of enemy patrol planes plus the submarines, there was little doubt that the Japanese knew the American carrier forces were in the neighborhood of Guadalcanal. Finally in the late morning a PBY attached to *Mackinac* (AVP 13) reported sighting enemy ships: transports, cruisers, and destroyers. At approximately 350 miles to the northwest they were beyond the immediate reach of TF 61, but the range was closing. The Catalina crew had located Captain Raizo Tanaka's Guadalcanal Reinforcement Force, bringing 1,500 Japanese troops of the Kawaguchi Unit from Truk to Guadalcanal, intending to land them in the early morning of the 24th.[70]

Once Tanaka's transport group had been sighted and its position plotted, Fletcher laid plans to destroy it. He gave *Saratoga* the attack assignment, and Captain Ramsey launched thirty-one SBDs and six TBFs at 1445. As duty carrier on the 23d, *Enterprise* had responsibility for the morning and afternoon long-range searches. *Enterprise*'s fighter pilots also maintained the CAP over the task forces, assisted by *Wasp*'s Wildcats. Kinkaid was anxious to get into the action, and an hour before *Saratoga*'s launch he requested permission to send a search-attack mission from *Big E* to the northwest. Instead he was ordered to use his scout bombers for 200-mile sector searches, 290 degrees through north to 070 degrees. But

---

[68] Morison, vol. 5, *The Struggle for Guadalcanal, August 1942–February 1943* (1949), 79–82; Spector, *Eagle Against the Sun*, 196–97.

[69] TCK oral history, 197–98; Stafford, *Big E*, 118–19.

[70] TF 16, War Diary, 20–23 Aug 1942; Stafford, *Big E*, 117–19; Tanaka, "Struggle for Guadalcanal," 160–66; Dull, *Battle History IJN*, 205–10.

neither *Saratoga*'s nor *Enterprise*'s air activity brought results. Tanaka had turned his transport group northwest at 1300 and was lucky enough to run into soupy weather. Both *Saratoga*'s 1445 strike and a small attack force of Marine SBDs sent from Guadalcanal at 1645 failed to contact the enemy. Because of the distance from the carriers to the assumed intercept point the *Saratoga* pilots were ordered to land at Guadalcanal and spend the night there. Kinkaid's searchers also turned up nothing, but they were able to return to their flat-top by 1615. The day ended with expectations on both sides that the 24th would be a day of decision.[71]

Toward the close of air operations on the 23d, Admiral Fletcher made a decision that was to seriously influence events the next day. Aware that the three task groups needed to refuel their ships regularly, Admiral Ghormley had suggested to Fletcher that he initiate refueling at this time by sending one group at a time to the oiler rendezvous.[72] Fletcher gave Admiral Noyes's *Wasp* task group (TG 61.3/TF 18) orders to leave the area and then released them at 1830 on the 23d. His decision was helped by a dispatch from CINCPAC a few hours earlier, estimating that all Japanese carriers were north of Truk. To his dismay, Frank Jack learned differently the next morning.

The Japanese transport group and its escorting cruiser-destroyer force, sighted the previous morning, was being covered by an impressive naval force. The transports were bringing the 1,500 troops of the Kawaguchi Unit, and they had their own naval escort with the light cruiser *Jintsu* and eight destroyers. About 100 to 200 miles to the east of Tanaka's transports were four more Japanese naval groups, hoping to bring Fletcher's task forces to action. Ahead of all these ships were a half-dozen submarines set up in a northeast to southwest scouting line. Many others were scattered around the Solomons, and all had scouting and attack missions. Out ahead of the surface forces as they steamed south from Truk was a Supporting Force of six cruisers, six destroyers, and the seaplane carrier *Chitose*. Following this cruiser-destroyer force was the powerful Vanguard Group, commanded by Rear Admiral Hiraoki Abe, which consisted of two battleships (*Hiei*, *Kirishima*), four cruisers, and six destroyers. The Japanese believed the Vanguard Group and the Supporting Force were more than adequate to meet in surface action any combination of battleships and cruisers that the Americans and Australians had in the area. But there were more. To the rear steamed a Striking Force of the fleet carriers *Shokaku* and *Zuikaku* and

---

[71] CTF 61 to COMSOPAC, "Preliminary Report of Actions, 23–24 Aug 1942," 6 Sep 1942, OA (hereafter CTF 61 Preliminary Action Report for 23–24 Aug 1942); TF 16, War Diary, 23 Aug 1942; ONI Combat Narrative: *Solomon Islands*, 46–47; Morison 5:82–84; Hammell, *Carrier Battles*, 94–100.

[72] COMSOPAC to CTF 61, 8/220910Z, Command Summary; Lundstrom, *First Team and Guadalcanal*, 104–5.

the light carrier *Ryujo* plus seven destroyers, all commanded by Vice Admiral Chuichi Nagumo, the commander of the Pearl Harbor strike force. *Shokaku* and *Zuikaku* were the two surviving carriers of that December attack. On the morning of the 24th the Japanese had divided their carriers, and a separate group, consisting of *Ryujo* and the heavy cruiser *Tone* plus two destroyers, was now steaming 100 miles south and west of Nagumo's Striking Force. With Rear Admiral Tadaichi Hara in command the *Ryujo* force mission was to support the transports and to bomb Henderson Field on Guadalcanal in company with Eleventh Air Fleet units from Rabaul. It is also probable that the *Ryujo* group was placed to the west of the Striking Force to serve as bait.[73] If the Americans launched deck-load strikes at *Ryujo*, *Shokaku* and *Zuikaku* would be clear to pounce on Fletcher's flat-tops without fear of retaliation.[74]

Kinkaid's task force was again responsible for the morning searches on the 24th, and at 0630 *Enterprise* launched twenty-three Dauntlesses to search 200 miles from 290 degrees through north to 090 degrees. Though these scouts found little to report, PBYs attached to *Mackinac* began in mid-morning to report sightings of Japanese cruisers approaching the Solomons from the northeast. Fletcher could do little because *Saratoga*'s bombing and torpedo squadrons that had spent the night at Guadalcanal had not yet returned. Kinkaid's SBDs were still returning from the morning searches. Both admirals waited for more information, particularly as to whether any Japanese carriers were in the area.[75] Finally at 1140 a Catalina reported a carrier, two cruisers, and a destroyer heading south. Unfortunately it gave no location. At about the same time *Saratoga*'s attack units arrived on board from CACTUS. A destroyer bombardment had resulted in a restless night for the aviators. Now able to launch an attack Fletcher still held *Saratoga*'s airmen while awaiting further sightings.

Following lunch and a shower *Enterprise*'s scouts were again sent out; this time sixteen SBDs and seven TBFs searched 250-mile sectors west through north to east. But for Fletcher and Kinkaid time was running out. If the enemy carrier could not be located by the early afternoon or if it were too far north, the squadrons could not attack and return for daylight recoveries by the carriers. Few of the pilots were truly competent at night carrier landings, and accidents could seriously weaken a squadron's attack capability.

At 1400 with no information coming from the *Big E*'s scouts, Fletcher decided to send an attack group toward an estimated position for the Japanese carrier. The admiral later described his situation: "This attack was launched on the most meager information which was three hours

---

[73] Dull disagrees in *Battle History IJN*, 198.
[74] Ibid., 197–8; Morison 5:79–84; Hammell, *Carrier Battles*, 484–87; Stafford, *Big E*, 117–19.
[75] CTF 61 Preliminary Action Report for 23–24 Aug 1942; Stafford, *Big E*, 120–21.

old and had never been confirmed."⁷⁶ At 1550 the *Ryujo* force was located both by some *Enterprise* pilots and by *Saratoga*'s attackers. It did not take long for *Sara*'s thirty dive bombers and eight torpedo planes to mortally damage *Ryujo*, but they were unable to hit any of the other ships. While the *Saratoga* and *Enterprise* airmen were ganging up on the hapless Japanese carrier, two pilots from *Big E*'s Bombing Six, one of them the commanding officer, stumbled onto the Striking Force's fleet carriers, *Shokaku* and *Zuikaku*. After signaling the location at 1530, both pilots unhesitatingly dove on *Shokaku*. Both managed damaging near misses, but the Pearl Harbor survivor again survived. The two pilots, Lieutenant Ray Davids and Ensign Robert C. Shaw, also escaped.

Communications were extremely poor, and neither *Saratoga* nor *Enterprise* received Davids's contact report, but other aircraft and screening vessels did receive it and relayed the report to the flagship. Fletcher was now caught in a terrible dilemma. Because of atmospherics he had been unable to reach the *Saratoga* strike force en route to *Ryujo*'s location and direct part of them against Nagumo's Striking Force. He also knew that the Japanese had his carriers pinpointed because of the large number of snoopers that had been in the area. Most had been shot down, but it was reasonably certain that they had gotten off contact reports before their destruction. Unable to do any better, Fletcher pulled together a twenty-five-plane strike group from the remaining SBDs and TBFs on board the two carriers and sent them on their way around 1620. They would not find *Shokaku* and *Zuikaku*, but the five Avengers and two Dauntlesses from *Saratoga* located the Japanese advance force of six cruisers, five destroyers, and the seaplane carrier *Chitose*. The torpedo planes missed their targets, but the two dive-bomber pilots placed near misses close enough to knock *Chitose* out of action and force its return to Japan for repairs.⁷⁷

Once the second strike was clear, Kinkaid and Fletcher had to prepare for the inevitable Japanese counterattack. The wait was mercifully short. Launched from their carriers at 1507 and 1600, the attackers began appearing on the American radars at 1602, distance 90 to 100 miles and boring in from the northwest.⁷⁸ Receiving this information, Kinkaid ordered all boilers in all ships placed on line and speed increased to 27 knots. Task Forces 16 and 11 were now steaming in formation I–V, the circular formation used when under air attack, with each carrier in the center of the defensive circle. *Portland* and *Atlanta* were stationed broad on the port and starboard bows of *Enterprise*, distance 2,000 yards, and *North Carolina* rolled along in the flat-top's wake. The six destroyers were

---
⁷⁶ CTF 61 Preliminary Action Report for 23–24 Aug 1942.
⁷⁷ Morison 5:92, 101–2.
⁷⁸ CTF 61 Preliminary Action Report for 23–24 Aug 1942; Morison 5:92–93.

also placed at 2,000 yards from the carrier, filling in the circle. As the Japanese approached, Kinkaid used the short-range talk between ships voice circuit to communicate with the task force. Finally at 1700 he ordered bent on the flag hoist the signal, "Follow my movements; prepare to repel attack from bearing 305 True."[79]

Because the *Enterprise* task force was the first encountered and the *Saratoga* group was 15 miles away, Kinkaid's force received the undivided attention of the Japanese. *Enterprise* was the target of almost every Japanese pilot, though a few tried to hit the battleship. *Saratoga*'s fighter pilots helped to beat off the enemy dive bombers and torpedo planes. From his location in *Balch*, ahead of the carrier, Captain Sauer, Commander Destroyer Squadron 6, had a splendid view of the attack as it began at 1711 from 12,000 feet. His action report was quite graphic:

> At about 1711, the first Jap plane started its dive and simultaneously the A.A. batteries (heavy and light) commenced firing. The action for the next six minutes became a confused picture of enemy dive bombers, one at a time, diving steeply (50–70 degrees) for the ENTERPRISE from bearing 330 degrees to 020 degrees (T); of released bombs directed at the carrier; of intense short range weapon fire and relatively light 5″ firing; of Jap planes disintegrating in midair with whole wings and bits of plane falling to the water; of Jap planes falling in flames around the ENTERPRISE brought down by 1.1 and 20 mm batteries; of bombs hitting the carrier or detonating close aboard; of a huge mass of smoke and flame erupted by the detonation of a close hit; of a skillfully maneuvered carrier turning and twisting to dodge the lethal downpour; of a surrounding screen of surface ships turning and twisting with the ENTERPRISE and pouring out streams of small caliber bullets; of a carrier being obscured by the dense smoke of the fire on board and the smoke of bombs detonating alongside; and of numerous 5″ A.A. projectile fragments raining on deck or splashing in water close aboard.[80]

Of the thirty or so Vals that dove on *Enterprise*, three hit the carrier and three obtained damaging near misses; only an estimated four or five Vals escaped destruction. None of the torpedo planes launched by the Japanese managed to penetrate the fighter screen and gunfire wall surrounding the task force.

For the first time in the war Kinkaid felt enemy bombs strike his flagship. The first hit came at 1714; the second, less than a minute later. Both 500-kilogram bombs struck in the vicinity of the aft (#3) elevator on the starboard side. The first penetrated the flight and hangar decks

---

[79] CTF 16 to CINCPAC, "Report of Action, 24 Aug 1942," 27 Aug 1942, encl. to CTF 16 to CINCPAC, "Report of Action, 24 Aug 1942," 9 Sep 1942.

[80] CTG 16.4 (COMDESRON 6) to CINCPAC, "Japanese Air Attack on U.S. *Enterprise*, 24 Aug 1942 . . . Action Report of," 28 Aug 1942, encl. to CTF 16 to CINCPAC, "Report of Action 24 Aug 1942."

and exploded on the third deck aft; the second burst in a 5-inch gun position below the starboard edge of the flight deck aft. A third bomb, estimated to be 250 kilograms, hit just forward of the previous two at 1716 and detonated on contact with the flight deck.[81] The carrier bucked mightily under this hammering. Kinkaid and his staff were tossed around the flag bridge but no one in his vicinity was seriously injured. In *Enterprise*'s bowels and gun mounts there was death and destruction, but the damage was controllable and the flat-top barely slowed. Inspection revealed the center (#2) and aft elevators were inoperable, but fortunately they were immobilized in the raised position. The aft corner of the flight deck on the port side had sprung upward 2 feet, and the aft 50 feet of the hangar deck also pushed upward 2 feet; but both areas could eventually handle aircraft. On the third deck there was extensive fire and explosion damage, but again repairs were possible.[82]

By 1725 the attack had ended and the enemy planes had fled northwest, pursued by those Wildcats with sufficient ammunition and fuel to engage in the chase. The Japanese pilots who managed to land back on board their carriers must have felt confident that they had mortally wounded the *Big E*. For a few minutes during the attack flames and smoke had engulfed the area aft of the island, but by 1740 the fires were under control and the smoke had dissipated. Forty minutes later Captain Art Davis turned the ship into the wind, worked up to 26 knots, and commenced recovering the carrier's brood. Unable to strike planes below with elevators #2 and #3, *Enterprise*'s plane handlers parked all they could on the flight deck and then asked *Saratoga* to recover the rest. At 1843, in the midst of landing aircraft, *Enterprise* lost steering control and began careening through the task force. The five flag ("Breakdown") flew out from the carrier's hoist and several blasts on the whistle warned all ships of the danger. Forty minutes later, after almost running down *Balch*, *Enterprise* again responded to its helm.[83]

When the final score was compiled, Task Forces 11 and 16 had not done too badly in what was to be named the Battle of the Eastern Solomons. A Japanese carrier (*Ryujo*) had been sunk, and a seaplane carrier (*Chitose*) had been knocked out of action. *Enterprise* had been hurt badly enough to require major work at Pearl Harbor, but would return to battle in six weeks. The damage to the Japanese was more insidious and longer lasting. More than seventy aircraft and air crews had been shot down during the attacks against TF 16. These pilots and crew members, all experienced, would be very difficult to replace in the weeks before the

---

[81] Hammell, *Carrier Battles*, 177–80.
[82] CTF 16 Action Report for 24 Aug 1942.
[83] Ibid.

next engagement with the American task forces. The Japanese also failed in their mission to reinforce their troops on Guadalcanal. The morning of the 25th long-range bombers from Espiritu Santo and dive bombers from Guadalcanal attacked Admiral Tanaka's Guadalcanal Reinforcement Force. His flagship, *Jintsu*, was heavily damaged; the transport *Kinryu Maru* and destroyer *Mutsuki* were sunk. Tanaka and his surviving troop carriers gave up the game and retired.[84] Japanese reinforcements would be forthcoming, but not immediately. The Marines would have time, a precious commodity, to strengthen their tenuous grip on Guadalcanal.

With the conclusion of the Japanese attacks Fletcher ordered TF 61 to withdraw in a southeast direction. He was not anxious to engage the enemy battleship-cruiser force at night, so the move seemed prudent. Believing that the Americans were badly hurt, Admiral Nobutake Kondo sent destroyers prowling to the south, looking for Fletcher's force, but it had moved out of harm's way. Equally unwilling to expose his own surface forces to retaliatory air attack with daylight, Kondo called his destroyers north to rejoin the main body and withdrew from the area.[85] By noon the next day, the 25th, Kinkaid was able to report *Enterprise*'s condition. He had thirty aircraft on board, mostly SBDs, and eleven planes at Guadalcanal. *Saratoga* had another thirty on board. Though two elevators were jammed, he believed the carrier could operate up to fifty planes in an emergency. But he and Captain Davis knew that the *Big E* would be at great risk were the Japanese to force another engagement.[86]

Kinkaid's report on the damage to *Enterprise* resulted in the dismantling of TF 16. In the early evening of the 25th Fletcher ordered *North Carolina, Atlanta, Gwin, Grayson*, and *Monssen* detached from TF 16 to report to himself as Commander TF 11. Kinkaid's truncated command now consisted of *Enterprise, Portland, Balch, Ellet*, and *Maury*.[87] It was clear that the carrier would be returning to Pearl Harbor, possibly even the West Coast, but the flat-top's squadrons would remain in the area. The CACTUS Air Force badly needed reinforcements, and the *Big E* loaned it the eleven scout bombers and crews that had not returned from their late afternoon launch against the Japanese. They stayed a month and proved a godsend to the Marines. Another seventeen Dauntlesses and Avengers with crews were sent ashore to Efate in the New Hebrides to provide backup for Guadalcanal or the carrier task forces remaining in the area. The thirty or so planes that landed on *Saratoga* after the engagement of the 24th remained with Sister Sara. *Maury* transferred the pilots' personal gear and medical and pay records. When the transfers

---

[84] Dull, *Battle History IJN*, 202–3; Morison 5:102–7; Hammell, *Carrier Battles*, 227–30.
[85] Dull, *Battle History IJN*, 202.
[86] CTF 16 to CTF 61, 8/242325Z, Command Summary.
[87] TF 16, War Diary, 25 Aug 1942.

were completed, only six Wildcats and six Dauntlesses remained to provide a minimum CAP and intermediate patrol for the task force.[88]

While Kinkaid awaited final orders for TF 16, Fletcher ordered him to remain in the reasonably secure area between New Caledonia and the New Hebrides. These instructions were superseded by Ghormley's orders to take *Enterprise* and its entourage to Tongatabu for inspection and evaluation of the carrier's damage.[89] Kinkaid thought this action would be a waste of time. Confident that the carrier was seaworthy, he radioed Ghormley that he believed he should sail directly to Pearl. He had just enough fuel and provisions in his force for the passage.[90] By leaving immediately and not awaiting the arrival of the light cruiser *San Juan* (CL 54) at Tongatabu, the carrier's time out of service would be significantly reduced. His message never reached Ghormley. Lacking any alternative instructions, the admiral took his force to Tongatabu where divers inspected *Enterprise*'s hull and did some minor patching. At 0800 on 3 September Kinkaid's force sortied for Pearl Harbor with *San Juan, Flusser* (DD 368), and the oiler *Platte* as new additions to the task force.

The passage to Pearl was uneventful and gave Kinkaid the opportunity to catch up on his correspondence, personal and official. While in Nukualofa, the admiral received the best antidote for a grouchy outlook that a sailor could receive—eighteen letters and several packages from his wife. She had been to Washington and had much to report. As usual she seemed to know more about events and decisions that would directly affect him than he did. For instance, she had found out that Vice Admiral Halsey was again physically fit for duty and would be returning to his carrier task force command. Kinkaid didn't officially receive that information for another week until he was back at CINCPAC headquarters.[91] From his letters it is clear that Tom Kinkaid felt cut off from "what was really going on" inside the Navy Department. The war news that the ships received over the armed forces network was about the country and the world, but Kinkaid's world was the Navy, and little information filtered down to Guadalcanal, Noumea, and Tongatabu that Kinkaid missed by his absence from Pearl Harbor and Washington.

With a week of little to concern him before arrival in Pearl, Tom had the leisure to read the action reports forwarded to him by his subordinate commanders and compose his own for the Battle of the Eastern Solomons. Most important, with his staff managing the task force, he could devote some undisturbed thought to the lessons the action provided. Unfortunately his action report for 24 August 1942 was little more than a few sum-

---

[88] Ibid., 25–27 Aug 1942.
[89] Ibid., 26 Aug 1942; COMSOPAC to CTF 16, 8/261812Z, Command Summary.
[90] CTF 16 to COMSOPAC, 8/262137Z, Command Summary.
[91] TCK to HSK, *Enterprise*, 3 Sep 1942; TCK to HSK, Pearl Harbor, 12 Sep 1942.

Enterprise *Task Force* 263

mary comments drawn from the reports of Admiral Tisdale, Captain Sauer, and the ship commanders in his task force. Subjects that were to become critical two months later were not even addressed. Perhaps, knowing that Fletcher would have to prepare a full report for TF 61, Kinkaid left the thornier questions for his old friend to answer.

The two points that Kinkaid dealt with most fully concerned gunfire defense of the task force and direction of the force's fighter planes and other aircraft when the ships were under attack by enemy planes. Integrating the battleship *North Carolina* into task force operations was a subject the admiral had to consider early on. He was quite positive on this topic, believing that the big ship's antiaircraft batteries had made a substantial contribution to the defense of the group, at least in the beginning. Admiral Tisdale observed that from his flag bridge in *Portland*, "her [*North Carolina*'s] broadsides appeared as solid sheets of flame." Kinkaid and Tisdale estimated that *North Carolina* had knocked down at least ten enemy planes. Both admirals, however, noted that once the task force began maneuvering in excess of 27 knots, the battleship began to be outdistanced. With twenty 5-inch, 38-caliber guns, it was valuable; Kinkaid wondered if it was really worthwhile for the carrier to steam at more than 27 knots when taking evasive action.[92]

In his evaluation of the antiaircraft gunfire defense of his task force, the admiral had been impressed by the 5-inch fire. *Atlanta* and *Portland* had laid a rapid-fire barrage at about 10,000 feet, just below the "push over" point of the enemy dive bombers, that had been effective in disrupting the attacks. Captain Laurance T. DuBose, skipper of *Portland*, concluded, "It is felt that it was the fire of the five inch batteries that frustrated the attack, thus providing the carrier her greatest protection from damage."[93]

Throughout Kinkaid's action report and the enclosures from the other commanders was recognition that most of the enemy aircraft knocked down by the ships' batteries had fallen to 20-mm and 1.1-inch gunfire, close in and after they had released their bombs. The 5-inch batteries had prevented most of the pilots from making effective dives.

As an ordnance specialist, it was natural for Kinkaid to be interested in antiaircraft weapons, but he was also concerned with the control and direction of the task force's fighter defense. He was well aware that Fletcher's inability to communicate with *Saratoga*'s attacking squadrons once they had reached the vicinity of *Ryujo* had cost them the opportunity to get at *Shokaku* and *Zuikaku*. This problem was due to inadequate equipment and cluttered circuits. Equally serious had been the inability of *Enter-*

---

[92] CTF 16 Action Report for 24 Aug 1942.
[93] CO *Portland* to CINCPAC, "Air Attack Made upon U.S.S. *Enterprise* by Japanese 24 Aug 1942," 30 Aug 1942, encl. to CTF 16 to CINCPAC, "Report of Action 24 Aug 1942" (hereafter CO *Portland* Action Report for 24 Aug 1942).

prise's FDO to utilize his CAP more effectively. Part of his problem was the undisciplined chatter of the pilots in combat that clogged the control frequencies. A third serious problem had been the cluttering of airspace near the carrier and on the ship's radar by aircraft returning from search and attack missions. Kinkaid summarized the problem as follows:

> During and immediately after the attack [on the *Enterprise*] the presence of many friendly aircraft in close proximity to the formation was confusing to the fighter director and imposed a great and unnecessary burden on ship and fire control personnel. It is certain that at least one friendly plane was damaged and possibly another was shot down by our own AA fire. The large number of our own planes in the immediate vicinity is accounted for by the fact that the attack developed almost immediately after the launching of our own attack group and coincident with the return of the scouting flights to the ENTERPRISE.

The admiral recommended that, when the carrier was under attack, returning aircraft should fly to an alternate location to await the end of the battle. Returning scouts that might lead enemy attack squadrons back to *Enterprise* should try to land at a shore base or fly to an alternate rendezvous point, at least 30 to 50 miles from the carrier and orbit there until it was safe to return to the flat-top.[94]

While Kinkaid's TF 16 steamed toward Tongatabu and then Pearl Harbor, disaster continued to dog the South Pacific carriers. During the morning watch of 31 August, Japan's submarine *I–26* sent one torpedo into *Saratoga*. The hit was not fatal, but the big carrier was again knocked out of the war for a couple months. So was Admiral Fletcher. Slightly wounded, he returned to the United States for recuperation and then took command of the Northwestern Sea Frontier. Most of *Saratoga*'s pilots flew to island shore bases, including Guadalcanal, where they continued to carry the fight to the enemy.[95] Two weeks later, on 15 September, while covering a convoy of troops headed for Guadalcanal, *Wasp* was torpedoed. Struck by three torpedoes, *Wasp* burned furiously and eventually sank. *North Carolina* and *O'Brien* (DD 415) were also holed. *North Carolina* would be out of action for several months; *O'Brien*, after temporary repairs, broke up trying to reach the West Coast.[96]

Enterprise arrived in Pearl Harbor at 1030 on 10 September to begin a five-week stay in the navy yard. Much needed to be done to repair the bomb damage. Most important, the 1.1-inch antiaircraft guns would be replaced by the superb Bofors 40-mm quadruple-mounted automatic

---

[94] CTF 16 Action Report for 24 Aug 1942.
[95] Morison 5:110–12; "Saratoga," *DANFS* 6:340–41.
[96] Morison 5:130–7.

weapons. These guns could blast attacking dive bombers before they released their deadly cargoes. With the flat-top in the hands of the yard workers, there was time for rest and recreation for the crew, including the task force commander.[97]

As usual, the admiral checked in with Helen as soon as he could get a reservation to make a telephone call. He finally got through three days after arrival. By chance Helen was visiting Martha Fletcher at Araby, the Fletcher home in La Plata, Maryland, and Tom was able to reassure Martha that Frank Jack had not been badly hurt. Tom had hoped for some leave for himself, but that was now out of the question. Because of censorship he couldn't explain why, but Helen could figure it out. Through the service grapevine Kinkaid had received notes from Rear Admirals Wilder Baker and Theodore Wilkinson that they had seen Helen in Washington and that she had been well and cheerful. The phone call helped confirm this.[98]

The month required to get *Enterprise* in shape for combat again gave Kinkaid an opportunity to tie up many loose ends in his personal affairs and to rest thoroughly. Bureaucratic slowness and censorship requirement meant Kinkaid had not yet received his Distinguished Service Medal (DSM) for the Coral Sea action. Nimitz visited *Enterprise* on 15 September and made twenty-seven awards, Kinkaid's among them. Tom's official citation did not describe what he did on 8 May:

> For exceptionally meritorious and distinguished service to the Government of the United States in a position of great responsibility as Cruiser Division Task Force Commander of Task Force ELEVEN, in the Battle of the Coral Sea, May 4–8, 1942. Due to Rear Admiral Kinkaid's aggressive leadership and determined action, and through the skill and courageous devotion to duty of the units under his command, heavy losses were inflicted on attacking air groups, thereby contributing unmeasurably to the ultimate success of our forces in these notable engagements.[99]

The loss of *Lexington* and Kinkaid's superb choreographing of the rescue operation for the carrier's crew were not mentioned. The citation better describes the reason for his DSM that followed the Eastern Solomons battle.

When not attending awards ceremonies, or taking care of routine business at his cabin in *Enterprise,* the admiral had a good deal of free time. Afternoon swims at Waikiki Beach followed by a drink on the way back to the ship became *de rigueur*. Though one cocktail was usually his

---
[97] Stafford, *Big E*, 146–48; Polmar, *Aircraft Carriers*, 256.
[98] TCK to HSK, Pearl Harbor, 12 Sep 1942.
[99] TCK Personnel File.

limit, his letters began to reflect a bit of guilt because his waist was again expanding. Weekends again were regularly spent at the Damian House, the rest house for senior officers on Kaneohe Bay. Mess attendants, including his own steward's mate Torre, made sure that Tom and his associates ate well, and local people had them in for cocktails regularly.

This month of inactivity was restful, but Kinkaid continued to fret because there was indecision about his next command. After Midway there had been a dearth of flag officer aviators who could command carrier task forces, and he was therefore tapped to relieve Spruance with TF 16. Now with only two carriers capable of action and *Enterprise* unable to sail until 15 October, Nimitz found himself with an abundance of experienced talent. Tom knew where he stood and told Helen several times that he was ready to return to his old billet as a screen commander. "I will be very sorry to leave this address [*Enterprise*] as it has been extremely interesting and I feel that I have gotten a lot out of it. There is something new to learn on every expedition."[100] Kinkaid understood Nimitz's problem. Admiral Halsey was in Pearl, anxious to take some carrier task forces to sea, but too senior to command a single carrier task force or even a force made up of two carrier task groups. There were also senior flag officers like John McCain, Jake Fitch, and Leigh Noyes to be placed. Even the most senior naval aviator, Rear Admiral John H. Towers, wanted to trade his Bureau of Aeronautics desk for an action billet in the Pacific. Because of the large number of carriers under construction and many due to be commissioned in 1943, the flag officer selection boards had begun to promote more aviators; there were Ted Sherman, Charles A. Pownall, John W. Reeves, Marc Mitscher, and a few others that could receive seagoing commands. But in the end Kinkaid's luck again held.

Nimitz was reluctant to replace Kinkaid because he was both experienced and successful. Working with Halsey, who was temporarily holding the billet of Commander Aircraft, Pacific Fleet (COMAIRPAC), the admiral decided to send Kinkaid back to the South Pacific with the *Enterprise* task force while Halsey flew ahead and investigated for Nimitz the situation in Guadalcanal and the status of the South Pacific command. Once TF 16 arrived in the South Pacific, Nimitz had planned to have Halsey take it over, and Kinkaid would relieve Rear Admiral George Murray of TF 17 and fly his flag in *Hornet*. Both carriers would then come under Halsey's direct command as TF 61. Tom was satisfied with this arrangement and wrote Helen, "I am glad it has come out this way because there are a lot of aviators in the offing and there is some inclination to push them ahead of us ordinary mortals."[101] Kinkaid left Pearl on the 16th of October expecting to follow this plan, but

---

[100] TCK to HSK, Pearl Harbor, 12 Sep 1942.
[101] Ibid., 8 Oct 1942.

Enterprise *Task Force* 267

Vice Admiral Robert L. Ghormley, left, speaks with Admiral Chester W. Nimitz after Ghormley's return from his South Pacific Command, circa 1943.

on the 17th (18th in New Caledonia); Halsey arrived in Noumea and received radio orders to relieve Ghormley as COMSOPAC. Tom would now remain in *Enterprise* and, because of his seniority, would become Commander TF 61 once TF 16 joined up with Murray's TF 17.

Before taking TF 16 to the South Pacific, Kinkaid managed to find five days for operations training at sea. This period was critical since the admiral would be working with a new destroyer squadron (DESRON 5) and with a new battleship. *North Carolina* was still under repair, but an even newer battlewagon, Captain Thomas L. Gatch's *South Dakota*, was ready for action. Having just emerged from the Pearl Harbor Navy Yard, where it had underwater damage repaired, it now bristled with a new load of 40-mm gun batteries. Once the task force arrived in the South Pacific area, it would be joined by an old friend, *Portland*, and a relative newcomer, antiaircraft cruiser *San Juan*. Of equal concern to Kinkaid was the new air group that would be fighting from *Enterprise*. So between 10 and 14 October, Commander John Crommelin, the air officer of the *Big E*, and Commander Richard K. Gaines, the air group commander, kept the squadrons busy practicing for their next encounter with the Japanese. Combat air patrols were flown by the fighters, long-range and intermediate searches were launched daily, and the VT–10 pilots made dummy runs against the task force. The fighter director officer and his gang tracked VB–10 pilots as they approached the carrier for dive-bombing practice and sent Lieutenant Commander James H. Flatley's V–10 fighters to intercept. And practically every minute that planes were aloft, *Enterprise*'s gunnery officer was instructing the crew on the new quad-40s as well as the rest of the ship's antiaircraft armament. Despite the intense air operations not a single plane was lost to an accident. Every ship in the task force followed an intense training schedule similar to *Enterprise*'s. At the end of this breaking-in period, Kinkaid and TF 16 were ready for action.[102]

On 16 October at 0830 TF 16 sortied from Pearl Harbor and Kinkaid began his fourth trip to the South Pacific. Three and a half hours later Captain Davis turned *Enterprise* into the southeast wind and recovered Air Group 10. Once the aircraft were on board, the helmsman swung the carrier to 216 True, the initial course for the task force's rendezvous with TF 17. Kinkaid quickly fell into the underway routines that had become so familiar to him. He now had a large staff, numbering a dozen, so management of the daily operations could be left to Sherm Burroughs. Because he wanted to stay on the bridge whenever action was likely to take place, the admiral had a bunk built into his sea cabin. With a wash basin and commode as well, there was scarcely room for the admiral, but he could now lie down during the day if he felt like it. It is un-

---

[102] TF 16, War Diary, 10–14 Oct 1942; TCK oral history, 199–201; Stafford, *Big E*, 147–49; Hammell, *Carrier Battles*, 58, 318–19.

likely that the Bureau of Ships had been asked to approve the addition, but Tom did believe that rank had at least a few privileges. Knowing that he would have plenty of free time, he laid in a stock of magazines and books, including Elliot Paul's *The Last Time I Saw Paris* and Joseph Davies's *Mission to Moscow* from Helen. And while there was little he could report, the admiral continued to write to his wife every other day.

The first few days out of Pearl, *Enterprise*'s pilots engaged in operational exercises, scouting, and attacks against the task force. Such work also provided the gunners on all of the ships an opportunity to practice. But starting on the 20th, air operations were severely limited because they slowed the speed of advance of the task force which was scheduled to rendezvous with *Sabine* (AO 25) and *Stack* (DD 406) on the 23d. *Portland* and *San Juan* and their escorts also joined them at this point. At the rendezvous the task force fueled through the day and night, a difficult operation, and at noon on the 24th TF 17 hove into sight. With the arrival of *Hornet* wearing the flag of Rear Admiral Murray, Task Force 61 was assembled under Kinkaid's command.[103] Its mission, spelled out by Vice Admiral Halsey, was "to proceed around the Santa Cruz Islands to the North. Thence proceed southwesterly and east of San Cristobal to area in the Coral Sea and be in position to intercept enemy forces approaching Guadalcanal-Tulagi area."[104]

Task Force 61, once formed, did not have to wait long for an opportunity to meet the enemy. At 1250 (local time) on 25 October, Kinkaid received a contact report from one of *Curtiss*'s (AV 4) Catalinas that there were two Japanese aircraft carriers and escorts at 8°51′S, 164°30′E heading on course 145 degrees at 25 knots. TF 61 was around 360 miles east-southeast of this reported position, steaming at 22 knots on course 295.[105] The presence of the Japanese task force was not a surprise since a carrier task force, probably containing *Zuiho*, had been spotted two days earlier about 250 miles north of the 1250 sighting.[106] These contacts plus many others in the last few days made it evident that the Japanese were about to commence a major operation to oust the Marines from Guadalcanal. Based on communications intelligence at Nimitz's headquarters it had been estimated that the Japanese "zero day" was to be 23 October, but that day had come and gone without a major movement of troop-laden transports and a naval support force toward Guadalcanal.[107]

---

[103] TF 16, War Diary, 16–24 Oct 1942.

[104] Ibid., 24 Oct 1942.

[105] CO *Enterprise* to CINCPAC, "Report of the Battle of Santa Cruz, 26 Oct 1942," 10 Nov 1942, encl. to CINCPAC to COMINCH, "Solomons Islands Campaign, Battle of Santa Cruz–26 Oct 1942," 6 Jan 1943 (hereafter CINCPAC Action Report, Battle of Santa Cruz).

[106] COMSOPAC to COMINCH, 10/250216Z, Command Summary.

[107] CINCPAC Action Report, Battle of Santa Cruz.

Task Force 61, October 1942

CTF 61 RADM Thomas C. Kinkaid

Task Force 16
    CTF 16 RADM Kinkaid
        CV *Enterprise* (flagship)   CAPT Arthur C. Davis to 10/21/42
                                        CAPT Osborne B. Hardison from 10/21/42

    COMCRUISERS TF 16 RADM Mahlon S. Tisdale
        BB *South Dakota*   CAPT Thomas L. Gatch
        CA *Portland* (flagship)   CAPT Laurence T. DuBose
        CLAA *San Juan*   CAPT James E. Maher

    COMDESRON 5 CAPT Charles P. Cecil
        DDs *Porter* (flagship), *Mahan, Cushing, Preston, Smith, Maury, Conyngham, Shaw*

Task Force 17
    CTF 17 RADM George D. Murray
        CV *Hornet* (flagship)   CAPT Charles P. Mason

    COMCRUISERS TF 17 RADM Howard H. Good
        CA *Northampton*   CAPT Willard A. Kitts III
          (flagship)
        CA *Pensacola*   CAPT Frank L. Lowe
        CLAA *San Diego*   CAPT Benjamin F. Perry
        CLAA *Juneau*   CAPT Lyman K. Swenson

    COMDESRON 2 CDR Arnold E. True
        DDs *Morris* (flagship), *Anderson, Hughes, Mustin, Russell, Barton*

SOURCES: Hammell, *Carrier Battles*, 488–89; Morison, 5:204–206.

Because the distance to the Japanese was too great, even assuming they continued to head toward TF 61, Kinkaid increased the force's speed to 27 knots and held his aircraft on deck for almost two hours. At 1430 he ordered *Enterprise* to launch twelve Dauntlesses to search 200-mile sectors between 280 degrees and 010 degrees. Unwilling to wait for a contact report, Kinkaid ordered a strike group of eleven Wildcats, twelve Dauntlesses, and six Avengers to head out 150 miles on course 325 degrees True, a median course of the sectors being searched. If no contact was made, the twenty-nine aircraft were to return to the carrier. *Hornet* was to stand ready to launch a full deck-load follow-up strike if a contact report came in. Shortly after the second group had departed, another contact report arrived from *Curtiss*'s patrol plane. The Japanese had turned north; it was now clear that neither *Enterprise* group would reach the enemy. Since radio silence was being observed within the task force no attempt was made to recall the two groups. Returning after dark and low on fuel, pilots in the second group met with disaster. Kinkaid later wrote:

> The striking group, through excess zeal of its leader, proceeded out to 200 miles and then searched 80 miles [more] to northeastward in the hope of making contact. They returned to the ENTERPRISE after dark and low on fuel. As pilots were not qualified for night landings, the group was landed with difficulty and with the loss of six planes through deck crashes and water landings. This was a serious loss as earlier in the day five planes had been damaged on deck by the first deck crash which had occurred since GROUP TEN came on board.[108]

Had *Enterprise* not been carrying extra aircraft in the hangar deck space that were to be flown to Guadalcanal at the appropriate time, the carrier would have been in deep trouble when it came time to defend itself.[109]

During the night of 25–26 October Kinkaid took TF 61 to the north in order to close the Japanese forces. Kinkaid and Murray agreed that *Hornet* should remain in strike readiness through the night in case the PBYs should locate the Japanese carrier force. Although *Hornet's* pilots had no battle experience with night attacks, at least they were qualified for night operations. *Enterprise's* airmen had demonstrated that they were not. The two task force commanders also agreed that the *Big E* would again be the duty carrier on the 26th. It meant that Captain Charles P. Mason in *Hornet* would not have "to break the spot," that is, change the arrangement of the aircraft on his carrier's flight deck in order to send out morning searches and intermediate patrols.[110] Just after midnight *Enterprise* received a Catalina report that a Japanese force was about 300 miles northwest of the carrier. When the ships' crews were called to general quarters for the usual dawn alert, there was little doubt in either flat-top that this would be a day to remember.[111]

It would have been easier for Kinkaid to decide on a course of action if the 0111 contact report had included the composition, course, and speed of the enemy force, and if he had been able to count on the Japanese holding to that course and speed. But the plane that made the contact did not stay to develop it. The admiral was again left with the battle conundrum: Do you estimate where the enemy ships might be and launch a deck-load strike designed to take them by surprise, or do you send out your scouts,

---

[108] CTF 61 to CINCPAC, "Report of Carrier Action North of the Santa Cruz Islands, 26 Oct 1942," 20 Nov 1942, encl. to CINCPAC Action Report, Battle of Santa Cruz (hereafter CTF 61 Action Report for 26 Oct 1942).

[109] Hammell, *Carrier Battles*, 324–28.

[110] CTF 61 Action Report for 26 Oct 1942.

[111] CO *Enterprise* Action Report for 26 Oct 1942.

272 Kinkaid of the Seventh Fleet

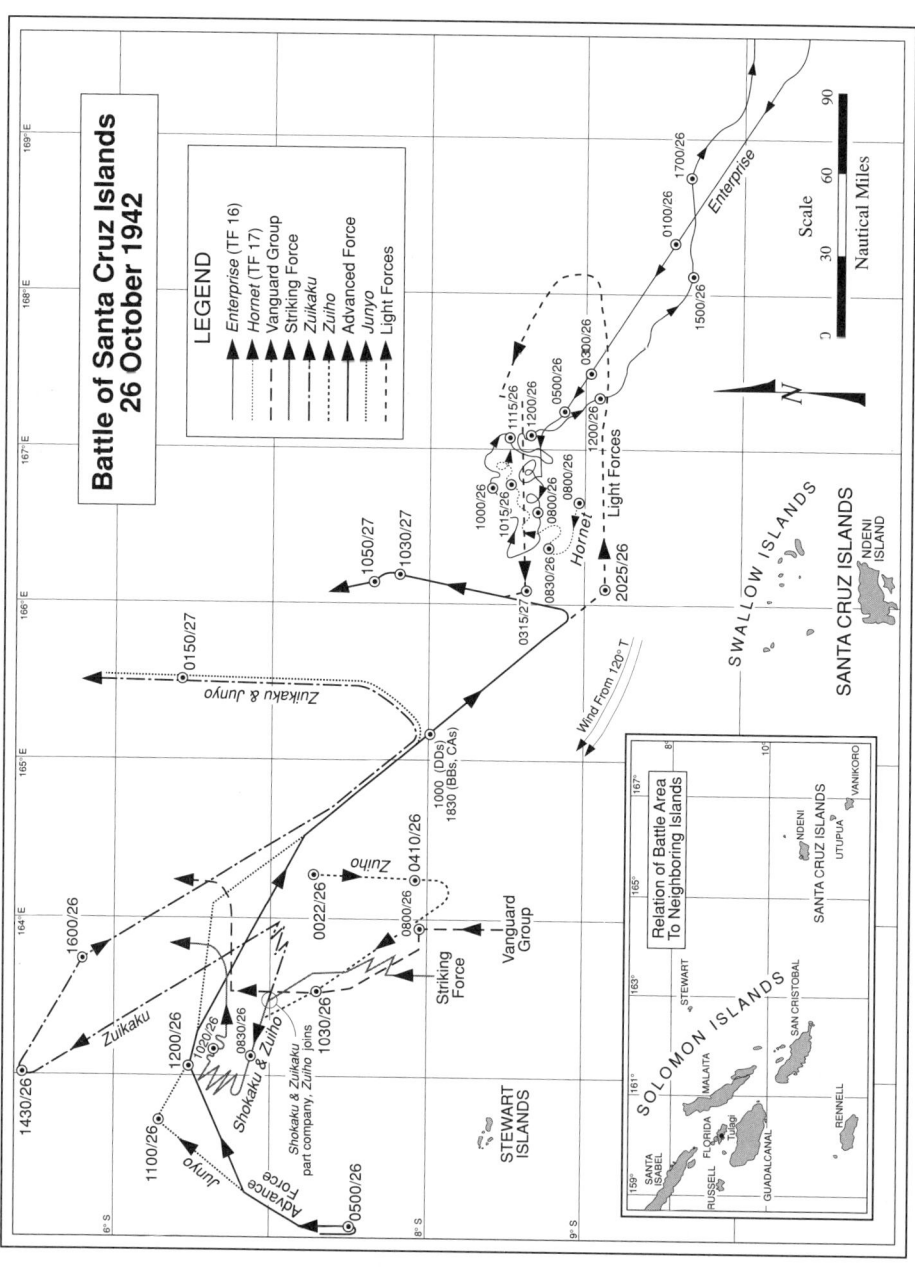

verify the enemy's position, and then hit him? Further complicating Kinkaid's assessment was the recently received message from COMSOPAC (Halsey), still ringing in his ears: STRIKE—REPEAT—STRIKE.

But lacking further information from the night-flying Catalinas, Kinkaid and his staff chose the second option. At 0600, a half hour before sunrise, *Enterprise* began launching sixteen SBDs, each carrying a 500-pound bomb. Searching in pairs, they would cover eight sectors between 235 degrees and 000 degrees to a distance of 200 miles. *Hornet*, within visual signaling distance, stood ready to strike if the scouts turned up the enemy. It was an unstated assumption that, if any pair of SBDs found the Japanese carriers, they would inform the flagship and the rest of the searchers and then make the best use of their 500-pounders.[112]

At this time, just after 0600, it became evident that fate was not going to consistently bless Kinkaid and his command. The admiral received from *Curtiss* a contact report he should have received two hours earlier. It had originally been sent at 0410 by a Catalina crew using a frequency not monitored by *Enterprise*. An enemy carrier task force was at 7°55′S and 164°15′E, headed south at 10 knots.[113]

Kinkaid's staff could see that at 0410 the Japanese had been about 200 miles, bearing 290 degrees from TF 61. If the Japanese had held to their course, then they were now, at 0620, to the west-southwest with the distance opening. If the weather did not interfere, the staff anticipated that *Enterprise* scouts should locate the Japanese in one of their sectors. Again Kinkaid had to decide whether to launch *Hornet*'s deck-load of eager pilots toward an estimated position, to send them along a median course of the sectors being searched, or to hold the aircraft in place until a confirmed position came in. He could also break radio silence and shift his searchers toward the new estimated position. If he guessed right, the sixteen searchers could become a sixteen-plane attack group, and *Hornet*'s aircraft could be a follow-on strike. But Kinkaid chose to maintain radio silence and let his scouts get a fresh location of the Japanese carrier force. At 0630 there was no evidence that the Japanese had located TF 61, so the admiral still hoped to surprise them. It is probable that Kinkaid and his staff were remembering the great success that Admiral Spruance had in surprising the Japanese at Midway.[114]

The first report from the *Enterprise* scouts came in at 0730. They had found two battleships, a heavy cruiser, and seven destroyers, but no carri-

---

[112] Ibid.; CTF 61 Action Report for 26 Oct 1942; Potter, *Bull Halsey*, 164; Merrill, *Admiral Halsey's Story*, 121. Frank, in his well-researched *Guadalcanal*, 335–36, 711, makes a convincing argument that Halsey's radio to Kinkaid read "Strike-Repeat-Strike," and not "Attack-Repeat-Attack" as stated in Halsey's memoirs and by his biographers. Lundstrom also makes this point, 349.

[113] CTF 61 Action Report for 26 Oct 1942.

[114] Ibid.; CO *Enterprise* Action Report for 26 Oct 1942; Hammell, *Carrier Battles*, 329–36.

ers. This Japanese force was 170 miles from TF 61 on a bearing of 275 degrees True. A second report from another pair of SBDs arrived at 0750. They had sighted two carriers and some escorts at 200 miles, bearing 300 degrees True from TF 61. On receiving this information Kinkaid ordered Admiral Murray to hit with everything he had in *Hornet*. The Japanese carriers were to be the primary objective. He also ordered Captain Osborne B. Hardison to put together whatever he could from *Enterprise* to join the attack. Both carrier skippers were to retain a portion of their Wildcats for combat air patrol. The fighter director officer in *Enterprise*, new to the position since Admiral Halsey had taken the renowned Lieutenant Commander Dow for his staff, would control the CAP for both carriers. At 0831 *Hornet* began launching its first wave, consisting of fifteen SBDs with 1,000-pound bombs, six TBFs with torpedoes, and eight F4F–4s for escort. Once the deck was clear, a second strike was brought up from the hangar deck and sent on its way. It had nine SBDs with 1,000 pounders, nine TBFs with four 500 pounders apiece, and seven Wildcats. The last of *Hornet*'s strike was clear of the carrier by 0910.[115]

Because most of *Enterprise*'s SBDs were looking for the Japanese or flying the intermediate antisubmarine patrols for both task forces, its strike was not well constituted for such a dangerous mission. Captain Hardison sent Air Group Commander Gaines in a TBF, plus three SBDs, eight TBFs, and a fighter escort of eight F4F–4s. This group got underway between the first and second waves from *Hornet*.

From their action reports it is evident that Kinkaid, Murray, Mason (*Hornet*), and Hardison (*Enterprise*) had not figured out the numbers and locations of the Japanese forces their squadrons were attacking. The Japanese had come down from Truk in two groups, both under the command of Vice Admiral Nobutake Kondo. A three-carrier Striking Force commanded by Vice Admiral Chuichi Nagumo and led by Rear Admiral Hiroaki Abe's Vanguard Group was to the west-northwest of TF 61. With two battleships (*Hiei* and *Kirishima*), four cruisers, and seven destroyers, Abe's group was ready to give surface battle if the American carriers were neutralized. About 80 miles to the northeast of Abe, at the time *Enterprise*'s scouts flushed them, was Admiral Nagumo's carrier group with *Shokaku* (sixty-one aircraft), *Zuikaku* (seventy-two aircraft), and *Zuiho* (twenty-four aircraft), accompanied by a cruiser and eight destroyers. One hundred miles west of the Striking Force, and beyond the reach of Kinkaid's carriers and their scouts, was Admiral Kondo's Advance Force. When concentrated, it had two battleships (*Kongo* and *Haruna*), five

---

[115] CO *Hornet* to SECNAV and CINCPAC, "Report of Action 26 Oct 1942, and subsequent loss of U.S.S. *Hornet*," 30 Oct 1942, encl. to CINCPAC Action Report, Battle of Santa Cruz; CO *Hornet* Action Report for 26 Oct 1942; CTF 61 Action Report for 26 Oct 1942.

cruisers, and twelve destroyers that could operate as a surface battle group. Also a part of this Advance Force was a carrier task group, commanded by Rear Admiral Kakuji Kakuta, which consisted of the light carrier *Junyo* (fifty-five aircraft) and two destroyers. Had Kondo and Nagumo concentrated their forces, they would have been in a position to annihilate the Americans, particularly if the surface forces were able to come to meet them. Fortunately it never occurred.

One of the advantages of sending scouts armed with bombs is that they occasionally have an opportunity to use them. The first contact with the Japanese carriers was by VS–10's skipper, Lieutenant Commander James R. (Bucky) Lee. He alerted TF 61, and then he and his wingman dived on the carriers. Although they missed, their attack drew off the Japanese CAP. In the meantime two more VS–10 Dauntlesses arrived above the Japanese carriers. Lieutenant Stockton B. Strong had heard Lee's contact report and decided to stretch his fuel to try for a hit. Followed by his wingman, Strong dived on what he thought was *Shokaku* or her twin, *Zuikaku*. He and Ensign Charles B. Irvine each hit *Zuiho*, damaging the flight deck aft of the island and shutting down flight operations on the battered flat-top. *Zuiho* was to be out of action for several months. The smoke from the flight deck became a beacon for some of *Hornet*'s pilots.[116]

About two hours after Strong and Irvine's daring attack on *Zuiho*, *Hornet*'s first strike arrived. The torpedo pilots got lost, but VB–8 and VS–8 Dauntless pilots fought their way through a "cloud of Zeros" to attack. Led by Lieutenant James E. Vose after Lieutenant Commander William J. (Gus) Widhelm was shot down, *Hornet*'s pilots got at least four hits on *Shokaku*, sending it back to Japan for nine months of repairs. The third carrier in the task force, *Zuikaku*, escaped detection and attack because of a convenient area of rain and low clouds. Once the Americans left, *Zuikaku* recovered the surviving aircraft that returned from attacking Kinkaid's carriers.[117]

Enterprise's twenty-plane group should have been the next to hit the Japanese carriers, but it was deflected by a vicious ambush. A large strike that the Japanese had launched toward the Americans passed close aboard *Hornet*'s first wave without attacking it. But when it encountered the *Big E*'s aircraft, escorting Zeros peeled off and wreaked havoc. Half of the torpedo planes and Wildcats were either shot down or so severely damaged that they had to return to their carrier. The surviving pilots pressed ahead, but, short on fuel, they chose to attack the battleships

---

[116] CTF 61 Action Report for 26 Oct 1942; CO *Enterprise* Action Report for 26 Oct 1942; Hammell, *Carrier Battles*, 344–47; Stafford, *Big E*, 154–56; VADM James H. Flatley, "The Bravest Man I Ever Knew," *Shipmate*, Dec 1978, 16–18.

[117] COMBOMBRON 8 to CO *Hornet*, "Action on 26 Oct 1942," 29 Oct 1942, encl. to CO *Hornet* Action Report, 26 Oct 1942, all enclosed in CINCPAC Action Report, Battle of Santa Cruz; Morison 5:213–14; Hammell, *Carrier Battles*, 362–67.

and cruisers they had stumbled upon. This attack by three Dauntlesses and four Avengers resulted in two bomb hits on the old battleship *Kirishima*, but the hits did little to impair it.[118]

Hornet's second strike, like *Enterprise*'s, did not reach the Japanese carriers. Instead it also pounced on the battleship-cruiser force of Admiral Kondo. Led by a junior officer (Lieutenant John J. Lynch), nine SBDs from VB–8 and VS–8 attacked the cruiser *Chikuma* and severely damaged it with four hits by half-ton bombs. Lynch's efforts were appreciated, but the two Dauntless squadron commanders, Vose and Widhelm, were bitter. Because the radio equipment was too primitive to pick up three different contact or attack reports, Lynch's group missed the opportunity to finish off *Zuiho* and *Shokaku*. Had Lynch or one of his squadron mates picked up any of the reports, they could have made a little more history.[119]

Even before the *Hornet* and *Enterprise* pilots subjected the Japanese flat-tops to their ordeal by fire, Kinkaid's task force was in trouble. At 0940 *Hornet*'s outbound second wave passed a large group of Japanese carrier aircraft obviously headed for TF 61. The Americans passed the word that twenty-four enemy dive bombers were about 60 miles from Kinkaid's force at 12,000 feet on a bearing of 280 degrees True. Receiving this information, at 0945 Kinkaid ordered by both light and flag hoist, "Prepare to repel air attack." Both carriers quickly recovered, serviced, and sent their CAPs aloft again. By 1000 there were at least twenty-five Wildcats in the air under the control of the FDO in *Enterprise*. To meet the incoming attack with the maximum firepower and concentrate the fighters for defense, at 1002 Kinkaid ordered Admiral Murray to close TF 16 with TF 17. The sea room had gradually been increasing between them as Kinkaid moved northeast, and Murray held his force into the wind on a general southeast bearing. As the *Hornet* force moved toward Kinkaid's, which had moved into the cover of a rainstorm, the Japanese struck at 1010.[120]

Hornet's fighters engaged the Japanese and tried desperately to prevent the deadly Vals from diving on their carrier in coordination with torpedo attacks by accompanying Kates. Despite heroic efforts by the fighters and outstanding gunnery from TF 17's ships, the Japanese were not to be repelled. Admiral Kinkaid later reported the attack:

---

[118] CO *Enterprise* Action Report for 26 Oct 1942; Hammell, *Carrier Battles*, 368–70; Stafford, *Big E*, 160–61.

[119] COMSCORON 8 and COMBOMBRON 8 to CO *Hornet*, "Action Report of 26 Oct 1942 with Enemy Japanese Fleet-Solomon Islands Area," 2 Nov 1942, encl. to CINCPAC Action Report, Battle of Santa Cruz; Morison 5:214.

[120] CTF 17 to CINCPAC, "Preliminary Report of Action, 26 Oct 1942," 30 Oct 1942, encl. to CINCPAC Action Report, Battle of Santa Cruz; CO *Hornet* Action Report for 26 Oct 1942; CTF 61 Action Report for 26 Oct 1942.

Japanese D3A "Val" dive bomber makes a crash dive on *Hornet* (CV 8) during the Battle of the Santa Cruz Islands, 26 October 1942. Note antiaircraft burst just off the carrier's starboard side, with its shrapnel striking the water below. A B5N "Kate" torpedo bomber is flying above, and another Val is off *Hornet*'s bow.

At 1010 a well coordinated attack by 15 dive bombers and 12 torpedo planes came in on the HORNET. At 1013 fires were started by a plane which dove into the ship. At 1015 HORNET was hit by two torpedoes and lost all power. At about the same time additional fires were started by two 500 pound bomb hits and other hits followed. There being no power on the ship, bucket lines were formed [to fight the fires] and destroyers were called alongside to fight the fires. By 1100 all fires were under control. . . . Efforts were made to tow the HORNET.[121]

As *Northampton* began to rig a tow line to *Hornet*, the Japanese switched their attention to *Enterprise*. Providentially hidden by a rain squall when the first Japanese wave arrived, *Big E*'s luck ran out at 1115. The Japanese air group commander was overheard by Kinkaid's communicators, reporting that he had sighted a second American carrier and directing an attack toward it.[122]

---

[121] CTF 61 Action Report for 26 Oct 1942.
[122] Ibid.

At 1115 *Enterprise*'s gunners spotted the first Vals, but by then they were already in their dives. Captain Hardison maneuvered the flat-top like a broken-field runner escaping for a touchdown, but *Enterprise* did not escape. During the four minutes that the Japanese bombers were successively peeling off and hurtling down in 65-degree dives, the carrier received three jolting blows. The first bomb hit well forward on the flight deck, passed through the forecastle, and exited through the ship's skin at the bows where it exploded. At least 160 shrapnel holes were counted later, but the damage was relatively light. This hit was followed by a 500-pounder that struck the flight deck dead center just aft of the forward elevator, and then detonated on the hangar deck. A portion of the bomb continued through the hangar deck and tore up the forward areas on the third deck. Captain Hardison described the third bomb's results:

> A third bomb detonated close aboard near frame 129 starboard, cracking the after bearing pedestal on No. 2 H.P. turbine, opening a seam in the side plating to a maximum of three inches extending from frame 123 to frame 135, flooding two empty fuel tanks, and opening a third tank which was full. The ship shook violently as a result of this explosion. Planes parked in Fly I were bounced clear off the deck and the farthest one forward on the starboard side fell over the side. One plane in Fly III was bounced into the starboard 20 mm battery.[123]

On Kinkaid's flag bridge each explosion tossed the admiral and staff around like bowling pins in an alley. Fortunately for them the shrapnel was confined to the flight deck and lower levels in the ship.

Once the Vals had completed their dives, the ship's radar operators reported the approach of torpedo planes from astern at 1135. Guns that had been pointed upward, desperately trying to follow the diving Vals, now trained outward and began picking off the Kates. Fourteen planes managed to work their way through the screen and then divided to attack toward each bow. Possibly as many as nine dropped their one-ton torpedoes, but *Enterprise* proved too nimble for them. No hits were scored and all of the attackers were splashed, either by gunfire or by defending aircraft. Captain Hardison's action report crisply described the maneuvering necessary to survive such an attack:

> An estimated 14 additional torpedo planes were then seen to divide into two groups which attempted to gain favorable approach positions forward on both sides, outside our screen. Heavy AA was brought to bear from ENTERPRISE as well as from vessels of the screen, but approximately nine torpedoes were launched, five from the starboard side and probably four

---

[123] CO *Enterprise* Action Report for 26 Oct 1942.

A bomb explodes close aboard *Enterprise* during the Battle of the Santa Cruz Islands, 26 October 1942.

from the port side. . . . Three torpedo tracks close together were observed coming at the ship from 20 [degrees] forward of the starboard beam. The rudder was immediately put over hard right and the ship passed inside the three tracks by an estimated fifty yards. The rudder was then reversed to avoid collision with SMITH which was aflame forward. ENTERPRISE was turning left when a plane was observed to drop its torpedo from ahead. The track of this torpedo was not seen until it was less than 800 yards away. It appeared that ENTERPRISE bow would be past the torpedo track, so hard right rudder was put on and the stern swung left. The torpedo passed the ship to starboard almost parallel to it and within 100 feet. . . .[124]

At 1220 *Enterprise*'s radar reported that the torpedo planes were gone, but a minute later the flat-top was again under attack, this time by dive bombers. This attack came in two waves. The earlier 1010 attack on *Hornet* and the 1115 one on *Enterprise* had come from *Shokaku*, *Zuikaku* and *Zuiho*; now it was time for *Zuikaku* and *Junyo*'s pilots to try their skills. Unlike the earlier Val pilots, who plunged down in steep-angled dives, *Junyo*'s Vals

---

[124] Ibid.

made their dives at 45 degrees or less. They probably chose the shallower dive because they were less skillful than the earlier attackers, or perhaps they felt it would increase their chances of hitting the *Big E*. Whatever their reasons for choosing the long, shallow approach it proved enormously beneficial to TF 16. The antiaircraft gunfire setups were simpler and the barrage was extremely effective. Only one attacker got through to *Enterprise* and his bomb bounced off the starboard side forward and detonated as a near miss. While dishing in plates and opening some voids, the damage was relatively negligible. Then at 1230 another group of Vals, fifteen in all from *Junyo* and *Zuikaku*, started their dives. Again the task force gunfire was cruelly effective: no hits scored, at least ten shot down.[125]

With only a few enemy aircraft surviving the Wildcat defenders and the ships' gunners, the Japanese had almost shot their bolt. But there was still a long afternoon ahead for Murray and Kinkaid. Murray, of course, had the most pressing problem because *Hornet* was grievously damaged. The bombs and torpedoes that had struck the carrier left it burning and dead in the water, but excellent damage control brought the fires under control and reduced the possibility of sinking. After two tries *Northampton* succeeded in taking the carrier in tow at 1550. But a half hour later enemy torpedo planes arrived, and the cruiser was forced to drop the tow line. The attackers failed to torpedo *Northampton*, but one managed to plant its torpedo in *Hornet*'s starboard side. Already in extremis the flattop was pounced on by four dive bombers and received another hit. With the ship now listing heavily to starboard and in danger of capsizing, Captain Mason ordered the ship abandoned at 1650. A few minutes later a final attack was made when nine horizontal bombers (Bettys) dropped their loads. Fortunately only one bomb hit and the misses were on the side away from the crew members in the water. *Hornet* was now a burning derelict, and Admiral Murray decided no further effort should be made to save it. He detailed destroyers *Mustin* and *Anderson* to sink the ship with torpedoes and gunfire, but they could not put the carrier under. With a surface battle force rapidly approaching, the destroyers turned southeast at 2140 to rejoin TF 17, which had already cleared the area. Concluding that salvage of the vessel was impossible, the Japanese fired four of their "Long Lance" torpedoes into the hulk and finished what the American torpedoes had failed to accomplish. *Hornet* went under at 0235 on 27 October 1942—Navy Day.[126]

Kinkaid's afternoon was equally packed with action and decisions. With *Enterprise* damaged and *Hornet* dead in the water, recovery of the

---

[125] Ibid.

[126] CO *Hornet* Action Report for 26 Oct 1942; CTF 17 Preliminary Action Report for 26 Oct 1942; CTF 61 Action Report for 26 Oct 1942; CINCPAC Action Report, Battle of Santa Cruz; Hammell, *Carrier Battles*, 475–78.

air groups from both carriers became the first of Kinkaid's concerns. He could not afford to lose the surviving aircraft and their crews. Once the Japanese attacks against *Enterprise* ceased, around 1235, the carrier began recovery of the *Hornet* and *Enterprise* strikes that had been launched against the Japanese earlier in the day. With the forward elevator jammed in the raised position, the flight deck crew still managed to park almost all the planes that returned. The flight deck was now fully occupied from the bow to the arresting gear wires aft of the #3 elevator. To give the packed carrier some breathing space, Kinkaid ordered thirteen SBDs flown to Espiritu Santo to reinforce the CACTUS Air Force on Guadalcanal or to replace aircraft sent earlier to that island. Thus by careful management of parking space, and judicious use of elevators two and three, the flight deck officer was now able to provide sufficient space forward to launch combat air patrols through the afternoon, but these pilots guarded only the *Big E*. Herein lay one of the major controversies of Kinkaid's career.

In a preliminary action report dated 3 November 1942, Kinkaid tersely described the period of attacks:

> During the attacks on the HORNET task force SIXTEEN continued on courses in general away from the approaching planes and took advantage of cover in three or four rain squalls. Attacks on the HORNET were followed by four separate attacks on the ENTERPRISE between 1115 and 1234. Between attacks and after the last attack ENTERPRISE recovered her own and HORNET planes and retired on southeasterly courses to clear the area.[127]

Kinkaid had actually ordered TF 16 to continue in a generally southeasterly direction once recovery operations were completed. With launch or recovery actions taking place once or twice during every hour and with the prevailing wind from the southeast, the task force would have been carried away from *Hornet*'s position unless attempts were deliberately made to remain nearby. In retreating from the scene of the battle, Kinkaid recognized that he was abandoning *Hornet*. In the TF 16 war diary his staff partially explained his decision:

> With the HORNET out of action, the extent of damage to the ENTERPRISE not fully determined, and the probability that there were one or two undamaged enemy carriers in the battle area which had not been sighted by our forces, the decision of Commander Task Force 61 to retire at high speed to the southeast was made without hesitation.[128]

---

[127] CTF 61 to CINCPAC, 2 Nov 1942, first endorsement to CTF 17 Secret ltr A16–3(11t), ser 0050, 30 Oct 1942; all enclosed in CINCPAC Action Report, Battle of Santa Cruz.

[128] Quoted in Miller, *Cactus Air Force*, 173.

An undocumented, but perfectly evident fact was that Kinkaid was riding the last operational American carrier in the Pacific. With its load of aircraft, and if its battle wounds were not too disabling, *Enterprise* would be a vital part of Admiral Halsey's arsenal in his struggle to maintain control of Guadalcanal. There is little doubt that Kinkaid felt heartsick when he informed Murray that the *Enterprise* fighters, a good number of which had come from *Hornet*, would remain over TF 16. Perhaps some of Jimmy Flatley's Wildcats could have prevented that last torpedo from being launched into *Hornet*, but it was still a stricken and powerless vessel awaiting a tow, and attempting to salvage it in submarine-infested waters would have endangered the remaining ships of both task forces. Both Kinkaid and Murray also knew there was an enemy surface battle force lurking nearby, hungry for a night engagement. Kinkaid now realized how it felt to wear the same mantle of responsibility worn by Frank Jack Fletcher while en route to Wake Island.[129]

By the time Captain Mason gave the order to abandon *Hornet*, Kinkaid had TF 16 heading southeast on the safer route to the east of the New Hebrides and then around to Noumea. Murray's TF 17 without *Hornet*, of course, would rendezvous with Kinkaid the next morning. During the early part of the night the two task forces were shadowed by aircraft from Admiral Abe's surface Vanguard Group. The Japanese scout planes dropped flares and float lights to keep track of the retreating Americans, but by midnight the Japanese gave up the chase and both task forces were clear of danger. Tom could finally get a good night's sleep.[130]

The four-day trip to Noumea gave the admiral a chance to think about the battle and begin preparing his action report. Because he was separated from Admiral Murray, he wrote a preliminary report as Commander Task Force 61.[131] Later he would write a fuller report and endorsements to reports by Murray and other subordinates. From what he had experienced in the battle and learned later from Admiral Halsey's staff, he believed that his task force had performed creditably and that the Japanese had taken a beating. Always careful of what he wrote to his wife, Kinkaid summed up the recent activities for her: "This has been a strenuous week. . . . The Japs have made a strenuous effort to retake Guadalcanal but at the moment are licking their wounds and probably planning another effort."[132]

He of course did not mention TF 61's "wounds": *Hornet* sunk; *Enterprise* damaged by bomb hits; *South Dakota* damaged from a bomb hit on a

---

[129] Ibid., 173–4.

[130] CTF 61 Action Report for 26 Oct 1942; CTF 17 War Diary (Chronology), 24–27 Oct 1942, encl. to CTF 17, Preliminary Action Report for 26 Oct 1942; Morison 5:222–23.

[131] CTF 61 Preliminary Action Report for 26 Oct 1942.

[132] TCK to HSK, *Enterprise*, 31 Oct 1942.

turret and its captain wounded; *Porter* (DD 366) sunk; *San Juan* damaged by a bomb hit; and *Smith* (DD 378) severely damaged forward from a Kate crashing on board. Except for *Hornet* all the damaged vessels had been in Kinkaid's TF 16. His screen commander, Rear Admiral Tisdale, thought the task force had come through remarkably well.

> I consider the fact that no more damage was suffered by vessels of this force [TF 16], especially the carrier, to reflect a marvelous spirit, determination and ability on the part of all concerned. This was probably the most sustained attack a U.S. Task Force had undergone without suffering serious damage. At least the PORTLAND people say so, and they have actually engaged in all four [carrier battles].[133]

The damage inflicted on the Japanese was considerable, though the extent was not completely clear to Halsey or Nimitz until war's end. *Shokaku* had taken four bomb hits that destroyed its flight and hangar decks and forced its retirement. The after part of *Zuiho*'s flight deck had been badly ripped up by hits from two 500-pounders and it too required repairs in Japan. *Hornet*'s Dauntlesses hit the cruiser *Chikuma* with four bombs and sent it back to Empire waters.[134]

Although the damage inflicted on the Japanese carriers was important for the continuing struggle for Guadalcanal, the loss of approximately one hundred Japanese carrier aircraft and most of their crews was of vital significance to the immediate and future war in the Pacific. These experienced pilots were almost irreplaceable. Neither were American carrier aircraft losses light. Seventy-four planes were lost, around twenty in combat and the rest due to fuel exhaustion and operations accidents. Only twenty-three pilots and ten rear seat men were killed. Loss of shipboard personnel was much heavier.[135]

Kinkaid himself, after almost a year in command and having survived five major operations, was beginning to show signs that he was starting to wear out. His boss, Halsey, summed up Kinkaid's work in a letter to Admiral Nimitz: "As soon as I can get some flag officers, I would like to send Tom back to the states for a rest. He has done a noble job and has been at it a long time."[136]

Kinkaid and Task Forces 16 and 17 arrived in Noumea on 30 October. Halsey and Kinkaid decided that *Enterprise* would be patched up by local facilities, meaning the repair ship *Vestal* (AR 4) and the *Big E*'s own crew. The carrier needed an overhaul at Pearl Harbor, but, though damaged, *Enter-*

---

[133] CTF 16 to CINCPAC, "Report of Action 26 Oct 1942," 29 Oct 1942, encl. to CINCPAC Action Report, Battle of Santa Cruz.
[134] Morison 5:214–15; Dull, *Battle History IJN*, 232–33.
[135] CINCPAC Action Report, Battle of Santa Cruz.
[136] Halsey to Nimitz, Noumea, 17 Nov 1942, Nimitz Papers.

prise could still handle an air group, and thus remained with Halsey. It was unthinkable to leave the South Pacific command without a carrier while the Japanese were still proceeding with operations to retake Guadalcanal.

By the time the task forces arrived in Noumea, Captain Mason of *Hornet* and Admiral Murray had completed their action reports and then made them available to Kinkaid. Both reports had an unstated underlying theme: *Hornet* had been lost because of flawed decisions made by Kinkaid. Both argued that TF 17 should not have been tied to TF 16 and operated in a tactical situation by a single officer in tactical command. Murray believed that the operations of the two task forces should have been coordinated by a senior officer based ashore (Commander South Pacific Force) until the task forces came under attack or attacked the enemy. Then each task force commander should have taken charge and controlled the battle action of his force. Mason and Murray were also in complete agreement that it had been wrong to have the fighter director officer in *Enterprise* control activities of the combat air patrols of both carriers. *Hornet*'s FDO should have worked with Flatley's VF–10. Captain Mason stated his conclusions forthrightly:

> It is recommended that carrier task forces operate singly or at least well separated. When enemy contact is made, communications can be established on normal radio frequency channels. It is firmly believed that each carrier should conduct its own fighter direction at all times. It is believed that single carrier task forces operating separately are more efficient than when two or more are operating together as one force.[137]

Admiral Murray was equally direct:

> Two carrier task forces cannot be operated with maximum battle efficiency and remain in visual touch under one OTC when contact with the enemy is sought. . . .
>
> When two carrier task forces are operated in company, the coordination of the movements of one to conform to the operations of the other introduces unacceptable delays when offensive action against an enemy is of paramount importance. . . .
>
> Each task force commander must exercise direct control of combat air patrols and carrier air group of own task force.[138]

In his endorsement of Admiral Murray's 30 October report, Kinkaid responded directly to Murray and inferentially to Captain Mason. He agreed with much of what the two had recommended, such as better armor pro-

---

[137] CO *Hornet* Action Report for 26 Oct 1942; Frank, *Guadalcanal*, 401–2.
[138] CTF 17 Preliminary Action Report for 26 Oct 1942.

tection from torpedoes for carriers and larger fighter squadrons. He also positively endorsed their recommendations that a carrier screen have at least twelve destroyers, both for their firepower and their antisubmarine capabilities. But he disagreed with their gunnery recommendations. Both Murray and Mason denigrated the 20-mm guns as being too short-ranged since they knocked down aircraft only after the aircraft had dropped their bombs or torpedoes. Murray also concluded that the 5-inch guns were useless against dive bombers and almost as useless against torpedo planes. The two would replace the 20-mm and 5-inch guns with the new quadruple-mounted 40-mm batteries. These rapid-fire weapons could break up air attacks before drops were made. Murray and Mason, of course, had been in *Hornet*; Kinkaid's perspective came from a ship that had survived. "Commander Task Force SIXTY-ONE does not agree that the 40 mm gun is the only weapon which has given promise of breaking up dive bombing and torpedo attacks. The 20 mm batteries on the ENTERPRISE have been remarkably effective in this and previous attacks." Kinkaid believed the new 40-mm mounts in *Enterprise* had done well, but the number that could be installed was limited. He summed up his position:

> They [40-mm batteries] can reach out to take attacker planes under fire before they reach the release point for bombs or torpedoes, but after the planes reach a certain point volume of fire is of paramount importance and that is supplied by 20 mm guns. The answer to this particular problem is to install as many 40 mm guns as practicable and to fill up every available remaining space with 20 mm guns.[139]

Concerning the subject of operating several carriers or carrier task groups together, Kinkaid met Mason and Murray head-on:

> I do not concur in the categorical statements . . . that the operations of two carrier task forces within visual touch causes delays or reduces battle efficiency. On the contrary, by having two carriers together one carrier can take care of all routine flying while the other maintains her full striking group spotted and ready to launch on short notice. If the carriers are separated, then each must fly its own inner air patrol and combat air patrol and make its own search. Exactly the same number of turns into the wind are required, the spot must be frequently broken and the maximum striking force is not available.
>
> Separate control of combat air patrols and carrier air groups of carriers in close proximity would fail to achieve the maximum of effectiveness that results from coordination by one command.[140]

---

[139] CTF 61 to CINCPAC, 3 Nov 1942, first endorsement to CTF 17 ltr of 30 Oct 1942; CTF 61 to CINCPAC, "Comments on U.S.S. *Hornet* Report of Action, 26 Oct 1942," 6 Nov 1942, encl. to CINCPAC Action Report, Battle of Santa Cruz.

[140] CTF 61 to CINCPAC, Comments on *Hornet* Action Report for 26 Oct 1942.

In endorsing the reports of Kinkaid and Murray, Admiral Halsey managed to straddle the subject of combined carrier operations. Concerning Admiral Murray's recommendations, he wrote:

> ComSoPacFor is of the opinion that when two carriers with their screening vessels are operating in close mutual support to one another, they should be combined into a single disposition and so operated until separation is desirable due to impending air attack.[141]

Because fighter aircraft control and direction seemed likely to come up again, Halsey tried to settle the matter. Perhaps his endorsement pleased someone.

> If, and when, carriers become separated by more than ten miles, then it is considered that the controlling director should immediately turn control of a proportionate number of fighters over to the separated carriers. In the event the direction of approach is definitely known, control of all fighters should be vested in the carrier nearest the direction of approach.[142]

Halsey's views were based on the admiral's personal experience in operating task forces with two carriers and in his expectations for the future. With the large number of flat-tops under construction, it was inevitable that multicarrier task forces would become the preferred arrangement for battle operations in the years ahead. He also knew that improvements in very high frequency and the arrival of ultra high frequency radio equipment would mean vastly improved control of aircraft from the carriers. Given his outlook, he did not want to fully accept the recommendations of Captain Mason (soon to become rear admiral) or Admiral Murray. Yet he did understand another source of their discontent. These men were naval aviators; Kinkaid was not. It was almost inevitable they would believe that no naval aviator would have left *Hornet* so poorly defended by the fighter cover available.

For the rest of the war Admiral John Towers, now Commander Aircraft, Pacific Fleet, would blame Kinkaid for the loss of *Hornet*.[143] Kinkaid would take the *Enterprise* task force to sea again in a few weeks, but it would be the last operation in which a carrier task force was commanded by a nonaviator.

---

[141] COMSOPAC to CINCPAC, 2d Endorsement to CTF 17 ltr, A16–3(11t), ser 0050, 30 Oct 1942; all enclosed in CINCPAC Action Report, Battle of Santa Cruz.

[142] COMSOPAC to CINCPAC, 3d Endorsement to CO *Hornet* ltr, CV8/A16–3 (5), ser 00101, 3 Nov 1942, all enclosed in CINCPAC, Action Report, Battle of Santa Cruz.

[143] Clark G. Reynolds, *Admiral John H. Towers: The Struggle for Naval Air Supremacy* (Annapolis: Naval Institute Press, 1991), 409, 609 n. 7, 611 n. 55.

While writing his action reports and keeping an eye on repairs to vessels in his Task Force 16, Kinkaid tried to let Helen know that he had survived the recent engagement. He was concerned that the release of news about the battle, including information that *Porter* had been sunk and "an American aircraft carrier severely damaged," would cause her worry. After several tries he did get another *sans origine* cable off to Philadelphia. Like the one after the Coral Sea battle, it was brief: "Well and going strong." It arrived on 4 November and had the desired effect; Helen was reassured.[144]

At Pearl Harbor Nimitz was furious. News of the Santa Cruz Islands battle was released at the same time the loss of *Wasp* hit the headlines. He was not sure the Japanese had known that *Wasp* had sunk. That news plus *Hornet*'s loss, which they did know about, provided them with too much information on American carrier weakness in the South Pacific. King understood, but the problem in this case was traceable to a censor in Noumea and, coincidentally, to presidential politics.[145]

For the first ten days after his arrival in Noumea, Kinkaid had a fairly relaxed schedule. Once his action reports and endorsements were nearly completed, he released most of the TF 16 staff to rejoin Halsey. He then took on a new group, headed by Captain Edward P. Moore and again including Lieutenant Commanders David Gladney as his flag secretary and Robert Taylor as his flag lieutenant. The latter was destined to spend many more months with the admiral. Kinkaid also received a new title to go with that of Commander Task Force 16. At the end of November he was named Commander Cruisers, Pacific Fleet, an administrative and type (cruisers) command. Admiral Fletcher had worn this hat prior to his detachment; now it would be Tom's.[146]

The admiral visited with flag and general officers in New Caledonia, rode around in one of Halsey's jeeps, and awarded decorations to Smith's crew. They had done a splendid job of saving their ship while continuing to defend *Enterprise*, and Kinkaid gave them more than the traditional "Well done!"

Ever interested in his next operation, Kinkaid regularly visited with Halsey and caught up on COMSOPAC's planning. He told Helen that his boss "seems to have recovered his health but looks very old." Perhaps Halsey had reasons to look or feel old. Although the Japanese striking force had left the area, it did not mean they had lost interest in Guadalcanal. At Pearl Harbor Nimitz's staff had recently drawn an estimate of the situation and predicted, "For the month of November we conclude that

---

[144] TCK to HSK, Noumea, 31 Oct 1942, 1 Nov 1942, cable 2 Nov 1942.

[145] *Los Angeles Times*, 27 Oct 1942; CINCPAC to COMINCH, 10/290311Z; CINCPAC to COMINCH, 11/012115Z, Command Summary; Potter, *Nimitz*, 219.

[146] TCK to HSK, Noumea, 5 Nov 1942; TCK Personnel File.

the most probable [enemy] move continues to be the recapture of the Southern SOLOMONS, and the extension of control in New Guinea."[147]

On 8 November the staff estimated that in the week ahead the enemy would be mounting a new "grand scale offensive" in which the following vessels were available to them and to Halsey:

Japan	U.S. Navy
4 battleships	2 battleships (one damaged)
2 fleet carriers	1 fleet carrier (damaged)
5 heavy cruisers	4 heavy cruisers
6 light cruisers	4 light cruisers
21 destroyers	33 destroyers (some required for escort)[148]

This Japanese order of battle and information about plans to land heavy reinforcements on Guadalcanal were based on code-breaking efforts in Pearl and Washington. By 9 November the only missing piece concerning the anticipated operation was "Zed Day," the actual day the transports would arrive. In his Top Secret radio to Halsey Nimitz provided information on the transports, troops, destinations, and supporting naval vessels, but still no date. He closed, "While this looks like a big punch, I am confident that you with your forces will take their measure."[149] One wonders whether Bill Halsey was as confident as he sounded in his last letter to Nimitz: "We are not in the least downhearted or upset by our difficulties, but obsessed with one idea only, to kill the yellow bastards and we shall do it." After he had read this letter, CINCPAC wrote in the margin for the benefit of his staff, "This is the spirit desired."[150]

Halsey did not need many messages from CINCPAC to prod him into action. He was quite aware that the Japanese were steadily reinforcing their garrison on Guadalcanal by the so-called Tokyo Express—destroyer runs to the island at night.[151] To begin derailing this delivery system, he abolished Task Forces 17 and 61 and continued TF 16, a single-carrier task force built around the damaged *Enterprise*, the only flat-top available to him. Kinkaid remained in command of the task force.

Halsey also created TF 65, a force of six cruisers and fourteen destroyers, and gave its command to Rear Admiral Daniel J. Callaghan. Admiral Willis A. Lee's Battleship Division 6 plus a couple destroyers would later operate separately from TF 16 and be known as TF 64.[152]

---

[147] "Estimate of Enemy Capabilities, 1 Nov 1942," Command Summary, 1149.
[148] Ibid., 1158.
[149] CINCPAC to COMSOPAC, 11/092107Z, Command Summary.
[150] Halsey to Nimitz, Noumea, 31 Oct 1942, Nimitz Papers.
[151] Morison 5:226.
[152] Ibid., 231–33.

Task Force 16, November 1942

CTF 16 RADM T.C. Kinkaid
    CV *Enterprise* (flagship)   CAPT O. B. Hardison

COMBATDIV 6 RADM W. A. Lee
    BB *Washington* (flag)   CAPT G. B. Davis
    BB *South Dakota*   CAPT T. L. Gatch

COMCRUDIV 5 RADM H. H. Good
    CA *Northampton* (flag)   CAPT W. A. Kitts
    CLAA *San Diego*   CAPT B. F. Perry

COMDESRON 2 CDR H. R. Holcomb
    Morris (DD 417), *Russell* (DD 414), *Mustin* (DD 413),
    Benham (DD 397), *Walke* DD 416), *Clark* (DD 361)

SOURCE: Morison, *The Struggle for Guadalcanal, August 1942–February 1943*, 231–33.

On 11 November Halsey gave Kinkaid two hours' notice to take TF 16 to sea. Slightly late, Kinkaid got the *Enterprise* force underway at noon and landed its air group on board an hour later. The ship was by now capable of operating at full power, but its aircraft were limited to thirty-eight Wildcat fighters, thirty-one Dauntless scouts and bombers, and nine Avenger torpedo planes.[153] The number of planes was larger than might be expected with elevator #1 still inoperable in the raised position and #3 now giving problems. Once clear of Noumea Halsey had ordered TF 16 to arrive in the vicinity of 14°S and 161°30′E by 0800 on the 13th and to "be prepared to strike targets CACTUS area."[154] In the haste to depart *Enterprise* took with it a contingent of surprised artisans from *Vestal* and some of the Noumea Seabee battalion who had been at work on the elevators.[155]

As TF 16 steamed north toward the neighborhood of Guadalcanal, the anticipated Japanese moves soon developed into a series of night actions followed by bombing attacks from Henderson Field against the enemy. Because of his distance from the field of action Kinkaid would be able to do little more than read the intercepted dispatches between Halsey and his cruiser admirals and wait for orders from Noumea. Enjoined to radio silence so knowledge of his task force would be hidden from the enemy, Kinkaid was forced to play a waiting game.

---

[153] CO *Enterprise* to CINCPAC, "Report of Action Against Japanese Forces Attempting to Recapture Guadalcanal, 13–14 Nov 1942," 19 Nov 1942, OA (hereafter CO *Enterprise* Action Report for 13–14 Nov 1942).
[154] COMSOPAC to COMINCH, 11/090347Z; COMSOPAC to CTF 16, 11/102102Z, Command Summary.
[155] TCK oral history, 208–9; Eric Hammell, *Guadalcanal: Decision at Sea* (New York: Crown Publishers, 1988), 295.

The night of 12–13 November was a critical one for Halsey's command and the Marines ashore on Guadalcanal. A Japanese heavy bombardment force under Rear Admiral Hiroaki Abe had been ordered to knock out the island's Henderson Field. If this step was accomplished, then eleven troop-laden transports could probably land their reinforcements and arms. American transports that had been unloading on the 12th pulled clear and their protective cruiser force turned to block the enemy bombardment forces. In the ensuing night action, Rear Admirals Daniel Callaghan and Norman Scott were killed along with most of their staffs, and the damage to their force was extensive. Of the five cruisers in Callaghan's force, the light cruisers *Atlanta* and *Juneau* (CL 52) were lost, and the heavy cruisers *San Francisco* and *Portland* were badly mauled. Four destroyers were sunk. The Japanese lost two destroyers, and the battleship *Hiei* was so badly torn up it became an easy target for the CACTUS Air Force to sink.[156]

Kinkaid's task force was too far south of Guadalcanal to actively support the island with *Enterprise*'s air group. Dauntlesses were launched northward on search and attack sorties, but no Japanese ships were encountered. The only way Kinkaid could contribute was to order nine Avengers and six Wildcats to land at CACTUS and help out. Once in the area they joined in the attack on *Hiei* and eventually had the satisfaction of seeing it sink. That evening those *Enterprise* pilots remained at Guadalcanal.[157]

As Kinkaid steamed north, his force was strengthened on the 13th by the addition of heavy cruiser *Pensacola* (Captain Frank L. Lowe) wearing the flag of Rear Admiral Tisdale and escorted by destroyers *Gwin* and *Preston* (DD 379). Together with Admiral Lee's two battleships, TF 16 was for a few hours a powerful surface battle group.[158] But with another bombardment force spotted en route to Guadalcanal, Halsey ordered Lee to depart TF 16 at 1900 and head for the area with his battleships. Unfortunately the distance was too great; Lee could not arrive in time to prevent a cruiser bombardment of Henderson Field.[159]

While the Japanese were battering the Guadalcanal airfields, Kinkaid continued north with TF 16. To protect his carrier from a surprise attack, morning searches were launched to the north and northwest. Upon receiving early contact reports from Henderson Field scouts and then from *Enterprise* pilots, Kinkaid ordered the remainder of the air group to attack. These planes landed at CACTUS after dropping their ordnance and continued to operate from the island base. The eleven transports and escorts ap-

---

[156] Morison 5:239–54; Hammell, *Decision at Sea*, 130–250.
[157] CTF 16 Action Report for 12–15 Nov 1942; CO *Enterprise* Action Report for 13–14 Nov 1942.
[158] TF 16 War Diary, 13 Nov 1942; CTF 16 Action Report for 12–15 Nov 1942.
[159] Halsey to Nimitz, Noumea, 17 Nov 1942.

proaching Guadalcanal became the target of every American aircraft at Halsey's command. Between *Enterprise*'s pilots and the shore-based Marine squadrons, the pickings were good. The heavy cruiser *Kinugasa* was sunk and three other cruisers and destroyers were damaged. Seven transports were sunk with heavy troop losses; four transports were beached and added to the shipping losses. Of the more than 13,000 troops the Japanese brought to Guadalcanal, it is estimated that about 2,000 made it ashore.[160]

The night of 14–15 November ended with a shootout between Admiral Lee's battleship task force and a Japanese bombardment force consisting of the battleship *Kirishima*, four cruisers, and nine destroyers. Kinkaid's classmate won. The Japanese lost *Kirishima* and a destroyer. On the American side two destroyers were sunk; two destroyers and *South Dakota* were heavily damaged. Most important, the Japanese were again turned back, their reinforcement effort almost completely frustrated. This was to be their last serious effort to retake Guadalcanal.[161] A few days after Admiral Lee's great battle, Halsey wrote to Nimitz: "It is my belief that we handed the Nips a crushing blow and defeat during his last go at it. I am of the opinion that his back is beginning to break."[162]

While Admiral Lee was battling around Savo Island, Kinkaid and the *Enterprise* force were steaming back to Noumea. Once the air group had launched at 0830 on the 14th, there was no reason to further expose the crippled carrier. Halsey ordered it south, and at 1530 Kinkaid decided it was time to go. The next day COMSOPAC directed Admiral Tisdale to take *Pensacola*, *Northampton*, and three destroyers to Espiritu Santo. Finally on the 15th at 1440, *Enterprise* dropped the hook at Noumea.[163] Kinkaid's tour as a carrier task force commander was now completed. To Helen he summed up the previous five months: "I hate to leave my present job because I feel I know it well and have had considerable success in it."[164]

According to the official record, Tom Kinkaid had indeed had "considerable success" as a task force commander. His actions during the Eastern Solomons battle in August brought a second Distinguished Service Medal with a citation that applauded his "keen leadership, determined action and outstanding resourcefulness in driving off and destroying a large attacking force."[165] After the Santa Cruz Islands engagement, Admiral Halsey recommended a third DSM and Nimitz concurred, but due to a technicality the award was never made. After the war was over, Kinkaid sought a DSM for the Santa Cruz Islands battle, but instead a new citation was issued for

---

[160] Morison 5:282; Miller, *Cactus Air Force*, 194–208.
[161] Morison 5:277–82; Hammell, *Decision at Sea*, 337–86; Halsey to Nimitz, Noumea, 17 Nov 1942.
[162] Ibid.
[163] CTF 16 Action Report for 12–15 Nov 1942; TF 16 War Diary, 14–16 Nov 1942.
[164] TCK to HSK, Noumea, 23 Nov 1942.
[165] CINCPAC to SECNAV, Pearl Harbor, 9 Dec 1942, TCK Personnel File.

Kinkaid's second DSM, rewritten to include the October battle and the 14–15 November "action to the southwest of Guadalcanal."[166]

Despite these awards, Kinkaid's career was to be dogged by the loss of *Hornet*. In time he became sensitive to anything he considered critical of his handling of the *Enterprise* force. When the Office of Naval Intelligence published several pamphlets about the Solomons Campaign, Kinkaid wrote to correct a statement suggesting that he had held *Hornet*'s strike force on deck too long after *Enterprise* scouts had sighted the enemy on 26 October. In 1944, Kinkaid even boiled over to a visiting British admiral about inaccuracies concerning TF 61 in Fletcher Pratt's *The Navy's War*. He disliked being blamed for decisions that had clearly been Admiral Fletcher's.[167]

With TF 16 back in Noumea, Kinkaid wrote more action reports and prepared for a change of duty. Admiral Halsey had concluded that it was time to put TF 16 into the hands of an aviation admiral. Rear Admiral Ted Sherman, now available in Noumea, relieved Kinkaid on 23 November.

The next day Kinkaid took command of Task Force 67. This command consisted of all the South Pacific Force cruisers that were still capable of operating at sea. Recognizing that his ships had fought in a disorganized manner during several of the night surface actions, Halsey wanted Kinkaid to take charge and bring order to the cruisers. He knew that Tom would only be with him a few days or weeks, but if he could at least write a plan of operations for fighting the Tokyo Express, it would be a major contribution.[168] Kinkaid moved to the cruiser base established at BUTTON (Espiritu Santo), wrote a plan, and was relieved on 28 November by Rear Admiral Carlton H. Wright. His plan was adopted by Wright, but the admiral's first encounter with the Japanese turned out to be a disaster. Kinkaid, however, had left the area and was en route to Pearl Harbor when his relief fought the Battle of Tassafaronga.[169]

Upon detachment from command of TF 67 and his return to Pearl Harbor on 2 December, Kinkaid's South Pacific tour was completed. Now staying with Nimitz, Tom wrote to Helen that "in the past eleven months I have steamed about 91,000 miles and have just finished flying about 3,500 miles."[170] He had also participated in eight naval operations, six of which had brought him into direct contact with the enemy. He would now wear four battle stars on his Asiatic-Pacific ribbon, a Dis-

---

[166] TCK to ADM F. J. Horne, New York, 26 Feb 1946; VADM Louis Denfeld to TCK, Washington, 2 May 1946, TCK Personnel File.

[167] Fletcher Pratt, *The Navy's War* (New York: Harper & Brothers, 1944); Paul G. Halpern, ed., *The Keyes Papers: Selections from the Private and Official Correspondence of Admiral of the Fleet Baron Keyes of Zeebruge*, 3 vols. (London: George Allen and Unwin, 1981), 3:282, 358.

[168] TCK Personnel File; Halsey to Nimitz, Noumea, 17 Nov 1942.

[169] Morison 5:293–97.

[170] TCK to HSK, Pearl Harbor, 2 Dec 1942.

tinguished Service Medal with a gold star denoting a second award, and the Presidential Unit Citation with a star marking his ride on *Enterprise* into the battles where the citation was earned. Professionally speaking, Kinkaid had been fortunate. He was at hand when a commander was needed for the *Enterprise* task force. It was a lucky ship, a survivor. Tom Kinkaid too was both lucky and a survivor, though his skills were well grounded in self-discipline and the ability to make correct decisions when they counted. Above all, and this counted with his superiors, he delivered the goods when in command.

Chapter 12

The Aleutians, 1943

Tom Kinkaid left the South Pacific area with mixed feelings. He had found command of the *Enterprise* task force exhilarating and professionally rewarding. His immediate superior, Bull Halsey, had been generous when endorsing his detachment orders, stating, "You have commanded carrier task forces operating in this area with skill and effectiveness. You inflicted great damage upon the enemy in repeated engagements. . . . I desire to pay full tribute to your superb work." Kinkaid wasn't sure what his next duty would be, but he did expect that it would result in a trip to Washington and, above all, a chance to see Helen again. "That is what counts more than anything."[1]

Upon arrival at Pearl Harbor Kinkaid received several surprises. For openers he was to relieve Rear Admiral Theobald as Commander North Pacific Force (COMNORPACFOR), with headquarters on Kodiak Island. He also discovered that he would not be visiting Washington but would spend several weeks on the West Coast. Serious planning for approaching operations in the Aleutians was starting, and he needed to take part in this work. First though he would spend almost a week with Admiral Chester Nimitz and his staff preparing for his new command. With flag officer quarters in short supply, Nimitz kindly invited Tom to stay in his quarters on Makalapa Hill. This was common practice on the part of CINCPAC and undoubtedly helped in the creation of his "band of brothers" as the war dragged on.[2]

As Kinkaid began to dig into the correspondence and dispatch files concerning the North Pacific Force (Task Force 8) and its testy commander, he was baffled by the complex command arrangements that had developed during the year of war. Nimitz was not only CINCPAC, but also Commander Pacific Ocean Areas, and thus responsible for the North Pacific Area, yet he did not command the 72,000 Army troops in the Alaskan Defense Command. Those soldiers served under Major General Simon Bolivar Buckner and were ultimately controlled by Lieutenant General John L. DeWitt, Commander Western Defense Com-

---

[1] TCK to HSK, at sea, 23, 25 Nov 1942; ADM W. F. Halsey to RADM T. C. Kinkaid, CTF 16, 23 Nov 1942, TCK Personnel File; Task Force 8, Pacific Fleet, War Diary, 24 Nov 1942, OA.

[2] TCK oral history, 213–14; TCK to HSK, Pearl Harbor, 2 Dec 1942.

mand, with headquarters in San Francisco. On the other hand, there were about 14,000 Army Air Corps aviators, crew members, and ground support personnel commanded by Brigadier General William C. Butler who would report to Kinkaid for operations. The naval bases and their attached seagoing units composed an Alaskan Sector of Rear Admiral Charles S. Freeman's Thirteenth Naval District, itself a part of Vice Admiral Frank Jack Fletcher's Northwestern Sea Frontier command.

Although "unity of command" for operational purposes had been established under Commander TF 8, all other matters had to be managed through cooperation between General Buckner and Admiral Theobald, or between their superiors, Admiral Nimitz and General DeWitt. Kinkaid somewhat exasperated Nimitz when, for three days in a row, he admitted that reading the files had not enhanced his understanding of the command channels in the Alaskan-Aleutian region. He said that Nimitz finally shook a finger at him and threatened to cancel his orders if he again admitted that he could not understand these matters.[3]

It did not take Kinkaid long to discover that he was being sent to relieve Theobald because the latter had displayed a remarkable penchant for nonproductive controversy with his opposite numbers in the Army. After a summer of receiving quarrelsome reports concerning operations, material, the weather, and even some doggerel written by Buckner, General George Marshall and Admiral Ernest King concluded that Buckner, Butler, and Theobald would all have to be relieved and reassigned. But it is clear that Marshall had more confidence in Buckner than King had in Theobald. By 1 November, after a particularly exasperating exchange of correspondence with Theobald concerning King's rather tactful criticism of Theobald's management of relations with the Army, COMINCH had had enough. He understood Buckner's problems: Theobald was impossible. King let Marshall know that he need not change Army commanders; the thin-skinned Theobald would be leaving.[4]

Why King and Nimitz decided to send Kinkaid north is not clear. It appears that he simply was available at the moment COMINCH reached the limit of his patience with Theobald. Kinkaid had proven to be a capable carrier task force commander, and since Admiral King personally approved all flag officer assignments, he was aware of Kinkaid's availability. He also knew that plenty of flag officers were available to take over

---

[3] TCK oral history, 213–14; Maurice Matloff and Edwin M. Snell, *Strategic Planning for Coalition Warfare, 1941–1942* (Washington: Department of the Army, 1953), 356–57; memo for the Secretariat, Joint Chiefs of Staff, by ADM E. J. King, Washington, 8 Oct 1942, Ernest J. King Papers, OA.

[4] Morton, Strategy and Command, 423–27; Forrest C. Pogue, *George C. Marshall: Organizer of Victory, 1943–1945* (New York: Viking Press, 1973), 150–55. Admiral Theobald's epistolary battles with General Buckner and Admiral King may be traced in the Robert A. Theobald manuscripts at the Hoover Institution, Stanford, CA, and in the FADM Ernest J. King manuscripts in the Office of Naval History at the Naval Historical Center.

the cruiser training responsibilities that were central to the TF 67 assignment. Given Admiral King's personality, it is quite likely that he wanted to send a combat-experienced officer who had proven to be offensive-minded to deal with Generals Buckner and DeWitt. Both officers had filled the files with memoranda and dispatches urging General Marshall and the Joint Chiefs of Staff to let them proceed with the business of driving the Japanese out of Attu and Kiska. Whatever the reason for sending Tom Kinkaid to the North Pacific command, it turned out to be the most fortuitous assignment of his flag officer career.[5]

After almost a week at CINCPAC headquarters, Kinkaid and Nimitz left Pearl Harbor for a flight to the West Coast. Nimitz would be meeting Admiral King on 11 December for their bimonthly meeting, this time at Twelfth Naval District offices in San Francisco. Kinkaid was to sit in as Alaskan affairs were discussed, but he also had other business to initiate. He was to meet General DeWitt and get his ideas concerning the approaching invasion of Amchitka Island and his planning for the seizure of Kiska. More important from Tom's point of view was the opportunity to see Helen, who had managed to get a reservation for a train trip to San Francisco once she knew her husband's plans. Even more remarkable was that in the midst of war, the Kinkaids had gotten reservations at the St. Francis Hotel for their reunion. It would be a year to the day since their last farewell.

The admiral's sojourn on the West Coast was busy. He had hoped to have a couple of weeks of leave on the East Coast, mostly in the Philadelphia area, but that had been scratched. His three weeks free of Navy concerns were reduced to a few days with Helen in the San Francisco Bay area; then it was back to business with the arrival of Admiral King and his entourage. These COMINCH-CINCPAC conferences had begun in April 1942 and continued on a bimonthly basis during the rest of the year. Usually the two commanders would meet in San Francisco, but as the war progressed King would occasionally travel to Pearl Harbor. Wherever they met, the most serious problems of strategy, operations, or personnel were dealt with quickly and with remarkable thoroughness. Occasionally flag officers who had just concluded an operation or were about to take over a new command would be invited to participate in the meetings. At this particular conference Kinkaid not only heard both King's and Nimitz's ideas about future operations in the Alaskan-Aleutian area, but he was also deputed to convince General DeWitt of a needed change in the plans for some Army troops up north. It was not the most auspicious beginning for Tom Kinkaid's relations with the Commanding General, Western Defense Command.[6]

---

[5] Samuel Eliot Morison to TCK, Harvard, 19 Feb 1962; TCK to Morison, Washington, 21 Feb 1962, TCK Papers; Morton, *Strategy and Command,* 421–28.

[6] COMINCH–CINCPAC Conferences (microfilm), San Francisco, 1–13 Dec 1942, OA; Potter, *Nimitz,* 68–69, 112–15, 186–88, 210–11.

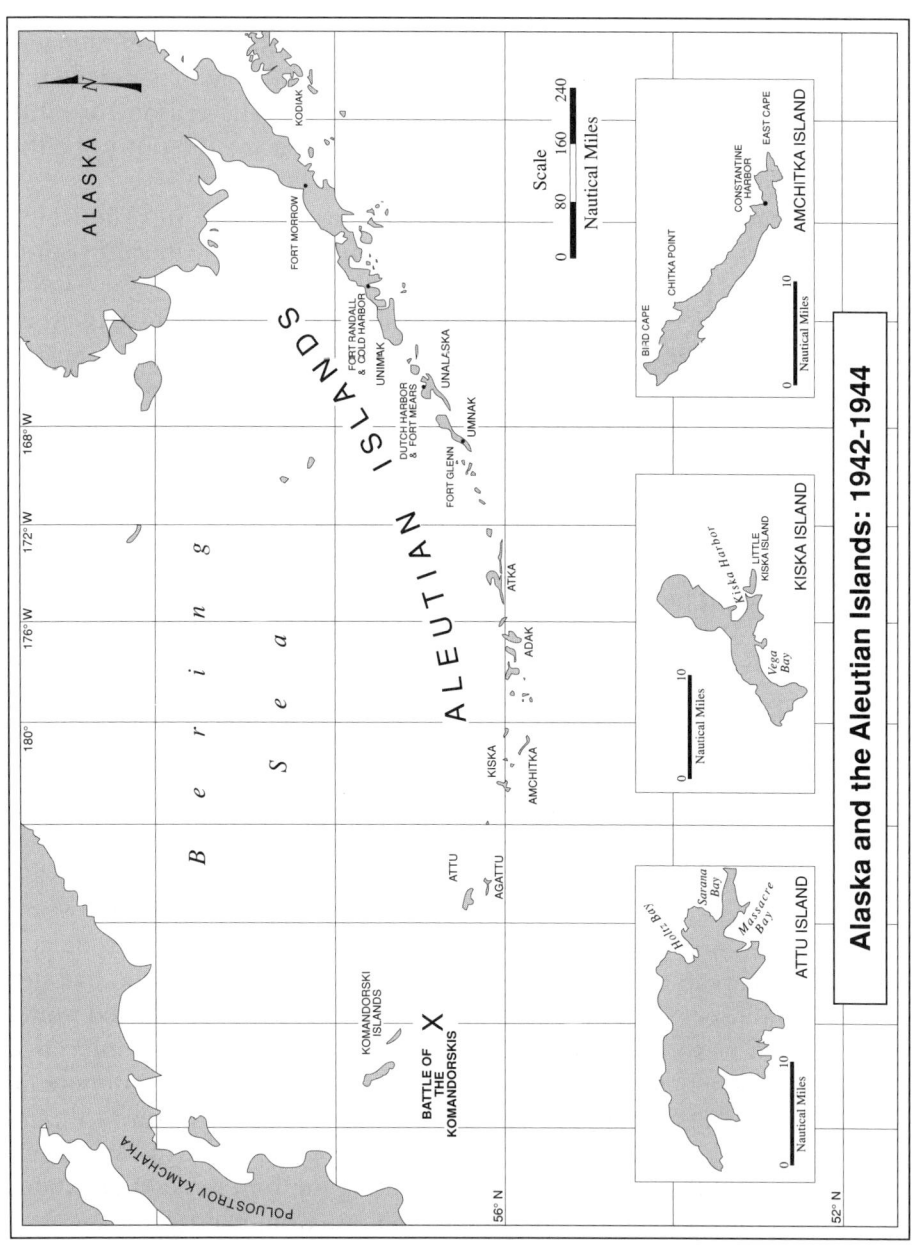

Not too long before Kinkaid was selected to relieve Fuzzy Theobald, King and Nimitz had reversed a major strategical decision that had stood since the Japanese capture of Attu and Kiska. Once the Japanese were emplaced, the JCS quickly recognized that they were not a major menace to Alaska. In fact maintenance of their forces in the Aleutians became a steady drain on Japanese resources in terms of personnel, material, and supplies and the naval forces to deliver them. Except for the irritation of having an enemy occupying American territory, naval planners could see no pressing need to root them out. And as the campaign against the Japanese in the Solomon Islands began to absorb the Navy's attention, and planning for the invasion of North Africa claimed the time of General Marshall and Admiral King, little thought was given to the Aleutians. Yet, given their responsibility for the security of the area and their failure to prevent the Japanese lodgment, Generals Dewitt and Buckner had steadily pressed since early July for the authority and the resources to mount a campaign to remove the enemy from American soil. But little had been accomplished by the first part of November 1942.[7]

Earlier, at DeWitt's initiative and with his assurances that he could handle the operation with forces already in Alaska, General Marshall and the JCS had approved the occupation of Tanaga Island and the construction of an air base there. However, Admiral Theobald had torpedoed the plan. Arguing that Tanaga would pose serious logistic problems because it lacked an adequate harbor, he proposed instead that Adak Island be occupied and developed. Both islands were almost 500 miles closer to the enemy in Kiska than Dutch Harbor was, and either would be a good block to any farther moves eastward by the Japanese. Either island would also be important as a staging base once the move against Kiska began. Theobald won the argument and Adak was occupied by General Buckner's troopers at the end of August.[8]

Two months later reconnaissance provided information that the Japanese were increasing their activities in the Aleutians. The garrison on Attu had been enlarged and there were signs that the enemy planned to occupy Amchitka Island, about 50 miles east of Kiska and then build an airfield on it. Given this evidence of Japanese plans for expansion, Nimitz directed Theobald to prepare preliminary plans to seize Amchitka in January and Kiska in May 1943.[9]

In San Francisco King and Nimitz confirmed that Amchitka should be occupied in early January and the Kiska assault should be moved up to March. Kinkaid was to get General DeWitt's acquiescence. King, Nimitz,

---

[7] Matloff and Snell, *Strategic Planning . . . 1941–1942*, 312, 371; Morton, *Strategy and Command*, 426.
[8] Conn, *Guarding the United States*, 270–72, 274–75; Morison, vol. 7, *Aleutians, Gilberts and Marshalls, June 1942–April 1944* (1950) 12–13; Garfield, *Thousand-Mile War*, 156–57.
[9] Command Summary, 10, 11, 17, 30 Nov 1942; TF 8 War Diary, 17 Nov 1942.

and Kinkaid were agreed that the Army should forget about Tanaga and use the troops gathered in Adak for the Amchitka operation (CROWBAR). Kinkaid approached the general gingerly but found him easy to deal with. According to the admiral, "His whole interest was in getting at the Japs. He didn't care how we got at them." Tanaga was scrapped, and DeWitt was ready to help in any way possible with the Amchitka movement, Kinkaid reported to his bosses.[10]

General Marshall fell into line, though he did insist that any plans for the invasion of Kiska be postponed until May at the earliest and that nothing be done beyond planning until troop needs throughout the world for 1943 had been determined. CROWBAR was a go; all Kinkaid would need was good weather, something difficult to obtain in the western Aleutians.[11]

Once the King-Nimitz conference had concluded, Kinkaid traveled south to San Diego to meet with Rear Admiral Francis W. (Skinny) Rockwell, who commanded the Pacific Fleet's amphibious training center. Although the Amchitka operation would be mounted with troops already in the theater, the Kiska assault would require at least one division prepared by the amphibious training command. Skinny Rockwell had been a classmate of Kinkaid's, but he was now senior to him by three and one-half months and seven numbers on the rear admiral seniority list. There had been more than a year's separation between them as captains. For Rockwell the difference was important; not so for Kinkaid. Rockwell spent several days introducing Tom to the operation and saw to it that he met and worked with Brigadier General Holland M. Smith, a Marine who would be assisting with the planning and training of the Kiska troops. Based on later difficulties that arose between Rockwell and Kinkaid, it is probable that Rockwell expected to command the Kiska operation in its entirety. In reporting his San Diego visit to Nimitz, Kinkaid concluded, "I find both DeWitt and Smith willing and ready to be helpful in every way and believe they will work well together."[12]

Tom and Helen, who had been in San Diego with him, returned to San Francisco for a few more days of business, mostly involving General DeWitt and the fresh directive from the JCS to capture Amchitka.[13] They then traveled north to Seattle. Again the admiral managed to mix business with pleasure. His old friend, Frank Jack Fletcher, now Commander Northwestern Sea Frontier, was delighted to have the Kinkaids as house guests during the Christmas holidays. Because Tom would be operating in areas of direct concern to Fletcher, he was happy to have the opportunity to learn all he could from his former mentor.

---

[10] COMINCH–CINCPAC Conference, San Francisco, 11 Dec 1942; TCK oral history, 214–15; Morton, *Strategy and Command*, 427.
[11] Pogue, *Marshall: Organizer of Victory*, 155.
[12] TCK to Nimitz, Seattle, 30 Dec 1942.
[13] LTGEN DeWitt to CINCPAC, 12/192048Z and 12/252050Z, Command Summary.

Expecting that her husband would soon be leaving for his new headquarters on Kodiak Island, Helen left Seattle by train on 28 December for Philadelphia. The admiral unfortunately was forced by weather to spend three more days at Frank Jack's offices before he could start the long journey to relieve Admiral Theobald. After two days in Juneau, again waiting for safe flying weather, he was flown to White Horse in Canada's Yukon Territory. Following another overnight stay, it was on to Fairbanks and, later that day, to Kodiak.[14] The weather in Juneau was not unlike Seattle's, but Fairbanks at minus 40 degrees was breathtaking. Throughout the Seattle-Kodiak trip and while traveling on the West Coast, Kinkaid was again accompanied by his aide and flag lieutenant, Lieutenant Commander Robert Taylor. The indispensable Taylor had served with the admiral's Cruiser Division 6 staff, then in *Enterprise*, and briefly when Kinkaid had taken over as Commander TF 67. Now they would be in Alaska together.

Kinkaid arrived on Kodiak Island late in the afternoon of 3 January 1943. Generals Buckner and Butler and Major General Charles H. Corlett had made the trip to the airfield with Admiral Theobald to welcome their new boss. Major General Buckner commanded all Army forces in Alaska and the Aleutians when they were not under the active command of the Commander North Pacific Force. As a graduate of the Class of 1908 at the Military Academy, Buckner was a contemporary of Kinkaid's. The "Silver Stallion of the North" had now served several years in Alaska and was familiar with the environment. Brigadier General Butler commanded the Army Air Corps units in Alaska, including the Eleventh Air Force, and, under the Commander North Pacific Force, he controlled both the Navy's and Air Corps's squadrons. He had found it difficult to relate to either Theobald or Buckner. General Charles Corlett commanded the Army forces at Fort Greeley on Kodiak.

Fuzzy hosted the group for dinner that evening, and General Butler did the honors the next evening. Because of the weather, Theobald was unable to leave Kodiak for Pearl Harbor until the 7th. To his wife Kinkaid admitted, "I must say it is a relief to have him go because he is anything but a restful person. He is continually arguing or reciting his woes in contentious fashion." Tom had also decided by that time that he could get along with his Army confreres: "So far, I have been very favorably impressed with the Army people and do not expect to have to row with them as Fuzzy did. There will be many bones of contention but I believe they can be handled by means other than open rowing."[15]

The basic structure of Kinkaid's new command had been set by Theobald in June 1942. He had been sent north from Pearl Harbor with a

---

[14] TCK to HSK, Juneau, AK, 31 Dec 1942, 1 Jan 1943; Kodiak, AK, 5 Jan 1943.
[15] TCK to HSK, Kodiak, 5, 7 Jan 1943.

small task force to meet an expected Japanese attack that was part of the Midway operation. In the course of their northern diversionary movement the Japanese launched carrier aircraft strikes against Dutch Harbor on 3 and 4 June and then occupied Attu and Kiska islands on the 6th. Admiral Theobald had been at sea with his TF 8 while these attacks were occurring. Cut off from his Army and Navy squadrons ashore by radio silence, Theobald was unable to locate the Japanese force or effectively coordinate any of the retaliatory activity. Learning from that lesson, the admiral moved ashore and established his headquarters on Kodiak Island, some 600 miles east of Dutch Harbor.[16] Here he had good communications equipment, comfortable housing, and a new administration building that he shared with the Army. Rear Admiral Poco Smith would command his ships at sea; Theobald as North Pacific Commander would coordinate and command the joint effort to deny the area to the Japanese.[17]

When Kinkaid relieved Theobald on 4 January, he realized that he was too far from the front to be an effective commander. To meet this problem, plans were already in motion to move his headquarters to Adak Island, about 1,000 miles to the west in the Aleutian chain. First, though, he had to deal with CROWBAR, the occupation of Amchitka Island.

As in so many operations during World War II, Pacific Fleet headquarters' interest in occupying Amchitka began as a reaction to evidence that the Japanese were considering the same move. Throughout the summer and fall of 1942 the Japanese had strengthened their foothold in the Aleutians. The garrison on Kiska was gradually increased from 1,250 to around 5,400 by early 1943, but the attempt to develop an air base or a naval operating base was frustrated by regular American air and surface attacks. Attu, originally occupied by 1,200 Japanese, was evacuated in September 1942 and then reoccupied toward the end of the year. By February 1943 there were about 1,400 enemy troops on Attu, and this number was slowly increased by 1,000 by May 1943. The gradual troop additions, the building of barracks on Attu and Kiska, and some harbor development on both islands left the American commanders with the impression that the enemy might be considering further moves to the east, perhaps as far as Dutch Harbor. Actually the Japanese strengthening of Kiska and Attu was designed to prevent American recapture and use of the islands for bombing missions against their bases in the Kurile Islands.[18]

At Pearl Harbor, Nimitz was now convinced that the Japanese would not be driven out of Kiska by a strategy of blockade and siege. In its Command

---

[16] Garfield, *Thousand-Mile War*, 28–52.
[17] "Command History, NORPACFOR," 108–11, OA.
[18] United States Strategic Bombing Survey (Pacific), *Interrogations of Japanese Officials*, 2 vols. (Washington: USSBS, 1947), 1:102–4, 110; 2:365–67; *Guarding the United States,* 259; Matloff and Snell, *Strategic Planning . . . 1941–1942,* 370.

Summary for 30 November, the CINCPAC staff noted, "In the ALEUTIANS the enemy moves are not clear. It seems probable that convoys now en route to the western ALEUTIANS are bringing in reinforcements and replacements. Photos show that the enemy is there to stay until ousted by troops." Two weeks later, after evidence had arrived that mines had been laid around Kiska, the Command Summary again commented, "These fields are just one more indication that the Japs are there to stay until thrown out."[19]

At their December conference Nimitz convinced Admiral King that the Amchitka-Kiska operation should be undertaken. Kinkaid, in agreement with Nimitz's plan, persuaded General DeWitt to use the troops slated to occupy Tanaga Island (60 miles west of Adak) for the Amchitka operation. Now convinced that positive action could finally be taken in the Aleutians, COMINCH sold the concept of the Amchitka-Kiska operation to General Marshall and then to the JCS. Concerned that there were already more than 85,000 troops in the Alaskan Theater, the Army Chief of Staff insisted that only troops already in Alaska be used to seize Amchitka. He then set two more provisos: 1) the operation could only go forward if it were clear that an airfield could be constructed on Amchitka, in a brief period of time; and 2) planning for the seizure of Kiska would not go beyond the planning stage.[20] A survey team flew to Amchitka, and, after spending several days examining the island and digging test holes in the soil, they informed Buckner and DeWitt on 20 December that a fighter strip, 150 by 3,000 feet, could be constructed in two or three weeks. That was enough for DeWitt and Nimitz; three days later CROWBAR was set in motion.[21]

By the time Kinkaid relieved Theobald on 4 January, CROWBAR was nearly ready to commence. Theobald and Buckner had wanted to use two regiments in the operation, but the limited number of transport vessels available forced them to scale down the troop requirements to about 5,000. Only one combat-loaded transport, *Arthur Middleton* (APA 25), could be spared by CINCPAC; smaller cargo vessels and destroyer transports would have to fill the other needs. At the request of Theobald, CINCPAC did add *Indianapolis* and four destroyers to strengthen the protective forces of TF 8.[22] Assuming their security had not been compromised, Kinkaid and Buckner expected that the Japanese would be

---

[19] TF 8 War Diary, 17 Nov 1942; Command Summary, 17 and 30 Nov, 16 Dec 1942.
[20] CINCPAC to COMINCH, 8 Dec 1942, Command Summary; COMINCH–CINCPAC Conference, San Francisco, 11 Dec 1942; TCK to Nimitz, Seattle, 30 Dec 1942, TCK Papers; Morton, *Strategy and Command*, 427–28.
[21] COMWDC to CINCPAC, 12/202304Z, Command Summary; CINCPAC to CTF 8, 12/232215Z, Command Summary, TCK Papers; Conn, *Guarding the United States*, 275.
[22] COMNORPACFOR to CINCPAC, 12/212238Z, Command Summary; COMWDC to CINCPAC, 12/252050Z, Command Summary; CTF 8 to CINCPAC, 12/210215Z, Command Summary; CINCPAC to CTF 8, 12/232215Z, Command Summary.

unable to interfere seriously with the amphibious landing on Amchitka.[23] The weather, though, was another matter; fortunately it worked as much against the Japanese as it did against Kinkaid's forces.

In preparing for CROWBAR, Admiral Kinkaid put his own stamp on the plans originated by his predecessor. Knowing that he would have to remain in Kodiak with his communications, he prepared his operations orders to his task group commanders in language that would allow them maximum personal freedom in making decisions at the scene of action. His flag secretary spelled out this principle in the TF 8 War Diary several times:

> The Task Force was informed that in the execution of tasks assigned . . . it is the intention of the Task Force Commander to issue necessary orders to the Commanders . . . in such terms as to allow the senior officer of the group or unit to make spot decisions when necessary. (6 Jan 43)

> Commander Task Group 8.6 [Covering Group, Rear Admiral C. H. McMorris] was advised that it is the intention of the Task Force Commander to issue broad flexible orders in the execution of the CROWBAR Operation and that Commander Task Group 8.6 has full authority to make necessary decisions on the spot whenever the time element does not permit obtaining a decision from the Task Force Commander. (9 Jan 43)

By delegating his authority Kinkaid believed that he had eliminated the need to establish an advance base headquarters where members of his staff might act for him. Having experienced fairly tight control from Admiral Halsey while commanding the *Enterprise* task force, Kinkaid now demonstrated that he had learned one valuable lesson: trust your subordinates until they prove unworthy of that trust. In theory at least he was also following the same instructions that Admiral King had issued when he was Commander in Chief of the Atlantic Fleet in 1941.[24]

Because he did not intend to take personal charge of the naval forces at Amchitka, Kinkaid designated Rear Admiral Soc McMorris to command the attack force. The Army troops would be led by Brigadier General Lloyd E. Jones, personally selected by Buckner. On 6 January Kinkaid asked General Jones to set the date and hour for sending his troops ashore. After conferring with the transport group commander and the skippers of several of the smaller vessels, Jones set 11 January to be D-day and 1030 (local time) as H-hour.[25] On the 10th, after discussing the matter with McMorris, Jones recommended and Kinkaid agreed that D-day be delayed for one day. With seas still running high and fog heavy

---

[23] COMWDC to CINCPAC, 12/252050Z, Command Summary.
[24] TF 8 War Diary, 6, 9 Jan 1943; Buell, *King*, 131–32, 521–23.
[25] TF 8 War Diary, 6–8 Jan 1943.

throughout the area, McMorris passed the word to start the landings during the morning of the 12th.[26]

The first troops to land were put ashore in Constantine Harbor by the destroyer *Worden*. In trying to leave the harbor, the destroyer was swept by heavy currents and wind onto a hidden pinnacle that ripped the vessel's bottom. His ship impaled, Commander William G. Pogue called for assistance. *Dewey*, a sister ship in the *Farragut* class, attempted to pull *Worden* free, but the towing cable snapped. *Worden* pivoted, foundered, broke in two, and sank. Fortunately the troops had made shore, but fourteen of the destroyer's crew were drowned. *Worden* had been with Kinkaid at Coral Sea, Midway, and battles around Guadalcanal, usually as a plane guard with the *Enterprise* Task Force. It was like losing an old friend when *Worden* went under.

Later in the day the transport *Arthur Middleton* grounded, broached, and came to rest hard aground in the harbor. Though leaking badly, the transport survived to be later hauled off and repaired. The ship's supplies for the troops ashore and the earth-moving equipment for airstrip construction had to be landed through the surf largely by muscle power. It took almost a month to empty the vessel. The Army engineers had hoped to complete the airstrip in two to three weeks, but the weather and problems in landing their heavy machinery conspired against them. However the first detachment of fighters, eight P–40s from Adak, did land on Amchitka on 16 February.[27]

At the end of the first day of CROWBAR Kinkaid wrote to Admiral Nimitz,

> I am somewhat aghast at the amount and seriousness of storm damage to ships operating in this area. It is particularly serious in a small force like this with no replacements in sight. . . . It is unusual, to say the least, to conduct our type of operations in this area at this time of year. Our ships operate under vicious conditions and our personnel take it on the chin.[28]

Almost daily during the next ten days COMNORPACFOR's War Diary and the Command Summary at CINCPAC headquarters listed some form of ship damage traceable to the miserable Aleutian weather. In late December *Wasmuth* (DMS 15) was mortally damaged in the Gulf of Alaska when two depth charges broke free in a gale and detonated beneath the ship's stern. Despite heroic assistance from an escorted oiler, the destroyer minesweeper was lost. Its commanding officer, Lieutenant

---

[26] Ibid., 10 Jan 1943; Garfield, *Thousand-Mile War*, 191–92.
[27] TF 8 War Diary, 12 Jan 1943; TCK to Nimitz, Kodiak, 12 Jan 1943, TCK Papers; Command Summary, 19 Jan 1943; Conn, *Guarding the United States*, 276.
[28] TCK to Nimitz, Kodiak, 12 Jan 1943.

Commander Joseph W. (Bill) Leverton, soon returned to become Kinkaid's flag secretary. On 18 January *Chandler* (DMS 9) and *Kane* (APD 18) were reported as leaking badly after riding out a gale. Motor torpedo boats that Kinkaid had hoped would be available to protect Amchitka were all damaged beyond local repair capabilities.[29] Since his North Pacific Force, even after augmentation by CINCPAC for CROWBAR, consisted of just three cruisers and eight destroyers, it is easy to understand Kinkaid's concerns about ship damage.

Once Amchitka was occupied and the airstrip operational, Kinkaid quickly put the island to the use anticipated by Nimitz and DeWitt. Fighters from Amchitka could now beat down any aircraft that might be launched from Kiska; they could intercept enemy planes coming from Attu or the Japanese base at Paramushiro in the Kurile Islands; and they could escort Eleventh Air Force medium and heavy bombers as they approached Kiska for bombardment. When the strip at Amchitka reached its full length, 200 by 5,000 feet, medium and heavy bombers could be launched against Kiska or Attu with heavier loads than was possible from Adak or bases farther east. With surface and submarine units from TF 8 patrolling for enemy ships approaching from the west, and Patrol Wing 4's far-ranging PBYs operating from Amchitka and Adak, the Japanese found it increasingly difficult to reinforce or even to bring supplies to the garrisons on Kiska and Attu. And although plenty of bombing sorties had been launched against the Japanese-held islands before January 1943, the pace now quickened.

Except when bad weather made flying too risky even for seasoned pilots, daily strikes were sent against Kiska. These strikes weren't in the same league as the huge multigroup or multiwing raids flown from English bases against German targets; neither were they opposed with the vigor of the Luftwaffe's fighter squadrons. But the antiaircraft fire over the target area, occasional float Zeros, and the ever-changing weather made a trip from Adak or Amchitka to Kiska something more than a milk run. Typical of the February raids was the one reported for the 13th. About noon at Kiska five B–24 Liberators (heavy bombers) and six B–25 Mitchells (medium bombers), escorted by ten P–38 Lightnings (fighters), struck Kiska. "Hits were observed on enemy installations. Three float Zeros were shot down." These aircraft came from Adak.[30] Because of impenetrable weather, there were fewer raids during March, but on the 8th Attu was hit for the first time. The sorties from Adak rarely were larger than ten or twelve bombers during February, March, and April, but they were often

---

[29] TF 8 War Diary, 12, 17, 18, 20 Jan 1943; Command Summary, 19 Jan 1943.
[30] Command Summary, 13 Feb 1943.

supplemented by raids from Amchitka, usually consisting of six or eight P–40 Tomahawks (fighters), each carrying a 500-pound bomb.[31]

The Japanese on Kiska soon learned that a heavy fog layer did not protect them from bombardment. When the bomber squadrons found their target shrouded in fog, they simply made a "calculated run" to the target using dead reckoning and radar navigation from their last sure position. This type of bombing psychologically harassed the Japanese more than when they could see the aircraft and the falling bombs, but at Pearl Harbor Nimitz's staff was not impressed. In early April, after ten heavies out of Adak struck Kiska, Captain J. M. Steele wrote in the daily Command Summary: "These 'calculated run' attacks cannot be expected to produce good results. Even using a bombsight the planes had little success in knocking out enemy installations."[32] Captain Steele was correct up to a point. Although physical destruction to Kiska and Attu was not heavy, it did have a degrading effect on Japanese troop morale. More important, combined with the naval surface blockade, the blockading aerial squadrons made it too risky for the Japanese to hazard their diminishing numbers of naval and cargo vessels to supply the island garrisons with needed food, munitions, and troop reinforcements. Occasional submarines brought in a few high-priority personnel and munitions, but they could not carry enough to be of any real assistance to the beleaguered Japanese.[33]

The blockade of Kiska and Attu was only a part of the operations preliminary to the actual invasion and seizure of Kiska. Once relieved by Kinkaid, Admiral Theobald went to Pearl Harbor for interim duty with CINCPAC before becoming Commandant First Naval District. When at Pearl, Theobald suggested that Kinkaid at first bypass Kiska and invade Attu. Kiska was much more heavily defended than Attu, and, of almost equal significance to Theobald, Aleutian weather moved from west to east. Control of Attu would confer important advantages when deciding D-days and H-hours.[34] During the few days that he and Kinkaid had been together, there is little doubt that Fuzzy had made the same suggestion to him. Two months later, Kinkaid formally suggested to Nimitz that Attu be taken before Kiska.[35]

As was often the case with Kinkaid, his proposal to substitute Attu for Kiska followed some strong hints originating in CINCPAC headquarters. And as usual with Nimitz, what he could do was controlled by the resources estimated to be available after needs in the European theater had

---

[31] Ibid., 17 Apr 1943.
[32] Ibid., 2 Apr 1943.
[33] *Interrogations of Japanese Officials* 1:104, 109.
[34] TF 8 War Diary, 17 Nov 1942; Worall Reed Carter, *Beans, Bullets and Black Oil* (Washington: Naval History Division, 1952), 75.
[35] TCK to Nimitz, Kodiak, 2 Mar 1943, TCK Papers.

been met. At the order of COMINCH in early February five attack transports and five attack cargo vessels were transferred from the Pacific to the Atlantic to support the July invasion of Sicily. Captain Steele recognized the significance to Kinkaid immediately: "This [transfer] hamstrings our KISKA effort for the present. Remaining APAs are sufficient to move only one reinforced regiment. No AKAs remain."[36] That same day Nimitz wrote a personal letter to Kinkaid, raising the possibility of laying Kiska under an air siege rather than invading it. He wondered if an airfield might not be built on Agattu or on the Semichi Islands, both almost 40 miles southeast of Attu. From there and Amchitka, bombing raids could be mounted against Kiska, 150 miles to the east.[37] As he often did, on 2 March Kinkaid radioed his suggestion to CINCPAC that Attu become the next operation, and he sent a lengthier letter at the same time. In it he dealt with the most important reason for shifting from Kiska to Attu:

> I have recommended to you that consideration be given to going after Attu and building an air field on Shemya [Semichi Islands]. This was prompted by a feeling that the ships at Rockwell's disposal are not adequate for training and execution of the Kiska job, that additional ships would not become available in time to be useful and that we could fritter away the good weather without getting anything done.[38]

The central problem was the number of Japanese on Kiska. Kinkaid's staff estimated, incorrectly as it turned out, that there were 500 Japanese troops on Attu and more than 6,000 on Kiska. He thought he could handle Attu with a reinforced regiment, but Kiska would take at least a division. He knew that there was not enough sealift available for a division, so he suggested that he switch targets.[39]

The next day Nimitz informed his North Pacific Force commander that his staff had studied this possibility in January and felt the attack on Attu was feasible. Once assured that Attu (JACKBOOT) could be taken with the forces then available to Kinkaid and Buckner, including elements of the Army's Seventh Division then training at Fort Ord in California, Nimitz pressed COMINCH and the JCS for the change. By 18 March the Attu operation (LANDCRAB) had the necessary approvals, and Nimitz set 7 May as D-day for Attu.[40]

---

[36] Command Summary, 5 Feb 1943.
[37] Nimitz to TCK, Pearl Harbor, 5 Feb 1943, Nimitz Papers.
[38] CTF 8 to CINCPAC, 3/030405Z, Command Summary; TCK to Nimitz, Kodiak, 2 Mar 1943, TCK Papers.
[39] "Command History, NORPACFOR," 118–20; TCK oral history, 219–20; Morison 7:20–21.
[40] "Command History, NORPACFOR," 118–20; COMINCH to COMWDC and CINCPAC, 03/111221Z, Command Summary.

Planning for a Kiska operation had been underway in San Diego since January; now with the substitution of Attu, it intensified. Overseen by General DeWitt and led by Admiral Rockwell, a team had been put together consisting of staff officers from the North Pacific Force (TF 8), Buckner's Alaskan Defense Command, DeWitt's Western Defense Command, and Rockwell's Pacific Fleet Amphibious Force Training Command (TF 3). Kinkaid's chief of staff, Captain Oswald S. (Ozzie) Colclough, and his air officer, Commander Douglas T. Day, represented the admiral at the beginning of planning, but they were later replaced by Captain Frederic I. Entwistle and Commander George F. O'Keefe, operations officer and maintenance and engineering officer, respectively. Entwistle eventually took the lead in planning as Colclough's work became more demanding. As their expertise was needed, others from Kinkaid's staff would take a quick trip to San Diego or San Francisco to help with the planning and to enjoy a rest.[41] With the decision to switch the target from Kiska to Attu, the staff found its work simplified. Fewer troops meant fewer ships and less dependence on resources from outside the Aleutians area.

During the planning period Admiral Kinkaid moved his headquarters from Kodiak to Adak. The move in many ways was a dramatic one—somewhat akin to leaving civilization for a frontier region. Although the weather on Kodiak was harsh and disagreeable, the island had taken on the characteristics of a small town. The city of Kodiak was close to the naval base, and there were civilian shops and businesses in it. Construction on the army post and naval base was done with permanence in mind. Thus Kinkaid's quarters and office areas were comfortable, adequate in space, and reasonably warm. The only real problem with Kodiak was that it was 1,000 miles east of the war. So on 13 March Ozzie Colclough and most of the staff sailed for Dutch Harbor and eventually Adak. Kinkaid and his two aides, Taylor and Leverton, planned to remain at Kodiak a few more days and then fly to Adak, but weather forced a delay until the 21st.[42] During the delay the admiral loafed in Kodiak, and Colclough and the staff managed the war to the west. It was just as well that he had been delayed, for Kinkaid found the paint still damp in his new quarters when he finally arrived. In anticipation that the weather would be different, he arrived freighted down with clothing, which he described to Helen:

> I wish you could see the collection of clothing I have drawn in preparation for the hop to my next ice floe, or rather mud floe, to be more exact. The climate will be milder than this but the mud will be terrible. Against that I have overshoes, galoshes, rubber boots, shoe pack (same as Maine hunt-

---

[41] "Command History, NORPACFOR," 114–17; Morton, *Strategy and Command*, 428–31; RADM J. Wilson Leverton to author, Whispering Pines, NC, 28 Feb 1977.

[42] "Command History, NORPACFOR," 165–69; TF 8 War Diary, 13, 18, 20, 21 Mar 1943.

Rear Admiral Kinkaid at Kodiak, Alaska, February 1943. The admiral is wearing his "tea cosy," a gift from the Marines.

Author's collection

Joint staff dining at Adak, Alaska, April 1943. Clockwise from left: Lieutenant Colonel Cole, USA, Lieutenant Commander R. H. Taylor, Lieutenant Commander L. G. Shaffer, Commander C. F. O'Keefe, Lieutenant Commander W. T. Jenkins, Lieutenant Colonel Parker, Lieutenant Commander J. W. Leverton, Colonel Crawford, USA, Captain O. S. Colclough, Rear Admiral Kinkaid, Major General S. B. Buckner, USA, Brigadier General E. D. Post, USA.

ing shoes) and high lace leather boots. Against the rain and cold I have oil skins and sou'easter, a cloth uniform rain coat, a uniform overcoat, a fur-lined flying suit, a fur-lined water repellent aviator's overcoat with fur collar, and fur-lined three-quarter length parka complete with hood.[43]

The admiral didn't mention the Marine fur hat, which he usually referred to as his tea cosy, that he had acquired a few days after landing in Kodiak.

The move west to Adak, which Admiral Nimitz had urged from January, had the benefit of bringing Kinkaid's command together with those of Generals Buckner and Butler. A few weeks later Commodore Leslie E. Gehres, who commanded the patrol wings, also brought his headquarters to Adak.

At Buckner's suggestion a joint mess was established where the two staffs shared all their meals. It was the beginning of a strong friendship

---

[43] TCK to HSK, 11, 20, 22 Mar 1943.

between Kinkaid and Buckner that lasted until the general's death on Okinawa. The admiral liked the messing arrangement and referred to it often in letters to Helen: "The senior members of Buckner's staff and mine make a total of fourteen and our mess room is a well lighted quonset hut with one end shut off for kitchen, laundry, etc." The Navy provided the mess stewards, and "not being equipped for roughing it ashore, we brought along the cabin china, silver, table cloths, etc., so we are respectable." Later, when interviewed for his oral history, the admiral recalled how they had all sat at a long table with him and General Buckner sitting opposite one another in the middle. "We educated a lot of people there at the table. We got to know each other a lot better, which was a very fine thing. As I say, I give Buckner credit for that."[44]

Compared with his Seventh Fleet staff of 1944 and 1945 Kinkaid's North Pacific Force staff was not a large one, yet it was considerably larger than his sea-going staffs in *Enterprise* or *Minneapolis*, and almost all of the senior members were professionals, graduates of the Naval Academy. Besides Robert Taylor, whom the admiral brought to be his aide and flag lieutenant, the rest of his staff, with one exception, consisted of people who had served Admiral Theobald and a few who had been ordered to the Aleutians in the course of changing duty stations.

Arriving at Kodiak about the same time as Kinkaid, Captain Colclough had come from commanding TF 8's submarines to be chief of staff. Hard working and somewhat formal, even formidable, Ozzie Colclough ran a taut ship. Everything came to him and a large portion of the answers came from him. Access to the admiral was closely guarded, except for the senior officers and Kinkaid's aides.[45] After the war Colclough became the Navy's Judge Advocate General. The senior commander (soon to become a captain), who reported to Colclough as operations officer, was Entwistle. He worked as the plans officer for the staff and spent a good deal of early 1943 traveling between the Aleutians, Pearl Harbor, and San Diego to coordinate activities with the Pacific Fleet Amphibious Training Command. Commander O'Keefe, the staff maintenance and engineering officer, found his work both challenging and interminable. The Aleutian environment, with its treacherous weather, gale-driven seas, and hazard-strewn waters almost guaranteed that ship maintenance would be the command's most pressing problem. Equally time-consuming, given the three assault landings between January and August 1943, was the work of the staff gunnery officer, Lieutenant Commander Walter T. (Jenks) Jenkins. Procurement, storage, and distribution of fleet munitions were a steady business; but so was the provision of facilities for antiaircraft and

---
[44] TCK to HSK, Adak, 1, 9 Apr 1943; TCK oral history, 244.
[45] CAPT Walter T. Jenkins to author, Radnor, PA, 29 Apr 1977.

shore bombardment training. Jenkins later noted that he saw little social life or recreation at Kodiak and Adak.[46] Kinkaid's flag secretary, as was typical of such officers on any staff, had a load of collateral duties thrust his way. Lieutenant Commander Bill Leverton managed the admiral's mess, a job which took on considerable importance once they moved to Adak and joined General Buckner's group. Of equal importance to the admiral, and probably of greater interest to Leverton, was his work as the North Pacific Force public information officer. Because the staff was based ashore and it was clear that operations were heating up in the Alaskan theater, there was a steady stream of reporters and public figures who came north to observe the war. Kinkaid needed help in dealing with these visitors, and this plus the censorship of news copy became the most important of Leverton's many activities.[47] Lieutenant Commander Leland Shaffer had served previously with the admiral as the communications officer of his Cruiser Division 6 staff and, like Taylor, was selected by Kinkaid for his new staff. When asked if there was any particular reason why the admiral brought Taylor and Shaffer north with him, another staff member from this period answered, "Kinkaid brought them with him to NorPac, I think, for the same reason he took Shaffer and me with him to SoWesPac—he wanted someone around who knew him well, who he trusted and who he liked."[48]

Given the operations ahead of them, Kinkaid and his staff were too busy to be bored. The admiral's routine was fairly simple. He rose each morning around 0730 and was at his desk by 0900. He took an hour for lunch and then returned to the office until 1730. Then, as he described his day to Helen, "5:30–7:00 clean shirt, radio [for news], drink; 7:00 dinner; 8:00–9:30 to 11:30 office; then home to bed. I usually get to bed by 9:30 or 10:00 and read." Leverton remembered that his own day began earlier with reading the overnight dispatches before breakfast. "Evenings were spent in the office until 9 o'clock or later, it was then we usually had staff meetings. . . . The admiral kept the same hours as did the rest of us." Mercifully, from the point of view of busy staff officers, meetings were rare. Most business that would have been raised in a staff meeting was managed at meals.[49]

For recreation there was little available. The admiral occasionally fished with Buckner or hiked around Adak; he played some bridge and attended movies now and then, but mostly wrote letters and read detective stories. Perhaps trying to improve his literary interests, Helen regu-

---

[46] Ibid.
[47] Leverton to author, 28 Feb 1977.
[48] Leverton to author, 2 Oct 1977.
[49] TCK to HSK, Kodiak, 26 Feb 1943; Leverton to author, 28 Feb 1977; Jenkins to author, 29 Apr 1977.

larly sent him books she received through the Book-of-the-Month Club or bought locally, and he had subscriptions to a few magazines, which eventually caught up with him. He was happy to exchange reading materials with members of his staff and often sent books he had completed to libraries on the island or to Soc McMorris's ships.

Kinkaid had regular "visiting firemen" from Washington, Pearl Harbor, San Diego, and San Francisco, and although he grumbled to Helen about the visits and the incessant "gabbing," he obviously enjoyed the news they brought. But his wife's four letters a week were still his best tie to the outside world. In Philadelphia she regularly saw Rear Admiral Milo Draemel and his wife at the navy yard and passed along the service gossip they provided. Almost every four to six weeks she would visit the Washington area and then her letters would be rich with new assignments, promotions, retirements and the trivia of service activity. On such junkets Helen would regularly visit the wives of long-time service friends such as Rear Admirals Tip Merrill, Spec Purnell, or Reggie Kauffman, and their gossip further enriched her letters. Occasionally she would shock her husband by mentioning an operation or new command assignment that he believed was not supposed to be known by the public. On the whole, though, Helen was extremely careful about passing along her husband's views on matters public or private. It was also during her Washington visits that Helen looked in on Tom's family and reported the news. On 28 March his mother died and Helen helped his Aunt Fannie with the necessary arrangements. Later she would deal with the lawyers concerning probate matters. Mary Tyler Urquhart, Tom's niece by his sister Helen Heiner, provided assistance to Helen and Fannie.[50] At times the strain of looking after her husband's affairs; taking care of her own father, who was now a house-bound invalid; and making time for a few hours a week of volunteer work as an observer with the Philadelphia Interceptor Command, got to Helen and Tom would feel guilty.

As planning and training for the Attu attack moved forward in California, Kinkaid's command maintained and intensified its siege of Kiska and Attu. To prevent the Japanese from divining that Attu would be the next assault point, the Eleventh Air Force bombed Kiska much more often than Attu. Until May Attu was attacked only once from the air. The results of the concentration on Kiska became evident by the middle of April when CINCPAC's Command Summary noted, "There are beginning to be signs of enemy distress from these attacks."[51] No Japanese surface craft had been able to penetrate the blockade since February, and

---

[50] TCK to HSK, Adak, 3 Mar; 12, 14 Apr 1943; Louise Merrill to TCK, Washington, 4 Apr 1943.
[51] Command Summary, 17 Apr 1943.

the troops on Kiska and Attu were beginning to go on shortened rations. Though submarines occasionally made it through, their cargoes were not large enough to replace the antiaircraft ammunition or the rations consumed by the occupation forces.[52]

In mid-February weather severely limited bombing operations. Kinkaid decided to raise the pressure on the Attu garrison when a patrolling submarine (S 28) signaled that Holtz Bay on Attu contained several merchant vessels. Already at sea with his Covering Task Group (TG 8.6), Admiral McMorris was directed to attack the harbor. Flying his flag in the light cruiser *Richmond* (CL 9) and accompanied by the heavy cruiser *Indianapolis* and four destroyers, McMorris reached the island at 1430 in the afternoon of the 18th and opened fire. No ships were in the harbor, but Soc laid on a bombardment of those shore installations around Holtz Bay and Chichagof Harbor that were visible through the ever present fog. The damage inflicted—six killed or wounded and three wooden barracks destroyed—was hardly worth the ammunition expended, but live firing at enemy targets always gave a boost to the morale of those enduring Aleutian Sea patrols.[53]

Kinkaid sought to make his blockade of Kiska and Attu more effective by improving his intelligence-gathering sources. Approaching Japanese convoys or individual ships were normally detected, if at all, by Commodore Gheres's patrol planes flying out of Amchitka and Adak or by submarines patrolling designated geographic areas. To enhance his intelligence net, the admiral wanted to set up a communications intelligence unit at Kodiak that would include the usual code breakers and Japanese language specialists. He thought such a unit could provide more timely intelligence than the staff at Pearl Harbor and could respond to special needs such as planning for the Attu operation. But Nimitz would have none of it. He believed the intelligence effort should be concentrated in Pearl and Washington with their results distributed by radio as was then the practice. The personnel with Kinkaid's command, in CINCPAC's opinion, were better used at sea in other areas.[54]

To assist task force commanders like Kinkaid, CINCPAC's staff distributed estimates of enemy forces based throughout the Pacific area. In early March Nimitz's combat intelligence unit estimated that the Japanese had two cruisers and four destroyers at Paramushiro and that they would be guarding a convoy being formed to reinforce Kiska and Attu

---

[52] *Interrogations of Japanese Officials*, 1:104.
[53] TF 8 War Diary, 18, 19 Feb 1943; *Interrogations of Japanese Officials*, 2:367; Office of Naval Intelligence, Combat Narrative: *The Aleutians Campaign, June 1942–August 1943* (Washington, 1943) 24–25 (hereafter ONI Combat Narrative: *Aleutians*).
[54] TF 8 War Diary, 18–20 Jan 1943.

with troops and material.⁵⁵ Using this intelligence, Kinkaid ordered McMorris to take his Covering Group to the west of Attu to intercept this convoy. With *Richmond*; the heavy cruiser *Salt Lake City*; and destroyers *Bailey* (DD 492), *Coghlan* (DD 606), *Dale* (DD 353), and *Monaghan*, Soc anticipated meeting the Japanese on even terms. He might even have an advantage with the radar gun directors on his ships—provided, of course, that CINCPAC's Ultra intelligence was on the mark.⁵⁶

The Ultra intelligence was only partially correct; McMorris's small force did make the anticipated interception at 0730 on 26 March about 180 miles west of Attu and 100 miles south of Medny Island in the Komandorski Islands. But the Ultra intelligence was incorrect concerning the size of the naval escort for the convoy: it outnumbered TG 16.6 almost two to one. Instead of two cruisers, the Japanese had two heavy cruisers (*Nachi* and *Maya*) and two light cruisers (*Tama* and *Abukuma*). There were also four destroyers plus two heavily armed merchant cruisers (*Asaka Maru* and *Sakito Maru*). Another destroyer, escorting a slow cargo vessel, was north of the group.⁵⁷ Despite the poor odds, McMorris decided to attack and the Battle of the Komandorski Islands began. Kinkaid was immediately notified of the interception, and both he and McMorris hoped that General Butler's bombers on Adak could lend a hand. But TG 16.6 was on its own.

The battle, from the Navy's point of view, was a victory of a mixed sort.⁵⁸ In the course of the three-and-a-half-hour engagement McMorris's task group stood on the brink of extermination. *Salt Lake City* was holed and dead in the water, and some of its turrets were inoperative; it appeared that it would sink. With *Salt Lake City* gone, nothing could save the lighter gunned *Richmond*. In desperation McMorris ordered a heavy bank of smoke laid by all ships. Then a gallant charge by Captain Ralph S. Riggs's destroyers inflicted some minor damage on the enemy and, most important, bought some time for *Salt Lake City*. During the destroyer attack Captain Bertram J. Rodgers managed to get his cruiser's boilers back on line and the vessel underway. And finally, miraculously to some, Vice Admiral Boshiro Hosogaya decided to break off the action and herd his ships back to Paramushiro. Soc wisely decided that his force was not in any condition to seek further action. From a strategic viewpoint he had already won: Hosogaya's convoy could not get through.

---

⁵⁵ Holmes, *Double-Edged Secrets*, 132–33.

⁵⁶ John A. Lorelli, *The Battle of the Komandorski Islands, March 1943* (Annapolis: Naval Institute Press, 1984), 12, 116.

⁵⁷ Ibid., 10–13; Morison 7:23–24. On 15 March 1943, Task Force 8 became Task Force 16 of the Pacific Fleet.

⁵⁸ For an account of the Battle of the Komandorski Islands, see Morison 7:22–36; Lorelli, *Battle*, 43–107; and Garfield, *Thousand-Mile War*, 200–208.

When Attu was invaded two months hence, those troops and munitions in the Japanese ships would not be there to greet the Americans.[59]

But Kinkaid still had the bitter taste of frustration in his mouth. He appreciated the fact that McMorris had won a strategic victory for the North Pacific Command, but he wanted some Japanese ships put down. He had not come to the Aleutians to stand on the defensive. He had worked to infuse his forces with the spirit of the offensive and believed he was succeeding;[60] but at this critical moment the Army Air Corps had let him down. When McMorris's contact report arrived at Adak, Eleventh Air Force bombers were preparing to hit Kiska with loads of fairly light, general-purpose bombs. General Butler estimated he could have the planes rearmed with armor-piercing munitions in two hours, and Kinkaid agreed to the delay. But it was more than four hours before the sorties were away. Though guided by PBYs that had arrived at the scene of action earlier, the Army planes lacked the range to reach the retreating Japanese force.[61]

Years later, when interviewed about the battle, the admiral concluded it would have been wiser to send Butler's airmen with the general-purpose bombs already on the planes.[62] No one has ever made a point of it, but Kinkaid's lack of knowledge concerning air operations was evident here. It is doubtful that he asked Commodore Gehres for his opinion about rearming the bombers, and his own staff air officer, Commander D. T. Day, was in San Diego helping plan Operation LANDCRAB. The admiral made his own decision based on the best guess of General Butler, and he and TG 16.6 had to live with it.

During the first three months of 1943, while Rear Admiral Rockwell and Major General Holland Smith, USMC, were planning and preparing Army troops for the Attu assault, Nimitz and DeWitt were awaiting a final "go" signal for the operation. The JCS had been reluctant to set a date for Attu until a Pacific Military Conference had met and finished its deliberations. Representatives from the Southwest Pacific Command (MacArthur), South Pacific Command (Halsey), and Pacific Ocean Areas (Nimitz) traveled to Washington for the meeting, which opened on 12 March. They heard from the JCS about future operations in North Africa and Sicily and about requirements for troops, ships and material. The bottom line was that South and Southwest Pacific operations in 1943 would be modest. Halsey could initiate minor campaigns in the Solomons, and MacArthur was expected to begin movement along the north coast of New Guinea in Papua. Given this situation there was no

---

[59] Morison 7:30–33; Lorelli, *Battle*, 83–102; ONI Combat Narrative: *Aleutians*, 64.
[60] RADM C. A. Lockwood to Nimitz, Kodiak, 3 Apr 1943, copy in TCK Papers.
[61] TCK to Nimitz, Adak, 28 Mar 1943, Nimitz Papers; Lorelli, *Battle*, 111, 116; Morison 7:34; Garfield, *Thousand-Mile War*, 204–5.
[62] TCK oral history, 233–34.

reason why a low-requirements operation could not be mounted in the North Pacific Area. The conference ended on 28 March, and three days later General Marshall and Admiral King signaled DeWitt and Nimitz that D-day for LANDCRAB was to be 7 May.[63]

DeWitt and Nimitz issued their joint directive to Kinkaid on 31 March. Its opening clearly set the mission of the North Pacific Force:

> OBJECTIVE: Reduction and occupation of Attu and occupation most suitable airfield site in Near Islands at earliest possible date.
>
> PURPOSE: To sever enemy's lines of communication to Western Aleutians; to deny the Near Islands to the enemy and to construct an airfield thereon for air operations against enemy forces; to render Kiska untenable and to create base of operations for possible future reduction and occupation of Kiska.
>
> TASKS: A) To reduce and occupy Attu;
>
> B) To occupy the most suitable airfield site in the Near Islands and to build airfield thereon.
>
> COMMAND: Supreme Command CTF 16. COMAMPHORPAC [Commander Amphibious Force, Pacific] to operate under CTF 16 and command amphibious operations until landing phase completed.[64]

The directive also allocated naval forces (TF 16 and TF 51) and designated which elements of the Seventh Division would be committed to the operation. One heavily reinforced regimental combat team (RCT), built around the Seventeenth Infantry Regiment, would make the initial assault. The Thirty-Second Infantry Regiment, similarly built up to RCT status, would constitute the floating reserve. Altogether the two RCTs would have approximately 11,000 troops. The landing force would be commanded by Major General Albert E. Brown, a career Army officer whose last experience under fire had been as a major in World War I. The Seventh Division itself had been trained as a motorized force for African desert operations, but it had now been "de-motorized" for the Aleutians.[65]

There was a steady buildup of naval forces in the Aleutians during April. Following the repulse of the Japanese attempt to reinforce Kiska and Attu, Kinkaid believed the enemy would return again, possibly with large ships and carriers. From Paramushiro to Attu was only two days' steaming distance for the Japanese Fifth Fleet, and Kinkaid did not think that his small command was in shape to meet it. The weather in early

---

[63] Morton, Strategy and Command, 390–99, 428–31; Maurice Matloff, *Strategic Planning for Coalition Warfare, 1943–1944* (Washington: Department of the Army, 1959), 101–2.
[64] CINCPAC to CTF 16 and COMAMPHORPAC, 3/311841Z, Command Summary.
[65] Ibid.; Conn, *Guarding the United States*, 282–83; Garfield, *Thousand-Mile War*, 224–25.

April had become violent and further damaged his cruiser-destroyer force. With the Attu landings less than six weeks ahead, the admiral radioed CINCPAC a wish list of surface forces he would like to have at his disposal. The list included two battleships immediately and another soon after, and more cruisers to help reinforce Soc McMorris's beat-up Covering Group. A couple of fleet submarines were also badly needed, four if possible. Another squadron of destroyers would make him a lot more comfortable, particularly with the battleships to screen. And although he didn't need an aircraft carrier at the time, he greatly desired a torpedo squadron and a dive-bombing squadron to base on Amchitka.[66]

Kinkaid already knew he was going to have three old battleships, *Pennsylvania*, *Nevada*, and *Idaho* (BB 42), but he was pleasantly surprised to learn three days later that Rear Admiral Robert C. Giffen would bring heavy cruisers *Wichita* (CA 45), *San Francisco*, and *Louisville*, plus four destroyers.[67] Kinkaid's submarine force also received reinforcement with the addition of seven S-boats that had been reconditioned after service out of Brisbane, Australia. The change of environment for these crews was, at the least, shocking. It appeared to some that their "main effort was put into physical survival rather than striking the Japanese."[68]

As the various groups arrived, Kinkaid immediately put them to work. On 12 April Rear Admiral Howard F. Kingman with Battleship Division Two reported that he was en route, and Kinkaid ordered him to transit Amukta Pass and then proceed to Kulak Bay on Adak. Following their arrival on the 16th, the battlewagons were dispatched the next day to operate northwest of Attu, "to intercept and destroy enemy shipping, keeping well clear of Attu and Komandorski Islands." Kinkaid wanted the protection provided by the big ships, but he also wanted to keep their presence unknown to the Japanese.[69] Nimitz was pleased to find some action for these older and slower battleships, two of which (*Pennsylvania* and *Nevada*) had been heavily damaged at Pearl Harbor. He commented to Kinkaid about their future:

> I am glad that the older battleships are going to have some really useful employment. It will buck up their ships' companies. I have reached the conclusion, which has been concurred in by higher authority, that these ships from now on should be employed in operations against the enemy in this war, and not be modernized for use in a far off future. Of course, you will understand they are not to be squandered.[70]

[66] CTF 16 to CINCPAC, 3/310313Z, Command Summary.
[67] CINCPAC to COMINCH, 3/130151Z; CINCPAC to CTF 16, 4/022341Z, Command Summary.
[68] Blair, *Silent Victory* 1:391–2.
[69] TF 16 War Diary, 12, 16, 17 Apr 1943.
[70] Nimitz to TCK, Pearl Harbor, 20 Apr 1943, Nimitz Papers.

A week later Giffen arrived at Kulak Bay with his heavy cruisers and departed on 25 April to relieve the battleships patrolling the area northwest of Attu. The big ships then headed for Cold Bay at the tip of the Alaska Peninsula to participate in final rehearsals for the attack on Attu.[71]

While the visiting battleships and heavy cruisers were being introduced to the rigors of the Aleutian environment, the light cruiser Southern Covering Group maintained its own patrol west and southwest of Attu. Now operating with *Richmond* (F), *Detroit* (CL 8), and *Santa Fe* (CL 60) plus six destroyers, Soc McMorris received orders on 25 April to bombard Holtz Bay and Chichagof Harbor on Attu the next morning. After making a night approach, the group opened fire at 0815 and completed action by 0840. Much of the gunfire was supposed to fall on shore installations that could impede the invasion, but McMorris had also been directed to create the impression that the airfield was the primary target. Upon returning to Adak, Soc expressed the opinion that the attack had been more successful than the one in February, but it probably did little more than inconvenience the Japanese. Although the heavy bombers out of Adak could probably do more lasting damage to Kiska and Attu, the omnipresent stormy weather and pea-soup fogs made it unlikely that either aerial or ship bombardments would do more than temporarily distress the enemy.[72]

During late March and much of April, Kinkaid found a great deal that fretted him in the plans that were drawn for LANDCRAB. Basic to his concerns was the fact that he was to command an operation where he was not, in terms of lineal standing in grade, the senior officer. Rockwell ranked Kinkaid as a rear admiral by several months and seven numbers. Rear Admiral Giffen, who was commanding the heavy cruiser group, had graduated from the Naval Academy a year ahead of Rockwell and Kinkaid and was senior to both of them on the admirals list. But Giffen was not a problem; he had arrived with orders from Admiral Nimitz to report and place himself under Kinkaid's command.[73] On the other hand, although Nimitz and DeWitt's directive of 31 March had identified Commander Task Force 16 as the "Supreme Command," Rockwell acted as though he and Kinkaid were co-equals who were simply coordinating their activities. Because the joint planning staff was working in San Diego at Rockwell's headquarters, Kinkaid learned little about the plans for LANDCRAB as they were being developed, and he only received a full operation plan in the middle of April when Captain Entwistle brought it from the meetings.[74] What he found in the plan irritated him considerably and he wrote to Nimitz that same day. His central concerns were spelled out in detail:

---

[71] TF 16 War Diary, 25 Apr 1943.
[72] Ibid.; Command Summary, 26 Apr 1943; ONI Combat Narrative: *Aleutians*, 65–67.
[73] CINCPAC to CTF 16, 4/022341Z, Command Summary.
[74] TCK to Nimitz, Adak, 14 Apr 1943.

I regret very much having to write this letter. Entwistle arrived this morning with the proposed Operation Plan for LANDCRAB and he confirms my worst fears regarding Rockwell's attitude toward that operation.

I have felt sure that Rockwell did not appreciate that he and Task Force Fifty One units were placed under my command for the LANDCRAB operation, in every sense of the word. He has consistently avoided giving me information regarding the development of plans although I have made repeated requests for it. Apparently he was particularly annoyed at my suggestion that he get out of the PENNSYLVANIA and into the Transport Group with the Commanding General of the Landing Force, feeling that I was interfering with his privilege of using any of his own ships as a Flagship. In the organization he has insisted upon the integrity of his force being maintained with the idea he will conduct the assault and landing and then return to San Diego with Task Force 51. What happens after that he considers is not his concern, apparently, including the occupation of Shemya and building of the airfield on that island. General [Eugene] Landrum arrived with Entwistle and has just been in to see me. He confirmed the above including inferences drawn....

If Rockwell leaves this area after three or four days with all of Task Force 51 we will have an inadequate force to cover Attu and Shemya and protect our supply lines. It is my idea that ships of Task Force 51 leave this area just as soon as possible, but during the first several days only some of the empty transports and cargo vessels should leave with a minimum of escorting destroyers. The PENNSYLVANIA with Rockwell in her should leave too or Rockwell should transfer to a transport, but I want to hold on to the IDAHO and NEVADA and as many destroyers as possible until developments indicate that they are no longer needed.

I am sure that the above is not in accord with Rockwell's ideas and, as previously noted, I have reason to doubt that his interpretation of my being in "supreme command" is sound. I consider it vitally important that the question of command be made perfectly clear. Buckner, Landrum and McMorris have stated to me that they, also, consider this vitally important.[75]

After five days reviewing the operation plan that Rockwell had forwarded, Kinkaid radioed a few changes he considered vital. He also reasserted his authority by inserting two sentences: "By order higher authority supreme command vested in COMNORPACFOR. COMTASKFOR 51 (COMAMPHORPAC) will operate under COMNORPAC, commanding amphibious operation until landing phase completed." Two days later, on 23 April, General DeWitt arrived at Adak and immediately "informed interested commands that Rear Admiral T. C. Kinkaid, U.S. Navy, was ordered to assume supreme command of the LANDCRAB Operation."[76]

---

[75] TCK to Nimitz, Adak, 16 Apr 1943.
[76] COMNORPACFOR to CTF 51, 4/210802Z, Command Summary; TF 16 War Diary, 23 Apr 1943.

Kinkaid would probably have liked to order Rockwell to move into a transport with General Brown and command the assault phase from there, but Rockwell had warned him that such a change would require serious rewriting of the plan and thus require a delay of D-day. Experience with the North African landings led Kinkaid and the Army staff to believe Brown and Rockwell plus their staffs should be loaded in a vessel that would not be required for another immediate use. Kinkaid, particularly, was worried that the Japanese might send a strong naval force to break up the landing and he would have to use Rockwell's command ship, the battleship *Pennsylvania*, as part of a fighting task group. Rockwell insisted that the old battleship had better communications and radar equipment, necessary for control of the operation, than any of the transports. He would stay in *Pennsylvania*.[77]

Kinkaid also tried to get the transport submarines *Nautilus* (SS 168) and *Narwhal* (SS 167) deleted from the operation. They were to carry a company of Alaskan Scouts to a beach northwest of Holtz Bay. The admiral believed it dangerous to have American subs operating this close to Attu because it would inhibit his orders that all submarine contacts were to be attacked immediately. Nimitz and Rockwell both rejected Kinkaid's arguments and the two submarines carried out their missions successfully.[78]

One other issue arose between Kinkaid and Rockwell that was to carry over into the postaction reports. The gunfire support plan for the battleships called for firing at ranges of 14,000 to 18,000 yards (seven to nine miles). Kinkaid tried to convince Rockwell to move in closer: "The gun power you have available in the battleships and destroyers should be ample to blow hell out of the Jap installations if the ships can get in *close enough to hit their targets*" [emphasis in original]. He noted that light cruisers had bombarded Holtz and Chichagof bays from 8,000 or 9,000 yards and destroyers had worked in even closer. There were no large-caliber coastal guns on Attu, so there was no danger from the enemy. Again Rockwell followed his own counsel. Later the Army was to criticize these long-range bombardments.[79]

Aleutian weather, which Kinkaid regularly described as "vile" or "vicious," played its part when it was time to commence LANDCRAB. It had originally been scheduled for 7 May with an H-hour of 0740W (local time), but stormy seas and then fog at Attu forced Rockwell and Kinkaid to reset the time of attack several times. Finally, despite a heavy blanket

---

[77] CTF 16 to CTF 51, 4/020400Z; CTF 51 to CTF 16, 4/022120Z, Command Summary; Memo, LTCOL Lynn D. Smith to GEN DeWitt, 28 Mar 1943, TCK Papers.

[78] COMNORPACFOR to CTF 51, 4/260124Z; CTF 51 to CTF 16, 4/262351Z; CINCPAC to CTF 16, 4/270135Z, Command Summary.

[79] TCK to F. W. Rockwell, Adak, 5 May 1943, Nimitz Papers; BGEN W. H. Lynd to CINCPAC, Elmendorf Field, 19 May 1943, enclosure in COMINCH–CINCPAC Conferences, 28 May–1 Jun 1943.

of fog, on 11 May at 1615W boats began landing troops at the invasion sites.[80] All ship-to-shore movements were unopposed. The Japanese had decided to fight from prepared inland positions rather than contest the initial landings.

The largest body of troops came ashore at Massacre Bay on the southeastern end of Attu and moved slowly inland. After an advance of a mile and a half on the semifrozen muskeg, these troops began receiving heavy enemy fire. The Japanese were dug into the upper slopes of the hills that enclosed three sides of the two valleys leading inland from Beaches Yellow and Blue on Massacre Bay. Unable to move and position their artillery quickly on the unfamiliar and soggy terrain, the troops were forced to dig in and wait for assistance. It meant spending the night in foxholes that filled with icy water. The units that landed on Beach Red on the northwest tip of Holtz Bay had to advance over rocky and hilly ground, then over an escarpment just beyond the beach, but at least they could move. The same was true of the Alaskan Scouts company that had paddled ashore earlier in the day from *Narwhal* and *Nautilus* onto Beach Scarlet.

Because of the fog enshrouding the eastern end of Attu, plans for prelanding aerial and ship bombardments were unfulfilled. The battleships *Idaho* and *Nevada* worked over Chichagof Harbor with radar-directed fire, but the bombardment was not effective. The fighters from the escort carrier *Nassau* (CVE 16) contributed very little on the first day as a result of the fog and low clouds. In fact a PBY had to lead the fighters to the beach area. In the following days, through the 20th, the "jeep carrier" would regularly launch its aircraft for ground support missions. Lacking TBF Avengers, which could carry fairly heavy bomb loads, the Wildcat fighters had to handle the bombing and strafing where directed. Rockwell liked the results of having an escort carrier squadron at hand for close support operations and later recommended that at least three be present, two with fighters and a third with bombing or torpedo planes.[81]

True to his ideas about command, Kinkaid and his staff remained in Adak throughout the Attu operation. He believed that the overall commander of a joint operation should remain close to his communications and out of the way of those in command at the scene of action. He remembered the trouble that overtook Admiral Theobald when he went to sea during the Japanese raids on Dutch Harbor the previous June. Kinkaid later observed that he had stayed so close to communications

---

[80] TF 16 War Diary, 4, 7, 8, 11 May 1943. Basic information concerning preparations for and the Battle of Attu was taken from Conn, *Guarding the United States*, 277–95; Garfield, *Thousand-Mile War*, 224–99; and ONI Combat Narrative: *Aleutians*.

[81] Y'Blood, *The Little Giants*, 30–33.

that he had never taken the opportunity to fish for the Dolly Varden trout that were so abundant in the streams of Adak.[82]

During the planning and at the inception of LANDCRAB neither Kinkaid nor anyone else in the higher command echelons expected the operation to take more than three or four days. The estimate of the number of Japanese on Attu varied from 500 to 1,800 during the planning, but no one expected the 2,380 that were actually there on 11 May.[83] In mid-March Admiral Nimitz had believed that the "seizure and occupation may turn out much easier than the subsequent logistic supply." Continuing in that optimistic vein he concluded, "It is quite possible that air operations from the NEAR ISLANDS, plus those from positions now under construction [Amchitka and Adak], will cause the enemy more difficulties than he can accept, thus making the large scale attack to capture KISKA unnecessary."[84] At Pearl and in Washington and Adak it was inconceivable that the 11,000 American troops could not quickly dispose of the Japanese.

Once the troops were ashore, Kinkaid's principal concern was to complete the operation as quickly as possible. Five days before the landings he had received information from CINCPAC's code breakers that the Japanese appeared to be accumulating a task force, possibly including the Fifth Fleet, at Paramushiro, and this new fleet might be heading for the Aleutians.[85] If the Japanese brought a strong surface force to Attu, Kinkaid had to be sure that the forces available to him would meet the enemy with at least equal strength. He had already lost two destroyers on the 10th when *Sicard* (DM 21) and *MacDonough* (DD 351) had collided in the fog off Attu. *Sicard*, a destroyer minelayer, had been forced to tow *MacDonough* to Adak.

On the 12th Admiral Rockwell received a reminder that his flagship was in a fairly exposed position when a Japanese submarine penetrated the area and fired two torpedoes at *Pennsylvania*. They missed, and destroyers *Farragut* and *Edwards* (DD 619) counterattacked and eventually drove off the intruder, which was sunk two days later by *Frazier* (DD 607). On the 15th another submarine fired torpedoes at the flagship, and again it was missed.[86] If Japanese accuracy improved, it was clear to everyone that the capital ships might be damaged and removed from Kinkaid's force. These big ships were also developing another problem that concerned Kinkaid. By the 15th they had completely expended their large-caliber high-capacity

---

[82] Comments by TCK on Office of Military History Manuscript, "Guarding the U.S. and Its Outposts," written in Apr 1959, series 6, TCK Papers.
[83] Conn, *Guarding the United States*, 295.
[84] Nimitz to TCK, Pearl Harbor, 16 Mar 1943.
[85] Command Summary, 6 May 1943.
[86] TF 16 War Diary, 12 and 15 May 1943; Morison 7:44–45; W. J. Holmes, *Undersea Victory: The Influence of Submarine Operations on the War in the Pacific* (Garden City, NY: Doubleday, 1966), 226–27.

bombardment ammunition. The forces ashore wanted them to begin using their AP (armor piercing) shells on enemy installations, but Rockwell demurred. Were his ships to begin firing their 14-inch AP ammunition, they would be in no shape to meet any enemy fleet that might appear.[87]

Kinkaid recognized that LANDCRAB was tying up a lot of ships that Admiral Nimitz would be needing elsewhere. If the operation became protracted, he would not only be in CINCPAC's bad graces, but he would also be upsetting COMINCH and the JCS as well. It is little wonder therefore that Kinkaid grew restive when on the 14th he received a radio from Rockwell that General Brown wanted more troops brought to Attu. Brown already had most of the troops from the Seventeenth and Thirty-Second Infantry Regiments ashore, but he needed more. The Fourth Regiment was in Adak awaiting deployment at Shemya along with an engineering regiment. The Fourth was, of course, the last reserve for the Seventh Division. Rockwell had no reason to deny General Brown's request except that the Massacre Bay beaches were too congested, in his judgment, to receive any more troops or equipment in the near future.[88] Several hours later Kinkaid let Rockwell know that he was "in entire accord with views regarding not putting more troops into Massacre until congested condition is relieved." He then revealed what was really bothering him:

> There are no escorts here for bringing additional reinforcements. We must be ready to meet strong enemy naval force probably assembling in the North Pacific. The time during which we can expect to be free of enemy efforts to save Attu is rapidly waning. Impress upon Brown the necessity for prompt action.[89]

The next day, 15 May, Kinkaid fired off an "eyes only Rockwell" message that was ominous for General Brown's future. He stated that General Buckner had received a message from General Brown,

> ... requesting large shipment heavy engineer road building equipment [which] indicate that Brown has stopped fighting and intends to consolidate his present position in MASSACRE BAY for an indefinite period. Evidently he does not intend to move his front line or to use his vastly superior numbers vigorously and aggressively until provided with a road net. This procedure would jeopardize the entire LANDCRAB operation. Brown's mission is based on necessity for speedy capture of VOLUBLE [Shemya] and construction of airfield thereon. . . . The view that reduction of ATTU will be slow is not acceptable.

---

[87] Morison 7:46–47; Garfield, *Thousand-Mile War*, 261, 267.
[88] CTF 51 to COMNORPACFOR, 5/142352Z, series 6, Message File, TCK Papers (hereafter TCK Msg File).
[89] COMNORPACFOR to CTF 51, 5/150233Z, TCK Msg File.

Kinkaid then asked Rockwell for his opinion whether General Brown had the necessary "stamina and aggressive spirit" to drive home the attack. If not, he planned to relieve him with Major General Eugene M. Landrum who was then at Adak. He concluded, "DeWitt and Buckner concur."[90]

In two separate messages Rockwell attempted to provide all the information he had concerning Brown's situation. But he still had to conclude that the general insisted that he needed the Fourth Regiment and other troops as well. He summarized, "Brown states . . . all present forces committed. Does not have sufficient strength to take Attu." He added that General Brown requested a conference with Kinkaid and General DeWitt.[91] Rockwell himself never suggested the general's relief.

Undoubtedly impatient with both Brown and Rockwell, Kinkaid radioed CINCPAC a few minutes after midnight, information to COMINCH: "I regret the necessity but feel compelled to have commander landing force superseded. Accordingly General Landrum will proceed by plane to JACKBOOT [Attu] May sixteen to relieve General Brown."[92]

Rockwell immediately sent one more message urging Kinkaid to hold off on relieving Brown until he had met with him personally, but Kinkaid declined to do this.[93] Based on the information he had at Adak, which was all radio traffic, Kinkaid felt he had to act. He still took another ten hours to review the situation with Buckner and DeWitt before he instructed Rockwell to inform General Brown that he was to be relieved.[94]

The general was dismayed. In the late afternoon of the 16th, he radioed Kinkaid that "if Landrum is relieving me because of failure I request investigation on the ground before action is taken. Progress to successful completion of our mission is being made." Two hours later Kinkaid replied that "time does not permit investigation on the ground."[95] Ironically, General Brown was correct. His Massacre Valley force had finally linked up with those that had landed on Beaches Red and Scarlet, and the campaign had entered the mopping up phase, which still lasted another two weeks.[96] But Brown was finished.

From Attu the general immediately flew to Adak and there confronted Kinkaid, DeWitt, and Buckner. They met in Kinkaid's hut, had a drink, and then got down to business. Kinkaid reviewed with Brown the reasons he had relieved him and then invited the general to read the file of dispatches that had formed the basis for his action. He later described

---

[90] COMNORPACFOR to CTF 51, 5/160400Z, Command Summary.
[91] CTF 51 to COMNORPACFOR, 5/160602Z, TCK Msg File.
[92] COMNORPACFOR to CINCPAC, 5/161013Z, Command Summary.
[93] CTF 51 to COMNORPACFOR, 5/161016Z, Command Summary.
[94] COMNORPACFOR to CTF 51, 5/162045Z, TCK Msg File.
[95] CTF 51 to COMNORPACFOR (forwarding GEN Brown's message), 5/170246Z; COMNORPACFOR to CTF 51 (for GEN Brown), 5/170500Z, TCK Msg File.
[96] Conn, *Guarding the United States*, 293–94.

the situation: "After carefully studying the despatches, Brown said that if he had been in my place with only that information available, he would have taken exactly the same action that I did take."

In writing to Chief of Staff General Marshall, General DeWitt described the meeting with General Brown in similar language, including Brown's statement that he would have done the same as Kinkaid. General DeWitt stated to Marshall that Brown was "by no means licked. He is not a failure." He recommended that Brown be "assigned to the command of a division or corps at the earliest possible date. He can be depended upon to do well. He has got what it takes and can take it."[97]

General Landrum took command just as it became clear that his troops would prevail. The brutal fighting would last until the end of May, but there was no way that the Japanese could hold on until relief might arrive. On the 22d and 23d bombers attacked from Paramushiro, but their efforts proved fruitless. Little damage was done to the ships or to the troops, and most of the Japanese aircraft were damaged or destroyed. Admiral Kinkaid sent a "well done" to the Air Corps fighter squadron that had turned back the attackers. Finally, on 30 May, Kinkaid ordered the troops to occupy Shemya and start construction of an airfield for heavy bombardment squadrons. Kiska would now be pounded from all sides.[98]

Writing eight years after the action, historian Samuel Morison concluded, "The operation succeeded, although clumsily executed."[99] Compared with later landings that benefited from the lessons learned at Attu, he was correct. It was not a thing of beauty, and this fact was evident to all who had planned and executed LANDCRAB. Because he had been charged with the planning and commanded the attack force, Admiral Rockwell had a long list of reasons for the problems that arose. In his action report he complained:

> From the inception of the operations in the Aleutians there were many factors which hampered orderly planning, and which prevented the thorough and complete training of forces involved that was desired. The reduction in forces [from two divisions to one], the change of objective, the lack of suitable ships [no attack cargo ships], the physical separation of commanders and forces involved, inadequate intelligence and proper preliminary reconnaissance, and the uncertainty and lateness of definite commitment to the operation are some of the factors referred to. All these factors had their bearing on the ultimate conduct of the operation.

---

[97] Comments by TCK... April 1959; LTGEN J. L. DeWitt to GEN G. C. Marshall, Adak, 18 May 1943, TCK Msg File.
[98] TF 16 War Diary, 22, 23 May 1943; Command Summary, 30, 31 May 1943.
[99] Morison 7:50.

Rockwell said as much and more in a report sent to Admiral Nimitz before the latter met with Admiral King in San Francisco on 28 May.[100]

An Air Corps observer assigned to Rockwell's staff, Brigadier General William H. Lynd, wrote a more pointed report to CINCPAC while the battle was still heated. He believed there was "unity of command between the Army and Navy in Task Force 51 by order, but little unity of thought." He still believed six or seven days after the event that Rockwell should have moved his battleships in much closer in order to provide more effective bombardments. As might be expected, he was much more critical than Rockwell when it came to discussing training flaws:

> It is strongly recommended that the Kiska operation be handled by commanders here, familiar with the Aleutian terrain and weather conditions. Also, that the planning of the entire action be done here, also, if possible, that the troops utilized be given at least a month's training in the Aleutian area.[101]

From his correspondence with his wife and others it is clear that Kinkaid was pleased with the outcome of the Attu operation. He did believe that the troops should have had training in the Aleutians before being committed to action. He recognized that terrible mistakes had been made in outfitting the troops because Brown's and Rockwell's staffs were unfamiliar with the muskeg and seemed unwilling to ask for advice from those who had been in the area for some time. The soldiers arrived with leather logger-type boots rather than the rubber-coated, waterproof "shoe pack" that was commonly used in the Aleutian theater. But the problems with Rockwell were set aside once the battle was won. Writing to Helen, the admiral mentioned that he had received "a very pleasant letter from Nimitz today in which he congratulated me on the complete success of the Attu operation. I was satisfied with it myself but was glad to know he felt that way about it." Kinkaid had good reason to be pleased. Nimitz said he had recommended him for promotion to vice admiral and Admiral King was "favorably disposed" to the promotion. Always a pragmatist, Kinkaid could feel at ease with his work at Attu, particularly since King did not hand out promotions to bumblers.[102]

Kinkaid interpreted his mission as Commander North Pacific Force to clear the Japanese out of the Aleutians. It was to be a three-step process. The first step was completed by 1 June when he declared Attu secure. There were still Japanese to be rounded up or killed, but this was now

---

[100] "Command History, NORPACFOR," 122; Memo by RADM F. W. Rockwell, May 1943, encl. in COMINCH–CINCPAC Conferences notes, 28 May–1 Jun 1943.

[101] BGEN W. H. Lynd to CINCPAC, Elmendorf Field, 19 May 1943. Enclosure in ibid.

[102] TCK to HSK, Adak, 8 Jun 1943; COMINCH–CINCPAC Conferences, 29 May 1943.

Author's collection

Joint staff planning for the invasion of Kiska, summer 1943. Seated from right are: Major General G. R. Pearkes (Canada), Brigadier General W. C. Butler, Lieutenant General S. B. Buckner, Major General C. H. Corlett who was to command the landing force, Vice Admiral Kinkaid, Rear Admiral F. W. Rockwell, and Lieutenant General J. L. DeWitt, Commander, Western Defense Command.

considered minor mopping up. The second step began at the end of May with the occupation of Shemya and the start of construction on its air strips. With a 10,000-foot runway and shorter cross-runways the Eleventh Air Force could launch heavy bombers against Kiska or send them on long-range strikes against the Japanese bases in the Kurile Islands. The final step to clearing the Japanese from Aleutian soil would be the amphibious assault of Kiska. For Operation AMATEUR (earlier COTTAGE) the planning was well along.[103]

The joint planning team that had developed the Attu attack had actually started plans for a Kiska assault until Kinkaid recommended a change of target. Now with the experience of Attu behind it, a joint team again began planning a Kiska attack despite a lack of enthusiasm from General Marshall and some of the JCS planning staff.[104] The Joint Chiefs had decided to re-

---

[103] Nimitz to TCK, Pearl Harbor, 20 Apr 1943, Nimitz Papers; Morton, *Strategy and Command*, 431–33.
[104] Matloff, *Strategic Planning . . . 1943–1944*, 195–96.

take Kiska and sold the concept to the Combined Chiefs of Staffs at the Trident Conference in Washington. This English-American meeting concluded on 25 May with adoption by President Roosevelt and Prime Minister Churchill of a broad plan for the defeat of the Axis Powers. Included in the plan for Japan's defeat was the task of ejecting the Japanese from the Aleutians.[105] Desirous of keeping the pressure on the enemy, Admirals King and Nimitz now believed that the Attu campaign should be followed by AMATEUR. They were strongly supported by General DeWitt, who had wanted to commence active planning for AMATEUR in April. He and Nimitz had gotten JCS permission in May to move ahead, but a target date for the attack had to await the conclusion of the Trident Conference.[106]

Once active planning for Kiska began, it moved along smartly. Admiral Rockwell was to again command the attack force and oversee the drafting of a plan of operations. His apparent reluctance to work under Kinkaid had been discussed by Admirals King and Nimitz in San Francisco at the end of May and then with Rockwell in San Diego. With Kinkaid's promotion to vice admiral, the problem of seniority had been obviated, though it is doubtful that Rockwell was pleased. He did secure agreement from Nimitz and Kinkaid that he would again use *Pennsylvania* as his flagship. King and Nimitz even agreed to some structural modifications to the old battlewagon that would make it more comfortable for a joint staff to be embarked.[107]

At DeWitt's suggestion Major General Charles Corlett was named to command the landing force. As Commander Amphibious Training Group 9 with headquarters at Fort Ord, Corlett oversaw the preparation of the troops and would then command them during the assault on Kiska. Unlike General Brown he was familiar with the Alaskan-Aleutian environment. Anticipating that the Japanese garrison was 9,000 to 10,000 strong, Rockwell's planning called for using about twice as many troops as had initially landed on Attu. This time the 34,000 attackers would include a Canadian brigade of about 4,800 troops.[108]

Between the conclusion of LANDCRAB and the commencement of AMATEUR, Kinkaid had at hand a large number of ships to employ. This situation was of some concern to Admiral Nimitz, and he asked Kinkaid what his plans for employment were. He recognized that support of operations for Attu and Shemya would require some naval ships, but what else did the North Pacific commander have in mind?[109] Kinkaid still believed

---

[105] Ibid., 144; Morton, *Strategy and Command*, 648–49; Hayes, *History of JCS*, 402–9.
[106] TCK to Nimitz, Adak, 26 Apr 1943, TCK Papers; CWDC to CINCPAC, 5/192327Z; CINCPAC to COMINCH, 5/210247Z; COMINCH to CINCPAC, 5/241336Z, Command Summary.
[107] COMINCH to CINCPAC, 6/091256Z; CINCPAC to COMNORPACFOR, 6/150121Z, Command Summary.
[108] Conn, *Guarding the United States*, 295–96.
[109] CINCPAC to COMNORPACFOR, 6/080057Z, Command Summary.

that the Japanese navy could mount a major raid against Attu, possibly including battleships; thus he had to be prepared for such an eventuality. He also intended to lay on surface bombardments of Kiska at the appropriate times. And there were still regular contacts with enemy submarines that were best met by escorting destroyers and by patrols. To meet his estimated needs the admiral said he would like to keep three battleships, four to six heavy cruisers, four light cruisers, and at least two squadrons of the ever useful destroyers. This number of ships would allow him to rest crews and provide tender maintenance for at least one-third of the force at any time. Nimitz agreed to these proposals but asked that the battleships not be unnecessarily risked.[110]

With the forces allowed him Kinkaid established a fairly tight blockade of Kiska and also laid siege to the island. The cruisers and battleships, operating as several task groups, patrolled out to 200 miles from Attu on an arc that extended from the southwest to the northwest. This patrolling was made more effective by using radar-equipped Catalinas and Venturas in support of the surface ships. Closer in his destroyers established a tight cordon around Kiska to prevent enemy submarines or surface vessels from bringing in troops or supplies. Although not completely impenetrable, the blockade severely limited submarine access to the island and made it virtually impossible for surface convoys to approach the area. The last surface attempt to break through was discovered on 10 July when a PBY located four enemy cargo vessels about 300 miles southwest of Attu. Guided by this and two other Catalinas, B–25s from Amchitka and B–24s from Attu found the convoy and attacked. Although not completely effective these aircraft did sink one vessel, heavily damaged another, and sent the other two at flank speed toward the Kuriles.[111] When the Japanese commander at Paramushiro attempted to send in supplies and evacuate troops by submarines, he lost seven of the thirteen I–class boats committed to the task. The resupply and evacuation operation was abandoned, though single submarines still managed to penetrate the cordon and an estimated 820 troops were evacuated by this means.[112]

The actual siege of Kiska was carried out through bombardment by both aircraft and surface forces under Kinkaid's command. The Eleventh Air Force sent Lightnings, Mitchells, and Liberators against the installations on the island any time weather permitted, and Navy Venturas often joined the raids. COMNORPACFOR reported the daily raids to CINCPAC, and they were duly recorded in CINCPAC's Command Summary. Typical entries read:

---

[110] CINCPAC to COMNORPACFOR, 6/120021Z, Command Summary.
[111] TF 16 War Diary, 10 Jul 1943.
[112] Blair, *Silent Victory*, 1:390–91; Dull, *Battle History IJN*, 265; Holmes, *Undersea Victory*, 232–34; Masataka Chihaya, "Mysterious Withdrawal from Kiska," *Proceedings* (Feb 1958): 35.

11 June. COMNORPAC dropped 29.4 tons bombs North Head, South Head, main camp, runway, Gertrude Cove area, and barges in KISKA harbor. Many hits on all targets. Bombing done from low altitude. 3 medium bombers damaged and 2 Lightnings and 1 Ventura lost.

3 July. Belated information from the North Pacific states that a total of 48.7 tons of bombs were dropped on KISKA on 2 July, with damage to three of our planes and three officer crew members wounded.

1 August. Air activity was confined to one radar controlled raid on KISKA because of weather.[113]

Because of the prevalence of fog in the Aleutians during the late spring and summer, bombings could be conducted on only about 50 percent of the days. Occasionally, when planes were launched and then found Kiska smothered in fog, the pilots would either use their radars to seek out targets, or they would simply make a dead-reckoning run and hope they did some damage. This aerial bombardment of Kiska undoubtedly hampered the Japanese ability to develop an air strip or improve their harbor facilities, but loss of lives was held to a minimum by good shelters and good discipline during raids.

The last serious surface vessel bombardment of Kiska had occurred almost a year before the anticipated assault on the island. On 7 August 1942, Rear Admiral W. W. Smith had led a formidable cruiser-destroyer force out to Kiska. The four cruisers and seven destroyers had given the enemy camp and installations twenty minutes of indirect fire and then departed for Dutch Harbor. The Japanese had suffered considerable damage to their installations, but a lot of good targets were never seen.[114] During the preparation for the Attu operation, Kiska was bombed regularly, but no surface ship attacks were made against it. The surface bombardment ammunition was saved for Attu. On 6 July, Kinkaid ordered his TG 16.7, which was in the vicinity of Kiska, to proceed immediately to the island and bombard the coastal batteries at North Head, South Head, the Main Camp, Gertrude Cove area and Little Kiska Island. Admiral Giffen responded instantly and had his three heavy cruisers *Wichita*, *San Francisco*, and *Louisville*, the light cruiser *Santa Fe*, and four destroyers ready to fire by 1200. With no Japanese aircraft on Kiska the ships were now able to use their SOCs for spotting. Giffen's force laid down an impressive barrage. Because of its high volume of fire Giffen selected *Santa Fe* to concentrate on the coastal battery installations on Little Kiska. For unknown reasons none of the coastal batteries returned the fire. The 100 tons of munitions that rained on Kiska again tore up the wooden buildings of

---

[113] Command Summary, 11 Jun, 3 Jul, 1 Aug 1943.
[114] Morison 7:9–12.

the Main Camp area, but the total damage wrought was unimpressive for the ammunition expended.[115] A few days later Giffen suggested another go at Kiska, if for no other reason than that it would be good practice for his spotter aircraft. Kinkaid appreciated Giffen's aggressive spirit but the stock of high-capacity ammunition available was not large enough for a repeat performance at that time.[116]

Once Admiral Giffen began the bombardments, the Japanese received almost daily attention from Kinkaid's ships. Starting on 11 July the destroyers *Monaghan*, *Aylwin*, *Farragut*, and *Hull* (DD 350), usually singly but occasionally in pairs, would fire 100 to 200 rounds of 5-inch ammunition per night at the Japanese. If nothing else, these nocturnal bombardments disturbed the enemy's sleep. To the extent that there is justice in such activities, Kinkaid was repaying the enemy for the night bombardments that had harassed the Marines during their first five months on Guadalcanal.[117]

These destroyer attacks were interrupted on 22 July when Kinkaid sent two task groups to pay their respects. Admiral Giffen's cruiser-destroyer group (four cruisers and five destroyers) was to approach from the south and fire on Gertrude Cove, the Main Camp, Bukhti Point, and Little Kiska. Rear Admiral Robert M. Griffin with the battleships *New Mexico* and *Mississippi*, the heavy cruiser *Portland*, and four destroyers had orders to approach from the northeast and attack North Head, South Head, Reynard Cove, and the island's submarine base. The air was crystal clear, so SOCs were launched to spot for their ships. With the battleships present, the twenty-one-minute cannonading was a thundering one. The 120 rounds of 14-inch high-capacity ammunition shook the Japanese targets mightily, but again enemy casualties were light. Wooden structures burned brightly, but the coastal batteries were not destroyed. Kinkaid's war diary was much more sanguine than later investigations justified: "Combined reports from all aircraft in flight over the target during and after the bombardment indicate considerable damage on target installations and extensive fires."[118]

With a target date of 15 August for the invasion of Kiska, Kinkaid ordered two more heavy bombardments of that island. On 2 August a cruiser-destroyer group led by Rear Admiral Wilder D. Baker and a battleship-destroyer group under Rear Admiral Howard Kingman followed approximately the same operation order used for the 22 July attack; only the ships were different. Baker brought three old light cruisers (*Richmond*, *Raleigh* [CL 7], and *Detroit*) and two heavies (*Indianapolis* and *Salt Lake City*) plus the usual five destroyers. Kingman had the battleships *Tennessee* and *Idaho* and four destroyers. The afternoon bombardment

---

[115] TF 16 War Diary, 6 July 1943; ONI Combat Narrative: *Aleutians*, 94–95.
[116] TF 16 War Diary, 10–11 Jul 1943.
[117] Ibid., Jul–Aug 1943.
[118] TF 16 War Diary, 22 Jul 1943; ONI Combat Narrative: *Aleutians*, 95–96; Morison 7:55–56.

was coordinated with another one by eighteen Liberators out of Adak and lasted almost an hour. The final task group bombardment took place on 12 August at 0400 when Admiral Baker's cruisers thought they were holding an early reveille for Kiska's occupiers. The American forces would soon learn that there was no one to be awakened. For this final night bombardment the cruisers expended 85 rounds of 8-inch, 450 rounds of 6-inch, and 800 rounds of 5-inch ammunition.[119]

Kinkaid took to heart many of the lessons learned from Attu. Concerned that one of the assault regiments, the Eighty-Seventh Infantry, would not have had as much training at Adak as the rest of the forces, he proposed to Nimitz that the invasion be delayed nine days. The admiral said the proposal was "unacceptable"; the attack would be on the 15th. The final countdown to D-day began on 8 August when Kinkaid issued Operation Plan 6–43. The task was stated simply: the forces were "to seize and occupy Kiska and Little Kiska, in order to destroy the last remaining hostile forces in the Aleutians, to deny Kiska and Little Kiska to the enemy, and to create a base for future operations against the enemy in the North Pacific."[120] On the 15th at 0611 the flash arrived at the admiral's headquarters that the First Special Service Regiment was ashore at Quisling Cove on Kiska. By 0745 the first and second waves had landed at Beach Scarlet and were moving inland.[121] To the consternation of Kinkaid and the Army and Navy staffs, and to the enormous relief of the troopers jammed in the landing craft and ships, there was no enemy on Kiska. Evidence indicated that the Japanese had evacuated the island several weeks before.

It was not until after the war that the full story of the Japanese evacuation of Kiska became known. Initially Kinkaid and others believed it must have been accomplished by submarines, but such was not the case. The Japanese high command decided on 19 May that their situation in the Aleutians was hopeless and ordered the Fifth Fleet commander, then Rear Admiral Shiro Kawase, to remove the Kiska garrison. Rear Admiral Masatomi Kimura organized the operation and used two cruisers (*Abukuma* and *Kiso*) and seven destroyers for the mission. After an abortive try in early July, Kimura's force worked their way through a heavy fog on 28 July and located Kiska harbor. The garrison embarked within an hour and the ships were away without having been spotted by Kinkaid's blockading vessels or any aircraft.[122]

---

[119] TF 16 War Diary, 31 Jul, 2, 11 Aug 1943; ONI Combat Narrative: *Aleutians*, 98–99.
[120] TF 16 War Diary, 8 Aug 1943.
[121] Ibid., 15 Aug 1943.
[122] Chihaya, "Mysterious Withdrawal," 31–47.

AMATEUR was an anticlimax for Kinkaid's command. It could only be considered a large and expensive amphibious training exercise. Brigadier General Sherwood Lett of the Canadian army, who had been at Adak as an observer, summed up a common view: "I am sorry the outcome of the operation was not more to your liking but there is no doubt much valuable training and experience has been acquired which will be of benefit in future operations."[123]

Good experience possibly, but Kinkaid was chagrined and suspected that others senior to him were also disappointed that the Japanese had gotten away cleanly. Assistant Secretary of War John J. McCloy had come to Adak with General DeWitt to view the assault. When he left, Kinkaid asked him to see if people in Washington were upset at the outcome of the operation. McCloy's reply was somewhat noncommittal. He noted that the recently concluded Quebec Conference had knocked Kiska out of the news. He cheered Kinkaid with the comment, "The newspaper account has generally been very good."[124] Kinkaid probably would not have been surprised to find that Admiral King's personal correspondence showed his displeasure. To a former aide King wrote, "Of course, we are all glad that we did not have to fight for Kiska, but you will not be surprised to know that I am not satisfied in that they were allowed to evacuate without being 'hampered.'"[125]

Kinkaid's own account of the operation, written to Helen, is unusually detailed:

> Your radio today told you that we have gotten the Japs out of the Aleutians and have occupied Kiska. . . . We had been collecting a strong force for the past two months but when it arrived at Kiska the Japs had gone. The pounding that we had given them for several weeks, both from the ships and from the air, combined with what had happened on Attu and the fact that they were cut off from supplies made them see the light and they evacuated.
>
> We destroyed the radio station on Kiska at the end of July and from then on, at my request, no news was published regarding Kiska. Up to that time there had been great activity on the island—building roads, trenches, fox holes, etc.—and the antiaircraft fire was heavy. After that activity was considerably reduced but we were hitting them hard and it was a great surprise to find that they were gone on August 15. It was, of course, an anticlimax when our force landed and found no one there.
>
> However, our objective of ridding the Aleutians of Japs had been accomplished. The stratagem of taking Attu in order to weaken their hold on Kiska succeeded beyond all expectations and Kiska fell of its own weight.

---

[123] BGEN Sherwood Lett, Canadian Army to TCK, Ottawa, Canada, 20 Aug 1943, TCK Papers.
[124] John J. McCloy to TCK, Washington, 26 Aug 1943, TCK Papers.
[125] ADM E. J. King to CAPT R. E. Libby, Washington, 31 Aug 1943, King Papers.

I am disappointed at not having caught more of them as they got away but the fog was with them. . . . Nimitz sent a "well done" to all concerned stating that the operations which preceded the final operations on Kiska made possible its accomplishment and the accomplishment of our purpose with a minimum loss of life. He also said that the Japanese evacuation was not displeasing as it put us several weeks ahead of schedule.[126]

Nimitz had indeed sent a "well done" on the 20th. Kinkaid was grateful, and in forwarding CINCPAC's message to all units involved in the Kiska operation, he tacked on his own "well done" for the "excellent state of training achieved in the minimum of time, which made it possible to undertake the assault and occupation of Kiska on schedule."[127]

In later years the admiral occasionally explained a few points about Kiska that puzzled people. Many wondered why it wasn't evident that the Japanese were gone, given the regular bombing sorties that were sent over the island. Also since some people had begun to suspect that the Japanese were gone or had seriously reduced their garrison, why hadn't any of the blockading forces discovered and intercepted the departing Japanese convoy?

In an oral history interview some eighteen years after AMATEUR, Kinkaid stated that the reports from the pilots who had bombed Kiska after 28 July regularly mentioned they were receiving return fire. The War Diary of the North Pacific command bears out the admiral's statement.

BEFORE THE JAPANESE EVACUATION

15 July. "Received intense, accurate, heavy AA fire. One plane slightly damaged."

22 July. Eight B–25s "received intense, accurate, heavy AA fire . . . with damage to 2 B–25s."

27 July. Five B–24s "received moderate, accurate AA fire, causing damage to one plane."

AFTER THE JAPANESE EVACUATION

2 Aug. Eight B–24s reported "no AA fire . . . numerous new buildings in main camp area and about 50 new tents. . . ."

Eight P–38s strafing the target area "received moderate, accurate, automatic weapons fire."

Eight B–25s dropped 161 100-lb. bombs and received "light, inaccurate automatic weapon fire."

---

[126] TCK to HSK, Adak, 21 Aug 1943.
[127] TF 16 War Diary, 20 Aug 1943.

11 Aug. A Navy PBY at night "received meager, trailing AA fire."

Sixteen A–24s dive bombing the island reported "meager automatic weapons fire."

Seventeen B–25s "dropped propaganda leaflets. Received meager small arms fire."

13 Aug. Fifteen A–24s dive bombing. One plane reported "small arms fire from Little Kiska."

Given this type of reporting, it is little wonder that Kinkaid and his staff continued to believe that Kiska was still occupied. Perhaps the Japanese were only keeping their heads down during the bombing raids. It is obvious now that pilots engaged in low-level strafing or low-level bombing by B–25s, or dive bombing by A–24s, were observing gunfire ricochets from their own and accompanying aircraft. Or the A–24 pilots might have been flying into shrapnel from bombs dropped by their own or preceding planes. Unless gunners in the B–24s were observing other gunners clearing their machine guns, it is difficult to understand their reports of small-arms fire. The Japanese had left no one on the island, nor had they set up guns to fire by timing devices. The pilots simply reported people shooting at them because that is what they expected.[128]

As D-day for Kiska approached, many around Kinkaid began to wonder if the Japanese were still on the island. Several factors made them suspicious: The island's radio had not been heard since 28 July; the volume of return fire during bombing attacks was greatly reduced; and there was silence from the shore during naval bombardments. Captain Russell S. Berkey, then commanding *Santa Fe*, had become suspicious, and he sent Kinkaid an "estimate of the situation," concluding that the landing would not be opposed. But the admiral's staff buried it with a brief note to Berkey that his exercise was "very interesting."[129]

Kinkaid had a different interpretation of the facts. He concluded that the Japanese were following the same pattern they had used on Attu: "I believed that the Japs on Kiska had destroyed all installations not already destroyed by our planes and ships and that they were digging in the hills for a last stand, although I could not get concrete evidence of this."[130]

Generals Buckner and Smith suggested to Kinkaid that a small party of Alaskan Scouts be put ashore by rubber boat from a submarine to have a look around before D-day. The admiral said no. He didn't want to risk the lives, or the ship. "If the Japs were still on the island we were

---

[128] Ibid., 15 Jul, 15 Aug 1943; Garfield, *Thousand-Mile War*, 326–27; TCK oral history, 237–39.
[129] ADM Russell S. Berkey, USN (Ret.), interview with author, Old Lyme, CT, 31 Aug 1976.
[130] Comments by TCK . . . Apr 1959, TCK Papers.

fully prepared for them. If they were not, our landing would be a super dress rehearsal, good for training purposes but with a let-down for the highly keyed assault troops."[131] Having been at war for almost two years, Kinkaid was not accustomed to thinking in terms of the cost of the invasion, or the money that would be saved if a smaller number of soldiers actually made the landing.

As to why the Japanese had gotten away without detection, the situation had almost been beyond Kinkaid's control. The Japanese had waited until 28 July, for the protection of fog to make the final run to Kiska harbor. By coincidence the blockading cruiser force that would have been to the southwest of Attu had moved to a sector southeast of the island to rendezvous with an oiler. Between 28 July and 1 August, Kiska was either blanketed with fog or a very low overcast. Kinkaid's war diary entry for 30 July was typical: "Searches from Attu and Amchitka were cancelled due to weather. . . . All other attack missions were cancelled due to weather."[132]

Based on information radioed from Adak, CINCPAC's Command Summary has an entry for 29 July that undoubtedly would have irritated Kinkaid had he seen it at a later date: "July 29. Activity in the Alaskan area was greatly curtailed because of weather. Patrol plane radar contact disclosed 7 possible ships southwest of Attu at 53–26N, 167–30E. Fog prevented any sightings. This may be an attempt to reinforce KISKA."[133]

There is little doubt that these ships were loaded with the Japanese garrison from Kiska and en route to safety in the Kuriles. As with the pilots in Adak, it was again a case of incorrectly interpreting the data. Instead of wondering if these ships were en route to reinforce Kiska, the question could have been raised whether they might not have been evacuating the island. Unfortunately a question asked is often the product of preconceptions concerning the answer.

With the Kiska operation behind him, Kinkaid's pace slowed noticeably as a result of indecision, both in Washington and at Pearl Harbor, about future operations in the North Pacific Area. The Japanese were gone, and it did not appear that the Aleutian bases would be in any danger in the foreseeable future. Except for the casualties caused by friendly fire (21 killed, 121 wounded) during the first days of movement on Kiska and the deaths of 70 when the destroyer *Abner Read* (DD 526) lost its stern to a mine, AMATEUR had left the attack force largely unscathed. There were now more than 54,000 amphibiously trained troops immediately available for another operation. Within the North Pacific command there were more than 130,000 soldiers and airmen awaiting action.

---

[131] Ibid.
[132] TF 16 War Diary, 30 Jul 1943.
[133] Command Summary, 29 Jul 1943.

Several weeks before D-day at Kiska General DeWitt had written to General Marshall (and through him to the JCS), presenting his ideas about the next operations in the North Pacific. He believed it was time to plan the invasion of Japanese soil by seizing the two northernmost of the Kurile Islands, Paramushiro and Shimushu. As he saw it, such an operation could be launched in the spring of 1944.[134] Admirals Nimitz and King saw DeWitt's memorandum at their bimonthly conference in San Francisco at the end of July, where the general also discussed his views with them. Although sympathetic, they recognized that Kinkaid's naval force had to be substantially reduced as soon as AMATEUR was completed in order to use the ships for operations in the South Pacific area. It was highly unlikely that an assault against the Kurile Islands could be undertaken in the spring of 1944.[135] From San Francisco General DeWitt went to Adak and became one of the many observers during the final days before the attack on Kiska. It is quite evident that he sold Admiral Kinkaid on invading the Kuriles.

On 21 August the admiral radioed CINCPAC and made a case for taking Paramushiro and Shimushu in November 1943. Using arguments similar to those that had supported the landing on Amchitka, Kinkaid noted, "COMNORPAC is strongly impressed by the fact that PARAMUSHIRO-SHIMUSHU Area is now in early stages of development which is progressing rapidly. Its capture and occupation would be far less costly now than in the spring." He concluded by predicting that such a movement against the Kuriles would undoubtedly precipitate a violent naval reaction, possibly leading to a major fleet action between the Pacific Fleet and the Imperial Japanese Navy. He was sure that Nimitz and King would now welcome such an engagement.[136]

Nimitz was not buying. In fact on the 19th and 20th he had been ordered by Admiral King to return the First Special Service Force to the United States and to send the Seventh Division to Hawaii.[137] Perhaps wanting to maintain a ready force in case an opportunity did arise to move against the Kuriles, Nimitz did instruct Kinkaid to continue training troops for amphibious operations in the North Pacific area. To that end he ordered Admiral Rockwell to move his planning and training staff to Adak and place their operation under Kinkaid's command. COMAMPHORPAC now became Commander Ninth Amphibious Force and in two months the Northern Pacific Force would become the Ninth Fleet.[138] Finally, noting the relative inactivity in Kinkaid's area, Nimitz told him to start planning the Kuriles operation, but to do so with two

---

[134] Morton, *Strategy and Command*, 530; Conn, *Guarding the United States*, 299.
[135] COMINCH–CINCPAC Conference Notes, 31 Jul 1943.
[136] COMNORPAC to CINCPAC, 8/220847Z, 8/220936Z, Command Summary.
[137] COMINCH to CINCPAC, 8/191758Z, 8/210820Z, Command Summary.
[138] CINCPAC to COMNORPAC, 8/240341Z, Command Summary.

different assumptions: that the USSR would be a full ally, and that the USSR would be scrupulously neutral.

At that time no one in the JCS or in COMINCH's headquarters believed that American forces could maintain themselves in Paramushiro and Shimushu unless the Russians provided bases and assistance from the Kamchatka Peninsula. To many planners trying to maintain a foothold in the Kuriles would be like the Japanese trying to hang on in the Aleutians.[139]

But any ideas that Kinkaid or DeWitt might have had about mounting an operation against Paramushiro in 1944 were ended in September. Because of a shortage of trained troops for other operations in 1944, including the invasion of Europe (OVERLORD), General Marshall proposed that troops in the Alaskan theater be reduced to 80,000 during 1944. General DeWitt, Rear Admiral John W. Reeves (representing Vice Admiral Fletcher), General Buckner, and Captain Colclough (representing Kinkaid) traveled to Washington to discuss the proposal with the JCS planners and argue for new operations in the North Pacific. As might be expected, Marshall's views prevailed. There would be no Kuriles operation before mid-1945; troop strength in Alaska would be drastically lowered. The area obviously was to become a backwater command, though a major operating base for "very long range" bomber squadrons and their B–29s was being prepared on Shemya.[140]

As operations slowed down and Kinkaid was faced with a mountain of paperwork, he began to grow restless. His letters to Helen revealed his dislike for administrative routine. He became concerned with his waist and tried cutting down on his eating. He began walking more, but was never very serious about it. He let Nimitz know that he could use some leave, and in letters to both Nimitz and Helen, he began to wonder if he was going to stay in Alaska or go to a new command. He did not want to go to Washington for duty, nor was he interested in a naval district or sea frontier job. Nimitz teased him by sending a cribbage board. Kinkaid wondered if that was to be his future—playing cribbage in Adak.[141] Also the days were getting shorter and much colder. He didn't want to spend another winter on his Aleutian mud flat.

Finally, on 27 September, Kinkaid received a dispatch from Nimitz ordering him to Washington for temporary duty and authorizing him to request leave. Unfortunately, he was to return to his post as COMNORPAC-FOR. But the thought of being with Helen was enough to add a new

---

[139] CINCPAC to COMNORPAC, 8/250215Z Command Summary; "Command History, NORPACFOR," 135–36; Morton, *Strategy and Command*, 530–31.

[140] Ibid.; Conn, *Guarding the United States*, 299–300; Pogue, *Marshall: Organizer of Victory*, 155–59; Hayes, *History of JCS*, 482–87; COMINCH–CNO to CINCPAC, COMNORPAC, 10/221625z, Command Summary.

[141] TCK to HSK, Adak, 23 Sep 1943.

Vice Admiral Kinkaid reads his orders detaching him as Commander North Pacific Force while his relief, Vice Admiral Frank Jack Fletcher, stands by, October 1943. Those assembled are senior members of Kinkaid's joint staff and commanders of units and groups under his command.

lightness to his letters. Ever practical, he planned to have his teeth repaired, including a new denture, and this would call for a couple of weeks. After that he would take leave. "There is no great hurry to get back that I know of at the moment."[142] Then on 4 October he received new orders. He would be permanently detached and travel to Washington for temporary duty and then a new assignment. A few days later he learned that his relief would arrive on the 11th to take over immediately. Unhappy, but resigned to his duty, Frank Jack Fletcher would relieve Kinkaid.

Kinkaid departed for Washington on the 12th. He had no idea where he would be going, whether to take winter or khaki uniforms, or even whether he would retain his rank as a temporary vice admiral, but he was not particularly worried. The Aleutian tour had been a good one. He had accomplished his mission—the Japanese were off American soil. He had also demonstrated that the Army and Navy could cooperate suc-

---

[142] Ibid., 27 Sep 1943.

cessfully. When it appeared that the Attu campaign was about to sink into the muskeg, he had acted decisively. And he had been supported by the senior Army commanders even though he had summarily relieved one of their own. On the day before the Kiska landings, he had written to Helen that "the Time correspondent has sent in a 'cover article' on me so do not be surprised if before long you see my countenance staring at you from the news stands."[143] Kiska might have been a success in terms of its goal, but it was certainly not a headline-grabbing operation; Kinkaid did not become a *Time* cover story. But it hardly mattered to the admiral; he was headed home.

---

[143] Ibid., 14 Aug 1943.

Chapter 13

Commander Seventh Fleet, November 1943–October 1944

At a press conference on 26 October 1943 Secretary of the Navy Frank Knox let the cat out of the bag. There was to be a shuffling of naval commanders in the Southwest Pacific; Vice Admiral Thomas Kinkaid would replace Vice Admiral Arthur S. Carpender as Commander Seventh Fleet. To the public, however, Tom Kinkaid would be the commander of "MacArthur's Navy." By chance the admiral was present at the conference. Just two weeks earlier he had left his command in the stormy Aleutians for a well-earned leave. Now he was to take over an equally tempestuous command preparing for a year of intense operations against the Japanese. General Douglas MacArthur was accelerating the pace of his drive toward the Philippines, and he was turning more and more to his Seventh Fleet to carry him there.[1]

When Admirals Ernest King and Chester Nimitz met for their bimonthly conference in San Francisco in September 1943, Admiral Kinkaid was on their agenda. Asked twice by MacArthur that his naval commander be relieved,[2] King knew what he needed: an aggressive battle-experienced admiral with a demonstrated ability to work with the Army. Tom Kinkaid seemed to fill the bill nicely. The admirals decided to move Kinkaid from Alaska to Australia.[3]

Following briefings in Washington, where Admiral King made sure that the new Seventh Fleet commander understood his views on strategy in the Pacific for the year ahead, Kinkaid flew to San Francisco and then immediately to Pearl Harbor. There he was briefed thoroughly again, this time on problems between the Navy and MacArthur as seen by CINCPAC. As a house guest of Admiral Nimitz he not only relaxed with

---

[1] *New York Times*, 27 Oct 1943.

[2] COMINCH–CINCPAC Conference, San Francisco, 25 Sep 1943; Buell, *King*, 319–20; D. Clayton James, *A Time for Giants: Politics of the American High Command in World War II* (New York: Franklin Watts, 1987), 110; Paolo E. Coletta, "Daniel E. Barbey, Amphibious Warfare Expert," in William M. Leary, ed., *We Shall Return! MacArthur's Commanders and the Defeat of Japan, 1942–1945* (Lexington: University of Kentucky Press, 1988), 220–21.

[3] Gerald E. Wheeler, "KINKAID, Thomas Cassin," in Roger J. Spiller et al., eds., *Dictionary of American Military Biography*, 3 vols. (Westport, CT: Greenwood Press, 1984), 2:567; James, *MacArthur* 2:358.

the Pacific Fleet Commander, but also had the opportunity to visit with Nimitz's staff and get some idea of the operations ahead.

With the briefings completed, Kinkaid, now fairly well rested from his travels, climbed in General Millard F. (Miff) Harmon's personal transport for a flight to Admiral William Halsey's South Pacific command headquarters in Noumea, New Caledonia. There he received the admiral's views on MacArthur's command and the news that Halsey was to visit Brisbane and would be pleased to introduce him to MacArthur.

Kinkaid was not shy about meeting his new boss, but he did have reason to wonder how he would be greeted.[4] Secretary Knox had announced Kinkaid's appointment to the command of Allied Naval Forces, Southwest Pacific Area, without General MacArthur's blessing. The Australian press had picked up the news of the appointment immediately and spread the word approvingly—a "fighting admiral" was on the way.[5]

General MacArthur's radio to General George Marshall was restrained, but direct. He had not been consulted and, more important, neither had the Australian government of Prime Minister John Curtin. Kinkaid would be working for MacArthur, and Australian forces would be included in his command. Prior consultation had been expected. Admiral King provided the formula to smooth the general's feathers: It was the Navy Department's intention to replace Vice Admiral Carpender with Vice Admiral Kinkaid, but the latter had received no orders as yet. Would he be acceptable? In forwarding this less-than-candid information, General Marshall added his own thoughts:

> Kinkaid has performed outstanding service against the Japs as naval commander in the North Pacific. His relations have been particularly efficient and happy with Army commanders, and he had the admiration of both services in that theater. I think you will find him energetic, loyal and filled with desire to get ahead with your operations. I think he is the best naval bet for your purpose.[6]

The *amende honorable* having been proffered, and accepted, Kinkaid's passage to the realm of Commander in Chief, Southwest Pacific Area (CINCSWPA) was now clear. But it was probably lucky that he had the legendary Bull Halsey for an escort. Kinkaid arrived in Brisbane on 23 November, two days before Thanksgiving. He was given a temporary room in Lennon's Hotel where almost all the senior officers associated with MacArthur's command were quartered. Once Admiral Carpender

---

[4] TCK to HSK, San Francisco, Honolulu, Brisbane, 17–27 Nov 1943.

[5] *The Courier Mail* (Brisbane), 27 Oct 1943; *The Telegraph* (Brisbane), 27 Oct 1943.

[6] CINCSWPA to Chief of Staff, USA, Brisbane, 27 Oct 1943; Chief of Staff to CINCSWPA, Washington, 27 Oct 1943, George C. Marshall Papers, Marshall Library, Lexington, VA (hereafter Marshall Papers).

left for his new assignment as Commandant Ninth Naval District, Kinkaid would move into his vacated suite at the hotel. In the meantime he began to settle in, meet his staff and General MacArthur's, and arrange for official calls on Australian and American civilian officials he needed to know. Because of the press of Halsey's business, he met only briefly with the general on a couple of occasions. He did, though, have a chance to visit with Rear Admiral Ralph W. Christie, his submarine force commander, who normally operated out of the naval base on the other side of the continent at Perth-Fremantle. Carpender had felt it important that Christie be in Brisbane to meet his new boss.

As luck would have it, Kinkaid had his first meeting with the general when he returned to his office from his first press conference and found Christie and MacArthur both waiting for him. For the submarine force commander this seemed a good omen. He wanted more awards for his submariners, and the general had said he merely had to ask. Christie thought Kinkaid agreed.[7] Later the ebullient Christie confided to his diary, "This is a happy day for the 7th Fleet! A new, fresh, good-natured attitude has come over the staff." Kinkaid was to learn soon that Christie was just one of several headstrong subordinate commanders he would have to manage.[8]

MacArthur and Kinkaid finally had a serious meeting the day after he formally relieved Carpender on Friday, 26 November. He described this first session to Helen:

> This morning I had a long talk with the General and he was extremely cordial. He told me all of his troubles in detail and we discussed the situation here. He asked for suggestions from me not only regarding the Navy but concerning any other phases of operations in this area. He said that his door is always open to me and that he would like me to come to see him often and keep him informed. I could not have asked for a more cordial reception.

This was Saturday. On Sunday he again wrote Helen about the general: "This morning I transacted my first business with the General and I must say I could not ask for greater consideration."[9] He found, however, that MacArthur worked every day, including most weekends, and expected his senior staff to maintain the same pace, which included the Navy. Kinkaid was no "sun-downer," but he must have projected a good image when the general learned that the new commander had dined with his senior staff on Thanksgiving and used the meal to learn more about Seventh Fleet affairs.

---

[7] VADM R. W. Christie to author, Honolulu, 11 Nov 1976.
[8] Blair, *Silent Victory*, 1:476.
[9] TCK to HSK, Brisbane, 27, 28 Nov 1943.

Kinkaid knew when he arrived in Brisbane that he would be wearing two hats. One hat would be that of Seventh Fleet commander and therefore under Admiral King's direct command. His other hat was that of MacArthur's naval commander, formally Commander Allied Naval Forces, Southwest Pacific Area. As such he commanded all U.S. naval forces plus those of Australia, New Zealand, and the Netherlands operating in the area. Except for operations involving selected individual units, each of the non-American naval forces was commanded by its own nation's officers. As a vice admiral Kinkaid was senior to all the naval officers in the SWPA with the exception of Admiral Sir Guy Royle, RN, who commanded Australia's naval forces, and Vice Admiral Conrad E. L. Helfrich, Commander in Chief, Netherlands East Indies Navy. By agreement among all concerned, Kinkaid was granted the authority to command, even though he lacked a fourth star on his collar and a fourth stripe on his dress blues. He liked Sir Guy almost immediately and found him "perfectly willing to fall in with our plans." He didn't particularly care for Helfrich for a militarily snobbish reason. As he explained to his wife, "I am interested only in the Allied Naval Forces when they are in contact with the enemy."[10] Australia had cruisers and destroyers working with the Seventh Fleet against the Japanese on New Guinea's north coast; the Dutch did not. This early opinion was to change over the next eighteen months.

In 1943 and early 1944 American flag officers were not too common in the Seventh Fleet. Among those present Rear Admiral Daniel E. Barbey was clearly the most important after the commander himself. As Commander Seventh Fleet Amphibious Force, designated Task Force 76 for operations purposes, Barbey had spent almost all of 1943 organizing, equipping, and training the naval force that would carry SWPA land forces into battle. Because of the role he played, he came into closest contact with General MacArthur's troop commanders and the general's air boss, Lieutenant General George C. Kenney. Before Kinkaid arrived in Brisbane, Barbey's TF 76 had the reputation at MacArthur's headquarters of being the fighting part of the Seventh Fleet. The fleet commander and his staff were simply rear echelon people whose jobs were to keep TF 76 fighting. Kinkaid quickly learned that "Uncle Dan" Barbey had done little to correct this impression. He concluded early that his principal subordinate was "ambitious" and "political," both being pejorative terms in the lexicon of the sea services.[11]

By design Admiral Kinkaid's headquarters were located in Brisbane's AMP Building, the same place that MacArthur had chosen for the gen-

---

[10] TCK to HSK, Brisbane, 11, 15 Jan 1944.
[11] Memo: Comments and Recommendations submitted . . . by CAPT R. C. Hudson, Pt. Moresby, 18 Nov 1943, Commander Seventh Fleet (COM7THFLT) Files, OA; TCK oral history, 357, 420; Coletta, "Barbey," 228–29.

eral headquarters (GHQ). This meant that the general could see, on a daily basis if desired, the commanders of the Allied Naval Forces (Kinkaid) and the Allied Air Forces (Kenney). The commander of the Allied Land Forces, General Sir Thomas A. Blamey, an Australian, was not so favored. With headquarters elsewhere he lacked the daily contact with MacArthur that might have led to significantly different relations between the Australian and American fighting forces. As a result of these physical arrangements, the American GHQ was dominated by the general and the Army, with little meaningful participation in planning or control of operations by non-American military leaders. MacArthur, of course, saw it differently. A few months before Kinkaid reported, the general had described his GHQ and the philosophy underlying its structure:

> Complete and thorough integration of ground, air, and naval Headquarters within General Headquarters is the method followed with marked success in the Southwest Pacific Area rather than the assembly of an equal number of officers from those components into a General Headquarters staff. Land, air and naval forces each operate under a commander with a completely organized staff.... General Headquarters is, in spirit, a Headquarters for planning and executing operations, each of which demands effective combinations of land, sea, and air power. General Headquarters has successfully developed an attitude that is without service bias.[12]

A GHQ "without service bias" probably existed only in the mind of General MacArthur; it certainly was not a reality, at least as viewed by the Navy. The quarreling among the Army, Navy, and Army Air Corps staff members in Brisbane persisted throughout the war and had grown to epidemic proportions by the time Kinkaid was ordered to SWPA. Coming from a command where operations with the Army and its Air Corps had called for joint planning and joint operations, with unity of command being exercised at sea and ashore, he was astounded to find such practices almost nonexistent in MacArthur's command. Admiral Barbey also recognized this problem and noted that in 1943 and most of 1944 operations were carried out by "mutual cooperation" rather than "unity of command" practices. Kinkaid and Barbey both chafed at their lack of input when GHQ was working up an operation. They became further irritated when amphibious operations were planned by General Walter Krueger's staff, after GHQ had made the broad plans, and all of this with

---

[12] Dudley McCarthy, *South-West Pacific Area—First Year, Kokoda to Wau: Australia in the War of 1939–1945*, 7 vols., series one: *Army* (Canberra: Australian War Memorial, 1959), 5:27–29; Charles A. Willoughby, comp., *Reports of General MacArthur: The Campaigns of MacArthur in the Pacific*, 2 vols. (Washington: Department of the Army, 1966), 1:109; James, *MacArthur* 2:313–15. See also, Stanley L. Falk, "Douglas MacArthur and the War Against Japan," 10, and D. M. Horner, "Blamey and MacArthur, The Problem of Coalition Warfare," 23–24, 28 in Leary, *We Shall Return*.

minimum interest in the Navy's views or concerns. The inevitable result, in the past, had been foot-dragging by Admirals Fairfax Leary and Arthur Carpender when they believed the Army's plans were unwise or not feasible. It was clear to Kinkaid that this source of friction could not be alleviated until MacArthur ordered changes in Army planning practices.[13]

Another source of what Kinkaid called chronic belly-aching among the services was traceable to the traditional wartime malaise that overtakes an operation during its period of build-up. MacArthur and his staff, a large one with plenty of senior officers, were in Australia to prepare for and carry out operations that would defend the continent and, in time, carry them back to the Philippines and possibly Japan. The tasks ahead were many, and the resources slender and maddeningly slow in arriving. GHQ was dominated by the "Bataan Gang" and driven by the same demon that tormented the general—the desire to avenge the defeat in the Philippines. Headed by Lieutenant General Richard K. Sutherland as Chief of Staff, this Praetorian Guard protected the general from outsiders (non-Army types) and controlled public knowledge of affairs in the SWPA by censorship of all news reporting. Aware that the Navy's contribution was receiving little space in SWPA communiqués, Kinkaid tried to add his own press officer to MacArthur's staff. A lieutenant commander, he was badly outranked and unwanted by the general's public relations staff. He quickly found a new billet in Admiral Halsey's staff in Noumea, and Kinkaid released him.[14]

The Navy in Australia, as Kinkaid later analyzed the situation, had serious problems with its organization and command relationships that tended to exacerbate relations with the Army. The Seventh Fleet in theory was a typical fighting organization. It possessed two air wings of patrol aircraft, a submarine force divided between the east and west coasts of Australia, a small cruiser force, four squadrons of destroyers and ten motor torpedo boat squadrons. It also possessed a large number of ships and smaller craft appropriate for amphibious assault operations.[15] In all, "MacArthur's Navy" was a good-size command for a vice admiral, but Kinkaid had two bosses. His operations orders came from General MacArthur, who was close at hand to see that they were carried out. But Seventh Fleet's personnel and material, including ships, came from Admiral King in Washington. When he created the Seventh Fleet in February

---

[13] VADM Daniel E. Barbey to Philip A. Crowl, Olympia, WA, 9 Nov 1953, Daniel E. Barbey Papers, OA (hereafter Barbey Papers); Administrative History: COMSOWPAC, 70–79 (written by CAPT A. D. Turnbull, USNR) [manuscript], OA; TCK to CAPT A. D. Turnbull, New York, 8 Jun 1949, TCK Papers.

[14] RADM Raymond D. Tarbuck, interview by John T. Mason, Jr., 1973, 117–33, USNI Oral History, Annapolis (hereafter Tarbuck oral history); RADM Joseph Leverton to Author, Whispering Pines, NC, 2 Oct 1977.

[15] Seventh Fleet Confidential Notice 3CN–44: U.S. Seventh Fleet Organization, 1 Feb 1944, OA.

1943, King kept it under his personal command as COMINCH, rather than adding it to Admiral Nimitz's Pacific Fleet. It is significant that Admiral King wrote Kinkaid's fitness reports, not MacArthur or Nimitz. It is also significant that all admirals were assigned to their commands by King. In short the Seventh Fleet commander had two very difficult bosses to keep happy with his work in the SWPA.

His first contacts with MacArthur were pleasant and reassuring, but there was an underlying tension that Kinkaid could do little to lessen. The general was anxious to get his show on the road and he needed more naval support than was at hand. Along with his new fleet commander, MacArthur had hoped that he would soon receive carriers, cruisers, and possibly some battleships. Kinkaid quickly set him straight on this point. There would be no carriers except those loaned by CINCPAC for specific SWPA operations. A bit daringly, if we are to believe the admiral's oral history, he even let the general know that he didn't believe these larger units should be given to the Seventh Fleet. Operating in the SWPA, they would not be facing the Japanese Combined Fleet, but they would be at risk from all of the land-based bombers in the area. If held in Sydney, Melbourne, or Brisbane for future use, these cruisers, carriers, and battleships would be returning very little for the heavy investment in their construction.[16] Kinkaid felt the same way about any British units the general might be able to obtain. Such vessels should be used directly against the Japanese navy, and that meant placing them with Halsey in New Caledonia or with Nimitz for Central Pacific operations. Kinkaid's views notwithstanding, the general did expect to acquire British naval units to strengthen his command and, more optimistically, probably a significant increase in U.S. naval vessels. Given these expectations, MacArthur offered Bill Halsey command of Allied Naval Forces, SWPA. Halsey said he was flattered by the offer, but he quickly turned it down.[17]

As MacArthur's naval commander Kinkaid suffered from the general's deep frustration over his relationships with the Navy. By the time Kinkaid arrived in Brisbane, it had become clear to his new boss that there was little chance that he would be able to change the basic strategy of the war against Japan, and the Navy appeared to be the principal source of resistance to change.

The current strategy called for an approach to the Philippines and China coast along two lines of advance. One axis had already been established with MacArthur's operations in New Guinea and Halsey's South Pacific command operations in the Solomon Islands. In time these lines of operations were expected to eliminate the Japanese in Rabaul and

---

[16] *The Sunday Mail* (Brisbane), 28 Nov 1943; TCK oral history, 81–82, 253–64.
[17] Potter, *Bull Halsey,* 259; Halsey and Bryan, *Admiral Halsey's Story,* 186.

Kavieng in the Bismarck Archipelago, take control of New Guinea, and then push on to Mindanao, and eventually Luzon in the Philippines.

The second axis of advance would be through the Central Pacific as had been projected in "Orange" War Plans since the 1920s. This strategy required seizing control of those island areas that Japan had occupied since the end of World War I, the so-called Pacific Mandates. These islands, lying north of the equator and formerly belonging to the German Empire, included the Marshall Islands with their major bases at Kwajalein and Eniwetok; the Caroline Islands, which included the bastion at Truk and a potentially great naval base at Ulithi; the Marianas with bases on Saipan and Guam; and the Palau Islands, which included the heavily fortified Peleliu. According to the prewar plan these islands would each have to be seized, one after the other, moving east to west. By 1943 they were fortified aviation and naval bases. To Admirals King and Nimitz it was unthinkable to leave them under Japanese control. As seen by King and somewhat concurred in by Nimitz, these island bases were an ongoing threat to the right flank of General MacArthur and Admiral Halsey, and they must be removed. This general strategy of a Central Pacific drive had been laid down by the English-American Combined Chiefs of Staff and the American Joint Chiefs of Staff in January and May 1943. It had been reaffirmed at Quebec in August 1943 and again in December 1943.[18]

What made this general Pacific strategy so galling to MacArthur was the obvious primacy of the Central Pacific drive over the SWPA line of advance. American shipyards were now sending out a steady stream of *Essex*-class 27,000-ton carriers, *Independence*-class light carriers built on cruiser hulls, and swift battleships and cruisers that could move with the new carrier task groups, but these new vessels were going to Nimitz's Pacific Fleet, not to the SWPA.

MacArthur's operations had been built on the premise that his forces would be covered by General Kenney's land-based Fifth Air Force whenever they grappled with the enemy. The schedule of operations set for Nimitz's forces, for instance at Kwajalein or Saipan, would require that the invasion forces be protected by carrier task forces at sea and over the beaches until airfields could be seized or constructed. Once air bases were available on the islands, Marine squadrons or Air Corps squadrons would be brought in. Because of planned operations in the Pacific, Mediterranean, and Atlantic during 1943–1944, there simply were not enough combat vessels constructed to supply everyone, so "MacArthur's Navy" came last.

---

[18] Potter and Nimitz, eds., *The Great Sea War*, 278–79, 310–13; Robert Ross Smith, *War in the Pacific: The Approach to the Philippines*, subseries vol 3 (Washington: U.S. Army Office of Military History, 1953), 1–6; Hayes, *History of the JCS*, 403–9, 415–17, 488–94; Morison, vol. 6, *Breaking the Bismarcks Barrier, 22 July–1 May 1944* (1950), 3–8; and vol. 8, *New Guinea and the Marianas, March 1944–August 1944* (1953), 3–10; Matloff, *Strategic Planning for Coalition Warfare, 1943–1944*, 453–55.

Admiral Kinkaid understood the problem and did not particularly like the results for his command. But he was a team player and did the best he could with what he received. General MacArthur, abetted by his SWPA staff, believed firmly that the wrong team (i.e., the Pacific Fleet) was being rewarded with the usufruct of America's shipbuilding industries.

MacArthur had been fighting the Japanese in New Guinea since mid-1942, had bested them at Buna and other places in Papua, and was ready to begin ejecting them from all of New Guinea. By the time Kinkaid took command of the Seventh Fleet, Admirals Carpender and Barbey had completed their preliminary planning for the opening operations in MacArthur's campaign to eliminate Rabaul as the most important Japanese bastion in the Southwest Pacific Area. Since their seizure of the Bismarck Archipelago in January 1942, the Japanese had turned Rabaul into the linchpin for defense of their conquered territories in the Solomons, Bismarck, and Admiralty islands and the north coast of New Guinea, all constituting a so-called Bismarck Barrier. For the Americans to move northwest toward the Philippines, it was necessary to clean out the Japanese on the north coast of New Guinea, from the Huon Gulf in the east to the westernmost tip of the great island, the aptly named Vogelkop. Before the U.S. forces could pass Cape Cretin and use the Dampier and Vitiaz Straits, the Japanese in their stronghold on New Britain in the Bismarck Archipelago had to be neutralized or eliminated. Making this task doubly difficult was the presence of the Japanese naval base, and its network of protective air bases, at the northeastern tip of New Britain. The first direct step in the assault on Rabaul was to be the invasion of southwestern New Britain at two points, Arawe on 15 December 1943 and Cape Gloucester eleven days later, on the day after Christmas, Boxing Day for the Australians. Admiral Barbey's Seventh Amphibious Force, of course, would do the lifting.[19]

Though the planning for assaults on Arawe and Cape Gloucester was well advanced when he arrived, Admiral Kinkaid found plenty of opportunities to add his own ideas and seek modifications of existing decisions. Probably the most serious problem brought to the admiral came from his amphibious commander, Dan Barbey. Kinkaid had visited him at Milne Bay and found him worried about possible Japanese air reaction during the two amphibious operations. Based on past history he was concerned that General Kenney's airmen wouldn't provide the air coverage when it was most needed. The critical period was when the assault vessels were in restricted waters and unable to maneuver or when

---

[19] Walter Krueger, *From Down Under to Nippon: The Story of the Sixth Army in World War II* (Washington: Combat Forces Press, 1953), 26–36; John Miller, Jr., *Cartwheel: The Reduction of Rabaul* (Washington: Department of the Army, 1959), 1–5; James, *MacArthur* 2:341–42; Willoughby, comp., *Reports of MacArthur* 1:100–101, 128–31.

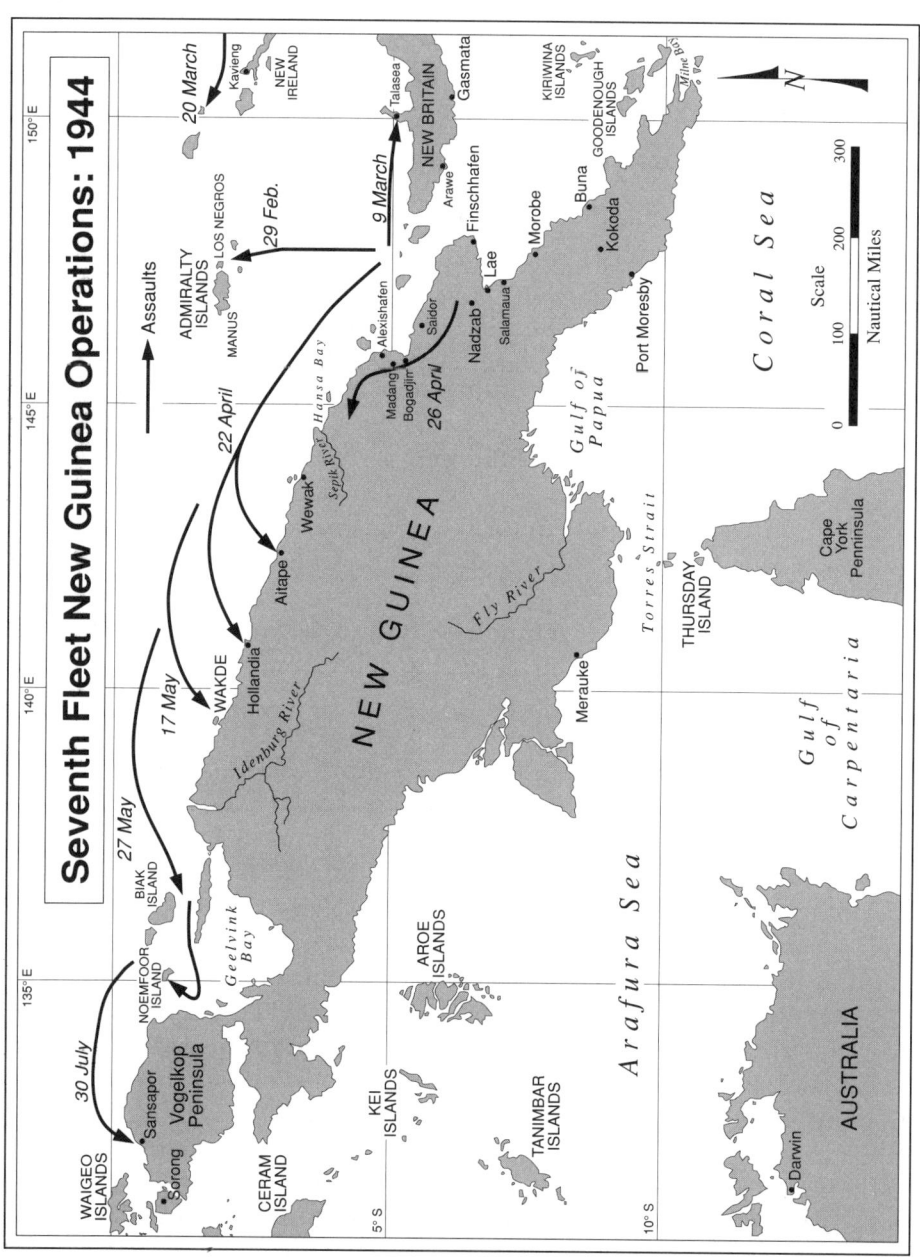

beached. Faced with a series of operations, the Seventh Amphibious Force could not afford to lose many of its ships. Kinkaid was also aware that the Army people believed that Leary and Carpender had been unnecessarily chary of risking ships on New Guinea's north coast.

The admiral's approach was to sit down on General MacArthur's veranda at Port Moresby and explain his problem forthrightly. He noted that Army fighter squadrons preferred to wait on the ground and then "scramble" when the enemy was reported inbound. The Navy preferred to keep a fighter CAP orbiting above its ships when an operation was being protected by carriers. He also noted that Army runways can be repaired when suffering bomb hits; ships often sink when struck by bombs. MacArthur understood and promised that Barbey would receive more fighter coverage than he had ever seen before. General Kenney's fighters filled MacArthur's promise admirably, but they were unable to prevent the loss of *Brownson* (DD 518) and damage to *Lamson* (DD 367), *Shaw* (DD 373), *Mugford*, and LSTs *66* and *202* due to air attacks at Cape Gloucester.[20]

Neither Kinkaid nor Barbey was satisfied with past command arrangements during operations. General Krueger and his troop commanders believed that the Army officer charged with carrying out an amphibious landing should be in charge of the whole show. The Navy officer present, admiral or not, was there to drive the ships and see that they got to the right destination. Kinkaid had handled this situation differently in Alaska, and he proposed to MacArthur that a change be made. He wanted the attack force commander, the officer in charge of the naval forces, to remain in command until the troops were ashore and set up to command their own affairs. At that point the troop commander ashore would take charge, and the amphibious commander would be concerned only with his ships. Again MacArthur saw the point and all operation plans, starting with Arawe's (Op Plan 3A–43), contained a transfer of command paragraph. Barbey also pressed to have the amphibious commander charged with coordinating the planning process for an operation, but here the Army dug in its heels. It wasn't until four months later that Kinkaid was able to convince the general that Admiral Barbey, or a designated attack force commander, should coordinate planning for an operation. Such plans were, of course, to be reviewed by MacArthur, Krueger, Kenney, and Kinkaid.[21]

During the first days of the Cape Gloucester operation, General Krueger became concerned that the schedule for amphibious shipping was too

---

[20] TCK oral history, 273–76; Daniel E. Barbey, *MacArthur's Amphibious Navy: Seventh Amphibious Force Operations, 1943–1945* (Annapolis: Naval Institute Press, 1969), 122.

[21] Administrative History: COMSWPA, 67–69, OA; TCK oral history, 85; Miller, *Cartwheel*, 316–17; COM7THFLT to CINCSWPA, Brisbane, 4 Apr 1944, TCK Papers.

tight, and he proposed that the landing at Saidor not be carried out on 2 January as planned. The assault area, about 110 miles west of Finschhafen, was important to MacArthur's plans because he hoped to trap a large number of Japanese troops who were retreating toward Saidor from Finschhafen. A delay might mean the Japanese would escape. Kinkaid joined MacArthur in the argument against Krueger. He promised the Sixth Army commander that the Navy would see that his supplies and troops arrived safely and on schedule. He agreed with MacArthur that SWPA forces were developing momentum and he didn't want to see it lost. He did not use the argument related by Admiral Barbey that Army commanders were often uncomfortable unless they were sure the beaches could be piled high with supplies within a few hours of landing, even if it was impossible to move the pile for several days. In the end Krueger's troops hit Saidor on schedule, and the Navy delivered the supplies as promised.[22]

While MacArthur's forces were invading New Britain and Saidor, Kinkaid remained at the advanced base headquarters in Port Moresby. He had accompanied the general north from Brisbane on 12 December and remained with him until their return on 4 January. In Port Moresby the admiral lived comfortably. His large tropical house was open, screened all around, with a broad shaded veranda on three sides. He and his aide, Lieutenant David F. Freeman, had separate bedrooms with attached showers, plus a bedroom for "visiting firemen." His office area was on the porch. The dining area would seat a dozen and was handy for staff meetings. Malaria had been pretty much eradicated from the area, but everyone took atabrine daily as a precaution and slept under mosquito netting. The "huts" for his staff were close to his house and the whole compound was enclosed by a fence. MacArthur's house was about 200 yards to the east; both faced the harbor. The admiral's personal steward, "the indispensable Ho," traveled with him and oversaw his meals and wardrobe.

This was the second time the admiral had moved up to the front, the earlier trip being to Barbey's headquarters at Milne Bay. Kinkaid's assistant chief of staff, Captain Roy C. Hudson, believed that Admiral Carpender had not spent enough time visiting his forces in New Guinea, and he had urged his new boss to get out of Brisbane and become known to his troops in the field. Several times during his second trip to the New Guinea area Kinkaid dropped in at Goodenough Island where General Krueger's soldiers were preparing for the landings at Arawe and Cape Gloucester.

While at this advanced outpost with MacArthur and Krueger, they were visited by Army Chief of Staff George Marshall and Rear Admiral Charles M. (Savvy) Cooke who were taking the long route back to

---

[22] Miller, *Cartwheel,* 299; VADM D. E. Barbey to CAPT Bern Anderson, Olympia, WA, 19 Oct 1952, Barbey Papers.

Washington from the Great Powers summit meetings at Teheran and Cairo. Cooke, Admiral King's deputy chief of staff, briefed Kinkaid on affairs in Washington and let him know that King was pleased with his work in the SWPA.

Kinkaid disliked the bother of hosting "visiting firemen," but he did the job with only private grousing to his wife.[23] He told Helen that he preferred to be closer to the action than Brisbane. In Australia he was perpetually spending time that he could ill afford on matters that contributed little to defeating the enemy. Visits from "Bill and his roughnecks" (Admiral Halsey and his staff) or from "Big Fire Chief" (Admiral Nimitz), or people at the level of General Marshall, he accepted as part of the job. But he was not pleased to see Raymond Clapper (a nationally prominent journalist and radio commentator), Robert E. Sherwood (an Office of War Information director and presidential speech writer), or even major Australian officials dropping in from Canberra and Brisbane itself. Though Port Moresby was 250 miles from Milne Bay or Goodenough Island, an hour and a half flight time in his R5D (C–54), he told Helen that he still preferred "to stay here with plenty of forces at my disposal and move on to the northwestward." On staying in Brisbane he wrote, "This business of living in a hotel in a city and at the same time being mixed up in war operations is incongruous. On my mud flat at Adak everything seemed to fit into the picture. I would rather be farther forward pushing this war towards its end."[24]

Planning and operations in the SWPA did not always move ahead in an orderly manner. There had to be a certain degree of flexibility that permitted General MacArthur to make use of fresh opportunities. One such opportunity came between the Arawe and Cape Gloucester landings when Admiral Halsey proposed that his forces move against the Green Islands around 15 February. Lying about 75 miles northwest of the Solomons, air bases and patrol torpedo (PT) boat bases in the Green Islands would make it easier to control the air over Rabaul and Kavieng. If the Admiralty Islands were seized (that is, Manus and Los Negros), the Japanese in the Bismarcks could be pounded from the east and west. SWPA planners already had Manus on their schedule of invasions but had thought it should be taken after Hansa Bay in New Guinea some time in the late spring of 1944. MacArthur agreed to the Green Island operation and Halsey's planners moved ahead.[25]

---

[23] Hudson Memorandum, 18 Nov 1943; TCK to HSK, Brisbane, 2, 15, 20 Dec 1943.

[24] TCK to HSK, Brisbane, 31 Dec 1943, 7 Feb 1944, 26 Mar 1944; Paul F. Foster to RADM C. E. Van Hook, Washington, 24 Dec 1943, Clifford E. Van Hook Papers, Hoover Institution (hereafter Van Hook Papers).

[25] Miller, *Cartwheel*, 312–13.

Vice Admiral Kinkaid and General Douglas MacArthur on the flag bridge of *Phoenix* during the preinvasion bombardment of Los Negros Island, 28 February 1944.

In mid-February General Kenney provided his own suggestion for seizing an opportunity. Photographs from bombing and reconnaissance flights over Manus and Los Negros had convinced him that the Japanese had evacuated the Admiralty Islands, or at least had removed most of their troops. On 23 February he recommended to MacArthur and Kinkaid that Los Negros be seized immediately and then Manus. They decided to use about 800 troops from the 1st Cavalry Division for a landing on 29 February and to call it a "reconnaissance in force." If there were too many Japanese on the island, the assault force would be withdrawn. Kinkaid agreed to the operation and directed Barbey to use three APDs (destroyer transports) with an escort force of four destroyers. The planning, according to Kinkaid, was accomplished "in just four days." By the time the "reconnaissance in force" left Oro Bay, the number of troops had grown to 1,026. Because General MacArthur wanted to observe the operation, Kinkaid brought in the light cruisers *Phoenix* (CL 46) and *Nashville* plus another division of destroyers. He and the general rode *Phoenix* to the scene of action, and MacArthur experienced at close quarters his first naval bombardment in support of an assault. He was "extremely impressed." In fact Kinkaid later reported that the general became such a naval gunfire enthusiast that Kinkaid occasionally "had to emphasize to [him] the things that naval gunfire could *not* do."[26]

In the afternoon of the first day of the Los Negros operation MacArthur, Kinkaid, and several of the general's staff went ashore to observe the action first hand. Though the enemy had pulled back into the bush and MacArthur and his party had military escorts, he could have been struck down by a mortar round, artillery shell, or an errant round of rifle fire. The general was apparently unconcerned about his personal safety. He was doing what he had always believed a military leader should do: let his troops see him in the presence of the enemy. Along with General Krueger, who felt quite strongly that MacArthur should not even have been on board *Phoenix,* Kinkaid probably deplored this whole exercise in military bravado. He had told MacArthur that he did not believe Krueger should have been at several of the landings. For Kinkaid the rule was that the senior commanders should be close to their communications and the fighting should be in the hands of less senior flag officers. On the other hand, the admiral believed that a ship's captain, and even a flag officer on board a vessel under fire, had to demonstrate to the crew and staff that his mind was on the battle and not his own personal safety. So Kinkaid made the rounds on Los Negros with the general, probably wondering how he would explain to Admiral King were a Japanese sniper to wound MacArthur.

The admiral's attitude was caught in a candid photo near the Momote airfield where they had come upon a couple of dead Japanese. MacArthur had seen plenty of dead enemy soldiers in his career. While not smiling or prancing around, he let those present know, "That's the way I like to see them." Kinkaid's countenance was what one might expect from an admiral who had never seen a dead Japanese soldier: stunned and revolted. He was happy to get back to his flagship.[27]

MacArthur's presence at Los Negros, and Kinkaid's as well, was probably necessary. MacArthur had stuck his neck out in ordering the early seizure of Los Negros. As he stated candidly, "I was relying almost entirely upon surprise for success and, because of the delicate nature of the operation and the immediate decision required, I accompanied the force aboard Admiral Kinkaid's flagship." The decision was to stay, and the general directed Kinkaid to have the reinforcements brought up. There were actually more than 4,000 Japanese troops on Los Negros,

---

[26] Miller, *Cartwheel,* 320–36; Barbey, *MacArthur's Amphibs,* 144–48, 151–53; George C. Kenney, *General Kenney Reports: A Personal History of the Pacific War* (New York: Duell, Sloan & Pearce, 1949), 358–62; TCK to HSK, Pt. Moresby, 1 Mar 1944; James, *MacArthur* 2:380–83; Walter Karig, Russell L. Harris and Frank Manson, *Battle Report: The End of an Empire,* vol. 4 (New York: Rinehart, 1948), 167, 172.

[27] Krueger, *Sixth Army,* 49; James, *MacArthur* 2:384–87 and photo section; and photo section in Clark Lee and Richard Henschel, *Douglas MacArthur* (New York: Henry Holt, 1952).

though they were somewhat bomb-happy from the pounding they had received in the past month. It required some desperate fighting by Major General William C. Chase's cavalrymen to turn a shoestring operation into a complete success. It was the last amphibious assault that MacArthur was to order where the defenders would outnumber the attackers throughout the first day of fighting.[28]

Historians have noted that General MacArthur's decision to risk an early assault on the Admiralty Islands was grounded in a larger issue of grand strategy. Briefly, during the first six weeks of 1944, the general had believed that his strategic vision had a good chance of acceptance by the Joint Chiefs of Staff and the Combined Chiefs of Staff. He had dared to hope that the Solomons–New Guinea–Philippines route to Japan would become the only line of action against Japan and that he would gain supreme command of all armed forces in the Pacific war.[29] In late January Sutherland, Kinkaid, and Kenney, assisted by senior members of their staffs, flew to Pearl Harbor for a Pacific Strategy Conference on 27–28 January. From General Kenney's viewpoint, the 27th was "a regular love feast." Except for Vice Admiral Soc McMorris, Nimitz's chief of staff, the principal naval leaders, including Nimitz, Kinkaid, and Vice Admiral John Towers, Commander Naval Air Forces, Pacific (COMAIRPAC), fell in with MacArthur's plans as presented by Sutherland. Once the conference closed, General Sutherland and Rear Admiral Forrest P. Sherman (Nimitz's war plans officer) flew to Washington to sell the package to the JCS. Reporting to MacArthur, Kenney thought "the scheme was in the bag." Though pleased, MacArthur preferred to see how Sutherland made out in Washington.[30]

It was well that General MacArthur had reserved his enthusiasm, for his chief of staff "ran into a stone wall named King." He also found that General Henry H. (Hap) Arnold, the Army Air Corps Chief of Staff, was firmly on the side of Admiral King and his plans to invade the Mariana Islands as a part of the Central Pacific thrust by the Navy. General Arnold now had B–29 Superfortresses to use against Japan, and he planned to launch them from Guam and Tinian. In the end MacArthur's move cost him nothing; in fact it provided an opportunity to have his ideas on Pacific strategy considered at the highest military levels in Hawaii and Washington. On the other hand, both Nimitz and Kinkaid dropped in the personal estimate of Admiral King.[31]

---

[28] Douglas MacArthur, *Reminiscences* (New York: McGraw-Hill, 1964), 187–89; Miller, *Cartwheel*, 325–32; *Reports of MacArthur* 1:136–40.

[29] Potter, *Nimitz*, 282; Edwin Hoyt, *How They Won the War in the Pacific: Nimitz and His Admirals* (New York: Waybright & Talley, 1970), 329; Spector, *Eagle Against the Sun*, 276.

[30] Hayes, *History of the JCS*, 343–52; Kenney, *Reports*, 347–49; Clark G. Reynolds, *The Fast Carriers: The Forging of an Air Navy* (New York: McGraw-Hill, 1968), 116–19.

[31] Potter, *Nimitz*, 280–83; Buell, *King*, 440–47.

Staff officers attending the 27–28 January 1944 Pacific Strategy Conference at Pearl Harbor, left to right: Captain C. D. Glover, Jr., Major General Richard J. Marshall, Lietanant General George Kenney, Lieutenant General Richard K. Sutherland, Vice Admiral Kinkaid, Rear Admiral Forrest P. Sherman, Major General Stephan J. Chamberlin.

By the end of February MacArthur was looking for an opportunity to further demonstrate the soundness of his strategic thinking. Having received hints from Washington that his New Guinea campaign might be slowed while forces were built up for invasions of Kavieng and the Admiralties, he seized the initiative with the "reconnaissance in force" into Los Negros. Now, after that success, he proposed to bypass Hansa Bay and jump to Hollandia, farther west on the north coast to New Guinea. Since the Marianas invasion could not be mounted before June, he thought it possible to have the Pacific Fleet support his next move. He might not be the supreme commander of the Pacific, but he would try to use the Pacific Fleet as if he were.[32]

---

[32] Hayes, *History of JCS*, 554; Smith, *Approach to the Philippines*, 1–12; James, *MacArthur* 2:381–82; D. M. Horner, *High Command: Australia and Allied Strategy, 1939–1945* (Boston: George Allen & Unwin, 1982), 307–8.

Probably the most important product of the Pearl Harbor and Washington Pacific strategy meetings was the creation of a new JCS operations timetable for the forces under Nimitz and MacArthur. This schedule was laid out in JCS document 713/1, dated 10 March 1944 and issued on 12 March. In it three important problems were addressed that were of great concern to MacArthur and Kinkaid: (1) Was the final advance across the Pacific to be by the Admiralties–New Guinea–Mindanao–Luzon route, General MacArthur's proposal; or by a Marshalls–Marianas–Palaus–Formosa route, Admiral King's proposal? (2) What was to be the target area in the Far East? and (3) What was to be the schedule of operations?

The debate over the route to the target area (Luzon or Formosa) was finally concluded in JCS 713/1: Both routes would be used. The question of a single commander in chief for the final stages in the Pacific was finessed by the JCS. By formally establishing a two-axis approach, MacArthur and Nimitz would continue as before, and the JCS would exercise supreme command over both. Nimitz was not concerned; MacArthur was not pleased. The document did make it clear that priority in shipping and naval construction would still be given to Nimitz's forces; but it was equally obvious that Pacific Fleet carriers and battleships would be used in support of SWPA operations.

From the early March discussions in Washington, and JCS 713, one can conclude that there were two target areas under discussion. The ultimate goal of the whole Pacific war was the final destruction of the "Japanese Citadel," made up of Korea, Manchuria and Japan. To accomplish this, Japan's support from the Southern Resources Area (the East Indies and mainland Southeast Asia) had to be eliminated. This required control of the Luzon–Formosa–China coast line. Admiral King believed that gaining control of Formosa, and possibly bypassing Luzon, would be the most efficacious means of severing Japan's lines of communication (LOC) to Southeast Asia. General MacArthur was equally convinced that seizure of the Philippines would also lead to severance of these LOCs. Silent on a campaign to take Luzon, JCS 713/1 did point MacArthur's command toward Mindanao. The general would "return," and he undoubtedly believed that his momentum would carry him north to Luzon.

The schedule of operations, including what would be captured and what would be bypassed, also emerged in JCS 713/1. For Nimitz the decision was finally made that Truk would be bypassed, and the southern Marianas (Guam, Tinian, Rota, and Saipan) would be assaulted by 15 June. Then Yap and Palau islands would follow by 15 September. With U.S. naval bases and bomber fields at Eniwetok in the Marshalls, on Guam, and in the Palau Islands, the Japanese naval bastion at Truk would become useless. And with the mid-Pacific area and New Guinea in American control, the Japanese forces in the Solomons and Bismarcks would be cut off in their tropical bases. The SWPA timetable was reasonably simple: Hollandia by 15 April and Mindanao by 15 November. During the seven months in between SWPA forces were expected to proceed to the Vogelkop and capture whatever intervening objectives were needed to allow them an unobstructed campaign against Mindanao. For Admiral Kinkaid's forces it meant five major amphibious assaults before the landings in the Philippines at Leyte.[33]

While Manus was being cleared of its Japanese defenders and the Joint Chiefs were arguing over the next moves for Nimitz and MacArthur, the general provoked a crisis in Army-Navy relations in the SWPA. He had received from Nimitz a copy of the admiral's proposal to the JCS to have Admiral Halsey's Seabees build a great naval base in Seeadler Harbor on Manus for the Seventh Fleet and Nimitz's forces. MacArthur was furious at his further proposal that Halsey and his Seabees do this work under Nimitz's direction. The general saw Nimitz's move as a backdoor means of taking control of a base within the SWPA and also of reasserting command over an admiral (Halsey) who worked for MacArthur. The general would have none of it; in fact, he would close Seeadler Harbor to all but the Seventh Fleet and other ships under his command.

Recognizing the foolish nature of the issue, Admiral Kinkaid got MacArthur to invite Halsey to Brisbane to thrash out the problem. At three sessions on 3 and 4 March, the general expostulated at length on these attacks on his authority, leadership, and even honor. Eventually Kinkaid, Halsey, and SWPA staffers reached an agreement to let Nimitz and the JCS know that they believed the naval base should be under SWPA control but open for use by all naval forces.[34]

It is hard not to conclude that General MacArthur's concern about control of the Seeadler Harbor naval base was simply another instance of vanity and ego overriding sound military judgment, or even common sense. To Kinkaid, this was another instance of Army paranoia over naval proposals. Occasionally he let off steam about these matters in letters to his wife: "Working in an Army organization is extremely difficult. . . . I try to fit in with their methods and organization but they are a bunch of horse traders and horse thieves and don't know the meaning of cooperation. They do not cooperate among themselves and therefore cannot be expected to cooperate with others." A few weeks later, he again lamented:

---

[33] Hayes, *History of the JCS*, 551–60; Smith, *Approach to the Philippines*, 9–12; James, *MacArthur* 2:391–95; King and Whitehill, *Fleet Admiral King*, 443–44; Matloff, *Strategic Planning*, 455–59.

[34] Potter, *Bull Halsey*, 265–66; James, *MacArthur* 2:388–91; Miller, *Cartwheel*, 349–50; Forrest C. Pogue, *George C. Marshall: Organizer of Victory*, vol. 3 (New York: Viking Press, 1973), 441–42; Halsey and Bryan, *Admiral Halsey's Story*, 188–90.

I am shocked at the things I find here. It has taken me five months of talking fast to convince MacArthur that I am not trying to steal the Army's shirt every time I make a suggestion. At least he claims he is convinced. But the small boys all the way down the line are suspicious of everything. I often wonder if they spend more time on studying how to put something over on the Navy than how to lick the Japs.[35]

Captain Ray D. Tarbuck, a Navy captain assigned to the war plans division of MacArthur's staff, provided an interesting perspective on Army-Navy relations in mid-1944:

The Army staff was very suspicious of the Navy. As a UP [United Press] man told me in Brisbane, "The war between the Yanks and the Japs is only exceeded by the war between the Army and the Navy." I would have no part of it. Biggest anti-Army agitator was Captain Cruzen on Kinkaid's staff. Biggest anti-Navy agitator was General Kenney. The arrival of Kinkaid started a new policy of co-existence, but he soon fell under the influence of the system. . . .[36]

Captain Tarbuck was wrong when he suggested that Kinkaid fell in with the prevailing attitudes and joined the internecine warfare. In his almost daily letters to his wife he would occasionally explode about a person, or "the system," but he worked to develop a cooperative spirit among the services. General Kenney did exasperate him, but even there he tried to keep the waters calm.

In time, when all of them were in the field, particularly in Hollandia and Tacloban, they found it much easier to conduct business among themselves. Perhaps men like Sutherland, Kenney, and Charles A. Willoughby were reacting to Brisbane and the war in the same manner as Kinkaid whose letters indicated that he found Brisbane dull, dirty and sterile. Except for a few families that he got to know well, he considered the people distinctly unattractive. He didn't understand the politics, particularly the Socialist positions, and the ability of labor unions to strike despite the pressures of war outraged him. Though he often had free time, the admiral did not go to the symphony, ballet, opera, or plays when they were available. About the only socializing he did was attend dinner parties, or occasionally give small ones in his apartment at Lennon's Hotel, but these too bored him. His cultural life before the war had been managed by his wife, but Helen was 9,000 miles away in Philadelphia. Able to go anywhere he wished in Australia, Kinkaid never went to Melbourne, made only one overnight trip to Sydney, and flew across the continent to Perth on just one occasion.

---

[35] TCK to HSK, Brisbane, 27 Apr 1944; Pt. Moresby, 3 May 1944.
[36] Tarbuck to Barbey, 19 May 1961, Barbey Papers.

Perhaps what bothered Admiral Kinkaid, more than any issue with which he had to deal, was the fact that he missed Helen—they had been apart for more than two years. For the Kinkaids, who had no children and depended on one another for support, wartime separation was particularly frustrating. At their age (he was fifty-six in April 1944) they did not want to waste precious years. This was a burden particularly for the older serviceman at war. Many of those who had been with MacArthur from the beginning of the war—the Bataan Gang—shared these problems with Kinkaid. Their inability to get along with non-Army types is understandable. In today's argot many in the SWPA leadership suffered from burnout.

The successful assault against the Admiralty Islands, in itself an opportunistic venture, led General MacArthur to propose other alterations to the JCS schedule of operations in the SWPA. On 4 March he requested permission to bypass the Wewak–Hansa Bay region and make Humboldt Bay–Hollandia–Tanemerah Bay the next target for 15 April. This operation, code-named RECKLESS, would include a simultaneous landing at Aitape, about 120 miles east of Hollandia. Because landings at Tanemerah Bay and Humboldt Bay would be beyond the reach of Fifth Air Force fighter squadrons, MacArthur stated that he would need carrier aircraft support from the Pacific Fleet to defend the beachheads. The request was necessary because the Seventh Fleet had no carriers of its own. The JCS approved this proposal and simplified the operations by canceling the mid-April assault on Kavieng. It was believed that aircraft from Los Negros, Emirau in the St. Matthias Islands, and the Green Islands could prevent any aerial interference at Hollandia from the Japanese in Rabaul or Kavieng.[37]

Planning for the three landings was left to the staffs of Admiral Barbey and General Krueger, but the precise naval assistance from Admiral Nimitz's Pacific Fleet was a matter for negotiation. Dissatisfied with responses he had received from CINCPAC's staff, Kinkaid proposed to MacArthur that Admiral Nimitz be invited to Brisbane for consultation. Because Sutherland, Kenney, and Kinkaid had made the trip to Pearl Harbor in January, Kinkaid told the general that it was Nimitz's turn to do the visiting. He had a message prepared to extend the invitation and MacArthur agreed with the idea. Nimitz accepted immediately and, a few days later, set the date.[38]

Most would agree that this visit of state by the Commander in Chief, Pacific Ocean Areas to the Supreme Commander Southwest Pacific Area was a complete success. The admiral and his retinue arrived on 25 March and MacArthur and Kinkaid were at the seaplane dock to greet them. Nimitz

---

[37] Willoughby, comp., *Reports of MacArthur* 1:142–3; Smith, *Approach to the Philippines*, 13–20; Morison 8:61–64.

[38] TCK oral history, 261–63; dispatches, MacArthur to Nimitz, 3/1501152, and Nimitz to MacArthur, 15 Mar 1944, Douglas MacArthur Papers, MacArthur Museum, Norfolk, VA (hereafter MacArthur Papers).

came bearing gifts: orchids for Mrs. MacArthur, candy and a playsuit for young Arthur. The general laid on a grand dinner at Lennon's with forty-eight of the highest ranking officers in the area in attendance. The second evening Kinkaid's stewards prepared a Chinese dinner for the general and his wife; Admiral Nimitz; Rear Admiral Forrest Sherman (CINCPAC's plans officer); Rear Admiral Clifford E. Van Hook, Deputy Commander Seventh Fleet; Rear Admiral Robert B. Carney, Halsey's chief of staff; and Commodore Homer W. Graf, Kinkaid's chief of staff. Both dinners went well, as did the small dinner that the general gave in his apartment on the third evening. By the end of the visit Kinkaid had had his fill of conferences, but he had to admit that much had been accomplished.[39]

There was no hesitancy on CINCPAC's part about furnishing carrier support for RECKLESS; the problem was how long they could stay. Until the Hollandia area airfields could be seized and put into operation, land-based fighter planes would find it difficult to protect the beaches and the ships. Their bases were too far east. Task Force 58, which then included a dozen of the Pacific Fleet's fast carriers, would be raiding the Palau Islands three weeks before the Hollandia operation. This raid should eliminate any Japanese aircraft that might move down to western New Guinea (the Vogelkop) and then against Hollandia. After the Palau raid Vice Admiral Marc Mitscher would bring TF 58 to the New Guinea coast to sweep the area of Japanese planes and assist in whatever way it could. But Nimitz did not want his fast carriers being held in one place for too many days. They would be sure to attract all of the land-based bombers and torpedo-carrying aircraft the Japanese could send. To assist the Seventh Fleet, once the fast carriers departed on the second day, two "jeep carrier" groups (eight CVEs) would remain in the area for at least another week.

As his part of the negotiation, General Kenney promised that his Fifth Air Force squadrons would eliminate the estimated 300 or so aircraft to the west of the Hollandia area before the operation. Kenney's word was as good as gold in this matter, but MacArthur was about the only one present who had confidence in his statement. To provide a margin of safety, the landing at Aitape was designed to capture an airfield that could be used by Kenney's fighter squadrons. The assumption was that the air base could be taken and made operational on the first or second day.[40]

As the date of the Hollandia operation approached, now postponed to 22 April, MacArthur and several of his senior staff departed on 18 April for Port Moresby and then Finschafen, where he would board *Nashville* and participate in RECKLESS. Kinkaid didn't believe that both

---

[39] James, *MacArthur* 2:399–402; Potter, *Nimitz*, 389–92; Reynolds, *Fast Carriers*, 146; TCK to HSK, Brisbane, 25, 26, 27, 28 Mar 1944.

[40] James, *MacArthur* 2:400–401; Potter, *Nimitz*, 389–92; Smith, *Approach to the Philippines*, 16–26; Barbey, *MacArthur's Amphibs*, 158–66; Kenney, *Reports*, 377.

the Supreme Commander and General Krueger needed to be at the scene of action, but he probably was not consulted. Kinkaid himself didn't move to Port Moresby until the 20th, and he remained there, close to his communications, throughout the whole operation. A few weeks later he explained in a memorandum for the general why he felt Krueger (and MacArthur by inference) should not take a destroyer to the next operation, an assault on Wakde Island:

> I can see no earthly reason why the Commander, Attack Force, should be saddled with this additional hazard [the presence of Krueger]. It is a definite hazard for, in addition to taking a badly needed destroyer from the scene the presence of General Krueger is a mental hazard both to the Commander, Attack Force, and the Commander, Landing Force; he does interfere despite his protests to the contrary and the best of intentions; and some day there will be a flare-up which is distinctly not desirable and might actually be detrimental to operations.[41]

Given the fact that General MacArthur observed the prelanding bombardment of the beaches in Humboldt Bay from *Nashville* and then went ashore to see for himself how the operation was going, it is ironic to read Kinkaid's 21 April letter to Helen:

> There is one thing about being here [in Port Moresby] that is definitely an asset. Except on occasion when dispatches have to be acted on, a full night's rest is assured. At my age . . . there is nothing that can do as much toward keeping fit and feeling good as turning in early.[42]

The admiral, of course, was eight years younger than his boss.

Despite its complicated nature the Hollandia operation went exceptionally well from Kinkaid's perspective. Mitscher's raids on the Palau Islands had eliminated a large number of Japanese aircraft that might have replaced those destroyed by Kenney's airmen. The raids had also driven the Japanese surface forces farther west, taking them out of range for any realistic attempt to interfere with the landings. As a result of these prior activities, Kinkaid could release Mitscher's fast carriers after two days, though eight CVEs would remain for another week—Carrier Division 22 under Rear Admiral Van H. Ragsdale: *Sangamon* (CVE 26), *Suwannee* (CVE 27), *Chenango* (CVE 28), *Santee* (CVE 29); and Carrier Division 24 under Rear Admiral Ralph E. Davison: *Natoma Bay* (CVE 62), *Coral Sea* (CVE 57), *Corregidor* (CVE 58), *Manila Bay* (CVE 61).

---

[41] TCK, "Memo General MacArthur," 3 May 1944, Kinkaid Papers; James, *MacArthur* 2:450; TCK to HSK, Pt. Moresby, 20 Apr 1944.
[42] TCK to HSK, Pt. Moresby, 21 Apr 1944.

Control over the Hollandia area and its three airfields was established more quickly than expected. On the other hand, the landings at Aitape led to a prolonged battle with the Japanese who were caught between SWPA armies to the east and those that had just landed. Unfortunately for the Japanese, Navy control of the sea off New Guinea meant that fresh troops and supplies could be fed to the U.S. Army ashore while the Japanese depleted their munitions and food resources. Time obviously was on the side of the SWPA troopers.[43] General MacArthur's communiqué of 24 April, although premature in terms of the Aitape area, accurately summarized the bleak future of the cut-off Japanese:

> The operation throws a loop of envelopment around the enemy's Eighteenth Army dispersed along the coast of New Guinea in the Madang, Alexishafen, Hansa Bay, Wewak sectors, similar to the Solomons and Bismarck loops of envelopment. To the east are the Australians and Americans, to the west Americans; to the north the sea controlled by our Allied naval forces; to the south untraversed jungle mountain ranges; and over all our Allied air mastery. The enemy is now completely isolated.[44]

The purpose behind the seizure of the Hollandia area was to provide a major base of operations for the final six-month drive toward the Philippines. From its field headquarters at Port Moresby, MacArthur's staff finished planning its next moves against Wakde Island, Biak Island, Noemfoor Island, and Sansapor, all a part of the New Guinea campaign. Planning actually went on constantly in GHQ, Kinkaid's headquarters, Barbey's command ship, and General Krueger's headquarters at Finschhafen. With the pace of operations accelerating, plans for future ones were drafted before a current campaign had been concluded.

Because there had been a considerable troop buildup on New Guinea as divisions were moved from the Solomons or arrived from stateside, there were periods of rest for the soldiers. Not every regiment had to take part in every landing. On the other hand, though staffs grew in size, those in the planning and logistics divisions worked steadily. The same was true for the fighting ships. The same cruisers, destroyers, and landing craft were called on week after week. This constant use meant the crews could not be properly rested and maintenance on the vessels was kept to a minimum. Drydocking for repairs and exterior hull cleaning was done by Seventh Fleet Service Force floating drydocks and repair ships, but it was hard to spare the time for the vessels to go to Brisbane

---

[43] Smith, *Approach to the Philippines*, 53–83, 103–205; Morison 8:49–90; Willoughby, comp., *Reports of MacArthur* 1:146–49; James, *MacArthur* 2:445–54; Krueger, *Sixth Army*, 56–75.

[44] Willoughby, comp., *Reports of MacArthur* 1:146–47.

or Sydney for the traditional rest and recreation. Recreation for troops and naval crews therefore had to take place in the field. Movies, athletics, and visiting troupes of entertainers sent by the ubiquitous United Services Organization were the most organized approaches. There were of course occasional "beer busts," but cargo space was still too precious to provide the amount of beer and soft drinks required.[45]

Following the Hollandia operation, SWPA forces began preparations to seize Wakde and Biak islands. Plans for both operations had been roughly laid out by the time troops splashed ashore for RECKLESS. When RECKLESS had appeared to be going so well on the first day, General MacArthur proposed that the reserve force, floating offshore, immediately be sent to seize Wakde. Admiral Barbey said that he was ready to go, but Krueger was hesitant and General Eichelberger was hostile to the plan. He believed the Japanese could cause some serious problems around Lake Sentani and the reserve might be needed. In the end MacArthur deferred to his field commanders. It is probably just as well that Wakde wasn't attacked on 23 April. Records later showed that the Japanese had more troops at the island and on the shore near it than were present three weeks later when Wakde was attacked.[46]

At one point between the Hollandia and Wakde operations, Kinkaid and MacArthur remained in Port Moresby, which was only an hour and a half from Krueger's headquarters at Finschhafen and 700 miles from the action at Hollandia and Aitape. Communications to the field and to Brisbane were excellent, and there were regular flights to Brisbane for mail purposes. When time was available, Kinkaid visited the general's porch to exchange ideas or simply to smoke. On 30 April, during such a visit, the admiral was startled when MacArthur bared his political soul. On the previous day he had issued a public statement that he had never been a candidate for the presidency, and, were the nomination offered to him, he would refuse it. As he smoked with Kinkaid he elaborated on his views. Kinkaid reported this to his wife:

> I have never mentioned politics to him because I thought it was none of my business, but this morning he opened the conversation by saying that he was annoyed by "these political things." He said that he had never been in the running and had tried to make it clear but that everything he said was turned around and misconstrued, etc. He said that it was obvious that a general at the front in time of war could not be a candidate for such a

---

[45] TCK to HSK, Pt. Moresby, 2 May 1944; Krueger, *Sixth Army*, 77–78.
[46] Barbey to CAPT Bern Anderson, Olympia, WA, 8 Aug 1952; Anderson to Barbey, Newport, RI, 11 Aug 1952, Barbey Papers. In his personal account of Seventh Amphibs operations, Barbey ignored the information Captain Anderson provided and argued that an earlier attack would have been easier. See Barbey, *MacArthur's Amphibs*, 190–91; also Morison 8:94.

position, that he had no qualifications for the job unless it was that of honesty and he would be like putty in the hands of the politicians who do not go in strong for honesty, that he thought a 42 year old ex-District Attorney [Thomas Dewey of New York] did not have much chance against Roosevelt that because of the war situation he thought the President should be reelected although he did not approve of him or believe that any man should have a fourth term in the White House.[47]

That was the only time Kinkaid mentioned anything concerning MacArthur and politics. It is doubtful that the admiral seriously believed that General MacArthur would be "putty in the hands" of anyone.

In early May, when the Wakde plans were in the distribution stage and the Biak planning was well advanced, Kinkaid returned to Brisbane. The Wakde operation (STRAIGHT LINE) was scheduled for 17 May with the HORLICKS Biak operation ten days later. Wakde and its airfield plus two airfields on nearby New Guinea were needed for two reasons: for basing aircraft to support the Biak invasion, and for keeping the Japanese from using the airfields against the Hollandia area. The seizure of Wakde, about 115 miles west of Humboldt Bay and lying two miles off the coast, was estimated to be a quick operation. Wakde and Biak had been bombed regularly during the buildup for Hollandia, and Mitscher's carriers had given them some attention when TF 58 was in the area. Because Admiral Barbey was on leave, Rear Admiral William M. Fechteler oversaw STRAIGHT LINE and Captain Albert G. Noble commanded the attack force that put troops ashore opposite Wakde on 17 May. The next day small craft carried the invaders to the island. The defenders were quickly wiped out, and the Wakde airfield was ready to handle its first fighter squadrons on 21 May. The runways were immediately lengthened so that B–24s could be based there for reconnaissance and bombing missions against Japanese concentrations in the Vogelkop, the Palau Islands, and air bases on Yap and Woleai.[48]

Prior to the Wakde operation Kinkaid decided it was time to visit his forces in western Australia. Taking only his aide, Lieutenant David Freeman, with him, he flew the eleven hours overnight and landed at Perth in the morning of 13 May. Admiral Christie saw that he was properly fed and had a good visit to the submarine base at Fremantle. Kinkaid liked what he saw of the city.

> Perth is just as lovely as everyone has said it is. It is a sprawling city with wide streets, attractive houses . . . and is spotlessly clean. The residential

---
[47] TCK to HSK, Pt. Moresby, 30 Apr 1944; James, *MacArthur* 2:422–40.
[48] Smith, *Approach to the Philippines*, 206–8; Willoughby, comp., *Reports of MacArthur* 1:150–52; Barbey, *MacArthur's Amphibs*, 185–91.

Author's collection

Lieutenant David F. Freeman, aide to Admiral Kinkaid, shares a smoke with natives at Port Moresby, New Guinea.

section up on a hill is charming and has a lovely view of the city and the river. The water front is clean and attractive. . . . It is so different from Brisbane with its unattractive houses and muddy river.[49]

Kinkaid's trip to Australia's west coast was timed to permit a visit to Exmouth on the 14th and 15th. Located 750 miles north of Perth-Fremantle, the naval operating base on Exmouth Gulf was used by Christie's submarines as a refueling stop when departing for or returning from patrols to the South China Sea. Earlier in the war a predecessor of Christie's had tried to establish a submarine operating base on Exmouth Gulf, but it proved ill-conceived. Kinkaid and Christie found a large portion of the British Eastern Fleet at Exmouth, including the carrier *Illustrious* and America's venerable *Saratoga*. *Sara* had already participated in a strike on Sabang in Sumatra a month earlier, and now the fleet was preparing to hit Soerabaya. The strike was designed to coincide with the Wakde landing and thus discourage the Japanese from sending a naval force to interfere with MacArthur's operation. Kinkaid, Christie and Commodore C. J.

---

[49] TCK to HSK, Perth, 13 May 1944.

Pope, RAN, the naval officer in charge at Exmouth, rode out to the battleship *Queen Elizabeth* and visited with Admiral Sir James F. Somerville, the commander in chief of the Eastern Fleet. It was little more than a social call, but Kinkaid apparently believed it was worth the trip. The attack on Soerabaya two days later was reasonably successful though it did not seem to influence Japanese behavior toward the Wakde and Biak invasions.[50]

The landings at Biak on 27 May began an operation that provided a change of pace for the Seventh Fleet. For a year SWPA amphibious operations had taken place without significant enemy naval opposition. Occasional Japanese submarines would enter an area where an assault was occurring, or land-based naval aircraft would make sporadic appearances, but on the whole the Japanese navy had remained clear of the New Guinea coast from Milne Bay to Wakde. With evidence pointing to an assault against Biak, leaders of the Imperial Navy felt it had to take action. The SWPA's purpose in seizing Biak was to use its three airfields for operating heavy bombers against the Palau Islands and Halmahera on the road to Mindanao, and also to assist the Central Pacific Force (Fifth Fleet) when it attacked the Mariana Islands. The Japanese needed Biak to operate as an air base protecting the Palau Islands and to block any American approach into the Celebes Sea region south of the Philippines and north of the Celebes Islands. Used effectively, Biak could help block farther westward movement by MacArthur's forces.

When the Americans landed on Biak, the Japanese navy decided to reinforce the garrison by rushing some 2,500 soldiers to the island by cruisers and destroyers. Rear Admiral Naomasa Sakonju used two cruisers and three destroyers to ferry the troops, and his force was covered by the battleship *Fuso* plus two cruisers and five destroyers. The Japanese had sufficient naval power to fight their way to Biak, and the expedition had an air umbrella of almost 200 fighters and bombers specially assembled for the operation. While en route, on 3 June Sakonju's force was sighted and reported by Seventh Fleet submarines and reconnaissance aircraft. Convinced that surprise was necessary for success, the Japanese admiral withdrew his force that evening.[51]

At the time of the original landings on Biak the Seventh Fleet provided two covering forces: Force A (TF 74) was commanded by Rear Admiral Victor A. C. Crutchley, RN, and consisted of the Australian heavy cruisers *Australia* and *Shropshire* and four destroyers, two of which were Australian. The other covering force, Force B (TF 75), was commanded by Rear Admiral Russell S. Berkey and included the light cruisers *Phoenix, Nashville,*

---

[50] Blair, *Silent Victory*, 2:600–602; Reynolds, *Fast Carriers*, 307–10; G. Hermon Gill, *Royal Australian Navy, 1942–1946*, series two, vol 2 (Adelaide: Griffin Press, 1968), 416–17.
[51] Dull, *Battle History IJN*, 302–303.

and *Boise* plus six destroyers. These covering groups alternately provided night coverage of the Biak area and withdrew toward Hollandia at daylight. On 2 and 3 June they were attacked vigorously by Japanese aircraft from the Noemfoor and Vogelkop airfields. Because American fighter planes were grounded at Wakde due to weather, the covering force had to protect itself with gunfire and by maneuvering.

On 3 June intelligence estimates convinced Admiral Kinkaid that the Japanese would try again to reinforce Biak, perhaps as early as 4 June. He ordered Crutchley and Berkey to replenish at Humboldt Bay on 3 June and then depart to arrive off Biak by sunset on 4 June. Task Forces 74 and 75 were combined into one force under Crutchley in *Australia*. *Shropshire* was now en route to Sydney for refit, so the combined force consisted of four cruisers and fourteen destroyers. Its orders were to guard Biak at night and withdraw eastward during daylight hours. The force was expected to be within interception distance if adequately warned of a Japanese daylight attempt to reinforce Biak.

During the first day's operation (4 June) Crutchley's force was attacked and *Nashville* suffered waterline damage from a near miss. The vessel stayed on station for the first night's operation, but then withdrew to Humboldt Bay for repairs. After Crutchley's Force patrolled the waters off Biak for four nights, occasionally attacked by Japanese aircraft when the moonlight was bright enough, Kinkaid informed Crutchley on 7 June that another Japanese reinforcement convoy was headed for Biak. Admiral Sakonju was en route with two cruisers and six destroyers with 2,500 soldiers on board or being towed in barges. At midday B–25s from Hollandia attacked the Japanese and sank one destroyer and badly damaged another. But the Japanese continued toward Biak. Just before midnight Sakonju learned the size of the American force awaiting him and decided again that retreat was the better part of valor. Then ensued the Battle of Biak, a three-hour stern chase that did little for Crutchley's force except expend its fuel and ammunition and increase its frustration. His ships were ready for a fight, but the Japanese were not.

For the Army ashore on Biak, the action was a success. They did not need any more Japanese added to the bitterly resisting forces there. Unlike the Wakde operation, HORLICKS took almost a month to conclude. In fighting to the bitter end, the Japanese kept the U.S. Navy from using Biak against them during the Marianas invasion and the resultant Battle of the Philippine Sea.[52]

To Kinkaid's Seventh Fleet, particularly its Seventh Amphibious Force, the conclusion of fighting on Biak simply meant that it was free for the

---

[52] Gill, *RAN* 2:416–17, 420–34; Morison 8:117–30; Blair, *Silent Victory* 2:607–12; *Interrogations of Japanese Officials* 2:45–54.

next westward movement of MacArthur's SWPA forces. Once it recognized that Biak would not be taken easily and that there would be considerable damage to the airfields, GHQ decided to move swiftly against Noemfoor, an island having three airfields and lying about 60 miles west of Biak. Besides denying its airfields to the Japanese, occupation of Noemfoor would make it possible to bring forward more medium-bomber and fighter groups to use against enemy bases on Vogelkop and Halmahera Island. It was also planned to concentrate B–24 squadrons on Biak once the mopping up phase was completed. The invasion date for Noemfoor was set for 30 June and later 2 July.

Kinkaid quickly issued his operation order on 17 June. Barbey's staff, currently working for Admiral Fechteler, finished its planning within a week. Kenney's bombers began daily bombardments on 20 June with no opposition except for ground fire. By the time of the landings 800 tons of bombs had rained on the abandoned Japanese. The invasion force, some 7,100 troops built around the 158th Regimental Combat Team, was covered by three cruisers and ten destroyers, which were led by Admiral Berkey in *Phoenix* and Commodore John A. Collins, RAN, in *Australia*. The latter had relieved Admiral Crutchley on 13 June, making it the first time a major Australian naval group was led by an Australian. Another fourteen destroyers, constituting fire support and escort groups, were present should there be some form of enemy naval resistance. But the landing was unopposed. By 6 July the first airfield was ready for use.[53]

The final New Guinea campaign, the one against the Japanese in the Vogelkop, was anticlimatic compared with the other operations since Kinkaid had taken over the Seventh Fleet the previous November. The Japanese navy, badly bloodied in the great Philippine Sea Battle of 19–21 June, had withdrawn to anchorages near Singapore (Lingga Roads), the Philippines, (Tawi-Tawi) and home waters. The Japanese army and navy air flotillas had been decimated in defending the Palaus and western New Guinea and in fighting with Mitscher's carriers off Saipan. As a result of these military calamities, Japanese air bases in the Vogelkop were almost empty of aircraft. Defense of the area was left in the hands of the Japanese troops left behind. Recognizing these realities, and mindful of Vogelkop geography, MacArthur set his next invasion for the western side of the peninsula at Sansapor and Mar. Major concentrations of enemy forces were 160 miles distant on the eastern side of the region at Manokwari, 40 miles west of Noemfoor, and 80 miles to the southwest of Sansapor, at Sorong. Without water transport neither Japanese group could move to the Sansapor area in a timely manner. Unopposed landings were made on

---

[53] Smith, *Approach to the Philippines*, 397–424; Gill, *RAN* 2:441–43; Barbey, *MacArthur's Amphibs*, 205–11; Morison 8:134–40.

30 July. Engineering troops immediately set about constructing two air bases in the area and both were operational by 3 September in time for the planned assault on Morotai on Halmahera islands.[54]

On a much smaller scale the Morotai operation (TRADEWIND) was a rehearsal for the anticipated landing on Mindanao at Sarangani Bay. For the first time since Hollandia, Pacific Fleet carriers would provide air cover over the beachhead and the invasion force. Also available should they be needed were the fast carriers of Rear Admiral John McCain (Task Group 38.1) and their deadly air groups. Though covering the Palau landings on the same date as the Morotai assault (15 September), other carrier task groups of Task Force 38 would be in the open sea between the two areas. The Seventh Fleet, as usual, supported the operation with Admiral Berkey's two task units commanded by himself and Commodore Collins and consisting of the two Australian heavy cruisers (*Australia* and *Shropshire*), the three American light cruisers (*Phoenix, Nashville,* and *Boise*), and ten destroyers, including the Australian *Arunta* and *Warramunga*. The landings were unopposed and the almost 20,000 troops in the assault had little trouble mopping up the less than 400 or so Japanese present.

The purpose in seizing Morotai was to provide airfields for operations against the southern Philippines and Japanese bases west and south of the island. It was planned to have a fighter strip available on D + 2 of the operation. Though unable to meet that deadline, a major airfield was constructed on the south side of Morotai and was operational in time to provide assistance to the Leyte assault in the third week of October.[55]

Before turning to the immense Leyte operation, it would be useful to look at the results of Admiral Kinkaid's ten months at the helm of the Seventh Fleet. Two points that can be made are that naval operations in SWPA had moved ahead with precision and without delay, and that interservice relations were better than when he took over. In some ways these points are interrelated.

The objectives of SWPA operations and the timetables for achieving them were planned by General MacArthur and the Joint Chiefs of Staff. The feasibility of projected operations would depend on the availability of shipping to bring troops and material to the SWPA, the number of amphibious ships and craft to carry the troops to the assault area, the number of Seventh Fleet naval vessels to support and protect the operation, and the ability of the Pacific Fleet to lend ships to protect or cover an operation if needed. By the time Kinkaid arrived in Brisbane, a calen-

---

[54] Smith, *Approach to the Philippines,* 425–49; Morison 8:140–44; Barbey, *MacArthur's Amphibs,* 211–16.

[55] Smith, *Approach to the Philippines,* 450–56, 475–79, 490–93; Morison, vol. 12, *Leyte, June 1944–January 1946* (1958), 19–29; Barbey, *MacArthur's Amphibs,* 220–28; U.S. Seventh Fleet, Seventh Amphibious Force, *Command History, 10 January 1943–23 December 1945* (Shanghai, 1945), passim; *Reports of MacArthur* 1:174–78.

dar for operations had been laid out for the next seven months. The schedule started well and then began to speed up, especially after the Hollandia landings were moved forward.

Admiral Barbey's staff carried the burden of operational planning, dealing directly with General Krueger's staff to lay out assault details, but Kinkaid's staff (and GHQ) did the negotiating for Pacific Fleet assistance and for the support services and material from Australia, Hawaii, or the United States. Given his can-do, will-do personality Admiral Barbey, with Kinkaid's backing, met all requests laid on the Seventh Fleet Amphibious Force.

The same spirit was demonstrated in the Seventh Fleet Submarine Force. Admiral Christie managed submarine operations capably and Kinkaid left him alone to do so. Long after their service together in Australia Admiral Christie commented on Kinkaid's style: "Kinkaid did delegate authority to his Task Force Comdrs. to a remarkable degree. I never experienced any interference from K in my submarine operations."[56] Kinkaid and Christie did come into conflict later, but it was over management details, not operations. Seventh Fleet and GHQ intelligence centers provided Christie with a steady flow of "Ultra" (ultrasecret) intelligence based on code breaking and radio direction-finding operations. This intelligence enabled the submarine force to locate enemy ships and convoys and to attack them with precision. By destroying Japanese merchant shipping and naval vessels, Christie's submarines (and those of the Pacific Fleet) mortally damaged Japan's ability to support its conquered territories and maintain its navy at sea. Christie's submarines also regularly penetrated the Philippine Islands and East Indies to deliver supplies to guerrilla units or to land agents from GHQ to deal with guerrilla leaders. Though the missions were extremely hazardous Seventh Fleet submarines met most requests from GHQ.[57]

Obviously convinced that his staff was competent, though he had selected very few of them, the admiral did what he should have—he let the division heads manage with minimum interference from him. A senior captain, the assistant plans officer, evaluated his position:

> As far as Admiral Kinkaid and his relationship with his staff is concerned, we operated very much as a family as far as the senior officers were concerned. It must be remembered that we had a very large staff. [Captain] Dick Cruzen was the 'old timer' and as operations officer he accepted responsibility very readily and didn't hesitate to initiate operations orders to various units under our command.[58]

---

[56] VADM R. W. Christie to author, Honolulu, 19 Oct 1976.

[57] Blair, *Silent Victory*, provides detailed coverage of submarine operations and use of Ultra intelligence. See also Lewin, *American Magic*, 224–31, 248–54.

[58] RADM C. J. Maguire to author, Paradise Valley, AZ, 28 Oct 1977.

From his own experience and proclivities, Kinkaid instinctively knew that people are more content and work more productively when they are well informed about events that concern them. To make sure that his staff was constantly current on all operations, Kinkaid tried to meet daily with his flag officers and staff captains. He had seen the benefits of such meetings in Alaska and at Nimitz's headquarters, so he continued the practice in his own command.[59]

Admiral Kinkaid was sent to MacArthur's command with firm instructions to restore peace between the Army and Navy. He also knew that he had to uphold the Navy's interests, "not give away the shop," if he was going to satisfy Admirals King and Nimitz. There were many issues that had contributed to poor Army-Navy relations in Brisbane, but Kinkaid only tried to correct those that he could influence. He recognized that there was little he could do to change Kenney's attitude toward the Navy. He later related, "General Kenney... was a little difficult to deal with because he was an old Billy Mitchell flier, and he thought 'Damn-Navy' was one word." In time he thought he detected some improvement in his dealings with the airmen, but it was slow going.[60]

On one critical issue that had fouled relations between his predecessors and GHQ, Kinkaid could and did contribute to real improvement. The Army had consistently criticized Admirals Leary and Carpender for being too timid in the operations of Seventh Fleet vessels. Neither Kinkaid nor Barbey deliberately hazarded their ships and smaller craft, but they did see that they did the jobs expected of them. Kinkaid had been in operations during 1942 when aircraft carriers and cruisers were lost in considerable numbers, and this experience might have made it easier for him to risk lesser vessels. He also had confidence in Barbey as an amphibious commander. Kinkaid also let MacArthur know his position concerning control of the planning process for amphibious operations and by the time of the Morotai operation the Navy process was followed. Barbey coordinated the planning with constant review from Kenney, Krueger, and Kinkaid.

One of the matters Kinkaid chose to ignore was the resentment in the Seventh Fleet over GHQ's system of issuing communiqués that seemed to ignore the Navy. Although he enjoyed receiving recognition for his accomplishments, he could go without it. So he let Nimitz and King do what they could. It is possible that he didn't understand how much of an impact the GHQ system had on morale in his command.

Finally there was a personal matter that had exacerbated relations between Carpender and MacArthur that Kinkaid managed to finesse neatly.

---

[59] *SWPA Command History*, 21.
[60] TCK oral history, 361; TCK to HSK, Pt. Moresby, 28 Dec 1943.

His predecessor, despite being a part of MacArthur's command, had insisted that he should be able to communicate directly with Admirals Nimitz and King. MacArthur had insisted that all communications go through him,[61] and he considered Carpender's attitude insubordinate, possibly "disloyal." At a minimum he was suspect. Kinkaid followed the chain of command for operational matters, but, like most of the flag officers in the Pacific Ocean, he regularly wrote private "Dear Chester" letters to Nimitz in which he felt free to discuss matters of personnel, operations, or material. Later MacArthur accepted the idea of receiving carbon copies of routine official correspondence between his Seventh Fleet Commander and his naval seniors. In a letter to Helen, Kinkaid summed up his general philosophy for dealing with MacArthur's command:

> My two predecessors . . . [went] about things in quite a different manner from the one I am used to. They both had a chip on their shoulders and put up strong arguments where, in my opinion, they [were] not necessary or desirable. . . . This is an Army set-up and it is up to the Navy to fit into it just as in the Aleutians the Army had to fit into the Navy organization. Everyone likes to do things his own way, but there is no use in butting your head against a stone wall.[62]

Kinkaid was also responsible for a few changes in the area of fleet operations. One change was the result of his experiences as a cruiser division commander working with carrier task forces, and then as a carrier task force commander. In those positions he had learned first hand the importance of fighter director officers to force defense. In Alaska he had insisted that his naval forces develop fighter direction capabilities. So it was natural for him to have his cruisers and a few destroyers learn how to use their radars for tracking aircraft aloft. Once a ship developed fighter direction teams, he requested that General Kenney have his squadrons provide practice for the ships. The admiral hoped, in time, to have his shipboard teams control air force squadrons when assault operations were underway. Initially Kenney was cool to the idea. The concept of keeping a fighter cover over the fleet and directed by officers in a ship was alien to him. Eventually he did agree to shipboard fighter direction, provided the officer calling the shots was an air force pilot.[63]

Another change that Kinkaid initiated was based on his prewar service as a naval attaché in Rome where he had developed an abiding interest in intelligence matters. He was well aware of the invaluable service provided by

---

[61] James, *MacArthur* 2:358.
[62] TCK to HSK, Brisbane, 6 Dec 1943.
[63] COM7THFLT to TF, TG and Cruiser and Destroyer Commanding Officers, 13 Dec 1943, 7th Fleet Records, 1942–44, RG 65, NA.

the cryptanalysts to Nimitz's intelligence staff. He had on his staff as fleet intelligence officer Captain Arthur H. McCollum, who was a trained Japanese linguist. Starting in December 1942 the captain had developed a fleet intelligence staff of enormous importance to both GHQ's land operations and the Seventh Fleet's submarine and air operations. In May 1944 the admiral approved McCollum's proposal that a Seventh Fleet Intelligence Center (SEFIC) be established separate from the staff. Captain McCollum became its head as well as continuing as Kinkaid's staff intelligence officer. By the time planning for Leyte began in Hollandia, SEFIC had approximately 150 officers and more than 200 enlisted men engaged in intelligence activities. McCollum's headquarters remained in Brisbane until early October 1944 when it moved to Hollandia. In February 1945 it moved to Tolosa, Leyte.[64]

Early in September 1944 Kinkaid and his staff moved from Brisbane to Hollandia, a move that the admiral did not regret. MacArthur and his staff moved a week later, though a substantial number of GHQ members were left behind to take care of logistics and personnel matters. For Kinkaid it meant not only that he was at the front, but also that he would now take a more direct interest in planning operations.

When they set up shop on a hillside overlooking Lake Sentani, the Morotai operation was ahead of them, and they expected next to seize the Talaud Islands, midway between Morotai and southern Mindanao. But all of that was to change. Two weeks after arriving at Hollandia, he exulted to his wife: "These are busy times. The Jap seems to be in difficulties and it is our purpose to keep him that way. Everyone feels much better now that things are going on and we have gotten out of Brisbane."[65] The "busy times" alluded to a change in plans concerning future operations. Instead of invading the Talauds on 15 October and Sarangani Bay (southern Mindanao) on 15 November, MacArthur's forces would land on Leyte in the central Philippines on 20 October.

In the official history of General MacArthur's operations, printed in Tokyo in 1950 but not released for publication until 1966, the first chapter dealing with the Leyte campaign begins, "The Philippine Islands constituted the main objective of General MacArthur's planning from the time of his departure from Corregidor in March 1942 until his dramatic return to Leyte two and one half years later."[66]

Once the security of Australia was assured by the defeat of the Japanese in eastern New Guinea (Papua) and on Guadalcanal, MacArthur submitted the first of his long-range plans for driving the Japanese from New Guinea and recapturing the Philippines. It was RENO I, dated 25 February

---

[64] COM7THFLT to CNO OP–20–G, 1 Sep 1945, 7th Fleet Records, RG 65, NA.
[65] TCK to HSK, Brisbane, 2 Sep 1944; Hollandia, 17 Sep 1944.
[66] Willoughby, comp., *Reports of MacArthur* 1:166.

1943. There were to be five variants of the plan, with RENO V emerging on 6 June 1944, but all had the same end: the invasion of Luzon and the final elimination of Japanese power in the archipelago. The intermediate places to be seized and the dates of specific operations changed as each new RENO plan emerged, but the focus on Luzon never wavered. When it was obvious that the Pacific Fleet had plans beyond the Philippines, RENO IV stated that control of Luzon (and the rest of the islands) would make it possible to move against Formosa or the China coast in the future.[67]

With the end of the New Guinea campaign in sight, on 10 July 1944 GHQ released MUSKETEER, its master plan for operations against the Philippines. It projected a landing in southern Mindanao at Sarangani Bay on 15 November, then one on the east coast of Leyte on 20 December. MUSKETEER II followed on 29 August, in which the major landing on Luzon was set for Lingayen Gulf on 20 February 1945.[68]

Between the issuance of the two MUSKETEER plans MacArthur fought a successful engagement against the Navy. It had become progressively more obvious throughout 1944 that Admiral King did not believe the invasion of Luzon was necessary. He wanted to bypass Luzon and move against Formosa. From Formosa he would move to the China coast, set up air bases protected by the Chinese armies, and then send the B–29s against Japan. But in Pearl Harbor Admiral Nimitz and his staff were not eager to assault Formosa. They foresaw another difficult campaign with heavy casualties. Nimitz preferred to move to the China coast once Leyte was in hand. Nimitz and King discussed the matter at their bimonthly meeting in San Francisco in May 1944. Nimitz, with Halsey kibitzing as a visitor, insisted that at least Mindanao be invaded. If the Philippines were totally bypassed, it might raise a greater controversy than would be acceptable. In July at Pearl Harbor King again suggested bypassing Luzon. He thought Guam would be a better logistic base than Manila Bay, and that Eniwetok could serve as a fleet anchorage. Also, were underway re-provisioning operations extended, then the dependence on bases could be lessened further. Nimitz listened, but he was not in complete agreement with his superior.[69] MacArthur's hostility to bypassing the Philippines was quite clear. He had again spelled out his views in an 18 June radio to General Marshall for the JCS. He made three basic arguments: the Philippines were necessary as a base for future operations; the United States had been defeated by Japan in the Philippines and that stain on its honor had to be removed; and America owed a debt to the Filipinos who were suffering

---

[67] Ibid., 168–70; M. Hamlin Cannon, *Leyte: The Return to the Philippines* (Washington: Department of the Army, 1954), 1–4.

[68] *MacArthur Reports* 1:172.

[69] COMINCH–CINCPAC Conferences, San Francisco, 6 May 1944; Pearl Harbor, 13–22 Jul 44, OA; Buell, *King*, 466–68; Potter, *Nimitz*, 310–14.

greatly under Japanese control. On 26–27 July, in the presence of President Franklin Roosevelt at Pearl Harbor, MacArthur and Nimitz argued out the merits of invading Formosa or the China coast without taking Luzon. The general, who had been irritated at the necessity of visiting Oahu, won the argument easily.[70] Luzon would follow Leyte, though an actual operations order would have to await the blessing of the JCS.

The change in the schedule of operations, including the abandonment of the Sarangani Bay operation, came with the Morotai and Palau invasions. To reduce the possibility of Japanese air or naval interference with the two amphibious assaults, Admiral Halsey's Third Fleet, spearheaded by TF 38's fast carriers, bombed and strafed enemy air bases on Morotai, the Palau Islands, Yap, Mindanao, and the Visayan Islands (including Leyte) in the central Philippines. The Japanese response seemed unexpectedly weak to Halsey's staff. The damage was awesome. The number of aircraft destroyed in the air and on the ground exceeded 200 and might have been double that. By 13 September, after a week of such marauding activities, Halsey and Mitscher concluded there was little worth attacking in the central and southern Philippines. Following discussions with his staff, Halsey on 13 September radioed Nimitz that many of their planned operations could be abandoned. Given the evident enemy weakness, he recommended that the invasions of Yap, Morotai, the Palau Islands, and Sarangani Bay be scrapped. He believed that Leyte could be invaded immediately with the troops already en route to the planned invasions and that the Third Fleet could cover the operation. Nimitz agreed with most of Halsey's ideas, though he believed that the Palau Islands expedition was still necessary. He forwarded Halsey's views, plus his own and added the Third Amphibious Force and the XXIV Army Corps, which could be diverted to Leyte from its planned invasion of Yap. CINCPAC's radio went to the JCS who were then meeting with their British counterparts in Quebec. Also present were Prime Minister Churchill and President Roosevelt. After discussions among themselves, the JCS sought General MacArthur's views. But the general was riding *Nashville* to the Morotai landing and was observing radio silence. His chief of staff, Lieutenant General Sutherland, answered the query enthusiastically. SWPA forces would be ready to hit the beaches at Leyte on 20 October. The JCS then approved the modification. In reducing the time before the invasion of Leyte by two months, the JCS were also reducing the time available to the enemy to strengthen his positions in the central Philippines, a desirable decision from the point of view of everyone except the Japanese.[71]

---

[70] Cannon, *Leyte*, 4–6; Morison 12:9–11; Potter, *Nimitz*, 317–19.

[71] Cannon, *Leyte*, 8–9; Morison 12:12–16; Reynolds, *Fast Carriers*, 247–48; Potter, *Halsey*, 276–78; Merrill, *A Sailor's Admiral*, 133–37.

Author's collection

Admiral Kinkaid, wearing his trademark pith helmet, sits with senior officers of the Seventh Fleet staff and Commander Support Aircraft Seventh Fleet and staff, on board *Wasatch* (AGC 9) during the Leyte-Philippine operation, 14 October–2 November 1944.

Kinkaid now moved into high gear since the two-month advancement in the target date for the Leyte landing meant that there would be less time for planning. The environment was almost ideal. Located where they were, Kinkaid and his staff could easily meet at General Krueger's headquarters on Humboldt Bay, about an hour's jeep ride away, or visit Admiral Barbey's flagship nearby. It was an enormous improvement over earlier operations that had found Kinkaid and Kenney in Brisbane, Barbey in Milne Bay, and Krueger often 500 miles west of Barbey. MacArthur and his staff were on a higher hill about a half-mile from Kinkaid. On 17 September Vice Admiral Ping Wilkinson, Commander of Amphibious Forces, Third Fleet, arrived at Kinkaid's headquarters to participate in the planning. Originally scheduled to bring the Army's XXIV Corps from Oahu to Yap, he was now to deliver it to Leyte. Wilkinson, an old friend, was invited to share Kinkaid's Quonset apartment. He stayed for seventeen days. During that time Kinkaid's mess, which included several of the Seventh Fleet flag officers and most of his senior staff officers, doubled in size due to the staffs of Wilkinson and other visiting admirals. Fortunately, nearby Quonsets, erected for captains' quarters, could accommodate the visitors. After the war, Kinkaid looked back on that period of manic activity:

> It was the only time during the Pacific War that I had adequate time to plan. It was the only time that I saw plans properly made. We had the ideal physical setup. Everyone was there. . . . We were able to get together and work out an excellent plan while looking over each other's shoulder. Each man had a chance to get in his oar.[72]

The planning had probably not gone as smoothly as Kinkaid remembered. For Dan Barbey and his staff it was an exceptionally frantic period. The Seventh Amphibs were still engaged in resupply activities associated with Morotai, some of the troops they would carry to Leyte were in the Admiralty Islands far to the rear of Humboldt Bay, and some of their craft were yet to arrive from the Pacific Fleet. As Uncle Dan later noted, some of the troops would be carried in slow-moving LSTs and would have to leave Manus by 4 October. This date was about the same time that the plans for KING II (the Leyte landings) were completed. He summarized the worries in Hollandia:

> Often there would be concern on the part of MacArthur's senior commanders as to whether planes, ships, and troops could be readied on the required date for the next operation. But there was never any uncertainty on MacArthur's part. He gave the orders, confident that what he directed to be done would be done.[73]

The question concerning the command of the Leyte attack force had been settled in mid-August. Because Leyte was scheduled for December, Kinkaid had plenty of time to think about personnel. In late July he had told CINCPAC's staff that he expected Admiral Barbey to command the attack force and that Barbey should have three Pacific Fleet amphibious commanders who were junior to him. After briefly considering it, Nimitz forwarded Kinkaid's ideas to COMINCH, with the observation that "this would place the largest amphibious operation in the Pacific to date under Barbey, assisted by Fechteler, Cecil, Connolly, Royal, and Reifsnider." More serious to CINCPAC would be the fact that "Turner, Wilkinson, Hill, Fort, and Blandy with their experienced staffs would be unemployed between STALEMATE (Palau Operation) and CAUSEWAY (Formosa Operation)." He recommended that, if large ships and forces from the Pacific Fleet were to be lent to Kinkaid, some of the experienced commanders should go with them.[74]

---

[72] Karig, *Battle Report* 4:308–9; Krueger, *Sixth Army*, 136–41.
[73] Barbey, *MacArthur's Amphibs*, 233.
[74] Nimitz to King, Pearl Harbor, 31 Jul 1944, Nimitz Papers.

Admiral King recognized what was bothering Nimitz, and on 17 August he proposed a solution to Kinkaid: "I assume that you will command, under MacArthur, all the Naval Forces involved directly in the operation, and that you will coordinate their activities with Admiral Halsey as Commander of the Third Fleet Covering Force." King then suggested that Barbey command one major part of the attack force and that Wilkinson command the other major part. He further assumed that Barbey and Wilkinson would each have a group of rear admirals working under his command. Kinkaid, as the attack force commander, would have Barbey and Wilkinson reporting to him. He would, of course, continue to command the entire Seventh Fleet. These arrangements meant that Barbey, a rear admiral, would not be under Wilkinson's command, nor would Kinkaid have to request that Wilkinson, a vice admiral, serve under Barbey. The relevant correspondence suggests that Admiral Nimitz would have preferred to have Ping Wilkinson serve as the attack force commander at Leyte. He considered Wilkinson more experienced than Barbey in managing large and complicated operations. But Nimitz was also aware that MacArthur had great confidence in Uncle Dan and would not like to see him under a Pacific Fleet commander.[75]

By the end of August, Kinkaid had made all command arrangements. Neither MacArthur nor Nimitz had objections. Kinkaid would be seeing Halsey in Manus on 4 September to work out their plans for coordinating activities and to borrow his Amphibious Force, including Wilkinson. There were disappointments, particularly for Barbey, but he flung himself and his staff into planning the Leyte operation, unaware that his workload would become infinitely heavier once Halsey's proposals were adopted.

From its earliest considerations, GHQ had believed that the invasion of Leyte should be a two-corps assault, four divisions in the original landings and two divisions reserve. This decision was based on the estimate of Japanese strength on Leyte and the number of troops that could be brought in as reinforcements during the first week of operations ashore. Information about the Japanese on Leyte and in the rest of the Philippines had come regularly from guerrilla units operating throughout the islands. Intelligence estimated that there were 180,000 Japanese soldiers throughout the Philippines with 80,000 in Luzon, 50,000 in Mindanao, and another 50,000 in the Visayan Islands (central Philippines). In Leyte, itself one of the Visayans, the best figure available in September 1944 was 21,700 Japanese troops, about half being service troops. It was also estimated that there were 100 to 120 military airfields in the Philip-

---

[75] King to TCK, Washington, 17 Aug 1944; TCK to Barbey, Brisbane, 26 Aug 1944; TCK to King, Brisbane, 27 Aug 1944; Barbey to TCK, Hollandia, 31 Aug 1944, TCK Papers; ADM Richard L. Conolly, interview by John T. Mason, Jr., 1960, 253–55, USNI Oral History, Annapolis, MD (hereafter Conolly oral history).

pines with anywhere from 700 to 1,500 aircraft available. These were July estimates before Halsey's TF 38 bombed the region in early September.[76] GHQ planned eventually to commit about 202,500 ground troops to seizing Leyte by eliminating Japanese forces there. General Krueger's Alamo Force, which had fought the New Guinea campaigns, was now the Sixth Army. It would consist of the X Corps (1st Cavalry Division, 24th Infantry division) with about 53,000 troops, and the reserve of the 32d and 77th Infantry Divisions with a total strength of about 28,500 soldiers. Along with these major units, totaling about 133,000 troops, there would be almost 70,000 troops in Corps battalions, special units such as tank battalions, artillery, engineer, amphibian truck and tractor battalions, signal companies, hospitals, etc.—a staggering accumulation of people to organize, lift to the beaches, supply, and protect.[77]

The immediate task assigned to the forces of the Southwest Pacific, supported by the Third Fleet, was to seize and control the Leyte Gulf–Surigao Strait area in order to establish air bases and logistic bases that would support further operations in the Philippines.[78] The initial target area for this task was the east coast of Leyte between the cities of Tacloban and Dulag. Once ashore the troops' first objective was to take control of the half-dozen or so airfields and air strips in the vicinity of the two cities. By A + 5 (five days after invasion), General MacArthur's Operation Order 70–44 called for establishing sufficient airfield capacity to hold two fighter groups (six squadrons) plus a night fighter squadron; and ten days later (A + 15) there should be room for seven more squadrons ashore and three Navy patrol squadrons based on tenders off the beaches of Leyte.[79] Once the necessary airfields were seized or constructed, it was expected that General Kenney's squadrons could take over the air defense of the area and the Navy's aircraft carriers could be returned to the Pacific Fleet.

Admiral Kinkaid's Operations Order 13–44 created three task forces under him as Commander Central Philippines Attack Force (CTF 77). The admiral would directly command four task groups: 77.1, 77.2, 77.3, and 77.4. Task Group 77.1 was created by Kinkaid's new chief of staff, Commodore V. H. (Val) Schaeffer. It was a flagship group consisting of the fleet flagship, *Wasatch* (AGC 9), the light cruiser *Nashville*, which would embark General MacArthur, and four destroyers. It was assumed that once in Leyte Gulf, the flagship group would maneuver as a unit and have sufficient firepower to defend itself under air attack. Task Group 77.2 was the bombardment and fire support group under Rear Admiral Jesse B. (Oley) Oldendorf. Lent by the Pacific Fleet, Task Group 77.2

---

[76] Cannon, *Leyte*, 22.
[77] Ibid., 26–27.
[78] Ibid., 23.
[79] Willoughby, comp., *Reports of MacArthur* 1:184–89.

consisted of six old battleships, all reconditioned survivors of the Pearl Harbor attack; three heavy cruisers; four light cruisers, including *Nashville*, and twenty-one destroyers. Task Group 77.3, the close covering group under Rear Admiral Berkey, consisted of the cruisers *Phoenix, Boise*, HMAS *Australia,* HMAS *Shropshire*, and seven destroyers. Task Group 77.4, commanded by Rear Admiral Thomas L. Sprague, consisted of sixteen CVEs (escort carriers) on loan from the Pacific Fleet plus an accompanying nine destroyers and twelve destroyer escorts. The CVEs were organized into three task units: TU 77.4.1 (Thomas Sprague) with four carriers; TU 77.4.2 (Rear Admiral Felix B. Stump) with six carriers; and TU 77.4.3 (Rear Admiral C. A. F. [Ziggy] Sprague) with six carriers. These task groups also made up a "scratch" battle force for the Seventh Fleet in case it was necessary to confront a portion of the Imperial Navy.[80]

Task Group 77.5 was the minesweeping and hydrographic group, Task Group 77.6 consisted of the seven beach demolition groups, and TG 77.7 was made up of Service Force Seventh Fleet vessels such as oilers, ammunition ships, provision ships, water tankers, net tenders, and salvage vessels. Task Groups 77.2, 77.3, and 77.4 were to be divided into smaller groupings in support of the Third and Seventh Amphibious Forces during their assaults.

Task Force 78 was Rear Admiral Barbey's Seventh Amphibious Force, for this operation designated the Northern Attack Force. Barbey's job was to land the X Corps (Major General Franklin C. Sibert) on the Leyte beaches, roughly in the three miles south of the Tacloban airport. He divided his force into two attack groups, each landing a division of the X Corps. Task Group 78.1, the Palo Attack Group, landing to the south, would be under his personal command. It would carry the 24th Infantry Division (Major General Frederick A. Irving) and land it on Red Beach. Task Group 78.2, the San Ricardo Attack Group under Admiral Fechteler's command, would land the 1st Cavalry Division (Major General Verne D. Mudge) on White Beach in the area between the 24th Division and Tacloban. Fire support for Barbey's assault would be provided by Rear Admiral George L. Weyler with the battleships *Mississippi, Maryland* and *West Virginia* plus a handful of destroyers and Admiral Berkey's cruisers, if needed.

Task Force 79, the Southern Attack Force, came to the Leyte operation from the Pacific Fleet and with it came Vice Admiral Wilkinson as its commander. Unlike Dan Barbey, Ping Wilkinson preferred to leave the management of his two assault groups to the experienced amphibious commanders he brought with him. Wilkinson's groups had the task of landing the XXIV Corps (Major General John R. Hodge) on the beaches between the small cities of San Jose and Dulag. As with the Northern Force the two attack

---

[80] Morison 12:415–23.

Vice Admiral Theodore S. Wilkinson, Vice Admiral Kinkaid, and Rear Admiral Daniel E. Barbey at Seventh Fleet headquarters for a meeting with officers of the Third and Seventh fleets to plan the invasion of Leyte, circa October 1944. Wilkinson and Barbey were to command the two invasion forces.

groups would each be responsible for landing a division. Attack Group Able (TG 79.1), led by Rear Admiral Richard Conolly, would land the 7th Infantry Division (Major General Archibald V. Arnold) on Orange and Blue Beaches. Attack Group Baker (TG 79.2), commanded by Rear Admiral Forrest B. Royal, would be responsible for putting the 96th Infantry Division ashore on Violet and Yellow Beaches. Prelanding bombardment and fire support during the assault would come from Rear Admiral Oldendorf's battleships and cruisers. Heavy bombardment would be provided by the 14-inch guns of the battleships *Tennessee, California,* and *Pennsylvania,* supplemented by the heavy cruisers *Louisville* (Oley's flagship), *Portland,* and *Minneapolis* and the light cruisers *Honolulu, Denver* (CL 58), and *Columbia* (CL 56). Again there was a substantial thirteen-destroyer screen for the larger vessels. Another innovation that Commodore Schaeffer inserted into Kinkaid's plan was the addition of an air support officer (Captain Richard F. Whitehead) to the Seventh Fleet staff in *Wasatch*. All requests for air strikes from the CVEs would come to Captain Whitehead and he would call upon the individual carriers for action. Kinkaid's chief of staff had resisted apportioning the CVEs to each task group commander, but almost the same result was achieved by having each of the three task units of TG 77.4 primarily responsible for supporting a sector of the beachhead.[81]

Before the two attack forces entered Leyte Gulf, Kinkaid's plan of operations required seizing certain islands in the Surigao Strait–Leyte Gulf area to prevent enemy interference with the landings. Under Admiral Oldendorf's direction in the absence of Kinkaid, Army units were to seize Suluan, Homonhon, and Dinagat islands on 17 and 18 October. During the three days before the actual landings on Leyte were to begin, Oldendorf would also oversee the sweeping of mines from Leyte Gulf, the clearance of any underwater obstacles in the approaches to the landing beaches, and the elimination by bombardment of enemy gun emplacements, fortified points of resistance, and any other military targets worthy of a 4-inch destroyer bullet or 14-inch battleship high-capacity shell. Though General MacArthur ordered his forces to avoid unnecessary damage to Filipino cities by aerial or ship bombardment, it was not always possible to comply. In protecting underwater demolition teams at work on the beach at Dulag, naval gunfire destroyed the city two days before the main assault.[82]

Although Kinkaid's reinforced Seventh Fleet was designed to escort, protect en route, and defend in Leyte Gulf the more than 700 vessels that constituted the Central Philippines Attack Force, he did anticipate assistance from Admiral Halsey. The expected actions of the Third Fleet were spelled out in SWPA's 70–44 of 21 September and in CINCPAC's Operation Plan 8–44 of 27 September. Third Fleet was to cover and support the Leyte operation by

(1) Containing or destroying the Japanese Fleet.

(2) Destruction of hostile air and shipping in the Formosa, Luzon, Visayas and Mindanao area during the period A − 9 through A − 3 and from A-Day through A + 30 as necessary to maintain their continued neutralization.

(3) Destruction of ground defenses and installations and shipping in the objective and adjacent enemy supporting areas from A − 2 until the escort carriers assumed the mission of direct support.

(4) Providing direct support of the landing and subsequent operations by fast carrier aircraft as required.[83]

---

[81] Ibid.; *Command History Seventh Amphibs* 1:8–9, sheet 16; Barbey, *MacArthur's Amphibs*, 232–36; Cannon, *Leyte*, 31–34; Morison 12:415–23.
[82] CINCSWPA to CINCAAF and CINCPOA, Brisbane, 9 Sep 1944, MacArthur Papers; COM7THFLT to COMINCH, "Report of Action for the Capture of Leyte Island . . . ," 31 Jan 1945, OA.
[83] Willoughby, comp., *Reports of MacArthur* 1:184.

These general tasks were made more specific in Nimitz's plan and in Halsey's own orders to his force. Nimitz broadened the scope of operations for the Third Fleet when he added, "In case opportunity for destruction of major portion of the enemy fleet is offered or can be created, such destruction becomes the primary task." As we shall see, this sentence became central in controlling Halsey's activities once the Japanese decided to attempt the destruction of the Leyte expeditionary force.[84] It should be noted here that Nimitz's orders to Admiral Halsey were dated six days after those of General MacArthur. It should also be remembered that MacArthur controlled the Seventh Fleet through Kinkaid; but Admiral Nimitz was Halsey's immediate superior. If the general wanted Bull Halsey to do anything not spelled out in Nimitz's orders, he would have to pass his request through Pearl Harbor. At the scene of action in the Leyte Gulf area there were two independent fleet commanders working cooperatively, with no one in a position to directly command both of them.

Before putting to sea and heading for Leyte, Kinkaid in early October reviewed the whole KING II plan with all of his senior commanders and their staffs. Kinkaid and Krueger started the briefings and were followed by Wilkinson and Barbey. Then each of the task group commanders reviewed his responsibilities and tasks. In this way everyone was informed about the total operation and the role of each subordinate commander. Oldendorf later commented that KING II was the first time he had been able to discuss a major operation before implementing it. Admiral Stump, one of the CVE task unit commanders (TU 77.4.2), was surprised to be there, particularly since he was the only representative from TG 77.4. Each "jeep carrier" carried nine torpedo planes (TBM/TBF) and eighteen fighters (FM/F4F), and each was allocated six torpedoes. Stump decided to carry more in his six carriers, and he later was glad he had ignored staff suggestions. Captain Richard W. (Rafe) Bates, who was Oley's chief of staff and a specialist in battle analysis, later mentioned to Kinkaid that he admired his calm, straightforward approach when briefing his flag officers. Bates felt it inspired great confidence in his commanders.[85]

Perhaps to put his own mind at ease, Kinkaid flew to Manus for a last conference with his Third Amphibious Force commanders on board Wilkinson's command ship, *Mount Olympus* (AGC 8). After another review of the Leyte plans, Wilkinson laid on a light buffet for all of the admirals, the XXIV Corps generals, and one lone colonel. The effort left a

---

[84] Quoted in Morison 12:57–58.

[85] ADM Felix B. Stump, interview by John T. Mason, Jr., 1964, 181–85, Columbia University Oral History, New York (hereafter Stump oral history); TCK oral history, 278–86, 292–93; R. W. Bates to TCK, 13 Aug 1945, RADM Richard W. Bates Papers, Naval War College (hereafter Bates Papers).

good feeling about Kinkaid among the Third Fleet types. Admiral of the Fleet Sir Roger J. B. Keyes, RN, who had been sent to the area as an observer for Prime Minister Churchill, found the proceedings interesting and the dinner good fun even though no liquor was served. But for Kinkaid the high point of the trip to Manus appeared to have been the evening movie, *The Mark of Zorro*, with Linda Darnell and Tyrone Power.[86]

---

[86] Halpern, ed., *The Keyes Papers*, 3:283–84; VADM Theodore S. Wilkinson, Diary, 10 Oct 1944, Wilkinson Papers, MD–LC (hereafter Wilkinson Papers).

Chapter 14

Commander Seventh Fleet, October 1944–November 1945

Wasatch, with Kinkaid, General Walter Krueger, and their senior staffs on board, departed Humboldt Bay at 0622 on 15 October. The last leg on the return to the Philippines had begun, and Kinkaid was pleased to be at sea again. He started his daily letter to Helen, "It is good to feel the throb of the engines again and to be away from the dust and insects." Avoiding details he continued, "Things are popping as you probably have been told by your radio. Today's developments forced me to make an important decision. That is what goes with three stars."[1] The decision made had indeed been serious. The question was whether the movement to Leyte should be delayed for a day or two until it became clearer what the Japanese were about to do.

The KING II plan had called for the Third Fleet to attack the Formosa, Luzon, Visayans, and Mindanao areas on days A − 9 through A − 3 before the Leyte landings. On 13 October Admiral Halsey reported that on the 12th and 13th "the entire Formosa–Pescadores area was thoroughly bombed with concentration on airfield installations, utilities, shipping installations and oil dumps." The score had been 396 aircraft destroyed and 14 transports and cargo vessels sunk.[2] The Japanese reaction to Halsey's raids was rigorous. Task Force 38's ships were attacked, with *Houston* (CL 81) and *Canberra* (CA 70) torpedoed and crippled. A variety of combat vessel sightings were reported from Brunei Bay, Borneo, to the Bungo Strait, between the Japanese main islands of Kyushu and Shikoku, leaving Admiral Nimitz's staff with the impression that the Imperial Navy was beginning a concentration preliminary to battle.[3] Halsey took action to fuel and position his own fleet preparatory to meeting whatever threat came from the Japanese. In reporting his dispositions, he also ominously advised Nimitz and Kinkaid that "no fast carriers will be available for the KING II operation until further notice."[4]

[1] TCK to HSK, *Wasatch* (AGC 9), 15 Oct 1944.
[2] COM3RDFLT to CINCPAC, 10/130955Z, Command Summary, 12 Oct 1944.
[3] CINCPAC to COM3RDFLT and COM7THFLT, 10/142219Z, Command Summary, 14 Oct 1944.
[4] COM3RDFLT to CINCPAC, 10/150149Z, Command Summary, 14 Oct 1944.

Halsey's messages were given to Kinkaid around noon during his first day out of Hollandia. Within three hours Kinkaid decided that there would be no delay in KING II, but he did "request assistance from the fast carriers as soon as possible, consistent with developments."[5] Given the fact that the attack force was observing radio silence, Kinkaid had to make this decision with no one to consult except his own staff. So they continued. As might be expected, the *Wasatch* war diary recorded that antiaircraft firing drills were held twice that day by the ship's crew.[6]

Some years later Kinkaid explained the basis for his decision to move ahead despite the possibility that the Third Fleet might not be available to assist them. He wrote to the head of the battle analysis group at the Naval War College:

> When the 3rd Flt dispatch was received on the morning of 15 Oct., I still believed that the Japs would not be able to oppose our landing with major surface ships.... I believed that we had adequate forces to effect a landing in Leyte Gulf without direct support from the 3rd Fleet, *provided* that the Japanese fleet did not interfere. If the 3rd Fleet could bring the Japanese fleet to action, the latter would not be able to interfere with our invasion. If the imminent fleet action did not come off, the 3rd Fleet would support us as planned. The risk of proceeding with the operation was not too great.[7]

As the massive convoy ploughed northwestward, the seas began to roughen and the barometer began to fall. From their position in the typhoon belt, and with the reports pouring in, it was clear that the attack force was in for heavy weather. Before departure, a plan had been decided for such an eventuality. If practical all ships in the convoy would gradually turn to the west and then continue to the south and then east in a large circle, arriving back at the starting point twenty-four hours later. By such action the whole operation plan could be followed as set down, with only the date set back. On the 16th (A−4) Wilkinson's force joined with Kinkaid's and they were able to compare meteorological guesses. The decision was to continue on course.[8]

On the 18th (A−2) *Nashville*, with General MacArthur on board, fell in with Kinkaid and Wilkinson's groups. From the flag bridge, Kinkaid had a message flashed by light: "Welcome to our city. Information from Leyte indicates operations all going well. Weather prediction for A-Day is good.... Fast carrier groups now supporting KING TWO in accordance

---

[5] COM7THFLT to CINCPAC, 10/150542Z, Command Summary, 14 Oct 1944.
[6] *Wasatch* War Diary, 15 Oct 1944, OA.
[7] TCK to Commodore R. W. Bates, Washington, 7 Jun 1952, Bates Papers.
[8] TCK to HSK, *Wasatch*, 16 Oct 1944; VADM Theodore S. Wilkinson, Diary, 18 Oct 1944, Wilkinson Papers; TCK to Commodore Bates, Washington, 7 Jun 1952, Bates Papers.

with commitments. Kinkaid." *Nashville's* flag bridge flashed back, "Thanks for your message. Glad indeed to be in your domicile and under your flag. It gives me not only confidence but a sense of inspiration. As Ripley says, believe it or not we are almost there. MacArthur."[9]

In the early morning of 20 October (A-Day), the command ships, transports, cargo carriers, and escorting combatant vessels passed boldly into Leyte Gulf. At daylight bombardments began on all the beaches to be assaulted and the landing craft were lifted out and filled. Following aerial bombardments and a final pulverizing of the beaches by rocket-firing LCIs (landing craft infantry), the troops hit the beaches at 1000 and scrambled inland. Casualties were few since the prelanding cannonading had driven most of the enemy away from the beaches. As at Biak and Peleliu, and later Okinawa, the Japanese had decided to mount their principal resistance inland. Overhead the air was practically free of enemy aircraft. In the two days before, and on A-Day itself, Halsey's carrier groups had returned to the business of decimating the Japanese squadrons in the central Philippines and to the north. There were plenty of planes left to attack the invaders, but the Japanese were holding these for the great counterattack that they called Plan SHO-I.

The planes now overhead were from the CVEs and two of TF 38's task groups. General MacArthur decided it was officially time "to return." In the early afternoon, accompanied by some of his senior staff, the general took a motor whaler from *Nashville* and stopped at the transport *John Land* (AP 167) to pick up the Philippine president, Sergio Osmeña, the Philippine secretary of national defense, General Basilio Valdez, and the president's aide, Brigadier General Carlos Romulo. The distinguished passengers were set ashore on Red Beach, near the city of Palo. After wading ashore and visiting a bit, MacArthur, Osmeña, and Romulo delivered radio messages to the Filipino people. The general's began, "People of the Philippines, I have returned. By the grace of Almighty God our forces stand again on Philippine soil."[10]

The general visited other beaches on the 21st and 22d and then led a procession of senior officers and Philippine officials to the steps of the provincial capitol building on Monday, 23 October. Kinkaid, Ping Wilkinson, and Dan Barbey represented the naval forces, and about a dozen Army officers were part of MacArthur's entourage. The ceremony was brief but meaningful. Civil self-government was restored to the Filipinos. President Osmeña immediately appointed Colonel Ruperto Kangleon, the guerrilla

---

[9] Messages in MacArthur Papers.
[10] Morison 12:130–38; James, *MacArthur* 2:550–57; Carlos Romulo, *I See the Philippines Rise* (Garden City, NY: Doubleday, 1946), 90–95; Paul Rogers, *The Bitter Years: MacArthur and Sutherland* (New York: Praeger, 1991), 177–79.

chief of Leyte, as acting governor of Leyte. Although the Osmeña government could only operate in those areas where the Japanese had been driven out, it was still good to have Filipinos in charge of their own affairs again.[11]

Kinkaid regretted the two and a half hours taken up by the Tacloban ceremonies. Recent dispatches had indicated that the Japanese were moving. At 0700 that morning messages had come from several of Admiral Christie's submarines that two groups of enemy ships, traveling north to the west of Palawan, had been attacked and four cruisers had been sunk or badly damaged. Most important, it was now clear to Kinkaid and Halsey that a major force was probably headed for the Sibuyan Sea and the San Bernardino Strait between Luzon and Samar.[12] This large force, commanded by Vice Admiral Takeo Kurita, consisted of five battleships, ten heavy cruisers, two light cruisers, and sixteen destroyers. In keeping with the SHO-I Plan, the First Striking Force, led by the 18-inch gun battleships *Yamato* and *Musashi*, was to transit San Bernardino Strait during the night of 24–25 October, steam south down the coast of Samar, and enter Leyte Gulf. Here, of course, the Japanese expected to destroy the American invasion forces. By daylight on the 24th Kurita's striking force had lost the cruisers *Atago*, *Maya*, and *Takao* to submarine attacks. *Takao* was badly damaged, and returned to Brunei. Now in the Sibuyan Sea Halsey's TF 38 fell on them.

Another Japanese force, led by Vice Admiral Shoji Nishimura, had departed Brunei Bay after Kurita on 22 October. On the 23d it had transited the Sulu Sea and entered the Mindanao Sea, destination Surigao Strait. This so-called Southern Force had the battleships *Yamashiro* (flagship) and *Fuso*, the heavy cruiser *Mogami*, and four destroyers. It was to be joined during the night of 24–25 October by a cruiser force led by Vice Admiral Kiyohide Shima. Not under Nishimura's command but operating cooperatively, Shima's group included the heavy cruisers *Nachi* (flag) and *Ashigara*, the light cruiser *Abukuma*, and seven destroyers. The mission of the Nishimura-Shima force was to enter Leyte Gulf by way of the Surigao Strait and, simultaneously with Kurita's First Striking Force, annihilate Kinkaid's central Philippines Attack Force. As was the case with Kurita's Force, Halsey's flyers located Nishimura's ships at about 0900 on the 24th and attacked them. Because of the route he took from the north, Shima's cruisers escaped detection and attack en route to the Surigao Strait.

The flash from the submarine *Darter* concerning Kurita's striking force did not surprise Kinkaid and his staff. For months his fleet intelligence officer, Captain Arthur McCollum, had been keeping track of the Japanese

---

[11] Vicente Albano Pacis, *Osmena*, 2 vols. (Quezon City, Philippines: Phoenix Press, 1971), 2:243–46; Teodoro A. Agoncillo, *The Fateful Years: Japan's Adventure in the Philippines, 1941–45*, 2 vols. (Quezon City, Philippines: R. Garcia Publishing, 1965), 2:850–53; Wilkinson Diary, 23 Oct 1944, Wilkinson Papers; TCK to HSK, Leyte, 23 Oct 1944; MacArthur, *Reminiscences*, 234–35; Romulo, *I See the Rise*, 127–30.

[12] TCK to HSK, Leyte, 23 Oct 1944; Blair, *Silent Victory* 2:724–31.

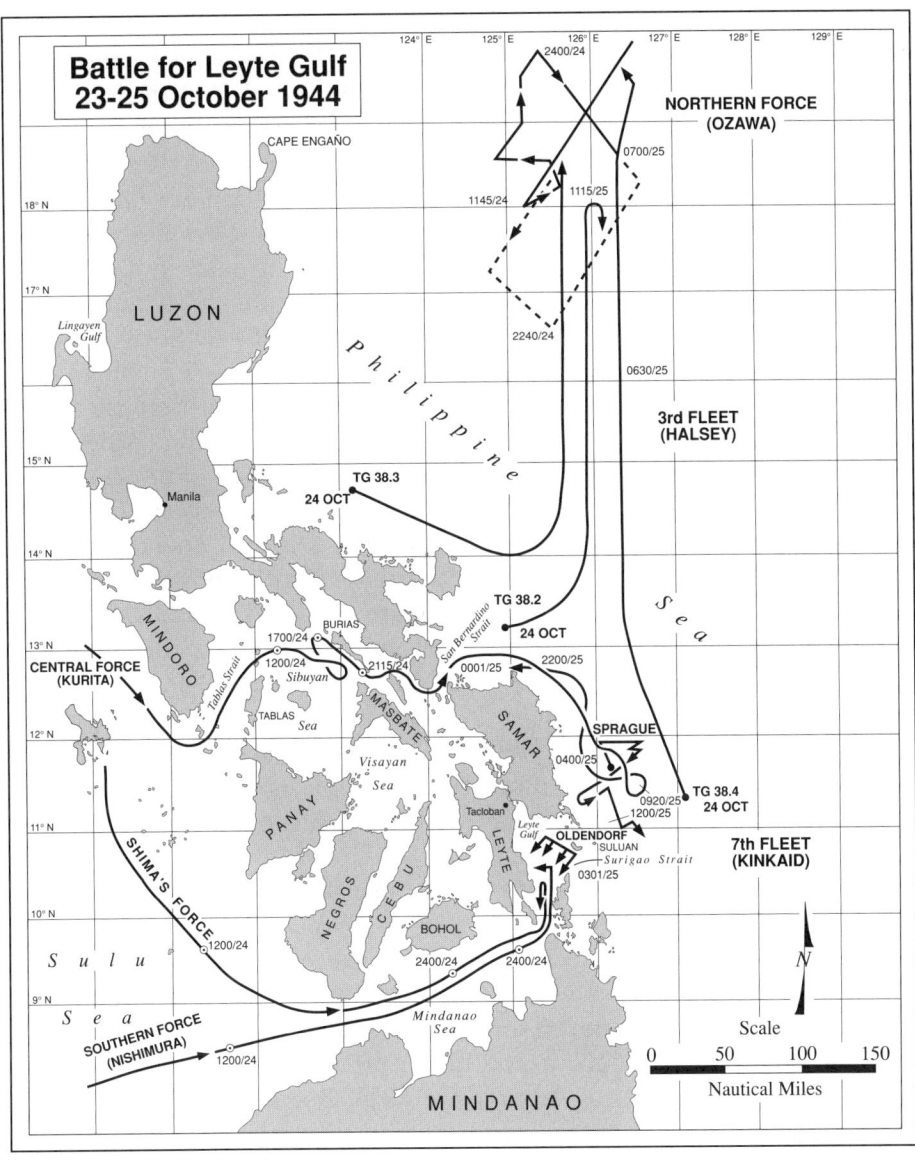

naval order of battle. The staff knew how many battleships, carriers, and cruisers existed and where most of them were. To help with location and tracking, General MacArthur had asked the Fourteenth and Twentieth Air Force squadrons to search Japanese anchorages in Singapore, Borneo, Indochina, Formosa, and the Bungo Suido area. He had also directed General Kenney to have his own air units search the Philippines for signs of Japanese fleet movements. To the Seventh Fleet staff it was fairly obvious that their CVEs should continue attacks on enemy airfields in the central Philippines area and provide combat air patrol over the gulf and beaches. Since there were only two passages into Leyte Gulf—by Surigao Strait from the south and from the open ocean to the east—the battleships, cruisers, and CVEs under Kinkaid would provide a last defense if the Third Fleet were unable to stop the Japanese. With the submarine sighting reports, it was fairly clear on the 23d that Kurita's force would approach by way of the San Bernardino Strait. But still a mystery was the location of the Japanese carriers, if they were at sea, and how they would attack. At this point there was no evidence that a Southern Force existed.

On the 23d, Halsey's carrier task groups (TGs 38.2, 38.3, 38.4) had been concentrated to the northeast of Samar, providing the "strategic cover" called for in KING II. During the night of 23–24 October the groups moved to a position about 125 miles east of central Luzon. Here, during the forenoon watch (0800–1200) three waves of enemy land-based aircraft, consisting of more than fifty planes in each group, attacked Rear Admiral Ted Sherman's TG 38.3. Although suffering enormous losses, the Japanese did manage to damage irreparably the light carrier *Princeton* (CVL 23). In trying to save the ship, the light cruiser *Birmingham* (CL 62) and the destroyers *Morrison* (DD 560) and *Irwin* (DD 794) were damaged by explosions in the carrier. *Birmingham* suffered 236 dead and 400 wounded, more than twice the losses in *Princeton*. *Princeton* was ordered sunk in the late afternoon.[13]

While Sherman's task group was under attack Rear Admiral Ralph E. Davison's TG 38.4 and Rear Admiral Gerald F. Bogan's TG 38.2, cruising off Samar, sent out morning search missions to the west to locate the enemy forces known to be at sea. They found them. At 0905 Davison's searching Helldivers (SB2C) spotted Nishimura's Southern Force and called for assistance from TG 38.4's *Franklin* (CV 13), *Enterprise*, *San Jacinto* (CVL 30), and *Belleau Wood* (CVL 24). At about the same time Bogan's search planes located Kurita's First Striking Force a few miles

---

[13] Morison 12:177–83; Edwin Hoyt, *The Battle for Leyte Gulf: The Death Knell of the Japanese Fleet* (New York: Weybright & Talley, 1972), 107–24; James A. Field, Jr., *The Japanese at Leyte Gulf, The Sho Operation* (Princeton University Press, 1947), 43–56; C. Vann Woodward, *The Battle for Leyte Gulf* (New York: Macmillan, 1947), 12–17, 20–24, 33–35. This chapter was completed and printed before the publication of Thomas J. Cutler's excellent study, *The Battle of Leyte Gulf, 23–26 October 1944* (New York: Harper Collins, 1994).

east of Mindoro in the Sibuyan Sea. Given the size of this fleet, Halsey ordered all three of the task groups, including Sherman's beleaguered TG 38.3, to attack Kurita's force. He also ordered Vice Admiral McCain's TG 38.1, currently en route to Ulithi for rest and recreation with the carriers *Wasp* (CV 18), *Hornet* (CV 12), *Monterey* (CVL 26), *Cowpens* (CVL 26), and *Bunker Hill* (CV 17) from Bogan's group, to return to the fray.[14]

The air attacks on the 24th were disastrous for the Japanese, but they were not the "knockout blows" reported by Halsey's pilots. Before being ordered to concentrate on the ships in the Sibuyan Sea, Davison's squadrons had dealt remarkably light damage to Nishimura's ships in three morning attacks. The Japanese ships were unimpeded in their progress toward Surigao Strait. Shima's force, although spotted several times during the 24th, was never attacked.[15]

Kurita's force, as might be expected, received almost the full attention of all three task groups. When ordered to join the attacks against Kurita's ships, Sherman was also directed to have his carriers search to the north and northeast for the missing enemy carriers. Bedeviled by his own problems, Sherman's searches did not get off until the afternoon. At 1540 a small force consisting of the two hermaphrodite battleship-carriers, *Ise* and *Hyuga*, plus light forces, was spotted and an hour later the carrier force was located, approximately 190 miles north of Sherman's task group. This carrier force consisted of the fleet carrier *Zuikaku* and the three light carriers *Zuiho*, *Chitose*, and *Chiyoda* plus two light cruisers and assorted destroyers. It was not immediately evident that only twenty-nine aircraft remained on the carriers. During that day, 24 October, the carrier fleet commander, Vice Admiral Jisaburo Ozawa, had sent over 130 planes on a one-way trip against Sherman's task group. The few survivors of the attacks then flew on to airfields in northern Luzon.[16]

During 24 October, while Admiral Halsey's carrier groups were locating the enemy forces and engaging them with their aircraft, Admiral Kinkaid and his small operations staff were planning their own reception for the Japanese. The admiral had brought with him in *Wasatch* a few senior officers, among whom were Commodore Val Schaeffer, his chief of staff; Captain David S. Crawford, the plans officer; Captain Richard H. Cruzen, the operations officer; Captain Arthur H. McCollum, the fleet intelligence officer; and Commander Leland G. Shaffer, the communications officer. Once the Southern Force of Admiral Nishimura was identified and its probable destination established—which occurred by 0915—the staff moved into action. The estimate was made that this enemy force would probably arrive in the Surigao Strait around 0200 on the 25th. The

---

[14] Reynolds, *Fast Carriers*, 264–65.
[15] CTF 77 Action Report, 31 Jan 1945, 14; Morison 12:190–91; Field, *Japanese at Leyte Gulf*, 54–55.
[16] Morison 12:192, 319; Sherman, *Combat Command*, 250–52, 263–66.

Rear Admiral Jesse B. Oldendorf, Vice Admiral Kinkaid, Rear Admiral T. E. Chandler, Rear Admiral Russell S. Berkey, and Commodore V. H. Schaeffer, November 1944. Schaeffer had just been presented the Legion of Merit award he earned when commanding *Bataan* (CVL 29) during the Battle of the Philippine Sea in June 1944.

chief of staff then notified all units in the gulf, by talk between ships, that a night action was anticipated. He also requested that all task group commanders come to *Wasatch* by 1200. To speed their arrival, patrol torpedo boats picked them up and returned them to their commands. Prior to the arrival of the task group commanders, preliminary plans were made by the staff under Schaeffer's guidance and then discussed with Kinkaid. During this same morning General Krueger, still operating from *Wasatch*, was informed of the pending activities. He quickly moved ashore with his staff. Kinkaid personally informed General MacArthur of the coming events and urged him to move ashore from *Nashville*. The general rejected the suggestion; he had never been in a sea battle and wanted to experience one. He later changed his mind.[17]

Kinkaid's meeting with his group commanders lasted less than an hour. Assignments were made orally, with dispatch orders to follow. Admiral Jesse Oldendorf, commander of TG 77.2, was to command the battle group that

---

[17] RADM V. H. Schaeffer to author, Coronado, CA, 3 Apr 1978; Rogers, *Bitter Years*, 187.

would meet the Japanese in Surigao Strait. He would have the six old battleships, three heavy cruisers, and two light cruisers that had come with him from the Third Fleet plus a mixture of twenty-six Third and Seventh Fleet destroyers. Kinkaid had also ordered Rear Admiral Russell (Count) Berkey, with his two light cruisers and one heavy cruiser, to serve under Oldendorf's command. Thirty-nine Seventh Fleet PT boats were also added. Oldendorf's command appeared sufficient to deal with the Nishimura-Shima force of two battleships, three heavy cruisers, one light cruiser, and eleven destroyers—forty fighting ships (plus thirty-nine PT boats) against seventeen. Rear Admiral Tommy Sprague's sixteen CVEs (TG 77.4), with their destroyer escorts, were disposed about 50 miles east of the gulf entrance in three groups within supporting distance of one another. The CVEs were expected to keep the area clear of Japanese aircraft and submarines and to be ready to attack the enemy ships if called upon to do so. All transport and cargo vessels that were unloaded were gathered into a convoy, allocated a couple of escorts, and sent out of the gulf toward Manus. Finally, the three amphibious command ships present—*Wasatch*, *Blue Ridge* (AGC 2) (Barbey), and *Mount Olympus* (Wilkinson)—plus *Nashville* (with General MacArthur still on board), and twenty-eight Liberty ships at the north end of Leyte Gulf were all pulled together and allocated a screen of destroyers and patrol craft. With dispositions made, the conference closed. Kinkaid let Halsey know by dispatch that the Seventh Fleet could handle the Southern Force and he expected the Third Fleet to take care of the Center Force, the term used for what was later identified as Kurita's First Striking Force.[18]

By 1600 on the 24th Admiral Halsey was fairly confident that he had already defeated Kurita's fleet, the Center Force. From 1030 to 1600 his carrier groups had launched 259 sorties against the Japanese. The enemy air cover was ineffective and easily brushed aside; their guns were numerous, but the fire brought down relatively few attackers. With better attack discipline the carrier strikes might have immobilized the whole Japanese force. Instead, only the super battleship *Musashi* was sunk and the heavy cruiser *Myoko* damaged severely enough to force its return to Brunei. Hits had been made on three other battleships, but all were able to continue. However, the TF 38 airmen gave such glowing reports of their accomplishments that Admirals Marc Mitscher and Halsey were convinced that a major naval victory had been won in the Sibuyan Sea. The clincher, from Halsey's perspective, came at 1600 when a flyer from *Intrepid* (CV 11) observed the fleet turn westward, apparently leaving the field of battle. What wasn't seen was the Center Force again countermarching at

---

[18] RADM Schaeffer to author, 3 Apr 1978; CTF 77 Action Report, 31 Jan 1945, 14–17; Morison 12:198–99.

1715 and shaping course for San Bernardino Strait. Halsey was convinced that the Japanese were no longer a threat to Kinkaid's fleet. By 1700 he had turned his attention to the carriers to the north of him.[19]

While TF 38 was mauling Kurita's Center Force, the Seventh Fleet was preparing a trap for Nishimura's Southern Force. Oldendorf had already spent a week in Leyte Gulf, and he had expended considerable thought on how best to use his battleships and cruisers to defend it. Not knowing what the Japanese intended to do, he and his chief of staff (Rafe Bates) concentrated on what they were capable of doing. The enemy had enough surface ships to attack in strength through the Surigao Strait or enter the gulf from the east or do both. So Oley had his battleships steam each night on an east-to-west line across the area where the Surigao Strait debouches into Leyte Gulf. That plugged one entrance. Were the Japanese to appear in force from the east, he assumed that air searches would give him time to move his line the hour's steaming distance to the opening. These evening steaming formations would allow Oldendorf to quickly set a battle plan. After the conference with Kinkaid, Oley had Bates draft the operations order and then he had his subordinate flag officers report to his flagship, *Louisville*, for conference. The battle plan was simple. The battleship line would steam across the end of the Surigao Strait on an east-west line. To the south of the line would be two cruiser groups, a left and right flank unit, also steaming on an east-west line. South of the cruisers, close to the shores on each side of the straits, would be thirteen groups of three motor torpedo boats (MTB) each. The MTBs would give the first warning of the enemy's presence and then attack; next the destroyers would attack with torpedoes; and finally the cruisers and battleships would open fire when reasonably sure of scoring a high percentage of hits. The battleships were short of armor-piercing 14- and 16-inch shells and did not want to waste any by firing too early. Kinkaid later reported that "fire was to be held until the destroyers had launched torpedoes and the enemy had closed to within 17,000 to 20,000 yards of our battleline."[20]

As Halsey's strikes against Kurita's Center Force were reaching a climax, the admiral had to make plans for the next phase. If Kurita were turned back, TF 38 aircraft would continue attacks the next day until the survivors were beyond the reach of the carrier planes. If Kurita continued eastward through San Bernardino Strait, a surface engagement was likely. To prepare for this contingency, Halsey flashed a preparatory dispatch at 1512 to all task group commanders in TF 38, designating the four battleships and their supporting cruisers and destroyers that were to become a surface bat-

---

[19] Morison 12:183–89; Reynolds, *Fast Carriers*, 265–66; Hoyt, *Leyte Gulf*, 125–55.
[20] CTF 77 Action Report, 31 Jan 1945, 14–15; ADM Jesse B. Oldendorf, "The Battle of Surigao Strait," *Blue Book* (Mar 1948), 38–40; Morison 12:198–202; VADM J. B. Oldendorf to CAPT A. A. Burke, San Francisco, CA, 4 Dec 1947 (copy), TCK Papers.

tle group. Vice Admiral Willis (Ching) Lee would command this TF 34, if it were formed. To make sure TF 38 understood that this was only a preparatory dispatch, Halsey informed his commanders by TBS, "If the enemy sorties, Task Force 34 will be formed when directed by me." An hour and half after his 1512 dispatch Halsey finally had solid information that an enemy carrier force was at sea to the north of him. This was Vice Admiral Ozawa's two-part Northern Force. Following a couple hours of indecision, Halsey sent a dispatch to Kinkaid: "Central Force heavily damaged according to strike reports. Am proceeding north with three groups to attack carrier force at dawn." From Bull Halsey's flag bridge in *New Jersey* it appeared that Kurita's force was no longer a genuine threat, so he was now turning north toward a foe worthy of a carrier task force's attention.[21]

Halsey's decision to attack an enemy carrier force to the north did not particularly worry Kinkaid. His radio crew had intercepted Halsey's 1512 radio concerning TF 34. He and his staff now assumed that Halsey had turned north with three carrier groups (TGs 38.2, 38.3, and 38.4), leaving Admiral Lee's TF 34 to guard San Bernardino Strait. By the time Halsey turned north, Kinkaid had informed him of the coming night battle with the Japanese Southern Force. Kinkaid's chief of staff remembered:

> We notified Halsey of our expected night engagement with the enemy Southern Force and that we would be able to take care of them without any assistance from him if he could handle the Jap Center Force. . . . At this point we were not at all concerned as to the outcome of an encounter with the oncoming forces of the Jap Fleet. As a matter of fact we rather relished the idea of taking part in a major naval battle which this was promising to be.[22]

The night battle in Surigao Strait was a smashing success for the Seventh Fleet. Nishimura's force was almost totally destroyed. Shima's force, steaming in Nishimura's wake, reversed course to prevent total destruction. The big guns and torpedoes of Oldendorf's forces sank two battleships and two destroyers in the main engagement. During the pursuit by the cruisers another destroyer was sunk, and the heavy cruiser *Mogami*, too damaged to keep up with Shima's fleeing cruiser-destroyer force, was sunk by the Japanese. Though Admiral Shima's smaller force escaped major damage in the gun battle, fuel shortage limited its speed and range of movement, and two of its cruisers were destroyed by air attack in the next ten days. Of the Nishimura-Shima forces only the heavy cruiser *Ashigara* and four destroyers escaped from the Battle of Surigao Strait.[23]

---

[21] Fleet Admiral William F. Halsey, Jr., "The Battle for Leyte Gulf," *Proceedings* (May 1952): 488–90; Morison 12:193–94.

[22] RADM V. H. Schaeffer to author, Coronado, CA, 3 Apr 1978.

[23] Morison 12:233–40; USSBS, *Interrogations* 1:235–44.

During both the preparatory period and the battle itself Kinkaid and his staff remained in *Wasatch*, close to their communications. There was little they could do once the battle dispositions had been made. During the afternoon and evening they received a stream of reports, some delayed, from Halsey about the carrier attacks against Kurita's Center Force. All times given are local (GCT plus 9).

24/1512—Enemy hurt and milling aimlessly in Sibuyan Sea. TF 34 set up but not ordered to be formed.

24/2004—Report of strikes on Central Force which now has reversed course to 270 degrees. Third Fleet concentrated off San Bernardino Strait entrance.

24/2024—Gave 1925 position of enemy in Sibuyan Sea; three groups of TF 38 now going north against enemy carrier force.

24/2115—Part of enemy force sighted by night fighter ("snooper") between Burias and Masbate Islands. [This was east of the 2024 report.]

There was nothing in these reports to make Kinkaid or his staff anxious, unless it was recognition that the damaged Center Force had moved to the area between Burias and Masbate islands, a position 25 miles east of its 1935 position. As they kept the watch through the night, monitoring reports from the Surigao Strait area, Kinkaid decided to reinforce a previously ordered search of the San Bernardino Strait entrance. At 1225 Kinkaid had sent a dispatch to the commander of VPB–33, a Catalina (PBY–5) squadron based on the tender *Half Moon* (AVP 26) in Leyte Gulf, and had ordered that three of his patrol planes search at night the sector 341 to 017 degrees to a distance of 600 miles from Tacloban, but starting through the entrance to the gulf. No reports had come in from the planes during the evening. At 0156 (the 25th) the admiral, by dispatch, ordered Commander TG 77.4 Tommy Sprague to have his CVEs make a dawn search of sectors 340 to 030 degrees to a distance of 135 miles from Suluan Island, at the entrance to Leyte Gulf.[24] This search, like that ordered of VPB–33, would take in the entrance to San Bernardino Strait.

Finally, after spending most of the night together, Kinkaid asked his staff if there was anything they had overlooked. Captain Cruzen, the staff operations officer, raised the point, "We've never asked Halsey directly if Task Force 34 is guarding the San Bernardino Strait." Kinkaid ordered a dispatch sent, and at 0412 the question was asked. Despite its urgency it was not answered for several hours.[25]

---

[24] COM7THFLT to COMINCH ("King's Eyes Only"), 12/160202Z, King Papers.

[25] COM7THFLT to COMINCH, 12/160202Z; CTF 77 Action Report, 31 Jan 1945, 25; TCK, "Communications Breakdown at the Battle for Leyte Gulf," in *The Pacific War Remembered: An Oral History Collection*, ed., John T. Mason, Jr. (Annapolis: Naval Institute Press, 1986), 271–73.

During the two hours between the message asking Halsey if TF 34 was guarding the San Bernardino Strait and sunrise at 0614, Admirals Oldendorf and T. L. Sprague began operations to pursue the defeated Nishimura-Shima forces. Given the slowness of the old battleships, the surface pursuit was a cruiser-destroyer action. Sprague was commander of the three "Taffies" as well as commander of Task Unit 77.4.1 (Taffy 1) with its four CVEs: *Sangamon* (CVE 26), *Suwanee* (CVE 27), *Santee* (CVE 29), and *Petrof Bay* (CVE 80). Taffy 1 loaded torpedoes or armor-piercing 500-pound bombs into its planes in preparation for early strikes. On board *Wasatch*, Kinkaid read a detective story and the staff relaxed as it awaited further developments. More than 200 miles to the north Admiral Halsey's TF 38 was about to hold reveille for Admiral Ozawa's carrier force.

At 0647 a plane on antisubmarine patrol from *Kadashan Bay* (CVE 76), a part of Rear Admiral Felix Stump's TU 77.4.2 (Taffy 2), reported being fired upon by an unidentified group of ships. It included battleships and cruisers and bore about 340 degrees, distance 20 miles, from Rear Admiral C.A.F. (Ziggy) Sprague's TU 77.4.3 (Taffy 3). The three Taffies of TG 77.4 lay about 60 miles offshore and were strung out in three groups from north (Taffy 3) to south (Taffy 2, then Taffy 1), with about 30 miles between each group. Ziggy Sprague's Taffy 3, lying 60 miles north-northeast of Suluan Island, became the only group whose ships directly engaged the Japanese force, Admiral Kurita's Center Force, in surface combat. At 0658 the enemy commenced firing on Taffy 3, and three minutes later Admiral Sprague called for support. Six escort carriers were no match for four battleships, six cruisers, and eleven destroyers. Kinkaid received the contact report at 0704. It was now quite obvious that TF 34 was not guarding San Bernardino Strait.

Kinkaid and his staff quickly moved to bring all assistance within their command to the aid of the carriers. They recognized that the Japanese force, including the battleships, had the advantage of speed over all of the CVEs and could, if not deterred, wipe out all of TG 77.4's sixteen carriers. Three actions were quickly taken by Kinkaid. At 0707 he informed Halsey of the situation and requested assistance at all possible speed. He directed Captain Richard Whitehead, who was the air support commander and on board *Wasatch*, to have the aircraft from all of the Taffies concentrate against the attacking Center Force. And lastly at 0725 he ordered Admiral Oldendorf to concentrate his battle line at the eastern entrance to Leyte Gulf. As Oley was gathering his heavy ships, Kinkaid also provided him with the light cruiser *Nashville* and nine destroyers from inside Leyte Gulf, and even recalled several destroyers escorting a convoy of empty transports and cargo ships toward Manus.[26]

---

[26] CTF 77 Action Report, 31 Jan 1945, 26–27; Morison 12:289–94.

In directing Oldendorf to prepare for action, Kinkaid had to deal with some dissenting views within his staff. As a former battleship officer (gunnery officer of *Arizona* and executive officer of *Colorado*), Kinkaid's first thoughts were to have Oldendorf place his battle line across the entrance to Leyte Gulf and force the Japanese to steam into it. As at Surigao Strait it would be a "T" situation with the battle line able to concentrate broadside fire on an approaching column or columns of vessels that could only use forward-firing turrets. On the other hand, this meant sacrificing the Taffies, since nothing would be done to prevent the swifter Japanese from destroying the CVEs. Kinkaid's chief of staff, Commodore Schaeffer, argued heatedly with his boss about this problem. A former carrier captain (*Bataan*) and a naval aviator, Val Schaeffer felt it would be seriously wrong to leave the escort carriers to be annihilated. He later wrote,

> when the time came (and there was no time to lose) to order Oldendorf out of the gulf to engage the Jap Center Force in support of our escort carriers, Kinkaid hesitated and questioned whether he should risk the destruction of battleships and cruisers, which take a long time and are expensive to build, to protect CVEs that were rapidly being built by the hundreds. . . . There was no question in my mind but that we should send our combatant forces, TG 77.2, out to help our CVEs before Kurita destroyed them all and with their destruction, the destruction of our air power. We had no Army Air and the fast carriers were now hundreds of miles away.[27]

Kinkaid accepted Schaeffer's arguments, but temporized briefly. At 0953 he directed Oldendorf to take his force out to meet Kurita and then canceled the order. Finally, at 1127, Kinkaid again directed his battle group commander to take his whole force out, but by then Admiral Kurita had decided to retreat back through San Bernardino Strait.[28]

It has never been clear why the Center Force commander reversed course and left the field of battle, thus terminating the Battle off Samar. Certainly there is little doubt that the stout resistance he met from the Taffies and the damage inflicted by their airmen and destroyermen played a significant part in Kurita's decision. It is also believed that the submarine attacks and the loss of his flagship on the 23d, and then the heavy air assaults and losses in the Sibuyan Sea on the 24th, shook the Japanese admiral's resolve. Vice Admiral McCain, whose TG 38.1 was en route to the battle area off Samar, believed that, when his inbound aircraft appeared on *Yamato*'s radar, Kurita must have realized that additional help for the CVEs was on the way. Ozawa's Northern Force was a decoy and his ships were expendable, but Kurita expected to join forces

---

[27] RADM V. H. Schaeffer to author, Coronado, CA, 26 Apr 1978.
[28] Oldendorf, "Battle of Surigao Strait," 47; Morison 12:295–96.

with Admirals Nishimura and Shima. So the destruction of the Southern Force contributed to ruining the SHO-I operation for Kurita.

Whatever the reasons for the Japanese retreat, Ziggy Sprague looked upon it as a heaven-sent dispensation. *Gambier Bay* (CVE 73) and *St. Lo* (CVE 63) had been sunk and it had looked like nothing could save Taffy 3. And among Oldendorf's warriors there were probably few tears shed at missing a second gun battle in one day. Oley's battleships and cruisers were low in the number of armor-piercing projectiles on board after their previous fight. This shortage could have caused trouble in a protracted gun fight with the Center Force.

Halsey's attack on Ozawa's Northern Force was as successful as Oldendorf's battle in the Surigao Strait. His flyers quickly sank a destroyer and three of the four carriers that had been the lure for TF 38. The battleship-carriers *Ise* and *Hyuga* had been lightly damaged and were chased back to Formosan waters. The fourth carrier and another destroyer were attacked and sunk by cruiser fire. Because of Kinkaid's insistent calls for assistance for the Taffies, Halsey finally turned his battleships south at 1115, and then at 1622 sent a special task group (TG 34.5) under Rear Admiral Oscar Badger racing ahead. Air cover along the way was provided by Admiral Bogan's TG 38.2. But none of the big ships reached the San Bernardino Strait area in time to attack Kurita's retiring force. Halsey's TF 38, in fighting the Battle off Cape Engaño, had won another victory over the Japanese at no cost in ships.[29]

The three-day multifaceted Battle for Leyte Gulf was a major victory for the Seventh and Third Fleets. The vessels sunk, including those in Admiral Sherman's TG 38.3 battle against the land-based air attacks on the 24th, are as follows:[30]

Ship Types Sunk	Japan	U.S.
Large Carriers (CV)	1	0
Light Carriers (CVL)	3	1
Escort Carriers (CVE)	0	2
Battleships (BB)	3	0
Heavy Cruisers (CA)	6	0
Light Cruisers (CL)	4	0
Destroyers/Destroyer Escorts (DD/DE)	9	3
Motor Torpedo Boats (MTB)	0	1

Though there was glory enough for all involved and perhaps a special place in the Pantheon of naval heroes for the officers and men of *Johnston* (DD 557), *Hoel* (DD 533) and *Samuel B. Roberts* (DE 413), who so

---

[29] Halsey, "Battle for Leyte Gulf," 491–95; Potter, *Halsey*, 293–304; Morison 12:317–32.
[30] Woodward, *Battle for Leyte Gulf*, 229.

ably defended the CVEs off Samar, the Battle for Leyte Gulf sparked more than fifty years of controversy about the actions of Admirals Halsey and Kinkaid. Kinkaid and almost all the naval commanders in Leyte Gulf or in the Taffies believed that Halsey should not have taken Task Force 38 north against the decoy Northern Force of Admiral Ozawa. Had he remained on guard at San Bernardino Strait, they argued, he could have smashed Kurita's Central Force and the Taffies would merely have joined the attack.

Halsey, of course, disagreed. He cited the paragraph in his instructions from Nimitz that stated, "In case opportunity for destruction of major portion of the enemy fleet offers or can be created, such destruction becomes the primary task." Halsey had had a "major portion of the enemy fleet" at hand in the Center Force, but when he heard of Ozawa's Northern Force with its aircraft carriers, that force became the "major portion" to be attacked. Once that decision had been made, the decision to let Kinkaid worry about Kurita's Center Force became a matter of assumptions and rationalizations. Halsey and his staff assumed that Kurita's force had been heavily damaged and significantly weakened by TF 38's airmen in the Battle of the Sibuyan Sea. He further assumed that Oldendorf's battleships would be finished with the Surigao Strait action in time and in shape to meet and defeat Kurita. He also assumed that the sixteen CVEs in TG 77.4 could provide the necessary striking power to assist significantly in stopping the Center Force and to defend against shore-based enemy aircraft.

Halsey's rationalizations came later. None of the troubles that beset the CVEs would have occurred had Kinkaid not mistakenly assumed that TF 34 had been formed and had he ordered proper surveillance of San Bernardino Strait by Seventh Fleet aircraft. Even if Kurita had broken into Leyte Gulf, his force could not have significantly damaged the American beachhead. And had there been a single person in overall command, instead of the two fleet commanders operating without a coordinating authority, communication between Halsey and Kinkaid would have been clear. The latter would have known that TF 34 had never been formed and left behind when Halsey took TF 38 north to attack Ozawa.[31]

In the evening of 25 October, Admiral Halsey sent a dispatch addressed to Nimitz, MacArthur, Kinkaid, and Ernie King that opened, "So that there be no misunderstanding concerning recent operations of the Third Fleet." He then stated that once Ozawa's carrier force was located, "to statically guard San Bernardino Strait until enemy surface and carrier air attacks could be coordinated would have been childish." So he had gone north to

---

[31] COM3RDFLT to CINCPAC, 10/251317Z, Command Summary; Potter, *Halsey*, 305–7; Morison 12:193–96. The views of Admirals Kinkaid and Halsey are given at length in Hanson W. Baldwin, *Sea Fights and Shipwrecks: True Tales of the Seven Seas* (Garden City, NY: Hanover House, 1955), 165–82.

strike the enemy at dawn, but his chance to destroy the enemy was aborted. "Com Seventh Fleet's urgent appeals for help came at a time when the enemy force was heavily damaged and my overwhelming [battleship] force was within forty-five miles of the cripples. I had no alternative but to stand off from my golden opportunity and head south to support Kinkaid although I was convinced that this force [Kinkaid's] was adequate to deal with an enemy force that was badly weakened by our attacks of the 24th, a conviction justified by later events off Leyte."[32] Without being asked, Halsey had stated his case. Some people, including Admiral Nimitz, believed Halsey must have felt "that he is in a defensive position in this matter."[33]

It wasn't until 11 December that Admiral King asked Kinkaid for explanations about the Battle for Leyte Gulf. He asked specifically what arrangements Kinkaid had made to assure himself that the Japanese Center Force had not passed through the San Bernardino Strait during the night of 24–25 October and was heading toward Leyte Gulf. In his reply Kinkaid explained that he had ordered a night search by aircraft from TG 77.4. He told of intercepting Halsey's message concerning the formation of TF 34 off San Bernardino Strait and assuming it had been left at the strait when Halsey took his three carrier task groups north. He noted that the PBY search had led to nothing and that the CVE search had not gotten off in a timely manner.[34] To his credit, Kinkaid placed no blame on Admiral T. L. Sprague for not seeing that the CVE morning search was pressed, nor on Admiral Stump, commander of Taffy 2, from whose CVEs the dawn search should have originated. Kinkaid had been urged by Admiral Wilkinson and his chief of staff, Commodore Paulus P. Powell, to specifically order Admiral C.A.F. Sprague to be prepared for morning air attacks against the Japanese battleships and to do some dawn searches. In describing this incident on board *Wasatch*, Powell noted, "I suggested that such an order was good enough for Felix [Stump] and Tommy Sprague, but not enough for 'Dopey' [C.A.F. Sprague]. Tom got very annoyed with me because I insisted that he had to tell 'Dopey' to do some night scouting and be ready to launch everything he had at dawn."[35]

With more reflection Kinkaid later concluded that the real source of the trouble that overtook his CVEs off Samar was Halsey's unwillingness to stick to the mission he had been assigned by Nimitz and MacArthur. In 1960 Kinkaid spelled out his views in an oral history interview for Columbia University:

---

[32] COM3RDFLT to CINCPAC, et. al., 10/251317Z, Command Summary.

[33] Nimitz to King, Pearl Harbor, 28 Oct 1944, Nimitz Papers; RADM Forrest Sherman, "Notes on Conference with CINCSWPA," 3 Nov 1944, Sherman Papers, OA.

[34] COMINCH to "Eyes Only Kinkaid," 12/111504Z, King Papers; COM7THFLT to COMINCH ("King's Eyes Only"), 12/160202Z, TCK Papers.

[35] RADM Paulus Powell to Commodore R. W. Bates, New York, 3 Nov 1953, Bates Papers.

> As commander of the Seventh Fleet, I was to transport the landing forces to Leyte Gulf beaches, establish them ashore, and see that they were covered and stayed ashore. The Third Fleet under Halsey was to give us protection during the landing and during whatever actions might take place afterwards. His was a strategic cover, mine was a direct cover and the protection of landing forces. It's a very important point that I have brought out frequently, because I had a mission and Admiral Halsey had a mission. In spite of the fact that we did not have a common superior, I have frequently said that if both Halsey and I had carried out our respective missions correctly there would have been no confusion. . . . It has always been my opinion . . . that one commander would not have been better than two where each of us had his mission . . . very clearly stated. . . .
>
> For Halsey, an aviator, the main Japanese force was the force that [had] carriers in it. Actually Ozawa's was not the strongest force, but it was the only one that had air power. So I think, combining that with the paragraph in his original orders from Nimitz, he felt justified in taking everything up north after Ozawa, neglecting his obligation to cover and support the Leyte operation.[36]

Despite the controversy that has surrounded the actions (or lack thereof) of Admirals Kinkaid and Halsey, the Battle for Leyte Gulf remains one of the U.S. Navy's greatest sea fights. The area that was encompassed; the fighting of four engagements (Sibuyan Sea, Surigao Strait, Samar, and Cape Engaño); the "crossing of the T" in the Surigao Strait; the drama of the Taffies' predicament; the heroics of the destroyermen; and the immense damage to the Japanese navy all helped to raise this battle above all others in the Pacific war. Samuel Eliot Morison, the great historian of U.S. naval operations in World War II, stated his conclusion on this epochal battle: "However you look at it, the Battle for Leyte Gulf should be an imperishable part of our national heritage."[37]

Four days after this great sea battle, Admiral Kinkaid in *Wasatch* joined a convoy returning ships to Ulithi, Manus, and Hollandia. During the five days' passage to his New Guinea headquarters, he had time to reflect on past battles and give some thought to action reports and operations ahead. Because of the excellent communication facilities in his command ship, the admiral was able to keep in touch with his ships in Leyte Gulf and with MacArthur's headquarters, but the flow of dispatches was not comforting.

Enemy air attacks, both Special Attack Corps (suicide) and regular operations, were unrelenting against the Seventh Fleet. The Navy's problem was traceable to the fact that General George Kenney had been unable to

---

[36] Mason, *Pacific War Remembered*, 267, 274–75.
[37] Morison 12:338.

bring sufficient fighter aircraft to the Leyte Gulf area. Soggy ground had made it impossible to build firm runways and taxi strips where they were needed. MacArthur had stated that the Fifth Air Force would have its fighters ready to defend Leyte by 27 October, but Kinkaid had his doubts. On the 27th he requested that Halsey provide two carrier task groups for air defense and suppression of the Visayan airfields. This was especially needed since the CVEs had to refuel on the 28th and their squadrons would be out of action. Nimitz wanted Halsey to withdraw and give his carriers a chance to rest their pilots and take care of replenishment, but he and Halsey agreed to leave one task group, usually two large (CV) and two light (CVL) carriers and supporting vessels.[38] Admiral Nimitz's Command Summary, sometimes referred to as the "Grey Book," reported the situation at Leyte Gulf in its record of 31 October:

> At 1437 on 1st [at Leyte] CTG 77.1 reported his group under attack. *Abner Read* (DD–526), while screening the damaged *Claxton* (DD–571), was hit by an aerial torpedo, blew up, and sank. At 1603 CTF 77 [Kinkaid] reported our air situation in Leyte Gulf Area to be deteriorating owing to constant enemy reinforcement and withdrawal of fast carrier task groups. Only 60 Army fighters were in the area. Resumption of carrier strikes in the Manila and Visayan areas was requested. At 2057 CTF 77 reported that on the 1st 1 DD had been sunk by enemy air attacks, and at least 4 other DDs damaged.[39]

Experience had demonstrated that aerial interception of incoming Japanese squadrons could never be totally effective, and that those who broke through could not be entirely destroyed by shipboard fire power. It was quite conceivable therefore that the Japanese could drive the Seventh Fleet from Leyte Gulf or so damage it that the next operations would have to be reconsidered. To Kinkaid and his staff the answer was obvious. The Japanese squadrons in the islands to the west of Leyte and those on Luzon had to be eliminated along with their bases. On 1 November, while still en route to Hollandia, Kinkaid advised MacArthur to request CINCPAC to order Halsey's fast carriers to attack the Japanese airfields around Manila and in the Visayans, and to continue those attacks until the Fifth Air Force could do the job from bases in Leyte. On 2 November the general radioed Admiral Nimitz that he needed "early strikes in Luzon area from fast carrier groups." Significantly, he also requested that TG 38.3 continue in close support of Leyte with its carriers *Essex* (CV 9), *Lexington* (CV 16), and *Langley* (CVL 27).[40] Halsey immedi-

---

[38] CTF 77 to COM3RDFLT, 10/270221Z; CINCPOA to COM3RDFLT, 10/282242Z, Command Summary.
[39] Command Summary, 31 Oct 1944.
[40] CINCSWPA to CINCPOA, 1 Nov 1944, file SOPAC 547, MacArthur Papers.

ately informed Nimitz that he could begin two days of attacks on Luzon airfields commencing 5 November, but he would have to let the Leyte Gulf area shift for itself. He suggested that Kinkaid simply empty the area of all but the most necessary, and maneuverable, shipping.[41]

True to his promise Halsey sent three of TF 38's fast carrier task groups to attack Visayan and Luzon airfields on 5 and 6 November. The carriers continued their destructive sorties for the rest of November.[42]

Once in Hollandia, Kinkaid and his staff began the final planning for the amphibious assault on the southwest coast of Mindoro (LOVE-3 or L-3) scheduled for 5 December, and for the great invasion of Luzon at Lingayen Gulf (MIKE-1 or M-1), targeted for 20 December 1944. The two operations were closely related. The purpose of invading Mindoro was to construct air bases from which Fifth Air Force fighter and bomber squadrons could attack Japanese air bases and their squadrons in Luzon and the neighboring islands. Those aircraft suppression attacks would make it possible for the Lingayen attack force to reach the gulf without hindrance from shore-based Japanese aviation. Aircraft from Leyte were supposed to cover the invasion force in the Mindanao Sea and part way to Mindoro, but their short range required that squadrons operating from the vicinity of Mindoro cover the balance of the trip to northern Luzon.

At MacArthur's order, Kinkaid flew to Tacloban on 15 November for a conference with the general and his staff. From staff conversations and personal experience he learned that the situation was still not completely in hand. Japanese airpower had not been silenced. The Navy people in Leyte, which included Admiral Nimitz's plans officer, were agreed that the Mindoro and Lingayen operations, still scheduled for 5 and 20 December, should be delayed until the Fifth Air Force had full control of the air over Leyte and the Sulu Sea, thus ensuring safe passage to the landing sites. MacArthur strongly disagreed with the postponement.

On 16 November, with Kinkaid on hand, the general sent a long dispatch to Nimitz, indicating that he intended to stick to his plans. He radioed:

> The obvious intention of the enemy to make strong fight for the Philippines can best be frustrated by immediate attack in strength to prevent his preparations for the defense of Luzon which he is pushing at top speed at the present time. For that reason I intend to adhere to the present target dates for the L-3 [Mindoro] and M-1 [Luzon] Operations.

MacArthur went on to admit that Kenney's air bases were not far enough along to "saturate enemy airfields and beat down enemy air

---

[41] COM3RDFLT to CINCPOA, 11/020315Z, file SOPAC 549, MacArthur Papers.
[42] Reynolds, *Fast Carriers*, 286–88; Morison 12:354; COM3RDFLT to CINCPOA, 11/110245Z.

strength in Luzon and the Visayan area." He therefore requested further Third Fleet attacks throughout Luzon and the Visayans preliminary to the two operations ahead.[43]

Nimitz's reply the next day created a genuine problem for the general. He understood the need to assist General Kenney's airmen in seizing control of the air prior to the Mindoro landing, and to continue assistance until the shore-based squadrons in Leyte and Mindoro could handle the situation. But Halsey's carriers and their squadrons had to have at least two weeks of rest and replenishment before the Mindoro operation in December.[44] The problem for MacArthur, of course, was to get Kenney's Fifth Air Force into Leyte in such strength that Halsey's carriers could leave the Philippine area by 26 November. Unfortunately, neither the weather nor the Japanese was under the command of the general.

Kinkaid returned to Hollandia on 17 November with a copy of Nimitz's radio in his briefcase, and three days later he boarded *Wasatch* for the five-day passage back to Leyte Gulf. On 21 November General Kenney's planners informed General Walter Krueger about Fifth Air Force capabilities to cover his troops when they landed on Mindoro. If the Navy's carriers could handle the air defense of Leyte and protect the convoys on the first day to Mindoro, then his pilots could cover the rest of the operation. But here was a major proviso: Kenney's operations would depend on being able to base ashore ten day-fighter squadrons, one night-fighter squadron, and one Navy medium-bomber squadron.[45] But that was the rub; airfield space for twelve squadrons could not be developed in time to cover the Mindoro convoys that would depart on 2 December. Kinkaid received a copy of this memorandum when he arrived at Tacloban on 25 November.

Once ashore, Admiral Kinkaid received more bad news, this time from Rear Admiral Arthur D. Struble, who would command the amphibious landing at Mindoro. He had drafted an estimate of the situation for Kinkaid, and it was filled with dire predictions and conclusions. He stated that Japanese air power was sufficient to launch strong attacks against the Mindoro expedition and that the number of Japanese aircraft available for attacks was growing as planes were staged into Luzon from Formosa. Given the weakness in Army air coverage for the expedition, Admiral Struble recommended that "Naval Air provide air cover for the convoys and over the beach area if the Army is unable to provide such cover."[46]

---

[43] CINCSWPA to CINCPAC, 11/160101Z, file Navy 573, MacArthur Papers.
[44] CINCPOA to CINCSWPA, 11/170200Z, TCK Papers.
[45] Memo, Chief of Staff, Fifth Air Force to COMGEN Sixth Army, 21 Nov 1944, TCK Papers.
[46] Memo for TCK by RADM A. D. Struble, "Estimate of the Situation-LOVE THREE Operation," 24 Nov 1944, TCK Papers.

As if to underscore the accuracy of Struble's estimate, Third Fleet carriers off Luzon suffered serious damage during the afternoon of 25 November, Kinkaid's first day back in Leyte Gulf. Kamikazes struck Task Groups 38.2 and 38.3 and damaged four of the nine fast carriers. The next day Admiral Halsey had had enough. He cancelled further strikes in the Visayans and Luzon and sent three of his four task groups back to Ulithi to repair damage and rest the crews. Like most naval aviators, he considered his fast carrier task force too important to jeopardize them through continuous operations within striking range of shore-based Japanese air fleets and special attack squadrons.[47]

On 26 November, the same day Halsey sent his fast carriers back to Ulithi, MacArthur called a meeting to lay out the final details for assaulting Mindoro on 5 December. In his opening remarks the general made it clear that he planned to stay on schedule. General Kenney estimated that his Fifth Air Force could handle its mission. General Krueger simply stated that his troops were ready to go. Admiral Kinkaid and his chief of staff, Commodore Schaeffer, were the wet blankets. After a few generalizations, Kinkaid asked Schaeffer to give his estimate. The chief of staff was honest and painted a grim picture of the air menace to the Mindoro attack force. Pressed for a percentage estimate of damage to transports and landing ships, Schaeffer (a naval aviator) guessed 25 percent. General Krueger said that he could not accept such casualties, particularly if he was going to meet General Tomoyuki Yamashita's armies in Luzon after another amphibious expedition. MacArthur then tossed the ball back to Kinkaid and asked if the Navy could send some escort carriers to provide its own air cover for the Mindoro force. The answer was yes. Kinkaid would pull together a small task force of six escort carriers and provide them and the convoys with antiaircraft and heavy gunfire support from three battleships, three light cruisers, and eighteen destroyers. The escort carriers would protect the whole force from air attacks, and the battleships and cruisers would provide the carriers with antiaircraft barrages when needed. MacArthur applauded Kinkaid's willingness to shoulder this serious responsibility. In a letter to his deputy commander a few weeks later, Kinkaid wrote that he had told the general that "I was not pleased and felt that the decision had been forced upon me."[48]

Back on board *Wasatch*, Kinkaid and his staff began having second thoughts about the wisdom of their decision to hit Mindoro on schedule. Particularly concerned were Commodore Schaeffer; Rear Admiral Struble, who would command the invasion force; Rear Admiral Theodore D. Rud-

---

[47] Reynolds, *Fast Carriers*, 288; Morison 12:357–60.
[48] TCK to RADM C. E. Van Hook, 10 Dec 1944, Van Hook Papers; RADM V. H. Schaeffer to author, Coronado, CA, 16 Nov 1977.

dock, who was to command the heavy support group made up of battleships, cruisers, and destroyers; and Rear Admiral Stump, who would command the six CVEs.

On 29 November, three days before the Mindoro expedition was scheduled to depart, Struble and Ruddock proposed in separate memoranda that the whole Mindoro-Lingayen plan be reconsidered. Both had been shocked by successful attacks on the big ships in Leyte Gulf. Struble commented that "the two recent attacks on the battleship force are not indicative to me of a waning Jap air power in the Philippine Area." With the Japanese in control of the air, even if the Mindoro force got through and was landed on 5 December, he doubted that the resupply convoy could get through six days later. He concluded, "I do not consider the L–3 operation sound at this time, and recommend L–3 be converted to a much shorter thrust into Jap territory."[49] Ruddock's paper was similar to that of Struble's. Scrawled in pencil and in obvious haste, it warned that damage incurred by the Mindoro expedition could be of such magnitude that the Luzon (Lingayen) effort would be hazarded. The next morning he sent a second penciled memorandum stating the same points, but in greater detail.[50]

Kinkaid now faced the same dilemma that had beset his predecessor as Commander Naval Forces, Southwest Pacific Area. Vice Admiral Chips Carpender had evoked the wrath of MacArthur and his staff during 1942 and 1943 because he did not want to risk naval vessels in dangerous waters along the New Guinea coast.[51] Now Kinkaid was being ordered into an expedition that his subordinate commanders considered too dangerous under the existing timetable. His principal flag officers and his staff understood clearly the menace to their forces when operating in restricted waters without adequate air coverage. From reports of the Battle off Samar, Struble knew how little it took to sink a CVE. As Leyte Gulf defense force commander, Ruddock had experienced suicide attacks against his large ships. To these officers, and to Kinkaid also, it appeared that MacArthur was letting vanity stand in the way of sound judgment. He wanted to stick to the Joint Chiefs of Staff timetable and would not permit a delay in the Mindoro operation until Japanese airpower had been more thoroughly smashed.

The climax to the controversy came on 30 November, when the Seventh Fleet commander confronted General MacArthur twice. The admiral's career now hung in the balance. In the morning Kinkaid went to the general's headquarters in Tacloban and had a two-hour discussion

---

[49] Memo, RADM A. D. Struble to TCK, 29 Nov 1944, TCK Papers.
[50] Memo, RADM T. D. Ruddock to TCK, 29, 30 Nov 1944, TCK Papers.
[51] James, *MacArthur* 2:231–32, 242, 282.

with him and Lieutenant General Richard Sutherland, his chief of staff. He had prepared a long memorandum arguing his case and proposing cancellation of the Mindoro and Lingayen operations and substituting short moves to nearby islands. Kinkaid presented these ideas orally, but did not leave the paper. The admiral made no progress. He later related, "The General insisted upon not delaying the operation and that Jap air was weak and would cause very little trouble. He said he could not change the plans at that late date."[52]

Frustrated, and determined to take the only action he could under such circumstances, Kinkaid returned to his command ship and drafted a dispatch to Admiral King, Commander in Chief, U.S. Fleet. In this message Kinkaid explained his concerns and MacArthur's refusal to give them credence. He stated candidly:

> General MacArthur declines to accept my evaluation of present conditions and my strong recommendation that the Mindoro operation be not, repeat not, conducted now. General MacArthur believes that we must push forward now. I believe that it is not possible from the naval and air standpoint at the present time and that it would be disastrous to do so. I am under orders to carry out the operation. To meet the scheduled date of 5 December the convoy and its covering force, including CVE's, pass through Surigao Strait the night of 2–3 December. I regret the necessity for sending this dispatch but as COM 7th Fleet it is my duty to do so. I can find no alternative. I request immediate action on this dispatch.[53]

Marked for information to MacArthur and Nimitz, this dispatch could hardly have failed to ignite explosions at general headquarters in Tacloban, on Makalapa Hill in Pearl Harbor, and at Main Navy in Washington. Fortunately for Kinkaid, the message was not sent and the alternative that he had been unable to find was brought to him by his communications officer.

Admiral Nimitz understood the box Kinkaid was in because he had heard about it from Admiral Halsey and probably from his plans officer, Rear Admiral Forrest Sherman, who very had recently returned to Pearl from Tacloban. To meet Halsey's need to give his carriers time for repairs and rest, Nimitz sent a dispatch to MacArthur that arrived, fortuitously, after Kinkaid had left in the morning of 30 November. In this message CINCPAC called attention to the dangers for naval vessels operating in restricted waters where the Japanese could still strike through the air. He noted that Halsey's carriers had spent a long period on the line and needed time to recover. Task Force 38's carriers could go again immedi-

---

[52] TCK to Van Hook, 10 Dec 1944, Van Hook Papers.
[53] COM7THFLT to COMINCH, n.d., marked "not sent," TCK Papers.

ately, but their striking power was greatly diminished. Given a longer period in Ulithi, the fast carriers could come back and thoroughly smash the Japanese air bases and make the landings at Mindoro and Lingayen a sure success. Nimitz said that Halsey had given him some suggestions and he was forwarding that message separately to the general.[54]

Kinkaid's communications staff had received Nimitz's radio message for the general, and he sent a copy ashore with his intelligence officer. At 1700 hours the admiral again went ashore to GHQ. He took his long and carefully drafted estimate and delivered it personally to the general. "I fully expected that my detachment would be requested but I could find no other justifiable course of action," Kinkaid later wrote to his deputy. Another two-hour argument ensued, and then they went to dinner.[55] Kinkaid found it hard to enjoy the meal, but the general entertained everyone present with a full recital of his discussions with Kinkaid. To the admiral's dismay, the audience contained several distinguished newspaper publishers, including Cyrus L. Sulzberger of the *New York Times*.[56]

Halsey's dispatch, which Nimitz had forwarded, arrived for dessert. In his message Halsey said his carriers would be much more effective if there was at least a ten-day delay.[57] After the meal MacArthur and Sutherland withdrew for a short conference and returned to announce that the Mindoro expedition would be delayed ten days, until 15 December, and the Lingayen assault for twenty days, until 9 January 1945.[58] A much relieved Kinkaid returned to *Wasatch* and buried in the files his unsent dispatch to Admiral King.

The ten-day respite was a godsend to the Navy and equally important to General Krueger. Still unable to finish off the Japanese in the monsoon-soaked terrain of northwest Leyte, Krueger staged two landings on the west coast of the island during the extra time allowed. Carried in Admiral Struble's amphibious craft, the landings at Baybay (4 December) and Ormoc Bay (7 December) finally permitted the Sixth Army to surround and eventually destroy the Japanese. But those operations did not come cheaply for the Navy. As if to drive home Kinkaid's predictions, during the week beginning 5 December three destroyers were sunk, six were heavily damaged, several large landing craft were destroyed, and a Liberty ship was sunk, all

---

[54] CINCPOA to CINCSWPA, 11/292349Z, file Navy 576, MacArthur Papers.
[55] TCK to Van Hook, 10 Dec 1944, Van Hook Papers.
[56] James, *MacArthur* 2:605–7.
[57] COM3RDFLT to CINCPAC, 11/290400Z, file Navy 576, MacArthur Papers.
[58] TCK to Van Hook, 10 Dec 1944, Van Hook Papers. Sergeant Rogers, the personal secretary to Generals Sutherland and MacArthur, was present when Kinkaid faced his superior. Rogers concluded MacArthur was disappointed and irritated by the actions of both Kinkaid and Halsey. Concerning Halsey's request for time to refresh and replenish his carrier squadrons, MacArthur was reported to have growled to Rogers: "It's the first time the old blowhard has talked like this." Rogers, *The Bitter Years*, 208–10. See also Paul Rogers, *The Good Years: MacArthur and Sutherland* (New York: Praeger, 1990), 241.

by air attack. On the other hand, with a strong escorting force present, Struble's passage to Mindoro was almost trouble free. On 14 December, as his assault force began its final approach to the island, Halsey's fast carriers returned for three days of attacks on everything that flew or moved in Mindoro and central and southern Luzon. When Struble passed the word to "land the landing force," the sky overhead was not free of Japanese planes, but command of the air clearly was in American hands.

Admiral Struble's 15 December landing on Mindoro was a complete success. More than 27,000 Army combat and engineering troops quickly eliminated the 1,000 Japanese and took control of the island. Airfields were promptly constructed, and by 20 December the first squadrons began operations. Mindoro had been seized to provide air coverage over the last half of the 800-mile route between Leyte and Lingayen Gulfs and, above all, to make it possible to protect the Lingayen area during the assault phase. Fortunately for all, the soil and rainfall were such that airfield construction did not suffer the delays experienced by the engineers in Leyte. However, because the island faced the South China Sea, the American bases and airfields were exposed to surface and air raids by the enemy, as were the convoys sent to resupply the bases.[59]

The danger from Japanese air raids against Mindoro had been reduced prior to the invasion by three days of Third Fleet air attacks against airfields on Luzon. Some ninety-nine installations were bombed and strafed during 14–16 December, and Halsey estimated that 373 planes had been destroyed or damaged. Later he raised the count to 461. The cost to TF 38 was seventy-one planes destroyed and twenty-three pilots lost. Struble's expedition was covered by six CVEs of Admiral Stump. The "jeep" carriers, not built for battle against land-based squadrons or other carriers, managed to destroy sixty-six aircraft in the course of protecting the expeditionary force. Only one of Stump's pilots was lost.[60] This destruction of enemy aircraft was significant for the future, but the air raids against Mindoro continued. The first resupply convoy arrived on 22 December, running a gauntlet of air attacks. Two LSTs were damaged. On the last day of the year, another resupply convoy lost three ships and two others were damaged. In early January two Liberty ships were heavily damaged and an ammunition ship was blown up by conventional and kamikaze air attackers. But the Air Force squadrons on Mindoro rode out the harassment and provided vital air cover when the Lingayen expedition hove into sight.[61]

---

[59] Robert Ross Smith, *The History of the War in the Pacific: Triumph in the Philippines*, Subseries, vol. 10 (Washington: Office of Chief of Military History, 1963), 43–49; Morison, vol. 13, *The Liberation of the Philippines, 1944–1945* (Boston: Little, Brown, 1959), 17–32.
[60] Command Summary, 17 Dec 1944.
[61] Command Summary, 22, 31 Dec 1944, 3–4 Jan 1945.

On the day after Christmas a Navy PB4Y (Liberator) spotted a Japanese cruiser-destroyer force about 180 miles, bearing 290 degrees from San Jose, Mindoro. At first reported as the battleship *Yamato*, a cruiser, and six destroyers, the force turned out to be the heavy cruiser *Ashigara*, the light cruiser *Oyodo*, and six destroyers, all commanded by Rear Admiral Masatomi Kimura. Given the warning, all fighters and B–25s on Mindoro scrambled to join the local torpedo boats in repelling the marauders. From Leyte, Admiral Kinkaid sent Rear Admiral Theodore E. Chandler with two heavy cruisers and two light cruisers plus ten destroyers to intercept and destroy the Japanese force, but they were too late. After lobbing a few salvos into San Jose, and a few at the air base, Kimura turned west. In the running fight he lost one destroyer to a PT boat's torpedoes and all of his force suffered damage from the Mindoro aircraft but no other Japanese ships were sunk.[62]

While the Army fought to bring Mindoro under American control, the largest amphibious operation in the Pacific to date was taking shape. The SWPA's Leyte operation had simply been the overture in the program; the main event was to be the invasion of Luzon. MacArthur's GHQ had been planning this campaign since 1942, and certain features, such as the landing on Leyte, had long been decided upon. Where to land on Luzon had also been considered carefully. During his prewar years in the Philippines, MacArthur had devoted a good deal of time to planning a defense of Luzon against a Japanese invasion. He knew that such an invasion must come by way of Lingayen Gulf and the central Luzon plain that ran from the gulf south to Manila Bay. Given MacArthur's knowledge of the terrain and information from guerrilla sources on the disposition of Japanese forces on Luzon in 1945, there was no reason why his forces should not follow the same route that the enemy had used so successfully. He even had the advantage of knowing the mistakes that had been made, by both sides, in 1941 and early 1942.

From Admiral Kinkaid's viewpoint, the general outline of the Navy's role in the coming campaign was not significantly different from what it had been for Leyte. Even the planning took on some aspects of déjà vu. Upon his return to Hollandia on 3 November, Kinkaid found Wilkinson and Oldendorf ready to finish the plans for the Luzon operation. Like the Seventh Fleet, the Third Fleet staff had been at work on their own plans. Now with Kinkaid on hand some of the final questions could be answered. Vice Admiral Wilkinson reopened the question of leadership, suggesting that he should command the attack force, as Kinkaid had done at Leyte, and that the latter should exercise broad strategic command over all of the Seventh Fleet naval forces, including the attack

---

[62] Command Summary, 25–26 Dec 1944; Morison 13:37–43.

force. Perhaps it was a measure of their close friendship that Kinkaid was not offended by Wilkinson's suggestion; but he had no intention of accepting it. He understood, as perhaps Wilkinson did not, that the general still did not wish to place his amphibious commander, Vice Admiral Barbey, under a Third Fleet commander. It is also possible that MacArthur wanted to ensure that everyone knew that this was an SWPA show, not Nimitz's or Halsey's. It was amazing that, given the problems at Leyte, the issue of a single commander for all naval forces—Third and Seventh Fleets—did not emerge. Halsey and Kinkaid would still have to work cooperatively, with no single person in command at the scene of action.[63]

As Commander Luzon Attack Force (TF 77), Admiral Kinkaid would command all Army troops and naval vessels, in the expeditionary force until General Krueger took command ashore. Two Army Corps (I and XIV), consisting of four divisions and a plethora of supporting units, would be immediately landed on 9 January (S-Day) and followed by service troops. Some 203,000 troops would land in the first two days. With later landings by Lieutenant General Robert L. Eichelberger's Eighth Army, ground forces on Luzon would soon swell to almost 400,000 soldiers. In December GHQ had estimated that there were 152,000 Japanese troops of all categories on Luzon. Unless there were massive enemy reinforcements from outside the Philippines, MacArthur would be bringing enough troops with him to subdue the Japanese.[64]

Sixth Army plans called for landing the two corps (four divisions) abreast on the beaches of Lingayen Gulf. To accomplish this, Kinkaid created two attack forces. The San Fabian Attack Force (TF 78), led by Vice Admiral Barbey, was to land I Corps (Major General Innis P. Swift) near the village of San Fabian in the southeast corner of the gulf. Barbey's force was further divided: TG 78.1, commanded by Barbey, would land the 43d Infantry Division (Major General Leonard F. Wing) on White Beach, the farther east of the two; TG 78.5, commanded by Rear Admiral William Fechteler, was to carry the 6th Infantry Division (Major General Edwin D. Patrick) to Blue Beach.

Vice Admiral Wilkinson's Lingayen Attack Force (TF 79), charged with landing XIV Corps (Major General Oscar W. Griswold), also consisted of two assault groups. Rear Admiral Ingolf N. Kiland would command TG 79.1 and be responsible for the 37th Infantry Division (Major General Robert S. Beightler); Rear Admiral Forrest B. Royal, commanding TG 79.2, would land the 40th Infantry Division (Major General Rapp Bush). Wilkinson's groups would go ashore on the beaches between the small cities of Dugupan and Lingayen in the southwest corner of the

---

[63] Wilkinson to VADM R. K. Turner, Hollandia, 7 Dec 1944, Wilkinson Papers.
[64] Smith, *Triumph in the Philippines*, 26–30.

gulf. Admiral Barbey's I Corps came largely from the New Guinea area, but Wilkinson had to collect the XIV Corps' 37th Division at Bougainville in the Solomons and the 40th at Cape Gloucester on New Britain. Once packed aboard the attack transports, cargo carriers, and LSTs, during 10–12 December they sailed to Huon Gulf in Eastern New Guinea for rehearsal landings and then to Manus for a repeat during Christmas week. Finally, on New Year's eve, the XIV Corps began its nine-day voyage to Lingayen by way of Leyte. The total distance sailed was approximately 3,500 miles in hot tropical waters.[65]

In another parallel to the Leyte experience, Kinkaid established a variety of task groups from his naval forces to handle the many missions that were vital to the success of the assault. Vice Admiral Oldendorf was again given TG 77.2, the Bombardment and Fire Support Group, consisting of six Pacific Fleet old battleships, six cruisers, and eighteen destroyers. Again following previous experience the Beach Demolition Group was placed under Oldendorf. Now a Seventh Fleet fixture, Rear Admiral Count Berkey commanded TG 77.3, the Close Covering Group. His command consisted of three light cruisers and six destroyers. For TG 77.4, the Escort Carrier Group (Rear Admiral Calvin T. Durgin), Admiral Nimitz again lent eighteen CVEs plus twenty-seven destroyers and destroyer escorts. Durgin's carriers not only provided air cover for the huge convoys from New Guinea to Lingayen Gulf, but the CVEs were also expected to provide antisubmarine coverage, and at the gulf their air groups would attack targets ashore when called upon. For his own purposes Kinkaid set up a Fleet Flagship Group (TG 77.1), which consisted of *Wasatch*, *Boise*, and four destroyers.[66]

Strategic cover for the Lingayen attack force would come from several sources. Most important was Admiral Halsey's Third Fleet and its highly mobile Fast Carrier Task Force (TF 38). Third Fleet air strikes in support of the Mindoro operation had been vital to its success. Halsey now agreed on 19 December to raid Formosa and Luzon airfields for six days before the 9 January landings.[67] In addition to Halsey's assistance, MacArthur also asked Lord Louis Mountbatten, Supreme Commander Southeast Asia Command, to provide diversionary actions a few days before S-Day at Lingayen. He was concerned that the Japanese surface forces in the Singapore area might seek to interfere in Luzon as they had in Leyte. The general suggested that action against enemy Malay Peninsula bases might force them to keep their ships in that area.[68] In addition to his own Fifth

---

[65] Morison 13:308–11; Smith, *Triumph in the Philippines*, 54–57; Willoughby, comp., *Reports of MacArthur* 1:254.
[66] Morison 13:303–14.
[67] COM3RDFLT to CINCSWPA, 12/190930Z, Command Summary.
[68] CINCSWPA to SUPCOMSEAC, 11/290842Z, Command Summary.

and Thirteenth Air Force missions against Philippine targets in support of S-Day, MacArthur asked General Claire L. Chennault to have his Fourteenth Air Force suppress hostile air forces and shipping in the Hong Kong–Canton area for the period S − 10 to S + 10. Finally the general requested the Joint Chiefs of Staff to have the Twentieth Air Force bombers (B–29s) strike Japanese air bases in Formosa, the Ryukyu Islands (Okinawa), and the home island of Kyushu in the two weeks before S-Day.[69]

While there had been serious concern about possible enemy air attacks against the Leyte beachhead during the KING II planning period, the planners for MIKE I had hard experience in dealing with enemy attackers, particularly the kamikaze pilots. In choosing the convoy route to Lingayen Gulf, the decision to go by way of the Mindanao and Sulu seas was based on the conclusion that better air coverage could be provided. The alternative, to approach by way of northern Luzon and the Formosa Strait, would allow attacks from Formosa and Luzon, where enemy aircraft were most heavily concentrated.[70]

Despite the decision to use the more protected route, Admiral Oldendorf had the most concerns among those who did the planning. In a memorandum to Kinkaid written about three weeks before S-Day, he expressed the view that not enough attention had been paid to potential damage to the ships from mines, heavy artillery, and air attack. To him the Mindoro expedition had been too easy; they could expect a much more dangerous response in Lingayen Gulf from Japanese aviation. He speculated that heavy damage to battleships and CVEs could make MIKE I unfeasible. "It would be of interest to know that provisions are being made to handle damaged ships in the long run to Lingayen and who will determine whether the operation is feasible, once a number of ships have retired."[71] Kinkaid didn't answer this memo, but when Oley raised similar questions at the large predeparture briefing session in Leyte, his answer was very direct. "Once we get underway for Lingayen, we keep going. There is no turning back. A damaged ship, unable to proceed under her own power, must be taken in tow on a course for Lingayen."[72] Kinkaid's plans officer remembered that Oldendorf also asked that if the situation became serious and there was a question of whether to continue or withdraw, did Kinkaid want Oldendorf to make the decision or radio him for instructions. Captain Charles J. Maguire recalled Kinkaid's reply: "Oldendorf you don't have to worry about that, you are going to Lingayen. Now are there any other questions?"[73]

---

[69] CINCSWPA to COMFEAF, 20th Air Force, etc., 12/230010Z, TCK Papers.
[70] CINCPAC to COMINCH, 11/062241Z, Command Summary.
[71] Memorandum for TCK, 19 Dec 1944, TCK Papers.
[72] TCK to Donald Kennecott, ed., *Blue Book Magazine*, 11 Mar 1949, TCK Papers.
[73] RADM C. J. Maguire to author, Paradise Valley, AZ, 28 Oct 1977; TCK oral history, 387–89.

Oldendorf's TG 77.2 sortied for Lingayen on 3 January in company with some of the CVEs and soon became a lightning rod for the Japanese Special Attack Squadrons. On 4 January, 40 miles west of Panay, a twin-engine kamikaze struck and mortally damaged *Ommaney Bay* (CVE 79). Unable to save the burning carrier, Oley ordered the vessel sunk by a screen destroyer's torpedo. The next day saw no sinkings in the convoy, but kamikaze hits damaged two cruisers, including Oldendorf's flagship, *Louisville*, the escort carrier *Manila Bay* (CVE 61); and three lighter vessels.

On the 6th TG 77.2 entered Lingayen Gulf and was met by the full fury of the "Divine Wind," as the Special Attack Squadrons were called. The battleships *New Mexico* and *California* were struck, and Rear Admiral Theodore E. Chandler was fatally wounded on board *New Mexico*. The Australian heavy cruiser *Australia* had been struck on the 5th, and it now took two more kamikaze hits, as did the cruisers *Louisville* and *Columbia*. Nine lighter vessels were also hit and among them a destroyer minesweeper, *Long* (DMS 12), was sunk. It is little wonder that Oldendorf, after surviving the attacks on his flagships, sent a pessimistic dispatch to Admiral Kinkaid.

> Additional damage may seriously and adversely affect this as well as important subsequent operations. More damage may invite action by the Japanese fleet for which this command is becoming progressively less prepared. Should suicide bombers attack transports, results might be disastrous. Recommend Fifth Air Force be informed seriousness of situation and need for more air support. Recommend Third Fleet be ordered this area immediately [to] provide additional air and surface cover urgently needed. Consider this matter of such serious import as to warrant serious consideration of present plans.[74]

Oldendorf's dispatch must have given Kinkaid and his staff a dash of cold water, especially since *Wasatch* had left Leyte's secure anchorage just a few hours earlier. Forgetting the niceties of command relationships, Kinkaid radioed Halsey directly and requested assistance from the "Big Blue Fleet," a favorite name around Pearl Harbor for the Third/Fifth Fleet. Kinkaid not only asked that enemy airfields in northern Luzon be smothered, but further requested that consideration be given "to moving Third Fleet to westward of Luzon to give direct air support objective area [Lingayen Gulf] which will be specially required during period loaded transports in that area."[75] By noon the next day, Kinkaid had a new worry, causing him to send a second dispatch. He had learned from the American Naval Group in China that a "major Japanese surface

---

[74] TG 77.2 to COM7THFLT, 1/061210Z, Command Summary.
[75] COM7THFLT to COM3RDFLT, 1/061842Z, Command Summary.

force" from Empire waters was at sea west of Kyushu. It could easily reach Lingayen Gulf by S-Day.[76]

The reply to Kinkaid's first dispatch came in a radio from Nimitz to MacArthur. CINCPOA reminded the general that the Third Fleet would have other commitments soon and could not be tied to Lingayen affairs too long. He then asked MacArthur if his staff had studied the problem of air defense closely enough, particularly whether the Fifth Air Force and the CVE squadrons could keep Japanese air attacks in hand. From this radio and subsequent dispatches between Halsey and Nimitz, it is clear that they believed that Third Fleet attacks on Formosa, Okinawa, and perhaps the China coast would be as effective in protecting the gulf as parking TF 38 in the area. It also appears that CINCPAC's staff thought that Kinkaid had a slight case of operational jitters. Nimitz ended his message to MacArthur with the suggestion that, unless the situation were urgent, he preferred to hear from Commander in Chief, SWPA, and not directly from subordinate commanders [such as Commander Seventh Fleet].[77]

Despite the grimness of the 6th, Japanese air attacks were diminishing. Oley's minesweepers went about their dangerous business and had the vital areas of the gulf cleared by S-Day. The bombardment vessels found that real targets were scarce. As at Peleliu and Leyte, the Japanese had evacuated the beach areas in order to prepare defenses to the rear. The same lack was evident when the underwater demolition teams looked for beach obstacles.[78] On the 7th only two ships—both minesweepers—were sunk. On S − 1, 8 January, the Japanese again came in force and hit six ships. Kamikazes twice rammed *Australia*, and two CVEs, *Kadashan Bay* and *Kitkun Bay* (CVE 71), suffered extensive damage but remained on station. Unknown to the Luzon Attack Force, the Japanese had shot their bolt. Halsey's attrition operations, and the destruction of enemy aircraft over the convoys and in Lingayen Gulf by the CVE squadrons and Fifth Air Force fighters, had reduced Japanese aviation to near impotence. They had shaken Kinkaid and his commanders badly, but General MacArthur's return to Luzon was not to be stopped.[79]

Assurances came from Filipinos ashore, air reconnaissance, and those on Oley's ship that the Japanese were not emplaced at the Lingayen Gulf beaches. Nonetheless, TG 77.2 did the usual thorough job of bombarding the shore before the troops landed. The first soldiers were on the beach at 0927, and by sunset some 65,000 troops had come ashore. The Japanese kamikazes came, but their efforts were pitifully weak. Despite

---

[76] COM7THFLT to COM3RDFLT, CINCPAC, etc., 1/070342Z, Command Summary.

[77] CINCPAC to CINCSWPA, 1/070322Z; COM3RDFLT to CINCPAC, 1/071044Z, Command Summary. Nimitz meant Kinkaid in his reference to subordinate commanders.

[78] Smith, *Triumph in the Philippines*, 67–69.

[79] Morison 13:111–19.

Vice Admiral Kinkaid watches landing operations in Lingayen Gulf from the bridge of *Wasatch*, 9 January 1945. Mrs. Kinkaid reported that this was the admiral's favorite photograph of himself.

the enormous number of ships in the gulf, they managed to hit only four, and only the light cruiser *Columbia* was seriously damaged. *Australia* experienced her fifth hit, fortunately a glancing blow with no personnel casualties. Around 1400, General of the Army MacArthur and a handful of his senior staff left *Boise*, the cruiser they had ridden to the gulf, and visited the troops near San Fabian. Forgoing the opportunity to step ashore via a makeshift pier, the general opted for his traditional wade. As his best biographer has noted, "the Barrymore side of MacArthur's personality could not resist another big splash of publicity and surf."[80]

On S+2 (11 January) the general's contentment with the MIKE I operation was disturbed by a dispatch from Admiral (now Fleet Admiral) Nimitz. CINCPOA officially reminded CINCSWPA that the Pacific Fleet ships on loan to Seventh Fleet had to be returned. They were to be used for DETACHMENT, the invasion of Iwo Jima, and were scheduled to be in Ulithi by S+10 (19 January).[81] The next day, after conferring with Kinkaid, MacArthur answered Nimitz. His greatest concern was to protect the Lingayen beachhead from attack by a Japanese surface force. He justified his situation:

> The extremely limited strength of the Seventh Fleet unless augmented is entirely inadequate for such purposes and is barely sufficient for escort duty to and from the beachhead. To withdraw the Third Fleet and the elements which have temporarily augmented the Seventh Fleet will completely expose Lingayen to naval surface attack and would plainly invite disaster.

Like any military commander worth his stars, the general then added, "Under these circumstances what is your suggested solution to comply with the naval mission of the basic directive of the Joint Chiefs of Staff with regard to the Luzon Operation?" Nimitz's reply had Admiral King, a member of the JCS, as an information addressee.[82] It appears that COMINCH had already been apprised of the situation and suggested that Nimitz have Halsey's Third Fleet continue its protection of Lingayen by operating to the west of Luzon. From such a covering position Halsey could intercept any surface force coming from Formosa or Empire waters. With alert reconnaissance activity he could also intercept a force coming from the direction of Singapore.[83] Nimitz complied with King's "suggestion" and let MacArthur know that the Third Fleet would continue its protective mission until the threat of surface attack was eliminated.[84]

---

[80] James, *MacArthur* 2:620–21; Morison 13:326; Smith, *Triumph in the Philippines*, 73–76.
[81] CINCPOA to CINCSWPA, 1/110216Z, Command Summary.
[82] CINCSWPA to CINCPOA, 1/121252Z, Command Summary.
[83] COMINCH to CINCPAC, 1/121241Z, Command Summary.
[84] CINCPOA to COM3RDFLT, 1/121606Z; CINCPOA to CINCSWPA, 1/130850Z, Command Summary.

The remnants of the Japanese fleet, scattered as they were, still constituted a menacing "fleet-in-being" for Kinkaid and MacArthur. Memories of the three-pronged Japanese thrust toward Leyte Gulf less than three months before were still with them. Starting on 10 January, Admiral Halsey's operations in the South China Sea were designed to eliminate part of the enemy's surface power, and part of Kinkaid's worries. Hoping to catch the elusive *Ise-Hyuga* battleship group, Halsey sent the fast carriers of TF 38 on a 12 January raid against Camranh Bay in French Indochina. His quarry was not present, but Bogan's squadrons found enough shipping for a decent target practice. Four days later the fast carriers visited Hong Kong with equally destructive behavior, but the two battleships were not in sight. In fact they were still at Lingga Roads, preparing for a dash to home waters.[85]

As Halsey was blasting Hong Kong on 16 January, Nimitz let COMINCH know that he was planning to leave four of the six old battleships at Lingayen Gulf. With eight U.S. cruisers, fifty destroyers, and the four battleships CINCPAC was sure that the Seventh Fleet could handle any surface force sent against it. He noted there were two battleships in the Lingga-Singapore area (*Ise* and *Hyuga*) and four in Empire waters (*Kongo, Haruna, Nagato* and *Yamato*), plus a possible light carrier or two, but he could not imagine the two groups could combine against the Seventh Fleet.[86] MacArthur didn't share this confidence. A few days earlier he had alerted General Kenney to intelligence information that *Ise* and *Hyuga* might be steaming northeast paralleling the coast of Borneo and Palawan. He directed that air searches over this route be made. Now, on the 17th, he reiterated to Nimitz his concern that Kinkaid would not have enough battleships: "I therefore strongly urge the retention of his six old battleships until the situation has clarified." Concerned that Kinkaid might give in too easily, the general told his Seventh Fleet commander that all traffic concerning the return of the battleships would be handled by MacArthur himself.[87]

In the end a compromise was developed. Nimitz received back his two most heavily damaged battleships, *California* and *New Mexico*, so they could receive repairs at Ulithi. They departed the gulf on 22 January. Heavy cruisers *Portland* and *Minneapolis* were to remain with Kinkaid, along with enough destroyers to bring his total to fifty-seven, until 5 February. It was assumed that Fifth Air Force bombers, operating out of Clark Field, would be able to provide the extra firepower to defend Lingayen Gulf against surface forces. Kinkaid actually released the Pacific Fleet ships on 10 February; by then Nimitz had made other arrangements for battleships off Iwo Jima. Kinkaid felt that he had been thor-

---

[85] Morison 13:164–72.
[86] CINCPAC to COMINCH, 1/161836Z, Command Summary.
[87] CINCSWPA to COMAAF, 1/131511Z; CINCSWPA to CINCPOA, 1/171229Z, Command Summary.

oughly whipsawed between his two superiors, but he saved his complaints for his oral biography in 1961.[88]

Despite the concerns of Kinkaid and MacArthur, it appears that the *Ise-Hyuga* force had only one operational interest in early February, and that was to get back to home waters. On 9 February an "Ultra" dispatch alerted Kinkaid that the two battleships were loading drums of gasoline at Singapore and would be underway soon. At first light on the 11th the two hermaphrodite battleships sortied with the heavy cruiser *Ashigara* and three destroyers and turned northeast. By then Kinkaid had ordered his Seventh Fleet Submarine Force commander, now Rear Admiral James Fife, to have his subs intercept and attack. Kinkaid also got the Fifth Air Force to prepare search and attack missions against the enemy task force.

Aware that Kinkaid had no battleships to use on the 10th, Rear Admiral Berkey, then on the Mindoro-Lingayen defense line, requested permission to intercept the Japanese with his cruiser-destroyer force. Count Berkey was described by Kinkaid's chief of staff as "the race horse of the Seventh Fleet," and his dispatch to MacArthur and Kinkaid suggests a real fighting heart:

> There is presented to the naval forces under your command the opportunity for a decisive naval action that may be the last of our time. The light cruisers and destroyers now with me can destroy . . . the attack force if permitted to intercept them at midnight 13–14 Feb. . . . I earnestly beseech that the naval forces long ordained for such action be given the opportunity to strike a decisive blow.[89]

Kinkaid appreciated Berkey's gesture but decided to stick to the current operations plan, which called for the cruiser force to support landings on Corregidor and Mariveles Point in Manila Bay on 15 February. He explained to MacArthur, who had supported Berkey's proposal, that submarines and the Fifth Air Force were waiting for the Japanese and that Berkey's force would only get in the way. He summarized his position: "The proposed operations for the light cruiser force do not appear to be sound or to be warranted by the probable strategic results."[90]

In the case of this operation (CRUSADER) the weather gods smiled benevolently on the Japanese. Plagued by storms, fog and low clouds, Kenney's bomber pilots never located the *Ise-Hyuga* task force. Fife had stationed fifteen submarines along the projected route, and, though a few tried, none could stop the enemy vessels. Once through the Luzon Strait

---

[88] CINCPOA to CINCSWPA, 1/181812Z; CTF 77 to CTG 77.2, 1/210838Z; CINCPOA to CINCSWPA, 2/060758Z; CINCSWPA to CINCPOA, 2/080314Z, Command Summary; TCK oral history, 393–95; RADM V. H. Schaeffer to author, Coronado, CA, 29 Dec 1977.

[89] CTG 77.3 to CTF 77, 2/101155Z, TCK Papers.

[90] COM7THFLT to CTG 77.3, 2/101840Z; CINCSWPA to COM7THFLT, 2/110043Z; COMANF to CINCSWPA, 2/110927Z, TCK Papers.

there were eleven Pacific Fleet submarines deployed on orders from Pearl Harbor, but none made contact. The two battleship-carriers made it safely back to the Kure Naval Base. In late July 1945 TF 38 pilots finally located the two old hermophrodites and sank them at their moorings.[91]

As at Leyte, Admiral Kinkaid's operations in Lingayen Gulf involved constant personal danger. From the day he left the anchorage off Tacloban until S + 5 (14 January) in Lingayen Gulf, his flagship's war diary reported air attacks on his ship and those around him, but *Wasatch* was never struck by bombs, torpedoes, or kamikazes. Earlier in the war, when *Enterprise* had been his flagship, Kinkaid had felt the jolt of bombs hitting his flight deck, but the island structure had been spared. Of the four Navy Distinguished Service Medals that he had been awarded, three recognized that he had earned them in the crucible of combat. Only in the Aleutians had he not actually been under fire. Now in Lingayen Gulf, by 19 January the greatest danger to his fleet was the possibility of surface force attack. Japanese air attacks were almost finished; it appeared that aircraft in Formosa and the Ryukyus were being husbanded against anticipated amphibious operations. In an estimate of future Japanese activities following his South China Sea raids, Admiral Halsey wrote:

> Japs know they are licked in the Philippines [and] will not attempt serious reinforcement in the face of our air, surface and ground superiority. . . . He has written off the Philippines [and] will not engage in dubious counterattacks and risk further loss to dwindling defense forces.[92]

Toward the end of the month Kinkaid took *Wasatch* down the west side of Luzon to observe Admiral Struble's management of a 29 January assault near the city of San Antonio on the Zambales Province coast. His task force landed almost 40,000 XI Corps troops of Lieutenant General Eichelberger's Eighth Army from Leyte. Though unopposed, the operation was replete with fire support vessels—CVEs for close air support and fighter squadrons overhead to eliminate intruding enemy aircraft. From their landing sites the troops were expected to strike due east and cut off any possible movement into the Bataan Peninsula by Japanese forces retreating before General Krueger's Sixth Army. Two days after Struble's operation Kinkaid looked in on a smaller assault, also a Seventh Amphib operation. Rear Admiral Fechteler, Barbey's subordinate, was landing several Eighth Army units on the south Luzon coast at Nasugbu in eastern Batangas Province. Only 55 miles south of Manila these forces would drive toward the city and force the Japanese to hold troops in place that

---

[91] Memo, RADM James Fife to TCK, 17 Feb 1945, 7th Fleet Files, OA; Blair, *Silent Victory* 2:821–24; Dull, *Battle History of IJN*, 347; Tarbuck oral history, 182–88.
[92] CINCPAC to COMINCH, 1/191730Z, Command Summary.

might otherwise have moved north to oppose the main American force coming down from Lingayen Gulf. Destroyers provided the principal gunfire support for the landing, though Struble's larger force was close enough to lend assistance should it be needed. Both assaults were accomplished with the precision that had come to be expected of Admiral Barbey's amphibious groups.[93]

Upon his return to *Wasatch*'s anchorage off Tolosa in Leyte Gulf, Kinkaid moved into his fairly new Seventh Fleet headquarters. His spaces had been briefly occupied by his old friend and classmate, Rear Admiral Kauffman, Commander Philippine Sea Frontier. A good organizer and somewhat aggressive in maintaining control of his territory, Reggie quickly took command of port facilities, operating bases, and many of the service functions that were vital to the Seventh Fleet. In time the Sea Frontier, which had been established on 28 November 1944, would itself be an operational command charged with defense of the Seventh Fleet operating area against stray elements of the Japanese navy.[94] Because Tolosa was to be his headquarters until he could move into Manila, Kinkaid brought his staff forward from Hollandia, including the few members who had remained in Brisbane. Though Tolosa was 400 miles from Manila, it was an appropriate location for Kinkaid's headquarters because Seventh Fleet operations now turned to eliminating the Japanese from areas in the Philippines and Borneo that SWPA forces bypassed as they took control of Leyte, Samar, and Luzon.

During most of 1945 Vice Admiral Barbey's Seventh Amphibious Force operated with three attack groups, each commanded by a rear admiral. Admirals Fechteler, Struble, and A. G. Noble were regular members of the Seventh Amphibs command and Rear Admiral Forrest B. Royal was a "loaner" from the Pacific Fleet's Third Amphibious Force. These four group commanders carried out more than twenty major and minor amphibious assaults, starting with the difficult Corregidor and Mariveles Point landing of 15 February and ending with the capture of Balut Island off the southernmost tip of Mindanao on 20 July. Barbey's command was, of course, a part of the Seventh Fleet, but he operated with a very loose rein held by Kinkaid. All of Barbey's operations came at the order of MacArthur through Kinkaid, but they did not originate with the JCS. It had been the intention of the Joint Chiefs to bypass the central and southern Philippines after Luzon was taken, but the general would not have it. He considered it a sacred obligation to free all Filipinos from Japanese control as quickly as possible, not wait for libera-

---

[93] Smith, *Triumph in the Philippines*, 310–14, 221–23; Morison 13:185–90; Barbey, *MacArthur's Amphibs*, 302.

[94] Administrative History: COMSWPA, chap. 4.

Liberated Navy nurses with Vice Admiral Kinkaid in Manila, 23 February 1945. A week later, he held a special dinner in their honor.

tion to come with a final surrender on some distant day. Kinkaid and Barbey simply carried out the general's commands.[95]

The weeks and months passed slowly for Kinkaid in Tolosa. MacArthur remained in Manila, close to the operations of the Sixth and Eighth Armies as they slowly liquidated General Yamashita's last troops. Kenney and most of MacArthur's staff were also there, so the admiral was the senior officer in the Leyte area. His letters to his wife regularly echoed the same themes: He was buried in paperwork; he had a constant stream of "visiting firemen"; and he really needed some home leave. He expected to get leave in March, then April, and finally in May. Barbey could handle the amphibious operations without his assistance. He knew that plans were being considered in Pearl Harbor and Washington for the invasion of Japan, or possibly Formosa or the China Coast, but the Seventh Fleet had received no orders to start planning. So Tom kept up with the reports, swam daily until the gulf became too polluted, pitched horseshoes, fed monkeys that visited his veranda, attended dances held by the Army nurses and Women's Army Corps officers, read detective stories each

---

[95] James, *MacArthur* 2:737–39.

NHC

Newly promoted Vice Admiral James L. Kauffman, Commander Philippine Sea Frontier, and Admiral Kinkaid, Commander Seventh Fleet, pin their new stars upon each other, at Philippine headquarters, 6 April 1945.

night, and wrote daily letters to Helen. On 6 April there was a pleasant break in routine when Kinkaid and Reggie, who had been Naval Academy roommates for four years, pinned new collar devices on each other. Kinkaid now wore the four stars of an admiral and Kauffman the three of a vice admiral. Tom opened his letter to Helen on 3 April, the admiral's fifty-seventh birthday, with a summary of his current status:

> It is hard to realize that I am fifty-seven years old today. That definitely is old age but I do not feel it. My hair is thin and grey, my belly is fat, my wind is short, my corns hurt and my teeth are old and brittle, but I look to the future with anticipation of interesting and pleasant times and I look forward to seeing my sweetheart again with the same keen pleasure as I did thirty odd years ago.[96]

Kinkaid still had to wait another month, but on 5 May he finally received a dispatch ordering him to Washington for consultations with Ad-

---

[96] TCK to HSK, Tolosa, 3 Apr 1945.

miral King and his staff. Following the meetings he was authorized six weeks delay before returning to his command. He had last seen Helen in November 1943. The eighteen months of separation seemed like an eternity, but she was in Washington to meet him when his command transport set down at Naval Air Station, Anacostia, on 12 May.[97]

Upon returning from leave, Kinkaid spent two weeks catching up on reading dispatches and preparing for the move to Manila. His new headquarters, built on the old polo field, were spacious and just a few hundred yards from his residence. He shared his official house with his new chief of staff, Rear Admiral Thomas S. Combs; his deputy chief of staff, Commodore Penn L. Carroll; and their aides. His sitting room and sleeping quarters were air conditioned, a genuine status symbol in the bombed-out Manila of July 1945. He quickly discovered that having a residence and headquarters in Manila meant that his hordes of visiting firemen would also be his luncheon and dinner guests. But he apparently was a good host, enjoyed visiting with those who were fresh from Washington, and only complained to his wife when they stayed too long.

Since Kinkaid's promotion there had been a change in the command responsibilities in the Pacific. With the invasion of Okinawa the war had been brought to Japan's doorstep. The division of the Pacific into a Southwest Pacific Area, South Pacific Area, North Pacific Area, and Central Pacific Area was no longer justified. In April the JCS decided there should be one commander for all naval forces in the Pacific (Nimitz) and one commander for all Army forces in that area (MacArthur). They had wanted to appoint a single commander for the final invasion of Japan but could not reach agreement. The Joint Chiefs did decide that Nimitz, or a commander under him, would plan and carry out the amphibious assault operation in cooperation with General MacArthur's designated commander. Once ashore all land forces and aviation in support of the land forces would be under MacArthur. Kinkaid learned about these developments from visits to Nimitz's headquarters on Guam and while in Washington. He also learned that the Seventh Fleet was now under CINCPAC's direct command rather than COMINCH's, but he and his fleet would continue to serve MacArthur.[98]

The last two weeks of the war found Kinkaid buried in paper and impatient to see it all come to an end. He was living comfortably, perhaps too much so, for even the daily movie after dinner had begun to pall on him. Having a group in the house to see the movie meant that he could not escape either from the movie itself or from the senior officers who were killing time by watching it. For a change of pace, he occasionally

---

[97] COMINCH to TCK, 5 May 1945, TCK Personnel File; TCK to HSK, Tolosa, 5 May 1945.
[98] Hayes, *History of JCS*, 686–95, 701–7.

took a jeep and drove himself around Manila, but it is evident from his letters that he did that only rarely. Despite his rank and position as a fleet commander, he knew little more about the negotiations to end the war than what appeared in the news summaries he received and the speculations in the Far East edition of *The Stars and Stripes*. He closed his 1 August letter to Helen with observations that probably could have been found in almost any senior officer's correspondence:

> The war with Japan is in its last phase. The statement of the three powers regarding Japan's unconditional surrender may have the desired effect in Japan. If not, destruction from the air and sea followed by invasion will end it. To end the war and get home is the immediate objective of all of us out here.[99]

The tenor of Kinkaid's letters changed rapidly after 6 August. His first reaction to the use of the atomic bomb reflected how little he knew about it: "The President's announcement regarding the atomic bomb is timely and will give the Japs something to think about. After they have felt one or two they will think even harder."[100] The admiral had obviously heard more about the bomb the next day: "Usually I do not pay much attention to things that might be classed as 'gadgets.' This bomb is not in that class. Its destruction is widespread and it comes at a time when its use is most potent politically." In speaking of the bomb's political potency, Kinkaid was thinking of Japan, not the Soviet Union. His views would change in the next couple of months, but in early August he still looked on the "Ruskies" as allies who could help shorten the war against Japan. On the day the second bomb was dropped, this time on Nagasaki, Kinkaid's letter became considerably more optimistic about an end to the war:

> Russia's entry into the war just about tops off Japan's grief. That and the atomic bomb may make the face-saving formula that the Japanese government needs to find before telling the Japanese people and the rest of the world that it is impossible to go on with the war.[101]

Like many others the admiral believed the war was over on the 10th when the Japanese made a surrender offer. Rumors became news, and news became fact. Manila had a noisy celebration, and Kinkaid invited all of the Navy's flag officers in Manila to come to a dinner on the 11th and bring their aides. In all thirty-two were present. Kelly Turner, now wearing four stars, came as did Vice Admiral Wilkinson, seven rear admi-

---

[99] TCK to HSK, Manila, 1 Aug 1945.
[100] TCK to HSK, Manila, 7 Aug 1945.
[101] TCK to HSK, Manila, 9 Aug 1945.

rals, and twelve commodores. Kinkaid served cocktails in his personal air-conditioned rooms before dining. He thought most of them enjoyed the evening, if only because of the air-conditioning. But Ping Wilkinson was disappointed: "I thought it would be a Victory Dinner or at least a jolly affair but it was rather stiff and soon over. A two course dinner."[102]

With Japan's final agreement and acceptance of surrender terms on 14 August, the whole Navy in the Pacific shifted gears. Planning for an invasion of Japan gave way to planning for its occupation and acceptance of the surrender of its armed forces throughout the Pacific and in Japan, Korea, China and Southeast Asia. On the 19th a team of senior Japanese officers flew to Manila to receive surrender instructions from MacArthur's staff and representatives of Admiral Nimitz. The series of meetings lasted into the early hours of the 20th, and the delegation was then hustled back to Japan. Kinkaid was not particularly concerned about the fate of the Japanese, but he was worried that MacArthur's people were rushing them too much. He expressed to Helen his views:

> I told Forrest Sherman that the Japs could not do the things they are going to be told to do in the time allowed. . . . We have nothing to gain by hurrying and we have a lot to lose if we rush things. Before we land in Japan the troops in the areas to be occupied should be disarmed and cleared out of the area. If that job is not thoroughly done, some one will pull a trigger and start a conflagration.[103]

A few days after the Japanese returned home, the admiral received orders for his next activities as Commander Seventh Fleet. He had anticipated going to Tokyo for the surrender ceremonies, but that was not to be. His ships would transport Major General John R. Hodge and the XXIV Corps to Korea and land the troops at Jinsen (Inchon) on the west coast. Once established ashore, Hodge and Kinkaid would go to Seoul and take the surrender of Japanese army and navy forces located south of the 38th parallel. Japanese north of that point would surrender to the senior Russian commander in the area.

Following the establishment of the occupation force in Korea, the Seventh Fleet was to show the flag along the China coast and land the Marine Third Amphibious Corps in Tientsin and Chefoo. Because of the limited number of transports available, once the XXIV Corps was lifted from Okinawa to Korea, Vice Admiral Barbey's ships would return to Okinawa and pick up the 1st Marine Division for transportation to Tientsin. With the 1st Division ashore, Uncle Dan would head for Guam to bring the 6th Marine Division to North China. While Barbey's ships were hauling troops, Kinkaid

---

[102] TCK to HSK, Manila, 12 Aug 1945; Wilkinson Diary, 11 Aug 1945.
[103] TCK to HSK, Manila, 19 Aug 1945.

Admiral Kinkaid signs the document accepting the surrender of Japanese forces in Korea, at Seoul, September 1945. To his right is Vice Admiral Daniel Barbey, to his left Major General Archibald V. Arnold.

planned to enter the Shanghai area and open the Yangtze River for navigation. Wherever the Seventh Fleet went, it was expected to help with the liberation of Allied prisoners of war and civilian internees. For assistance in this task Kinkaid included several hospital ships among his vessels.

Despite his concern about the rush Kinkaid and the Seventh Fleet moved rapidly once word came that it would be going to Korea and the China coast. On 26 August the admiral issued Operation Plan 13–45; the next day he moved out of his offices ashore and into *Minneapolis,* which would serve as his command ship until *Rocky Mount* (AGC 3) joined up. At 0900 on the 28th his fleet moved out and shaped course for Okinawa where it would be joined by the transports loaded with the First Marine Division. With *Minneapolis* underway Kinkaid's service under MacArthur's command effectively ended. He would continue as Commander Allied Naval Forces, Southwest Pacific Area until surrender documents were signed on 2 September in Tokyo Bay, but practically speaking there was little to do concerning that command. Now with his four-starred blue flag snapping in the wind, he was one of Admiral Nimitz's fleet commanders, preparing to reestablish America's standing naval presence in Eastern Asia.

The term Asiatic Fleet was no longer used, but its shadowy outline continued in the organization set forth in Kinkaid's Operation Plan 13–45.[104] The Seventh Fleet would consist of five operating forces and a large number of miscellaneous ships organized into supporting groups.

TF 71 North China Force, commanded by Rear Admiral Francis S. Low and consisting of seventy-five ships, constituted a powerful surface fighting force. Within TF 71 was Cruiser Division 16 with *Alaska* (CB 1) and *Guam* (CB 2), each ship carrying nine 12-inch rifles. These new large cruisers had been designed to outfight any commerce raider, heavy cruiser, or pocket battleship afloat. Also in the North China Force was Kinkaid's first flag command, Cruiser Division 6, under Rear Admiral Jerauld Wright with the four surviving *Astoria*-class heavy cruisers: *San Francisco, New Orleans, Minneapolis,* and *Tuscaloosa* (CA 37). The balance of TF 71 consisted of three destroyer divisions and a plethora of minesweepers, landing craft, and vessels designed to get harbors and rivers into condition for safe operations.

TF 72 Fast Carrier Force commanded by Rear Admiral Arthur C. Davis with *Antietam* (CV 36), *Intrepid,* and *Cabot* (CVL 28) was to provide the heavy air punch for the Seventh Fleet if needed. During its operations in North China TF 72 was to engage in aerial displays (fly-overs) to impress those tempted to interfere with the landings of the U.S. Marines or any other fleet operations.

TF 73 Yangtze Patrol Force under Rear Admiral C. Turner Joy represented an insensitive return to prewar thinking on the part of the Navy Department. Probably the last thing the government of Generalissimo Chiang Kai-shek needed was an active reminder to its citizens that it still could not control its own waterways. Whereas the Yang Pat Command of 1941 consisted of a half-dozen river gunboats and a few destroyers, Admiral Joy's powerful force in September 1945 was led by Cruiser Division 15's *Nashville* and *St. Louis* (CL 49), a destroyer division, seven gunboats, six fleet minesweepers, forty-eight infantry landing craft, and several command ships. The four groups of LCIs were to be used for embarking and transporting U.S. Marines or Chinese armies along the Yangtze River and China coast and for evacuating Japanese troops from the central China area.

TF 74 South China Force under Rear Admiral Elliott Buckmaster was totally unlike the prewar South China Patrol, a small command within the Asiatic Fleet. With six escort carriers (CVEs) and a dozen destroyer escorts, Admiral Buckmaster had plenty of firepower to deal with hold-out Japanese naval forces or maritime brigands who were already in operation. He was also strong enough to cover those units evacuating Japanese forces and transporting Chinese armies. For transport pur-

---

[104] COM7THFLT Operation Plan 13–45, 26 Aug 1945, TCK Papers.

poses the force had a dozen LCIs, seven LSTs, five cargo transports, and a handful of miscellaneous auxiliaries. The aircraft from the CVEs proved useful in locating prisoner-of-war camps in Formosa and in south China and dropping relief supplies to their inmates.

TF 78 Amphibious Force was still commanded by Vice Admiral Dan Barbey. It would draw its shipping from the various forces within the Seventh Fleet and from CINCPAC's pool of vessels. Though not so designated, Barbey was also the deputy commander of the Seventh Fleet and soon expected to relieve Kinkaid. TF 78's first job was to put the XXIV Corps ashore at Jinsen (Inchon) on the west coast of Korea.

As Kinkaid's Seventh Fleet stood out of Manila Bay on 28 August, it received a warm send-off from General MacArthur:

> As the Seventh Fleet leaves the Southwest Pacific Area, I desire to express my admiration and grateful acknowledgment for the magnificent manner in which all its fleet elements have performed their assigned tasks in the campaigns of this theater. To you and your officers and men who have with great gallantry, resourcefulness, and devotion to duty so fully upheld the highest traditions of our country's naval service, I send Godspeed.
>
> MacArthur

During the next ten days the Seventh Fleet proceeded at an almost leisurely pace to show the flag in the Yellow Sea and the Gulf of Chihli. Starting on 1 September Kinkaid's letters to Helen usually mentioned some form of naval demonstration: ". . . steamed in close to the entrance to Tsingtao . . . just to show ourselves" (1 September); "Our carrier planes made a demonstration over Shanghai this morning and will do the same thing over Korea tomorrow" (2 September); "The destroyers went in close enough to see the Chinese on the docks who were waving flags and signalled 'welcome'" (6 September).

Mail censorship ceased at this time, and on 7 September the fleet began steaming with normal night running lights and the ports open. After almost four years of "buttoning up" ship at sunset the crews could once again sleep comfortably at night.[105]

Kinkaid's fleet entered Jinsen harbor during the forenoon watch of 8 September. With a tidal range great enough to ground a whaleboat at lowtide, there was tension among the commanding officers until it was determined that the inner harbor had been dredged sufficiently for the deep-draft vessels to enter. Following three destroyers that kept a sharp lookout for mines, *Minneapolis* led a column of transports into the harbor and dropped anchor at 1145. Chiefs of staff for Kinkaid, Barbey and

---

[105] TCK to HSK, *Minneapolis*, 1, 2, 6 Sep 1945.

Hodge, quickly went ashore and met their Japanese counterparts to arrange the surrender ceremonies for the next afternoon in Keijo (Seoul). At the same time troops of the XXIV Corps began debarking and starting toward Seoul, about 25 miles to the east. Perhaps as a sign that they would find cooperation ashore, a signal flashed from the Inchon signal tower: "Welcome American Fleet."[106]

The surrender ceremony took place at the government building in Seoul, the former governor's palace. Kinkaid and Hodge made a formal entrance, followed by the rest of the Americans who would witness the signing of the documents. The Japanese then entered and sat at a long table opposite the Americans. Though it lacked the majesty of the ceremony on board *Missouri* a week earlier—after all there was only one MacArthur—Kinkaid did find the event "dignified and impressive." General Nobuyuki Abe, the governor-general of Korea, Vice Admiral Jisaburo Yamaguchi, and Lieutenant General Yoshi Kotsuki first signed the surrender documents, then Kinkaid and Hodge signed for the United States. At the conclusion the Japanese flag in front of the government building was lowered for the last time, and the American flag was run up in its place. Operating in the name of the wartime Allies, the American occupation of Korea, south of the 38th parallel, would continue until V–J Day, 15 August 1948.[107]

During the first month following Japan's surrender, Allied commanders throughout the Pacific were deeply involved in retrieving their prisoners of war. After assisting those freed in the Manila area, Kinkaid oversaw the recovery of POWs in Shanghai and north China, in Manchuria and Korea, and in Formosa. Because the Japanese had used prisoners for forced labor, these unfortunates were found throughout the many island and mainland areas that had been overrun. POWs were also scattered throughout Japan, including in cities that had been devastated by American bomber and carrier attacks. The first group of POWs the admiral encountered were those from the Mukden (Manchuria) area. The Russians took the Japanese surrender in Manchuria and sent Allied prisoners to the port of Dairen as they found them. Kinkaid was impatient with the Russians' slow pace in moving POWs, but there was little he could do except send destroyers into Dairen to bring them out, and perhaps to speed up the Russians by their presence. It took ten days for the main body of POWs to arrive in Dairen on 12 September, but there was plenty of transport available there, including hospital ships, to move them to Okinawa before embarkation for home.[108] Rear Admiral Dixwell (Dixie) Ketcham,

---

[106] TCK to HSK, Inchon, 8 Sep 1945; Barbey, *MacArthur's Amphibs*, 324–27.

[107] TCK to HSK, Seoul, 9 Sep 1945; Barbey, *MacArthur's Amphibs*, 327–28; Robert G. Babb, "Day We Lost the Admiral," *Leatherneck* (Sep 1976), 56–57.

[108] TCK to HSK, *Minneapolis*, 2 and 12 Sep 1945.

who commanded the CVE group ordered to retrieve POWs in Formosa, had better luck. Within two days he was able to bring 1,200 prisoners on board, many on stretchers, and begin moving them to Manila.[109]

In Seoul Kinkaid met 128 American Army, Navy, and Marine POWs who had survived since capture in the Philippines at the opening of the war. After two and a half years in Philippine camps the group had been shipped from Manila in December 1944 on board the *Oryuko Maru* as a part of some 1,600 American prisoners. Kinkaid related their story to Helen:

> This group lost 300 of their number when the *Oryuko Maru* was bombed and sunk in Subic last December. They were then put into another equally filthy ship and taken to Takeo on the southern tip of Formosa where they were bombed again and a large number killed. From there they went to a new prison camp at Fukuoka in southern Kyushu and finally across the straits to Fusan in Korea and on to Keijo (Seoul). It was winter and cold and they had very little clothing and very little food. By the time they reached Fukuoka their number was less then 600 and something less than 350 arrived at Keijo; 128 survived.[110]

The work in Korea concluded, the Seventh Fleet immediately began its next operations. Vice Admiral Barbey would bring the III Marine Amphibious Corps to north China to protect a variety of strategic locations while awaiting the arrival of Chinese government forces from the south. Admiral Kinkaid left this part of the fleet's operations to Barbey while he moved on to Shanghai. To his annoyance the admiral was prodded by his boss. Admiral Nimitz radioed Kinkaid from Guam that he did not understand why the Seventh Fleet was taking so long to reach Shanghai, particularly since "from both humanitarian and political considerations it is a matter of utmost urgency." Kinkaid explained that clearing the river approaches to Shanghai of Japanese and Allied mines was proving particularly difficult, but it had to be done.[111] Rear Admiral Joy was overseeing the mine-clearing operation and he had no intention of allowing one of Kinkaid's ships to be lost at this time. Particularly difficult to clear were the magnetic mines that had been dropped by American bombers to bottle up the enemy shipping in the Yangtze River and its approach waters.

The weather had also been uncooperative. An approaching typhoon caused the Seventh Fleet to seek shelter, particularly for the amphibious craft. But by 16 September the admiral's patience had run out. Accepting Admiral Joy's cautions about bringing his new flagship, *Rocky Mount*, up the Yangtze, Kinkaid planned an informal trip to Shanghai in a light

---

[109] Ibid., 5–6 Sep 1945.
[110] TCK to HSK, *Rocky Mount*, 11 Sep 1945.
[111] Nimitz to TCK, Guam, 9/082259Z; TCK to Nimitz, 9/090301Z, TCK Papers.

minesweeper. His more formal entry would come three days later when he could bring his larger vessels to anchorages off the Bund, the city's famous business area fronting on the river. Arriving in *YMS 49* with his aide, Lieutenant Commander David Freeman, and a staff captain, Lee F. Sugnet, who was the fleet navigation officer, the admiral was met by Rear Admiral Milton E. Miles, Commander Naval Group China. Wise to the ways of the Chinese theater Miles saw to it that Kinkaid immediately met the most important people in the Shanghai area. The worsening weather turned the admiral's "informal" trip into a two-day visit.[112]

Following a day and a half of receptions, grand meals, and a flurry of hastily arranged conferences with Shanghai officials, Chinese military leaders, and a few senior Army and Navy types, Kinkaid returned to his flagship to catch his breath. Two days later, in *Rocky Mount*, he led a representative number of Seventh Fleet vessels to their Shanghai anchorages. Because he controlled the port of Shanghai, Admiral Miles saw to it that *Rocky Mount* was moored to the number one buoy opposite the Bund. This was a not-too-subtle announcement that the British were no longer the dominant naval power in Chinese waters. Admiral Bruce A. Fraser, RN, the senior British naval officer in the Far East, was furious to find his flagship moored far upriver from the Royal Navy's traditional anchorage, but there was nothing he could do about it. When he raised the issue with Generalissimo Chiang Kai-shek, he was turned away with a few soft phrases. Fraser probably recognized that the Chinese were evening the score after the British had insisted on having the Japanese surrender in Hong Kong despite vigorous objections from the Chinese. Admirals Fraser and Kinkaid had both learned a lesson in the importance of "face" on the China Station.[113]

From the very beginning of what was to prove to be two months of unrelenting activity, the admiral regretted that "the lovely Helen" could not be there with him. "I wish my sweetheart were here to see Shanghai with me. We would enjoy it a lot and the Chinese are very hospitable and very pleasant . . . had you been here, I am quite sure you would be by this time playing bridge and palling around with some of these cute China dolls." There is little doubt that Helen would have thoroughly enjoyed being with her admiral husband. Even toward the end of her life she recalled with evident fondness their years together in Constantinople in the early 1920s when Lieutenant Commander Kinkaid had served on Admiral Bristol's staff; those exciting voyages to Europe in the early 1930s as part of the naval delegation to the World Disarmament Confer-

---

[112] TCK to HSK, Shanghai, 15, 16, 17 Sep 1945; banquet place card and memo, 16 Sep 1945, VADM Milton E. Miles Papers, Hoover Institution, Stanford, CA; Milton E. Miles, *A Different Kind of War* (Garden City, NY: Doubleday, 1967), 545–46.

[113] TCK to HSK, Shanghai, 20 Sep 1945; Chungking, 25 Sep 1945.

ence meetings; and the marvelous years abroad when both had felt they were at the center of vital international events, and it had been just plain fun. Now her husband again was in an exotic place, taking part in meaningful political affairs, and Helen was home in Philadelphia, caring for an ill and aged father. It hardly seemed fair to either of them.[114]

Admiral Kinkaid found it amazing that he was the senior American military officer in the Far East. Only Major General Patrick J. Hurley, the United States Ambassador to China, outranked him. The Army's Commanding General, China Theater, was Lieutenant General Albert C. Wedemeyer, a skilled strategic planner who had replaced the irascible General Joseph (Vinegar Joe) Stilwell in October 1944. Though senior to Wedemeyer, Kinkaid let him know early that he would follow Wedemeyer's lead in the politics of dealing with the Chinese. Fearing the problems that could be generated by a headstrong American admiral, Wedemeyer and the Chinese were clearly relieved at what they perceived as Kinkaid's eminent good sense.[115] Practically speaking there was little else the admiral could do. He no longer had MacArthur's large intelligence staff to provide him with political intelligence and analysis, and his own staff had little expertise in contemporary Chinese affairs. The best informed source immediately available to him was Admiral Miles, but he was disintegrating physically and psychologically from too many months of extremely demanding work under great pressure. Because of his close relations with certain controversial Chinese leaders, particularly the notorious General Tai Li, Miles was distrusted by General Wedemeyer and his staff, and this added to the pressure on him. Fortunately for the doughty Miles, Kinkaid recognized the value of his previous labors in China and prevented any severe damage to his reputation by the general's staff.[116]

Once Kinkaid and the Seventh Fleet headquarters were established in Shanghai, he called on Generalissimo Chiang Kai-shek at his capital in Chungking. In preparation for the visit the admiral would have preferred several serious meetings with Ambassador Hurley and General Wedemeyer, but this proved impossible. Wedemeyer was called to Washington in mid-September and stopped in Shanghai on the 19th while en route. He and Kinkaid managed about an hour's conversation on board *Rocky Mount* before both attended a reception and dinner hosted by the Mayor of Shanghai. The admiral seemed grateful for even this much time with the general: "I am very glad to have seen him before he went home. Lots

---

[114] TCK to HSK, 22 Sep 1945; Helen S. Kinkaid interview, Jan 1976.

[115] TCK to HSK, Shanghai, 18 Sep 1945; TCK to RADM F. D. Wagner, New York, 3 Nov 1947, TCK Papers.

[116] Miles, *Different Kind of War*, 549–64; Roy Stratton, *The Army-Navy Game* (Falmouth, MA: Volta, 1977), 237–45.

of little things can be straightened out in a few minutes conversation. Also broad matters of policy can be told in a few words and I learned from Wedemeyer what he and the Generalissimo were thinking."[117]

The next day, 20 September, Ambassador Hurley flew into Shanghai. He too was headed for Washington and a highly controversial resignation from his post. Kinkaid got a few words with him at a dinner given by General Tang En-po at the Cathay Hotel. The next morning the admiral called on the ambassador and they squeezed in an hour of conversation. Kinkaid told Helen that he had received "a lot of interesting background on China . . . am sorry that he is not going to stay on as Ambassador." The revelation that Hurley was to resign would have stupefied the State Department had those in charge read it. The ambassador did not announce his resignation until 26 November in Washington. Fortunately for Kinkaid, his wife never dropped this tidbit anywhere it could have become national news.[118]

A few days after conferring with Ambassador Hurley, Admiral Kinkaid flew to Chungking to call on the Generalissimo. The business end of the visit was not pressing; Kinkaid had a pretty clear idea of what the future operations for his Seventh Fleet would involve. But it seemed proper to Kinkaid as the senior American military officer in China to present himself to the Chinese head of state. His arrival almost destroyed many days of Chinese planning because the pilot landed at the wrong air base. A guard of honor and a few senior officers were hastily scraped together to greet the admiral but the real show had been laid on at the airport on the other side of the city. Lieutenant General George E. Stratemayer, Wedemeyer's deputy, managed to meet Kinkaid and fly with him to the other airfield where the planned reception ceremonies were held. From there the admiral was taken to the Generalissimo's compound for tea and informal talks with him and Madame Chiang.

From his letters to Helen it is clear that Kinkaid liked his hosts.

> They are both very impressive people and have attractive personalities. She is much lovelier than I had expected. She has gained fifteen pounds, so she said, and is very pretty. Her mind is quick as a flash. I got the impression that she and the Gissimo (as they call him for short) are good pals.[119]

---

[117] TCK to HSK, Shanghai, 20 Sep 1945.

[118] Ibid., 21 Sep 1945; George Curry, "James F. Byrnes," in Robert Ferrell, ed., *The American Secretaries of State and Their Diplomacy* vol. 14 (New York: Cooper Square Publishers, 1965), 163–65; Don Lohbeck, *Patrick J. Hurley* (Chicago: Henry Regnery, 1956), 414–27; Michael Schaller, *The U.S. Crusade in China, 1938–1945* (New York: Columbia University Press, 1979), 275–76; William Head, *America's China Sojourn* (Lanham, MD: University Press of America, 1983), 179–83.

[119] TCK to HSK, Chungking, 24 Sep 1945.

Admiral Kinkaid visits with Generalissimo and Madam Chiang Kai-shek in Chungking, 24 September 1945.

At the formal dinner for seventy that evening the Chiangs sat together with Kinkaid on Madame Chiang's right and the peripatetic Bishop Spellman on the Generalissimo's left. Both Americans gave short speeches, and joined all present in toasts to President Harry S. Truman and the Chiangs, but Kinkaid clearly was the guest of honor. As a further display of approval from the Chinese, the admiral was invited to stay at a guest cottage in the compound.

The next morning Kinkaid spent an hour discussing business with the Generalissimo. The admiral reported to his wife:

> We met in the Chiang's drawing room with an interpreter (K. C. Wu, former Mayor of Chungking) at 0930 this morning and soon got down to a very interesting conversation. It was centered about the 7th Flt operations in Chinese waters but had largely to do with the British Fleet (of which I have a group under my command) and the British in general. He let his hair down [?] and I got a pretty clear picture of the situation. It clarified my own position, which was needed as none of my bosses has seen fit to give me any policies or instructions of any sort. U.S. ships are welcome in Chinese ports at any time. I told the Gissimo what the 7th Fleet had been doing and planned to do and he was pleased. He even suggested that I keep a ship at all times in certain of the important Chinese ports which he named. He was particularly pleased when I told him that my ships immediately made contact with local Chinese naval and port authorities upon entering a Chinese port.[120]

Sixteen years later when interviewed for an oral history, Kinkaid retained a favorable impression of the Chiangs, based largely on that one visit to Chungking, since he never met them again. He told John Mason, the interviewer for Columbia University's Oral History Program:

> Well I have a higher estimate of Chiang and his character than most people have. He's certainly a man who has been through rough times. He has done things. He has stood up against great difficulties. Now, when people talk about Chiang Kai-shek, they start talking usually about his family, and the crookedness, the building up of wealth of the family, and so on. The crooked politics. Well, you have that, but you can see that in Philadelphia too. . . . He's a man of courage, a man of intelligence. I think he is patriotic. I myself have said, without any basis for it, that I don't believe he is crooked. I don't believe he is crooked even in money affairs. Now maybe that is wrong. But at any rate, he certainly condones it, because it goes on in the family.

In the same interview he was asked about Madam Chiang, and it is clear that in 1961 he had lost none of his admiration for her: "Quite a remarkable woman. All the men who ever met her, fell for her. She was

---

[120] Ibid., 25 Sep 1945.

attractive, charming, very intelligent and she knew the politics of the situation. She knew what was going on."[121]

Within a week of his visit to Chungking Kinkaid faced the consequences of his assurances to the Generalissimo concerning future activities of the Seventh Fleet. His letters to Helen told of being busy and pressured from several directions. Occasionally he would drop a hint that he was operating without clear policy guidance. What he didn't recognize was that actions taken or not taken at this time would bear significantly on the future of China and Chinese-American relations. As Admiral Barbey's units were preparing to land the Marine Corps' 6th Division on the north coast of the Shantung Peninsula, at Chefoo, Kinkaid wrote to Helen:

> The Navy out here is like a five-ring circus. The 7th Fleet has been landing the Army in Korea, the Marines at Tienstsin, another Marine force [the 6th Division] will land at another point at an early date, and we are about to start the movement of several Chinese armies from one point to another. At the same time we are in process of changing the organization of the Fleet, getting personnel and ships home for demobilization and setting up organizations to assist China Theater forces.[122]

A central concern of the admiral's was getting his two Marine divisions ashore in China. Between 26 and 30 September Barbey landed the 1st Division at the mouth of the Pai Ho and moved the troops upriver to Tientsin by small craft. All went smoothly and the local populace appeared happy to receive them. This proud division, with many still present who had waded ashore at Guadalcanal in August 1942, had hoped to lead a victory parade along the Ginza in Tokyo. Instead they were to keep order in the vital Tientsin-Peiping (Beijing) area, round up the remaining Japanese and disarm them, and generally maintain the status quo until Chinese Nationalist troops could arrive and relieve them. Were it not for the presence of Chinese Communist forces in the area Marine operations would have been relatively simple. But the Communist forces had no loyalty to Chiang Kai-shek, and they were determined to keep all of north China and Manchuria in their own hands.[123]

This determination was demonstrated when elements of the 6th Division were to land at Chefoo. Before the transports arrived from Guam, Barbey sent Rear Admiral Thomas G. W. Settle ahead with *Nashville* and a few destroyers to make arrangements for the landing. Settle was greeted

---

[121] TCK oral history, 414–18.

[122] TCK to HSK, Shanghai, 4 Oct 1945.

[123] Barbey, *MacArthur's Amphibs*, 330–32; "The Charge in China (Robertson) to the Secretary of State, Chungking, Oct 2, 1945," in U.S. Department of State, *Foreign Relations of the United States: Diplomatic Papers, 1945*: vol 7, *The Far East, China* (Washington: GPO, 1969), 573–74 (hereafter *FRUS, 1945*, 7).

in a friendly manner, even with studied politeness, but he quickly learned from the mayor of Chefoo, Commissioner Yu Ku-ying, that the Marines were unwelcome. A letter from Admiral Kinkaid, informing the mayor that he wanted no interference with the debarkation of the Marines, met with bureaucratic evasion. Mayor Yu had to wait for instructions from Chinese Communist headquarters in Yenan. He did point out to Settle, and the word was passed to Barbey and Kinkaid, that there were no Japanese in the area, the civil government was operating satisfactorily under Communist direction, and the Chinese Communist Army forces at Chefoo were perfectly capable of maintaining order.

On 7 October Barbey and the transports arrived off the port. Fresh meetings with the Chinese led Uncle Dan to conclude that the Americans might meet armed resistance from General Chu Teh's Eighth Route Army. After consulting with Rear Admiral Settle and Major General Keller E. Rockey, who was commanding the Marine III Amphibious Force, Barbey radioed their views to Kinkaid. They believed the Marines should be landed at Tsingtao, on the south side of the Shantung Peninsula. Barbey later explained his reasoning to a press correspondent: "Chefoo was in control of the 8th Route Army. The city is well policed and here are no disorders. As there are no Japanese and no prisoners of war and no American internees, there is no military reason for landing United States troops at this time."[124]

Kinkaid's decision to land the Marines at Tsingtao on 12 October, rather than at Chefoo, was grounded in common sense and basic instructions laid down by the Joint Chiefs of Staff in October 1944 and again in August 1945. In their directives to the Commanding General, United States Forces, China Theater, the JCS had stated:

[1] . . . You will not employ United States resources for suppression of civil strife except insofar as necessary to protect United States lives and property.

[2] All its [October 1944 directive] provisions apply only insofar as action in accordance therewith does not prejudice the basic U.S. principle that the United States will not support the Central Government of China in fratricidal war. [8–10–45]

[3] It is not proposed to involve U.S. ground forces in a major land campaign in any part of the China Theater. [8–10–45][125]

---

[124] Quoted in Herbert Feis, *The China Tangle* (Princeton University Press, 1953), 365–66; Barbey, *MacArthur's Amphibs*, 333–36; correspondence in VADM T. G. W. Settle Papers, OA; transcript of radio broadcast by TCK, Shanghai, 12 Oct 1945, TCK Papers.

[125] "The Joint Chiefs of Staff to the Commanding General, U.S. Armed Forces, China Theater (Wedemeyer), Washington, August 10, 1945," in *FRUS, 1945* 7:527–28.

To Kinkaid, Barbey, and Lieutenant General Stratemayer, the possibility of having the Marines shoot their way in to Chefoo seemed to contravene the existing JCS instructions, so the Marines went to the more interesting port of Tsingtao. Chefoo would have been a splendid port to use for ferrying troops across the Gulf of Chihli to Manchurian entry ports, but in October 1945 it did not seem worth a fight.

With the Marines ashore in China, the Seventh Fleet now turned to redistributing Chinese field armies from Indochina and south China to north China and Manchuria. The forces transported to north China were expected to relieve the Marines in Tsingtao, Tientsin, and Peiping. Armies entering Manchuria would replace the Russians, permitting them to depart by the agreed-on mid-November deadline. In theory all of these Chinese armies were going north to take control from the Japanese so that their repatriation could begin. To most Americans present, including General Wedemeyer, it was evident that the Chinese armies were to be moved to north China and Manchuria to prevent these critical areas from falling under the control of the Communist forces lead by Mao Tse-tung. Admiral Kinkaid certainly understood the situation as he explained to his wife:

> The redistribution of Central Government troops is intended to strengthen the Generalissimo's hand in the northern areas relative to the Communist forces and to provide an occupation force for Manchuria to move in as the Russians move out in accordance with their treaty.... These are delicate operations because we do not want to get involved in Chinese civil strife and the Communist factions in the north are already causing trouble. I have Barbey up north examining the ports of debarcation [sic] to see if we can land the Central Government forces without opposition.[126]

Unfortunately for the Generalissimo, Admiral Barbey had no more success putting Chiang's armies ashore in Manchuria than he had had at Chefoo. In early November approaches were made at Hu-lu-tao and Ying-K'ou to debark troops. In both cases the Russians washed their hands of the situation, stating that the Americans would have to deal with the local (Communist) forces in control of the ports. Again unwilling to risk an opposed landing, Barbey landed the Chinese troops at Chin-huang-tao, a few miles south of where the Great Wall is breached by the railroad at Shan-hai-kuan. This change in plans meant that the central government troops would have to move overland, probably against resistance, in order to reach Manchuria.

Kinkaid and Wedemeyer believed there was little the United States could do to influence the situation unless there was a specific change in policy

---

[126] TCK to HSK, Shanghai, 29 Oct 1945, 1 Nov 1945.

that would direct the Seventh Fleet and the III Marine Amphibious Corps to actively assist Chiang Kai-shek's forces against the Communists. By mid-November 1945 the Generalissimo had enough troops in north China to control and protect the region against hostile acts from the surrendered Japanese, but he did not have enough power to wage an offensive campaign against the Chinese Communists.[127] In Washington the decision was reached by the Secretaries of State, War, and Navy that the United States should not take sides in the internecine warfare between Generalissimo Chiang Kai-shek's forces and those of Chairman Mao Tse-tung.[128]

Fortunately, Admiral Kinkaid was spared the necessity of trying to implement any further decisions made in Washington and Chungking. In mid-October Helen had had a recurrence of an intestinal problem she had suffered in Rome. She had become depressed about her elderly father and further depressed that everyone seemed to be returning from the war except her husband.[129] Kinkaid's old friend, Rear Admiral Milo F. Draemel, Commandant of the Fourth Naval District, radioed him on 19 October that Helen had been operated on at the Philadelphia Naval Hospital. She had progressed satisfactorily for a week, but then had a relapse. Now there was concern that another operation might be necessary. Once it was clear that Helen's condition had stabilized, Draemel wrote a calming letter. Luckily, Admiral Nimitz learned of the situation and with Admiral King arranged for a change of duty. Admiral Kinkaid finally would return from the war.

Throughout their wartime correspondence, but particularly in the last six months of the war, the Kinkaids exchanged views on what his first postwar assignment would be. Tom was not interested in a desk job in Washington; Helen preferred a billet that carried a government house and servants. To the admiral it seemed that a tour as president of the Naval War College in Newport, Rhode Island, or as superintendent of the Naval Academy in Annapolis would be ideal. He particularly wanted the Academy and had regularly requested such duty whenever fitness reports were submitted concerning him. Unfortunately, Vice Admiral Aubrey Fitch was there and had several years left on his tour. There was even less chance of getting the War College. Vice Admiral William Pye, though retired in July 1944, had held the presidency through the war's end and was soon to be relieved. Kinkaid was fairly sure that either Admiral Raymond Spruance or Kelly Turner would get the post. He guessed correctly: Spruance relieved Pye on 1 March 1946.

---

[127] Barbey, *MacArthur's Amphibs*, 336–42; GEN Albert C. Wedemeyer, *Wedemeyer Reports!* (New York: Henry Holt, 1958), 344–49; "Commanding General U.S. Armed Forces, China Theater (Wedemeyer), to Chief of Staff USA (Marshall), Shanghai, Nov 5, 1945," *FRUS, 1945* 7:603–5; ibid., 14 Nov 1945, 627–28.

[128] "Minutes of Meeting of the Secretaries of State, War, and Navy, Washington, 6 Nov 1945," *FRUS, 1945*, 7:606–7, 646–67.

[129] RADM M. F. Draemel to TCK, Philadelphia, 5 Nov 1945, TCK Papers.

On 10 November Kinkaid's orders finally arrived. He was to relieve Admiral Royal E. Ingersoll as Commander Western Sea Frontier, with headquarters in San Francisco Bay. Kinkaid was nonplussed, but he put the best face on the job for Helen's sake. It offered a fine location, interesting responsibilities, a government house with a view, and plenty of servants. The problem, of course, was the distance from Wynnefield Avenue and Helen's father. By the time Tom's letter arrived in Philadelphia with the news, which Helen had already picked up from the *New York Times* on the 15th, he was homeward bound. His orders had been modified and he was now to report to the Chief of Naval Operations for temporary duty before relieving Ingersoll. He was also authorized two weeks delay before reporting to Washington. On the 19th Admiral Kinkaid's four-star blue flag was hauled down on board *Estes*, and Dan Barbey's three stars were run up. The brief change of command ceremony completed, Kinkaid boarded his Coronado command plane for the long flight home.[130]

There is little doubt that Admiral Kinkaid's service under General MacArthur's command was the most important of his naval career. He had been successful in Alaska, and the third star on his collar was solid recognition of that service. He was assigned to the SWPA Command because of his reputation for working smoothly and effectively with the Army, Air Corps, and Canadians. But service under MacArthur opened the door to potential professional disaster and future assignment to a backwater command. On the other hand, upon arrival in Brisbane, Kinkaid found the general ready to launch a series of amphibious operations designed to isolate the Japanese stronghold at Rabaul. He badly needed a senior naval commander who would exert positive leadership in carrying out SWPA plans.

Besides his battle-tested experience, Kinkaid brought to Brisbane judgment, a fund of common sense, and an understanding of how to deal with people, both superiors and subordinates. To many of his contemporaries he was colorless, but when asked, most agreed that he was a good listener and respectful of the opinions of those he consulted.

He also believed in delegating authority. Until subordinates proved otherwise, Kinkaid trusted them with as much authority and responsibility as he thought they could manage. He quickly recognized that Admiral Barbey was a "charger" who could produce handsomely. Kinkaid might have been annoyed with his pushiness, or occasional self-serving behavior, but Dan Barbey handled amphibious operations with consummate skill and that is what counted with Kinkaid. He found Count Berkey to be a dynamic leader, at times impulsive, but intelligently courageous. Like Barbey he enjoyed command under a loose rein. Admiral Oldendorf was another in whom Kinkaid placed a lot of trust. Less flashy than Barbey or Berkey,

---

[130] TCK Personnel File.

Oley was a solid, goal-oriented commander. He enjoyed responsibility, took early initiatives when he understood the whole picture, and saw projects through to completion. When he expressed reservations to a plan, as he did in preparing for Lingayen, Kinkaid knew how to keep him moving. Ironically, Kinkaid's staff was the source of the greatest criticism concerning him. He accepted its members as he found them, molded them to his approaches to problem solving, and kept most of them with him during 1944 and 1945. He clearly won their loyalty and at all times remained supportive of them. Many outsiders considered his staff second-rate. But seen with historical perspective, it is clear that they served him well and deserved the loyalty he gave them.

In an Army environment Kinkaid won the approbation of his fellow commanders through his performance under fire. He was present at both Leyte and Lingayen when the Japanese suicide pilots attacked his ships. Oldendorf and the Spragues met the enemy at close quarters, but Kinkaid was close enough to each engagement to command effectively and act in the interest of his subordinates. His type of leadership and personal courage were easily recognized by the general and his GHQ as being the hallmarks of a true master of naval warfare.

Finally, it is clear that Admiral Kinkaid's loyalty to MacArthur's leadership and plans was repaid in kind. Kinkaid was no sycophant. He knew that he was working for the Army, but when planned operations conflicted with his own professional naval judgment, he was willing to confront the general. In the Mindoro operation, Kinkaid risked MacArthur's anger almost to the point of possible recall. Fortunately, Admirals Nimitz and King recognized his dilemma and provided the necessary leverage to force a change in plans on the general. The success of the operations at Mindoro and Lingayen Gulf eliminated any lingering doubts in MacArthur's mind about the value of his naval commander. A few days after Kinkaid pinned on his fourth star, he visited MacArthur in Manila and thanked him for his assistance in receiving the promotion. MacArthur answered simply, "The four stars are due entirely to Tom Kinkaid."[131]

---

[131] TCK to HSK, Manila, 14 Apr 1945.

Chapter 15

The Postwar Years, 1946–1950

Once the guns were silent and the great fleets had returned to stateside ports, retirement was a natural action for many of the Navy's flag officers to take. Those who had reached retirement age during the war years, and remained on active duty, were expected to retire and most did. But in January 1946, Tom Kinkaid was only fifty-seven years old and would not reach mandatory retirement age until April 1950. He and Helen did not want to "turn in his suit" just yet, but neither did he want to "fleet down" to vice admiral for the few years to retirement. Most important, he did not want to give up his rank. Fortunately, the retirement rules had been changed during the war. Officers could retire at their highest held ranks, if they had served in that rank for two years. Those receiving combat decorations, a silver star or higher, would be advanced one rank at retirement, though they would receive the retired pay of their actual rank. Although Tom would retire as an admiral, he was a bit concerned about those years until April 1950.

During his temporary duty in Washington after returning from leave, Kinkaid managed to get his orders to the West Coast changed. Instead of relieving Admiral Ingersoll as Commander Western Sea Frontier, he was to relieve his old friend Fairfax Leary as Commander Eastern Sea Frontier (CESF) and Commander Sixteenth Fleet. Leary was a vice admiral, but the issue of rank did not arise. Kinkaid continued his service as an admiral. With the assignment went one of the finest houses under the Navy's control, the Commandant's Quarters in the New York Navy Yard. Designed by Charles Bulfinch (1763–1844) and first occupied in 1806, "Quarters A" occupied a hill within the yard. Helen Kinkaid remembered the house and Tom's years as the Eastern Sea Frontier Commander with great delight.[1]

The headquarters building for Kinkaid's command was 90 Church Street in New York City. Because he was "wearing two hats," the Sea Frontier command and the Sixteenth Fleet, Tom rated two staffs. The Sixteenth Fleet, which consisted of the Navy's vessels on the East Coast placed either in reduced commission or out of commission (in "mothballs"), was managed by his deputy. Sea Frontier affairs were ably looked after by his chief of staff.

---

[1] "The Commandant's Quarters, Navy Yard, New York," [leaflet, n.d.], 3, Naval Historical Center; Helen Kinkaid interview, 8 Jan 1976.

This situation suited Tom and Helen for they hoped to have four years of reasonably nondemanding duty, free from serious conflicts, and filled with interesting opportunities to entertain and be entertained. The admiral was, after all, a national hero. Once the older admirals retired, he would be number four on the admirals list and number two by his 1950 retirement.[2] Besides, he had spent three long years separated from his wife. Back in early 1943 he had written to Helen: "When the war is over and I am due ashore I want a nice quiet place. . . . If I have to spend a few hours in an office each day, all right, but I am not going to be looking for a busy job."[3]

A small dark cloud appeared in this era of blue skies, and Kinkaid had anticipated its coming. In a letter to Helen written from Shanghai, the admiral noted that the subject of unification of the armed services was appearing more regularly in the papers. He expected there would be a "long and acrimonious fight," but hoped he would not be too involved: "I would like to be consulted and say my say but wrangling over service politics is something I very much dislike."[4]

During the war, pressure began to rise in the Army and Army Air Force, as well as in Congress, to create a unified military service made up of Army, Navy, and Air Force, administered by a single civilian secretary and commanded by a single military person assisted by a general staff. Depending upon who was doing the proposing, the Marine Corps and its functions might be subsumed by the Army; and Marine and Navy aviation, except perhaps carrier aviation, might be taken over by the new Air Force. Most expected unification would lead to great financial savings in research and development, as well as acquisition of aircraft, armament, munitions, and possibly even uniforms. It was assumed that a unified high command would lead to better strategic direction, coordination, and command in wartime. President Truman and the Army high command (Army Chief of Staff General George Marshall and Commanding General Army Air Forces Henry Arnold) believed the concept of a unified military to be sound. The Air Force people, desiring above all to be independent of the Army, enthusiastically campaigned for the ideas. The Navy, however, let it be known that it was hostile to this line of thinking.[5]

---

[2] In January 1946, Fleet Admirals W. D. Leahy, E. J. King, C. W. Nimitz, and W. F. Halsey held the first four signal numbers. Halsey would leave active service in December 1946 and be listed as retired in the 1947 *Register*. Leahy, as Chief of Staff to President Truman, headed the active list of flag officers. King, from December 1945, remained on the active list, but without assignment, as was his right as a fleet admiral. Nimitz relieved King as CNO. In 1946 the list of four-star admirals included, in order of seniority, R. A. Spruance, J. H. Ingram, R. S. Edwards, H. K. Hewitt, T. C. Kinkaid, R. K. Turner, and J. H. Towers.

[3] TCK to HSK, Kodiak, 15 Feb 1943.

[4] TCK to HSK, Shanghai, 19 Oct 1945.

[5] Vincent Davis, *Postwar Defense Policy and the U.S. Navy, 1943–1946* (Chapel Hill: University of North Carolina Press, 1962), 50–53, 138–47, 225–26.

President Truman forced congressional action on 19 December 1945 by officially proposing a bill to unify the armed services. The House and Senate had been dilatory in taking action, and Truman now wanted results.[6] At first stymied by the President's insistence that the Navy Department support his proposal, Secretary of the Navy Forrestal convinced him that naval officers must be allowed to state their personal views before congressional committees.[7] On 9 July 1946 Admiral Kinkaid "had his say" before the congressional committee considering Senate Bill 2044, providing for armed services unification. As might be expected from a team player, Tom's testimony was not outside the mainstream of Navy thinking.

The admiral spoke strongly about lack of protection for service autonomy in the bill, the possible fatal damage to the Marine Corps if it were absorbed into the Army, and the possible elimination of Navy weapons research and development. His strongest arguments were directed against eliminating land-based patrol bombing squadrons from the Navy's order of battle. Drawing on his experience with General Kenney's airmen in the Southwest Pacific, Tom highlighted the failures of Army Air Corps squadrons in reconnaissance, protection of shipping, and attacks against enemy naval formations. His central thesis was that aviation in support of sea power activities must be under the control of Navy people, and that aviators in these missions must be Navy trained and indoctrinated.[8]

Tom's other trips to Washington during 1946 included professional duties other than congressional testimony. Probably the most distasteful occurred in March when he was ordered to Main Navy to sit on a flag officer "plucking board." Chaired by Fleet Admiral Halsey, the board included Admirals Spruance, Kinkaid, and Towers, and Vice Admiral Mitscher. As part of the postwar reduction in size of the Navy, Congress had decided that about fifty rear admirals and twenty commodores should be retired involuntarily. Theoretically this move would cut some flag officers who had become dead wood and open the way for new promotions to flag rank. Public Law 305, approved by the President on 21 February 1946, provided that officers "plucked" in this way would retire at their highest held permanent or temporary rank and receive the retired pay of that rank.[9]

Tom believed the involuntary retirement act was wrongheaded but he performed his duty as ordered. To him, 50 rear admirals out of 215 was "a drastic plucking"; he thought there were a lot of temporary vice admirals

---

[6] Harry S. Truman, *Memoirs by Harry S. Truman*, vol. 2, *Years of Trial and Hope, 1946–1952* (Garden City, NY: Doubleday, 1955), 48–50.

[7] Walter Millis, ed., *The Forrestal Diaries* (New York: Viking Press, 1951), 118–19.

[8] U.S. Congress, Senate, Naval Affairs Committee, *Hearings on S. 2044: Unification of the Armed Services*, 79th Cong., 2d sess., 9 Jul 1946, 261–76.

[9] *Army and Navy Journal*, 2, 9, 16 Mar 1946; Chief of Naval Personnel to TCK, Washington, 26 Feb 1946, TCK Papers.

who would soon revert to rear admirals and should be reviewed. To pluck twenty to thirty commodores was equally drastic and ill-considered; most commodores had been advanced to that rank because they were outstanding captains and thus did not deserve to be placed at risk. He thought it would be fairer to let some of the deserving officers revert to captain so they could continue their service until they reached thirty years or retirement age, then they would retire at flag rank. The board completed its work in ten days and forwarded its report on 3 April. However, this was not to be the last time Tom had to serve on a "plucking board."[10]

As a peacetime commander of the Eastern Sea Frontier in New York, Kinkaid found he was occupying a command in transition. During the war, his predecessors controlled antisubmarine activities in coastal waters and coordinated convoyed shipping from frontier ports; they also commanded a large number of activities related to defense of the eastern seaboard. Whereas Vice Admiral Leary's staff had numbered 226 officers and 156 enlisted in early 1945, Kinkaid's would drop to 26 officers and 46 enlisted at the end of 1946. CESF had much less to do in 1946 than had been the case in 1944 or 1945.[11]

What Kinkaid did find is that his job entailed a variety of tasks. During the war, naval district commandants on both coasts had steadily lost power to sea frontier commanders. After the war, CNO Fleet Admiral King decided this transfer of power was not a bad thing. In October 1945 he issued a directive prescribing the duties of the Commander Eastern Sea Frontier.[12] The commander would now have command and coordination authority over all commandants whose districts lay within the Eastern Sea Frontier. To better coordinate sea frontier and Atlantic Fleet operations, the CNO's directive called for CESF to become a task force commander within the Atlantic Fleet. Thus Kinkaid became Commander Task Force 70 under Admiral Jonas H. Ingram, Commander in Chief, Atlantic Fleet. Although all naval district craft were at his command, CTF 70 was to be concerned principally with logistic support of the Atlantic Fleet.

As Eastern Sea Frontier commander, Kinkaid also served on a variety of joint boards which included Army and Air Force representatives. Until mid-March 1946, the boundaries of the Sea Frontier and the Army's Eastern Defense Command were approximately conterminous, leading to regular interaction with the commanding general. After March 1946, the Army divided the Eastern Defense Command into a number of Army

---

[10] Kinkaid's orders to the Halsey Board, and memoranda concerning the work, except for the list of names, may be found in the Kinkaid Collection.

[11] "The Eastern Sea Frontier" (Draft article for *Army and Navy Journal*); "Narrative of Eastern Sea Frontier, 1 Sep 1945 to 1 Oct 1946," Commander, Eastern Sea Frontier to Office of Naval History, New York, 19 Dec 1946, TCK Papers (hereafter CESF)

[12] CNO to CESF, Washington, 18 Oct 1945, copy in TCK Papers.

Ground Forces command areas, and naval district people were used for the joint boards as needed. Kinkaid believed the Navy had the advantage in those joint boards where he was active because of his rank.[13]

In practical terms, the Eastern Sea Frontier was an anachronism by 1946, and Admiral Kinkaid carried more rank than the commander's billet deserved. But the Navy, unable in 1946 to anticipate its future operations in the Atlantic, decided to continue an existing command. Keeping track of merchant and naval ship movements in the Atlantic Coast and Gulf regions was harmless, but hardly necessary. Hurricane-tracking activities based in Miami, though useful, could have been administered through the Seventh Naval District. Air-sea search and rescue operations were monitored by Kinkaid's staff until July 1946, but were then transferred to the Coast Guard. In short, it was evident to Kinkaid (and to his successors) that the Eastern Sea Frontier was a self-liquidating command.

With commands that could be managed by deputies, the admiral was free to spend a great deal of time on public relations. Given the pressure for unification of the armed services, and the Navy's unwillingness to fall into line, it was important to the Department that its senior officers do everything possible to develop a positive attitude toward the Navy in the civilian community. Tom Kinkaid could work effectively toward this end. He was a national hero and a well-decorated flag officer who had earned his reputation as a "fighting admiral" under fire. At six feet, and still reasonably fit, with bushy eyebrows and a fair amount of greying hair, he was an imposing figure at a speaker's rostrum or in the middle of a cocktail party. Because he usually confined his presentations to subjects that drew on his combat experiences, his speeches were delivered forcefully and were well sprinkled with anecdotes that pleased his audiences.

During the transition period in January, Admiral Leary made certain that his old friend met a good number of the most influential people in the New York area. Using the occasion of a luncheon at the officers club at the Navy Yard on the 4th, Leary introduced Tom to Thomas J. Watson (IBM), Clarence Dillon (Dillon Read & Co.), Winthrop Aldrich (Chase Manhattan Bank), and a host of other business luminaries. Even Grover Whalen, former mayor of New York City and now its "official greeter," was present. Kinkaid's brief speech before this group introduced him to an important network of acquaintances and friends and opened the door to traveling the "chicken salad circuit."[14] By the admiral's own count, he gave 107 speeches during his first two years in New York.

---

[13] "Narrative" for 1 Sep 1945 to 1 Oct 1946.
[14] VADM Fairfax Leary to TCK, New York, 27 Dec 1945, TCK Papers.

Although the admiral preferred to speak about his wartime service, he did hold forth regularly on topics dealing with national defense, naval support of foreign policy, and, from February 1947 on, the internal and external threat of communism. Kinkaid supported the President in his call for universal military training (UMT),[15] and in 1947 tied this support to his Sixteenth Fleet, which had now become the Atlantic Reserve Fleet. Citizens participating in the Naval Reserve, or trained under UMT, could staff the 987 ships under his command or the 1055 vessels in the Pacific Reserve Fleet, thus helping preserve the naval power developed during the war. With such strength available to the United Nations, Kinkaid believed there was little likelihood of world peace being disturbed.[16]

In the early spring of 1947, Kinkaid invited fifty members of the New York State Society of Newspaper Editors to lunch on board the battleship *North Carolina* at the New York Navy Yard. After the newsmen had toured the vessel, then in the process of being moth-balled, the admiral addressed them in the officers wardroom. Noting the international tension that March, he opined that "without the Communist danger [internally] and without Russia this would be a pretty peaceful world right now." He noted: "We of the Western World are in danger from a most potent weapon—Communist infiltration. There seems to be no defense for it. We can defend ourselves from atomic warfare, but the only defense against this infiltration is to kill it."[17] Soviet expansionism and communist infiltration remained themes that the admiral used in public speeches during the rest of his tour in New York. The natural link between his reserve fleet, national military strength, and the containment of the Soviet Union was also a frequent topic. Addressing the Overseas Press Club in the summer of 1947, he warned, "If we fail to keep strong, there is a danger of another war; whereas if we build our military strength and contain Russian expansionism, a third world war will be avoided."[18]

A year later, in October 1948 before the Propeller Club, the admiral again warned about a new threat to America's security, "the subtle boring from within." To combat the spread of communism and subversive elements within our country, he believed in the "education of all our citizens in the true meaning of communism and what it stands for."[19] At a Flag Day observance in New York's City Hall Plaza, sponsored by the Sons of the American Revolution, Kinkaid told an audience of 500 that it was "particularly important that our children acquire knowledge and

---

[15] Harry S. Truman, *Memoirs by Harry S. Truman*, vol. 1, *Years of Decisions* (Garden City, NY: Doubleday, 1945), 510–11; and 2:54–55.
[16] *New York Times*, 6 Oct, 6 Dec 1946, 23 Feb, 25 Mar 1947.
[17] Ibid., 25 Mar 1947.
[18] Ibid., 3 Jul 1947.
[19] Ibid., 16 Oct 1948.

an understanding of the principles upon which our forefathers established our great republic." In this way they could learn "to recognize as enemies the forces intent upon destroying our freedom."[20]

Of all the ceremonial functions he attended or participated in, the most colorful came just a few months after Tom assumed command of the Eastern Sea Frontier. On 5 March 1946, Winston Churchill had startled the world by delivering his "Iron Curtain" speech at Westminster College in Fulton, Missouri, where he had been introduced by President Harry Truman. Ten days later the city of New York held a grand reception at the Waldorf Astoria to honor the former British Prime Minister. Two thousand people, including the Kinkaids, each paying fifteen dollars a plate to break bread with this historical figure, attended the party. Tom and Helen had an opportunity to visit with the guest of honor. Churchill greeted them, saying that the admiral had won "the greatest sea battle of the war." Kinkaid repaid the compliment by noting that he and his wife had visited the Gallipoli battlefield four times and that he believed the strategy was absolutely correct; only the execution was faulty. In his usual blunt manner, Churchill noted that, right or wrong, the campaign had cost him his job as First Lord of the Admiralty.[21]

A reading through Tom Kinkaid's postwar correspondence reveals that he was also engaged in quiet competition with others on the flag list to see who could accumulate the most decorations for wartime service. By the time the admiral returned from his Seventh Fleet command, he had been awarded four Distinguished Service Medals by the Navy (technically one medal and three gold stars, one for each subsequent award). During his visit to China, after the cessation of hostilities, Lieutenant General Wedemeyer decorated him with the Army version of the Legion of Merit award.[22] But what ate at the admiral, and did so for many years, was the bald fact that he had received no recognition from General of the Army MacArthur for the two years under his command. While it probably was an oversight by the general's staff, it still seemed a bit strange to Kinkaid.[23]

Tom opened his campaign to rectify the record with a letter to the Vice Chief of Naval Operations in late February 1946. He wondered what had become of Admiral Halsey's recommendation that he be awarded a DSM after the Santa Cruz Islands engagement. The decision in 1942 was that the DSM he received for the Coral Sea and the Solomons area battles had in-

---

[20] Ibid., 25 Mar 1947. The author wishes to acknowledge the assistance of Clayton Trost of Campbell, California, who as a graduate student undertook research concerning Admiral Kinkaid's public-speaking activities.
[21] Helen S. Kinkaid interview, 7 Jan 1976; *New York Times*, 16 Mar 1946.
[22] David F. Freeman, interview with author, Rumson, NJ, 6 Aug 1976; U.S. Forces, China Theater, General Order No. 233, Shanghai, 18 Nov 45, TCK Papers.
[23] TCK to ADM Frederick C. Horne, New York, 26 Feb 1946; Chairman Board for Review of Medals and Decorations to Secretary of the Navy, Washington, 15 Mar 1946, TCK File.

cluded the October battle. Apparently recognizing that there was a difference between the August battle of the Eastern Solomons and the October battle of the Santa Cruz Islands, the Board of Awards compromised. Instead of awarding a DSM as Halsey had recommended, it rewrote the citation for the 24 August battle to include that of 26 October. Tom received no fifth Navy DSM, only a slightly more fulsome citation for his earlier medal.[24]

In December, Kinkaid's attention was caught by a news story that Admirals Halsey, Spruance, and Turner had been awarded DSMs by the Army. He wrote to an old friend on the General Board inquiring about the DSM that General Krueger had recommended for him. By the time his friend replied, Tom had received a message from MacArthur: "I have recently learned that the senior naval commanders in the Pacific Ocean Area accepted the Army's DSM. I cannot see therefore why a similar award should not, repeat not, be made to you and accordingly have forwarded an appropriate recommendation to the War Department covering period November 23, 1943 to September 2, 1945."[25]

The admiral finally received his Army DSM on 10 April 1947 at Governors Island in New York Harbor. General Courtney Hodges read the citation to all assembled:

> Admiral Thomas C. Kinkaid, United States Navy, performed exceptionally meritorious and distinguished service to the Government in a position of great responsibility in the Southwest Pacific Area. . . . As Commander of the Allied Naval Forces supporting Sixth Army, he demonstrated a consummate mastery of all phases of joint Army-Navy activity as well as a conspicuously outstanding knowledge of strategic warfare and naval tactics as he directed the planning and execution of naval support of amphibious operations in the Admiralties and Philippine Islands. His employment of naval forces against the Japanese fleet in the Battle for Leyte Gulf resulted in disaster for the enemy and removed a threat to the entire plan for the liberation of the Philippine Islands. . . .[26]

The medals story might have ended on Governors Island, but in July 1948 Tom's friend and Naval Academy roommate, Rear Admiral Kauffman, decided that Tom should also have received the Navy Cross. In a letter to Kinkaid, Reggie noted that he had asked Fleet Admiral Nimitz to recommend Tom for the decoration. Although he had not mentioned names to Nimitz, Reggie commented to Kinkaid that Spruance, Turner, and even Carney had received Navy Crosses. Tom replied that

---

[24] TCK oral history, 363–65.
[25] TCK to RADM R. W. Hayler, New York, 19 Dec 1946; Hayler to TCK, Washington, 16 Jan 1947, TCK Papers; MacArthur to TCK, Tokyo, 27 Dec 1946, TCK to MacArthur, New York, 1 Jan 1947, MacArthur Papers.
[26] TCK File.

he was "only mildly interested," but he did feel the Philippine government should have given him some sort of an award. Nimitz did his part, but the Board of Awards invoked the three-year rule; too much time had elapsed.²⁷ Tom was philosophical, but Reggie was still irritated, perhaps embarrassed. Kinkaid had recently gotten the Navy Department to recognize that Kauffman's DSM had been earned under battle conditions, thus allowing Reggie to retire with the rank and pay of a vice admiral.²⁸

While Kinkaid did actively seek to increase the number of decorations for his wartime service, other recognition came unsolicited from appreciative foreign governments. Queen Wilhelmina of the Netherlands honored Kinkaid in December 1944, making him a Grand Officer in the Order of Orange Nassau (with swords). The award was made while the news of the victory at Leyte Gulf was still fresh in the mind of America's ally, but it took almost fourteen months for the medal and documents to catch up with Tom.²⁹

Kinkaid's trip to China not only yielded a Legion of Merit, but a grateful Chinese government awarded him the Grand Cordon Pao Ting (Tripod) medal of the Special Class. At the time of his return from the Pacific, in November 1945, the British government notified him that King George VI had made him an Honorary Companion of the Order of the Bath. This award had been made on the recommendation of the Prime Minister of Australia.³⁰ It was not until January 1948, on Australia Day, that the Australian Embassy in Washington arranged a luncheon and ceremony for the admiral, by that time having also made him an Honorary Commander of the Military Division of the Most Honourable Order of the Bath. Regardless of the title, it was still a very handsome award, and Tom looked quite dashing with his pink sash.³¹ The admiral's last two foreign decorations were awarded in March 1948 at the Belgian Embassy in Washington: he was made a Grand Officer of the Order of Leopold, with Palm, and he received the Croix de Guerre, with Palm.³² Though not in the same class as Fleet Admirals King, Nimitz and Halsey when it came to accumulating foreign decorations, the six that Kinkaid received put him ahead of Kelly Turner and Harold Stark, a fact that probably soothed his competitive soul.³³

---

²⁷ RADM J. L. Kauffman to TCK, Philadelphia, 14 Jul 1948; TCK to Kauffman, New York, 16 Jul 1948; FADM C. W. Nimitz to ADM L. E. Denfeld, 26 Jul 1948; Denfeld to Nimitz, Washington, 9 Aug 1948; Nimitz to Kauffman, 17 Aug 1948; TCK to Kauffman, New York, 25 Aug 1948, TCK Papers.

²⁸ RADM J. L. Kauffman to TCK, Philadelphia, 29 Jun 1948; TCK to Kauffman, New York, 25 Aug 1948, TCK Papers.

²⁹ Memo by RADM L. A. Davidson, Washington, 13 Jan 1945; CDR D. H. Northrup to TCK, Washington, 13 Nov 1945; LCDR W. C. Palmer to TCK, Washington, 21 Jan 1946, TCK File.

³⁰ H. W. Allen to TCK, Washington, 5 Nov 1945, TCK Papers.

³¹ Norman Makin to TCK, Washington, 17 Dec 1947, TCK Papers.

³² TCK to CHNAVPERS, New York 2 Mar 48, TCK File.

³³ *The Register of Alumni*, U.S. Naval Academy, lists the number of foreign decorations an officer has received. While not completely reliable, it does offer a basis for comparisons.

To suggest that Kinkaid's pursuit of additional American decorations and his accumulation of foreign decorations and medals were the actions of a selfish, narcissistic personality would be a serious misreading of his character, however. His personal papers, from the time he became a flag officer, are replete with examples of the assistance he gave others where there could be no possible quid pro quo. A former member of the admiral's Seventh Fleet staff, Captain Dick Cruzen, wrote in December 1946 to thank his former boss for a good word at the right time. Tom had helped him get a cruiser command, leading to Cruzen's selection for flag rank.[34] Though he had asked for Rear Admiral R. W. Christie's relief in 1944, Kinkaid wrote a strong letter on his behalf in 1947 when asked about his fitness to be Commander Submarines, Atlantic Fleet: "As Commander Submarines, SEVENTH FLEET, Christie did an extremely fine job. . . . His operations were well-planned, sound and highly successful. . . . If you take Christie as your submarine commander, you will have an excellent one."[35] Christie, however, did not get the job; CNO Denfeld had other ideas.

Kinkaid's generosity manifested itself most interestingly during early 1948. He had heard from acquaintances that the British were having a miserable winter. Food and fuel were scarce and being rationed, clothing was terribly expensive, and the weather had been dreadful. He and Helen began sending CARE-type (Cooperative for American Remittances Everywhere) packages to British officers they knew, and to friends of these friends. Helen emptied her wardrobe of unneeded clothing and rounded up more. From the letters they received in return, it is clear that the "tinned meats," chocolates, clothing and other items were received gratefully and without embarrassment.[36]

During his tour in New York, the admiral spoke occasionally about the Battle for Leyte Gulf, and even considered writing a magazine piece on it, but for most of this period he carefully avoided any critical comments concerning the parts played by others. When occasionally pressed by friends or acquaintances about Admiral Halsey's role in the battle, Tom's usual approach, after the summer of 1947, was to recommend reading C. Vann Woodward's *The Battle for Leyte Gulf,* or James A. Field's *The Japanese at Leyte Gulf.* Based on Japanese sources, both books state that Admiral Ozawa's Northern Force was a decoy and Admiral Halsey had left the San Bernardino Strait unguarded to attack it.[37]

---

[34] CAPT Richard Cruzen to TCK, at sea, 4 Dec 1946, TCK Papers.

[35] Blair, *Silent Victory,* 2:854; TCK to ADM W. H. Blandy, New York, 12 Mar 1947, TCK Papers.

[36] TCK to RADM Sir Richard Bevan, New York, 3 Feb 1948; Bevan to TCK, 13 Mar 1948; Mary Addison to HSK, Kent, England, 13 Apr 1948; Kathleen Parkam to HSK, Plymouth, England, 15 Jan 1949; Mrs. J. W. W. Brown to HSK, Sussex, England, 7 Nov 1948, TCK Papers.

[37] RADM T. L. Sprague to TCK, Washington, 25 Mar 1947; TCK to Lloyd Stark, New York, 20 Aug 1948, TCK Papers.

In the summer of 1947, Fleet Admiral Halsey publicly called into question Kinkaid's management of the Seventh Fleet during the battle, particularly when Admiral Kurita's Center Force was mauling Taffy 3 off Samar. Beginning 14 June, the *Saturday Evening Post* published nine articles that were eventually to become Halsey's memoirs. The first six pieces were innocuous enough and interesting to the civilian reader, but the seventh article in the 26 July issue concerned Leyte Gulf. It caught the attention of Tom Kinkaid and many other flag officers, including Fleet Admiral King. Bull Halsey never admitted that the Third Fleet had a protect-and-cover mission in its orders for the Leyte landings in October 1944. He only stated: "The Seventh Fleet was defensive; having convoyed MacArthur's transports to Leyte, it stood by to protect them. . . . The Third Fleet was offensive; it prowled the ocean, striking at will with its new battleships and fast carriers."[38]

Halsey indirectly criticized Fleet Admirals Nimitz (CINCPAC) and King (COMINCH) for having written orders that called for two separate fleet commanders to operate through coordination, rather than under a single commander.[39] The admiral also shifted the responsibility for keeping track of Kurita's fleet away from the Third Fleet and Task Force 38, which had engaged it, to Kinkaid and Rear Admiral C.A.F. Sprague: "I wondered how Kinkaid had let 'Ziggy' Sprague get caught like this, and why 'Ziggy's' search planes had not given him warning."[40] The admiral stated that his greatest regret was that he was not there to stop Kurita, but that he had turned his battleships back toward Leyte Gulf (too late to be useful) before they had engaged Ozawa's (depleted) carrier force. Finally, somewhat as an afterthought, he said he probably would have acted as Kinkaid had, if had been in his shoes at Leyte Gulf.[41]

Within a week of the article's appearance, King stated his own views to Halsey: "Personally, I must say that I did not like the tenor of the installment, neither as to Kinkaid, as to the phony dispatch [allegedly from Nimitz] nor as to the command set-up." King also thought that Halsey should review and rewrite the Leyte installment. Halsey did not agree: "I regret that your point of view and mine do not coincide."[42]

The article outraged Kinkaid, and Halsey's book, which followed a month later, intensified his anger. Although Kinkaid did not "go public," he evened the score through private channels. Probably anticipating

---

[38] Halsey and Bryan, *Admiral Halsey's Story*, 210–11; Fleet Admiral William F. Halsey with LCDR J. Bryan III, "Admiral Halsey Tells His Story, Part Seven," *The Saturday Evening Post*, 26 Jul 1947, 64, 68.

[39] Halsey, *Admiral Halsey's Story*, 210, 227; Halsey and Bryan, "Admiral Halsey Tells His Story" 64.

[40] Halsey, *Admiral Halsey's Story*, 219; Halsey and Bryan, "Admiral Halsey Tells His Story" 68.

[41] Halsey, *Admiral Halsey's Story*, 227; Halsey and Bryan, "Admiral Halsey Tells His Story" 71.

[42] King to Halsey, Washington, 30 Jul 1947; Halsey to King, 12 Aug 1947, William F. Halsey Papers, MD–LC. See also, Potter, *Halsey*, 371–72.

that there would be controversy when Halsey's memoirs reached Leyte Gulf, the editorial board of *Life* magazine approached Kinkaid and suggested that he write or assist with an article on the controversy surrounding the battle. Tom declined. Later he wrote to Captain Arleigh A. Burke, who had been chief of staff to Vice Admiral Mitscher, CTF 38:

> [I]n July I tried to persuade "Life" not to write an article on "the controversial issues of the Battle for Leyte Gulf." I told Mr. Longwell, Chairman of the Board of Editors, that I had kept quiet on the subject for nearly three years because I believed a controversy would do the Navy no good and I declined to talk to him about it until Halsey's seventh installment appeared in the Saturday Evening Post.[43]

But once Halsey was in print, Kinkaid agreed to assist Gilbert Cant of *Life* magazine with a "factual article."[44] He had hoped to write an article of his own, but the weekly picture magazine had done the job too well. What Gilbert Cant published was "Bull's Run: Was Halsey Right at Leyte Gulf?"[45]

Headed by photographs of a scowling Kinkaid and an intense Halsey, Cant's article could hardly have agreed more with Kinkaid's views. Cant early framed the focus of the piece: "The four-day, four-ring battle left one great question unanswered: was Admiral William F. ("Bull") Halsey right in dashing off to destroy the Japanese aircraft carriers instead of their battleships—or did he leave a fellow American admiral in the lurch?"[46] The author's judgment was gentle, but clear: Halsey should not have left San Bernardino Strait unguarded.

> No one can deny the brilliance of Halsey's leadership. But in the matter of Bull's run his judgment seems so questionable that even one of his most loyal former subordinates, after vigorously defending him, admitted, "Still, it's a damned shame it turned out the way it did, with all those battleships getting away."[47]

Although the *Life* magazine article probably offended Halsey, neither he nor Kinkaid reopened the subject for eighteen months. In April 1949 Tom spoke to a convention of the Reserve Officers Association meeting at the Ambassador Hotel in New York. The topic was Leyte Gulf and this time he stated forthrightly that Halsey had erred in leaving San Bernar-

---

[43] TCK to CAPT Arleigh Burke, New York, 4 Dec 1947, copy in Bates Papers.

[44] Gilbert Cant was an experienced author in naval affairs. See his *The Great Pacific Victory: From the Solomons to Tokyo* (New York: John Day, 1946).

[45] TCK to R. J. Abbott, New York, 18 Aug 1947, TCK Papers. Gilbert Cant, "Bull's Run: Was Halsey Right at Leyte Gulf? *Life*, 24 Nov 1947, 73–90.

[46] Cant, "Bull's Run," 73.

[47] Ibid., 90.

dino Strait unguarded while he moved to attack the Japanese carrier decoy force. The *New York Times* reported the speech fully, but a bit inaccurately. The *Army and Navy Register* picked up the *Times* story, error and all.[48] A few letters to Kinkaid applauded his speaking out, but time had passed and the Halsey-Kinkaid feud was not a hot topic even in the summer of 1949. King, however, decided that Kinkaid needed to be taken down a peg. He wrote the admiral on 3 August and said he had never received a reply to a query he had radioed to Kinkaid after the victory at Leyte Gulf. He had asked what specific orders the admiral had issued to his air units to make sure the Japanese had not transited San Bernardino Strait.[49] Tom sent the admiral a copy of the top secret, "for Admiral King's eyes only," dispatch 160202 of December 1944, which King's staff had evidently lost. It showed that Kinkaid had ordered the seaplane search to the north by VP–33, and that he had ordered the CVEs to conduct a dawn search of sector 340 to 030 degrees, which included the strait.[50] King remained obtuse. Perhaps his powers of concentration were weakening, as suggested by his biographer.[51] He terminated his correspondence with Kinkaid with this comment:

> From all the available information that I have gleaned . . . I have to conclude that, except for the five patrol planes available as "snoopers," no proper orders were given by you to any of the three escort carrier groups to search the whole area of the Sibuyan Sea down through the rest of the important strait to the open sea. Had such planes been on "search" even only from the earliest dawn, such planes could not have missed seeing the Japanese "middle" group if it were there, or could have remained aloft long enough to report nothing important was to be seen.[52]

Tom wrote one more lengthy letter to Admiral King, spelling out his position, but the admiral had made up his mind. In a conversation with Walter Whitehill while they were working on King's memoirs, the admiral commented: "If [Kinkaid] had not made that mistake in the Battle of Leyte Gulf . . . but that mistake was just natural to him."[53] There the matter rested for another five years until other writers chose to resurrect the question of whose views were correct.

---

[48] *New York Times*, 26 Apr 1949; *Army and Navy Register*, 7 May 1949. The *Times* reporter misunderstood Kinkaid and wrote that ADM Nimitz had ordered Halsey to guard the San Bernardino Strait.
[49] King to TCK, Portsmouth, NH, 3 Aug 1949, TCK Papers.
[50] TCK to King, New York, 19 Aug 1949, TCK Papers.
[51] Buell, *King*, 508.
[52] King to TCK, Portsmouth, NH, 22 Aug 1942, TCK Papers.
[53] "E. J. King Comments on Flag Officers," 31 Jul 1949, in Walter Muir Whitehill Papers, Naval War College, Newport, RI.

The other vexations for Tom Kinkaid during his four years in New York City were mostly minor ones, except for the issue of rank—reverting to a rear admiral or a vice admiral.[54] As noted before, there was no question that Kinkaid would retire as a four-star admiral. But in the summer of 1947, Congressman Walter G. Adams of New York, chairman of the House Armed Services Committee, introduced legislation designed to reduce the number of four-star officers on active duty. Rear Admiral Richard E. Byrd, then on special duty in the CNO's office, heard of this legislation and began passing the word to senior flag officers who might be affected. In the Navy, those who would probably have to fleet down or retire included Admirals Spruance, Hewitt, and Kinkaid. For Spruance, it was no serious matter; he would retire on the anticipated effective date, 1 July 1948. For Kent Hewitt, if he chose to retire, it would shorten his potential service life by eight months but would have no impact on his retired income. For Kinkaid, the legislation would not affect his retirement pay but would mean retiring twenty-two months early, at just age sixty.[55] It was a delicate matter because the generals and admirals involved could not openly lobby Congress; it would seem too self-serving. Unless invited to do so, the three military departments could not introduce legislation or speak out for the same reason. Seeking a nonpersonal alternative, Kent Hewitt suggested that a terminal date be set, far enough ahead to take in Kinkaid's 62d birthday, for reducing the admirals list to a fixed number.

A variety of public figures with access to congressmen and senators were approached privately and informed of the plight of the flag officers and generals. The case for continuation in four-star rank was made on the basis that the stars had been earned under battle conditions, and that the cost to the government would be a mere $1,700 per person for the few years involved. As a result of this pressure, Congress passed Public Law 804, which allowed a temporary increase (beyond the figure set in the Officer Personnel Act of 1947) in the number of admirals and generals, if the President so desired, until 1 July 1950. Once the President signed it, he issued an executive order, stating, "In accordance with Public Law 804, 80th Congress, Admirals Henry K. Hewitt and Thomas C. Kinkaid, U.S. Navy, shall be continued in the grade of Admiral on the Active List until July 1, 1950 unless sooner retired."[56]

---

[54] TCK to ADM D. C. Ramsey, New York, 10 Jun 1947; TCK to ADM H. K. Hewitt, New York, 18 Jun 1947, TCK Papers.

[55] RADM R. E. Byrd to TCK, Washington, 28 Jun 1947, TCK Papers.

[56] President Harry S. Truman to Secretary of the Navy, Washington, 2 Jul 1948. Navy Dept. file 1285–C, Truman Library.

Tom Kinkaid had one more serious brush with interservice politics before he retired. In the summer of 1949, a Navy Department civilian employee, Cedric Worth, triggered a congressional investigation of the Air Force's procurement and use of its intercontinental bomber, the B–36. Worth, an assistant to the Under Secretary of the Navy, had prepared a paper alleging that Secretary of the Air Force Stuart Symington and Secretary of Defense Louis Johnson had been improperly involved in letting contracts for purchasing the giant six-engined bomber. He then passed the paper to several congressmen; from them it reached the press. Chairman of the House Armed Services Committee Carl Vinson (D–Georgia), a good friend of the Navy, decided he had had enough of interservice bickering; he would use hearings as a means to investigate the ugly rumor and give the Navy a chance to air many of its grievances publicly. The hearings uncovered the fact that Worth's paper had been partly developed with information supplied by the Organizational Research and Policy Section (OP–23) of the office of the Assistant Chief of Naval Operations. But more embarrassing was the committee's finding that the charges in the paper were unfounded.[57] Secretary of the Navy Francis P. Matthews decided that someone should pay for this embarrassment and ordered Admiral Kinkaid to convene a formal court of inquiry to determine if any naval officers had acted illegally or unprofessionally by providing information to Mr. Worth. Though finding that a number of officers had supplied information to Worth, the court concluded that their actions had been open and blameless.[58]

While Kinkaid was engaged in the investigation, Vinson reconvened his committee to investigate unification, strategy, and the value of the B–36 as the principal weapon for defending the nation through airpower. The tone of the Navy's testimony, except for that of Secretary Matthews, was set on the opening day (7 October 1949) by Admiral Arthur W. Radford. Prepared with the help of the OP–23 team, his testimony was dramatic. Disagreeing with the "atomic blitz" approach to national strategy, he called it a "bad gamble with national security." He labeled the B–36, the backbone of the Air Force's strategic bombing policy, a "billion dollar blunder." Radford agreed with other flag officers that, because the Navy was suffering under a unification system which

---

[57] E. B. Potter, *Admiral Arleigh Burke* (New York: Random House, 1990), 321–22; Stephen Jurika, Jr., ed., *From Pearl Harbor to Vietnam: The Memoirs of Admiral Arthur W. Radford* (Stanford, CA: Hoover Institution Press, 1980), 161–64; Vincent Davis, *The Admirals Lobby* (Chapel Hill: University of North Carolina Press, 1967), 286–87; Paolo E. Coletta, *The United States Navy and Defense Unification, 1947–1953* (Newark: University of Delaware Press, 1981), 169–206.

[58] SECNAV to TCK, Washington, 25 Aug 1949, TCK Papers; Paolo E. Coletta, "Francis Matthews," in Paolo E. Coletta, ed., *American Secretaries of the Navy*, 2 vols. (Annapolis: Naval Institute Press, 1980), 2:813–14; Potter, *Burke*, 322; Coletta, *Navy and Defense Unification*, 170.

was not working fairly, Navy morale was at the lowest level in twenty years.[59] In the week that followed, a parade of naval witnesses buttressed Radford's views concerning strategic bombing, the worthlessness of the B–36, and the mistreatment of the Navy within the newly unified Department of Defense. Kinkaid wrote his own testimony; it proved completely acceptable to the people in OP–23 coordinating the presentations.[60] In his analysis, delivered to the committee on 12 October, he stressed the importance of carrier task forces in stopping the Japanese in 1942 and defeating them in 1944 and 1945. The mobility of the carriers and their ability to launch attacks against distant enemy shores made them vital in the nation's strategic arsenal. He also expressed his views of dependence on strategic bombing to defend the nation:

> Strategic bombing theories—the Douhet or other concepts—particularly when combined with ideas regarding the atomic bomb, may develop a false sense of security, a Maginot Line mentality, which would be fatal to our efforts to ensure our own security and to prevent civilization from being destroyed.[61]

Kinkaid's testimony was a strong call for building more and larger carriers of a supercarrier class, like the recently canceled *United States*, and a plea to reconsider national strategy based on strategic bombing.

Tom spent the winter and early spring of 1950 getting his affairs in order for retirement. One key decision had been made: Tom and Helen would live in Washington. They had wanted a home in Georgetown, but could not find what they wanted at an appropriate price. Instead, after dickering for one house on R Street in the northwest section, they bought another at 3124. In the East Coast tradition, it was a "semi-detached" structure of three stories with 10-foot ceilings on the ground floor.[62] Tom wrote to the pastor of Christ Church in Georgetown to let him know that he would be taking over and paying the rent for pew number 82, which had been formerly occupied by his aunt, Miss Fannie Cassin. The pew had been in the family since the days of Dr. Grafton Tyler, Jr., the grandfather of Kinkaid's mother.[63]

During this last winter on active duty, the admiral sat once more for a portrait. In May 1949 he had been invited to join the prestigious Union

---

[59] *New York Times*, 8 Oct 1949; Coletta, "Matthews," 798–801; Jurika, *Radford*, 181–82.
[60] CAPT A. A. Burke to TCK, Washington, 13 Sept 1949, TCK Papers.
[61] *New York Times*, 13 Oct 1949; "Statement of Thomas C. Kinkaid . . . Before the Armed Services Committee Investigating the B–36 and Related Matters" (typescript), TCK Papers.
[62] TCK to RADM A. G. Quynn, New York, 18 Aug 1949, TCK Papers; Helen S. Kinkaid interview, 6 Jan 1976.
[63] TCK to W. E. Miller, New York, 3 Apr 1950, TCK Papers.

Author's collection

Oil painting of Admiral Kinkaid by Albert Murray, official Navy combat artist. The painting was completed while the admiral was Commander Eastern Sea Frontier.

Club of New York City. He did so and remained a member until his death. Well-liked and admired by the members, he was asked to sit for a portrait, which would hang in the club's spaces. He groused a bit, but agreed to sit for Albert D. Smith (1886–1962), a well-known portraitist. General of the Army Dwight D. Eisenhower also sat for Smith. Both portraits hang in a corridor leading to the main dining room at the clubhouse on East 69th Street.[64] This was Kinkaid's fourth portrait sitting. The first time was in Constantinople when a Russian émigré, Nicolai

---

[64] Helen W. Allen to author, New York, 5 Apr 1989, 14 Apr 1989.

Becker, painted both Tom and Helen. His second portrait, done in late 1946 by Albert K. Murray (1906–1992), is in the art collection at the Naval Historical Center and was used as the frontispiece for Samuel Eliot Morison's Philippine liberation volume. Robert S. Sloan (1915–) painted the third portrait in March 1947 as part of a series of portraits of outstanding American military leaders of the war commissioned by International Business Machine Corporation. Those portraits were exhibited nationally, and IBM ultimately donated them to the National Portrait Gallery in Washington. Admiral Kinkaid's portrait has been on long-term loan to the Navy Art Gallery.[65]

As with most officers, the retirement process began with a letter from the Chief of Naval Personnel observing that his 62d birthday fell on 3 April and that he would have to retire on or before the first of May. A couple of weeks later, the Secretary of the Navy sent him retirement orders that included the usual requirement for a complete physical examination. As a result of this exam, Tom's retirement changed from the standard retirement for service to retirement for physical disability. The arteriosclerosis first observed a few years earlier was now 50 percent disabling. He would still retire at 75 percent of an admiral's pay with more than 40 years service ($716.06 per month, $8,593 per annum), but a percentage of that pension would now be tax-free.[66] Had he retired in 1990, his retired pay would have been $4,887.45 per month, or $58,650 annually.

Probably very few officers have retired with the amount of pomp and ceremony that attended Tom Kinkaid's departure from active duty. The admiral's retirement ceremonies were set for Friday, 28 April, but there were many parties before that date, the grandest taking place on 18 April at the Hotel Pierre in New York City. Laid on by the New York chapter of the Military Order of the World Wars, of which Tom was a longtime member, it was a glittering black-tie affair. Navy Secretary Matthews and General George Kenney joined the Kinkaids at the head table, as did Tom's predecessor as Commander Eastern Sea Frontier, Vice Admiral Fairfax Leary (Ret.), and his relief, Vice Admiral Oscar C. Badger. After all the speeches, he was presented with a bound volume of letters attesting to his service to his country, the Navy, New York City, and friends everywhere. Secretary of Defense Louis Johnson concluded, "Yours has been an inspired leadership from which younger officers of all military departments may draw lessons of noble service." His "old comrade-in-arms," General of the Army Douglas MacArthur, struck a note that always

---

[65] Mrs. James F. Shaw to TCK, New York, 25 Feb 1947; TCK to Mrs. James F. Shaw, New York, 26 Feb 1947, TCK Papers.

[66] VADM J. W. Roper to TCK, Washington, 21 Feb 1950; SECNAV to TCK, Washington, 7 Mar 1950; SECNAV to TCK, Washington, 27 Apr 1950, TCK Personnel File.

pleased Kinkaid: "I have known many sailors of many lands but never a sailor of greater fighting heart than Tom Kinkaid." Given his epistolary exchanges with Fleet Admiral King not too many months before, Tom must have been bemused a little to read his contribution:

> [H]e made his own name in the services, especially in the South Pacific, Alaska, and finally in the Southwest Pacific where General MacArthur believed Admiral Kinkaid to be one of the most important naval officers in the campaign from New Guinea to the Philippines. He topped off by managing for the Navy a great victory in the Philippines. He was always steady and always ready to carry on with whatever he had to do. In fact, he was one of those men who could be so reliable as to make the best of the situation and his best was very good indeed.[67]

Press coverage of the banquet prompted many New York area newspapers to run retirement stories or editorials about Kinkaid's imminent departure. The *Journal American* saw him as a "modest but unsurpassed warrior [whose name] will live in our history with the names of Farragut and Dewey."[68] The *New York Times* editorial was more personal; the editor was a friend:

> His courtly manner, wise judgment and friendly personality have won many friends during his regime here, friends not only for him but for the Navy. . . . New York, like the Navy, will be sorry to lose the active services of a man of whom it, too, is proud—Thomas Cassin Kinkaid, Admiral U.S.N.[69]

Friday, 28 April, became a day filled with ceremony. The most important started at 1030 on board *Enterprise* in the navy yard. Kinkaid arrived to side-boys, ruffles and flourishes, the "Admiral's March," and his flag broken at the main. To the official staffs, guests, and Admiral Badger, he spoke briefly about his battles on board the carrier, and then he read his retirement orders, ordered his flag hauled down, and listened for the last time to the cannonading of the seventeen-gun salute in his honor. Admiral Badger then read his orders, relieved Kinkaid, ordered his three-starred flag broken, and stood by for his fifteen-gun salute. Before departing the hangar deck, Tom received his four-star blue flag and draped it over his left arm. Halfway down the quarterdeck brow, Kinkaid took a farewell glance at his old flagship.

The official limousine took Tom, his staff, and Helen back to 90 Church Street where they transferred to the city's open touring cars that were used

---

[67] *New York Times*, 19 Apr 1950; "Retirement," TCK Papers.
[68] "Retirement of a Veteran" (editorial), *New York Journal American*, 25 Apr 1950.
[69] "An Admiral Retires" (editorial), *New York Times*, 24 Apr 1950.

Admiral Kinkaid salutes as he receives a seventeen-gun salute during his retirement ceremony at the New York Navy Yard, 28 April 1950.

Admiral and Mrs. Kinkaid ride through the streets of New York City during the admiral's retirement parade, 28 April 1950.

for city street parades. Leaving at 1200 with motorcycle escort, and preceded and followed by a variety of service and municipal bands, Tom and Helen got a real hero's parade up Broadway to City Hall. There Mayor O'Dwyer presented Tom with the Official Medal of the City and a scroll and gave a short speech. For a half hour, the Kinkaids and the denizens of New York were treated to a parade of marching groups and bands. As expected, the Army band played "The Caissons Go Rolling Along" and the Navy unit, "Anchors Aweigh," but the city's Sanitation Department band's rendering of "I'm in Love with a Wonderful Guy," was truly memorable. Twenty-six years later, Helen still recalled the parade and musical tributes with great pride and amusement.[70] The official close of the admiral's career came on 30 April with a fitness report remark written by Chief of Naval Operations Forrest Sherman: "Admiral Kinkaid has retired for age after an outstanding and distinguished career of service to his country."[71]

[70] "Retirement," TCK Papers; Helen S. Kinkaid interview, 8 Jan 1976.
[71] Fitness Report, 30 Apr 1950, TCK Personnel File.

Chapter 16

Retirement, 1950–1972

Retirement for many people, including naval officers, often begins with a vacation to break with the past and ease into the retirement status. For Tom and Helen, however, a vacation would have to wait; they were beginning to settle into their new R Street home in northwest Washington, and much work had to be done on the residence to make the house suitable for Helen's entertainment style. Tom had also agreed to sit on another "plucking board." Chaired by Fleet Admiral Nimitz, this board would review all flag officers with five or more years in grade and a minimum of thirty-five years of commissioned service. The number of those to be retained could not exceed 75 percent, nor could it be less than 50 percent. Stated more negatively, at least 25 percent of the Navy's flag officers would be "plucked" to retire. Beginning on 26 June 1950, the board concluded its work in two weeks, but the list was not approved by the President until 21 July.[1] By then Tom and Helen were enjoying a long-planned vacation at Point-au-Pic, Quebec, on the marvelously cool and scenic St. Lawrence River.

Once back from Canada, the Kinkaids began twelve active years of retirement. Helen entertained at least once a month. In the fashion of a true Washington hostess, Helen brought together a balanced group of military people, ambassadors, government officials, journalists, and even an occasional Supreme Court justice. Nonmilitary names that appeared regularly on the table seating plans included Allen Dulles, Alice Roosevelt Longworth, Arthur Krock, Walter Lippman, Dean Acheson, and Justices Stanley Reed and John Marshall Harlan. At first dinner parties were limited to eight or ten people at a time; the Kinkaid dining room couldn't handle many more. A year later, however, after Tom had become a member of The Alibi, a men's social club, on I Street, they did most of their entertaining in the club's spaces, which allowed for a dinner seating of 12 to 24. By entertaining on the scale they followed, Tom and Helen usually spent three or four evenings a week as either hosts or guests. They were both interesting people who kept abreast of international affairs and who

---

[1] VADM J. W. Roper to TCK, Washington, 6, 26 Jun 50; TCK to Roper, Washington, 7 Jun 1950, TCK File.

Tom and Helen Kinkaid enjoy an evening on the town, probably in Washington, early 1960s.

were still doing a lot of traveling, particularly after the admiral's appointment to the American Battle Monuments Commission in 1953. They adhered to this pace and lifestyle until 1962 when Tom's health failed.[2]

At the request of the Navy Department, Kinkaid traveled to Australia in the spring of 1951 to participate in the celebration of Coral Sea Week, a national holiday period in May. Admiral Arthur Radford and his wife, who participated in 1950, had made such a wonderful impression that the Australian government and the Australian-American Association had requested that another senior naval officer be sent.[3] With the Korean War underway, the Vice Chief of Naval Operations believed it more appropriate to send a retired officer, preferring Kinkaid.[4]

Tom and Helen's three weeks in Australia and New Zealand, beginning 28 April, were both gratifying and strenuous. The admiral gave four public speeches and was feted in Sydney, Canberra, Melbourne, and Brisbane. His speech in Sydney was recorded and broadcast nationwide during the week.[5] It was here, on 7 May, that the Kinkaids attended the Coral Sea Victory Ball, a black tie affair of the city's elite. At a luncheon in Melbourne on 2 May, Tom relaxed, pocketed his formal speech, and told sea stories for a full half hour. The guests, which included top government officials and military officers, were delighted with his informal approach. After two weeks of hearty Australian hospitality, the Kinkaids flew to New Zealand on the 14th. By the time they left on the 21st, Tom had his fill of public speaking, but American-Antipodean relations were the better for it.[6]

Shortly after the Kinkaid's return to Washington, the admiral discovered that good things, like a glorious trip to Australia, often had a way of requiring repayment. In June the 82d Congress passed the Universal Military Training and Service Act (Public Law 51), commonly referred to as the UMT Act, legislation that Truman had urged upon a reluctant Congress as early as 1946.[7] Admiral Kinkaid was appointed to the five-member commission of three civilians and two military members selected to implement the

---

[2] The Kinkaid papers contain guest lists and seating charts for many of the dinners given at the Alibi Club. They could entertain 24 guests for around $240 in 1954–1958.

[3] Jurika, *Radford*, 221–22; Herbert W. Gepp to TCK, Melbourne, 1 May 1950, TCK Papers.

[4] Memo, CNO to SECNAV, Washington, 1 Mar 1951; CNO to CHNAVPERS, Washington, 28 Mar 1951, TCK Personnel File; Norman Makin to President Harry S. Truman, Washington, 3 Apr 1951, file 480, Australia, Truman Library.

[5] Kinkaid's speeches are filed "Speeches," series 5, TCK Papers.

[6] "Australia Recalls Coral Sea Victory," *Pacific Neighbors* (Federal Journal of the Australian-American Association) (1951), 6:2; TCK, "Four Years of War," 123–24; Gepp to TCK, Melbourne, 4 Jun 1951, TCK Papers.

[7] Truman, *Memoirs* 1:510–12; Omar N. Bradley and Clay Blair, *A General's Life: An Autobiography by General of the Army Omar N. Bradley and Clay Blair* (New York: Simon & Schuster, 1983), 481–83; Russell F. Weigley, *The American Way of War: A History of United States Military Strategy and Policy* (New York and London: Macmillan, 1973), 395.

President Dwight D. Eisenhower meets with the National Security Training Commission at the White House, 14 December 1953. Commission Chairman General Julius Ochs Adler is seated with the President. Standing are, left to right, Admiral Kinkaid, Lieutenant General Raymond S. McLain, Warren Atherton, and Karl Compton.

act and to oversee its operation.[8] Kinkaid and Lieutenant General Raymond S. McLain, Comptroller General of the Army, represented the armed services. The civilians were Dr. Karl T. Compton, a former president of the Massachusetts Institute of Technology, former Under Secretary of State Will Clayton, and former Senator James W. Wadsworth. The *New York Times* concluded that the President had appointed "Five Able Men."[9]

The UMT Commission quickly adopted the name National Service Training Commission (NSTC) and got to work on 12 July. It was to meet continuously and to report to Congress in four months a set of policies dealing with the character of military training to be given, the nonmilitary training that was expected, the military rules the trainees would live under, the amount of moral and character education to be received, and the precise amount of money each trainee would receive in the event of death, injury, or disability during the first six months. When trainees

---

[8] The appointment process can be followed in NSTC file 109C, Truman Library.
[9] *New York Times*, 30 Jun 1951.

completed their national service training, they would be subject to the rules and regulations and pay tables of the regular armed forces.[10]

Tom found the commission's work interesting, and his colleagues equally so. Despite the oppressive heat outside, the group was comfortable enough in its Pentagon offices. Hearings, during which Kinkaid expressed his ideas regularly and fully, were held to allow church members, veterans groups, educators, and the armed services to present their views on UMT/NST. Kinkaid took seriously the idea that training would be universal and believed that the armed services could find a place for most of the physically handicapped. He set forth this principle during the second hearing: "I think we ought to go on record as hoping they will take them all in."[11] When Dr. Compton proposed that, like university students, the trainees govern and police themselves through their own courts, the admiral protested: "Surely you don't propose self-government in military organizations for enlisted men. You have got to have some discipline and military control." Compton was serious, but the rest of the commission agreed with Tom's view that "you don't want any too much of a commune in there."[12] When representatives from various religious denominations urged that liquor not be served in or near the training camps and that brothels be outlawed, the commission took refuge in the policy that training camp commanders would manage such matters.

The commission submitted its report to President Truman on 10 November and thereafter met only at the call of its chairman, Senator Wadsworth. National Service Training would not begin until national conscription ceased. With the Korean War underway and a draft of 18-year-olds in operation, many representatives believed there was no need for an NSTC and its staff.[13]

Upon entering office in January 1953, President Dwight Eisenhower accepted some commission resignations, appointed two new members, and asked General McLain and Kinkaid to continue on the NSTC. He also asked the commission to shift its focus to creating a fairer conscription system and stronger military Reserves.[14] Eisenhower wanted effective Army and Navy reserve forces built around people with recent discharges from two to four years in the armed services. With the passage of the Reserve Forces Act of 1955 (P.L. 305), which amended the 1951 NSTC Act, the armed services began taking in trainees who would follow

---

[10] Ibid.
[11] Minutes of Meeting of NSTC, 13 Jul 1951, RG 330:130, NA.
[12] Ibid.
[13] Harry S. Truman to LTGEN R. S. McLain, Washington, 26 Apr 1952, file 109C; McLain to TCK, Oklahoma City, 7 Jul 1952, TCK Papers.
[14] *Public Papers of the Presidents of the United States: Dwight D. Eisenhower, 1953* (Washington: GPO, 1960), 514–15.

Admiral Kinkaid, acting for the National Service Training Commission, interviews recruits at the Marine Corps recruit depot, Parris Island, S.C., 4 June 1956. With Kinkaid are Brigadier General Wallace Greene, USMC, head of the recruit training command, and Major General Homer L. Witzenberg, USMC.

six months' active duty with seven and one-half years in a ready reserve unit.[15] NSTC was expected to monitor the training of the reservists during active duty, but the armed services quickly took control of the training programs.

In November 1956, commission chairman David G. Sarnoff wrote a memorandum to President Eisenhower suggesting that the NSTC mission be changed or the commission shut down. That suited the President, who called for NSTC's abolition on 30 June 1957.[16] Tom had enjoyed his six years with the NSTC, but he was irritated at the total waste of effort. In his letter of resignation to the President, Kinkaid unloaded some of his anger: "During the six years that I have been a member of

---

[15] C. Joseph Bernardo and Eugene H. Bacon, *American Military Policy: Its Development Since 1775*, 2d ed.(Harrisburg, PA: Stackpole, 1961), 479–83; Russell F. Weigley, *History of the United States Army* (New York: Macmillan, 1967), 529–30.

[16] Memo, Status and Future of the National Security Training Commission, 22 Nov 1957, by David G. Sarnoff; President Dwight D. Eisenhower to Sarnoff, 25 Mar 1957, TCK Papers.

the Commission, I have been disappointed that the Congress did not follow through with its authorization of Universal Military Training."[17]

In the spring of 1953, as the NSTC approached extinction, the admiral received another offer for service that would be hard to refuse. President Eisenhower wanted him to serve on the reconstituted American Battle Monuments Commission (ABMC) charged with constructing and overseeing the nation's overseas military cemeteries and battle monuments.[18] There were fourteen World War II military cemeteries, with important monuments in each to be completed in the next ten years; monuments were also to be raised on each U.S. coast to commemorate those missing in action. For an admiral with a wife who thoroughly enjoyed European travel, this was "duty" made in Heaven. Tom accepted without delay.[19]

In addition to Kinkaid, the ABMC initially consisted of General of the Army George Marshall as chairman, Leslie A. Biffle, Joseph J. Foss, Forest A. Harness, Congressman John Phillips (R–Calif.), Senator Charles E. Potter (R–Mich.), General Carl Spaatz, General Alexander A. Vandegrift and Edith Willkie (Mrs. Wendell L. Willkie). In selecting commission members, Eisenhower had told General Marshall that he intended to add a "Negro veteran" and a second woman. Brigadier General Benjamin O. Davis, the first black general in American history, and Eleanor Alexander Roosevelt, wife of Brigadier General Theodore Roosevelt Jr. who died in the Normandy campaign, joined the commission. The thirteenth member and the commission's secretary was Brigadier General Thomas North. North supervised the operation of all overseas military cemeteries, and with his staff carried out the policies and orders of the commission as given by its chairman. At the first meeting, Kinkaid was elected vice chairman; he served in that position until he resigned fifteen years later. Between the commission's scheduled meetings Generals Marshall and North and Admiral Kinkaid constituted its executive committee. When Marshall's health began to decline seriously, Kinkaid chaired the commission meetings, directed its work, and after consultation with the general issued necessary orders and directives in Marshall's name.[20]

Before Kinkaid had barely settled into his new position, Marshall sent him and four other new members on an inspection tour of the ABMC's activities in Europe and North Africa. The group spent an exhausting month, including a voyage to Bremerhaven on board the transport *Gen-*

---

[17] TCK to President Dwight D. Eisenhower, 28 May 1957, TCK Papers.
[18] President Dwight D. Eisenhower to General of the Army George C. Marshall, 27 Apr 1953; Marshall to Eisenhower, 29 Apr 1953, Marshall Papers.
[19] Sherman Adams to TCK, 4 Jun 1953; TCK to Adams, Washington, 9 Jun 1953, TCK Papers; Marshall to TCK, 15 Jul 1953; TCK to Marshall, 17 Jul 1953, Marshall Papers.
[20] The work of General Marshall and Admiral Kinkaid on the ABMC can be followed in their papers. The records of the ABMC are deposited in the National Archives in Suitland, Maryland.

eral Rose, visiting most of the commission's World War I cemeteries and monuments and all of the World War II cemeteries. Tom and his colleagues, including Helen, also saw British, French, Italian, Belgian and German cemeteries or monuments, as well as several privately sponsored American memorials of the two wars. From their report, it is clear that they were overwhelmed by their experiences:

> The Committee found the World War I cemeteries and monuments, without exception, to be most impressive and worthy of their object. At Brookwood, to name but one, the simple, dignified design of the chapel can not fail to appeal to visitors of any epoch. . . .
>
> With the exceptions noted below, the Committee was deeply impressed by the simple beauty and appropriateness of all of the [World War II] cemeteries and memorials. This was especially so in the case of St. James (Manche, France), St. Laurent (Calvados, France), and Epinal (Vosges, France).[21]

These World War II "exceptions" were serious. The committee (and commission) found the mosaic mural at the Cambridge memorial grotesque and "a distinct shock." Bereaved visitors would find little consolation in the chapel. The architect agreed and made changes to his original design. At the cemetery in Hamm, Luxembourg, the commission found the 1948 memorial design "inappropriate to its purpose," and the associated sculpture "completely unsuitable . . . too modernistic" and impressionistic. Writing for commission members, General North expressed their uneasiness about the Hamm memorial:

> [I]ts character is alien. . . . The Commissioners believe that a majority of the visitors, particularly American, will not be able to appreciate the ideas or symbolism which such carvings are intended to convey. Many will come with a burden of grief and will find little consolation in sculptural problems; if any sculpture is necessary to the architecture its meaning should be reasonably obvious, and its forms recognizable and not unpleasing.[22]

Since 1953, the commission's work had been directed toward the summer of 1956 when six of the cemeteries and their monuments would be formally dedicated. Tom and most of the commission members made the trip to Europe; the admiral was selected to oversee ceremonies at the great Normandy cemetery. The first dedication was in England at the Cambridge cemetery on 16 July. Three days later, in Normandy, near the village of St. Laurent-sur-Mer, Kinkaid opened the dedication cere-

---

[21] ABMC, Memorandum for the Chairman, 1 Nov 1953, box 161, Marshall Papers.
[22] BGEN Thomas North to Ralph Walker, Washington, 17 Dec 1953; Walker to North, New York, 14 Jan 1954; North to ABMC, Washington, 8 Apr 1954, TCK Papers.

The Kinkaids picnic with friends in the Italian countryside, circa 1960s.

monies by calling attention to the 9,385 buried there: "They came to these shores as their countrymen had done two decades before them, without thought of conquest or reward. They came as the responsible heirs of our forefathers to defend the freedom which had been handed down to us as our most precious possession."

Secretary of the Army Wilber M. Brucker delivered the principal address. A poignant moment came when Mrs. Roosevelt laid a wreath at her husband's grave site and another at the grave of her brother-in-law, Lieutenant Quentin Roosevelt, killed in aerial combat during World War I. The commission moved to Brittany (St. James) the next day and two days later to Epinal. On 26 July, at Draguignon in the Rhone Valley, the smallest of the cemeteries was dedicated. Finally, on 30 July, the commission concluded its obligations at the Sicily-Rome Cemetery at Anzio. Admiral Kinkaid's report to Chairman Marshall simply noted that "all ceremonies were performed smoothly, without noticeable difficulty. Numerous compliments have been received upon their appropriateness and impressiveness."[23]

Work progressed steadily on the eight remaining cemeteries. In late 1959, following Marshall's death, General Jacob L. Devers was appointed

---

[23] Memorandum for the Chairman: Dedications, 1956, by TCK, 25 Sep 1956, TCK Papers; Howell Walker, "Here Rests in Honored Glory," *The National Geographic* (Jun 1957), 738–68.

ABMC chairman; Kinkaid continued as vice chairman. A new round of dedications took place in July 1960, and the commission had a month of hectic activity beginning with dedications at Hamm on 4 July with Grand Duchess Charlotte of Luxembourg present and then moved to the Margraten Cemetery in the Netherlands. With Queen Juliana present, Tom opened the ceremonies there.

> They and their allies fought for human values—values which distinguish men from beasts—for decency in human relations, integrity, charity, truth, and faith in almighty God. By their efforts they restored these values but no one generation has ever been able to preserve them for all time. These values flourish only in freedom which must be defended continuously or it will perish. Upon us of the present generation there rests the inescapable duty to preserve and to maintain for those who come after us the freedom, justice and democratic institutions for which they died.[24]

On the 16th Kinkaid opened a special ceremony at Brest at the restored naval monument destroyed by the Germans in July 1941. Secretary of the Navy William B. Franke dedicated the memorial commemorating the service of American seamen lost in European waters during both world wars. After the July ceremonies in Florence, Tom and Helen remained in Europe to see old friends in Rome, Berlin, and Salzburg. It was to be their last visit to the continent and they made the most of it.

The Kinkaids flew to San Francisco for the 29 November dedication of the West Coast Memorial to the Missing at the Presidio. Two of Tom's old friends, General John DeWitt and Fleet Admiral Chester Nimitz, each gave addresses memorializing the 412 servicemen whose names were engraved on the grey granite wall overlooking the Pacific. Following these ceremonies, Tom and Helen flew to Honolulu and then on to Manila, where Tom presided over the dedication ceremonies at the Fort McKinley Memorial Cemetery on the nineteenth anniversary of the Japanese attacks on Pearl Harbor and Manila (8 December). Generals Walter Krueger and Emmett O'Donnell spoke briefly, and Admiral Raymond Spruance delivered the dedicatory address.

Tom's last significant work with the ABMC came in the spring of 1963 when he chaired the dedication ceremonies at the East Coast Memorial in New York City's Battery Park. This impressive memorial consisted of eight granite tablets, 19 feet high, on which were inscribed 4,596 names of servicemen who had died in American coastal waters. Accenting these tablets, atop a low pedestal, was a 20-foot high bronze eagle in landing posture. An address by President John F. Kennedy and the rendering of

---

[24] Series VI, folder 7, TCK Papers.

Admiral Raymond Spruance, USN (Ret.), former ambassador to the Philippines, delivers an address at ceremonies dedicating the WWII cemetery and memorial at Fort William McKinley, Manila, 8 December 1960. Seated in the front row are, left to right, Ambassador Hickerson, Philippine President Carlos Garcia, Admiral Kinkaid.

the presidential and national salutes by destroyer leader *Mitscher* (DL 2) highlighted the ceremonies.[25]

Three years later, when the National Memorial Cemetery of the Pacific (The Punch Bowl) was dedicated on 1 May 1966, Tom's health was too poor to permit his participation. On 14 March 1968, with considerable regret, the admiral resigned from the Monuments Commission.[26] He had made a substantial contribution to its operations by providing leadership during his first six years while General Marshall's health deteriorated. Now Kinkaid was unable to travel or even attend the Washington meetings. President Lyndon Johnson's letter to the admiral succinctly summarized Tom's contribution to the commission: "The impact of your leadership, skill, thoroughness and proficiency can be seen in the beauty and dignity of the memorials."[27]

[25] *New York Times*, 23 May 1963.
[26] North to TCK, Washington, 30 Apr 1968, TCK Papers.
[27] President Lyndon B. Johnson to TCK, Washington, 11 Oct 1968, TCK Papers.

His work on the ABMC was not the only activity to occupy Kinkaid. During the early years of his retirement, Tom had tried his hand at writing a book with the working title "Four Years of War in the Pacific, A Personal Narrative." In September 1952 publisher Albert Knopf in New York City wrote the admiral that he would be interested in publishing his memoirs. Knopf suggested that New York agent Paul Reynolds handle the admiral's affairs and advise him about his manuscript.[28] After reading Tom's manuscript, Reynolds was less than sanguine. In fact, he saw too many problems in the writing, but urged Tom to get Knopf to read it.[29] By June, the publisher advised Tom to get an experienced writer to assist him. Knopf agreed with Reynolds that what Kinkaid had produced was neither a memoir nor a history, but an amalgam that just didn't work.[30]

The real problem with the manuscript was Tom Kinkaid, not the subject matter or its organization. He just could not bring himself to write about his friends, and himself, in the many interesting situations he described. Reynolds was clearly exasperated that Tom had spent several days visiting Admiral Kimmel after Pearl Harbor and had written nothing about how his brother-in-law had reacted to the tragedy that had overtaken him. Because he was neither a historian like Samuel Morison nor able to write with the abandon of Admiral Halsey, his "memoirs" were never published. The manuscript stops in the middle of the Battle of Savo Island. For historical reasons, it is unfortunate that Kinkaid did not carry the story to Leyte Gulf and clearly state his views on the battle.

Unable or unwilling to write about the Pacific War in a publishable way, the admiral, however, in late 1954 did take advantage of an opportunity to put some of his views in print. Hanson Baldwin, a nationally prominent and respected military affairs writer and a 1924 graduate of the Naval Academy, asked Kinkaid to critique a chapter on the Battle for Leyte Gulf for his latest manuscript titled "Sea Fights and Shipwrecks." Kinkaid's real interest lay in how Baldwin analyzed the Halsey-Kinkaid controversy surrounding "Bull's Run" to the north while the Seventh Fleet escort carriers engaged Admiral Kurita's Center Force. Tom noted to Baldwin that "the controversy" existed because of Halsey's need for self-justification; furthermore "the controversy has not been bitter for the simple and sole reason that I refused to get in a public brawl with Halsey. I have kept quiet for ten years—not so Halsey. He feels that he needs justification."[31]

Retaining the sense of Kinkaid's harshest comments and language, Baldwin wisely edited out most of his *ad hominem* comments about Hal-

---

[28] Alfred Knopf to TCK, New York, 11 Sept, 15 Oct 1952, TCK Papers.
[29] Paul Reynolds to TCK, New York, 4 Feb 1953; Reynolds to TCK, New York, 17, 20 Mar 1953, TCK Papers.
[30] Knopf to TCK, New York, 3 Jun 1953, TCK Papers.
[31] Notes on Manuscript, The Battle for Leyte Gulf—Baldwin, 13 Nov 1954, 7, TCK Papers.

sey. The special notes to the Leyte Gulf chapter, written by both Kinkaid and Halsey, make this portion of the text a particularly enlightening exposition on the battle. Tom thought Baldwin did an excellent job, and *Sea Fights and Shipwrecks* became another title, along with the works by C. Vann Woodward and James A. Field, that he recommended for information and proper analysis of the Leyte Gulf battle.[32]

In mid-1959 Kinkaid was asked to critique a chapter on Leyte Gulf from a manuscript history of sea war in the Pacific. The co-editors of the work, Professor E. B. Potter of the Naval Academy's history faculty and Fleet Admiral Nimitz, covered the full history of navies and naval warfare from the days of rowed galleys, but nearly half of the manuscript's pages (and later books) were devoted to World War II. When similarly asked to comment on the Leyte Gulf chapter, Admiral Halsey cut to what for him was the heart of the matter: his future reputation.

> I think, in general, your account is very good and very fair, but you fall down when you try to tell people what I was thinking. I do not intend to allow grossly wrong statements about my thoughts to go into a book which will be used to teach Midshipmen, without making trouble for you.
>
> I also think you make a great mistake in criticizing my strategical acts and categorically stating that they were wrong.[33]

Potter and Nimitz gave further thought to the chapter. In its final version they largely eliminated the judgments about Halsey's decisions; the editors believed these could be handled during classroom discussions of the textbook.

After Halsey's critique was in hand, Professor Potter asked Kinkaid to comment on the chapter as originally written.[34] Like Halsey, he found the chapter "well written, easy to read and [presenting] a clear picture of what happened at Leyte." But he believed that Potter and Nimitz had accepted too much of what Halsey had written.

> I do object strongly to the effort of one commander to justify his faults, particularly at the expense of another. Ever since Oct 1944, Halsey has attempted to justify his obvious errors, sometimes at my expense, first in his book, of which the *Saturday Evening Post* published extracts, then by a series of articles in the U.S. Naval Institute *Proceedings*, interviews, speeches, and newspaper articles, etc. Much of what he has said has been accepted

---

[32] Hanson W. Baldwin, *Sea Fights and Shipwrecks*, 134–82; TCK to H. Terry Morrison, Jr., 12 Feb 1958, TCK Papers.

[33] Halsey to E. B. Potter, New York, 27 Jun 1959, Halsey Papers, box 35, MD–LC; see also Potter, *Bull Halsey*, 380–81.

[34] Potter to TCK, Annapolis, 11 Aug 1959, TCK Papers; TCK to Potter, Washington, 15 Aug 1959, TCK Papers.

The now retired commanders of the Southwest Pacific celebrate their boss's birthday at the 26 January 1961 SWPA reunion, left to right: General Walter Krueger, USA, General George C. Kenney, USA, General of the Army Douglas MacArthur, Admiral Kinkaid. These reunions were held annually and MacArthur attended each between 1952 and 1962.

by his readers. Through the years some of these statements have become accepted facts by the casual reader.

Tom again rejected Halsey's argument that having two commanders at Leyte, and no overall commander, had resulted in the escape of Kurita's Center Force.

Of course it would have been sound practice and better to have an overall commander of naval forces.... However, the Third Fleet and the Seventh Fleet each had an assigned mission which, if fulfilled, would have resulted in the destruction of the Japanese fleet then and there. The question of an overall commander at the scene of action would have been purely academic. Most surely Nimitz's orders to Halsey did not contemplate the withdrawal of covering forces at the height of battle. "Divided Command" is not the key to what happened at Leyte. "Mission" is the key.[35]

---

[35] Copy, "Comments on Chapter 39, The Battle for Leyte Gulf, T. C. K.," in Potter to TCK, Annapolis, 19 Aug 1959, TCK Papers.

Kinkaid's reply to Professor Potter was written on 15 August, the day Fleet Admiral Halsey died of a heart attack. He appended a postscript to his letter: "The radio has just announced that Halsey died this morning at Fisher's Island. All of these comments were written before this announcement. I have no time to change them, nor do I desire to do so."[36]

The first decade of retirement for Admiral Kinkaid was about all he could have desired for a satisfying existence. He had things to do, mostly concerned with naval or government service, and they were worth the time invested in them. There was plenty of travel for him and Helen, both for business and for leisure. While not true "snow birds," who migrated south at the first frost, Tom and Helen spent several weeks, almost every year until 1962, vacationing in Florida or South Carolina. Captiva, on South Florida's Gulf Coast, was one of their favorite resorts. Here, with civilian and service friends, they would spend several weeks fishing, golfing, reading and playing bridge. When Washington became insufferable in the summer months, they escaped to New England or to Quebec and the Maritime Provinces. Wherever they went, there were friends who enjoyed seeing them. In retirement Tom and Helen were still an urbane pair, *au courant* with affairs in Washington and the world scene. And once the horrors of summer were survived, the parties and dinners began again at the R Street house and The Alibi, or at the residences of their friends.

As in most families, the quality of retired life is related directly to personal health, and Tom's was in decline. The year 1961, and early 1962, was to be his last period of full activity. He and Helen spent part of the summer on Cape Cod, at Harwich Port, and the following winter in Captiva. Tom was hospitalized twice in the summer and fall of 1962 with breathing and lung troubles associated with emphysema. Helen brought a nurse into the house to help manage, and with the installation of an elevator and the purchase of a portable respirator, Tom was reasonably mobile around the house. His activities became progressively more restricted, although he was not an invalid. Suspecting that the January 1962 gathering of MacArthur's staff in New York might be the last for the Old Soldier, he hated to miss it, but did. He had been there the previous year, and it had been a grand affair at the Waldorf Astoria. Krueger, Kenney, Kinkaid, MacArthur, and many other senior staffers were able to attend and the New York press had some great photo opportunities.[37] The January 1961 photograph of MacArthur and Kinkaid embracing revealed what time and failing health had wrought on the bodies of the former warriors.

In April 1962, Tom resigned as a vestryman at Christ Church in Georgetown. His financial advice had been sound, and he and Helen supported

---

[36] TCK to Potter, Washington, 15 Aug 1959, TCK Papers; also Potter, *Bull Halsey*, 406.
[37] *New York Times*, 27 Jan 1961.

Author's collection

Kinkaid and MacArthur embrace at the 1961 reunion.

the parish handsomely. The Cassin pew was still theirs, when the admiral was up to attending services.[38] By 1968, when he resigned from the Monuments Commission, his attendance at the Class of 1908 luncheons at the Army and Navy Club had ceased, but at sixty years out of the Academy, who would notice? He was one of the few "survivors."

After several hospitalizations in 1972, the admiral slipped away during the morning watch on Friday, 17 November, at the Bethesda Naval Hospital. In casting off, Kinkaid joined an impressive group of men who had died that year: former shipmates Vice Admiral W. T. Tarrant, Admiral H. R. Stark, Admiral H. K. Hewitt, Vice Admiral M. S. Tisdale, and Admiral T. L. Sprague, and classmates Commodore H. B. Mecleary, Captain N. W. Pickering, Captain J. W. Rankin, and Lloyd C. Stark, former Governor of Missouri.[39] The formal military funeral took place from the Fort Myer Chapel to the grave site in the Arlington Cemetery on Tuesday the 21st. The admiral's funeral had all of the trappings, honors, and dignity that a four-star admiral and national hero deserved.[40]

---

[38] TCK to Harry Tyson Carter, Washington, 27 Apr 1962, TCK Papers.

[39] *Shipmate*, Nov 1972, 88–90.

[40] *Baltimore Sun*, 22 Nov 1972; *Washington Post*, 22 Nov 1972.

Courtesy J. Urquhart

Helen Kinkaid and her great-niece Jennifer Urquhart at the christening ceremony of *Kinkaid* (DD 965).

In returning to their R Street residence, Helen was greeted by a large number of cables, telegrams, and letters from Tom Kinkaid's friends throughout the world. All, of course, were saddened by the admiral's death and offered sympathy. Many she treasured for their memories and graciously stated sentiments, but she clung to one in particular because she so deeply respected the writer as a friend and as a naval professional with a superb career. In writing to Helen Kinkaid, Admiral Arleigh Burke spoke not only for himself but for many of the Navy's senior officers:

> He is known as one of the greatest Naval Commanders in our Navy. He made his mark in history and his beloved country owes much to him for his great victories in combat.
>
> But his greatest contribution may very well be the example he set for his associates in the Navy, both senior and junior. He was what we all thought to be the ideal naval officer. He looked, acted and was a leader whom many generations will try to follow. He was inspiring. He was knowledgeable. He was skillful in his profession. He had high values. His warm-

hearted nature and his keen humor endeared him to his friends and associates. By just being the kind of man he was, he caused others to become better men than they otherwise would have been.[41]

The Navy's final honor for those it memorializes is to name a fighting ship after the person. On 1 June 1974, Helen Kinkaid sent *Kinkaid* (DD 965) down the ways at Ingalls Shipbuilding Corporation in Pascagoula, Mississippi. Two years later the vessel's commanding officer, Commander Howard J. Kerr, wrote the admiral's widow:

> The day for which you have long awaited is here and we regret that you could not be present to see this magnificent ship—named for your husband—commissioned. From Coral Sea, to Midway, the Aleutians, Leyte Gulf and finally to the homeland of the enemy, Admiral Kinkaid fought in every major battle in the Pacific. Those qualities which your husband so brilliantly displayed—steadfastness in battle and always true to his mission—we now pledge to emulate as USS *Kinkaid* joins the United States Pacific Fleet.[42]

---

[41] Arleigh Burke to HSK, Washington, 20 Nov 1972, TCK Papers.
[42] CDR Howard J. Kerr to HSK, Pascagoula, MS, 10 Jul 1976, TCK Papers.

Epilogue

If there is one phrase that characterizes the life of Admiral Kinkaid, it is "attention to mission." Throughout his service career and well into retirement, the admiral was goal-oriented. Because he graduated in the lower half of his class, he usually made lightly of his intellectual abilities. In 1961, while he was being interviewed by John Mason for his oral history, Mason commented that it took a lot of brains to be a great leader. Kinkaid demurred: "I don't think it takes too much brains. I'm a great believer in the average man—not having brains myself. I'm a great believer in the average man who will get down and work and who has judgment, good judgment, other than a very keen, very high I.Q."

When asked if good judgment in a leader didn't result from "a certain amount of gray matter," the admiral relented: "A certain amount is the key to what you said there. He's got to have a certain amount, but doesn't have to have gray matter completely filling his skull."

Kinkaid, of course, was describing how he saw himself. Annapolis men of his generation (and fifty years later as well) learned early to respect the star men in their classes and to expect that, on the average, they would move ahead more easily than those less academically accomplished. But it was also drilled into young Kinkaid and his classmates that solid day-in, day-out performance of duties would lead to steady promotions. With a Navy that expanded until well into the early 1930s, and in a culture that believed in the concept of progress, the Class of 1908 moved steadily ahead, and Tom Kinkaid with it.

Attention to duty, however, would not have been enough to turn Kinkaid into a flag officer. Working against him was the fact that he had less sea duty than every captain in his class. In addition, his many assignments to duty in Washington made him suspect to some of his contemporaries who saw him as a BUNAV "fixer." A couple of the Washington tours were BUORD assignments, and Kinkaid by training and experience was a card-carrying member of the Gun Club. To many, BUORD people appeared to have an inside track in the promotion sweepstakes.

The Navy, however, was larger than the Bureau of Ordnance. A careful planner when it came to his career, Kinkaid recognized the power of positive fitness reports, particularly when written by highly placed and respected seniors. As a lieutenant commander, he asked for duty under Rear Admiral Mark Bristol, a difficult but greatly respected flag officer.

Kinkaid not only served Bristol well, but it is clear that Helen Kinkaid's social *savoir-faire* made the Kinkaids good friends of the Bristols and the admiral's steadily rising chief of staff, Arthur J. Hepburn. After a quick turn in a destroyer command and another BUORD assignment, Kinkaid joined the staff of CINCUS Admiral Henry Wiley. Here he proved he could move a mountain of paperwork and also be creative in his thinking. The second highest ranking officer in the Navy was appreciative, and the Kinkaids and Wileys became good friends, a friendship that lasted until Wiley's death in 1943.

Kinkaid's assignment to the General Board was clearly the result of his service with Admiral Bristol. Although performing his duties as secretary of the board in an exemplary way, he almost went aground on two dangerous shoals, the London Naval Conference of 1930 and the World Disarmament Conference of 1931–1932. But the quality of his work was such that even the testy Bristol, who suspected that anyone connected with the nation's disarmament delegations was a fool or a traitor, had to admit in his fitness reports that Commander Tom Kinkaid was worthy of advancement. Able to choose his own billet in 1937, the captain chose to place himself in the center of the Battle Force with its hierarchy of flag officers overseeing his performance. The move paid off. Kinkaid commanded *Indianapolis* to everyone's satisfaction and also renewed an old friendship with Rear Admiral Walter S. Anderson, Commander Cruiser Division 4. As Director of Naval Intelligence, Anderson was to continue surveillance of his friend when Kinkaid moved to Rome. These assignments under important flag officers known to Kinkaid does not necessarily mean that he sought and received preference. Like most officers in the Navy, he simply preferred to serve someone he knew and respected, rather than work for a stranger.

There is another element that affected Kinkaid's career, especially as a flag officer, and that was pure and simple luck. Kinkaid was in the right place at the right time when opportunity knocked. He told his oral history interviewer, "I've often said I'd rather have luck than brains any day." Certainly his command of the *Enterprise* Task Force came about as the result of Admiral Halsey's misfortune. With no important seagoing assignment at hand, he was available when it was necessary to replace Admiral Theobald in Alaska. Attaining command of the Naval Forces, Southwest Pacific Area was attributable both to luck and his own success at working with the Army in the North Pacific Command. It was Vice Admiral Carpender's bad luck, and Kinkaid's availability and successful experience that made it possible for Kinkaid to leap past such classmates as Kelly Turner, Willis Lee, and Francis Rockwell. Life under General MacArthur's command was no bed of roses, but it did pay off in an admiral's four stars, ahead of everyone else in his Academy class.

Admiral Kinkaid's legacy is not something that can be quantified or photographed. The possibility that the Pacific War was shortened because of victory at Leyte Gulf is worth discussing but is not provable. The enhancement of the Navy's relations with the civilian community in the greater New York area was evanescent at best. Those splendid military cemeteries and monuments in Europe, Africa, and the Pacific, which were constructed during his postretirement years on the American Battle Monuments Commission, are indeed a lasting legacy, but few recognized Kinkaid's role in their creation. There is no question, however, that what the Navy gained of lasting value from the admiral's forty-six years of service was another role model for its officer corps. In 1941 the "Articles for the Government of the Navy" stated, "The commanders of all fleets, squadrons, naval stations, and vessels belonging to the Navy are required to show in themselves a good example of virtue, honor, patriotism, and subordination." The admiral probably smiled when he read the section; the regulation of "virtue" certainly was an Old Navy concept. On the other hand, courage in battle and attention to mission were traits absolutely necessary for the Navy's future commanders and would never become obsolete. Seen in retrospect, Admiral Kinkaid's career exemplified this value to both the Navy and the nation.

Abbreviations

AA	antiaircraft
ABDA	American-British-Dutch-Australian
AP	armor-piercing
ASW	antisubmarine warfare
BUNAV	Bureau of Navigation
BUORD	Bureau of Ordnance
CAP	combat air patrol
CINCLANT	Commander in Chief, Atlantic Fleet
CINCPAC	Commander in Chief, Pacific Fleet
CINCSWPA	Commander in Chief, Southwest Pacific Area
CINCUS	Commander in Chief, U.S. Fleet
CNO	Chief of Naval Operations
COMAIRPAC	Commander Aircraft, Pacific Fleet
COMAMPHORPAC	Commander Amphibious Forces Pacific
COMBATFOR	Commander Battle Force
COMCRUSCOFOR	Commander Cruisers, Scouting Force
COMINCH	Commander in Chief, U.S. Fleet, after December 1941
COMNORPACFOR	Commander North Pacific Force
COMSCOFOR	Commander Scouting Force
COMSOPAC	Commander South Pacific Area
CRUDIV	Cruiser Division
CTF	Commander Task Force
CTG	Commander Task Group
DESDIV	Destroyer Division
DESRON	Destroyer Squadron
DSM	Distingushed Service Medal
EOS	Estimate of the Situation
FDO	Fighter Director Officer
GHQ	General Headquarters

JCS	Joint Chiefs of Staff
LOC	lines of communication
LRBP	long range battle practice
ONI	Office of Naval Intelligence
OOD	Officer of the Day
OTC	Officer in Tactical Command
POW	prisoner of war
RCT	Regimental Combat Team
SEFIC	Seventh Fleet Intelligence Center
SRBP	short range battle practice
SWPA	Southwest Pacific Area
TAD	temporary additional duty
TBS	talk between ships

Bibliography

Primary Sources

Manuscript Materials

Admiral Thomas C. Kinkaid's personal papers were the most important source for this book. The admiral's widow, Helen S. Kinkaid, as specified by her husband, donated his papers to the Operational Archives, Naval Historical Center, Washington, DC, in 1973. Arranged by Mae C. Seaton in 1974, the ten series are most complete concerning the admiral's activities during World War II and until his retirement in 1950. Mrs. Kinkaid added to the collection more than 500 letters written to her during the war. Unfortunately, for the researcher, the admiral adhered to the rules of censorship and rarely wrote about planning and operations. The letters do give a full picture of an admiral at war and his reflections on non-operations subjects brought up by Mrs. Kinkaid in her letters. There are no letters from Mrs. Kinkaid to husband. To make biographical research as complete as possible, the Operational Archives arranged to have copied Admiral Kinkaid's orders files, correspondence files, and promotion files held by the Bureau of Naval Personnel (BUPERS). These records are now filed with the Military Personnel Records Center in St. Louis, Missouri. In the Kinkaid papers is a bound file of his orders and correspondence for the years 1908–1922. Some of those papers do not appear in his BUPERS official files.

Of transcendent importance for tracing the Pacific Fleet's operations, and Kinkaid's role within it, is "Captain Steele's 'Running Estimate and Summary,' Covering the Period 7 December 1941 to 31 August 1945." Held in the Operational Archives and available for purchase on three reels of microfilm through Scholarly Resources, Inc., this document contains radio correspondence between Admiral Chester W. Nimitz, Commander in Chief, Pacific Fleet, and his commanders, estimates of the situation, radio correspondence with Army high commands, reports of operations from task force and fleet commanders at sea, and secret and top secret radio traffic. These volumes are sometimes referred to by some historians as the "Grey Book."

The official record of almost any regular Navy officer who served between 1900 and 1941 began with admission to the U.S. Naval Academy. Following graduation from that institution, an officer's life may be traced through records of the Bureau of Navigation (later Bureau of Naval Personnel), the bureau in which he might have become a specialist (Aeronautics, Yards and Docks, Supplies and Accounts, etc.), the ships and stations in which he served, and in the individual officer's correspondence, orders, and promotion files. Unless there is cooperation from an officer's family, these files are not easily available. The basic daily record of a ship's operations, even when in drydock, can be followed in its log book. These log books are stored in the National Archives, Washington, DC. When operating in wartime, every vessel, aviation squadron, task unit, group, force or fleet, and shore base maintains a daily war diary. These are preserved in the Operational Archives, Naval Historical Center.

Archival and Special Collections

National Archives and Records Administration, Washington, DC.

RG 24: Records of the Bureau of Navigation and the Bureau of Naval Personnel

Ships' log books:

Arizona (BB 39), 1918–1919
Arkansas (BM 7), 1907
Astoria (CA 34), 1941
Colorado (BB 45), 1933–1934
Enterprise (CV 6), 1942
Hartford, 1905
Indianapolis (CA 35), 1937–1938
Isherwood (DD 284), 1924–1925
Machias (PG 5), 1914–1915
MacLeish (DD 220), 1923
Minneapolis (CA 36), 1942, 1945
Minnesota (BB 22), 1910–1913
Nebraska (BB 16), 1908–1910
Nevada (BM 8), 1905
Newark (C 1), 1906
Pennsylvania (BB 38), 1916–1918
Texas (BB 35), 1927–1929
Trenton (CL 11), 1924
Wainwright (DD 419), 1941
Wasatch (AGC 9), 1944

RG 59: Central Files. Department of State

RG 80: General Records of the Navy Department

RG 117: Records of the American Battle Monuments Commission

RG 330: Records of the National Service Training Commission

RG 405: Records of the U.S. Naval Academy

Naval Historical Center, Operational Archives, Washington, DC.
>Forrestal, James V. Diaries, 4 July 1944–16 September 1947. 8 vols. Microfilm.
>General Board Records:
>>Proceedings of the General Board
>>Hearings conducted by the General Board
>>Minutes of meetings of the General Board and its Executive Committee
>>Reports of the General Board
>Naval Operations Records:
>>World War II Action Reports, 1941–1945
>>Records (scattered) of task groups, task forces, and fleets
>>War Diaries for ships and flag staffs of task groups, task forces and fleets
>>Pacific Fleet, "Captain Steele's 'Running Estimate and Summary,' 7 December 1941 to 31 August 1945"

Oral Histories and Interviews

Columbia University, Oral History Projects Office, New York, NY (*Copies held in Operational Archives*).
>Anderson, Vice Admiral Walter S. 1962.
>Kinkaid, Admiral Thomas C. 1961.
>Kirk, Admiral Alan G. 1961.
>Stump, Admiral Felix D. 1964.

U.S. Naval Institute, Oral History Collection, Annapolis, MD (*Copies held in Operational Archives*).
>Conolly, Admiral Richard L. 1960.
>Dyer, Vice Admiral George C. 1969.
>Tarbuck, Rear Admiral Raymond D. 1973.

Interviews by author. Author's personal collection.
>Berkey, Admiral Russell. Old Lyme, CT. 1976, 1978.
>Burroughs, Rear Admiral Sherman E. Coronado, CA. 1988.
>DeLany, Vice Admiral Walter S. Washington, DC. 1977.
>Freeman, David F. Rumson, NJ. 1976.
>Grader, Jan. Washington, DC. 1976.
>Kimmel, Captain Thomas Kinkaid. Annapolis, MD. 1976.
>Kinkaid, Helen S. Washington, DC. 1976, 1977, 1978.
>Thornton, Captain Proctor. San Francisco, CA. 1977.
>Urquhart, Mary Tyler (Mrs. John). Chevy Chase, MD. 1976, 1978.
>Wheeler, Rear Admiral C. Julian. Menlo Park, CA. 1977.

Private Papers

Hoover Institution Archives, Stanford, CA.
   Cooke, Charles M.
   Gibson, Hugh
   Miles, Milton E.
   Theobald, Robert A.
   Van Hook, Clifford E.

Library of Congress, Manuscript Division, Washington, DC.
   Bristol, Mark L.
   Halsey, William F., Jr.

MacArthur Museum, Norfolk, VA.
   MacArthur, Douglas

Virginia Military Institute, Marshall Library, Lexington, VA.
   Marshall, George C.

Naval Historical Center, Operational Archives, Washington, DC.
   Barbey, Daniel E.
   King, Ernest J.
   Nimitz, Chester W.
   Settle, Thomas G.W.
   Sherman, Forrest P.

Naval War College Library, Newport, RI.
   Bates, Richard W.
   Kalbfus, Edward C.

Princeton University Library, Princeton, NJ.
   Dulles, Allen

Harry S. Truman Presidential Library, Independence, MO.
   Truman, Harry S.

U.S. Naval Academy Archives, Annapolis, MD.
   Brown, Wilson

Yale University Library, New Haven, CT.
   Lane, Arthur Bliss
   Stimson, Henry L.

U.S. Government Documents

Bureau of National Literature. *A Compilation of the Messages and Papers of the Presidents*. 20 volumes. New York: Bureau of National Literature, 1917.

U.S. Congress. House of Representatives. House Committee on Naval Affairs, *Hearings on Sundry Legislation Affecting the Naval Establishment, 1922–1923*. 67 Cong., 2d, 3d, and 4th sess., 1922–1923. Washington: GPO, 1923.

———. Joint Committee on the Investigation of the Pearl Harbor Attack. *Hearings*. 79th Cong., lst sess., 1945–1946. 39 vols. Washington: GPO, 1946.

———. Senate. *Journal of the Executive Proceedings of the Senate of the United States*. Vol. 82. 77th Cong., lst sess. Washington: GPO, 1942.

———. Naval Affairs Committee. *Hearings on S.2044: "Unification of the Armed Services."* 79th Cong., 2d sess. Washington: GPO, 1946.

———. Naval Subcommittee of Appropriations Committee, *Hearings on Navy Department Appropriation Bill, 1923*. 67th Cong. Washington: GPO, 1923.

U.S. Department of the Navy. *Register of the Commissioned and Warrant Officers of the Navy of the United States and of the Marine Corps to January 1, 1890*. Washington: GPO, 1890.

———. *Register of the Commissioned and Warrant Officers of the Navy of the United States and of the Marine Corps to January 1, 1896*. Washington: GPO, 1896.

———. *Register of the Commissioned and Warrant Officers of the Navy of the United States and of the Marine Corps to January 1, 1942*. Washington: GPO, 1942.

———. Office of Naval Intelligence, *Combat Narratives:*

The Aleutians Campaign, June 1942–August 1942. Washington; 1945, reprint, Naval Historical Center, 1993.

Battle of the Coral Sea. Consisting of the Actions at Tulagi, May 4th; off Misima, May 7th; and in the Coral Sea on May 8th, 1942. Washington, 1943.

The Battle of Midway, June 3–6, 1942. Washington, 1943.

Early Raids in the Pacific Ocean, February 1 to March 10, 1942: Marshall and Gilbert Islands, Rabaul, Wake and Marcus, Lae and Salamaua. Washington, 1943.

Solomons Islands Campaign, I: The Landing in the Solomons, 7–8 August 1942. Washington, 1943; reprint, Naval Historical Center, 1994.

Solomons Islands Campaign, II: The Battle of Savo Island, 9 August 1942; III: The Battle of the Eastern Solomons, 23–25 August 1942. Washington, 1943; reprint, Naval Historical Center, 1994.

Solomon Islands Campaign, V: Battle of Santa Cruz Islands, 26 October 1942. Washington, 1943; reprint, Naval Historical Center, 1994.

U.S. Department of State. *Papers Relating to the Foreign Relations of the United States, 1931*. Vol. 1. Washington: GPO, 1946.

———. *Papers Relating to the Foreign Relations of the United States, 1932.* Vol. 1. Washington: GPO, 1948.

———. *Foreign Relations of the United States: Diplomatic Papers 1932.* Vol. 4. Washington: GPO, 1948.

———. *Papers Relating to the Foreign Relations of the United States, 1945.* Vol. 7, *The Far East, China.* Washington: GPO, 1969.

U.S. Naval War College. *The Battle of the Coral Sea, May 1 to May 11 inclusive, 1942: Strategical and Tactical Analysis.* NAVPERS 91050 (1950).

———. *The Battle of Midway, Including the Aleutians Phase, June 3 to June 14, 1942: Strategical and Tactical Analyses.* 1948.

U.S. Strategic Bombing Survey (Pacific), *Interrogation of Japanese Officials,* 2 vols. Washington: GPO, 1947.

Willoughby, Charles A., comp., *Reports of General MacArthur: The Campaigns of MacArthur in the Pacific.* 2 vols. Washington: Department of the Army, 1966.

Autobiographies, Biographies, Memoirs, and Journals

Bradley, Omar N., and Clay Blair. *A General's Life: An Autobiography by General of the Army Omar N. Bradley.* New York: Simon and Schuster, 1983.

Buell, Thomas B. *Master of Sea Power: A Biography of Fleet Admiral Ernest J. King.* Boston: Little, Brown, 1980.

———. *The Quiet Warrior : A Biography of Admiral Raymond A. Spruance.* Boston, Toronto: Little, Brown, 1974.

Coletta, Paolo E. *Admiral Bradley A. Fiske and the American Navy.* Lawrence, KS: The Regents Press of Kansas, 1979.

———. *Patrick N.L. Bellinger and U.S. Naval Aviation.* Lanham, MD, New York, London: University Press of America, 1987.

Coontz, Robert E. *From the Mississippi to the Sea.* Philadelphia: Dorrance, 1930.

Dyer, Vice Admiral George Carroll. *The Amphibians Came to Conquer: The Story of Admiral Richmond Kelly Turner.* 2 vols. Washington: Naval History Division, 1971.

Evans, Robley D. *An Admiral's Log.* New York and London: D. Appleton, 1910.

Fiske, Bradley A. *From Midshipman to Rear-Admiral.* New York: Century, 1919.

Forrestel, Vice Admiral E. P. *Admiral Raymond A. Spruance, USN: A Study in Command.* Washington: Office of Naval History, 1966.

Gleaves, Rear Admiral Albert. *The Life of an American Sailor: Rear Admiral William Hemsley Emory, United States Navy.* New York: George H. Doran, 1923.

Halpern, Paul G., ed. *The Keyes Papers: Selections from the Private and Official Correspondence of Admiral of the Fleet Baron Keyes of Zeebrugge.* Vol. 3, *1939–1945.* London: George Allen & Unwin, 1981.

Halsey, Fleet Admiral William F., and Lt. Commander J. Bryan III. *Admiral Halsey's Story.* New York and London: Whittlesey House, McGraw Hill, 1947.

Hooker, Nancy Harvison, ed. *The Moffatt Papers: Selections from the Diplomatic Journals of Jay Pierrepont Moffatt.* Cambridge, MA: Harvard University Press, 1956.

James, D. Clayton. *The Years of MacArthur: Volume II, 1941–1945.* Boston: Houghton Mifflin, 1975.

Jurika, Jr., Stephen, ed. *From Pearl Harbor to Vietnam: The Memoirs of Admiral Arthur W. Radford.* Stanford, CA: Hoover Institution Press, 1980.

Kenney, George C. *General Kenney Reports.* New York: Duell, Sloan and Pearce, 1949.

King, Ernest J., and Walter Muir Whitehill. *Fleet Admiral King: A Naval Record.* New York: W. W. Norton, 1952.

Krueger, General Walter. *From Down Under to Nippon: The Story of the Sixth Army in World War II.* Washington: Combat Forces Press, 1953.

Layton, Rear Admiral Edwin T., with Captain Roger Pineau and John Costello. *"And I Was There": Pearl Harbor and Midway—Breaking the Secrets.* New York: William Morrow, 1986.

Lee, Clark, and Richard Henschel. *Douglas MacArthur.* New York: Henry Holt, 1952.

Leutze, James. *A Different Kind of Victory : A Biography of Admiral Thomas C. Hart.* Annapolis: Naval Institute Press, 1981.

Lowenheim, Francis L., Harold D. Langley, and Manfred Jonas. *Roosevelt and Churchill: Their Wartime Correspondence.* New York: Saturday Review Press/E. P. Dutton, 1975.

Lohbeck, Don. *Patrick J. Hurley.* Chicago: Henry Regnery, 1956.

MacArthur, General of the Army Douglas. *Reminiscences.* New York: McGraw-Hill, 1964.

Marks, Jeannette. *Life and Letters of Mary Emma Woolley.* Washington: Public Affairs Press, 1955.

Mears, Lieutenant Frederick. *Carrier Combat.* Garden City, NY: Doubleday, Doran, 1944.

Merrill, James M. *A Sailor's Admiral: A Biography of William F. Halsey.* New York: Thomas Y. Crowell, 1976.

Miles, Vice Admiral Milton E. *A Different Kind of War.* Garden City, NY: Doubleday, 1967.

Millis, Walter, ed. *The Forrestal Diaries.* New York: Viking Press, 1951.

Morison, Elting E. *Admiral Sims and the Modern American Navy.* Boston: Houghton Mifflin, 1942.

Pacis, Vicente Albano. *Osmena.* 2 vols. Quezon City, Philippines: Phoenix Press, 1971.

Phillips, William. *Ventures in Diplomacy.* London: John Murray, 1955.

Pogue, Forrest C. *George C. Marshall: Education of a General, 1880–1939.* New York: Viking Press, 1963.

———. *George C. Marshall: Ordeal and Hope, 1939–1942.* New York: Viking Press, 1966.

———. *George C. Marshall: Organizer of Victory, 1943–1945.* New York: Viking Press, 1973.

———. *George C. Marshall: Statesman, 1945–1959.* New York: Viking Press, 1987.

Potter, E. B. *Admiral Arleigh Burke.* New York: Random House, 1990.

———. *Bull Halsey.* Annapolis: Naval Institute Press, 1985.

———. *Nimitz.* Annapolis: Naval Institute Press, 1976.

Richardson, Admiral James O. *On the Treadmill to Pearl Harbor: The Memoirs of Admiral James O. Richardson, USN (Retired).* Washington: Naval History Division, 1973.

Rodman, Hugh. *Yarns of a Kentucky Admiral.* Indianapolis: Bobbs-Merrill, 1928.

Romulo, Carlos P. *I See the Philippines Rise.* Garden City, NY: Doubleday, 1946.

Sherman, Frederick C. *Combat Command: The American Aircraft Carriers in the Pacific War.* New York: Bantam Books, 1982.

Smith, Vice Admiral William W. *Midway: Turning Point of the Pacific.* New York: Crowell, 1966.

Stirling, Yates. *Sea Duty: The Memoirs of a Fighting Admiral.* New York: G.P. Putnam's Sons, 1939.

Taylor, Theodore. *The Magnificent Mitscher.* New York: W. W. Norton, 1954.

Truman, Harry S. *Memoirs by Harry S. Truman.* Vol. 1, *Years of Decisions*; Vol. 2, *Years of Trial and Hope, 1946–1952.* Garden City, NY: Doubleday, 1955.

Wedemeyer, General Albert C. *Wedemeyer Reports!* New York: Henry Holt, 1958.

Wheeler, Gerald E. *Admiral William Veazie Pratt, U.S. Navy: A Sailor's Life.* Washington: Naval History Division, 1974.

Wiley, Henry A. *An Admiral from Texas*. Garden City, NY: Doubleday, Doran, 1934.

Wilson, Eugene E. *Slipstream: The Autobiography of an Air Craftsman*. New York: McGraw Hill, 1950.

Wilson, Hugh R. *Diplomat Between Wars*. New York and Toronto: Longmans, Green, 1941.

Zogbaum, Rufus. *From Sail to Saratoga: A Naval Autobiography*. Rome: Tipografia Italo-Orientale, 1961.

Secondary Sources

Books, Monographs, and Treatises

Abbazia, Patrick. *Mr. Roosevelt's Navy: The Private War of the U.S. Atlantic Fleet, 1939–1942*. Annapolis: Naval Institute Press, 1975.

Bailey, Thomas A., and Paul B. Ryan. *Hitler vs Roosevelt: The Undeclared Naval War*. New York: Free Press, 1979.

Baldwin, Hanson W. *Sea Fights and Shipwrecks: True Tales of the Seven Seas*. Garden City, NY: Hanover House, 1955.

Baker, Ray Stannard. *Woodrow Wilson and World Settlement*. 3 vols. Garden City, NY: Doubleday, Page, 1922.

Barbey, Daniel E. *MacArthur's Amphibious Navy: Seventh Amphibious Force Operations, 1943–1945*. Annapolis: U.S. Naval Institute, 1969.

Battle Stations! Your Navy in Action. New York: William H. Wise, 1946.

Bauer, K. Jack. *Ships of the Navy, 1775–1969*. Vol. 1, *Combat Vessels*. Troy, NY: Rensselaer Polytechnic Institute, 1969.

Beigel, Harvey M. *Battleship Country: The Battle Fleet at San Pedro-Long Beach, California, 1919–1940*. Missoula, MT: Pictorial Histories, 1983.

Belote, James H., and William M. Belote. *Titans of the Sea : The Development and Operations of Japanese and American Carrier Task Forces During World War II*. New York: Harper and Row, 1975.

Bernardo, C. Joseph, and Eugene H. Bacon. *American Military Policy, Its Development Since 1775*. 2d ed. Harrisburg, PA: Stackpole, 1961.

Blair, Jr., Clay. *Silent Victory: The U.S. Submarine War Against Japan*. 2 vols. Philadelphia and New York: J.B. Lippincott, 1975.

Cannon, M. Hamlin. *United States Army in World War II: The War in the Pacific: Leyte: The Return to the Philippines*. Washington: Office of the Chief of Military History, 1954.

Cant, Gilbert. *The Great Pacific Victory: From the Solomons to Tokyo.* New York: John Day, 1946.

Carter, Worrall Reed. *Beans, Bullets and Black Oil.* Washington: Office of Naval History, 1952.

Churchill, Winston S. *The Second World War.* Vol. 2, *Their Finest Hour.* Boston: Houghton Mifflin, 1949.

———. *The Second World War,* Vol. 6, *Triumph and Tragedy.* Boston: Houghton Mifflin, 1953.

Clephane, Lewis P. *History of the Naval Overseas Transportation Service in World War I.* Washington: Naval History Division, 1969.

Coletta, Paolo E., ed. *American Secretaries of the Navy,* 2 vols. Annapolis: Naval Institute Press, 1980.

———. *Sea Power in the Atlantic and Mediterranean in World War I.* Lanham, MD: University Press of America, 1989.

———. *The United States Navy and Defense Unification.* Newark, DE: University of Delaware Press, 1981.

Conn, Stetson, Rose E. Engleman, and Byron Fairchild. *United States Army in World War II: The Western Hemisphere: Guarding the United States and Its Outposts.* Washington: Office of Chief of Military History, 1964.

Costello, John. *The Pacific War.* New York: Rawson, Wade Publishers, 1981.

Craven, Frank Wesley, and James Lea Cate, eds. *The Army Air Forces in World War II.* Vol. 1, *Plans and Early Operations, January 1939 to August 1942.* Chicago: University of Chicago Press, 1948.

Cressman, Robert. *That Gallant Ship: U.S.S. Yorktown (CV-5).* Missoula, MT: Pictorial Histories, 1985.

Cutler, Thomas J. *The Battle of Leyte Gulf, 23–26 October 1944.* New York: Harper Collins, 1994.

Dallek, Robert. *Franklin D. Roosevelt and American Foreign Policy, 1932–1945.* New York: Oxford University Press, 1979.

Davis, George T. *A Navy Second to None: The Development of Modern American Naval Policy,* New York: Harcourt, Brace, 1940.

Davis, Vincent. *The Admirals Lobby.* Chapel Hill: University of North Carolina Press, 1967.

———. *Postwar Defense Policy and the U.S. Navy, 1943–1946.* Chapel Hill: University of North Carolina Press, 1962.

Dictionary of American Naval Fighting Ships, 9 vols. Washington: Naval Historical Center, 1959–1991.

Dull, Paul S. *A Battle History of the Imperial Japanese Navy (1941–1945).* Annapolis: Naval Institute Press, 1978.

Earle, Ralph. *Life at the U.S. Naval Academy: The Making of the American Naval Officer.* New York and London: G. P. Putnam's Sons, 1917.

Fahey, James C. *The Ships and Aircraft of the United States Fleet, 1939.* Annapolis: Naval Institute Press, 1976.

Feis, Herbert. *The China Tangle.* Princeton, NJ: Princeton University Press, 1953.

Ferrell, Robert H., ed. *The American Secretaries of State and Their Diplomacy.* Vol. 14. New York: Cooper Square, 1965.

Field, James A., Jr., *The Japanese at Leyte Gulf: The Sho Operation.* Princeton, NJ: Princeton University Press, 1947.

Frank, Patrick H. H., and Joseph D. Harrington. *Rendezvous at Midway: U.S.S. Yorktown and the Japanese Carrier Fleet.* New York: Stein and Day, 1967.

Frank, Richard B. *Guadalcanal.* New York: Random House, 1990.

Fuchida, Mitsuo, and Masatake Okumiya. *Midway: The Battle That Doomed Japan.* Annapolis: Naval Institute Press, 1955.

Garfield, Brian. *The Thousand-Mile War: World War II in Alaska and the Aleutians.* Garden City, NY: Nelson Doubleday, 1969, 1983.

Gill, G. Hermon. *Royal Australian Navy, 1942–1945.* Adelaide: Griffin Press, 1968.

Hailey, Foster. *Pacific Battle Line.* New York: Macmillan, 1944.

Hamersly, Lewis Randolph. *The Records of Living Officers of the U.S. Navy and Marine Corps.* New York: L. R. Hamersly, 1902.

Hammel, Eric. *Guadalcanal: The Carrier Battles.* New York: Crown, 1987.

———. *Guadalcanal: Decision at Sea, The Naval Battle of Guadalcanal, November 13–15, 1942.* New York: Crown, 1988.

Hart, Robert A. *The Great White Fleet: Its Voyage Around the World, 1907–1909.* Boston, Toronto: Little, Brown, 1965.

Hattendorf, John B., with B. Mitchell Simpson III, and John R. Wadleigh. *Sailors and Scholars: The Centennial History of the U.S. Naval War College.* Newport, RI: Naval War College Press, 1984.

Hayes, Grace Person. *The History of the Joint Chiefs of Staff in World War II: The War Against Japan.* Annapolis: Naval Institute Press, 1982.

Head, William P. *America's China Sojourn*. Lanham, MD: University Press of America, 1983.

Holmes, W. J. [Jasper]. *Double-Edged Secrets: U.S. Naval Intelligence Operations in the Pacific during World War II*. Annapolis: Naval Institute Press, 1979.

———. *Undersea Victory: The Influence of Submarine Operations on the War in the Pacific*. Garden City, NY: Doubleday, 1966.

Horner, D. M. *High Command: Australia and Allied Strategy, 1939–1945*. Sydney, London, Boston: George Allen & Unwin, 1982.

Housepian, Marjorie. *The Smyrna Affair*. New York: Harcourt Brace Jovanovich, 1966.

Hoyt, Edwin P. *The Battle of Leyte Gulf: The Death Knell of the Japanese Fleet*. New York: Weybright and Talley, 1972.

———. *Blue Skies and Blood: The Battle of the Coral Sea*. New York: Paul S. Ericksson, 1975.

———. *How They Won the War in the Pacific: Nimitz and His Admirals*. New York: Weybright and Talley, 1970.

———. *Japan's War: The Great Pacific Conflict, 1853–1952*. New York: McGraw Hill, 1986.

The Institute of Politics at Williamstown, Massachusetts: Its First Decade. Williamstown: The Institute of Politics, 1931.

James, D. Clayton. *A Time for Giants: Politics of the American High Command in World War II*. New York and Toronto: Franklin Watts, 1987.

Johnston, Stanley. *Queen of the Flat-Tops: The U.S.S. Lexington and the Coral Sea Battle*. New York: E. P. Dutton, 1942.

Karig, Walter, Earl Burton, and Stephen L. Freeland. *Battle Report*. Vol. 2, *The Atlantic War*. New York: Rinehart, 1946.

Karig, Walter, Russell L. Harris, and Frank A. Manson. *Battle Report: The End of an Empire*. Vol. 4. New York: Rinehart, 1948.

Larkins, William T. *U.S. Navy Aircraft, 1921–1941*. Concord, CA: Privately printed, 1961.

Leary, William M., ed. *We Shall Return! MacArthur's Commanders and the Defeat of Japan, 1942–1945*. Lexington: University of Kentucky Press, 1988.

Lewin, Ronald. *The American Magic: Codes, Ciphers and the Defeat of Japan*. New York: Farrar, Straus, Giroux, 1982.

Link, Arthur S. *Wilson: Confusions and Crises, 1915–1916*. Princeton, NJ: Princeton University Press, 1964.

---. *Wilson: The Struggle for Neutrality, 1914–1915*. Princeton, NJ: Princeton University Press, 1960.

Lord, Walter. *Incredible Victory*. New York, Evanston, London: Harper and Row, 1967.

Lorelli, John A. *The Battle of the Komandorski Islands, March 1943*. Annapolis: Naval Institute Press, 1984.

Love, William, Jr., ed. *The Chiefs of Naval Operations*. Annapolis: Naval Institute Press, 1980.

Lucky Bag 1908: A Chapter in the History of the United States Naval Academy. Vol. 15. Philadelphia: Hoskins Press, 1908.

Luey, A. T., and H. P. Bruvold. *The "Minnie" or the War Cruise of the U.S.S. Minneapolis*. Elkhart, IN: Bell Printing, 1946.

Lundstrom, John B. *The First South Pacific Campaign: Pacific Fleet Strategy, December 1941–June 1942*. Annapolis: Naval Institute Press, 1976.

---. *The First Team and the Guadalcanal Campaign: Naval Fighter Combat from August to November 1942*. Annapolis: Naval Institute Press, 1994.

---. *The First Team: Pacific Naval Air Combat from Pearl Harbor to Midway*. Annapolis: Naval Institute Press, 1984.

MacDonald, Scot. *Evolution of Aircraft Carriers*. Washington: Chief of Naval Operations, 1964.

Malone, Dumas, Robert Livingston Schuyler, and Eduard T. James, eds. *Dictionary of American Biography: Supplement Two*. Vol. 22. New York: Charles Scribner's Sons, 1958.

Matloff, Maurice. *United States Army in World War II: The War Department:Strategic Planning for Coalition Warfare, 1943–1944*. Washington: Office of the Chief of Military History, 1953.

Matloff, Maurice, and Edwin M. Snell. *United States Army in World War II: The War Department: Strategic Planning for Coalition Warfare, 1941–1942*. Washington: Office of the Chief of Military History, 1953.

Melosi, Martin V. *The Shadow of Pearl Harbor: Political Controversy over the Surprise Attack, 1941–1946*. College Station, TX & London: Texas A&M University Press, 1977.

Miller, John, Jr. *United States Army in World War II: The War in the Pacific: Cartwheel: The Reduction of Rabaul*. Series V, Vol. 4. Washington: Office of the Chief of Military History, 1959.

Miller, Roman J. *Around the World with the Battleships*. Chicago: A. C. McClurg, 1909.

———. *Pictorial Log of the Battle Fleet Cruise Around the World.* Chicago: A. C. McClurg, 1909.

Miller, Jr., Thomas G. *The Cactus Air Force.* New York: Harper and Row, Bantam Books, 1969, 1981.

Morison, Samuel Eliot. *History of United States Naval Operations in World War II:*

Vol. 1, *The Battle of the Atlantic, September 1939–May 1943.* Boston: Little, Brown, 1947.

Vol. 3, *The Rising Sun in the Pacific, 1931–April 1942.* Boston: Little, Brown, 1948.

Vol. 4, *Coral Sea, Midway and Submarine Actions, May 1942–August 1942.* Boston: Little, Brown, 1949.

Vol. 5, *The Struggle for Guadalcanal, August 1942–February 1943.* Boston: Little, Brown, 1954.

Vol. 6, *Breaking the Bismarcks Barrier, 22 July 1942–1 May 1944.* Boston: Little, Brown, 1950.

Vol. 7, *Aleutians, Gilberts and Marshalls, June 1942–April 1944.* Boston: Little, Brown, 1951.

Vol. 8, *New Guinea and the Marianas, March 1944–August 1944.* Boston: Little, Brown, 1953.

Vol. 12, *Leyte, June 1944–January 1945.* Boston: Little, Brown, 1958.

Vol. 13, *The Liberation of the Philippines, 1944–1945.* Boston: Little, Brown, 1959.

Morton, Louis. *United States Army in World War II: War in the Pacific: Strategy and Command: The First Two Years.* Washington: Office of the Chief of Military History, 1962.

O'Connor, Raymond G. *Force & Diplomacy: Essays Military and Diplomatic.* Coral Gables, FL: University of Miami Press, 1972.

———. *Perilous Equilibrium: The United States and the London Naval Conference of 1930.* Lawrence, KS: University of Kansas Press, 1962.

Polmar, Norman. *Aircraft Carriers: A Graphic History of Carrier Aviation and Its Influence on World Events.* Garden City, NY: Doubleday, 1969.

Potter, E. B., and Chester W. Nimitz, eds. *The Great Sea War: The Story of Naval Action in World War II.* New York: Bramhall House, 1960.

Prange, Gordon W. *At Dawn We Slept: The Untold Story of Pearl Harbor.* New York: McGraw Hill, 1981.

Prange, Gordon W., Donald M. Goldstein, and Katherine V. Dillon. *Miracle at Midway.* New York: McGraw Hill, 1982.

Rappaport, Armin. *Henry L. Stimson and Japan, 1931–1933.* Chicago & London: University of Chicago Press, 1963.

Reckner, James R. *Teddy Roosevelt's Great White Fleet*. Annapolis: Naval Institute Press, 1988.

Reynolds, Clark G. *Admiral John H. Towers: The Struggle for Naval Air Supremacy*. Annapolis: Naval Institute Press, 1991.

———. *The Fast Carriers: The Forging of an Air Navy*. New York: McGraw Hill, 1968.

Roscoe, Theodore. *United States Destroyer Operations in World War II*. Annapolis: United States Naval Institute, 1953.

Schaller, Michael. *The U.S. Crusade in China, 1938–1945*. New York: Columbia University Press, 1979.

Sherrod, Robert. *History of Marine Corps Aviation in World War II*. Washington: Combat Forces Press, 1952.

Shirer, William L. *The Rise and Fall of the Third Reich: A History of Nazi Germany*. New York: Simon and Schuster, 1960.

Smith, Robert Ross. *United States Army in World War II: War in the Pacific: The Approach to the Philippines*. Subseries, vol. 3. Washington: Office of Chief of Military History, 1953.

———. *United States Army in World War II: War in the Pacific: Triumph in the Philippines*. Subseries, vol. 10. Washington: Office of Chief of Military History, 1963.

Spector, Ronald H. *The American War with Japan: Eagle Against the Sun*. New York: Free Press, 1985.

Sprout, Harold, and Margaret Sprout. *Toward a New Order of Sea Power: American Naval Policy and the World Scene, 1918–1922*. Princeton, NJ: Princeton University Press, 1943.

Stafford, Commander Edward P. *The Big E*. New York: Random House, 1962.

Stratton, Roy. *The Army-Navy Game*. Falmouth, MA: Volta, 1977.

Sweetman, Jack. *The U.S. Naval Academy: An Illustrated History*. Annapolis: Naval Institute Press, 1979.

Tansill, Charles Callan. *America Goes to War*. Boston: Little, Brown, 1938.

Tate, Merze. *The United States and Armaments*. Cambridge, MA: Harvard University Press, 1948.

Trask, David F. *Captains & Cabinets: Anglo-American Naval Relations, 1917–1918*. Columbia: University of Missouri Press, 1972.

Trask, Roger R. *The United States Response to Turkish Nationalism and Reform, 1914–1939*. Minneapolis: University of Minnesota Press, 1971.

Turnbull, Archibald D., and Clifford L. Lord. *History of United States Naval Aviation*. New Haven: Yale University Press, 1949.

U.S. Naval Academy Alumni Association. *Register of Alumni, Graduates, and Former Naval Cadets and Midshipmen.* Annapolis: U.S. Naval Academy Alumni Association, 1986.

Vlahos, Michael. *The Blue Sword: Naval War College and the American Mission 1919–1941.* 1st ed. Newport, RI, Washington: Naval War College Press, GPO, 1980.

Walters, F. *A History of the League of Nations.* 2 vols. London, New York, Toronto: Oxford Press, 1952.

Watson, Mark S. *United States Army in World War II: The War Department: Chief of Staff: Prewar Plans and Preparations.* Washington: Office of Chief of Military History, 1950.

Webber, Lieutenant Richard H., ed. *Monitors of the U.S. Navy, 1861–1937.* Washington: Naval History Division, 1969.

Weigley, Russell F. *The American Way of War: A History of United States Military Strategy and Policy.* New York and London: Macmillan, 1973.

———. *History of the United States Army.* New York and London: Macmillan, 1967.

Wheeler, Gerald E. *Prelude to Pearl Harbor: The United States Navy and the Far East, 1921–1931.* Columbia: University of Missouri Press, 1963.

Willmott, R. P. *The Barrier and the Javelin: Japanese and Allied Pacific Strategies, February to June 1942.* Annapolis: Naval Institute Press, 1983.

Winton, John. *Ultra in the Pacific: How Breaking Japanese Codes and Cyphers Affected Naval Operations Against Japan, 1941–45.* London: Leo Cooper, 1993.

Wohlstetter, Roberta. *Pearl Harbor, Warning and Decision.* Stanford, CA: Stanford University Press, 1962.

Woodward, C. Vann. *The Battle for Leyte Gulf.* New York: Macmillan, 1947.

Y'Blood, William T. *The Little Giants: U.S. Escort Carriers against Japan.* Annapolis: Naval Institute Press, 1987.

Young, Alfred. *The Cruise of the U.S.S. Trenton.* (No publication data, c. 1925.)

Articles

Anderson, Rear Admiral Bern. "The High Commissioner to Turkey." U.S. Naval Institute *Proceedings* (January 1957).

———. "Bristol, Mark Lambart." In *Dictionary of America Biography, Supplement Two.* New York: Charles Scribner's Sons, 1946.

Babb, Robert G. "The Day We Lost the Admiral." *Leatherneck* (September 1976).

Beers, Henry P. "United States Naval Detachment in Turkish Waters, 1919–1924." *Military Affairs* (Spring 1943).

Buzanski, Peter M. "The Interallied Investigation of the Greek Invasion of Smyrna, 1919." *The Historian* (May 1963).

Cant, Gilbert. "Bull's Run: Was Halsey Right at Leyte Gulf?" *Life* (November 24, 1947).

Chihaya, Masataka. "Mysterious Withdrawal from Kiska." U.S. Naval Institute *Proceedings* (February 1958).

Curry, George. "James F. Byrnes." In *The American Secretaries of State and Their Diplomacy*, edited by Robert H. Ferrell. Vol. 14. New York: Cooper Square, 1965.

Detwiler, Donald S., and Charles B. Burdick, eds. "Eastern New Guinea Invasion Operations: Japanese Monograph No. 96." By H.Q. Far East Command, Military History Section, Special Staff Japanese Research Division, in *War in Asia and the Pacific, 1937–1949*. Vol. 5. New York and London: Garland, 1980.

Graybar, Lloyd J., "American Pacific Strategy After Pearl Harbor: The Relief of Wake Island." *Prologue* (Fall 1980).

Halsey, Jr., Fleet Admiral William F. "The Battle for Leyte Gulf." U.S. Naval Institute *Proceedings* (May 1952).

Halsey, Fleet Admiral William F., and Lieutenant Commander J. Bryan III, "Admiral Halsey Tells His Story," Part Seven. *The Saturday Evening Post* (July 26, 1947).

Hiatt, Walter. "Admiral Mark L. Bristol, American Naval Diplomat." *Current History* (February 1928).

Kincaid [sic.], Lieutenant Commander, Thomas C. "Naval Corps, Specialization and Efficiency." U.S. Naval Institute *Proceedings* (October 1921).

Kinkaid, Commander T. C. "Present Problems of Naval Reduction." U.S. Naval Institute *Proceedings* (July 1931).

Kinkaid, Lieutenant Commander T. C. "Probability and Accuracy of Gun Fire." U.S. Naval Institute *Proceedings* (October 1921).

Oldendorf, Admiral Jesse B. "The Battle of Surigao Strait." *Blue Book* (March 1948).

Richmond, Admiral Sir Herbert. "Immediate Problems of Naval Reduction." *Foreign Affairs* (April 1931).

Stankovich, Mike. "The Hardest Choice." *Naval History* (Winter 1988).

Tanaka, Raizo. "The Struggle for Guadalcanal." In *The Japanese Navy in World War II*, edited by David C. Evans. Annapolis: Naval Institute Press, 1986.

Walker, Howell. "Here Rests in Honored Glory." *The National Geographic* (June 1957).

Wheeler, Gerald E. "The United States Navy and War in the Pacific, 1919–1941." *World Affairs Quarterly* (October 1959).

Miscellaneous Papers

Cassin, Mary Margaret. "Genealogy of the Deakins, Cassin, Tyler and Kinkaid Families." Manuscript, undated in possession of Mary Tyler (Mrs. John) Urquhart of Washington, DC.

DeCola, Thomas G. "Roosevelt and Mussolini: The Critical Years, 1938–1944." Ph.D. diss., Kent State University, 1967.

Kinkaid, Admiral Thomas C. "Four Years of War in the Pacific: A Personal Narrative." Typescript, 1951–1952. 285 leaves. Kinkaid MSS, Operational Archives, Naval Historical Center, Washington, DC.

Kinkaid, Commander T. C. "Senior Class, 1930, Thesis: The Present Foreign Policies of the United States." Naval War College, Newport, RI, 26 April 1930.

Laning, Admiral Harris. "An Admiral's Yarn." Manuscript, Collection, Naval War College, Newport, RI.

[Turnbull, Captain A. D., USNR]. Administrative History: Commander, United States Naval Forces Southwest Pacific. Office of Naval History [1948–1949]. Microfilm.

U.S. National Archives. "Selected Naval Attache Reports Relating to the World Crisis, 1937–1943." (Microfilm) M–975.

U.S. Navy, Pacific Fleet, North Pacific Naval Force. "Command History, North Pacific Force." Typescript, Office of Naval History, 1945.

Newspapers

Annapolis Evening Capital. May 1911, August 1920.

Army and Navy Journal. April 1933, March 1946.

Army and Navy Register. May 1949.

Evening Bulletin (Philadelphia). April 1911.

San Francisco Examiner. July 1908.

Los Angeles Times. March 1933, October 1942.

New York Journal American. April 1950.

New York Times. June 1934, March 1939, February 1941, January 1946, April 1950, May 1967.

San Francisco Chronicle. November 1933, August 1937.

The Courier Mail (Brisbane, Australia). October 1943.

The Sunday Mail (Brisbane, Australia). November 1943.

The Telegraph (Brisbane, Australia). October 1943.

Index

Abe, Hiroaki, 145, 256, 274, 290
Abe, Nobuyuki, 435
Abner Read (DD 526), 338, 407
Abukuma, 316, 334, 393, 415
Acadia, 125
Acheson, Dean, 471
Achilles, 164, 183
Adak occupation, 299
Adams, Charles Francis, III, 51, 61, 64
Adams, Walter G., 462
Adler, Julius Ochs, 474
Ady, Howard P., 213
Ainsworth, Walden L. (Pug), 129
Aitape landings and seizure, 366
Akagi, 215
Alaska (CB 1), 433
Aldrich, Winthrop, 453
Aleutian Islands, battles
   See Amchitka Island occupation; Attu campaign; North Pacific Force (NORPACFOR), battles and campaigns
Alfonso XIII, King (of Spain), 120
Alibi Club, 471, 485
AMATEUR, operation, 329–30
Amchitka Island occupation (Jan 1943), 299–307
   See also North Pacific Force (NORPACFOR), battles and campaigns
American Battle Monuments Commission, 473, 477–481
Anderson (DD 411), 170, 193, 195, 280
Anderson, Walter S., 45, 121, 133, 490
Andrews, Adolphus, 88, 89, 90, 91, 101–2, 133
Antietam (CV 36), 433
ANZAC Squadron, 164, 169–70
Aoba, 145, 184
Arawe and Cape Gloucester operations, 351, 353
Arcadia conference, 152
Arctic (AF 7), 97
Arizona (BB 39), 21, 24–25

Arkansas (BB 33), 67
Arkansas (BM 7), 8
Arnold, Archibald V., 385, *432*
Arnold, Henry H. (Hap), 358, 450
Arthur Middleton (APA 25), 303
Arunta, 373
Asaka Maru, 316
Ashford, William H., 206
Ashigara, 393, 399
Astoria (CA 34), 95, 143, 155, 169, 198, 216, 219, 224, 249
Atago, 393
Ataturk, Kemal, 31
Athenia, 114
Atherton, Warren, *474*
Atlanta (CL 51), 213, 239, 248, 258, 261, 263, 290
Atomic bombs, 430
Attu campaign (May–Jun 1943), 307–29
   amphibious assault, 322–28
   campaign objectives, 318
   problems with RADM Rockwell, 320–22
   relief of MGEN Brown, 325–27
Augusta (CA 31), 67
Ault, William B., 169
Australia, 164, 170, 182, 185, 188–89, 370–72, 384, 419–20
Aylwin (DD 355), 333

Badger, Oscar C., 93, 99, 100, 466, 467
Bagley (DD 386), 169
Bagley, David W., 85
Bailey (DD 492), 316
Baker, Wilder D., 265, 333
Balch (DD 363), 218, 239, 248, 258, 259, 261
Baldwin, Hanson, 482–83
Barbey, Daniel E., 347, 346, 374, 381–82, 384–85, 391, 416, 426, 432, 434, 444, 446
Barney (DD 149), 25
"Bataan Gang" (MacArthur's GHQ), 348, 361–63, 375

Bates, Richard W. (Rafe), 387, 398
Battle for Leyte Gulf, The, 458
Battle of the Coral Sea, The, 199
Beck, Edward L., 196
Becker, Nicolai, 35, 465–66
Beightler, Robert S., 416
Belin, Ferdinand L., 33
Belleau Wood (CVL 24), 394
Bellinger, Patrick N.L., 234
Benes, Edward, 106
Benham (DD 397), 216, 218, 239, 248
Benson, William S., 5, 21
Berenson, Bernhard, 117
Berkey, Russell S., 337, 370, 384, 397, 417, 424
Biak operation, 367, 368, 370–71
Bidwell, Abel T., 120, 132
Biffle, Leslie A., 477
Birmingham (CL 62), 394
Bismarck Barrier, 351
Blamey, Sir Thomas A., 347
BLEACHER, operation, 252
Bloch, Claude C., 28, 94, 95, 99
Blue (DD 387), 143
Blue Ridge (AGC 2), 397
Bogan, Gerald F., 394
Boise (CL 47), 244, 371, 373, 384, 417
Bostwick, Lusius A., 43
Bowie, Mary M., 1
Bowie, Walter, 1
Breck (DD 283), 38
Brett, George H., 189
Briggs, Zeno E., 49
Bristol, Arthur L., 126
Bristol, Mark L.
 Commander U.S. Naval Forces in Turkish waters, 30–36
 recommends TCK as Secretary to General Board, 56–57
 relations with TCK, 30, 36–37, 105, 133, 489–90
 senior member General Board, 59, 64, 67
 U.S. High Commissioner to Turkey, 31–36
Brooklyn (CL 40), 127, 130
Brown, Albert E., 318, 325–27
Brown, Cecil, 116
Brown, Constantine, 117
Brown, Wilson, 141, 147, 158, 168, 175

Browning, Miles R., 213, 215
Brownson (DD 518), 353
Brucker, Wilber M., 479
Buckmaster, Elliott, 201, 218, 433
Buckner, Simon Bolivar, 223, 295, 301, 311–12, 326, 337, 340
Bullfinch, Charles, 449
Bunker Hill (CV 17), 395
Burdick, Charles B., 114n
Bureau of Ordnance, Department of the Navy, 25, 27–30, 42–45
Burke, Arleigh A., 460, 487–88
Burroughs, Sherman E., 236, 241, 268
Bush, Rapp, 416
Butler, Henry V., Jr., 47
Butler, William C., 301, 317
Byrd, Richard E., 462

Cabot (CVL 28), 433
CACTUS, operation, 250
California (BB 44), 46, 92, 385, 419, 423
Callaghan, Daniel J., 288, 290
Canberra (CA 70), 389
Canberra, 249
Cant, Gilbert, 460
Cape Engaño, Battle off, 395, 397, 398–99, 403
Cape Gloucester operations
 See Arawe and Cape Gloucester operations
Carney, Robert B., 364
Carpender, Arthur S., 120, 124, 132, 343, 348, 353, 354, 375, 411
Carrier raids (Feb–Mar 1942), 149–73
 Lae-Salamaua raid, 169–71
 Rabaul-Bougainville action, 164–68
 track chart, 162
Carroll, Penn L., 429
Carter, Worrall R. (Nick), 132
Case (DD 285), 38
Cassin, James Luke, 1
Cassin, Mary Margaret, 1n
Cassin, Virginia Lee, 1
 See also Virginia Lee Kinkaid
Cassin, William Deakins, 1
Cassin, Tree and Merritt, 1
Causeway, operation, 381
Chamberlain, Neville, 106
Chamberlin, Stephan J., *359*
Chandler (DMS 9), 306

Chandler, Theodore E., 415, 419
Chapline, Vance, 37
Charlotte, Grand Duchess (of Luxembourg), 480
Chase, Jehu V., 58, 64, *67*, 68
Chase, William C., 358
Chenango (CVE 28), 365
Chennault, Claire L., 418
Chester (CA 27), 97
Chiang Kai-shek, 437, 439–42
Chiang, Madame (Sung Mei-lin), 439–42
Chicago (CA 29), 92, 164, 170, 179, 188–89, 249
Chikuma, 217, 276, 283
Chillingworth, Charles E., 196
Chitose, 256, 258, 395
Chiyoda, 395
Chokai, 249
Christie, Ralph W., 345, 368, 374, 458
Churchill, Winston, 130–31, 378–79, 455
Ciano, Galeazzo, 109, 110, 112, 114, 115
Cimarron (AO 22), 131, 210, 225
Clapper, Raymond, 355
Clark, Frank H., 76
Clark, George R., 15, 184
Claxton (DD 571), 407
Clayton, Will, 474
Code breaking
 See Communications intelligence
Coghlan (DD 606), 316
Colclough, Oswald S., 309, 312, 340
Cole, C. W., *67*
Collins, John A., 372
Colorado (BB 45), 67, 69, 71–87
Columbia (CL 56), 385, 419
Combs, Thomas S., 429
COMINCH-CINCPAC conferences, 297, 339, 343
Communications intelligence ("Ultra," code breaking)
 and Aleutian Islands, 316
 and Battle of the Eastern Solomons, 252–53
 and Battle of Midway, 203–4
 and Guadalcanal operations, 230, 288
 and *Ise-Hyuga* sortie, 424
 and Japanese Port Moresby operation, 176–77
 and Seventh Fleet submarines, 374, 376–77

Compton, Karl T., 474, 475
Connecticut (BB 18), 11
Conolly, Richard L., 381, 385
Cook, Arthur B., 127, 129
Cooke, Charles M. (Savvy), 354
Coolidge, J. Calvin, 36, 50
Coontz, Robert E., 9
Coral Sea (CVE 57), 365
Coral Sea, Battle of (May 1942), 175–202
 battle chart, 183
 forces involved, 180, 183–84
 lessons, 200
 Lexington sunk, 192–96
 map, 183
 preliminary intelligence, 176–77, 183
 Tulagi attack, 184
Corlett, Charles H., 301, 330
Corregidor (CVE 58), 365
COTTAGE, operation, 329
Cowpens (CVL 26), 395
Crace, John G., 164, 169, 182, 183, 185, 188
Craft, Ralph P., 80, 81, 84, 86
Crawford, David S., 395
Crommelin, John G., 235, 268
CROWBAR, operation, 300
Cruiser Division 6, 135, 138, 148–234
 carrier raids with TF 11, 159–73
 in Coral Sea battle, 177–92
 cruiser division operations 153–54
 flagship change, 157
 in Midway battle, 206–22
 staff, 154
 in Wake Island relief operation (Dec 1941), 138–48
 TCK assumes command of, 148
 See also Carrier raids; Coral Sea, Battle of; Midway, Battle of
CRUSADER, operation, 424
Crutchley, Victor A. C., 370
Cruzen, Richard H., 374, 395, 400, 458
Cunningham, Winfield S., 139
Curtin, John, 344
Curtiss (AV 4), 269, 273

Daladier, Edouard, 106
Dale (DD 353), 169, 316
Daniels, Josephus, 84n
Darnell, Linda, 388
Darter (SS 227), 393
Davids, Ray, 258

Davies, Joseph, 269
Davis, Arthur C., 138, 246, 260
Davis, Benjamin O., 477
Davis, Norman H., 64–65
Davis, Ralph O., 82, 100
Davison, Ralph E., 365, 394
Day, Douglas T., 309, 317
Dayton, John H., 26
Deakins, Leonard, 1
Deakins, Tabitha Marbury, 1
Defrees, Joseph R., 52
Denebola (AD 12), 33–34
Denfeld, Louis E., 121, 458
Denver (CL 58), 385
Depression, Great, 94
DeSteiguer, Louis R., 40–41, 46
DETACHMENT, operation, 422
Detroit (CL 8), 320, 333
Devereux, James P.S., 138, 139
Devers, Jacob L., 479–80
Dewey (DD 349), 169, 193, 196, 305
Dewey, Thomas, 368
DeWitt, John L., 295, 326–27, 335, 339–40, 480
Dillon, Clarence, 453
Dixon, Robert E., 188
Dolbeare, Frederick, 33
Dominican Republic intervention (1915), 19–20
Doolittle, James H. (Jimmy), 179, *181*
Douglas, Archibald H., 155
DOVETAIL, operation, 242
Dow, Leonard J. (Ham), 236, 274
Draemel, Milo F., 147, 445
Drake, Waldo, 77
DuBose, Laurance T., 263
Dufilho, Marion W., 167
Dulles, Allen, 32, 33, 65, 471
Dunn, Arthur W., 33
Durgin, Calvin T., 417
DuVal, Miles, 39
Dyer (DD 84), 25
Dyer, George C., 99–100

Earle, Ralph, 28
Eastern Sea Frontier, Commander of
  See Kinkaid, Thomas C.
Eastern Solomons, Battle of the
  (Aug 1942), 253–64
  map, 254

Eberle, Edward W., 45
Edison, Charles, 95
Edwards (DD 619), 324
Edwards, R. S., 450n
Eichelberger, Robert L., 367, 416, 425
Eisenhower, Dwight D., 465, *474*, 475, 477
Eller, Donald T., 128
Ellet (DD 398), 239, 261
English, Robert H., 207
Enterprise (CV 6), 140, 156, 201, 209, 213, 217, 221, 223–25, 245–48, 255–61, 263, 268, 273, 278, 291, 394
  See also Enterprise Task Force
Enterprise Task Force (Jun–Oct 1942), 229–93
  controversy about joint carrier task force operations, 284–86
  damage to *Enterprise* and TF 16 return to Pearl Harbor, 261–62
  Eastern Solomons, Battle of the (Aug 1942), 253–64
  groups and ships of TF 16, 239–41
  Guadalcanal assault (Aug 1942), 230–52
  Nimitz continues TCK in command, 266–68
  Santa Cruz Islands, Battle of (Oct 1942), 269–83
  staff, 235–36
  TCK assumes command TF 16, 234
  TCK relieved of TF command, 291–92
  TF 16 continues operations around Guadalcanal despite *Enterprise* damage, 288–91
  TF 61 formed with TF 16 and TF 17, 269, 270
  withdrawal of task forces to New Caledonia and Hebrides area, 250–52
Entwistle, Frederic L., 309, 312, 320
Essex (CV 9), 407
Estes (AGC 12), 446
Evans, Margaret, 16
Evans, Myron T., 154

Farragut (DD 348), 185, 324, 333
Fechteler, William M., 368, 381, 384, 416, 425, 426
Fenner, Edward B., 91
Field, James A., 458, 483

Fife, James, 424
Fiske, Bradley A., 8
Fitch, Aubrey W. (Jake), 141, 143–45, 175, 177, 179, 192, 194, 196, 224, 234, 445
Flatley, James H., 268, 282
Fletcher, Frank Jack
  as Commander CRUDIV 6, 138
  as Commander Northwestern Sea Frontier, 296
  as Commander Wake Island relief expedition, 143–45
  as CTF 17 in Battle of Coral Sea, 177, 194
  as CTF 17 in Battle of Midway, 207
  as CTF 61 in Guadalcanal campaign, 234, 238–39, 263
  hosts TCK and Helen Kinkaid, 84, 300
  relieved of CRUDIV 6 command, 148
  relieves TCK as COMNORPACFOR, 341
  wounded in Battle of the Eastern Solomons, 265
Fletcher, Martha, 265
Florida (BB 30), 42
Flusser (DD 368), 262
Foss, Joseph J., 477
Franke, William B., 480
Franklin (CV 13), 394
Fraser, Bruce A., 437
Frazier (DD 607), 324
Freeman, David F., 354, 368, *369*, 437
Furutaka, 145, 184
Fuso, 393

Gaines, Robert K., 268
Gambier Bay (CVE 73), 403
Garcia, Carlos, *481*
Gatch, Thomas L., 268
Gehres, Leslie E., 311
General Rose, 477–78
George VI, King (of England), 457
George F. Elliott (AP 13), 247
Georgia (BB 15), 12
"Germany First" strategy, 151–52
Ghormley, Robert L., 56, 231, 237, 250
Gibson, Hugh, 60, 64, 66
Giffen, Robert C., 319, 320, 332
Ginder, John K. B., 196
Gladney, Donald W., 154, *157*, 202, 287
Glover, D. C., Jr., *359*

Goto, Aritomo, 145, 184
Goto, Eiji, 165
Graf, Homer W., 364
Admiral Graf Spee (BB), 109
Graybar, Lloyd J., 143n
Grayling (SS 209), 149
Grayson (DD 435), 239, 248, 261
"Great White Fleet" Cruise (1907–1909), 9–13, 16, 50
Green Islands operation, 355
Greene, Wallace, *476*
Greenslade, J.W., 67
"Grey Book," 407
Griffin, Robert M., 333
Griswold, Oscar W., 416
Guadalcanal campaign, 230–52
  amphibious assault, 245
  command structure (WATCHTOWER), 238
  estimates of Japanese plans, 287–88
  final Japanese offensive (Nov 1942), 288–91
  Japanese air attacks, 246–47
  MacArthur-Ghormley reservations, 237
  preliminary intelligence and plans, 230–33, 236
  rehearsal at Koro Island, 242
  Savo Island, Battle of, 249–50
  TF 16 organization chart, 289
  U.S. carrier withdrawals, 249–52
Guadalupe (AO 22), 210, 225
Guam (CB 2), 433
Guedalla, Phillip, 202
Gwin (DD 433), 239, 261, 290

Half Moon (AVP 26), 400
Halsey, William F., 450n
  chairman 1946 "Plucking Board," 451
  Commander Naval Air Forces Pacific, 266
  Commander Tokyo bombing operation, 179
  and controversy over Battle for Leyte Gulf, 404–5, 458–60, 482–85
  misses Midway and Guadalcanal operations, 205–6, 234, 266
  orders during Battle of Santa Cruz Islands, 273
  relieves Ghormley as COMSOPAC, 266–68

Task Force Commander, 143, 147, 158, 177, 199
and Third Fleet operations in Leyte campaign, 386–87, 398–99
urges earlier assault on Leyte, 379–80
visits MacArthur with TCK, 355
Hammann (DD 412), 170, 195, 222
Hammargren, Henning, 117
Hammond, Philip Houston, 16
Hara, Tadaichi, 184, 257
Harding, Warren G., 36
Hardison, Osborne B., 274, 278
Harlan, John Marshall, 471
Harness, Forest A., 477
Harsch, Joseph C., 116
Hartford (screw sloop), 6
Haruna, 217, 274, 423
Heim, Schuyler F., 10
Helfrich, Conrad E. L., 346
Helm (DD 388), 143
Henderson (AP 1), 97
Henley (DD 391), 143
Hepburn, Arthur J., 5, 32, 34, 62, 64, 66
Hewitt, H. Kent, 91, 93, 131, 450n, 462
Hewitt, R. S., 450n
Hickerson, Ambassador, *481*
Hiei, 256, 274, 290
Hiryu, 44, 215–17
Hitler, Adolf, 106, 107, 110
Hobart, 182, 183, 185, 188–89
Hodge, John R., 384, 431, 435
Hodges, Courtney, 456
Hoel (DD 533), 403
Hollandia landings, 365–66
Hollandia-Tanamerah Bay campaign
 Aitape landings and seizure, 366
 Hollandia landings, 365–66
 Pacific Fleet carrier support, 364–66
Holmes, Ralston S., 103, 121, 154
Honolulu (CL 48), 204, 385
Hoogewerff, John A., 23
Hoover, Herbert, 66, 71
HORLICKS, operation, 368
Hornet (CV 8), 179, 209, 213, 217, 221, 222, 223–25, 234, 269, 273, 274–75, 276–80
Hornet (CV 12), 395
Hosogaya, Boshiro, 316
Houston (CA 30), 96, 101
Houston (CL 81), 389

Howard, William L., 24
Hudson, Roy C., 354
Hughes (DD 410), 170, 218
Hughes, Charles Evans, 36, 50
Hughes, Charles F., 45–46, 58
Hull (DD 350), 333
Hull, Cordell, 107
Hunsaker, Jerome C., 44
Hurley, Patrick J., 438–39
Hyuga, 395, 403, 423

Iceland occupation (1941), 126
Ichiki, Kiyorao, 253
Idaho (BB 42), 127, 310, 319, 333
Illustrious, 369
Imbrie, Robert W., 36–37
Impero, 118
Indianapolis (CA 35), 91–103, *100*, 160, 169, 204, 303, 315, 333
Ingalls Shipbuilding Corporation, 488
Ingersoll, Royal E., 92, 101, 127, 446, 449
Ingram, Jonas H., 9, 127, 450n, 452
Inouye, Shigeyoshi, 184, 190–91, 202
Institute of Politics, Williams College (MA), 51–52, 54, 59
International Business Machine Corporation, 466
Intrepid (CV 11), 397, 433
Irvine, Charles B., 275
Irving, Frederick A., 384
Irwin (DD 794), 394
Ise, 395, 403, 423
Isherwood (DD 284), 37–41
Ives, E. L., 35

Jackboot, operation, 308
Jaime de Borbon, Prince (of Spain), 117
James, Jules, 130
Japanese at Leyte Gulf, The, 458
Japanese Citadel, 360
Jarrett, Harry B., 196
Jarvis (DD 393), 143, 247
Jenkins, Walter T. (Jenks), 312
Jintsu, 256, 261
John Land (AP 167), 391
Johnson, Louis, 463, 466
Johnson, Lyndon B., 481
Johnston (DD 557), 403
Jones, Lloyd E., 304
Joseph T. Dickman (AP 26), 131

Joy, C. Turner, 158, 433, 436
Juliana, Queen (of the Netherlands), 480
Juneau (CL 52), 290
Junyo, 206, 279

Kadashan Bay (CVE 76), 401, 420
Kaga, 215
Kajioka, Sadamichi, 139, 184
Kako, 145, 184
Kakuta, Kakuji, 275
Kalbfus, Edward C., 36, 37, 88, 92
Kane (APD 18), 306
Kangleon, Ruperto, 391
Kaskaskia (AO 27), 131, 171, 179, 224, 251
Kauffman, James L. (Reggie), 43, 314, 426, 428, 456
Kawase, Shiro, 334
Kazagumo, 217
Kellogg, Edward S., 44n
Kellogg, Frank B., 36, 50
Kennedy, John F., 480–81
Kenney, George C., 346, 356, 358, *359*, 362, 364, 376, 383, 406–7, 409, 466, *484*, 485
Kerr, Howard J., 488
Ketcham, Dixwell (Dixie), 435–36
Keyes (Admiral of the Fleet), Sir Roger J. B., 388
Kidd, Isaac C., 87
Kido Butai, 171, 176, 230
Kiland, Ingolf N., 416
Kimmel, Husband E., 102, 126, *137*, 138, 139, 140–41, 143, 159, 482
Kimura, Masatomi, 334, 415
KING II, operation, 381, 387, 389
King, Ernest J., 450n
  agrees to TCK promotion to VADM, 328
  command philosophy, 151
  as Commander in Chief, Atlantic Fleet, 126
  as Commander Aircraft Battle Force, 98
  criticizes Halsey's 1947 articles, 459
  decides to assign TCK to SWPA, 343
  Guadalcanal plans, 230–33, 237
  intervenes in Alaskan command squabble, 296
  Kiska campaign disappoints, 335
  named COMINCH, 141, 149
  opposes MacArthur's SWPA strategy, 358
  praises TCK on retirement, 467
  presses TCK about Leyte Gulf, 405, 461
  teaches at Naval Academy, 5, 30
Kingman, Howard F., 319, 333
Kinkaid (DD 965), xv, *487*, 488
Kinkaid, Helen Sherburne Ross (Mrs. Thomas C. Kinkaid), 2, 3
  attends Institute of Politics (Williamsburg, MA), 51–52, 59
  early years, 16–17
  illnesses, 36, 445
  social life with TCK, 93–94
  and TCK's mother, 135, 172, 205, 314
  travels with TCK, 30–31, 51, 60–61, 65–66, 91
  visits to TCK, 80, 135–36, 297, 300–301
  volunteer activities, 42, 314
Kinkaid, Susan Monahan, 2
Kinkaid, Thomas Cassin
  at Bureau of Navigation (1934–1937), 87–90
    detailing section duties, 87–88
    selection to captain, 88–89
  at Bureau of Ordnance (1919–1922), 25, 27–30
    chief of supply section, 28
    publishes two articles, 29
  at Bureau of Ordnance (1925–1927), 42–45
    argues for large caliber guns on battleships, 42–43
    passes promotion tests to commander
  as CINCUS Staff Gunnery Officer (1927–1929), 46–54
    and fleet gunnery training, 48–49
    relations with Wiley, 53–54
  as Commander CRUDIV 6 (1941–1942), 148–234
    arrives at Pearl Harbor, 136–38
    assumes command, 148
    staff, 154
  as Commander Cruisers Pacific Fleet (1942), 287, 292
  as Commander DESRON 8 (1941), 123–33
    command style, 129
    destroyers and staff, 127–29
    escort of British troop convoy WS–124, 130–31
    promotion to rear admiral

as Commander Eastern Sea Frontier
  (1946–1950), 449–69
 anticommunist speaking, 454–55
 and B-36 bomber investigation,
  463–64
 ceremony on *Enterprise* and parades,
  467–69
 and decorations for wartime service,
  455–57
 and Leyte Gulf controversy, 458–61
 named as commander, 449
 "plucking board" service, 451–52
 public relations activities, 453
 retention of rank legislation, 462
 retirement process and fetes, 466
 and unification of military branches,
  450–51, 463–64
 and universal military training,
  450–51, 454
as Commander *Enterprise* Task Force
  (1942), 234–92
 assumes command of TF 16, 234
 continues under Nimitz's command,
  266–68
 relieved of command, 291–92
 returns to Pearl Harbor, 261–62
 staff, 235–36
as Commander Naval Forces Southwest
  Pacific Area (1943–1945), 343–434
 See also Seventh Fleet operations
as Commander North Pacific Force
  (1942–1943), 295–343
 named to command, 295
 staff, 312–13
 See also North Pacific Force
  (NORPACFOR), battles and
  campaigns
as Commander Seventh Fleet
  (1943–1945), 343–446
 accepts surrender of Japanese forces
  in South Korea (Sep 1945), 431,
  434–35
 celebrates war's end (Aug 1945),
  430–31
 and Mindoro campaign plan
  change, 411–13
 relieved as commander, 446
 See also Seventh Fleet operations
as Commanding Officer *Indianapolis*
  (1937–1938), 91–103

 command style, 93–94
 gunnery exercises, 96, 98
 position with Battle Force, 91–92
 with presidential naval review, 101
 visits to Portland, OR, 94–95, 101–2
as Commanding Officer *Isherwood*
  (1924–1925), 37–41
 Caribbean exercises, 38–39
 training for naval reservists, 39–41
duty with U.S. Naval Forces in Turkish
  waters (1922–1924), 30–36
 assistant chief of staff and gunnery
  and engineering officer, 32
 relations with ADM Bristol
 Smyrna evacuation of Greeks
  (1922), 34
 social life in Constantinople, 32–33
as Executive Officer of *Colorado*
  (1933–1934), 69–86
 duties, 69–72
 gunnery exercises, 75–76, 79, 82
 Long Beach earthquake, 78–79
 personal qualities, 73, 86
and family
 Fannie Marby Cassin (aunt), 172,
  314, 464
 Helen Kinkaid Heiner (sister), 2,
  172, 314
 Dorothy Kinkaid Kimmel (sister), 3,
  172, 205
 Thomas Kinkaid Kimmel (nephew),
  xvi
 Thomas Wright Kinkaid (father), 1,
  2–4, 14, 29–30
 Virginia Cassin Lee Kinkaid
  (mother), 1–2, 135, 172, 205, 314
 Mrs. Ross, 172
 Grafton Tyler, 464
 Jennifer Urquhart (great-niece), 487
 Mary Tyler Heiner Urquhart
  (niece), xvi, 314
 See especially Kinkaid, Helen
  Sherburne Ross; and other
  individual listings
as General Board Secretary
  (1930–1933), 57–67
 Disarmament Conference activities,
  59–62, 64–66
 General Board in 1930, 57–59
 relations with Bristol, 57–58

as Midshipman and Passed Midshipman
    (1904–1910), 1–15
  Naval Academy years, 1, 4–8
  Passed Midshipman service, 9–15
    Minnesota (1910–13), 15–18
    Nebraska (1908–10), 9–15
as Naval Attaché in Rome (1938–
    1941), 105–22
  duties, 107–8, 114–15
  intelligence reporting, 108, 111,
    114–15, 119–20
  ONI briefing (1941), 123–24
  social activities, 108–10, 112, 116–17
  visits to Yugoslavia, 111–13, 117–18
at Naval War College (1929–1930),
    54–57
in postgraduate ordnance training
    (1913–1914, 1915–1916), 18–21
  Dominican Republic intervention
    (1914–15) (*Machias*), 19–20
promotions
  to admiral, 428
  to captain, 88–90
  to commander, 44–45
  to ensign, 15
  to lieutenant, 23
  to lieutenant commander, 24
  to lieutenant junior grade, 18
  to rear admiral, 132–33, 135
  to vice admiral, 328
in retirement (1950–1972), 471–88
  American Battle Monuments
    Commission (1953–1968), 473,
    477–81
  Australia-New Zealand trip (1951),
    473
  declining health and death, 485–86
  entertaining, 471, 485
  National Service Training
    Commission (1951–1956),
    473–77
  "plucking board" service, 471
World War I years and beyond (1916–
    1919), 21–26
  in *Arizona* (1918–1919), 24–26
  in *Pennsylvania* (1916–1918), 21–24
writing and publications, 29, 56,
    62–63, 482–85
Kinkaid, Thomas Wright, 1, 2
Kinkaid, Virginia Lee, 2

Kinkaid, William P., 1–2
Kinryu Maru, 255
Kinugasa, 145, 184, 291
Kirishima, 256, 274, 291
Kirk, Alan, 103, 123, 129
Kiska campaign, 329–34
  amphibious "assault," 334
  bombardments, 307, 314–15, 331–34,
    336–37
  Japanese evacuation, 334, 338
  planning, 330
Kiso, 334
Kitkun Bay (CVE 71), 420
Knopf, Alfred, 482
Knox, Dudley W., 9
Knox, Frank, 139–40, 343–44
Komandorski Islands, Battle of
    (Mar 1943), 316–17
Kondo, Nobutake, 261, 274
Kongo, 264, 423
Kongo Maru, 170
Koro Island, rehearsal at, 242
Kotsuki, Yoshi, 435
Krock, Arthur, 471
Krueger, Walter, 347, 365, 396, 409–10,
    416, 480, *484*, 485
Kurita, Takeo, 393, 402

Lae-Salamaua raid, 169–71
Lais, Alberto, 116
Lake Sentani headquarters, 377, 380
Lamson (DD 367), 164, 353
LANDCRAB, operation, 317
Landrum, Eugene M., 321, 326
Lane, Arthur Bliss, 111, 113, 117, 120
Lane, Cornelia, 111
Langley (AV 3), 94, 100
Langley (CVL 27), 407
Langsdorff, Hans, 109
Laning, Harris, 9
Lardner (DD 286), 38
Lark, Jacob A., 128
Layton, Edwin T., 176–77
Leahy, William D., 5, 89, 133, 450n
Leander, 164
Leary, Herbert Fairfax, 43–44, 154, 155,
    348, 375, 449, 453–54, 466
Lee, James R. (Bucky), 275
Lee, Willis A. (Ching), 89, 288, 291, 399,
    490

Legion of Merit award, 455
Leigh, Richard H., 78, 79
Lend-Lease Act of 1941, 126
Leonard Wood (AP 25), 131
Lett, Sherwood, 335
Leverton, Joseph Wilson, 305–6, 313, 348
Leviathan, 61, 65
Lewis, Thomas L., 129
Lexington (CV 2), 53, 76, 98, 140, 160, 165, 173, 178, 187, 191–96, *197*
Lexington (CV 16), 407
Leyte Gulf, Battle for
  Cape Engaño, Battle off
    Halsey takes TF 38 north, 397, 398–99
    Japanese Northern Force, 395, 403
  invasion, 391
  map, 393
  Samar, Battle off
    Japanese Center Force attacks TG 77.4, 401
    Japanese forces retreat, 402–3
  Sibuyan Sea, Battle of, 393
    TF 38 carriers attack Japanese Center Force, 393, 397, 399
  Surigao Strait, Battle of, 393–99
    battle, 398–99
    Japanese Southern Force, 393–94
    Seventh Fleet battle plan, 398
Leyte operation planning, 380–83, 384
  Army Air Corps role, 383
  Army forces involved, 382–83
  decisions about commands, 381–82
  Seventh Fleet task forces and groups, 383–86
  Third Fleet operation plan, 386–87
Lindsey, Eugene E., 215
Lingayen Gulf (Luzon) campaign
  14th Air Force support, 418
  kamikaze attacks, 419–22
  landings at Lingayen Gulf, 420–22
  TF and TG assignments, 416–17
Lippman, Walter, 471
Littorio, 119
London Naval Conference of 1930, 490
Long, Andrew T., 56–57
Long (DMS 12), 419
Long Island (AVG 1), 250, 253
Longworth, Alice Roosevelt, 471
Los Negros operation, 356–58

Louisville (CA 28), 169, 170, 204, 319, 332, 385, 398, 419
LOVE-3, operation, 408
Low, Francis S., 433
Lowe, Frank L., 290
Lowisch, Werner, 114
Lowry, Frank J., 198, 234
Lucas, L. C., 67
Luce (DD 99), 25
Lurline, 136
Luzon campaign
  See Lingayen Gulf (Luzon) campaign
Lynch, John J., 276
Lynd, William H., 328

MacArthur, Douglas A.
  agrees to Solomon's campaign, 233
  crisis in relations over Mindoro, 410–13
  discusses 1944 politics with TCK, 367–68
  and Los Negros assault with TCK, 356–57
  named Commander all Army forces in Pacific, 429
  named Supreme Commander for Japanese surrender and occupation, 431
  and Port Moresby headquarters, 354
  relations with TCK, 349
  and reservations about Guadalcanal plans, 237
  and retaining Third Fleet at Lingayen Gulf, 422
  in retirement, with TCK, 466–67, 485, 486
  and sea battle experience with TCK at Leyte Gulf, 391, 396
  and Seeadler Harbor use controversy, 361–62
  and Solomons campaign, 233
  and SWPA strategy supported by TCK, 358
  and TCK assigned to SWPA as COM7THFLT and COMNAVFORSWPA, 343–44, 346
  and TCK's completion of service, 432
  and TCK's DSM, 456
  and TCK's promotion to admiral, 447
  and views on retaking Philippines, 378
MacDonough (DD 351), 324

Machias (PG 5), 19–20, 167
Mackinac (AVP 13), 255
MacLeish (DD 220), 35
Madeira, Dashiell L., 129
Magruder, Cary W., 10, 16, 71–76
Maguire, Charles J., 418
Manila Bay (CVE 61), 365, 419
Manley (DD 74), 25
Mao Tse-tung, 444, 445
Marie, Princess (of Greece), 117
Marriner, Theodore C., 65
Marshall, George C., 149, 231, 237, 296, 300, 354–55, 450, 477
Marshall, Richard J., *359*
Marston, John, 126
Martin, Charles H., 95
Marumo, Kuninori, 184
Maryland (BB 46), 69, 384
Mason, Charles P., 271, 282, 284–85
Mason, John, 441, 489
Massey, Lance E., 215
Matthews, Francis P., 463
Matthews, Herbert, 116
Maury (DD 401), 216, 239, 261
Maya, 316, 392
Mayflower (PY 1), 13
Mayo, Henry T., 24
McCain, John S., 248, 373, 395, 402
McCloy, John J., 335
McClure, Lady Caroline, 109
McClure, H. A., 37
McClure, Sir Robert, 109
McClusky, Wade, 215
McCollum, Arthur H., 377, 393–95
McCrea, John L., 135
McDougal (DD 358), 101, 129
McKean, Josiah S., 24
McLain, Raymond S., 474, 475
McMorris, Charles H. (Soc), 136, 147, 304, 315, 320, 358
McNair, Laurance N., 124
McNamee, Luke, 76, 85
McVay, Charles B., 28, *67*
Merrill, A. Stanton (Tip), 33, 127, 314
Messersmith, George S., 30
Midway, Battle of, 203–27
   action chart, 214
   lessons, 225–26
MIKE-1, operation, 408, 422
Mikuma, 220, 222

Miles, Milton E., 437
Miles, Sherman, 33, 37, 123, 136
Mindoro campaign, 408–14
   Air Corps coverage problem, Leyte to Mindoro, 409
   Army hesitancy to risk troop transports, 410
   Japanese raid landing sites, 415
   TCK insists on plan change, 411–13
Minneapolis (CA 36), 98–99, 143, 154, 157, 167, 190, 193–98, 201, 209, 215, 217, 222, 223, 423, 432–34
Minnesota (BB 22), 15–18
Mississippi (BB 41), 333, 384
Missouri (BB 63), 435
Mitscher (DL 2), 481
Mitscher, Marc A., *181*, 213, 234, 266, 364, 379, 451
Mo, operation, 176, 184, 191
Moffat, J. Pierrepont, 33, 35, 60, 64, 105
Mogami, 220, 222, 393, 399
Monaghan (DD 354), 316, 333
Monssen (DD 436), 239, 261
Monterey (CVL 26), 395
Moore, Edward P., 287
Morison, Samuel Eliot, 145, 327, 406, 466
Morotai operation, 373
Morris (DD 417), 193, 195
Morrison (DD 560), 394
"Mothball Fleet" (16th Fleet), 449–50
Mount Olympus (AGC 8), 387, 397
Mount Vernon (AP 22), 131
Mountbatten, Lord Louis, 417
Mudge, Verne D., 384
Mugford (DD 389), 143, 353
Munroe, William R., 120, 132
Murray, Albert K., *465*, 466
Murray, George D., 234, 266, 276, 280, 284–85
Musashi, 393, 397
MUSKETEER, operation, 378
Mussolini, Benito, 106, 107, 110, 113, 114, 115, 116, 119–20
Mustin (DD 413), 129, 280
Mutsuki, 261
Myoko, 397

Nachi, 316, 393
Nagato, 423
Nagumo, Chuichi, 211, 257, 274

Narwhal (SS 167), 322
Nashville (CL 43), 127, 130, 204, 356, 364, 370–71, 373, 383, 390, 396, 402, 433, 442
Nassau (CVE 16), 323
Nasugbu landings, 425–26
National Service Training Commission (NSTC), 474
Natoma Bay (CVE 62), 365
Nautilus (SS 168), 322
Naval Militias, 17
Naval War College, 54–57
Navy's War, The, 292
Nebraska (BB 14), 9–14, 163
Neches (AO 5), 143, 158
Neosho (AO 23), 159, 171, 182, 185, 186, 187
Nevada (BB 36), 22, 319
Nevada (BM 8), 5
New Guinea operation control
  Biak operation, 367, 368, 370–71
  Lake Sentani headquarters, 377, 380
  map, 352
  Morotai operation, 373
  Noemfoor operation, 372
  Vogelkop operations, 372
  Wakde operation, 367–68
New Jersey (BB 62), 399
New Mexico (BB 40), 127, 333, 419, 423
New Orleans (CA 32), 178, 193, 195, 222, 433
New York (BB 34), 75
Newark (C 1), 8
Nicholson, Reginald F., 9
Nimitz, Chester W., 450n
  assists with Mindoro campaign, 412–13
  becomes CINCPAC, 141, 149
  and Coral Sea battle, 199
  dedicates West Coast Memorial, 480
  Guadalcanal plans, 230–34, 252, 288
  at Midway battle, 203, 220
  named commander of naval forces in Pacific, 429
  opposes Paramushiro-Shimushu plans, 339–40
  orders to Halsey before Leyte campaign, 387
  solves Seeadler Harbor use problem, 301–4
  supports MacArthur's SWPA strategy, 358
  and TCK, 135, 295, 340, 343, 376
Nishimura, Shoji, 393–94, 401
Noble, Albert G., 368, 426
Noemfoor operation, 372
North Carolina (BB 55), 239, 258, 261, 263, 264
North, Thomas, 477, 478
North Pacific Force (NORPACFOR), battles and campaigns
  Adak occupation, 299
  Alaska-Aleutians map, 298
  Amchitka operation (Jan 1943), 299–307
  Army and Navy cooperation, 309–12
  Attu campaign (May–Jun 1943), 307–29
  headquarters shift (from Kodiak to Adak), 309–11
  Kiska campaign, 329–34
  Komandorski Islands battle (Mar 1943), 316–17
  staff, 312–13
  strategy for the theater, 299, 303, 339–40
  TCK named Force Commander, 295
  and weather, 300, 305, 309, 318–19, 322–23
Northampton (CA 26), 67, 201, 215, 280, 291
Noyes, Leigh, 238–39, 256

O'Brien (DD 415), 264
O'Donnell, Emmett, 480
O'Hare, Edward H. (Butch), 167
O'Keefe, Arthur, 50
O'Keefe, George F., 309, 312
Oklahoma (BB 37), 22
Olch, Isaiah, xvi, 127, 129
Oldendorf, Jesse B. (Oley), 383, 396, 415, 417–18, 419, 446–47
Oliver, Robert J., 206
Ommaney Bay (CVE 79), 419
Oregon (BB 3), 4
Orizaba (AP 24), 131
Orme, Ruth, 1
Orr, Harry A., 23
Oryuko Maru, 436
Osmena, Sergio, 391
OVERLORD, operation, 340

Oyodo, 415
Ozawa, Jisaburo, 395, 458

Pacific Fleet carrier support, 364–66
Pacific Military Strategy Conferences, 317, 358, 360
Pasha, Mustafa Kemal, 31
Patrick, Edwin D., 416
Patterson (DD 392), 143, 169
Paul, Elliot, 269
Paul, Prince (of Yugoslavia), 111, 117, 120
Pearl Harbor Attack investigations, 140–41
Pell, H. C., 65
Pennsylvania (BB 38), 21, 22, 24, 25, 319, 322, 385
Pensacola (CA 24), 160, 169, 201, 216, 290, 291
Perkins (DD 377), 179
PESTILENCE, operation, 233
Peter, King (of Yugoslavia), 111
Petrof Bay (CVE 80), 401
Phelps (DD 360), 193, 196
Philadelphia (CL 41), 127
Philippines recovery campaign, 379
Phillips, Caroline, 116
Phillips, John, 477
Phillips, William, 107, 108, 114, 115, 121
Phoenix (CL 46), 356, 370, 372, 373, 384
Pinchot, Gifford, 202
Pinney, Frank L., 44–45
Pinta, 3
Pius XII, Pope, 112
Platte (AO 24), 251, 262
"Plucking Boards," 451–52, 471
Pogue, William G., 305
Pope, C. J., 369–70
Porter (DD 356), 283
Portland (CA 33), 224, 239, 248, 258, 261, 263, 268, 290, 333, 385, 423
Potter, Charles E., 477
Potter, E. B., 483–85
Powell, Paulus P., 405
Power, Tyrone, 388
Pownall, Charles A., 266
Pratt, Fletcher, 292
Pratt, William V., 5, 46, 53, 54, 58, 63, 80
Pray, Dudley, 40
Preston (DD 379), 290
Princeton (CVL 23), 394
Prisoners of war (POWs), 435–36

Purnell, William R., 132, 314
Putnam (DD 287), 38
Putnam, Paul A., 138
Pye, William S., 141, *142*, 143, 145, 147, 148, 159, 445

Queen Elizabeth, 370
Quincy (CA 39), 129, 131, 249

Rabaul campaign
  Arawe and Cape Gloucester operations, 351, 353
  Green Islands operation, 355
  Los Negros operation, 356–58
  Saidor operation, 354
Rabaul-Bougainville action, 164–68
Radford, Arthur W., 463–64, 473
Ragsdale, Van H., 365
Raleigh (CL 8), 333
Ralph Talbot (DD 390), 143
Ramsey, DeWitt C., 224
Ranger (CV 4), 98, 131
RECKLESS, operation, 363
Reed, Milton E., 19
Reed, Stanley, 471
Reeves, John W., 266, 340
Reeves, Joseph M., 49
Reichmuth, Ferdinand, 131, 132
RENO, operation, 377–78
Reserve Forces Act of 1955 (P.L. 305), 475–76
Reynolds, Paul, 482
Rhind (DD 404), 131
Richardson, James O., 67
Richmond (CL 9), 315, 333
Richmond, Sir Herbert, 62, 63
Riggs, Ralph S., 316
Robertson, Ashley, 50
Robison, Samuel S., 43
Rochefort, Joseph J., 176–77, 203
Rockey, Keller E., 443
Rockwell, Francis W., 300, 317, 325–28, 339, 490
Rocky Mount (AGC 3), 432, 436
Rodgers, Bertram J., 316
Rodgers, John, 9
Rolph, James (Sunny Jim), 78
Roma, 118
Romulo, Carlos P., 391
Roosevelt, Eleanor Alexander, 477, 479

Roosevelt, Franklin D., 78, 84, 92, 101, 110, 114, 115, 130–31, 231, 378–79
Roosevelt, Quentin, 479
Roosevelt, Theodore, 4, 13, 84
Roosevelt, Theodore, Jr., 477
Ross, Frances, 16
Ross, Helen Sherburne
　See Kinkaid, Helen Sherburne Ross
Rowcliff, Gilbert J., 101
Royal, Forrest B., 381, 385, 416, 426
Royle, Sir Guy, 346
Ruddock, Theodore D., 410–11
Russell (DD 414), 185, 198, 218
Ryujo, 206, 256, 258, 260

Sabine (AO 25), 269
Sadler, Frank H., 92, 96, 98, 99
Saidor operation, 354
St. Lo (CVE 63), 403
St. Louis (CL 49), 204, 433
Sakae, Noboru, 165
Sakonju, Naomasa, 370
Salt Lake City (CA 25), 201, 316, 333
Samar, Battle off, 401, 402–3
Samuel B. Roberts (DE 413), 403
San Diego (CL 53), 224
San Francisco (CA 38), 160, 169, 290, 319, 332, 433
San Jacinto (CVL 30), 394
San Juan (CL 54), 262, 268
Sangamon (CVE 26), 365, 401
Santa Cruz Islands, Battle of (Oct 1942), 269–83
　map, 272
Santa Fe (CL 60), 320, 332
Santee (CVE 29), 365, 401
Saratoga (CV 3), 53, 76, 94, 98, 140, 143, 146, 154–55, 223–24, 225, 255–59, 261, 263, 369
Sarnoff, David G., 476
Sauer, Edward P., 239, 259
Savannah (CL 42), 127
Savo Island, battle of, 249–50
　and TCK manuscript, 482
Schaeffer, Valentine H., 383, 385, 395, 402, 410–11
Scorpion (PY 3), 33
Scott, Norman, 290
Sea Fights and Shipwrecks, 483
Seattle (CA 11), 49

Seeadler Harbor (Manus) controversy, 361
Selfridge (DD 357), 143
Seligman, Morton T., 196
Sellers, David F., 79, 84
Settle, Henry T., 41
Settle, Thomas G. W., 442
Seventh Fleet operations
　(Nov 1943–Nov 1945)
　AMP Building headquarters, 346
　Hollandia-Tanamerah Bay campaign
　　Aitape landings and seizure, 366
　　Hollandia landings, 365–66
　　Pacific Fleet carrier support, 364–66
　Leyte Gulf, Battle for (Oct 1944)
　　Cape Engaño, Battle off
　　　Halsey takes TF 38 north, 397, 398–99
　　　Japanese Northern Force, 395, 403
　　Samar, Battle off
　　　Japanese Center Force attacks TG 77.4, 401
　　　Japanese forces retreat, 402–3
　　Sibuyan Sea, Battle of, 393
　　　TF 38 carriers attack Japanese Center Force (Kurita), 393, 397, 399
　　Surigao Strait, Battle of, 393–99
　　　battle, 398–99
　　　Japanese Southern Force, 393–94
　　　Seventh Fleet battle plan, 398
　Leyte invasion, 391
　Leyte operation planning, 380–83, 384
　　Army Air Corps role, 383
　　Army forces involved, 382–83
　　decisions about commands, 381–82
　　Seventh Fleet task forces and groups, 383–86
　　Third Fleet operation plan, 386–87
　Lingayen Gulf (Luzon) campaign
　　(Jan. 1945)
　　14th Air Force support, 418
　　kamikaze attacks, 419–22
　　landings at Lingayen Gulf, 420–22
　　TF and TG assignments, 416–17
　Luzon campaign
　　See Lingayen Gulf (Luzon) campaign
　and MacArthur's staff, 346–48
　Mindoro campaign (Dec 1944), 408–14

Air Corps coverage problem, Leyte to Mindoro, 409
Army hesitancy to risk troop transports, 410
Japanese raid landing sites, 415
TCK insists on plan change, 411–13
Nasugbu landings (Jan 1945), 425–26
New Guinea operation control
Biak operation, 367, 368, 370–71
naval engagement, 370–71
Lake Sentani headquarters, 377, 380
map, 352
Morotai operation, 373
Noemfoor operation, 372
Vogelkop operations, 372
Wakde operation, 367–68
Philippines recovery campaign (Oct 1944–May 1945)
Halsey recommends change from Mindanao to Leyte, 379
posthostilities activities (Aug–Nov 1945)
Chungking visit, 439
movement of Marines to North China, 433, 442–45
POW recovery, 435–36
Shanghai visit, 436–39
surrender of Japanese forces in South Korea (Sept. 1945), 431, 434–35
Rabaul campaign
Arawe and Cape Gloucester operations, 351, 353
Green Islands operation, 355
Los Negros operation, 356–58
Saidor operation, 354
Zambales coast landings (Jan. 1945), 425
Sexton, Walton R., 83
Shaffer, Leland G. (Jake), 154, *157*, 313, 395
Shafroth, Jack F., 102
Sharp, Alexander S., 103
Shaw (DD 373), 353
Shaw, Howland, 33
Shaw, Robert C., 258
Shepler, Dwight, ii
Sherman, Forrest P., 358, *359*, 364, 469
Sherman, Frederick C. (Ted), 166, 191, 194, 198, 266, 292, 394
Sherwood, Robert E., 355

Shima, Kiyohide, 184, 393, 395
SHO-I Plan, 391, 393
Shoemaker, William R., 36
Shoho, 184, 188, 189
Shokaku, 184, 190, 192, 256, 274, 275, 279, 283
Short, Walter C., 141, 159
Shropshire, 370, 373, 384
Sibert, Franklin C., 384
Sibuyan Sea, Battle of, 393, 397, 399
Sicard (DM 21), 324
Simard, Cyril T., 206
Simonds, George S., 66
Simpson, Edward, 18
Sims (DD 409), 170, 179, 182, 186, 187
Sims, William S., 15, 23, 24, 54
Sirius (AK 15), 87
Sloan, Robert S., 466
Smeallie, John M., 67, 92
Smith (DD 378), 283
Smith, Albert D., 465
Smith, Holland M., 300, 317, 337
Smith, Joseph C., 191
Smith, Oscar, Jr., 19
Smith, Walton W., 169
Smith, William W. (Poco), 169, 218, 230, 332
Smyth, William W., 60, 61
Solace (AH 5), 198
Solomon Islands, map, 232
  See also Eastern Solomons, Battle of the
Somerville, Sir James F., 370
Somigli, Admiral, 109
Soryu, 215
South Dakota (BB 57), 253, 268, 291
Spaatz, Carl, 477
Sperry, Charles S., 11
Spellman, Bishop, 441
Sprague, Clifton A. F., 384, 401, 405
Sprague, Thomas L., 384, 397, 400, 405
Spruance, Raymond A., 201, 205–6, 209, 219, 220–21, 230, 445, 450n, 451, 480, *481*
Stack (DD 406), 129, 269
STALEMATE, operation, 381
Standley, William H., 84, 85
Stark, Harold R., 140, 144, 147, 149, 457
Stark, Lloyd C., 95
Steele, James M., 140n, 229, 307
Sterrett (DD 407), 129

Stich, Francis S., 128
Stilwell, Joseph, 438
Stimson, Henry L., 63, 64, 66, 71, 141
STRAIGHT LINE, operation, 368
Strategy of Pacific War
  Aleutians strategy, 299, 317–18, 339
  in December 1941, 140, 141
  final campaigns against Japan, 429
  1942 plans, 149–52, 161
  post-Midway changes, 230–31
  for Southwest Pacific area, 318, 349–50, 358, 360, 378–79
Stratemayer, George E., 439, 444
Strong, Stockton B., 275
Struble, Arthur D., 409–11, 414, 425, 426
Stump, Felix B., 384, 387, 401, 405, 410–11, 414
Sugnet, Lee F., 437
Sulzberger, Cyrus L., 117, 413
Surigao Strait, Battle of, 393–99
  map, 393
Sutherland, Richard K., 348, 358, *359*, 379
Suwanee (CVE 27), 365, 401
Swanson, Claude, 64, 85
Swearingen, R. W., 154
Swenson, Lyman K., 131
Swift, Innis P., 416
Sykes, James B., *106*, 112–13
Symington, Stuart, 463

Tai Li, 438
Takagi, Takeo, 184, 186, 187
Takao, 393
Tama, 316
Tama Maru No. 2, 170
Tambor (SS 198), 220
Tanaka, Raizo, 255, 261
Tang En-po, 439
Tangier (AV 8), 141, 143
Tanikaze, 221
Tarbuck, Ray D., 362
Tarrant, William T., 91, 94–95, 96, 97, 99, 102, 133
Task Force 16, 208, 289
Task Force 17, 180, 208
Task Force 61, 270
Tatsuta, 184
Taussig, Joseph K., 56, 92, 100

Taylor, Robert H., 154, *157*, 202, 235–36, 287, 301, 312
Tennessee (BB 43), 75, 333, 385
Tenyo Maru, 170
Texas (BB 35), 46, 49–54
Thach, John S., 165, 170
Theobald, Robert A. (Fuzzy), 204, 206, 223, 296, 301, 307, 490
Thomason, Thaddeus, 106
Thornton, Louise, 112, 122
Thornton, Proctor M., 106, 111, 112, 122
Tippecanoe (AO 21), 179
Tisdale, Mahlon S., 230, 239, 246, 283, 291
Tokyo bombing attack, 179, 181
Tone, 215, 217
Toucey (DD 282), 38
Towers, John H., 266, 286, 358, 450n, 451
TRADEWIND, operation, 373
Train, Harold C., 120
Trammel, Webb, 33
Treadwell, R.C., 35
Trenton (CL 11), 36–37
Trost, Clayton, 455n
True, Arnold E., 196
Truman, Harry S., 450, 451, 455, 475
Tugwell, Rex G., 135
Tulagi
  See Coral Sea, Battle of
Turner, Richmond K., 64, 88, 89, 120, 132, 230, 238, 242, 250, 381, 430, 450n, 457, 490
Tuscaloosa (CA 37), 97, 433
Tyler, Grafton, Jr., 1, 464
Tyler, Mary Amelia (Mittie), 1

"Ultra," code breaking
  See Communications intelligence
Underway replenishment, 171
United States Naval Academy, 1, 4–5, 18, 445
United States Naval Forces in Turkish waters, 30–34
Universal Military Training and Service Act (P.L. 51), 473
Urquhart, Mary Tyler (Mrs. John), 1n
Utah (BB 31), 42

Valdez, Basilio, 391
Vandegrift, Alexander A., 242, 477
Van Hook, Clifford E., 364

Van Keuren, Alexander H., 64
Vestal (AR 4), 94, 283
Victor Emmanuel II, King (of Italy), 114
Victoria Eugenia, Queen (of Spain), 117, 120
Vincennes (CA 44), 129, 131, 201, 216, 249
Vinson, Carl, 463
Vixen (PG 53), 149
Vogelkop operations, 372
von Ribbentrop, Joachim, 110
Vose, James E., 275

Wadsworth, James W., 474, 475
Wainwright (DD 449), 127, 156
Wakde operation, 367–68
Wake Island relief operation, 138–39, 141–48
  plans and forces, 142–43
  recall of task forces, 145–48
  TCK's views on recall, 148
Wakefield (AP 21), 131
Waldron, John C., 215
Warramunga, 373
Wasatch (AGC 9), 383, 385, 390, 395–96, 417, 425
Washington Conference on the Limitation of Armament (1922), 28
Wasmuth (DMS 15), 305
Wasp (CV 7), 239, 245, 255–56, 264, 287
Wasp (CV 18), 395
Watchtower, operation, 233, *238*
Watson, Thomas J., 453
Wavell, Sir Archibald P., 152
Wedemeyer, Albert C., 438, 444, 455
West Point (AP 23), 131
West Virginia (BB 48), 69, 384
Wev, Bosquet N., 82
Weyler, George L., 384
Whalen, Grover, 453
Wheeler, Charles Julian, 33, 35
Whipple (DD 217), 185
Whitehead, Richard F., 385–86, 401
Whitehill, Walter, 461
Wichita (CA 45), 319, 332
Widhelm, William J. (Gus), 275
Wilbur, Curtis, 42
Wiley, Henry A., 5, 45, 46, 47, 48, 49, 52–54, 133

Wilhelmina, Queen (of the Netherlands), 457
Wilkinson, Theodore S. (Ping), 66, *67*, 89, 265, 380, 381–82, 384–85, 390–91, 405, 415–16, 430–31
Williams, E. M., 67
Williams, George W., 38
Williams College, Institute of Politics (MA), 51–52, 54, 59
Willkie, Edith (Mrs. Wendell), 477
Willoughby, Charles A., 362
Willson, Russell, 124
Wilson, Henry B., 23
Wilson, Hugh, 64, 65–66
Wing, Leonard F., 416
Winslow (DD 359), 128
Witzenberg, Homer L., *476*
Woodward, C. Vann, 458, 483
Woolley, Mary Emma, 65
Worden (DD 352), 305
World Disarmament Conference of 1931–1932, 62, 65, 66, 490
Worth, Cedric, 463
Wortman, Ward K., 41
Wright, Carlton H., 292
Wright, Jerauld, 433
Wygant, Benyaurd B., *70*, 71–80, 84, 86

Yamaguchi, Jisaburo, 435
Yamamoto, Isoroku, 171, 176–77, 203, 209, 220, 230
Yamashiro, 393
Yamato, 393, 423
Yarnell, Harry E., 76, 98
Yokohama Maru, 170
Yorktown (CV 5), 127, 129, 140, 158, 179, 182, 187, 192, 209, 211–12, 216–18, 222, 234
Yu Ku-ying, 443
Yubari, 184
Yugumo, 217

Zambales coast landings, 425
Zmaj, 117
Zog, King (of Albania), 111
Zuiho, 269, 279, 283, 395
Zuikaku, 184, 190, 192, 256, 274, 275, 279, 395

The Author

Following service during World War II as a naval aviator (airship) and air navigation instructor, Gerald E. Wheeler attended the University of California at Berkeley where he received his Ph.D. in history in 1954. During his academic career he taught at the U.S. Naval Academy, San Jose State University, and the University of the Philippines. He also was Fleet Admiral Ernest J. King Professor of Maritime History at the Naval War College, 1968–1969. His publications include *Prelude to Pearl Harbor: The U.S. Navy and the Far East, 1921–1931*; *Admiral William Veazie Pratt, A Sailor's Life*; and chapters dealing with Secretaries of the Navy Edwin Denby and Charles Francis Adams III in P. E. Coletta, ed., *The American Secretaries of the Navy*. A retired professor of history from San Jose State University, Dr. Wheeler resides in Los Gatos, California.

The **Naval Institute Press** is the book-publishing arm of the U.S. Naval Institute, a private, nonprofit society for sea service professionals and others who share an interest in naval and maritime affairs. Established in 1873 at the U.S. Naval Academy in Annapolis, Maryland, where its offices remain today, the Naval Institute has more than 85,000 members worldwide.

Members of the Naval Institute receive the influential monthly magazine *Proceedings* and discounts on fine nautical prints and on ship and aircraft photos. They also have access to the transcripts of the Institute's Oral History Program and get discounted admission to any of the Institute-sponsored seminars offered around the country.

The Naval Institute also publishes *Naval History* magazine. This colorful bimonthly is filled with entertaining and thought-provoking articles, first-person reminiscences, and dramatic art and photography. Members receive a discount on *Naval History* subscriptions.

The Naval Institute's book-publishing program, begun in 1898 with basic guides to naval practices, has broadened its scope in recent years to include books of more general interest. Now the Naval Institute Press publishes about 100 titles each year, ranging from how-to books on boating and navigation to battle histories, biographies, ship and aircraft guides, and novels. Institute members receive discounts of 20 to 50 percent on the Press's nearly 600 books in print.

For a free catalog describing Naval Institute Press books currently available, and for further information about subscribing to *Naval History* magazine or about joining the U.S. Naval Institute, please write to:

Membership & Communications Department
U.S. Naval Institute
118 Maryland Avenue
Annapolis, Maryland 21402-5035
Telephone: (800) 233-8764
Fax: (410) 269-7940